Political Ideologies

ST

Political Ideologies

A Reader and Guide

Edited by

Matthew Festenstein and Michael Kenny

OXFORD
UNIVERSITY PRESS

OXFORD

UNIVERSITY PRESS

Great Clarendon Street, Oxford OX2 6DP

Oxford University Press is a department of the University of Oxford.
It furthers the University's objective of excellence in research, scholarship,
and education by publishing worldwide in

Oxford New York

Auckland Cape Town Dar es Salaam Hong Kong Karachi Kuala Lumpur
Madrid Melbourne Mexico City Nairobi New Delhi Shanghai Taipei
Toronto

With offices in

Argentina Austria Brazil Chile Czech Republic France Greece
Guatemala Hungary Italy Japan South Korea Poland Portugal
Singapore Switzerland Thailand Turkey Ukraine Vietnam

Oxford is a registered trade mark of Oxford University Press
in the UK and in certain other countries

Published in the United States
by Oxford University Press Inc., New York

© Matthew Festenstein and Michael Kenny 2005

A catalogue record for this title is available from the British Library

Library of Congress Cataloging in Publication Data

Data available

ISBN 0-19-924837-0

10 9 8 7 6 5 4 3 2 1

Typeset by Newgen Imaging Systems (P) Ltd., Chennai, India
Printed in Great Britain
on acid-free paper by
Ashford Colour Press Ltd., Gosport, Hants.

Acknowledgments

We would like to express our gratitude to Carissa Honeywell both for her intellectual input and research assistance with this Reader. We decided at an early stage to seek advice from a number of experts in the fields covered within its pages, and have benefited greatly from the ideas of Andrew Dobson, Bob Eccleshall, Michael Freeden, Vincent Geoghegan, Roger Griffin, Jeremy Jennings, Noël O'Sullivan, and Judith Squires. The anonymous referees commissioned by OUP have been helpful and constructive through the different stages of the life of this volume, and have given us much food for thought. We ought to emphasize, however that none of these should be saddled with responsibility for the text that has resulted. Finally, we are indebted to the patience and hard work of the editorial staff at OUP who have worked on this project, particularly Angela Griffin, Sue Dempsey Ruth Anderson, and Nicola Rainbow.

Outline Contents

Contents

5 Nationalism   **257**

6 Feminism   **293**

Introduction

This volume brings together writings on the concept of ideology, statements which represent the principal ideological traditions, and reflections on possible futures for political ideology. Its purpose is to give the reader an understanding of debates about the concept, and a sense of the diverse, complex, and contested character of ideologies.

Both the concept of ideology and particular ideological terms are part of the common furniture of political discourse and argument. Politicians proudly announce their ideological convictions, or (in a different mood) condemn their opponents as merely ideological. Similarly, we may identify ourselves through one of the ideological traditions as a liberal, a conservative, a socialist, a feminist, or fascist. At the same time, the delusions of those who are unfortunate enough to disagree with us can be explained by reference to their soppy liberalism, the forces of conservatism, and so on.

Behind the divisions in everyday usage lies a sense that modern politics is the politics of an 'age of ideologies'. Ideologies and ideological conflict have profoundly shaped and reflected the turbulence, horror, and exhilaration of social and political change in the nineteenth and twentieth centuries. Indeed, the term 'ideology' was coined by Antoine Destutt de Tracy in revolutionary France at the same time as another momentous piece of political language emerged, the split between 'left' and 'right' (terms that originally referred to seating arrangements in the revolutionary assembly). Over the course of the nineteenth century, liberalism, socialism, and conservatism crystallized as crucial terms for understanding conflicting political loyalties and commitments. Indeed, one marker of this is the appearance of textbooks on these ideologies. At the beginning of the twentieth century, the British Home University Library commissioned a series of books, each covering one of these: there is an excerpt from L. T. Hobhouse's classic and influential statement *Liberalism* below [Reading 17]. At the same time, doctrines such as feminism, anarchism, and nationalism challenged these mainstream traditions from their different directions. The sense that modern politics was ideological politics intensified and was cemented by the emergence of the 'totalitarian' doctrines of fascism and communism between the world wars. After the Second World War, revulsion at where ideological politics was thought to lead, together with a sense that contemporary capitalist society was robust and flexible enough to heal the split between left and right, led to claims that ideology could finally and happily be laid to rest. Yet the rate of ideological production in the second half of the twentieth century hardly slowed, with revived forms of feminism and nationalism, more novel ideological positions such as ecologism emerging, together with more intense conflict along the traditional ideological borders. Recent experiences, above all the collapse of Soviet communism, have led to a renewed sense for some that the age of ideologies has finally ground to a halt. Yet whether what we are witnessing is the end of ideology or the realignment of ideological beliefs and commitments is hotly contested.

The concept of ideology itself was transformed as a part of this history. While de Tracy held out hopes that 'ideology' would be a science of ideas, which would help societies to put their beliefs on a firm and rational footing, the concept came to mean the opposite of clarity about ideas. Ideology became a term associated with dogma and the manipulation of belief. This was particularly so for those mid-twentieth century authors who saw in the violent and authoritarian politics of fascism, Nazism and communism a distinctively ideological component: the claim on the part of a privileged leadership or party to be a repository for political truth, which served to facilitate and justify the political extremism of these regimes. More generally, for many social scientists the salience of political ideologies in modern politics could be explained (or explained away) as the product of deeper structural transformations in modern societies, such as the traumas of industrialization and urbanization. Once these processes had reached fruition, the implication went, and ideology could safely disappear from the political scene. At the same time, the quintessential 'ideology' for this perspective, Marxism, could lay claim to having given ideology its specifically political content, with another, but also negative, meaning: the Marxist view of ideology as false consciousness sees it as offering distorted, illusory images that obfuscate hidden social realities and constitute the projected aspirations, and frustrations, of oppressed social classes. In a further twist there were those, such as the unlikely trio of Vladimir Ilyich Lenin, Antonio Gramsci, and Margaret Thatcher, who viewed ideology as an unavoidable feature of the political landscape, and who insisted on the need for the clear and self-conscious formulation of their own ideology in order to seize the beliefs and imaginations of their audiences and rout the competing ideological beliefs of opponents. On one side, then, there are those who hold that ideology is a form of distorted and mistaken belief which we would do well to be rid of, and, on the other side, there are those who view ideology as a part of political life that cannot be eliminated— and cutting across and within *each* of those sides, there is profound ideological conflict. For the former perspective, the prospect of an *end* to ideology is to be welcomed, since ideology is not only a pernicious but also a contingent and remediable feature of social and political life. For the latter perspective, the end of ideology is an incoherent idea, conceivable only, perhaps, with the disappearance of politics itself.

In a moment of ideological shift and uncertainty, it seems timely to gather together these readings on political ideology and to reflect on how useful or powerful the concept of political ideology and the particular ideologies are in helping us to understand politics. The concept of ideology and the political significance of the concept have been fiercely contested since its inception. The study of ideologies, no less than the ideologies themselves, takes many forms and is characterized by bitter disagreement from those involved. In particular, scholars of ideology are torn between different conceptualizations of ideology, different approaches to studying it, and different judgements of the significance of ideology for social and political thought: different views, we may say, of *what* ideology is, *how* it should be studied, and *why* it should be studied. To some degree, it is a concern of this volume to bring out these differences over what ideology is, how to study it, and why it is significant. In particular these are central concerns of Chapter 1, which gathers together and introduces key readings on the concept of ideology, and Chapter 11, which looks at some of the claims that ideology has 'ended', or that it is about to. It is not our intention to be too directive about how to navigate these thickets of controversy. However, in this introduction we want to offer a general orientation to the reader, spelling out some of our commitments in selecting and organizing the readings in this book in the way that we have, and offering up a conceptual outline of political ideology, and raising some of the central themes and concerns in what follows.

A glance down the contents page should raise some questions and suspicions in the mind of a reader. Unlike biology and sociology, ideology is not a branch of study but an object of study—and, for its students, part of the fabric of the social and political world. This collection contains writings representing liberalism, conservatism, socialism, nationalism, feminism, ecologism, anarchism, and fascism, as well as some writings that suggest new ideological directions. So a first question is: what do we mean by 'political ideology', and what ties such differing currents of thought together as 'political ideologies'? It is not satisfying just to notice that these categories (along with masochism, alcoholism, and atomism) are all labelled with words that end in '-ism'. By a political ideology is usually meant something more than merely an idea about politics. The excerpts below discuss or invoke a huge array of ideas, including the state, political parties, liberty, equality, rights, democracy, property, race, the nation, sex, political economy, nature, globalization, culture, gender, and so on. But this is not a book principally about those ideas but about what various ideologies *make of* them, that is, the different ways in which these ideas are fleshed out and given specific interpretations within the structures of particular ideologies. One way of putting this is that these concepts are 'essentially contested': that is, the particular meanings that one takes these concepts to have depends on one's broader commitments about politics, human nature, and society. For example, democracy may refer to a people's democracy dominated by the workers, to a national democracy dominated by the nation, to a pluralist democracy in which different social groups have a say in political decisions, to an elitist democracy in which popular involvement is minimal, and so on. The nation may refer to a group sharing racial or ethnic characteristics, cultural characteristics such as a language, common membership of the same state, or some other feature. For proponents of one definition, the others misuse the concept or offer up a bogus usage. What determines the specific content that one gives to a concept such as democracy or the nation, then, depends on a wider range of political commitments. Ideologies may be understood then as frameworks for interpreting these concepts, reflecting different basic commitments on the part of those who hold them.

It is also usual to distinguish an ideology from a theory or philosophy of politics. The latter are generally seen as possessing a logical or deductive structure, which attempts to achieve a maximal degree of clarity among different elements in it, while ideologies are closer to Henry James's characterization of the Victorian novel—'loose baggy monsters', which do not aspire to clarity and logical consistency in the same way that a theory does. Indeed, as a genre, ideology takes on a heterogeneous range of guises, not only in formal treatises but also in manifestos, political speeches, public documents, novels, poems, and autobiographies. We have representatives of each of these in our text below, although we have erred on the side of more formal statements. A technically more ambitious guide to political ideologies than this one could plausibly include pieces of music, film, photography, architecture, painting, posters, sculpture, and so on. We want now to turn to some more positive, but still quite general, observations about the structure and content of political ideologies, as they are understood here.

We can understand a political ideology as possessing some general structural or syntactic features. First, an ideology offers an account of human society and history. This offers an explanation of social and political phenomena: for example, why is there poverty or war?

A conservative may explain these by reference to unchanging features of the human condition (we are all sinners or fallible and self-seeking creatures who are bound to inflict misery on one another) while a socialist might explain these in terms of alterable features of the social and political world, such as private ownership of the economy, and the lack of democratic control of the state. A fascist may have her own explanation, in terms of racial mixing and alien conspiracies. This is not to say that there is an ideologically neutral agenda of questions or problems for which different ideologies give different explanations. Ideologies not only reflect but also in part intellectually construct the phenomena that they then account for: they offer a language in which experiences and phenomena can be articulated, as well as a language of explanation. So a nationalist may view a nation's failure to have its own state as a profound problem, a conservative may perceive a crisis of social order, an ecologist a problem with the human use of non-human natural resources, or a feminist a problem of gender inequality, each of which requires explanation using the terms offered by the ideological tradition, where a liberal may see none of these as phenomena that require explanation; indeed, he or she may not register these as phenomena at all.

Second, ideologies offer an evaluative perspective on existing social and political phenomena. A fascist may see war as a healthy opportunity for citizens to discover their national identity and loyalty to the state, while a liberal may see it as a retrograde and regrettable sign that properly cosmopolitan and rational principles of international relations have not yet been implemented. Different ideologies tend to offer different criteria for evaluating the social phenomena that they identify. For example, both some liberals and socialists identify, account for, and bemoan the inequality in capitalist-worker relations. Liberals, however, tend to emphasize their deleterious impact on freedom of individual workers, while socialists may appeal to the importance of equality in social relations or the collective good of the working classes (compare for example John Stuart Mill [Reading 15], T. H. Green [Reading 16], Karl Marx [Reading 41], Georges Sorel [Reading 42], and Alex Callinicos [Reading 51]).

Third, ideologies have an expressive dimension, offering a sense of identity to individuals and groups. Ideological commitments provide a sense of where a person belongs, how she relates to others, and who her friends and enemies are. Political identities that ideologies may render central include that of being a worker for socialists, a woman (or man) for feminists, as a member of the nation for a nationalist, or part of the non-human natural world for ecologists. In this respect, ideology offers not only a cerebral but an emotional appeal to its audience to view themselves and act as a member of a particular collectivity, nation, identity, or tradition with the loyalties and obligations of a member of that group (for different perspectives on this theme see the excerpts from Louis Althusser [Reading 4], Giovanni Sartori [Reading 5], Clifford Geertz [Reading 6], Kenneth Minogue [Reading 7], and Slavoj Žižek [Reading 9]).

Fourth, ideological writings tend to offer or to imply a view of political agency, although this may be very inchoate. This may advise doing very little, as in some quietist forms of conservatism. Or it may urge reform or radical action, to promote individual rights, rectify class or gender inequality, establish political self-determination for the nation, or defend the natural environment.

As the readings excerpted below bring out, ideologies are internally pluralistic, contested, complex, and overlapping. They are pluralistic in the sense that the identity of the ideology does not consist of a single set of consistent beliefs or doctrines. A single ideological tradition may contain diverse and incompatible elements, along all four of the dimensions of account, evaluation, identity, and agency. Nationalists agree that the nation is important, but disagree about what the nation is and why, about which groups count as nations, and about what should follow from this in legal and political terms. (Compare, for example, the excerpts from John Stuart Mill [Reading 55], Heinrich von Treitschke [Reading 56], and Marcus Garvey [Reading 59] in Chapter 5.) This is accompanied by internal differences in rhetoric, genre, and language, in the way that ideologies are expressed. Ideologies are contested in the sense that this pluralism gives rise to active disagreements within ideological traditions about their content and character. For example, from the second half of the nineteenth century, liberals notoriously came to disagree about the appropriate scope of state intervention in economic relationships (see the excerpts from Mill [Reading 15], Green [Reading 16], Hobhouse [Reading 17], John Dewey [Reading 18], and J. M. Keynes [Reading 21]). Green theorists disagree over whether their values are rooted in a 'deep' account of the centrality of non-human nature or a 'shallower' view of the natural world as valuable as a necessary condition for human life and flourishing (see the excerpts from Arne Naess [Reading 75] and Murray Bookchin [Reading 76]). It should be noted that for some scholars of ideology who identify with a fixed set of dogmatically held principles, to view ideologies as not only permitting internal disagreement and disharmony but as actually being constituted as the ideologies that they are by these phenomena, may be considered incoherent (see, for example, the excerpts from Sartori [Reading 5] and Minogue [Reading 7]). For others, however, this dissonance is a defining mark of ideological discourse (see the excerpts from Michael Freeden [Reading 8] and Slavoj Žižek [Reading 9]).

Ideologies are complex in that there is not a single simple set of concepts or claims at the core of each ideology. In an influential recent study, Michael Freeden brings out this feature of political ideologies by arguing for attention to what he calls the morphology of ideologies, that is the study of their form and structure (for an excerpt from Freeden's book, see Reading 8). Political ideologies, he argues, are made up of concepts, some of which lie at the core of the ideology, and others at the periphery. The study of ideologies must examine the ways in which ideologies are structured by the relationship among these concepts. Liberalism, for example, has liberty as a core concept, while the concepts of democracy and equality are closely related concepts 'adjacent' to the core, and the concept of the nation is located at the periphery of the ideology. Internal disagreements within an ideological tradition, of the sort that go to make up a tradition's pluralism, in part consist of disagreements about the relationships among these concepts.

Finally, political ideologies are not sealed boxes, each with its own set of concepts and concerns, but overlapping, porous, and interactive. The same concept may be important in different ways for different ideological traditions and be vested with a different meaning by them: for example, as we have already seen, nationalism may come with liberal or conservative inflections, and liberals may share concerns with socialists. Some overlaps or amalgams seem more natural than others: for example, liberal feminism as an ideological category (see the excerpts from Mill [Reading 63] and Susan Moller Okin [Reading 69]) trips off the tongue more readily than socialist conservatism: but even in the latter case, we can see areas of shared concern among some conservatives and some socialists, in scepticism about the free market and individualism and a concern for community, for example (and compare the excerpt from Anthony Giddens [Reading 101]).

These observations about the structure and content of political ideologies should not detract from the need to see them as historical products. Ideologies exist both in time and space. For example, liberalism changes in the course of the nineteenth century in Britain, and these changes in part reflect the specific problems and dilemmas for liberal thought posed by this changing society and culture. Liberalism also takes different forms in different national contexts (in Germany and in the United States of America, for example), each with its own distinct background of legal, social, and political forces and institutions with which liberal thought has to grapple. This is probably the most challenging source of variety for this book to do justice to, but we have tried to include both a range of different perspectives across space and time, and to draw attention to the specific problems and contexts lying behind particular ideological texts in the editorial material here.

These general statements, and the approach that we take here, do not rule the thought that some ideological beliefs may exhibit the negative features ascribed to them by those traditions of commentary that have held ideology to be blind prejudice, authoritarian manipulation, or false consciousness. Nor do they exclude the project of explaining away some ideological beliefs in terms of the traumas of class society, or of social and economic modernization. Yet this conception of ideology does suggest that political ideologies are not most usefully seen merely as one of these forms of distorted belief or as epiphenomena of deeper lying structural forces. Ideologies and ideological conflict reflect the various ways in which we can flesh out and give particular content to our political ideas, and persistent disagreement about how we should account for social, political, and economic life, how we should evaluate these phenomena, who we are and where our deepest loyalties lie, and what action we should take. This also gives us a reason grounded in the concept of ideology for scepticism about claims that ideology is going to end. For, given the open-ended, vague, and contestable character of the concepts that political ideologies flesh out with more specific meanings, ideological conflict will not disappear so long as there is scope for systematic differences in interpretation of political concepts. In this light, we may see the dream of the end of ideology, like the dream of the end of politics which was shared by Henri Saint-Simon [see Reading 38] and Marx, as constituting an intelligible and all-too-human attempt to impose a final settlement on disagreement along these four dimensions, one which tries its best to mask its own ideological content and character. The prospects for an end to ideologies in the twenty-first century seem as dim and ill-conceived as they were in the twentieth. The ideological shifts and realignments of contemporary politics only make the study of political ideologies and their past all the more important.

1   The concept of ideology

Introduction

The term 'ideology' was born in revolutionary France, at the end of the eighteenth century. Its originator, Antoine Destutt de Tracy (1754–1836), saw the need for a 'Newton of the science of thought', who could set the human understanding of ideas on a scientific footing. He aimed to show how simple physical sensations formed the building blocks for all ideas. As he developed this project in his *Eléments d'Idéologie*, written between 1801 and 1815, Tracy thought that this reconstruction of the origin of ideas could be the basis of a rational and just society. Briefly fêted by Napoleon, Tracy fell out of favour as the Emperor began to appreciate the virtues of tradition and established religion as a reliable source of social order. In failing to see the merits of tradition, Napoleon opined, the ideologues created a hazy metaphysics of no benefit to anyone.

The concept of ideology was invested with a specifically political meaning by Karl Marx and Friedrich Engels, in *The German Ideology* [Reading 1]. The originator of 'ideology', in other words, has his own term turned against him, as Marx and Engels, like Napoleon, used the term in a pejorative sense to refer to a realm of cloudy metaphysical falsehood. Indeed, Tracy himself was attacked both in the latter work and in Marx's *Capital* as a 'bourgeois doctrinaire', which may account for why Marx picks up this term and uses it in this critical fashion. The principal target of *The German Ideology*, however, is German idealist philosophy. Idealists such as the immensely influential G. W. F. Hegel (1770–1831), Marx and Engels argue, wrongly believe that the realm of consciousness can be studied independently of social relations and view history as primarily a matter of the unfolding logic of ideas. But this is not just a mistake, in their view. What makes this error specifically *ideological* is the particular relationship of the privilege that the idealists give to ideas over the *real* driving forces in human history. This reality consists in the processes of struggle between different economic classes in society over the ownership and control of the way material goods are produced. The idealists invert the true order of things, Marx and Engels think, since they picture ideas as fundamental to social and political life rather than as they really are, offshoots of underlying economic relationships. The topsy-turvy vision of the world is ascribed to the idealists by Marx from some of his earliest writing, such as the *Economic and Philosophical Manuscripts* (1844), onwards. Ideology exists in a perverse but intelligible relationship to the reality of class struggle, as the comparison of ideology to the 'camera obscura' in the excerpted passage suggests. A camera obscura reflects an upside-down image of what it points toward. So, while the vision of reality depicted in ideology is inaccurate, it corresponds to, and offers a definite image of, something in the real world. It follows that we can *decode* ideology—turn the picture that it offers the right way up—in order to find out about the real world of conflicting material interests, and that we can use our knowledge of the real world of conflict among social classes to work out why an ideology takes the particular form that it does.

Ideology not only offers a systematically misleading image of social reality, it also has a distinctive function, by misrepresenting the world in a particular way. Ideology papers over the real conflicts in society, making what is artificial and coerced appear natural and free. For example, religion presents earthly suffering as an inevitable way station on the path to heavenly reward. Alternatively, capitalist ideology presents a contract of employment as an agreement between two parties, each of whom freely accepts the terms offered. But the first of these conceals the reality that earthly suffering is the result of particular relationships of domination and exploitation, not an inevitable feature of the human condition, and the second masks the fact that the power of the individual employer to set the terms of the contract is far greater than that of the employee. As these examples suggest, for Marx and Engels ideology is instrumental in serving the interests of the ruling class, that is, of the particular group who exercises control over the production of goods in a society. 'The ideas of the ruling class are in every epoch the ruling ideas', since those who control economic production and distribution can also control the production and distribution of ideas. In this way the notion of ideology is extended by Marx and Marxism well beyond the attack on the specific intellectual system of idealism to encompass a whole panoply of ideas and practices that explain and justify class society to itself. For example, in *The Manifesto of the Communist Party*, Marx and Engels cast their net much more widely so that law, morality, and religion are described as 'so many bourgeois prejudices, behind which there lurk just as many bourgeois interests'. Particularly in their more directly political writings, Marx and Engels view ideology as produced on demand by paid mouthpieces of the bourgeoisie, the ruling class in modern capitalist societies, deliberately to cover up the reality of class war and exploitation. But they also allow (as the excerpt here suggests) that ideology need not be produced in this way, and that it may constitute an *unintentional* apologia for the status quo. Indeed, Engels later coined an influential phrase, 'false consciousness', to sum up the state of mind of ideology's producers. The latter are not cynical manipulators of ideas but unaware of the real driving forces and purposes behind their ideological production, for this view. As an instrument of class rule, ideology not only offers a distorted reflection of the reality of class conflict, it also plays an active role in *shaping* that reality. The law of contract offers not just a misleading image of the true relations between workers and employers, but is an institution or practice that controls their lives. In contrast to the mystifications of ideology, the materialist science of society reveals the truth, unmasking the ideological fictions that support the existing social order. Once this order is overthrown, and society is classless, the need for ideology evaporates. For Marx and for orthodox Marxism from the period after his death up to the First World War, just as for some twentieth century writers who diagnosed an 'end of ideology' (see the readings in Chapter 11), ideology will fade away once it ceases to serve a useful social purpose.

Karl Mannheim's *Ideology and Utopia* was published in 1929, in the political turmoil of the Weimar Republic [Reading 2]. For Mannheim, the critical view of ideology embodied in the Marxist approach is insufficiently self-conscious. He agreed with Marx that we can only understand ideas against the background of the society that gives birth to them. However, this 'sociology of knowledge' should not be, as he thinks it is in Marxism, only part of the intellectual armament of a particular political position, selectively used to undermine rivals. Rather, it has to be ruthlessly applied to all systems of thought, including Marxism itself, revealing the partial and limited character of the insights that each system offers. Mannheim distinguishes what he calls 'particular' and 'total' conceptions of ideology. We use a 'particular' conception when we aim to show how calculated bias or self-deception plays a role in the formation of beliefs: I can unmask the ideological elements in your thinking by demonstrating how the errors and nonsense that you spout are systematically related to (say) your economic interests. But this enterprise is limited to revealing the falsehood of particular beliefs. A 'total' conception of ideology is employed in a more subtle and ambitious project, of teasing out the presuppositions behind whole worldviews and showing how they are shaped by underlying social relationships. For Mannheim, Marxism tangles up the particular and total conceptions. It wants to show how capitalist ideology is the product of agents of the bourgeoisie and serves this group's interests. Yet it also tries to show how the capitalist view of the world (for example, the belief that employment relations are freely contracted to) reflects the reality of underlying social relationships.

The aim of Mannheim's sociology of knowledge is the 'total' project of grasping systems of ideas in their particular historical and social contexts, bringing out how those contexts give the ideas their meaning. To see all thought as historically conditioned in this way raises the spectre of relativism. If all thought is linked to the particular historical position of the thinker, there seems to be no standpoint from which a person can claim that her beliefs have objective or universal standing: for example, if the ideas of bourgeois political economy reflect the social circumstances of capitalism, then in the same way so do those of socialist political economy. But then this historical conditionality holds true for Mannheim's own beliefs about the sociology of knowledge. Mannheim tries to address this by appealing to the notion of a 'free' intelligentsia, the members of which are capable of compensating for the one-sidedness of any one system of thought by critically comparing it to its rivals, and so arriving at a kind of provisional objectivity: this is what he calls 'relationism' in the excerpt reproduced here. Both the persuasiveness of this escape route from relativism and the role assigned to intellectuals have been controversial themes. Perhaps more of concern for us here is whether by folding the notion of ideology into that of the sociology of knowledge Mannheim deprives the concept of ideology of any specific meaning: the ideological just corresponds to the whole realm of socially determined belief.

The Italian revolutionary Antonio Gramsci also grappled with the ambiguities of the Marxist conception of ideology, although he was concerned to regenerate rather than displace it [Reading 3]. The central category in Gramsci's thinking is not ideology but hegemony. By this, he means whatever social tools win the consent of the population (although he sometimes uses it to refer to both consent and coercion—whatever keeps people in line). Gramsci generally associates hegemony, especially ideological hegemony, with the realm of what he calls civil society, the sphere of non-state activity by organizations and individuals, which includes, for example, such entities as the media, churches, trade unions, and political parties. These serve to tie people to the state, and hence to capitalist society, by winning and moulding our consent. Ideology, then, is one aspect of a wider institutional phenomenon. The robustness of civil society, and hence of bourgeois hegemony, in Western Europe, he argued, helped to explain why the revolution in Russia was successful in 1917, while comparable upheavals in Germany and Italy failed.

As the excerpt below brings out, Gramsci in part wanted to redeem ideology from the predominantly negative view of it within the Marxist tradition. Ideology was necessary to organize 'human masses' and to help them acquire consciousness of their position in the class struggle. In believing that socialism required ideology, Gramsci could appeal to some distinguished support. In some texts, such as the *Preface to Contribution to a Critique of Political Economy* (1859), Marx himself seemed to allow that possibility. More importantly, V. I. Lenin in his famous pamphlet *What is to Be Done?* [Reading 46] argued for the necessity of an influential socialist ideology in order to protect the working classes from its bourgeois rival, which would otherwise infiltrate them via such mechanisms as trade unions. This Leninist point of view became orthodoxy in Marxist circles after the First World War, and Gramsci's reflections on hegemony should be seen in this light. For Gramsci, 'organic' intellectuals could help the working classes arrive at a clearer and more revolutionary picture of their place in society by building on and critically engaging with their 'common sense' understanding of the world. Where Mannheim wished to detach the intelligentsia from specific political positions, for Gramsci the only valid conception of intellectual life was both emphatically political and engaged in a tense and critical dialogue with forms of popular thought.

The apparent usefulness of the concept of ideology in explaining the difficulties experienced by the Marxist revolutionary project within the industrial heartlands of the West led to increasingly nuanced elaborations of the concept. While borrowing much from Gramsci's conception of hegemony, Louis Althusser [Reading 4] drew a much sharper line between science (by which he principally meant Marxist theory) and ideology. For Althusser, ideology was not identified with consciousness or products of the mind, but itself had a material existence in what he called the 'ideological state apparatus'. Like Gramsci's domain of hegemony-producing civil society, this includes such institutions as churches, trade unions, and schools. As the second of the two excerpts brings out, ideology plays a role in recruiting people as 'subjects', giving them a sense of their own identity. This is what he calls 'interpellating', and is described through the mini-drama of hailing a person. Here we should recall the view of ideology in *The German Ideology* as papering over the structural conflicts of real social life. In Althusser's view, this is the function of ideology at an individual level. An ideology gives us what he variously calls an 'imaginary', 'lived', or 'spontaneous' sense of ourselves as subjects. In the case of capitalist ideology, it makes us feel that we are individuals, each of us valuable, and free to choose or reject contractual relations. These feelings correspond to no facts: the reality is that I am embedded in a set of social structures and there is no choosing self who can step back from or get behind these structures. In an important sense for Althusser ideology is not in competition with theory or science, as it is for Marx and Engels in *The German Ideology*. For the function of ideology is not to represent the world, but to give people a sense of identity. Influenced by psychoanalysis—another theory that suggests our 'lived' or subjectively experienced sense of ourselves sits precariously on top of internal conflicts—Althusser came to see ideology as indispensable or 'eternal'. Indeed, he thought that it was a feature of a particular ideological outlook to imagine a society without ideology: that is, without a means of making people into subjects. This will be just as necessary in a communist society as in any predecessor, although in a communist society ideology would no longer perform the function of aiding the acceptance of a class-divided society. Although his conception of ideology proved influential, neither Althusser's confidence that in Marxism there exists a science of society on a superior footing to the flotsam of the rest of intellectual life nor his bleak structural determinism has worn very well.

From the perspective of much mainstream social and political science in the period after the Second World War, attempts such as Gramsci's and Althusser's to develop the Marxist model were themselves to be viewed as ideological. This was so not only in the sense that these analyses were 'value-laden', in the current jargon, flowing out of and representing a particular political position, but also in that the position that they represented was held to be the ideology *par excellence*. By contrast, it was felt that political inquiry needed to rid itself of particular partisan commitments in order to offer a 'value-free', and putatively scientific, way of explaining political phenomena. So the concept of ideology had to be shorn of evaluative connotations, either positive or negative, in order to take its place in the political scientist's analytical toolbox.

In one influential example, the article 'Politics, Ideology and Belief Systems', part of which is excerpted here [Reading 5], Giovanni Sartori argues for the usefulness of ideology as an explanatory concept. Ideological belief systems can be distinguished from pragmatic belief systems, he proposes. Pragmatic belief systems are practically-minded and open to revision in the light of experience, where ideological belief systems privilege the authority of theory over practice and are resistant to revision in the light of experience. They are also complex, possess a 'quasi-logical structure', and carry a strong emotional charge for adherents. These features make ideologies highly constraining, directing holders toward some social goals rather than others, but also mean that they are characteristically held by elites, since only the few can absorb their complexity, structure, and theoretical character. The masses, by contrast, tend to have simpler, more malleable and less sophisticated belief systems. Ideologies therefore are not only 'self-constraining' for the elites who have them but other-constraining (what Sartori called 'hetero-constraining') for the masses who 'need guidance', as he put it. Ideologies serve as a crucial tool of mass mobilization on this view. It is worth noting that, while officially value-free, this conception of ideology as rationalistic, close-minded, manipulative, etc., is laden with negative connotations, and that the examples of ideology in Sartori's article are Marxism, socialism, communism, and egalitarianism. By contrast, liberalism is acquitted of the charge of being an ideology. Ostensibly an attempt to come up with a value-free concept of ideology, Sartori's article expresses a sceptical attitude toward ideology as inherently totalitarian and potentially dispensable. This sceptical attitude also expressed the so-called 'end-of-ideology' thesis in the same period (see Chapter 11, especially Reading 99).

The anthropologist Clifford Geertz put forward his conception of ideology as part of an ambitious programme of social inquiry. In particular, he was concerned to establish the centrality of culture as a system of symbols to social understanding. For Geertz, ideologies are cultural maps, sets of symbols that help to render otherwise incomprehensible social situations meaningful for those experiencing them [Reading 6]. Ideologies are born and come into conflict where societies are in the throes of change, from revolutionary France to post-colonial states such as Indonesia and Morocco. No longer able to rely on spontaneous responses or on established images of social order, people in periods of social disruption require a way of orienting themselves to their social world that is at once independent of tradition (including myth and religion) but able to mobilize some of the collective beliefs and sentiments that tradition shaped and secured. Political leaders, and aspirant political leaders, invent national traditions and promote symbols that unify their countries. Understanding the meaning of these symbols often requires a complex process of interpretation, Geertz argues, akin to the analysis of a literary text. For Geertz, as for Althusser, ideology is a way in which an underlying functional problem of social dissonance is managed by and for people, but the causes of this dissonance are thought to lie in secularization and the breakdown of traditional order rather than in class conflict. As the end of this excerpt suggests, Geertz views ideology both as an indispensable component of modern political life, and also as subject to criticism from non-ideological perspectives.

A different version of the pejorative conception of ideology makes its presence felt in Kenneth Minogue's reflections on ideology after the collapse of communism [Reading 7]. For Minogue, an acolyte of the British political philosopher Michael Oakeshott, ideological think- ing is an inherent tendency of modern political thought. Ideology is characterized, first, by a claim to insight or revelation of total knowledge superior to all competitors, which makes it akin to religion. Second, like religion, it aims not just to make some empirical claims about the world but to define the criteria used to distinguish true and false claims. Third, it is the insight of a privileged group, elite, or party, which therefore has a 'tutorial' relationship to the mass of people sunk in false consciousness, that is, a relationship grounded in the pretensions of this group to superior insight. Fourth, ideologies tend to ride roughshod over the complexity of modern pluralistic societies. In modern liberal democratic states, Minogue argues, each person is, on the one hand, a citizen, and, on the other, a member of civil society, where civil society consists of an array of different attachments ('worker, Catholic, female, mother, Black, football supporter, etc. etc.'). It is characteristic of ideologies that they demand that their adherents privilege one component of their identities—as a worker, a woman, a member of a particular nationality or race—at the expense of the others, and that this privileged identity is made the basis of political organization. Once again, Marxism, at least in its Leninist form, is the exemplary ideology here, although Minogue also alludes to the 'ambitions of Islamic fundamentalism'. These four features of political ideology distinguish it from the more sober notion of a political doctrine. Doctrines such as feminism can take their place in the ordinary give and take of political discussion, Minogue suggests, provided that they do not attempt to adopt the authoritative standpoint of ideologies.

The authors of the final two extracts in different ways combine a sense that understanding ideology is essential to grasping the workings of power in social and political life, a belief that this requires the interpretation of cultural objects and practices, and a commitment to the indispensability of ideology. Michael Freeden is concerned to free ideology of the negative connotations that are attached to it by much of Marxism, on the one hand, and by writers such as Sartori or Minogue, on the other. The study of political ideology, he argues, is a distinctive way of examining political ideas that can be set apart from political philosophy and the history of political thought [Reading 8]. He follows Geertz in viewing political ideologies as symbolic and cognitive maps through which individuals and groups order their experience and which require interpretation, and, like Sartori, views ideologies as distinguished by peculiar internal structural features. According to Freeden's 'morphological' analysis, ideologies are complex bundles of political concepts arranged into discernible patterns, whose differing arrange- ments distinguish ideologies from one another. Freeden argues that ideologies characteristic- ally aim to 'decontest' the meanings of political concepts. By this he means that particular political concepts tend to be ambiguous and subject to deep squabbles among political philosophers about how properly to understand them. Does liberty consist of the absence of constraint or possession of the actual power to do what I want? Is equality a matter of equality of opportunity or of outcome? Ideologies present themselves as ways of establishing clarity and certainty about a particular group of concepts. So, for example, liberals share a concern with the individual, liberty, reason, and progress, but offer different 'decontestations' of these from, say, socialists. Ideologies compete with one another over which set of concepts is the most powerful for understanding society, and with one another over which meaning of a concept should prevail. There are family quarrels too within ideologies over the precise way to decontest a concept: so, for example, some liberals argue that respect for individual liberty requires an entrenched set of property rights, where others argue that it does not.

Slajov Žižek draws on Althusser to argue that ideology is not an illusion that masks the real state of things [Reading 9]. Rather, while ideologies present a necessary illusion, there is no reality behind this illusion with which to contrast it. Instead, ideology is characterized by the attempt to impose harmony over the inevitable trauma and dislocation of social life. Ideology creates a reality for us by masking a traumatic social division that cannot be symbolized, which he calls, following the French psychoanalyst Jacques Lacan, 'the real'. A sort of panic in the face of this unsymbolizable 'real' produces hostile fantasies that characterize ideological thought. For example, a society's inability to achieve its full identity as a harmonious community is projected in Fascist thought on to the figure of the 'Jew' who is seen as disrupting the integrity of the community. From this perspective, as for Freeden's, the project of 'decontestation', which attempts to fix a particular meaning on a term that is subject to multiple and conflicting interpretations ('being a Jew', 'British', 'one of us'), is the exemplary ideological move, but one doomed to failure in the face of the recalcitrance of the real.

FURTHER READING

Lucid starting points include Michael Freeden, *Ideology: A Very Short Introduction* (Oxford University Press, 2003) and David McLellan, *Ideology* (Open University Press, 1986). Other introductory volumes include Jorge Larrain, *The Concept of Ideology* (Hutchinson, 1979), Raymond Boudon, *The Analysis of Ideology* (Polity Press, 1989), Michele Barret, *The Politics of Truth* (Polity Press, 1991), and Terry Eagleton, *Ideology: An Introduction* (Verso, 1991). Raymond Geuss, *The Idea of a Critical Theory* (Cambridge University Press, 1981) and Michael Rosen, *On Voluntary Servitude: False Consciousness and the Theory of Ideology* (Polity Press, 1996) are important and accessible treatments of ideology as 'false consciousness'. Useful (but very different) anthologies of writings on the concept of ideology include David Apter (ed.) *Ideology and Discontent* (Free Press, 1964), Terry Eagleton (ed.) *Ideology* (Longman, 1993), and S. Žižek (ed.) *Mapping Ideology* (Verso, 1994).

1   **Karl Marx and Friedrich Engels, from *The German Ideology*,**
     in *Collected Works, vol. 5* (Lawrence and Wishart, 1976),
     pp. 35–7, 59–61

Karl Marx (1818–1883) was born into a middle class family in Trier in Germany and educated in Bonn and Berlin. A radical journalist, he became a communist from 1843, arguing for the central role of economic structure in understanding politics and history. In *The Manifesto of the Communist Party* (1848), which he wrote with Engels, he viewed history as a process of struggle among social classes, which would culminate in the triumph of working class and the abolition of capitalism. Exiled to London after the revolutions of 1848, he concentrated his intellectual efforts on political economy although only the first volume of his principal study *Capital* (1867) was published in his lifetime. He had a leading role in the International Working Men's Association, but only after his death did his theoretical ideas became central to working class parties in Europe. Marx was invoked in support of a range of dictatorial communist movements in Russia, China, and elsewhere in the twentieth century, usually with little regard for niceties of what Marx actually thought.

Friedrich Engels (1820–1895) was born into a wealthy family of factory owners in the Rhineland in Germany. He went to work for his family but was appalled at the factory conditions that he encountered. He collaborated with Marx on *The Holy Family* (1844), a scathing attack on German philosophy, and on subsequent works up to Marx's move to England. After Marx's death, he became the literary executor and interpreter of Marxism for the European Marxist political parties. *The German Ideology* was posthumously published in 1932.

The fact is, therefore, that definite individuals who are productively active in a definite way enter into these definite social and political relations. Empirical observation must in each separate instance bring out empirically, and without any mystification and speculation, the connection of the social and political structure with production. The social structure and the state are continually evolving out of the life-process of definite individuals, however, of these individuals, not as they may appear in their own or other people's imagination, but as they *actually* are, i.e., as they act, produce materially, and hence as they work under definite material limits, presuppositions and conditions independent of their will.

The production of ideas, of conceptions, of consciousness, is at first directly interwoven with the material activity and the material intercourse of men—the language of real life. Conceiving, thinking, the mental intercourse of men at this stage still appear as the direct efflux of their material behaviour. The same applies to mental production as expressed in the language of the politics, laws, morality, religion, metaphysics, etc., of a people. Men are the producers of their conceptions, ideas, etc., that is, real, active men, as they are conditioned by a definite development of their productive forces and of the intercourse corresponding to these, up to its furthest forms. Consciousness [*das Bewusstsein*] can never be anything else than conscious being [*das bewusste Sein*], and the being of men is their actual life-process. If in all ideology men and their relations appear upside-down as in a *camera obscura*, this phenomenon arises just as much from their historical life-process as the inversion of objects on the retina does from their physical life-process.

In direct contrast to German philosophy which descends from heaven to earth, here it is a matter of ascending from earth to heaven. That is to say, not of setting out from what men say, imagine, conceive, nor from men as narrated, thought of, imagined, conceived, in order to arrive at men in the flesh; but setting out from real, active men, and on the basis of their real life-process demonstrating the development of the ideological reflexes and echoes of this life-process. The phantoms formed in the brains of men are also, necessarily, sublimates of their material life-process, which is empirically verifiable and bound to material premises. Morality, religion, metaphysics, and all the rest of ideology as well as the forms of consciousness corresponding to these, thus no longer retain the semblance of independence. They have no history, no development; but men, developing their material production and their material intercourse, alter, along with this their actual world, also their thinking and the products of their thinking. It is not consciousness that determines life, but life that determines consciousness. For the first manner of approach the starting-point is consciousness taken as the living individual; for the second manner of approach, which conforms to real life, it is the real living individuals themselves, and consciousness is considered solely as *their* consciousness.

This manner of approach is not devoid of premises. It starts out from the real premises and does not abandon them for a moment. Its premises are men, not in any fantastic isolation and fixity, but in their actual, empirically perceptible process of development under definite conditions. As soon as this active life-process is described, history ceases to be a collection of dead facts, as it is with the empiricists (themselves still abstract), or an imagined activity of imagined subjects, as with the idealists.

Where speculation ends, where real life starts, there consequently begins real, positive science, the expounding of the practical activity, of the practical process of development of men. Empty phrases about consciousness end, and real knowledge has to take their place. When the reality is described, a self-sufficient philosophy [*die selbständige Philosophie*] loses its medium of existence. At the best its place can only be taken by a summing-up of the most general results, abstractions which are derived from the observation of the historical development of men. These abstractions in themselves, divorced from real history, have no value whatsoever. They can only serve to facilitate the arrangement of historical material, to indicate the sequence of its separate strata. But they by no means afford a recipe or schema, as does philosophy, for neatly trimming the epochs of history. On the contrary, the difficulties begin only when one sets about the examination and arrangement of the material—whether of a past epoch or of the present—and its actual presentation. The removal of these difficulties is governed by premises which certainly cannot be stated here, but which only the study of the actual life-process and the activity of the individuals of each epoch will make evident.

. . .

The ideas of the ruling class are in every epoch the ruling ideas: i.e., the class which is the ruling *material* force of society is at the same time its ruling *intellectual* force. The class which has the means of material production at its disposal, consequently also controls the means of mental production, so that the ideas of those who lack the means of mental production are on the whole subject to it. The ruling ideas are nothing more than the ideal expression of the dominant material relations, the dominant material relations grasped as ideas; hence of the relations which make the one class the ruling one, therefore, the ideas of its dominance. The individuals composing the ruling class possess among other things consciousness, and therefore think. Insofar, therefore, as they rule as a class and determine the extent and compass of an historical epoch, it is self-evident that they do this in its whole range, hence among other things rule also as thinkers, as producers of ideas, and regulate the production and distribution of the ideas of their age: thus their ideas are the ruling ideas of the epoch. For instance, in an age and in a country where royal power, aristocracy and bourgeoisie are contending for domination and where, therefore, domination is shared, the doctrine of the separation of powers proves to be the dominant idea and is expressed as an "eternal law".

The division of labour, which we already saw above . . . as one of the chief forces of history up till now, manifests itself also in the ruling class as the division of mental and material labour, so that inside this class one part appears as the thinkers of the class (its active, conceptive ideologists, who make the formation of the illusions of the class about itself their chief source of livelihood), while the others' attitude to these ideas and illusions is more passive and receptive, because they are in reality the active members of this class and have less time to make up illusions and ideas about themselves. Within this class this cleavage can even develop into a certain opposition and hostility between the two parts, but whenever a practical collision occurs in which the class itself is endangered they automatically vanish, in which case there also vanishes the appearance of the ruling ideas being not the ideas of the ruling class and having a power distinct from the power of this class. The existence of revolutionary ideas in a particular period presupposes the existence of a revolutionary class; about the premises of the latter sufficient has already been said above . . .

If now in considering the course of history we detach the ideas of the ruling class from the ruling class itself and attribute to them an independent existence, if we confine ourselves to saying that these or those ideas were dominant at a given time, without bothering ourselves about the conditions of production and the producers of these ideas, if we thus ignore the individuals and world conditions which are the source of the ideas, then we can say, for instance, that during the time the aristocracy was dominant, the concepts honour, loyalty, etc., were dominant, during the dominance of the bourgeoisie the concepts freedom, equality, etc. The ruling class itself on the whole imagines this to be so. This conception of history, which is common to all historians, particularly since the eighteenth century, will necessarily come up against the phenomenon that ever more abstract ideas hold sway, i.e., ideas which increasingly take on the form of universality. For each new class which puts itself in the place of one ruling before it is compelled, merely in order to carry through its aim, to present its interest as the common interest of all the members of society, that is, expressed in ideal form: it has to give its ideas the form of universality, and present them as the only rational, universally valid ones. The class making a revolution comes forward from the very start, if only because it is opposed to a *class*, not as a class but as the representative of the whole of society, as the whole mass of society confronting the one ruling class. It can do this because initially its interest really is as yet mostly connected with the common interest of all other non-ruling classes, because under the pressure of hitherto existing conditions its interest has not yet been able to develop as the particular interest of a particular class. Its victory, therefore, benefits also many individuals of other classes which are not winning a dominant position, but only insofar as it now enables these individuals to raise themselves into the ruling class. When the French bourgeoisie overthrew the rule of the aristocracy, it thereby made it possible for many proletarians to raise themselves above the proletariat, but only insofar as they became bourgeois. Every new class, therefore, achieves domination only on a broader basis than that of the class ruling previously; on the other hand the opposition of the non-ruling class to the new ruling class then develops all the more sharply and profoundly.

Both these things determine the fact that the struggle to be waged against this new ruling class, in its turn, has as its aim a more decisive and more radical negation of the previous conditions of society than all previous classes which sought to rule could have.

This whole appearance, that the rule of a certain class is only the rule of certain ideas, comes to a natural end, of course, as soon as class rule in general ceases to be the form in which society is organised, that is to say, as soon as it is no longer necessary to represent a particular interest as general or the "general interest" as ruling.

2   Karl Mannheim, from *Ideology and Utopia* (Routledge, 1936), pp. 69–74

Karl Mannheim (1893–1947) lived in Hungary, where he was a student of the great Hungarian Marxist Georg Lukacs, Germany and eventually England. *Ideology and Utopia*, his most influential work, was first published in German in 1929, with an English edition in 1936. Other work, including *Man and Society in an Age of Reconstruction* (1940), and *Diagnoses of Our Time* (1943) proved less influential, but his work on ideology and the sociology of knowledge remains an important point of reference for thinking in these areas.

At the present stage of our understanding it is hardly possible to avoid this general formulation of the total conception of ideology, according to which the thought of all parties in all epochs is of an ideological character. There is scarcely a single intellectual position, and Marxism furnishes no exception to this rule, which has not changed through history and which even in the present does not appear in many forms. Marxism, too, has taken on many diverse appearances. It should not be too difficult for a Marxist to recognize their social basis.

With the emergence of the general formulation of the total conception of ideology, the simple theory of ideology develops into the sociology of knowledge. What was once the intellectual armament of a party is transformed into a method of research in social and intellectual history generally. To begin with, a given social group discovers the "situational determination" *(Seinsge-bundenheit)* of its opponents' ideas. Subsequently the recognition of this fact is elaborated into an all-inclusive principle according to which the thought of every group is seen as arising out of its life conditions. Thus, it becomes the task of the sociological history of thought to analyse without regard for party biases all the factors in the actually existing social situation which may influence thought. This sociologically oriented history of ideas is destined to provide modern men with a revised view of the whole historical process.

It is clear, then, that in this connection the conception of ideology takes on a new meaning. Out of this meaning two alternative approaches to ideological investigation arise. The first is to confine oneself to showing everywhere the interrelationships between the intellectual point of view held and the social position occupied. This involves the renunciation of every intention to expose or unmask those views with which one is in disagreement.

In attempting to expose the views of another, one is forced to make one's own view appear infallible and absolute, which is a procedure altogether to be avoided if one is making a specifically non-evaluative investigation. The second possible approach is nevertheless to combine such a non-evaluative analysis with a definite epistemology. Viewed from the angle of this second approach there are two separate and distinct solutions to the problem of what constitutes reliable knowledge—the one solution may be termed *relationism*, and the other *relativism*.

Relativism is a product of the modern historical-sociological procedure which is based on the recognition that all historical thinking is bound up with the concrete position in life of the thinker *(Standortsgebundenheit des Denkers)*. But relativism combines this historical-sociological insight with an older theory of knowledge which was as yet unaware of the interplay between conditions of existence and modes of thought, and which modelled its knowledge after static prototypes such as might be exemplified by the proposition $2 \times 2 = 4$. This older type of thought, which regarded such examples as the model of all thought, was necessarily led to the rejection of all those forms of knowledge which were dependent upon the subjective standpoint and the social situation of the knower, and which were, hence, merely "relative". Relativism, then, owes its existence to the discrepancy between this newly-won insight into the actual processes of thought and a theory of knowledge which had not yet taken account of this new insight.

If we wish to emancipate ourselves from this relativism we must seek to understand with the aid of the sociology of knowledge that it is not epistemology in any absolute sense but rather a certain historically transitory type of epistemology which is in conflict with the type of thought oriented to the social situation. Actually, epistemology is as intimately enmeshed in the social process as is the totality of our thinking, and it will make progress to the extent that it can master the complications arising out of the changing structure of thought.

A modern theory of knowledge which takes account of the relational as distinct from the merely relative character of all historical knowledge must start with the assumption that there are spheres of thought in which it is impossible to conceive of absolute truth existing independently of the values and position of the subject and unrelated to the social context. Even a god could not formulate a proposition on historical subjects like $2 \times 2 = 4$, for what is intelligible in history can be formulated only with reference to problems and conceptual constructions which themselves arise in the flux of historical experience.

Once we recognize that all historical knowledge is relational knowledge, and can only be formulated with reference to the position of the observer, we are faced, once more, with the task of discriminating between what is true and what is false in such knowledge. The question then arises: which social standpoint *vis-à-vis* of history offers the best chance for reaching an optimum of truth? In any case, at this stage the vain hope of discovering truth in a form which is independent of an historically and socially determined set of meanings will have to be given up. The problem is by no means solved when we have arrived at this conclusion, but we are, at least, in a better position to state the actual problems which arise in a more unrestricted manner. In the following we have to distinguish two types of approach to ideological inquiry arising upon the level of the general-total conception of ideology: first, the approach characterized by freedom from value-judgments and, second, the epistemological and metaphysically oriented normative approach. For the time being we shall not raise the question of whether in the latter approach we are dealing with relativism or relationism.

The non-evaluative general total conception of ideology is to be found primarily in those historical investigations, where, provisionally and for the sake of the simplification of the problem, no judgments are pronounced as to the correctness of the ideas to be treated. This approach confines itself to discovering the relations between certain mental structures and the life-situations in which they exist. We must constantly ask ourselves how it comes about that a given type of social situation gives rise to a given interpretation. Thus the ideological element in human thought, viewed at this level, is always bound up with the existing life-situation of the thinker. According to this view human thought arises, and operates, not in a social vacuum but in a definite social milieu.

We need not regard it as a source of error that all thought is so rooted. Just as the individual who participates in a complex of vital social relations with other men thereby enjoys a chance of obtaining a more precise and penetrating insight into his fellows, so a given point of view and a given set of concepts, because they are bound up with and grow out of a certain social reality, offer, through intimate contact with this reality, a greater chance of revealing its meaning. (The example cited earlier showed that the proletarian-socialistic point of view was in a particularly favourable position to discover the ideological elements in its adversaries' thought.) The circumstance, however, that thought is bound by the social- and life-situation in which it arises creates handicaps as well as opportunities. It is clearly impossible to obtain an inclusive insight into problems if the observer or thinker is confined to a given place in society. For instance, as has already been pointed out, it was not possible for the socialist idea of ideology to have developed of itself into the sociology of knowledge. It seems inherent in the historical process itself that the narrowness and the limitations which restrict one point of view tend to be corrected by clashing with the opposite points of view. The task of a study of ideology, which tries to be free from value-judgments, is to understand the narrowness of each individual point of view and the interplay between these distinctive attitudes in the total social process. We are here confronted with an inexhaustible theme. The problem is to show how, in the whole history of thought, certain intellectual standpoints are connected with certain forms of experience, and to trace the intimate interaction between the two in the course of social and intellectual change. In the domain of morals, for instance, it is necessary to show not only the continuous changes in human conduct but the constantly altering norms by which this conduct is judged. Deeper insight into the problem is reached if we are able to show that morality and ethics themselves are conditioned by certain definite situations, and that such fundamental concepts as duty, transgression, and sin have not always existed but have made their appearance as correlatives of distinct social situations. The prevailing philosophic view which cautiously admits that the content of conduct has been historically determined, but which at the same time insists upon the retention of eternal forms of value and of a formal set of categories, is no longer tenable. The fact that the distinction between the content and the forms of conduct was made and recognized is an important concession to the historical-sociological approach which makes it increasingly difficult to set up contemporary values as absolutes.

Having arrived at this recognition it becomes necessary also to remember that the fact that we speak about social and cultural life in terms of values is itself an attitude peculiar to our time. The notion of "value" arose and was diffused from economics, where the conscious choice between values was the starting-point of theory. This idea of value was later transferred to the ethical, æsthetic, and religious spheres, which brought about a distortion in the description of the real behaviour of the human-being in these spheres. Nothing could be more wrong than to describe the real attitude of the individual when enjoying a work of art quite unreflectively, or when acting according to ethical patterns inculcated in him since childhood, in terms of conscious choice between values.

The view which holds that all cultural life is an orientation toward objective values is just one more illustration of a typically modern rationalistic disregard for the basic irrational mechanisms which govern man's relation to his world. Far from being permanently valid the interpretation of culture in terms of objective values is really a peculiar characteristic of the thought of our own time. But even granting for the moment that this conception had some merit, the existence of certain formal realms of values and their specific structure would be intelligible only with reference to the concrete situations to which they have relevance and in which they are valid. There is, then, no norm which can lay claim to formal validity and which can be abstracted as a constant universal formal element from its historically changing content.

To-day we have arrived at the point where we can see clearly that there are differences in modes of thought, not only in different historical periods but also in different cultures. Slowly it dawns upon us that not only does the content of thought change but also its categorical structure. Only very recently has it become possible to investigate the hypothesis that, in the past as well as in the present, the dominant modes of thought are supplanted by new categories when the social basis of the group, of which these thought-forms are characteristic, disintegrates or is transformed under the impact of social change.

Research in the sociology of knowledge promises to reach a stage of exactness if only because nowhere else in the realm of culture is the interdependence in the shifts of meaning and emphasis so clearly evident and precisely determinable as in thought itself. For thought is a particularly sensitive index of social and cultural change. The variation in the meaning of words and the multiple connotations of every concept reflect polarities of mutually antagonistic schemes of life implicit in these nuances of meaning.

Nowhere in the realm of social life, however, do we encounter such a clearly traceable interdependence and sensitivity to change and varying emphasis as in the meaning of words. The word and the meaning that attaches to it is truly a collective reality. The slightest nuance in the total system of thought reverberates in the individual word and the shades of meaning it carries. The word binds us to the whole of past history and, at the same time, mirrors the totality of the present. When, in communicating with others, we seek a common level of understanding the word can be used to iron out individual differences of meaning. But, when necessary, the word may become an instrument in emphasizing the differences in meaning and the unique experiences of each individual. It may then serve as a means for detecting the original and novel increments that arise in the course of the history of culture, thereby adding previously imperceptible values to the scale of human experience. In all of these investigations use will be made of the total and general conception of ideology in its non-evaluative sense.

3 **Antonio Gramsci, from *Selections from the Prison Notebooks* (ed. and trans. by Quintin Hoare and Geoffrey Nowell Smith; Lawrence and Wishart, 1971), pp. 12–13, 332–4, 376–7**

Antonio Gramsci (1891–1937) was born in Sardinia, in the south of Italy. He won a scholarship to study in Turin, where he became a member of the Socialist Party. He was the leading theorist of the 'factory council movement' in the revolutionary ferment that gripped the cities of the industrial north of Italy immediately after the First World War. He was a founder member of the Italian Communist Party when it broke from the Socialists in 1921, and went to Moscow in 1922–1923 as the Party representative to the Comintern. He was imprisoned by the Fascist government in 1926 and during this period wrote his so-called *Prison Notebooks*, elusive and immensely influential reflections on the revolutionary project in western Europe, which appeared in print after the Second World War. Always in poor health, he died awaiting release.

The relationship between the intellectuals and the world of production is not as direct as it is with the fundamental social groups but is, in varying degrees, "mediated" by the whole fabric of society and by the complex of superstructures, of which the intellectuals are, precisely, the "functionaries". It should be possible both to measure the "organic quality" *[organicità]* of the various intellectual strata and their degree of connection with a fundamental social group, and to establish a gradation of their functions and of the superstructures from the bottom to the top (from the structural base upwards). What we can do, for the moment, is to fix two major superstructural "levels": the one that can be called "civil society", that is the ensemble of organisms commonly called "private", and that of "political society" or "the State". These two levels correspond on the one hand to the function of "hegemony" which the dominant group exercises throughout society and on the other hand to that of "direct domination" or command exercised through the State and "juridical" government. The functions in question are precisely organisational and connective. The intellectuals are the dominant group's "deputies" exercising the subaltern functions of social hegemony and political government. These comprise:

1. The "spontaneous" consent given by the great masses of the population to the general direction imposed on social life by the dominant fundamental group; this consent is "historically" caused by the prestige (and consequent confidence) which the dominant group enjoys because of its position and function in the world of production.

2. The apparatus of state coercive power which "legally" enforces discipline on those groups who do not "consent" either actively or passively. This apparatus is, however, constituted for the whole of society in anticipation of moments of crisis of command and direction when spontaneous consent has failed.

. . .

The active man-in-the-mass has a practical activity, but has no clear theoretical consciousness of his practical activity, which nonetheless involves understanding the world in so far as it transforms it. His theoretical consciousness can indeed be historically in opposition to his activity. One might almost say that he has two theoretical consciousnesses (or one contradictory consciousness): one which is implicit in his activity and which in reality unites him with all his fellow-workers in the practical transformation of the real world; and one, superficially explicit or verbal, which he has inherited from the past and uncritically absorbed. But this verbal conception is not without consequences. It holds together a specific social group, it influences moral conduct and the direction of will, with varying efficacity but often powerfully enough to produce a situation in which the contradictory state of consciousness does not permit of any action, any decision or any choice, and produces a condition of moral and political passivity. Critical understanding of self takes place therefore through a struggle of political "hegemonies" and of opposing directions, first in the ethical field and then in that of politics proper, in order to arrive at the working out at a higher level of one's own conception of reality. Consciousness of being part of a particular hegemonic force (that is to say, political consciousness) is the first stage towards a further progressive self-consciousness in which theory and practice will finally be one. Thus the unity of theory and practice is not just a matter of mechanical fact, but a part of the historical process, whose elementary and primitive phase is to be found in the sense of being "different" and "apart", in an instinctive feeling of independence, and which progresses to the level of real possession of a single and coherent conception of the world. This is why it must be stressed that the political development of the concept of hegemony represents a great philosophical advance as well as a politico-practical one. For it necessarily supposes an intellectual unity and an ethic in conformity with a conception of reality that has gone beyond common sense and has become, if only within narrow limits, a critical conception.

However, in the most recent developments of the philosophy of praxis the exploration and refinement of the concept of the unity of theory and practice is still only at an early stage. There still remain residues of mechanicism, since people speak about theory as a "complement" or an "accessory" of practice, or as the handmaid of practice. It would seem right for this question too to be considered historically, as an aspect of the political question of the intellectuals. Critical self-consciousness means, historically and politically, the creation of an *élite* of intellectuals. A human mass does not "distinguish" itself, does not become independent in its own right without, in the widest sense, organising itself; and there is no organisation without intellectuals, that is without organisers and leaders, in other words, without the theoretical aspect of the theory-practice nexus being distinguished concretely by the existence of a group of people "specialised" in conceptual and philosophical elaboration of ideas. But the process of creating intellectuals is long, difficult, full of contradictions, advances and retreats, dispersals and regroupings, in which the loyalty of the masses is often sorely tried.

. . .

It seems to me that there is a potential element of error in assessing the value of ideologies, due to the fact (by no means casual) that the name ideology is given both to the necessary superstructure of a particular structure and to the arbitrary elucubrations of particular individuals. The bad sense of the word has become widespread, with the effect that the theoretical analysis of the concept of ideology has been modified and denatured. The process leading up to this error can be easily reconstructed:

1. ideology is identified as distinct from the structure, and it is asserted that it is not ideology that changes the structures but vice versa;

2. it is asserted that a given political solution is "ideological"—i.e. that it is not sufficient to change the structure, although it thinks that it can do so; it is asserted that it is useless, stupid, etc.;

3. one then passes to the assertion that every ideology is "pure" appearance, useless, stupid, etc.

One must therefore distinguish between historically organic ideologies, those, that is, which are necessary to a given structure, and ideologies that are arbitrary, rationalistic, or "willed". To the extent that ideologies are historically necessary they have a validity which is "psychological"; they "organise" human masses, and create the terrain on which men move, acquire consciousness of their position, struggle, etc. To the extent that they are arbitrary they only create individual "movements", polemics and so on (though even these are not completely useless, since they function like an error which by contrasting with truth, demonstrates it).

It is worth recalling the frequent affirmation made by Marx on the "solidity of popular beliefs" as a necessary element of a specific situation. What he says more or less is "when this way of conceiving things has the force of popular beliefs", etc. Another proposition of Marx is that a popular conviction often has the same energy as a material force or something of the kind, which is extremely significant. The analysis of these propositions tends, I think, to reinforce the conception of *historical bloc* in which precisely material forces are the content and ideologies are the form, though this distinction between form and content has purely didactic value, since the material forces would be inconceivable historically without form and the ideologies would be individual fancies without the material forces.

4 Louis Althusser, from (a) *For Marx* (Verso, 1969), pp. 232–4, and (b) *Lenin and Philosophy* (Monthly Review/New Left Books 1971), pp. 171–5

Louis Althusser (1918–1990) was born in Algeria, moving to France in 1930. He spent most of the Second World War as a prisoner of war, and joined the French Communist Party in 1948. He was a pupil of the historian of science Gaston Bachelard at the École normale supérieure, where he went on to work. He attempted to develop a rigorously anti-humanist and structuralist Marxism, claiming to offer a return to the authentic Marx, and his work reflects some of the political agonies that afflicted Marxism in the 1960s and after. Key works include *For Marx* (1965) and, with Etienne Balibar, *Reading Capital* (1967). In 1980, in a delusional state, he killed his wife Hélène, and was committed to a psychiatric hospital.

(a) And I am not going to steer clear of the crucial question: *historical materialism cannot conceive that even a communist society could ever do without ideology*, be it ethics, art or 'world outlook'. Obviously it is possible to foresee important modifications in its ideological forms and their relations and even the disappearance of certain existing forms or a shift of their functions to neighbouring forms; it is also possible (on the premise of already acquired experience) to foresee the development of new ideological forms (e.g. the ideologies of 'the scientific world outlook' and 'communist humanism') but in the present state of Marxist theory strictly conceived, it is not conceivable that communism, a new mode of production implying determinate forces of production and relations of production, could do without a social organization of production, and corresponding ideological forms.

So ideology is not an aberration or a contingent excrescence of History: it is a structure essential to the historical life of societies. Further, only the existence and the recognition of its necessity enable us to act on ideology and transform ideology into an instrument of deliberate action on history.

It is customary to suggest that ideology belongs to the region of 'consciousness'. We must not be misled by this appellation which is still contaminated by the idealist problematic that preceded Marx. In truth, ideology has very little to do with 'consciousness', even supposing this term to have an unambiguous meaning. It is profoundly *unconscious*, even when it presents itself in a reflected form (as in pre-Marxist 'philosophy'). Ideology is indeed a system of representations, but in the majority of cases these representations have nothing to do with 'consciousness': they are usually images and occasionally concepts, but it is above all as *structures* that they impose on the vast majority of men, not via their 'consciousness'. They are perceived–accepted–suffered cultural objects and they act functionally on men via a process that escapes them. Men 'live' their ideologies as the Cartesian 'saw' or did not see— if he was not looking at it—the moon two hundred paces away: *not at all as a form of consciousness, but as an object of their 'world'*—as their *'world'* itself. But what do we mean, then, when we say that ideology is a matter of men's 'consciousness'? First, that ideology is distinct from other social instances, but also that men *live* their actions, usually referred to freedom and 'consciousness' by the classical tradition, in ideology, *by and through ideology*; in short, that the 'lived' relation between men and the world, including History (in political action or inaction), passes through ideology, or better, *is ideology itself*. This is the sense in which Marx said that it is in ideology (as the locus of political struggle) that men *become conscious* of their place in the world and in history, it is within this ideological unconsciousness that men succeed in altering the 'lived' relation between them and the world and acquiring that new form of specific unconsciousness called 'consciousness'.

So ideology is a matter of the *lived* relation between men and their world. This relation, that only appears as *'conscious'* on condition that it is *unconscious*, in the same way only seems to be simple on condition that it is complex, that it is not a simple relation but a relation between relations, a second degree relation. In ideology men do indeed express, not the relation between them and their conditions of existence, but *the way* they live the relation between them and their conditions of existence: this presupposes both a real relation and an *'imaginary'*, *'lived'* relation. Ideology, then, is the expression of the relation between men and their 'world', that is, the (overdetermined) unity of the real relation and the imaginary relation between them and their real conditions of existence. In ideology the real relation is inevitably invested in the imaginary relation, a relation that *expresses* a *will* (conservative, conformist, reformist or revolutionary), a hope or a nostalgia, rather than describing a reality.

It is in this overdetermination of the real by the imaginary and of the imaginary by the real that ideology is *active* in principle, that it reinforces or modifies the relation between men and their conditions of existence, in the imaginary relation itself. It follows that this action can never be purely *instrumental*; the men who would use an ideology purely as a means of action, as a tool, find that they have been caught by it, implicated by it, just when they are using it and believe themselves to be absolute masters of it.

This is perfectly clear in the case of a *class society*. The ruling ideology is then the ideology of the ruling *class*. But the ruling class does not maintain with the ruling ideology, which is its own ideology, an external and lucid relation of pure utility and cunning. When, during the eighteenth century, the 'rising class', the bourgeoisie, developed a humanist ideology of equality, freedom and reason, it gave its own demands the form of universality, since it hoped thereby to enroll at its side, by their education to this end, the very men it would liberate only for their exploitation. This is the Rousseauan myth of the origins of inequality: the rich holding forth to the poor in 'the most deliberate discourse' ever conceived, so as to persuade them to live their slavery as their freedom. In reality, the bourgeoisie has to believe in its own myth before it can convince others, and not only so as to convince others, since what it lives in its ideology is *the very relation* between it and its real conditions of existence which allows it simultaneously to act on itself (provide itself with a legal and ethical consciousness, and the legal and ethical conditions of economic liberalism) and on others (those it exploits and is going to exploit in the future: the 'free labourers') so as to take up, occupy and maintain its historical role as a ruling class. Thus, in a very exact sense, the bourgeoisie *lives* in the ideology of *freedom* the relation between it and its conditions of existence: that is, *its* real relation (the law of a liberal capitalist economy) *but invested in an imaginary relation* (all men are free, including the free labourers). Its ideology consists of this play on the word *freedom*, which betrays the bourgeois wish to mystify those ('free men'!) it exploits, blackmailing them with freedom so as to keep them in harness, as much as the bourgeoisie's need to *live* its own class rule as the freedom of those it is exploiting. Just as a people that exploits another cannot be free, so a class that *uses* an ideology is its captive too. So when we speak of the class function of an ideology it must be understood that the ruling ideology is indeed the ideology of the ruling class and that the former serves the latter not only in its rule over the exploited class, *but in its own constitution of itself as the ruling class*, by making it accept the lived relation between itself and the world as real and justified.

But, we must go further and ask what becomes of *ideology* in a society in which classes have disappeared. What we have just said allows us to answer this question. If the whole social function of ideology could be summed up cynically as a myth (such as Plato's 'beautiful lies' or the techniques of modern advertising) fabricated and manipulated from the outside by the ruling class to fool those it is exploiting, then ideology would disappear with classes. But as we have seen that even in the case of a class society ideology is active on the ruling class itself and contributes to its moulding, to the modification of its attitudes to adapt it to its real conditions of existence (for example, legal freedom)—it is clear that *ideology (as a system of mass representations) is indispensable in any society if men are to be formed, transformed and equipped to respond to the demands of their conditions of existence*. If, as Marx said, history is a perpetual transformation of men's conditions of existence, and if this is equally true of a socialist society, then men must be ceaselessly transformed so as to adapt them to these conditions; if this 'adaptation' cannot be left to spontaneity but must be constantly assumed, dominated and controlled, it is in ideology that this demand is expressed, that this distance is measured, that this contradiction is lived and that its resolution is 'activated'. It is in ideology that the classless society *lives* the inadequacy/adequacy of the relation between it and the world, it is in it and by it that it transforms men's 'consciousness', that is, their attitudes and behaviour so as to raise them to the level of their tasks and the conditions of their existence.

. . .

(b) It follows that, for you and for me, the category of the subject is a primary 'obviousness' (obviousnesses are always primary): it is clear that you and I are subjects (free, ethical, etc. . . .). Like all obviousnesses, including those that make a word 'name a thing' or 'have a meaning' (therefore including the obviousnesses of the 'transparency' of language), the 'obviousness' that you and I are subjects—and that that does not cause any problems—is an ideological effect, the elementary ideological effect. It is indeed a peculiarity of ideology that it imposes (without appearing to do so, since these are 'obviousnesses') obviousnesses as obviousnesses, which we cannot *fail to recognize* and before which we have the inevitable and natural reaction of crying out (aloud or in the 'still, small voice of conscience'): 'That's obvious! That's right! That's true!'

At work in this reaction is the ideological *recognition* function which is one of the two functions of ideology as such (its inverse being the function of *misrecognition— méconnaissance*).

To take a highly 'concrete' example, we all have friends who, when they knock on our door and we ask, through the door, the question 'Who's there?', answer (since 'it's obvious') 'It's me'. And we recognize that 'it is him', or 'her'. We open the door, and 'it's true, it really was she who was there'. To take another example, when we recognize somebody of our (previous) acquaintance ((*re*)-*connaissance*) in the street, we show him that we have recognized him (and have recognized that he has recognized us) by saying to him 'Hello, my friend', and shaking his hand (a material ritual practice of ideological recognition in everyday life—in France, at least; elsewhere, there are other rituals).

In this preliminary remark and these concrete illustrations, I only wish to point out that you and I are *always already* subjects, and as such constantly practice the rituals of ideological recognition, which guarantee for us that we are indeed concrete, individual, distinguishable and (naturally) irreplaceable subjects. The writing I am currently executing and the reading you are currently performing are also in this respect rituals of ideological recognition, including the 'obviousness' with which the 'truth' or 'error' of my reflections may impose itself on you.

But to recognize that we are subjects and that we function in the practical rituals of the most elementary everyday life (the hand-shake, the fact of calling you by your name, the fact of knowing, even if I do not know what it is, that you 'have' a name of your own, which means that you are recognized as a unique subject, etc.)—this recognition only gives us the 'consciousness' of our incessant (eternal) practice of ideological recognition—its consciousness, i.e. its *recognition*—but in no sense does it give us the (scientific) *knowledge* of the mechanism of this recognition. Now it is this knowledge that we have to reach, if you will, while speaking in ideology, and from within ideology we have to outline a discourse which tries to break with ideology, in order to dare to be the beginning of a scientific (i.e. subject-less) discourse on ideology.

Thus in order to represent why the category of the 'subject' is constitutive of ideology, which only exists by constituting concrete subjects as subjects, I shall employ a special mode of exposition: 'concrete' enough to be recognized, but abstract enough to be thinkable and thought, giving rise to a knowledge.

As a first formulation I shall say: *all ideology hails or interpellates concrete individuals as concrete subjects*, by the functioning of the category of the subject.

This is a proposition which entails that we distinguish for the moment between concrete individuals on the one hand and concrete subjects on the other, although at this level concrete subjects only exist insofar as they are supported by a concrete individual.

I shall then suggest that ideology 'acts' or 'functions' in such a way that it 'recruits' subjects among the individuals (it recruits them all), or 'transforms' the individuals into subjects (it transforms them all) by that very precise operation which I have called *interpellation* or hailing, and which can be imagined along the lines of the most commonplace everyday police (or other) hailing: 'Hey, you there!'

Assuming that the theoretical scene I have imagined takes place in the street, the hailed individual will turn round. By this mere one-hundred-and-eighty-degree physical conversion, he becomes a *subject*. Why? Because he has recognized that the hail was 'really' addressed to him, and that 'it was *really him* who was hailed' (and not someone else). Experience shows that the practical telecommunication of hailings is such that they hardly ever miss their man: verbal call or whistle, the one hailed always recognizes that it is really him who is being hailed. And yet it is a strange phenomenon, and one which cannot be explained solely by 'guilt feelings', despite the large numbers who 'have something on their consciences'.

Naturally for the convenience and clarity of my little theoretical theatre I have had to present things in the form of a sequence, with a before and an after, and thus in the form of a temporal succession. There are individuals walking along. Somewhere (usually behind them) the hail rings out: 'Hey, you there!' One individual (nine times out of ten it is the right one) turns round, believing/suspecting/knowing that it is for him, i.e. recognizing that 'it really is he' who is meant by the hailing. But in reality these things happen without any succession. The existence of ideology and the hailing or interpellation of individuals as subjects are one and the same thing.

5   Giovanni Sartori, from 'Politics, Ideology and Belief Systems', *American Political Science Review* 63 (1969), pp. 400–3, 410–11

Giovanni Sartori (1924–) was born in Florence, in Italy, and graduated from the University of Florence in 1946. He is the Albert Schweizer Professor in Humanities at Columbia University. Among his influential publications on political concepts, comparative politics, and democratic theory are *Democratic Theory* (1965), *The Theory of Democracy Revisited* (1987), and *Comparative Constitutional Engineering* (1996).

If ideology is linked to "belief," it is readily apparent that the general class is "belief systems" and that ideology is the narrower conceptualization. Properly speaking, "a person's belief-disbelief system is really a political-religious-philosophic-scientific-etcetera system," i.e., a total and diffuse framework; whereas ideology indicates only the political *part* of a belief system. Whatever the psychological functions of a belief system, for the present discussion it can be simply defined as the system of symbolic orientations to be found in each individual. Correlatively, a *political* belief system consists of the set of beliefs according to which individuals navigate and orient themselves in the sea of politics.

It is not sufficient to say, however, that ideology is the political slice, or part, of a belief system. Under the a.c.p. (awaiting contrary proof) clause, I assume that ideology indicates a particular state, or structure, of political belief systems. By definition, then, not all political belief systems are ideological.

Two corollaries follow. First, pragmatism is also a state of belief systems. Indeed to contrast ideologism and pragmatism as representing, respectively, a belief versus a belief-less orientation toward politics is to preempt the issue from the outset. The first corollary is, therefore, that *both* ideologism and pragmatism are possible states of belief. Second, and conversely, the presence of beliefs does not suffice to qualify, per se, the ideological nature of such beliefs: the pragmatic actor also is belief-oriented. The second corollary is, then, that beliefs are, as such, a *common*, not a discriminating element. While not every polity need contain ideological publics, no polity can exist without publics that have beliefs.

A number of authors seemingly agree to the effect that not all political belief systems are ideological, but they founder on the reefs of definition by failing to provide a discriminating element. According to Talcott Parsons, for instance, ideology is "a system of beliefs, held in common by the members of a collectivity . . . which is oriented to the *evaluative integration* of the collectivity." But the discriminating power of the notion of evaluative integration and, in general, of having recourse to the value dimension, is almost nil. Beliefs are inextricably value-laden—they precede the analytical distinction between value and fact—and any belief system serves the purpose of integrating (analogically or otherwise) the belief collectivity. It is not without reason, therefore that I propose to search for structural elements of differentiation bearing on *how* one believes.

Speaking of belief systems, both the notions of "belief" and "system" must be taken seriously. Under the awaiting-contrary-proof clause a *belief* is neither an opinion nor an idea. Opinions include and characterize the more ephemeral and superficial level of discourse, and can be safely set aside, therefore, with reference to belief systems. On the other hand, in the strict sense ideas are *thought of*, they typically belong to the more self-conscious dimension of discourse, to reasoning and theorizing. If the sentence is understood *cum grano salis*, beliefs can be defined as "ideas that are no longer thought," to signify that beliefs are idea-clusters that routinize the cost of decisions precisely because they are taken for granted. Beliefs are *believed*—not explored, tested and held under the searchlight of consciousness.

As for the notion of *system*, a first obvious caution is that the system may have properties which are not exhibited by its parts. But it is more important to underline that a "belief system" points to a state of *boundedness*, to the fact that beliefs hang together. This belief-linkage is presumably what a number of authors have in mind when they define ideology as a more or less coherent set of ideas. Now, logical (or rational) attributes such as "coherence," "consistency," and the like, are hardly applicable to a belief-linkage.

Indeed the single belief-elements can be logically contradictory. But there is no question that beliefs are "bound together by some form of constraint or functional interdependence." Beliefs, then, cluster in *systems*, though not in rationally congruent and organized systems.

Having issued the caveat that the system should be taken seriously, no harm follows if one decomposes belief systems in a number of ways. Following Rokeach, one may distinguish between 1) primitive beliefs, 2) intermediate, and 3) peripheral regions of belief. I propose to dwell briefly on the intermediate region, and then to decompose the more peripheral regions of belief into single belief-elements.

The first problem is to pinpoint the discriminating element, the mentality (*forma mentis*) that qualifies an ideological structure of belief in its difference from a pragmatic structure of belief. Following Rokeach again, it appears that the crucial single factor resides in so-called "authority beliefs," and more precisely in the beliefs concerning cognitive authority: the beliefs that tip us off to what is true or false about the world and its events. More concretely one may say that the crucial factor is "the authorities," those on whom we rely for information.

Since nobody can avoid reliance on cognitive authorities, the difference must reside in how authorities are chosen and how the instructions emanating from these authorities are assessed. It is on this basis, in effect, that Rokeach draws the distinction between the *closed* and *open* mind. His initial basic definition is as follows: "A person's [belief] system is open or closed . . . [to] the extent to which the person can receive, evaluate and act on relevant information . . . on its own intrinsic merits." The closed mind is defined, accordingly, as a cognitive state in which a person does not discriminate substantive information from information about the source. Hence the more closed one's belief system, the more he is unable to evaluate relevant information on its own intrinsic merits. In substance, the closed mind relies on, indeed yields to, absolute authority, and is hardly in a position to select and to check its authorities.

Doubtless the association of the ideological mentality with the closed mind can be accused of representing an anti-ideological bias. However, ideological closedness is bad and pragmatic openness is good only according to an intellectual yardstick—and one could well say an intellectualistic prejudice. If we are reminded that the pertinent yardstick is "efficacy" the evaluation could be reversed, for reliance on absolute authorities does obtain the kind of efficacy praised by the man of action and is surely in keeping with the purpose served by ideologies. In short, the ideologist cannot have it both ways, he cannot claim at the same time an intellectual and a practical primacy.

The foregoing underpins nicely the common opinion according to which the ideological mentality represents a typically *dogmatic*, i.e., rigid and impermeable, approach to politics. On the other hand, it should be noted that a cognitive closed structure fails to justify the other characteristic generally imputed to the ideological mentality, namely, its typically *doctrinaire* bent. Should this characterization be dropped? Or does it draw from another source? I shall abide by the latter suggestion, thereby shifting the focus to the notion of *ideological culture*.

When we speak of ideology as a "culture"—or a cultural pattern—we are more or less implicitly referred to the anthropological notion of culture. Perhaps we may say that we are referred once again to the intermediate regions of belief, though no longer to the "authority-beliefs" but to the "processing-coding-beliefs." The simplest and closest analogy appears to be, however, the *Gestalt* analogy: a cultural pattern is characterized by the forms, or the matrixes, with and within which our mind stores and orders whatever it apprehends. For our purposes these processing-coding *Gestalten* will be labelled "rationalism" and "empiricism," and the assumption will be that these cultural matrixes help explain why only certain polities characteristically display, over time, an ideological patterning.

What strikes me in this connection is the extent to which the typically ideological *isms* of polities—marxism being the outstanding current example—were born and have developed (before being exported) in the cultural area qualified by the notion of *rationalism*, hardly in other cultural contexts, and surely not in the cultural area of *empiricism*. I find it equally striking that only the "rational ideologies"—I mean, the ideologies drawn from rationalistic philosophies and nurtured in a rationalistic soil—travel easily throughout the world. Hence my hypothesis is that ideology and pragmatism qua "political cultures" are related, respectively, to the "cultural matrixes" rationalism and empiricism.

Rationalism and empiricism are generally associated, respectively, with a "coherence" theory of truth as against a "correspondence" theory of truth. Oakeshott equally makes a good point when he writes that "Rationalism is the assertion that . . . practical knowledge is not knowledge at all." But, however sweepingly, let us attempt to qualify rationalism and empiricism in more detail, with the understanding that the following characterizations represent a syndrome, so that the full enumeration is required to appreciate the meaning of the separate assertions.

The *rationalistic* processing-coding tends to approach problems as follows: i) deductive argumentation prevails over evidence and testing; ii) doctrine prevails over practice; iii) principle prevails over precedent; iv) ends prevail over means; and v) perceptions tend to be "covered up," doctrine-loaded, typically indirect. Hegel's famous sentence "the rational is real" goes to the very heart of the rationalistic mind, for the rationalistic attitude is to argue that if the practice goes astray, there must be something wrong with the practice, not with the theory.

Conversely, and symmetrically, the *empirical* processing-coding can be described as follows: i) evidence and testing prevail over deductive argumentation; ii) practice prevails over doctrine; iii) precedent prevails over principle; iv) means prevail over ends, and, therefore; v) its perceptions tend to be more "direct." Consequently the empirical attitude is to argue that if the practice goes astray, something is likely to be wrong with the theory, not with the practice.

The *ad hoc* implications for our subject are that the rationalistic *Gestalt* is characterized (relatively speaking, of course) by openness to deductive axiomatization and deafness to empirical evidence, by low *practical* problem-solving flexibility and by high *theoretical* problem solving ability. Also, and consequently, the rationalistic mind soars at a higher level of explicitness and especially of abstraction than the empirical mind. This implies, in turn, that rationalism is able to embrace and to cover in terms of *Weltanschauung* a comparatively broader "space," either with long deductive chains or with acrobatic leaps—a quality that I shall call comprehensiveness.

The foregoing can be easily translated into a "cultural" characterization of the ideological mentality. If we assume ideologism to result from a rationalistic cultural matrix, it follows that to the extent that the ideological mentality is "open," it is open to rational, deductive argument, hardly to evidence: the sentence "experience proves" proves nothing to an ideologically-minded actor. An ulterior implication is that the ideological mentality identifies *par excellence* with highly "abstract" and "comprehensive" belief systems. In particular an important feature of the ideological mentality that neatly flows from its rationalistic matrix is that the central elements of an ideological belief system are necessarily "ends," not "means."

I shall revert to these characteristics later. For the moment let us simply retain that to the extent that the ideological mentality is characterized by the rationalistic cultural matrix, to the same extent it can be legitimately qualified as a typically principled and doctrinaire way of perceiving political problems and of constructing their solution. It should be clear that I am *not* saying: given a rationalistic cultural matrix, the ideological mentality necessarily follows. I am simply saying that a rationalistic culture is particularly vulnerable on this score. It should be equally clear that a number of individuals react to the culture to which they belong. Therefore, an ideological culture will contain non-ideological minority groups, just as an empirical culture will breed ideological minorities.

Bringing our two threads together, the ideological mentality now results in both a *personality trait* and a *cultural trait*, and the following conclusion appears reasonably warranted: ideologism can be legitimately understood to mean not only a rigid and dogmatic approach to politics, but also a principled and doctrinaire perception of politics. Needless to say, the two characterizations reinforce one another but can exist disjointly. However, for the simplicity of the argument in the following section, the ideological mentality will be reduced to a "closed" cognitive structure, and cognitive closedness will be defined as a state of dogmatic impermeability both to evidence and to argument. Conversely the pragmatic mentality will be simplistically identified with an "open" cognitive structure, and cognitive openness will be defined a state of mental permeability.

. . .

It was suggested earlier that mass publics are, in general, easily hetero-constrained, in the sense that poorly articulated believers need guidance not only for the horizontal inter-belief linkage, but also for the vertical event-principle linkage. But now the argument can be pinned down, according to the following three points.

First: The greater the centrality of the belief elements designating *ends*, the more a belief system will elicit normative, goal-oriented, if not futuristic or even chiliastic responses and behavior.

Second: The more *abstract* a belief system, the more "what follows from what" (inter-belief linkage), and "which event goes with which principle" (event-principle linkage) escape the grasp of mass publics and require elite guidance. Hence, the more abstract a belief system, the more it allows for elite manipulation and maneuvering.

Third and correlatively: The more a belief system transcends common sense spatial and temporal boundaries, that is, the more it obtains a totalistic *comprehensiveness*, the more it calls for elite interpretation and facilitates elite control.

The foregoing forcibly suggests, then, that the hetero-constraining potentiality of belief systems increases the more the system is ideological, and diminishes the more the system is pragmatic. In short, ideologies are the *hetero-constraining* belief systems par excellence. And this is the same as saying that ideologies are the crucial lever at the disposal of elites for obtaining political mobilization and for maximizing the possibilities of mass manipulation. This is, it seems to me, the single major reason that ideology is so important to us. We are concerned about ideologies because we are concerned, in the final analysis, with the power of man over man, with how populations and nations can be mobilized and manipulated all along the way that leads to political messianism and fanaticism.

6   Clifford Geertz, from 'Ideology as a Cultural System', in *The Interpretation of Cultures* (Basic Books, 1973), pp. 217–20, 230–3

Clifford Geertz (1926–) was educated at Harvard University and held academic posts at Chicago and Princeton. One of the most influential of post-war anthropologists, he argues that the task of anthropology is not discovery of laws or patterns but the reconstruction of the 'webs of significance' that make action meaningful to agents. He conducted influential fieldwork in Indonesia, Bali, and Morocco, producing numerous books including *The Religion of Java* (1960), *Agricultural Involution* (1963), *Peddlers and Princes* (1963), and *Islam Observed* (1968). His wider reputation is founded on two influential collections of theoretical reflections: *The Interpretation of Cultures* (1973) and *Local Knowledge* (1983).

The reason such symbolic templates are necessary is that, as has been often remarked, human behavior is inherently extremely plastic. Not strictly but only very broadly controlled by genetic programs or models—intrinsic sources of information—such behavior must, if it is to have any effective form at all, be controlled to a significant extent by extrinsic ones. Birds learn how to fly without wind tunnels, and whatever reactions lower animals have to death are in great part innate, physiologically preformed. The extreme generality, diffuseness, and variability of man's innate response capacities mean that the particular pattern his behavior takes is guided predominantly by cultural rather than genetic templates, the latter setting the overall psychophysical context within which precise activity sequences are organized by the former. The tool-making, laughing, or lying animal, man, is also the incomplete—or, more accurately, self-completing—animal. The agent of his own realization, he creates out of his general capacity for the construction of symbolic models the specific capabilities that define him. Or—to return at last to our subject—it is through the construction of ideologies, schematic images of social order, that man makes himself for better or worse a political animal.

Further, as the various sorts of cultural symbol-systems are extrinsic sources of information, templates for the organization of social and psychological processes, they come most crucially into play in situations where the particular kind of information they contain is lacking, where institutionalized guides for behavior, thought, or feeling are weak or absent. It is in country unfamiliar emotionally or topographically that one needs poems and road maps.

So too with ideology. In polities firmly embedded in Edmund Burke's golden assemblage of "ancient opinions and rules of life," the role of ideology, in any explicit sense, is marginal. In such truly traditional political systems the participants act as (to use another Burkean phrase) men of untaught feelings; they are guided both emotionally and intellectually in their judgments and activities by unexamined prejudices, which do not leave them "hesitating in the moment of decision, sceptical, puzzled and unresolved." But when, as in the revolutionary France Burke was indicting and in fact in the shaken England from which, as perhaps his nation's greatest ideologue, he was indicting it, those hallowed opinions and rules of life come into question, the search for systematic ideological formulations, either to reinforce them or to replace them, flourishes. The function of ideology is to make an autonomous politics possible by providing the authoritative concepts that render it meaningful, the suasive images by means of which it can be sensibly grasped. It is, in fact, precisely at the point at which a political system begins to free itself from the immediate governance of received tradition, from the direct and detailed guidance of religious or philosophical canons on the one hand and from the unreflective precepts of conventional moralism on the other, that formal ideologies tend first to emerge and take hold. The differentiation of an autonomous polity implies the differentiation, too, of a separate and distinct cultural model of political action, for the older, unspecialized models are either too comprehensive or too concrete to provide the sort of guidance such a political system demands. Either they trammel political behavior by encumbering it with transcendental significance, or they stifle political imagination by binding it to the blank realism of habitual judgment. It is when neither a society's most general cultural orientations nor its most down-to-earth, "pragmatic" ones suffice any longer to provide an adequate image of political process that ideologies begin to become crucial as sources of sociopolitical meanings and attitudes.

In one sense, this statement is but another way of saying that ideology is a response to strain. But now we are including *cultural* as well as social and psychological strain. It is a loss of orientation that most directly gives rise to ideological activity, an inability, for lack of usable models, to comprehend the universe of civic rights and responsibilities in which one finds oneself located. The development of a differentiated polity (or of greater internal differentiation within such a polity) may and commonly does bring with it severe social dislocation and psychological tension. But it also brings with it conceptual confusion, as the established images of political order fade into irrelevance or are driven into disrepute. The reason why the French Revolution was, at least up to its time, the greatest incubator of extremist ideologies, "progressive" and "reactionary" alike, in human history was not that either personal insecurity or social disequilibrium were deeper and more pervasive than at many earlier periods—though they were deep and pervasive enough—but because the central organizing principle of political life, the divine right of kings, was destroyed. It is a confluence of sociopsychological strain and an absence of cultural resources by means of which to make sense of the strain, each exacerbating the other, that sets the stage for the rise of systematic (political, moral, or economic) ideologies.

And it is, in turn, the attempt of ideologies to render otherwise incomprehensible social situations meaningful, to so construe them as to make it possible to act purposefully within them, that accounts both for the ideologies' highly figurative nature and for the intensity with which, once accepted, they are held. As metaphor extends language by broadening its semantic range, enabling it to express meanings it cannot or at least cannot yet express literally, so the head-on clash of literal meanings in ideology—the irony, the hyperbole, the overdrawn antithesis—provides novel symbolic frames against which to match the myriad "unfamiliar somethings" that, like a journey to a strange country, are produced by a transformation in political life. Whatever else ideologies may be—projections of unacknowledged fears, disguises for ulterior motives, phatic expressions of group solidarity—they are, most distinctively, maps of problematic social reality and matrices for the creation of collective conscience. Whether, in any particular case, the map is accurate or the conscience creditable is a separate question to which one can hardly give the same answer for Nazism and Zionism, for the nationalisms of McCarthy and of Churchill, for the defenders of segregation and its opponents.

. . .

The differentiae of science and ideology as cultural systems are to be sought in the sorts of symbolic strategy for encompassing situations that they respectively represent. Science names the structure of situations in such a way that the attitude contained toward them is one of disinterestedness. Its style is restrained, spare, resolutely analytic: by shunning the semantic devices that most effectively formulate moral sentiment, it seeks to maximize intellectual clarity. But ideology names the structure of situations in such a way that the attitude contained toward them is one of commitment. Its style is ornate, vivid, deliberately suggestive: by objectifying moral sentiment through the same devices that science shuns, it seeks to motivate action. Both are concerned with the definition of a problematic situation and are responses to a felt lack of needed information. But the information needed is quite different, even in cases where the situation is the same. An ideologist is no more a poor social scientist than a social scientist is a poor ideologist. The two are—or at least they ought to be—in quite different lines of work, lines so different that little is gained and much obscured by measuring the activities of the one against the aims of the other.

Where science is the diagnostic, the critical, dimension of culture, ideology is the justificatory, the apologetic one—it refers "to that part of culture which is actively concerned with the establishment and defense of patterns of belief and value." That there is natural tendency for the two to clash, particularly when they are directed to the interpretation of the same range of situations, is thus clear; but that the clash is inevitable and that the findings of (social) science necessarily will undermine the validity of the beliefs and values that ideology has chosen to defend and propagate seem most dubious assumptions. An attitude at once critical and apologetic toward the same situation is no intrinsic contradiction in terms (however often it may in fact turn out to be an empirical one) but a sign of a certain level of intellectual sophistication. One remembers the story, probably *ben trovato*, to the effect that when Churchill had finished his famous rally of isolated England, "We shall fight on the beaches, we shall fight on the landing grounds, we shall fight in the fields and in the streets, we shall fight in the hills . . . ," he turned to an aide and whispered, "and we shall hit them over the head with soda-water bottles, because we haven't any guns."

The quality of social rhetoric in ideology is thus not proof that the vision of sociopsychological reality upon which it is based is false and that it draws its persuasive power from any discrepancy between what is believed and what can, now or someday, be established as scientifically correct. That it may indeed lose touch with reality in an orgy of autistic fantasy—even that, in situations where it is left uncriticized by either a free science or competing ideologies well-rooted in the general social structure, it has a very strong tendency to do so—is all too apparent. But however interesting pathologies are for clarifying normal functioning (and however common they may be empirically), they are misleading as prototypes of it. Although fortunately it never had to be tested, it seems most likely that the British would have indeed fought on the beaches, landing grounds, streets, and hills—with soda-water bottles too, if it came to that—for Churchill formulated accurately the mood of his countrymen and, formulating it, mobilized it by making it a public possession, a social fact, rather than a set of disconnected, unrealized private emotions. Even morally loathsome ideological expressions may still catch most acutely the mood of a people or a group. Hitler was not distorting the German conscience when he rendered his countrymen's demonic self-hatred in the tropological figure of the magically corrupting Jew; he was merely objectifying it—transforming a prevalent personal neurosis into a powerful social force.

But though science and ideology are different enterprises, they are not unrelated ones. Ideologies do make empirical claims about the condition and direction of society, which it is the business of science (and, where scientific knowledge is lacking, common sense) to assess. The social function of science vis-à-vis ideologies is first to understand them—what they are, how they work, what gives rise to them—and second to criticize them, to force them to come to terms with (but not necessarily to surrender to) reality. The existence of a vital tradition of scientific analysis of social issues is one of the most effective guarantees against ideological extremism, for it provides an incomparably reliable source of positive knowledge for the political imagination to work with and to honor. It is not the only such check. The existence, as mentioned, of competing ideologies carried by other powerful groups in the society is at least as important; as is a liberal political system in which dreams of total power are obvious fantasies; as are stable social conditions in which conventional expectations are not continually frustrated and conventional ideas not radically incompetent. But, committed with a quiet intransigence to a vision of its own, it is perhaps the most indomitable.

7 Kenneth Minogue, from 'Ideology After the Collapse of Communism', in *The End of 'Isms'* (ed. Aleksandras Shtromas; Basil Blackwell for the Political Studies Association, 1994), pp. 8–10, 11–14

Kenneth Minogue (1930–) was born in New Zealand, and educated in Australia, and is now Emeritus Professor of Political Science at the London School of Economics. Among his works of political theory are *The Liberal Mind* (1963), *Nationalism* (1967), and *Alien Powers: The Pure Theory of Ideology* (1985). He has written and broadcast widely on political, social, and cultural affairs.

An ideology therefore radiates truth of a higher kind, and thus illuminates the darkness of that other sense of ideology as false belief. This is why the term 'correctness' springs easily to the lips of ideologists because at any moment there usually is an ideologically correct line. What this entails is a special kind of relationship between the believer on the one hand and the mass of people sunk in false consciousness on the other; it is a tutorial relationship, a relationship of correction. And this, as one would expect of people who spend so much time thinking about power, is unmistakably a power relationship.

Ideology is thus distinguished by a specific logic and it is this logic which determines the sociology of relations between insiders and outsiders; that relationship in turn shapes the regimes in which ideologists have come to power. An elite party, or vanguard, takes over all power and proceeds to tutor the population in how to think and to act. Ideology is, as Hannah Arendt remarked, the logic of an idea; an ideological regime is the following through of this idea. And as Marx himself remarked,

> Social life is essentially *practical*. All mysteries which mislead theory to mysticism find their rational solution in human practice and in the comprehension of this practice.

This famous remark is powerful but never totally conclusive evidence even from within the Marxist canon that the collapse of communism is the collapse of its ideology. However that may be, it certainly would seem difficult to deny the difference between a so-called one-party state in which a single doctrine is imposed on a society, and a liberal democratic state whose theories are institutionalized in the give and take of party debate and discussion in the media and throughout the country. Can it really be denied that there is a logical difference between the sets of beliefs involved in these two basically different situations?

Admittedly, reality itself is complicated by the fact that political doctrines adapt to the circumstances in which they find themselves. Communists living in a liberal democracy have had little option but to enter the discussion as one party among others.

Marxism is thus a model ideology and its regimes supply abundant evidence of the connection between theory and practice. Any regime to the extent that it is totalitarian will be based on a revelation of an ideological kind. Hence Nazism and fascism have been linked with communism as totalitarian ideologies, but religions may well function in a similar way. They are, after all, paradigm revelations, and the ambitions of Islamic fundamentalism in the modern world are certainly politico-tutorial in the way we have described. Indeed, anyone looking for religious analogues of the logic of ideology need go no further than early Christianity. For St. Augustine, the Christian revelation is criteriological in precisely the same way as ideology is for the ideological believer. It is what makes sense of everything and St. Augustine attacks pagan philosophers as dealers in mere ideas—as men prostituting their wits to their own fancies, as *fantastica fornicatio*. This is ideology *avant la lettre*.

In specifying other ideologies, one must remember the mixed and contingent character of actual human thought and argument, and thus not put our trust in names. Much feminism, for example, is purely ideological, especially as it develops in the protective colouring of universities; but the term 'feminism' also refers to a sequence of proposals for changing the law and conventions regulating relations between men and women. And proposals, backed by reasons, advanced against others recognized as rational beings rather than creatures sunk in false consciousness, are not the stuff of ideology. 'Anarchism', 'syndicalism' and 'libertarianism' are all names of a miscellany of doctrines sometimes presented in ideological form, and sometimes as a family of proposals and political principles. The interests of a variety of groups ranging from ethnic minorities to homosexuals or the disabled have been turned into ideologies by some intellectuals.

· · ·

Our concern so far has been with clarifying the character of ideology as the underlying logic of a variety of salvationist doctrines which have flourished in the last two centuries. We have taken Marxism as the paradigm of this type of doctrine, and extended our range of exemplification into ideologies current in liberal democratic societies today, leaving to one side such ideologies as fascism and racialism which would require special treatment. One of the central points about all these doctrines is that they are much more intellectual than political doctrines like liberalism and conservatism. At their core lies not advocacy but some theory of the human condition. In this lies their claim to superiority, even to science. And each specific ideology has historical conditions in which it may flourish, or disappear, as Marxism and syndicalism have fallen on evil days, while feminism and environmental forms of salvation have in recent decades flourished mightily.

Now the continuing currency of a variety of ideologies suggests that there is something in our civilization to which ideological doctrines correspond; indeed, that we may talk of 'ideology' in the singular not merely as the generalized character of a set of doctrines sharing a similar pattern of thought but as a real and influential movement in itself. It clearly speaks to very powerful tendencies in the modern world.

I propose now to consider ideology in this sense, in order first to locate it within the current intellectual world, and then to consider some of its contemporary ramifications. Our orientation point here lies in the fact that ideology is characterized by an insistence that human beings have a single basic identity: generically, no doubt, they are human beings but specifically they are workers, women, Blacks, colonials, nationals, participatory citizens or some similar idea. In this guise, the chosen class are constituted as the heroes of a melodrama, and appropriate corresponding abstractions filled in as evil figures.

We might call this 'identity-monism', because it corresponds to that other kind of monism, familiar in political theory, which seeks to understand a society in terms of some basic ideal—justice, democracy, welfare, community or some similar idea. Both forms of monism are attractive for the same reason: the implementation of *one* idea or criterion makes conflict logically impossible. A society in which both freedom and justice are valued, or in which community and individual welfare must be balanced against each other, constantly runs up against problems of coherence. Normative political philosophers these days spend much energy in trying to work out a set of coherent principles which would constitute, for example, a just society. The closer one gets to the real world, however, the more conflicts between values multiply.

The essence of a modern state is, then, as the American motto has it *e pluribus unum*. Out of a plurality of individuals and endeavours emerges, for limited purposes, a civil unity in which the government is authorized to act for us all. And the *unum* is constituted by the individual members of a civil association in their capacity of subjects and citizens.

They enjoy rights as subjects and they participate in public life as citizens. They are, however, *plures* in respect of their participation in what we now call (reviving Hegel) 'civil society', the arena of the family, the firm, the club and all the other emanations of private life. Not the least of the underlying changes in a modern state is the way in which 'civil society' understood as a social realm is insinuating itself massively between public and private life, demanding more and more public regulation on the one hand, and spreading itself down into the remoter reaches of privacy on the other.

A modern state is thus a set of human arrangements in which a vast plurality of individual endeavours cannot help but lead to conflicts which are resolved at the political level by a process generating laws and regulations. Such states have been immensely successful in the last two centuries at keeping the peace and indeed at facilitating increased prosperity along with the growth of things called 'rights'. Paradoxically, however, as the involvement of the state in every sphere of life has increased, it has also come to operate in terms of the redress of grievances, a process not unlike the way in which the enlightened despots of the past brought justice to their subjects. Perhaps the basic principle at work in this restless form of politics is equality. Civil society, as a vast complex of different occupations, intelligences, sexes, races, nationalities, enthusiasms, temperaments, opinions, religions etc. constantly produces inequalities from which grievances spring; out of these grievances emerge citizenly demands for redress; out of the resulting laws come new situations in which the same process is repeated.

Further, there are good reasons why this process should never culminate in a final solution and therefore why it is ceaseless. A population as varied as this will value justice, but not to the extent that it obliterates freedom; democracy but not so that it threatens order; welfare, but not so that it impedes prosperity, and so on. Politics is thus a continuing debate about diverse desirabilities which are largely incommensurable.

The essence of liberal democratic states is that they are associations of individuals in which each person is both a subject and citizen on the one hand, and a member of civil society on the other—worker, Catholic, female, mother, Black, football supporter etc. etc. on the other. The essence of ideology is to find the problem of politics precisely in this divergence. A so-called 'worker's state' is one in which everyone is a worker (alias 'comrade') and associated together in respect of one basic activity, namely membership of a community devoted to the satisfaction of needs. The *unum* of liberal democratic society, by contrast, is the limited and artificial role of subject and citizen, leaving a whole private realm in which individual initiative is at play and therefore free to cause unplanned and troublesome developments. The *unum* aspired to by an ideologicial community is of a *natural* not an artificial character—it is that of being a worker, a female, a needs bearing organism, a sexual desirer, a member of a race, or a nationality.

Ideology is thus an attempt to solve the problem of political conflict by a kind of amalgamation of the state and civil society in terms of a single, supposedly natural identity, and fights between ideologists (socialists vs. anarchist, communists vs. fascists etc.) are (when not about questions of which is to be master) intellectual disputes about *which* natural role is the proper candidate for this ultimate solution to the problem of politics. In all cases, a theory of humanity is involved. Marxists identified humanity with the sociable worker, feminists often see in women part of the human essence previously repressed and necessary for the flowering of a full community, and so on. Racists like

Hitler have a rather classical view of humanity as a hierarchy of desirable qualities, and regard the lower parts of the hierarchy (Jews and suchlike) as dispensable. But in all cases, actual human beings are essentially the *matter* out of which a real community can be constructed. A lot of them prove unsuitable and must be liquidated.

It is clear that things would be a great deal simpler (and there would be much less conflict and breakdown) if society could indeed be organized according to a single principle and many accounts of needs, rights, utilities, etc. have been provided to suggest what such a principle ought to be. If it could ever be discovered, its implementation would certainly (as Engels promised) abolish politics, because it would transform the problem of order into the technical issue of implementing the single principle. The only problem is that it could only really work if modern peoples were basically homogeneous. They are not and attempts to create societies of this kind have thus led to hideous slaughter and repression.

The history of the twentieth century does for this reason seem to have taught one widely accepted political lesson: that the more ambitious the social transformation a government embarks upon (and such governments are usually of recent origin through revolution) the more likely is the body count to rise. Western liberal governments, which have kept ideological ambitions at bay, have by contrast allowed most of their subjects to get through their lives without finding it necessary to kill many of them. Our question now becomes one of trying to formulate the basic difference between these two modes of government and of considering whether this distinction remains central to contemporary politics.

8 Michael Freeden, from *Ideologies and Political Theory* (Oxford University Press, 1996), pp. 75–82

Michael Freeden (1944–) is Professor of Politics at the University of Oxford. He has written extensively on the history of liberal political thought and the theory of political ideology, and he has staunchly defended and promoted the study of ideologies as a branch of social and political inquiry, both in his own writings and editorship of the academic journal *Political Ideologies*. His books include *The New Liberalism: An Ideology of Social Reform* (1978), *Liberalism Divided: A Study in British Political Thought, 1914–1939* (1986), *Ideologies and Political Theory: A Conceptual Approach* (1996), and *Liberal Languages: Ideological Imaginations and Twentieth Century Progressive Thought* (2004).

The analysis of ideologies may now be advanced by utilizing a three-tier formation: the components of a concept, a concept, and a system of concepts, just as by analogy we could talk about a level surface, a table, and a furnished room. So far we have been discussing the internal morphology of a single concept. Ideologies, however, are combinations of political concepts organized in a particular way. Here we alight on a major morphological distinction between political philosophies, at least as commonly perceived in ideal-type, and ideologies: the different methods by which they handle the problem of essential contestability. As we saw in Chapter 1, pure philosophical argument, judged by its own understandings rather than its practices, would have to engage one of two methods. It could explore and account for all logical adjacencies to a given ineliminable component of a concept, that is, trace the entire families of incompatible cultural connotations that the logical structure of a political concept can summon up. Alternatively, it could present a reflective, rationally and morally justifiable case for a choice among its components, in which case the conceptual end-product would not differ in form from that of an ideology, though the means of organizing that structure might. Contrary to the first method, ideologies will seek to maximize or optimize determinacy, if never entirely securing it. Contrary to the second method—while not necessarily ignoring logical adjacencies— ideologies will allow a socially situated and partisan value-arbitrated choice among adjacent components, by relying heavily on the notion of cultural adjacency, and the result will display various mixes of rational criteria, emotional inclinations, and cultural value-preferences. A similar process will also be at work in deciding how to organize the wide range of political concepts encompassed by any ideology and how to interlink them.

In parallel to philosophers and logicians, most linguists would challenge the attribution of a one-to-one relationship between signifier and signified. A word may be related to many meanings and to changing meanings. Ideologies, however, display precisely the converse features. They aim at cementing the word-concept relationship. By determining the meaning of a concept they can then attach a single meaning to a political term. Ultimately, ideologies are configurations of *decontested* meanings of political concepts, when such meanings are ascribed by methods at least partly foreign to those employed in currently predominant approaches of scientists, philosophers, linguists, or political theorists. Political philosophers, on the other hand, may claim not to decontest meanings at all when they are engaged in the clarification of concepts; and when they do engage in decontesting, they will attempt to do so by means which preserve accepted technical or moral standards of analysis.

In concrete terms, an ideology will link together a particular conception of human nature, a particular conception of social structure, of justice, of liberty, of authority, etc. '*This* is what liberty means, and *that* is what justice means', it asserts. Ideologies need, after all, to straddle the worlds of political thought and political action, for one of their central functions is to link the two. The political sphere is primarily characterized by decision-making, and decision-making is an important form of decontesting a range of potential alternatives. Thus, while the very nature of political concepts lies in their essential contestability, the very nature of the political process is to arrive at binding decisions that determine the priority of one course of action over another. Put differently, human thought-behaviour aspires to determine the meaning of political language, though any specific form this decontestation may adopt will, from the viewpoint of the analyst, necessarily fail to achieve finality. Ideologies serve as the bridging mechanism between contestability and determinacy, converting the inevitable variety of options into the monolithic certainty which is the unavoidable feature of a political *decision*, and which is the basis of the forging of a political identity. However, it is never possible to achieve total determinacy, and even an ostensibly clear-cut decision may retain ambiguities. For practical purposes, though, such indeterminacy may become insignificant. Furthermore, ideologies frequently adopt deliberately indeterminate statements, often because a political decision is to be avoided for whatever reason, or because a message is designed to appeal to a pluralist body of consumers. Political party manifestos tend to be such creatures, illustrating how the vagueness of language comes to the rescue of its political users. Even then, political language is employed to convey specific sets of meanings out of wider ranges.

It is plain to see why so many theorists of ideology connect that term with power, for the act of decontesting, of deciding, of closing options, and of forging a political identity, is an instance of power-wielding. Because ideologies involve concerted action, they relate to the sphere of organization; because they involve decisions, they relate to control; and because they involve language, they relate to the attempted injection of certainty into indeterminacy. Competing ideologies are hence struggles over the socially legitimated meanings of political concepts and the sustaining arrangements they form, in an attempt to establish a 'correct' usage. But it is equally plain that the nature of action-orientated thinking necessitates such decisions, so that to attribute a pejorative connotation to the power aspect of ideology, in the absence of an alternative, is a futile qualification. Likewise, social psychologists draw attention to the inevitable cognitive ordering of the perceived (political) world required by individuals in order to make it intelligible and increase its predictability. What *is* meaningful is why one specific decontestation, one ordering of the political world, prevails over another. This is where morphology is underwritten by culture and history.

Central to any analysis of ideologies is the proposition that they are characterized by a morphology that displays core, adjacent, and peripheral concepts. For instance, an examination of observed liberalisms might establish that liberty is situated within their core, that human rights, democracy, and equality are adjacent to liberty, and that nationalism is to be found on their periphery. The existence of concepts adjacent to the ideological core is essential to the formation of an ideology. The notions of logical and cultural adjacency, which we have explored within the framework of a single concept, are equally vital to the articulation of an entire ideology. On further examination of a specific case, for example, it would be evident that liberty may be given a particular meaning— self-determination—because of its close association with democracy, while conversely, democracy may be given a particular meaning—limited popular government—because of its structural interlinkage with liberty. So while the concepts of democracy and of liberty each have their ineliminable cores, they are filled out in a distinctive way due to their mutual proximity. This is a feature of the Western political tradition, in which the conventional path through the logical outreaches of liberty has become the one affiliated with democratic self-government, or with the kinds of equality that make self-government possible and that allow the generalization of liberty. Ideas drawn from equality and democracy have come in turn to create an ideational context that colours our understanding of liberty. In sum, all these skeletal or 'thin' concepts develop elements, both logically and culturally, that form overlapping and shared areas, which then react back on their separate ineliminable components to constitute full but mutually dependent concepts. These mutually influential relationships exist among the manifold concepts that make up an ideological system, and these structural networks give the ideology its distinguishing features. As with political concepts, an ideology will have concept-categories that are both culturally and logically necessary to its survival, though the particular instances of those categories are not.

In addition, an ideology will contain peripheral concepts that add a vital gloss to its core concepts. More specifically, ideologies have two kinds of periphery. The one exists on the dimension of significance, and will be referred to as the margin. The other exists on the interface with time and space, and will be referred to as the perimeter. The margin pertains to ideas and concepts whose importance to the core, to the heart of the ideology, is intellectually and emotionally insubstantial. Concepts may often gravitate from a more central to a marginal position, or vice versa. Natural rights gravitated from a core to a marginal position in liberal morphology, whereas violence gravitated from a marginal to a core position in the development of fascism. Hence modifications on the significance dimension will often be longer term arrangements, reflecting accumulative changes, though they may occasionally be triggered off by cataclysmic events in the non-ideational environment of an ideology, such as the impact of the collapse of the Soviet Union on the hitherto marginal role of markets in East European socialist ideologies. Sometimes the retention of a marginal concept or idea may be dysfunctional to the survival of an ideology and direct it to ideational dead ends, as increasingly became the case with nationalization in Western socialist programmes. Although no longer closely adjacent to the socialist core in many modern reformulations of socialism, dogged adherence to nationalization in its new marginal location proved costly to many West European socialist ideologies, and German and British socialists, for example, acted on that insight. In addition, some concepts may be marginal simply in the sense that other ideologies force them on the agenda, but the ideology in question relates to them only reluctantly and contingently. Xenophobia and its impact on immigration policies may serve as an example. It is of course the case that a concept marginal to one ideology, for instance social order to liberalism, may be at the core of another—conservatism.

The perimeter reflects the fact that core and adjacent concepts are located in historical, geographical, and cultural contexts. It refers to additional ideas and concepts that straddle the interface between the conceptualization of social realities and the external contexts and concrete manifestations in and through which those conceptualizations occur. It requires that, for an ideology to relate to, and emerge from, those contexts, indeed to avoid being couched at levels of generality that have no relevance to social and political worlds, it must conceive of, assimilate, and attempt to shape 'real-world' events. Through it a practice or institution or event is integrated into the macro-structure of the ideology. That process is essential to the specific decontestation and fleshing out of the abstractions which characterize core, and to a lesser extent adjacent, concepts. Whereas those abstractions enable ideologies to function on a long-term and wide-space basis, and hence permit the flexibility necessary to their survival, the relatively concrete perimeter concepts, ideas, and attitudes enable them to gain relevance for specific issues, to incorporate and identify significant facts and practices, to embrace external change, and to provide the greater degree of precision necessary to interpret the core and adjacent concepts.

Perimeter components of an ideology often are specific ideas or policy-proposals rather than fully fledged concepts, lacking the generalization and sophistication associated with a concept. They may also be applications of more general concepts to specific practices, as in the case of a concrete instance of censorship relating to the core concept of liberty. They may tend to be more ephemeral as well as particular, but that very specificity enables them to serve as the micro-ideological conduits of cultural constraints that impact on the macro-ideological structure, as well as conduits of structural and logical constraints already available in the ideological grouping in question, through which social facts and concrete events are construed. Their boundary location is crucial to the configuration, flow, and layering of meaning within the ideology and, unlike marginal concepts, is not to be regarded as a reflection of lesser or 'fallen' conceptual status within it. Nevertheless, any particular perimeter concept is peripheral in the sense that the existence of the total ideological morphology does not depend on its presence or absence. Of course, some perimeter concepts may be marginal concepts as well, while others may gravitate towards the ideological core. The impact of the practice of civil disobedience on conservative ideology has been marginal; while, conversely, free trade as a concrete set of practices moved away from both perimeter and marginal status to take on the features of an important adjacent concept to the nineteenth-century core of liberalism. By adopting an adjacent position, it no longer came under case-by-case scrutiny and thus was insulated from immediate and continuous change.

Here lies another significant morphological distinction between political philosophies and most ideologies. The former organize political concepts without much reference to perimeter ideas and practices. Their structure is controlled by the individual philosopher, or group of philosophers, producing them. Superficially, this constitutes a parallel with the subgroup of dogmatic and doctrinaire ideologies, whose structure is governed by powerful ideologues. However, philosophers adopt such an immunity to the perimeter for clarificatory reasons, or because they hope to maintain a high level of argument unsullied by less rational contributions, or because they focus on counterfactual or ideal propositions. Yet they remain open to internal conceptual rearrangements on the basis of logic or 'good' arguments. Doctrinaire and dogmatic ideologies, on the other hand, deliberately sever their links with key perimeter 'intrusions', thus isolating themselves from the external world and from the possibility of reflecting changes in their idea-environments, in order to ensure the relative immobilization of forced relationships among the components of their ideologies. Both need be contrasted with open ideologies which are partly perimeter-driven and shaped by notions and practices at the interface with political action.

Any specific belief item within an ideology will be identified by a particular route (among many possible ones) from the core, through adjacent concepts, to a perimeter one, as well as by the reverse movement. Thus, the assertion of the importance of a viable national health service may be decoded as encompassing a core belief about human welfare, decontested (and valued) as human flourishing; attached to adjacent concepts such as community, power, and responsibility (jointly decontested as involving state intervention to further the core belief), human rights (decontested as rights to social services), and the public interest (decontested as the maintenance of human capacities at their highest possible level); and rounded off by perimeter concepts linked to specific policy-proposals, such as pain and suffering (decontested as undesirable, especially when avoidable), and need (decontested as the provision of medical services to all who require them). Concurrently, travelling in the other direction of the interface, a financial crisis, or the lack of blood donors, may spark off a consideration of market-exchange relationships as an adjacent constraint on human flourishing, or genetic engineering may be identified as a relevant fact when interpreted through the prism of its potential danger to the equal rights principle involved in a national health service. The result could be the relocation of an adjacent concept within the ideological morphology, and in the longer run a potentially transformational impact on the core itself if, for instance, the responsibility for human flourishing would, through the economic and legal penalization of infirmity, shift to parents and experts. Conversely, the existing morphology could be reinforced as a consequence of such a prospect. In addition, perimeter concepts acting as conduits for cultural constraints could override logical constraints. The latter, after all, are internal rather than external and do not interface with the 'real' world. Thus, a 'national' health service could override its entailed universal and equal treatment by granting differential access to various groups, as a response to exigencies of funding and to preferences of allocation. This rudimentary scheme does not rule out other interpretations.

9   Slavoj Žižek, from 'Introduction' to *Mapping Ideology* (Verso, 1994), pp. 7–8, 10–15

Slavoj Žižek (1949–) is a Slovenian social and cultural theorist. Žižek has been particularly influenced by the psychoanalysis of Jacques Lacan as well as by Hegel and Althusser. He has produced a torrent of theoretical studies of subjects as diverse as Hegel and Alfred Hitchcock, including *The Sublime Object of Ideology* (1989), *Looking Awry* (1991), *Everything You Always Wanted to Know About Lacan (but were Afraid to Ask Hitchcock)* (1992), *The Metastases of Enjoyment* (1994), *The Ticklish Subject* (1999), *Did Somebody Mention Totalitarianism?* (2002).

In all these *ad hoc* analyses, however, we have already *practicized* the critique of ideology, while our initial question concerned the *concept* of ideology presupposed in this practice. Up till now, we have been guided by a 'spontaneous' pre-comprehension which, although it led us to contradictory results, is not to be underestimated, but rather explicated. For example, we somehow implicitly seem to know what is 'no longer' ideology: as long as the Frankfurt School accepted the critique of political economy as its base, it remained within the co-ordinates of the critique of ideology, whereas the notion of 'instrumental reason' no longer appertains to the horizon of the critique of ideology—'instrumental reason' designates an attitude that is not simply functional with regard to social domination but, rather, serves as the very foundation of the relationship of domination. An ideology is thus not necessarily 'false': as to its positive content, it can be 'true', quite accurate, since what really matters is not the asserted content as such but *the way this content is related to the subjective position implied by its own process of enunciation*. We are within ideological space proper the moment this content—'true' or 'false' (if true, so much the better for the ideological effect)—is functional with regard to some relation of social domination ('power', 'exploitation') in an inherently non-transparent way: *the very logic of legitimizing the relation of domination must remain concealed if it is to be effective*. In other words, the starting point of the critique of ideology has to be full acknowledgement of the fact that it is easily possible to *lie in the guise of truth*. When, for example, some

Western power intervenes in a Third World country on account of violations of human rights, it may well be 'true' that in this country the most elementary human rights were not respected, and that the Western intervention will effectively improve the human rights record, yet such a legitimization none the less remains 'ideological' in so far as it fails to mention the true motives of the intervention (economic interests, etc.). The outstanding mode of this 'lying in the guise of truth' today is cynicism: with a disarming frankness one 'admits everything', yet this full acknowledgement of our power interests does not in any way prevent us from pursuing these interests—the formula of cynicism is no longer the classic Marxian 'they do not know it, but they are doing it'; it is 'they know very well what they are doing, yet they are doing it'.

How, then, are we to explicate this implicit pre-comprehension of ours? How are we to pass from doxa to truth?

. . .

This logico-narrative reconstruction of the notion of ideology will be centred on the repeated occurrence of the already mentioned reversal of non-ideology into ideology—that is, of the sudden awareness of how the very gesture of stepping out of ideology pulls us back into it.

1. So, to begin with, we have ideology 'in-itself': the immanent notion of ideology as a doctrine, a composite of ideas, beliefs, concepts, and so on, destined to convince us of its 'truth', yet actually serving some unavowed particular power interest. The mode of the critique of ideology that corresponds to this notion is that of *symptomal reading*: the aim of the critique is to discern the unavowed bias of the official text via its ruptures, blanks and slips—to discern in 'equality and freedom' the equality and freedom of the partners in the market exchange which, of course, privileges the owner of the means of production, and so on. Habermas, perhaps the last great representative of this tradition, measures the distortion and/or falsity of an ideological edifice with the standard of non-coercive rational argumentation, a kind of 'regulative ideal' that, according to him, inheres in the symbolic order as such. Ideology is a systematically distorted communication: a text in which, under the influence of unavowed social interests (of domination, etc.), a gap separates its 'official', public meaning from its actual intention—that is to say, in which we are dealing with an unreflected tension between the explicit enunciated content of the text and its pragmatic presuppositions.

Today, however, probably the most prestigious tendency in the critique of ideology, one that grew out of discourse analysis, inverts this relationship: what the tradition of Enlightenment dismisses as a mere disturbance of 'normal' communication turns out to be its positive condition. The concrete intersubjective space of symbolic communication is always structured by various (unconscious) textual devices that cannot be reduced to secondary rhetoric. What we are dealing with here is not a complementary move to the traditional Enlightenment or Habermasian approach but its inherent reversal: what Habermas perceives as the step out of ideology is denounced here as ideology *par excellence*. In the Enlightenment tradition, 'ideology' stands for the blurred ('false') notion of reality caused by various 'pathological' interests (fear of death and of natural forces, power interests, etc.); for discourse analysis, the very notion of an access to reality unbiased by any discursive devices or conjunctions with power is ideological. The 'zero level' of ideology consists in (mis)perceiving a discursive formation as an extra-discursive fact.

Already in the 1950s, in *Mythologies*, Roland Barthes proposed the notion of ideology as the 'naturalization' of the symbolic order—that is, as the perception that reifies the results of discursive procedures into properties of the 'thing itself'. Paul de Man's notion of the 'resistance to (deconstructionist) theory' runs along the same lines: 'deconstruction' met with such resistance because it 'denaturalizes' the enunciated content by bringing to the light of day the discursive procedures that engender evidence of Sense. Arguably the most elaborate version of this approach is Oswald Ducrot's theory of argumentation; although it does not employ the term 'ideology', its ideologico-critical potential is tremendous. Ducrot's basic notion is that one cannot draw a clear line of separation between descriptive and argumentative levels of language: there is no neutral descriptive content; every description (designation) is already a moment of some argumentative scheme; descriptive predicates themselves are ultimately reified-naturalized argumentative gestures. This argumentative thrust relies on *topoi*, on the 'commonplaces' that operate only as naturalized, only in so far as we apply them in an automatic, 'unconscious' way—a successful argumentation presupposes the invisibility of the mechanisms that regulate its efficiency.

One should also mention here Michel Pêcheux, who gave a strict linguistic turn to Althusser's theory of interpellation. His work is centred on the discursive mechanisms that generate the 'evidence' of Sense. That is to say, one of the fundamental stratagems of ideology is the reference to some self-evidence—'Look, you can see for yourself how things are!'. 'Let the facts speak for themselves' is perhaps the arch-statement of ideology—the point being, precisely, that facts *never* 'speak for themselves' but are always *made to speak* by a network of discursive devices. Suffice it to recall the notorious anti-abortion film *The Silent Scream*—we 'see' a foetus which 'defends itself', which 'cries', and so on, yet what we 'don't see' in this very act of seeing is that we 'see' all this against the background of a discursively pre-constructed space. Discourse analysis is perhaps at its strongest in answering this precise question: when a racist Englishman says 'There are too many Pakistanis on our streets!', *how—from what place—does he 'see' this*—that is, how is his symbolic space structured so that he can perceive the fact of a Pakistani strolling along a London street as a disturbing surplus? That is to say, here one must bear in mind Lacan's motto that *nothing is lacking in the real*: every perception of a lack or a surplus ('not enough of this', 'too much of that') always involves a *symbolic* universe.

Last but not least, mention should be made here of Ernesto Laclau and his path-breaking approach to Fascism and populism, whose main theoretical result is that meaning does not inhere in elements of an ideology as such—these elements, rather, function as 'free-floating signifiers' whose meaning is fixed by the mode of their hegemonic articulation. Ecology, for example, is never 'ecology as such', it is always enchained in a specific series of equivalences: it can be conservative (advocating the return to balanced rural communities and traditional ways of life), etatist (only a strong state regulation can save us from the impending catastrophe), socialist (the ultimate cause of ecological problems resides in the capitalist profit-orientated exploitation of natural resources), liberal-capitalist (one should include the damage to the environment in the price of the product, and thus leave the market to regulate the ecological balance), feminist (the exploitation of nature follows from the male attitude of domination), anarchic self-managerial (humanity can survive only if it reorganizes itself into small self-reliant communities that live in balance with nature), and so on. The point, of course, is that none of these enchainments is in itself 'true', inscribed in the very nature of the ecological problematic: which discourse will succeed in 'appropriating' ecology depends on the fight for discursive hegemony, whose outcome is not guaranteed by any underlying necessity or 'natural alliance'. The other inevitable consequence of such a notion of hegemonic articulation is that etatist, conservative, socialist, and so on, inscription of ecology does not designate a secondary connotation that supplements its primary 'literal' meaning: as Derrida would have put it, this supplement retroactively (re)defines the very nature of 'literal' identity—a conservative enchainment, for example, throws a specific light on the ecological problematic itself ('due to his false arrogance, man forsook his roots in the natural order', etc.).

2. What follows is the step from 'in-itself' to 'for-itself', to ideology in its otherness-externalization: the moment epitomized by the Althusserian notion of Ideological State Apparatuses (ISA) that designate the material existence of ideology in ideological practices, rituals and institutions. Religious belief, for example, is not merely or even primarily an inner conviction, but the Church as an institution and its rituals (prayer, baptism, confirmation, confession . . .) which, far from being a mere secondary externalization of the inner belief, stand for *the very mechanisms that generate it*. When Althusser repeats, after Pascal: 'Act as if you believe, pray, kneel down, and you shall believe, faith will arrive by itself', he delineates an intricate reflective mechanism of retroactive 'autopoetic' foundation that far exceeds the reductionist assertion of the dependence of inner belief on external behaviour. That is to say, the implicit logic of his argument is: kneel down and *you shall believe that you knelt down because of your belief*—that is, your following the ritual is an expression/effect of your inner belief; in short, the 'external' ritual performatively generates its own ideological foundation.

What we encounter here again is the 'regression' into ideology at the very point where we apparently step out of it. In this respect, the relationship between Althusser and Foucault is of special interest. The Foucauldian counterparts to Ideological State Apparatuses are the disciplinary procedures that operate at the level of 'micro-power' and designate the point at which *power inscribes itself into the body directly, bypassing ideology*—for that precise reason, Foucault never uses the term 'ideology' apropos of these mechanisms of micro-power. This abandoning of the problematic of ideology entails a fatal weakness of Foucault's theory. Foucault never tires of repeating how power constitutes itself 'from below', how it does not emanate from some unique summit: this very semblance of a Summit (the Monarch or some other embodiment of Sovereignty) emerges as the secondary effect of the plurality of micro-practices, of the complex network of their interrelations. However, when he is compelled to display the concrete mechanism of this emergence, Foucault resorts to the extremely suspect rhetoric of complexity, evoking the intricate network of lateral links, left and right, up and down . . . a clear case of patching up, since one can never arrive at Power this way—the abyss that separates micro-procedures from the spectre of Power remains unbridgeable. Althusser's advantage over Foucault seems evident: Althusser proceeds in exactly the opposite direction—from the very outset, he conceives these micro-procedures as parts of the ISA; that is to say, as mechanisms which, in order to be operative, to 'seize' the individual, always-already presuppose the massive presence of the state, the transferential relationship of the individual towards state power, or—in Althusser's terms—towards the ideological big Other in whom the interpellation originates.

This Althusserian shift of emphasis from ideology 'in-itself' to its material existence in the ISA proved its fecundity in a new approach to Fascism; Wolfgang Fritz Haug's criticism of Adorno is exemplary here. Adorno refuses to treat Fascism as an ideology in the proper sense of the term, that is, as 'rational legitimization of the existing order'. So-called 'Fascist ideology' no longer possesses the coherence of a rational construct that calls for conceptual analysis and ideologico-critical refutation; that is to say, it no longer functions as a 'lie necessarily experienced as truth' (the sign of recognition of a true ideology). 'Fascist ideology' is not taken seriously even by its promoters; its status is purely instrumental, and ultimately relies on external coercion. In his response to Adorno, however, Haug triumphantly demonstrates how this capitulation to the primacy of the doctrine, far from implying the 'end of ideology', asserts the founding gesture of the ideological as such: the call to unconditional subordination and to 'irrational' sacrifice. What liberal criticism (mis)perceives as Fascism's weakness is the very resort of its strength: within the Fascist horizon, the very demand for rational argumentation that should provide grounds for our acceptance of authority is denounced in advance as an index of the liberal degeneration of the true spirit of ethical sacrifice—as Haug puts it, in browsing through Mussolini's texts, one cannot avoid the uncanny feeling that Mussolini had read Althusser! The direct denunciation of the Fascist notion of the 'community-of-the-people [*Volksgemeinschaft*]' as a deceptive lure that conceals the reality of domination and exploitation fails to take note of the crucial fact that this *Volksgemeinschaft* was materialized in a series of rituals and practices (not only mass gatherings and parades but also large-scale campaigns to help the hungry, organized sports and cultural activities for the workers, etc.) which performatively produced the effect of *Volksgemeinschaft*.

3. In the next step of our reconstruction, this externalization is, as it were, 'reflected into itself': what takes place is the disintegration, self-limitation and self-dispersal of the notion of ideology. Ideology is no longer conceived as a homogeneous mechanism that guarantees social reproduction, as the 'cement' of society; it turns into a Wittgensteinian 'family' of vaguely connected and heterogeneous procedures whose reach is strictly localized. Along these lines, the critiques of the so-called Dominant Ideology Thesis (DIT) endeavour to demonstrate that an ideology either exerts an influence that is crucial, but constrained to some narrow social stratum, or its role in social reproduction is marginal. At the beginnings of capitalism, for example, the role of the Protestant ethic of hard work as an end-in-itself, and so on, was limited to the stratum of emerging capitalists, whereas workers and peasants, as well as the upper classes, continued to obey other, more traditional ethical attitudes, so that one can in no way attribute to the Protestant ethic the role of the 'cement' of the entire social edifice. Today, in late capitalism, when the expansion of the new mass media in principle, at least, enables ideology effectively to penetrate every pore of the social body, the weight of ideology as such is diminished: individuals do not act as they do primarily on account of their beliefs or ideological convictions—that is to say, the system, for the most part, bypasses ideology in its reproduction and relies on economic coercion, legal and state regulations, and so on.

Here, however, things get blurred again, since the moment we take a closer look at these allegedly extra-ideological mechanisms that regulate social reproduction, we find ourselves knee-deep in the already mentioned obscure domain in which reality is indistinguishable from ideology. What we encounter here, therefore, is the third reversal of non-ideology into ideology: all of a sudden we become aware of a For-itself of ideology at work in the very In-itself of extra-ideological actuality. First, the mechanisms of economic coercion and legal regulation always 'materialize' some propositions or beliefs that are inherently ideological (the criminal law, for example, involves a belief in the personal responsibility of the individual or the conviction that crimes are a product of social circumstances). Secondly, the form of consciousness that fits late-capitalist 'post-ideological' society—the cynical, 'sober' attitude that advocates liberal 'openness' in the matter of 'opinions' (everybody is free to believe whatever she or he wants; this concerns only his or her privacy), disregards pathetic ideological phrases and follows only utilitarian and/or hedonistic motivations—*stricto sensu* remains an ideological attitude: it involves a series of ideological presuppositions (on the relationship between 'values' and 'real life', on personal freedom, etc.) that are necessary for the reproduction of existing social relations.

What thereby comes into sight is a third continent of ideological phenomena: neither ideology *qua* explicit doctrine, articulated convictions on the nature of man, society and the universe, nor ideology in its material existence (institutions, rituals and practices that give body to it), but the elusive network of implicit, quasi-'spontaneous' presuppositions and attitudes that form an irreducible moment of the reproduction of 'non-ideological' (economic, legal, political, sexual . . .) practices. The Marxian notion of 'commodity fetishism' is exemplary here: it designates not a (bourgeois) theory of political economy but a series of presuppositions that determine the structure of the very 'real' economic practice of market exchange—in theory, a capitalist clings to utilitarian nominalism, yet in his own practice (of exchange, etc.) he follows 'theological whimsies' and acts as a speculative idealist. . . . For that reason, a direct reference to extra-ideological coercion (of the market, for example) is an ideological gesture *par excellence*: the market and (mass) media are dialectically interconnected; we live in a 'society of the spectacle' (Guy Debord) in which the media structure our perception of reality in advance and render reality indistinguishable from the 'aestheticized' image of it.

2   Liberalism

Introduction

Liberalism is complicated, intricate, and pervasive. Its emergence as a name for a distinctive political position in the early nineteenth century is often taken to mark the birth of the 'age of ideologies', but it remains a notoriously tricky business either precisely to date its origins or to police its boundaries. For liberalism spills over into other ideological domains. There are liberal forms of feminism, nationalism, and even of socialism and sometimes conservatism. There is often a corresponding lack of clarity among liberalism's critics about whether they have come to bury the doctrine or to fulfil it: that is, about whether it embodies a wholly corrupt picture of human nature, society, and politics, or a basically sound ethical vision that needs liberating from the socially limited expression of it offered by particular liberals—from patriarchy for feminists, a misguided belief in private property and free exchange for social-ists, or from an excessive faith in the state as an agent of social justice, for libertarians. And, as with all the ideologies discussed in this book, liberalism is riven by significant internal divi-sions and arguments, and emerges through a variety of distinctive national discourses, prob-lems, and traditions. The term sets out as a description of a form of education, and as a term for certain personal traits of tolerance and broadmindedness. In the latter sense, it was used both as a compliment and as a rebuke—an ambiguity that still attaches to the term in contemporary discourse, notably in the United States of America. It emerges as a specifically political term in Spanish politics between 1810 and 1820, where the party of *liberales* sought to establish a secular constitution and a freedom of the press, but is soon used in English and French to refer to similar political movements.

The readings selected here bring out the important similarities and divergences within liberalism. In part, these differences reflect the contextual character of political ideology, as different historical moments and national contexts bring out different concerns. For example, one major fissure emerges through the changing attitudes toward capitalism among liberals from the second half of the nineteenth century. The assault on freedom of contract launched by a later generation of liberals in the name of individual liberty would have been inconceiv-able to an earlier generation. A second diagnosis of these divergences is not historical but conceptual. Debates within liberalism also offer prime examples of the 'essentially con-tested' character of political concepts, terms whose meanings are perennially vulnerable to debate. For example, if liberals are defined as fundamentally committed to individual liberty as the highest political value, this opens up a range of controversies about this value. Is lib-erty 'positive' or 'negative'? What are its limits? What are its social preconditions? Is a person's liberty constrained only by physical restraint, by threats, by social disapproval, or by some other means? These disagreements and shifts in ideological character within liberalism are not unique to this ideology, as we noted in the Introduction.

In spite of the divergences among liberals, certain continuities of concern among liberals can be identified, however differently these are interpreted by different liberals in different settings. For liberals, the individual human being is the central unit of ethical value, and the protection and promotion of individual interests form the bedrock criteria by which political arrangements are assessed. Central among these interests is individual freedom. This sets liberals against tyranny and arbitrary or absolutist government, which suppress individual freedom. The state is viewed as a human organization whose authority derives from its meeting the secular and purposes of the governed, rather than from divine right, tradition, or the charisma of political leaders. Accordingly, liberals support such constitutionalist devices as the separation of powers between the legislature, the judiciary, and the executive, due process, and protection of individual rights, such as freedoms of movement, occupation, and association, in order to constrain government to respect the interests of the governed. Liberals also tend to support representative government, as a mechanism for reminding governors of this responsibility. An important part of this liberal conception of the state is a resistance to the theocratic imposition of a single religious or doctrinal viewpoint, and support of toleration for a variety of ways of life and beliefs. While liberals tend to share a cautious attitude toward the state as a potential purveyor of intolerance and tyranny, important disagreements and differences of emphasis emerge from quite early in the history of the doctrine over whether the sources of constraint on individual freedom may not merely be political but also social, deriving from the conformist biases of public opinion or the operation of untrammelled individualism, and how liberals should treat social threats to freedom.

The first extract, from the second of John Locke's *Two Treatises of Government* pre-dates the crystallization of liberalism as an ideology. But Locke's work articulates a number of themes that were to shape the political imaginations of later generations of liberals, including the importance of reason, religious toleration, the significance of private property and a conception of the state as nothing more or less than an instrument through which citizens can enforce their rights and which is subject to their consent [Reading 10]. The extracts here focus on these last two aspects of Locke's thought. Locke's account of property rights is expressly rooted in a view of humans as a special sort of divine creation. The earth's bounty is initially made available to all by God. What gives rise to private property rights in some part of this is in the first instance the fact of having 'mixed labour' with some unowned portion of the world. Since natural resources, and particularly land, will tend wholly to fall into private ownership, he adds that even those without private property of this sort benefit in an economic system in which property is in private hands.

Political society is understood as the product of an act of consent on the part of those who are governed. Since humans are naturally free, they can only give up their freedom by agreeing to forgo their natural liberty and placing themselves under the control of political authority. (In most contemporary societies, Locke prudently and famously concedes, this consent need merely be tacit, taken as read from the behaviour of the governed.) This too, it is worth noting, is the result of an attempt to live according to the purposes God has assigned to humankind, since legitimate political authorities are legitimate precisely in that they can effectively judge and enforce the God-given natural law. The legitimacy of the government then depends on its legally enforcing the implications of the law of nature, and in particular in its protecting the 'life, liberty and estates' of those who are subject to it. Where the government fails to do so, the political bond between governors and governed is dissolved, and the subjects have a right to 'appeal to heaven', and to resist and replace their governors. While the people are the final judges of whether the government has become tyrannous, Locke emphasizes that relatively minor misdemeanours should be overlooked and that revolution aims to re-establish the political bond and restore a prior set of legitimate constitutional arrangements between governors and governed.

The following four extracts articulate different varieties of early liberal individualism. Each views the state as an indispensable source of security for the individual but at the same time as a potential interference, and emphasizes the need for limited and constitutional government. Benjamin Constant, writing at the moment when the term 'liberal' comes to designate a particular political stance, offers a famous statement of a liberal conception of individual liberty. His view of liberty rests on an account of the distinctive economic and social requirements of modern societies [Reading 11]. In his 1819 speech given at the Athénée Royale, from which an extract is included here, he sets out what freedom means in modern societies, and to explain why modern liberty has come to shape what is politically possible: 'we must have liberty', as he puts it, 'and we will have it'. According to Constant, liberty in ancient polities such as Athens, Sparta, and Rome meant political liberty, the liberty to participate in governing collective affairs, by deliberating in the public forum over whether to go to war, voting on laws, and in scrutinizing the actions of magistrates or the public accounts. This was compatible with individual subjection to public norms in matters of religion, opinion, and occupation. The populations of modern Europe by contrast have grown accustomed to liberty as civil liberty, freedoms of opinion, occupation, movement and association, and other rights, including political rights, that guarantee individual independence. The source of this difference was not only the size and complexity of modern states, which rendered the importance of the individual contribution to collective self-government negligible, but the demands of 'commercial society'. The ancient polities employed war to get what they wanted, where modern polities now see and are able to exploit the advantages of peaceful economic exchange in pursuit of the same goal. Cheaper and less hazardous than war, trade will tend to displace it as the principal mode of international relations (an extraordinarily optimistic judgement in the immediate wake of Europe's post-Revolutionary and Napoleonic wars). Private economic interests become the focus of individual lives, which have none of the leisure necessary for a sustained concern with public affairs. At the same time, commercial society promotes a love of independence from collective power, whose intervention in free exchange always seems inefficient and irritating. The attempt to resurrect a version of ancient liberty led to the violent excesses manifested in French Revolutionary Terror, but both Napoleonic and royalist forms of authoritarianism fail to respect modern liberty. Constant, it should be noted, locates a tension at the heart of modern liberty, between the individual drive to devote oneself to private affairs and the need for a degree of concern with the public good in order to defend the liberties of the moderns against a state that is only too happy to deprive its subjects of the right to share in political power. In the conclusion of his speech, he defends the need for some ancient public vigilance in the form of political representation if the liberties of the moderns were to be secured by the state, and indeed as an intrinsically worthwhile form of human activity.

One of the sources for Constant's appreciation of the significance of individuality was German romanticism. In the extract from *The Limits of State Action (Ideen zur einem Versuch, die Grünzen der Wirkskamkeit der Staats zu bestimmen)*, written in 1792 but only published in 1851, sixteen years after the death of its author, Wilhelm von Humboldt offers a powerful statement of the romantic conception of individuality as rational self-realization [Reading 12]. Liberalism was not a self-conscious movement in Germany until the 1840s, so it would be anachronistic to regard Humboldt as a fully fledged liberal. But this book was immensely influential, in Britain and France as well as in Germany. He celebrates originality, diversity, and the quasi-organic development of character through the interaction of the spontaneous self with a diverse and alterable environment. He ties this to a view of the minimal or 'night-watchman' state as the only political form that does not impede the organic development of individual selfhood: the principal purpose of the state is not to promote happiness, but to provide the conditions that allow individuality and excellence to flourish. This requires a minimal state, which allows each person to do as he wants, provided that he does not interfere with the liberty of others. A state that takes on too many roles saps the capacities for individual agency and judgement on the part of its subjects. It also erodes the social bonds and sense of mutual responsibility that naturally develop through the spontaneous arc of individuality.

The extract from James Mill's essay on *Government* displays a different sort of early liberal individualism, grounded in an egoistic psychology for which the principle of action is self-interest [Reading 13]. For Mill, government, like other social relationships and institutions, should be viewed in instrumental terms: it is essentially a means of reducing human insecurity in the light of the individual selfishness that Mill sees as the fundamental human motivation. For Mill (unlike Humboldt) the purpose of government is to promote the happiness of the individual and the whole community. The main way in which it does this is by providing for individual security and by constraining the extent to which some members of the community illegitimately live off the labour of others. In the absence of public authority, we would all be vulnerable to the unrestrained use of terror ('Terror is the grand instrument') on the part of those seeking to use us to advance their own interests and desires. A problem then arises with the authority that is set up in order to protect the individual, which he sets out in the extract here. Government is required since there is no limit to the terror that we are prepared to inflict on one another in pursuit of our chosen ends. Even that paragon, the English gentleman, when in possession of unchecked personal power over others, as in the case of the slaveholders in the West Indies, is capable of blood-freezing cruelty. However, given the uniformity of human motivation, any governors we set up over us will themselves be inclined to use their power in order to exploit the rest of the populace. The solution is to make governors representative, subject to election with short terms of office. As the extract here makes clear, Mill is optimistic about the extent to which the interests of those represented are harmonious, a position somewhat in conflict with the assumptions of self-interest and potential mutual antipathy from which he sets out. The interests of women happily converge with those of their husbands or fathers, for example, allowing the franchise to be restricted to men, and the interests of men beneath middle age and the very poor too also may be satisfactorily represented by others. All the same, it should be noted that Mill's proposals entail a radical extension of the franchise by contemporary standards.

Like Constant, Alexis de Tocqueville starts from what he takes to be the general social tendencies of the modern world, grounded in his momentous studies of America [Reading 14]. Modern society is defined by a democratic ethos of egalitarianism, for which no individual or group can claim an inherent superiority: it is a society in which careers are open and in which there is no social fixity or aristocracy. Such a society gives rise to various passions. One of these he calls '*individualisme*', a 'calm and considered feeling which disposes each citizen to isolate himself from the mass of his fellows and withdraw into the circle of family and friends'. In a fluid society with no fixed social hierarchy, we each rely on our own individual efforts to rise or fall in the world, and this leads to an individual focus on the private sphere and a devotion to commercial activity to the exclusion of wider public concerns. At the same time, the absence of accepted intellectual authority creates a vacuum that is filled by ill-informed majority opinion, since only weight of numbers can serve to give an idea legitimacy. The psychological dynamics of democratic society give rise to a stultifying sameness in public opinion and an unwillingness on the part of the majority to permit difference. This in turn supports popular government that may prove as insensitive to individual liberty as traditional absolutist rulers. This famous account of 'democratic despotism' is only part of a larger and highly refined account, which also discerns counter-tendencies to this despotism in the political decentralization and strength of voluntary associations in the United States. But Tocqueville sees these latter tendencies as relatively weak in a European state such as France, labouring under the historical legacies of feudalism and absolutist government, and which would be accordingly more subject to the threat of democratic despotism.

Tocqueville, Humboldt and James Mill were all profound influences on the latter's son, John Stuart Mill, who offers the most potent and enduring, if also elusive, statement of the liberal conception of individual liberty in *On Liberty* [Reading 15], in one 'very simple principle': 'the only purpose for which power can be rightfully exercised over any member of a civilized community, against his will, is to prevent harm to others'. For contemporaries, as well as subsequent legions of commentators, the principle appears not very simple at all, the critical issues being not only whether the principle is valid but, if it is, what we take to constitute harm to others. With Tocqueville, Mill in *On Liberty* stresses not only the political but social sources of oppression: he is concerned with the need to protect individuality from the social pressures that stifle non-conformity. As in the extracts from Locke and from the elder Mill, it is worth noting the shadow of imperial possession in Mill's account. His 'very simple principle' is not intended to apply where a population is uncivilized, childish, or backward: it has no grip on earlier stages of European society when despotism was a more appropriate form of government, and the despotic power of the East India Company over its subjects remains legitimate for Mill.

The second extract from Mill indicates a fissure within the liberal tradition that deepens as the nineteenth century wears on. For liberals in the early part of the century, tradition, the state, and even public opinion can be oppressive. The thought that the individual should be allowed to enter into whatever agreements he wishes and to dispose of his private property as he likes was central to the liberal emphasis on establishing the individual as the linchpin of political morality. But it was apparent, as socialists stressed, that private property may be used oppressively rather than beneficially or merely harmlessly, and in theory and practice it became a pressing concern for liberals whether restraints on freedom of trade or contract were justifiable within a liberal framework. In the late work *Chapters on Socialism*, Mill argues that the wage-labourer has little genuine choice over his choice of occupation or terms of employment. In the extract reproduced here, he stresses the conventional rather than natural character of property rights. Provided that equitable compensation is made, he concludes, 'society is fully entitled to abrogate or alter any particular right of property which on sufficient consideration it judges to stand in the way of the public good'.

The struggle for the soul of liberalism was sharpened in the later nineteenth century by the liberalism of the idealists and the development of 'New Liberalism', for which unchecked freedom of contract could be as tyrannous as state power. Where once it had seemed most important to free the entrepreneurial individual from oppressive government and tradition, it was now necessary to free the worker and consumer from the misuse of capital. For T. H. Green, the liberal value of freedom is only a substantive value when it designates not merely the negative absence of interference but a more complex value, 'the liberation of all men equally for contributions to a common good' or 'a positive power or capacity of doing or enjoying something worth doing or enjoying, and that, too, something we do or enjoy in common with others' [Reading 16]. Traditional liberal notions of freedom need to be refined in order to take into account the social context of human action, and to recognize that liberty requires an actual capacity to act. So, for example, my freedom to read a book requires not merely that no one stop me from putting it in front of my nose but that I have the requisite level of literacy. Further, there is a moral component in this conception of freedom: a person is only free if doing something worth doing. Finally, there is a social component: freedom must be enjoyed in common with others, which means that my freedom not only requires that I do not deprive others of their freedom, but that in acting freely I make some contribution to the good or well-being of others. The state can contribute to freedom, by laying down rules whose infringement is punishable, but which can be treated as a guide if followed freely, and by removing obstacles to free action that stem from the abuse of social, economic or political power, or from such factors as ignorance and poor environmental conditions. Liberalism should be distinguished from the uncritical embrace of *laissez-faire* therefore, and Green argues for such measures as health and safety legislation governing factories and tighter public control of drinking establishments. At the same time, Green expresses a concern that the state should not stifle individual self-direction.

Green's thought was influential for a subsequent generation of so-called New Liberals, along with ideas of the evolution of society towards increasing rational cooperation. Some New Liberal demands came to be expressed in the social policies of the Asquith government in Britain and by Progressive demands and policies of Roosevelt's New Deal in the United States. In the extract from L. T. Hobhouse's classic summation *Liberalism* [Reading 17], the 'social factor' in private property is stressed. The responsibility of a liberal society is, on the one hand, to maintain and stimulate personal effort—as socialism cannot, he believes—and, on the other hand, to ensure a just level of reward for each social function and to further public goods that the market fails to supply. Hobhouse also affirms the democratic character of liberalism, as expressive of the equality and solidarity of all social classes. He argues that although the internal politics of Britain are increasingly democratic this is incompatible with practice of imperial rule, which is damaging in its effects not only on colonies but on the internal politics of imperial powers. In the extract here, he sets out how he believes liberal internationalism is wedded to the principle of self-government. The overarching belief in Hobhouse's thought is the rational harmony of human experience and both these extracts here set out to show that apparently opposed principles are in fact reconciled in a properly understood liberalism.

For the American philosopher John Dewey the replacement of *laissez-faire* with intelligent social action is a requirement of the positive liberty in modern, industrial conditions

[Reading 18]. To will freedom as an end is to will its means, and these means now include a socialized economy, or what he calls (with a piece of contemporary sociological jargon) social control, a notion that commentators on both the right and the left came to think of as ominous. Dewey's intentions, however, are idealistic rather than authoritarian. A progressive and later a critic of the New Deal from the left, Dewey argues for democratic control over those social institutions that shape our character and dispositions—that are relevant to the development of individuality.

Max Weber offers a far more pessimistic prognosis for liberalism in the twentieth century [Reading 19]. For Weber the distinctive structures of modern social control raise profound problems for individual liberty and for the liberal aspiration to control the state in the interests of citizens. In the extract from 'Parliament and Government in a Reconstructed Germany', written in 1917, Weber anticipates the collapse of German imperial government and offers a diagnosis of its pathologies. He famously argues that bureaucratic organization is an indispensable feature of modern societies, found in the business corporation, the state, the army, political party, and church—indeed, one of his central criticisms of Marxist socialism was directed at the aspiration to overcome bureaucratic economic and political management. Bureaucracy is the supreme social expression of efficiency, a machine that can in principle be turned in any direction. However, it also has its own internal logic, and the hierarchy, rigidity, and routine imposed by the bureaucratic machine opens up a future of lifeless serfdom, and erodes the conditions for individual liberty. In an echo of earlier liberal concerns, he argues that unresponsive rule by officials, in collusion with cartelized industrial and agricultural interests, destroys the conditions for individual initiative, and in particular the context in which certain kinds of elite group—the independent politician, the entrepreneur—may develop and flourish and undermines the social credibility of the value of individual freedom. The future of liberal societies, if they have a future, is one of perpetual struggle to maintain liberal values and forms of life in the face of the countervailing social forces in modernity.

The following three readings in different ways mark out the distinctive liberal responses to the ideological conflicts of the first half of the twentieth century, and illustrate distinctive liberal preoccupations in the years after the Second World War. The economist John Maynard Keynes's essay 'The End of Laissez-Faire' offers an influential statement of the conditional acceptance of capitalism that characterizes many liberal thinkers. He seeks to stake out a middle ground between socialism and capitalism through endowing the state with the responsibility of regulating levels of saving and investment [Reading 20]. The aim is to leave capitalism intact while mitigating the chief defects of the marketplace, such as unemployment. A potent model for reconciling an extensive state with the principles of liberalism, 'Keynesianism' became a crucial target for New Right criticisms of state economic management, for figures such as Hayek (see Reading 32).

The United Nations Declaration of Human Rights, proclaimed in the General Assembly of the UN on 10 December 1948, as a 'common standard of achievement for all peoples and all nations' became a key document for post-war liberalism [Reading 21]. This expressed the post-war reaction to the horrors of the interwar period and the Second World War. The document enshrines a particular set of rights with universal applicability. On the one hand, this provided lawyers and human rights campaigners with a potent ideological weapon that could be used in criticizing particular regimes and abuses. On the other hand, the document was not legally binding, and states are not signatories to it. This has meant that while some argue that the UN Declaration is an important part of customary international law, providing a standard against which states must be legally assessed, others view it as political rhetoric, which is only effective when states choose to enforce it, or are able to.

Isaiah Berlin's 'Two Concepts of Liberty' is also an important document for charting the self-understanding of liberals in the post-war period [Reading 22]. The comparison of negative and positive liberty echoes Constant's discussion of the liberties of the ancients and the moderns in his speech in 1819, and there is some parallel too in their political purposes. Like Constant, Berlin seeks to show how the positive conception of liberty as self-mastery has allowed the concept of liberty to be employed as a justification for oppression. The element in positive liberty he rejects is the idealist view of freedom as rational self-direction, which he identifies with mastery of a 'lower self'—the ignorant bundle of contingent impulses—on the part of a 'higher self', which claims a more assured knowledge of which desires pass muster as rational. This picture of inner struggle between the higher and the lower self can easily be abused as a justification for the domination of *others* on the part of those who claim the requisite moral or social knowledge. So, if I have a positive view of liberty, 'I am in a position to ignore the actual wishes of men or societies, to bully, oppress, torture them in the name, and on behalf of, their "real" selves, in the secure knowledge that whatever is the true goal of man (happiness, performance of duty, wisdom, a just society, self-fulfilment) must be identical with his freedom'. Instead (and in contrast to a writer such as Dewey) he argues for the pluralism of values, such as freedom, democracy, and happiness. To achieve one of these is not to achieve the others, and there may be circumstances in which achieving one is incompatible with achieving the others. Berlin's essay was an important statement of Cold War liberalism and scepticism about grand political projects, and remains a touchstone and starting point for debates among political philosophers over the concept of liberty.

One way of understanding John Rawls's magisterial philosophical study *A Theory of Justice* is as a distillation of the moral basis of the social democratic politics inaugurated by Keynesian liberalism together with the confident sense that liberal values, including individual rights, are universally applicable and provide a common standard for judging all societies, which was expressed in the UN Declaration. The extracts here [Reading 23] focus on his statement of two basic principles of justice, and particularly on what he calls the 'difference principle', whereby only those unequal social arrangements are justified that work to the greatest benefit of the least advantaged societies. Reviving something like the Lockean notion of a social contract, Rawls asks us to imagine a hypothetical situation in which we have to arrive at a set of social arrangements that we find acceptable, while each of us lacks any knowledge of the particular place we will end up occupying—whether we will be talented, untalented, rich, poor, devout, faithless, and so on. He argues that, given certain assumptions about human rationality, these hypothetical choosers will opt, first, to protect a set of basic liberal rights, guaranteeing individual freedoms. Once these are in place, they will support the difference principle as the basis for distributing the society's assets. The idea is that any chooser in this hypothetical situation will be concerned about the prospect of ending up at the bottom of the social order, and will therefore pick a social arrangement that will best promote the prospects of the worst off. Rawls's theory proved immensely influential, has provoked a torrent of debate, discussion, and criticism, and has been credited by some with reviving the discipline of political philosophy. (Robert Nozick's libertarian account of distributive justice from which we have included an excerpt in Chapter 3 [Reading 36] is in very large part an attempt to rebut the Rawlsian account in the name of a narrower set of individual rights. For a brief statement of a socialist challenge to the kind of liberal egalitarian discourse inaugurated by Rawls, see the excerpt from Alex Callinicos [Reading 51].) A historical irony is that Rawls's statement of liberal social justice emerged at the point at which the social democratic politics of the welfare state entered a period of prolonged crisis from the nineteen-seventies and onwards.

Rawls's second extract expresses a rather more chastened vision of liberalism, for which his earlier confident universalism fails to recognize deeply enough the plurality of moral, religious, and philosophical doctrines in contemporary societies. Liberalism, Rawls argues, aims for a standpoint from which its values can be justified to all those who have to live under them. But, in contrast to what Rawls calls a comprehensive liberalism, a category in which he includes Mill among others, what he calls political liberalism seeks to avoid specific, controversial ethical and metaphysical commitments, such as a belief in the progressive self-development of the individual. Instead, it tries to craft a set of principles that could be the object of agreement between 'incompatible but reasonable comprehensive doctrines', that is, on which all members of a society (or at least all, as he importantly qualifies it, who are 'reasonable') can converge. Whether and why all should converge on a set of specifically liberal principles—and where this leaves the earlier Rawls's commitment to social justice, which, as we saw, rested on a specific conception of human rationality—are questions that have been the subject of intense consideration by political theorists. It is a sign of the continuing importance and influence of liberalism for ideological discourse generally that attempts to think about the need to incorporate social diversity into the politics of the modern state tend to be framed as challenges or reconstructions of liberal thought (see, for example, Readings 51, 68, 69, 95, 96 below).

FURTHER READING

There is a voluminous literature on liberalism. Useful texts which offer differing readings of liberalism's ideological trajectories include Guido de Ruggiero, *The History of European Liberalism* (trans. by R. G. Collingwood; Clarendon Press, 1924), Larry Siedentop, 'Two Liberal Traditions', in Alan Ryan (ed.), *The Idea of Freedom* (Oxford University Press, 1979), Gerald F. Gaus, *The Modern Liberal Theory of Man* (Croom Helm, 1983), Anthony Arblaster, *The Rise and Decline of Western Liberalism* (Basil Blackwell, 1986), John Gray, *Liberalism* (Open University Press, 1986) and *The Two Faces of Liberalism* (Polity Press, 2000), Richard Bellamy, *Liberalism and Modern Society* (Polity Press, 1992), and James T. Kloppenberg, *The Virtues of Liberalism* (Oxford University Press, 1998). As well as the previous works, the following are good starting points for understanding contemporary debates in liberal political theory: Michael Sandel (ed.) *Liberalism and Its Critics* (Basil Blackwell, 1983); Stephen Mulhall and Adam Swift, *Liberals and Communitarians* (second edition, Basil Blackwell, 1996); and Gerald F. Gaus, *Contemporary Theories of Liberalism* (Sage, 2004).

10   **John Locke, from *Two Treatises of Government* (ed. P. Laslett; Cambridge University Press, 1988), pp. 285–92, 412–16**

John Locke (1632–1704) was born into an established country family in Somerset, and educated, as a physician and a philosopher, at the University of Oxford. He joined the household of Anthony Ashley Cooper, the Earl of Shaftsbury, an association that led to exile in Holland during the reign of James II. He developed his mature philosophy and political theory in this period. After the Glorious Revolution of 1688 Locke returned to England, and the publication of *An Essay Concerning Human Understanding* in 1690 established his philosophical reputation. By contrast, the publication of his most important political work, *Two Treatises of Government*, in the previous year was anonymous: the theoretical vindication of revolution was still immensely controversial, and would most likely have been lethal for Locke had the book appeared earlier in the decade (historians dispute the precise date of composition). His other important social and political works include *Thoughts on Education* (1693), *The Reasonableness of Christianity* (1695), and another text important for the foundation of liberal values, *A Letter Concerning Toleration* (1689).

25. Whether we consider natural *Reason*, which tells us, that Men, being once born, have a right to their Preservation, and consequently to Meat and Drink, and such other things, as Nature affords for their Subsistence: Or *Revelation*, which gives us an account of those Grants God made of the World to *Adam*, and to *Noah*, and his Sons, 'tis very clear, that God, as King *David says, Psal.* CXV. xvj. *has given the Earth to the Children of Men*, given it to Mankind in common. But this being supposed, it seems to some a very great difficulty, how any one should ever come to have a *Property* in any thing: I will not content my self to answer, That if it be difficult to make out *Property*, upon a supposition, that God gave the World to *Adam* and his Posterity in common; it is impossible that any Man, but one universal Monarch, should have any *Property*, upon a supposition, that God gave the World to *Adam*, and his Heirs in Succession, exclusive of all the rest of his Posterity. But I shall endeavour to shew, how Men might come to have a *property* in several parts of that which God gave to Mankind in common, and that without any express Compact of all the Commoners.

26. God, who hath given the World to Men in common, hath also given them reason to make use of it to the best advantage of Life, and convenience. The Earth, and all that is therein, is given to Men for the Support and Comfort of their being. And though all the Fruits it naturally produces, and Beasts it feeds, belong to Mankind in common, as they are produced by the spontaneous hand of Nature; and no body has originally a private Dominion, exclusive of the rest of Mankind, in any of them, as they are thus in their natural state: yet being given for the use of Men, there must of necessity be a means *to appropriate* them some way or other before they can be of any use, or at all beneficial to any particular Man. The Fruit, or Venison, which nourishes the wild *Indian*, who knows no Inclosure, and is till a Tenant in common, mut be his, and so his, *i.e.* a part of him, that another can no longer have any right to it, before it can do him any good for the support of his Life.

27. Though the Earth, and all inferior Creatures be common to all Men, yet every Man has a *Property* in his own *Person*. This no Body has any Right to but himself. The *Labour*

of his Body, and the *Work* of his Hands, we may say, are properly his. Whatsoever then he removes out of the State that Nature hath provided, and left it in, he hath mixed his *Labour* with, and joyned to it something that is his own, and thereby makes it his *Property*. It being by him removed from the common state Nature placed it in, it hath by this *labour* something annexed to it, that excludes the common right of other Men. For this *Labour* being the unquestionable Property of the Labourer, no Man but he can have a right to what that is once joyned to, at least where there is enough, and as good left in common for others.

28. He that is nourished by the Acorns he pickt up under an Oak, or the Apples he gathered from the Trees in the Wood, has certainly appropriated them to himself. No Body can deny but the nourishment is his. I ask then, When did they begin to be his? When he digested? Or when he eat? Or when he boiled? Or when he brought them home? Or when he pickt them up? And 'tis plain, if the first gathering made them not his, nothing else could. That *labour* put a distinction between them and common. That added something to them more than Nature, the common Mother of all, had done; and so they became his private right. And will any one say he had no right to those Acorns or Apples he thus appropriated, because he had not the consent of all Mankind to make them his? Was it a Robbery thus to assume to himself what belonged to all in Common? If such a consent as that was necessary, Man had starved, notwithstanding the Plenty God had given him. We see in *Commons*, which remain so by Compact, that 'tis the taking any part of what is common, and removing it out of the state Nature leaves it in, which *begins the Property*; without which the Common is of no use. And the taking of this or that part, does not depend on the express consent of all the Commoners. Thus the Grass my Horse has bit; the Turfs my Servant has cut; and the Ore I have digg'd in any place where I have a right to them in common with others, become my *Property*, without the assignation or consent of any body. The *labour* that was mine, removing them out of that common state they were in, hath *fixed* my *Property* in them.

29. By making an explicit consent of every Commoner, necessary to any ones appropriating to himself any part of what is given in common, Children or Servants could not cut the Meat which their Father or Master had provided for them in common, without assigning to every one his peculiar part. Though the Water running in the Fountain be every ones, yet who can doubt, but that in the Pitcher is his only who drew it out? His *labour* hath taken it out of the hands of Nature, where it was common, and belong'd equally to all her Children, and *hath* thereby *appropriated* it to himself.

30. Thus this Law of reason makes the Deer, that *Indian's* who hath killed it; 'tis allowed to be his goods who hath bestowed his labour upon it, though before, it was the common right of every one. And amongst those who are counted the Civiliz'd part of Mankind, who have made and multiplied positive Laws to determine Property, this original Law of Nature for the *beginning of Property*, in what was before common, still takes place; and by vertue thereof, what Fish any one catches in the Ocean, that great and still remaining Common of Mankind; or what Ambergriese any one takes up here, is *by* the *Labour* that removes it out of that common state Nature left it in, *made* his *Property* who takes that pains about it. And even amongst us the Hare that any one is Hunting, is thought his who pursues her during the Chase. For being a Beast that is still looked upon as common, and no Man's private Possession; whoever has imploy'd so much *labour* about any of that

kind, as to find and pursue her, has thereby removed her from the state of Nature, wherein she was common, and hath *begun a Property*.

31. It will perhaps be objected to this, That if gathering the Acorns, or other Fruits of the Earth, *&c.* makes a right to them, then any one may *ingross* as much as he will. To which I Answer, Not so. The same Law of Nature, that does by this means give us Property, does also *bound* that *Property* too. *God has given us all things richly*, I Tim. vi. 17. is the Voice of Reason confirmed by Inspiration. But how far has he given it us? *To enjoy*. As much as any one can make use of to any advantage of life before it spoils; so much he may by his labour fix a Property in. Whatever is beyond this, is more than his share, and belongs to others. Nothing was made by God for Man to spoil or destroy. And thus considering the plenty of natural Provisions there was a long time in the World, and the few spenders, and to how small a part of that provision the industry of one Man could extend it self, and ingross it to the prejudice of others; especially keeping within the *bounds*, set by reason of what might serve for his *use*; there could be then little room for Quarrels or Contentions about Property so establish'd.

32. But the *chief matter of Property* being now not the Fruits of the Earth, and the Beasts that subsist on it, but the *Earth it self*; as that which takes in and carries with it all the rest: I think it is plain, that *Property* in that too is acquired as the former. *As much Land* as a Man Tills, Plants, Improves, Cultivates, and can use the Product of, so much is his *Property*. He by his Labour does, as it were, inclose it from the Common. Nor will it invalidate his right to say, Every body else has an equal Title to it; and therefore he cannot appropriate, he cannot inclose, without the Consent of all his Fellow-Commoners, all Mankind. God, when he gave the World in common to all Mankind, commanded Man also to labour, and the penury of his Condition required it of him. God and his Reason commanded him to subdue the Earth, *i.e.* improve it for the benefit of Life, and therein lay out something upon it that was his own, his labour. He that in Obedience to this Command of God, subdued, tilled and sowed any part of it, thereby annexed to it something that was his *Property*, which another had no Title to, nor could without injury take from him.

33. Nor was this *appropriation* of any parcel of *Land*, by improving it, any prejudice to any other Man, since there was still enough, and as good left; and more than the yet unprovided could use. So that in effect, there was never the less left for others because of his inclosure for himself. For he that leaves as much as another can make use of, does as good as take nothing at all. No Body could think himself injur'd by the drinking of another Man, though he took a good Draught, who had a whole River of the same Water left him to quench his thirst. And the Case of Land and Water, where there is enough of both, is perfectly the same.

34. God gave the World to Men in Common; but since he gave it them for their benefit, and the greatest Conveniencies of Life they were capable to draw from it, it cannot be supposed he meant it should always remain common and uncultivated. He gave it to the use of the Industrious and Rational, (and *Labour* was to be *his* Title to it;) not to the Fancy or Covetousness of the Quarrelsom and Contentious. He that had as good left for his Improvement, as was already taken up, needed not complain, ought not to meddle with what was already improved by another's Labour: If he did, 'tis plain he desired the benefit of another's Pains, which he had no right to, and not the Ground which God had given him in common with others to labour on, and whereof there was as good left, as

that already possessed, and more than he knew what to do with, or his Industry could reach to.

35 'Tis true, in *Land* that is *common* in *England*, or any other Country, where there is Plenty of People under Government, who have Money and Commerce, no one can inclose or appropriate any part, without the consent of all his Fellow-Commoners: Because this is left common by Compact, *i.e.* by the Law of the Land, which is not to be violated. And though it be Common, in respect of some Men, it is not so to all Mankind; but is the joint property of this Country, or this Parish. Besides, the remainder, after such inclosure, would not be as good to the rest of the Commoners as the whole was, when they could all make use of the whole: whereas in the beginning and first peopling of the great Common of the World, it was quite otherwise. The Law Man was under, was rather for *appropriating*. God Commanded, and his Wants forced him to *labour*. That was his *Property* which could not be taken from him where-ever he had fixed it. And hence subduing or cultivating the Earth, and having Dominion, we see are joyned together. The one gave Title to the other. So that God, by commanding to subdue, gave Authority so far to *appropriate*. And the Condition of Human Life, which requires Labour and Materials to work on, necessarily introduces *private Possessions*.

. . .

222. The Reason why Men enter into Society, is the preservation of their Property; and the end why they chuse and authorize a Legislative, is, that there may be Laws made, and Rules set as Guards and Fences to the Properties of all the Members of the Society, to limit the Power, and moderate the Dominion of every Part and Member of the Society. For since it can never be supposed to be the Will of the Society, that the Legislative should have a Power to destroy that, which every one designs to secure, by entering into Society, and for which the People submitted themselves to the Legislators of their own making; whenever the *Legislators endeavour to take away, and destroy the Property of the People*, or to reduce them to Slavery under Arbitrary Power, they put themselves into a state of War with the People, who are thereupon absolved from any farther Obedience, and are left to the common Refuge, which God hath provided for all Men, against Force and Violence. Whensoever therefore the *Legislative* shall transgress this fundamental Rule of Society; and either by Ambition, Fear, Folly or Corruption, *endeavour to grasp* themselves, *or put into the hands of any other an Absolute Power* over the Lives, Liberties, and Estates of the People; By this breach of Trust they *forfeit the Power*, the People had put into their hands, for quite contrary ends, and it devolves to the People, who have a Right to resume their original Liberty, and, by the Establishment of a new Legislative (such as they shall think fit) provide for their own Safety and Security, which is the end for which they are in Society. What I have said here, concerning the Legislative, in general, holds true also concerning the *supreame Executor*, who having a double trust put in him, both to have a part in the Legislative, and the supreme Execution of the Law, Acts against both, when he goes about to set up his own Arbitrary Will, as the Law of the Society. He *acts* also *contrary to his Trust*, when he either imploys the Force, Treasure, and Offices of the Society, to corrupt the *Representatives,* and gain them to his purposes: or openly pre-ingages the *Electors,* and prescribes to their choice, such, whom he has by Sollicitations, Threats, Promises, or otherwise won to his designs; and imploys them to bring in such, who have

promised before-hand, what to Vote, and what to Enact. Thus to regulate Candidates and *Electors,* and new model the ways of *Election,* what is it but to cut up the Government by the Roots, and poison the very Fountain of publick Security? For the People having reserved to themselves the Choice of their *Representatives,* as the Fence to their Properties, could do it for no other end, but that they might always be freely chosen, and so chosen, freely act and advise, as the necessity of the Commonwealth, and the publick Good should, upon examination, and mature debate, be judged to require. This, those who give their Votes before they hear the Debate, and have weighed the Reasons on all sides, are not capable of doing. To prepare such an Assembly as this, and endeavour to set up the declared Abettors of his own Will, for the true *Representatives* of the People, and the Law-makers of the Society, is certainly as great a *breach of trust,* and as perfect a Declaration of a design to subvert the Government, as is possible to be met with. To which, if one shall add Rewards and Punishments visibly imploy'd to the same end, and all the Arts of perverted Law made use of, to take off and destroy all that stand in the way of such a design, and will not comply and consent to besttray the Liberties of their Country, 'twill be past doubt what is doing. What Power they ought to have in the Society, who thus imploy it contrary to the trust that went along with it in its first Institution, is easie to determine; and one cannot but see, that he, who has once attempted any such thing as this, cannot any longer be trusted.

223. To this perhaps it will be said, that the People being ignorant, and always discontented, to lay the Foundation of Government in the unsteady Opinion, and uncertain Humour of the People, is to expose it to certain ruine; And *no Government will be able long to subsist,* if the People may set up a new Legislative, whenever they take offence at the old one. To this, I Answer: Quite the contrary. People are not so easily got out of their old Forms, as some are apt to suggest. They are hardly to be prevailed with to amend the acknowledg'd Faults, in the Frame they have been accustom'd to. And if there be any Original defects, or adventitious ones introduced by time, or corruption; 'tis not an easie thing to get them changed, even when all the World sees there is an opportunity for it. This slowness and aversion in the People to quit their old Constitutions, has, in the many Revolutions which have been seen in this Kingdom, in this and former Ages, still kept us to, or, after some interval of fruitless attempts, still brought us back again to our old Legislative of King, Lords and Commons: And whatever provocations have made the Crown be taken from some of our Princes Heads, they never carried the People so far, as to place it in another Line.

224. But 'twill be said, this *Hypothesis* lays a *ferment* for frequent *Rebellion.* To which I Answer,

First, No more than any other *Hypothesis.* For when the *People* are made *miserable,* and find themselves *exposed to the ill usage of Arbitrary Power,* cry up their Governours, as much as you will for Sons of *Jupiter,* let them be Sacred and Divine, descended or authoriz'd from Heaven; give them out for whom or what you please, the same will happen. *The People generally ill treated,* and contrary to right, will be ready upon any occasion to ease themselves of a burden that sits heavy upon them. They will wish and seek for the opportunity, which, in the change, weakness, and accidents of humane affairs, seldom delays long to offer it self. He must have lived but a little while in the World, who has not seen Examples of this in his time; and he must have read very little, who cannot produce Examples of it in all sorts of Governments in the World.

225. Secondly, I Answer, such *Revolutions happen* not upon every little mismanagement in publick affairs. *Great mistakes* in the ruling part, many wrong and inconvenient Laws, and all the *slips* of humane frailty will be *born by the People,* without mutiny or murmur. But if a long train of Abuses, Prevarications, and Artifices, all tending the same way, make the design visible to the People, and they cannot but feel, what they lie under, and see, whither they are going; 'tis not to be wonder'd, that they should then rouze themselves, and endeavour to put the rule into such hands, which may secure to them the ends for which Government was at first erected; and without which, ancient Names, and specious Forms, are so far from being better, that they are much worse, than the state of Nature, or pure Anarchy; the inconveniencies being all as great and as near, but the remedy farther off and more difficult.

226. Thirdly, I Answer, That *this Doctrine* of a Power in the People of providing for their safety a-new by a new Legislative, when their Legislators have acted contrary to their trust, by invading their Property, is *the best fence against Rebellion,* and the probablest means to hinder it. For Rebellion being an Opposition, not to Persons, but Authority, which is founded only in the Constitutions and Laws of the Government; those, whoever they be, who by force break through, and by force justifie their violation of them, are truly and properly *Rebels.* For when Men by entering into Society and Civil Government, have excluded force, and introduced Laws for the preservation of Property, Peace, and Unity amongst themselves; those who set up force again in opposition to the Laws, do *Rebellare,* that is, bring back again the state of War, and are properly Rebels: Which they who are in Power (by the pretence they have to Authority, the temptation of force they have in their hands, and the Flattery of those about them) being likeliest to do; the properest way to prevent the evil, is to shew them the danger and injustice of it, who are under the greatest temptation to run into it.

11   Benjamin Constant, from 'The Liberty of the Ancients Compared with that of the Moderns', in *Political Writings* (ed. Biancamaria Fontana; Cambridge University Press, 1988), pp. 310–15

Born in Lausanne in Switzerland, Benjamin Constant (1767–1830) was educated in Bavaria and Edinburgh, where he became acquainted with the Scottish political economy of Adam Smith, David Hume, and Dugdald Stewart. He spent the most momentous years of the French Revolution as a Gentleman of the Chamber in the Court of Brunswick, but moved to Paris in 1795. He had a public and political life, which included both fierce criticism of the Napoleonic regime and drafting of constitutional reforms to shore it up, as well as a literary career, including notably the publication of the novel *Adolphe* in 1806.

First ask yourselves, Gentlemen, what an Englishman, a Frenchman, and a citizen of the United States of America understand today by the word 'liberty'.

For each of them it is the right to be subjected only to the laws, and to be neither arrested, detained, put to death or maltreated in any way by the arbitrary will of one or more individuals. It is the right of everyone to express their opinion, choose a profession and practise it, to dispose of property, and even to abuse it; to come and go without permission, and without having to account for their motives or undertakings. It is everyone's right to associate with other individuals, either to discuss their interests, or to profess the religion which they and their associates prefer, or even simply to occupy their days or hours in a way which is most compatible with their inclinations or whims. Finally it is everyone's right to exercise some influence on the administration of the government, either by electing all or particular officials, or through representations, petitions, demands to which the authorities are more or less compelled to pay heed. Now compare this liberty with that of the ancients.

The latter consisted in exercising collectively, but directly, several parts of the complete sovereignty; in deliberating, in the public square, over war and peace; in forming alliances with foreign governments; in voting laws, in pronouncing judgements; in examining the accounts, the acts, the stewardship of the magistrates; in calling them to appear in front of the assembled people, in accusing, condemning or absolving them. But if this was what the ancients called liberty, they admitted as compatible with this collective freedom the complete subjection of the individual to the authority of the community. You find among them almost none of the enjoyments which we have just seen form part of the liberty of the moderns. All private actions were submitted to a severe surveillance. No importance was given to individual independence, neither in relation to opinions, nor to labour, nor, above all, to religion. The right to choose one's own religious affiliation, a right which we regard as one of the most precious, would have seemed to the ancients a crime and a sacrilege. In the domains which seem to us the most useful, the authority of the social body interposed itself and obstructed the will of individuals. Among the Spartans, Therpandrus could not add a string to his lyre without causing offence to the ephors. In the most domestic of relations the public authority again intervened. The young Lacedaemonian could not visit his new bride freely. In Rome, the censors cast a searching eye over family life. The laws regulated customs, and as customs touch on everything, there was hardly anything that the laws did not regulate.

Thus among the ancients the individual, almost always sovereign in public affairs, was a slave in all his private relations. As a citizen, he decided on peace and war; as a private individual, he was constrained, watched and repressed in all his movements; as a member of the collective body, he interrogated, dismissed, condemned, beggared, exiled, or sentenced to death his magistrates and superiors; as a subject of the collective body he could himself be deprived of his status, stripped of his privileges, banished, put to death, by the discretionary will of the whole to which he belonged. Among the moderns, on the contrary, the individual, independent in his private life, is, even in the freest of states, sovereign only in appearance. His sovereignty is restricted and almost always suspended. If, at fixed and rare intervals, in which he is again surrounded by precautions and obstacles, he exercises this sovereignty, it is always only to renounce it.

I must at this point, Gentlemen, pause for a moment to anticipate an objection which may be addressed to me. There was in antiquity a republic where the enslavement of individual existence to the collective body was not as complete as I have described it. This republic was the most famous of all: you will guess that I am speaking of Athens. I shall return to it later, and in subscribing to the truth of this fact, I shall also indicate its cause. We shall see why, of all the ancient states, Athens was the one which most resembles the modern ones. Everywhere else social jurisdiction was unlimited. The ancients, as Condorcet says, had no notion of individual rights. Men were, so to speak, merely machines, whose gears and cog-wheels were regulated by the law. The same subjection characterized the golden centuries of the Roman republic; the individual was in some way lost in the nation, the citizen in the city.

We shall now trace this essential difference between the ancients and ourselves back to its source.

All ancient republics were restricted to a narrow territory. The most populous, the most powerful, the most substantial among them, was not equal in extension to the smallest of modern states. As an inevitable consequence of their narrow territory, the spirit of these republics was bellicose; each people incessantly attacked their neighbours or was attacked by them. Thus driven by necessity against one another, they fought or threatened each other constantly. Those who had no ambition to be conquerors, could still not lay down their weapons, lest they should themselves be conquered. All had to buy their security, their independence, their whole existence at the price of war. This was the constant interest, the almost habitual occupation of the free states of antiquity. Finally, by an equally necessary result of this way of being, all these states had slaves. The mechanical professions and even, among some nations, the industrial ones, were committed to people in chains.

The modern world offers us a completely opposing view. The smallest states of our day are incomparably larger than Sparta or than Rome was over five centuries. Even the division of Europe into several states is, thanks to the progress of enlightenment, more apparent than real. While each people, in the past, formed an isolated family, the born enemy of other families, a mass of human beings now exists, that under different names and under different forms of social organization are essentially homogeneous in their nature. This mass is strong enough to have nothing to fear from barbarian hordes. It is sufficiently civilized to find war a burden. Its uniform tendency is towards peace.

This difference leads to another one. War precedes commerce. War and commerce are only two different means of achieving the same end, that of getting what one wants. Commerce is simply a tribute paid to the strength of the possessor by the aspirant to possession. It is an attempt to conquer, by mutual agreement, what one can no longer hope to obtain through violence. A man who was always the stronger would never conceive the idea of commerce. It is experience, by proving to him that war, that is the use of his strength against the strength of others, exposes him to a variety of obstacles and defeats, that leads him to resort to commerce, that is to a milder and surer means of engaging the interest of others to agree to what suits his own. War is all impulse, commerce, calculation. Hence it follows that an age must come in which commerce replaces war. We have reached this age.

I do not mean that amongst the ancients there were no trading peoples. But these peoples were to some degree an exception to the general rule. The limits of this lecture do not allow me to illustrate all the obstacles which then opposed the progress of commerce; you know them as well as I do; I shall only mention one of them.

Their ignorance of the compass meant that the sailors of antiquity always had to keep close to the coast. To pass through the pillars of Hercules, that is, the straits of Gibraltar, was considered the most daring of enterprises. The Phoenicians and the Carthaginians, the most able of navigators, did not risk it until very late, and their example for long remained without imitators. In Athens, of which we shall talk soon, the interest on maritime enterprises was around 60%, while current interest was only 12%: that was how dangerous the idea of distant navigation seemed.

Moreover, if I could permit myself a digression which would unfortunately prove too long, I would show you, Gentlemen, through the details of the customs, habits, way of trading with others of the trading peoples of antiquity, that their commerce was itself impregnated by the spirit of the age, by the atmosphere of war and hostility which surrounded it. Commerce then was a lucky accident, today it is the normal state of things, the only aim, the universal tendency, the true life of nations. They want repose, and with repose comfort, and as a source of comfort, industry. Every day war becomes a more ineffective means of satisfying their wishes. Its hazards no longer offer to individuals benefits that match the results of peaceful work and regular exchanges. Among the ancients, a successful war increased both private and public wealth in slaves, tributes and lands shared out. For the moderns, even a successful war costs infallibly more than it is worth.

Finally, thanks to commerce, to religion, to the moral and intellectual progress of the human race, there are no longer slaves among the European nations. Free men must exercise all professions, provide for all the needs of society.

It is easy to see, Gentlemen, the inevitable outcome of these differences.

Firstly, the size of a country causes a corresponding decrease of the political importance allotted to each individual. The most obscure republican of Sparta or Rome had power. The same is not true of the simple citizen of Britain or of the United States. His personal influence is an imperceptible part of the social will which impresses on the government its direction.

Secondly, the abolition of slavery has deprived the free population of all the leisure which resulted from the fact that slaves took care of most of the work. Without the slave population of Athens, 20,000 Athenians could never have spent every day at the public square in discussions.

Thirdly, commerce does not, like war, leave in men's lives intervals of inactivity. The constant exercise of political-rights, the daily discussion of the affairs of the state, disagreements, confabulations, the whole entourage and movement of factions, necessary agitations, the compulsory filling, if I may use the term, of the life of the peoples of antiquity, who, without this resource would have languished under the weight of painful inaction, would only cause trouble and fatigue to modern nations, where each individual, occupied with his speculations, his enterprises, the pleasures he obtains or hopes for, does not wish to be distracted from them other than momentarily, and as little as possible.

Finally, commerce inspires in men a vivid love of individual independence. Commerce supplies their needs, satisfies their desires, without the intervention of the authorities. This intervention is almost always—and I do not know why I say almost—this intervention is indeed always a trouble and an embarrassment. Every time collective power wishes to meddle with private speculations, it harasses the speculators. Every time governments pretend to do our own business, they do it more incompetently and expensively than we would.

12   W. von Humboldt, from *On the Limits of State Action* (ed. J. W. Burrow; Cambridge University Press, 1969), pp. 16–19, 25–7

Wilhelm von Humboldt (1767–1835) was born into a Prussian aristocratic family. He served as Minister for Education in Prussia, in which role he created an influential unified school system and founded the University of Berlin. He was also the Prussian representative at the Congresses of Prague (1813) and Vienna (1815). He was an eminent philosopher of language as well as political theorist, and, with Goethe, a representative of Weimar classicism, hoping to revive German culture along lines inspired by ancient Greece.

The true end of Man, or that which is prescribed by the eternal and immutable dictates of reason, and not suggested by vague and transient desires, is the highest and most harmonious development of his powers to a complete and consistent whole. Freedom is the first and indispensable condition which the possibility of such a development presupposes; but there is besides another essential—intimately connected with freedom, it is true—a variety of situations. Even the most free and self-reliant of men is hindered in his development, when set in a monotonous situation. But as it is evident, on the one hand, that such a diversity is a constant result of freedom, and on the other hand, that there is a species of oppression which, without imposing restrictions on man himself, gives a peculiar impress of its own to surrounding circumstances; these two conditions, of freedom and variety of situation, may be regarded, in a certain sense, as one and the same. Still, it may contribute to clarity to point out the distinction between them.

Every human being, then, can act with only one dominant faculty at a time; or rather, our whole nature disposes us at any given time to some single form of spontaneous activity. It would therefore seem to follow from this, that man is inevitably destined to a partial cultivation, since he only enfeebles his energies by directing them to a multiplicity of objects. But man has it in his power to avoid this one-sidedness, by attempting to unite the distinct and generally separately exercised faculties of his nature, by bringing into spontaneous cooperation, at each period of his life, the dying sparks of one activity, and those which the future will kindle, and endeavouring to increase and diversify the powers with which he works, by harmoniously combining them, instead of looking for a mere variety of objects for their separate exercise. What is achieved, in the case of the individual, by the union of the past and future with the present, is produced in society by the mutual cooperation of its different members; for, in all the stages of his life, each individual can achieve only one of those perfections, which represent the possible features of human character. It is through a social union, therefore, based on the internal wants and capacities of its members, that each is enabled to participate in the rich collective resources of all the others. The experience of all, even the rudest, nations, furnishes us an example of a union formative of individual character, in the union of the sexes. And, although in this case the difference as well as the longing for union, appears more marked and striking, it is still no less active in other kinds of association where there is actually no difference of sex; it is only more difficult to discover in these, and may perhaps be more powerful for that very reason. If we were to follow out this idea, it might perhaps lead us to a clearer insight into those relations so much in vogue among the ancients, and more especially the Greeks, among whom we find them engaged in even by the legislators themselves: I mean those so frequently, but unworthily, given the name of ordinary love, and sometimes, but always erroneously, that of mere friendship. The effectiveness of all such relations as instruments of cultivation, entirely depends on the extent to which the members can succeed in combining their personal independence with the intimacy of the association; for whilst, without this intimacy, one individual cannot sufficiently possess, as it were, the nature of the others, independence is no less essential, in order that each, in being possessed, may be transformed in his own unique way. On the one hand, individual energy is essential to both parties and, on the other hand, a difference between them, neither so great as to prevent one from comprehending the other, nor so small as to exclude admiration for what the other possesses, and the desire to assimilate it into one's own character.

This individual vigour, then, and manifold diversity, combine themselves in originality; and hence, that on which the whole greatness of mankind ultimately depends—towards which every human being must ceaselessly direct his efforts, and of which especially those who wish to influence their fellow-men must never lose sight: individuality of energy and self-development. Just as this individuality springs naturally from freedom of action, and the greatest diversity in the agents, it tends in turn directly to produce them. Even inanimate nature, which, proceeding according to unchangeable laws, advances by regular steps, appears more individual to the man who has been developed in his individuality. He transports himself, as it were, into nature itself; and it is in the highest sense true that each man perceives the beauty and abundance of the outer world, in the same degree as he is conscious of them in his own soul. How much closer must this correspondence become between effect and cause—this reaction between internal feeling and outward perception—when man is not only passively open to external sensations and impressions, but is himself also an agent?

If we attempt to test these principles by a closer application of them to the nature of the individual man, we find that everything in the latter, reduces itself to the two elements of form and substance. The purest form beneath the most delicate veil, we call idea; the crudest substance, with the most imperfect form, we call sensuous perception. Form springs from the combinations of substance. The richer and more various the substance that is combined, the more sublime is the resulting form. A child of the gods is the offspring only of immortal parents: and as the blossom ripens into fruit, and from the seed of the fruit the new stalk shoots with newly clustering buds; so does the form become in turn the substance of a still more exquisite form. The intensity of power, moreover, increases in proportion to the greater variety and delicacy of the substance; since the internal cohesion increases with them. The substance seems as if blended in the form, and the form merged in the substance. Or, to speak without metaphor, the richer a man's feelings become in ideas, and his ideas in feelings, the more transcendent his nobility, for upon this constant intermingling of form and substance, or of diversity with the individual unity, depends the perfect fusion of the two natures which co-exist in man, and upon this, his greatness. But the intensity of the fusion depends upon the energy of the generating forces. The highest point of human existence is this flowering. In the vegetable world, the simple and less graceful form seems to prefigure the more perfect bloom and symmetry of the flower which it precedes, and into which it gradually expands. Everything hastens towards the moment of blossoming. What first springs from the seed is not nearly so attractive. The full thick trunk, the broad leaves rapidly detaching themselves from each other, seem to require some fuller development; as the eye glances up the ascending stem, it marks the grades of this development; more tender leaves seem longing to unite themselves, and draw closer and closer together, until the central calyx of the flower seems to satisfy this desire. But destiny has not blessed the tribe of plants in this respect. The flower fades and dies, and the germ of the fruit reproduces the stem, as rude and unfinished as the former, to ascend slowly through the same stages of development as before. But when, in man, the blossom fades away, it is only to give place to another still more beautiful; and the charm of the most beautiful is only hidden from our view in the endlessly receding vistas of an inscrutable eternity. Now, whatever man receives externally, is only like the seed. It is his own active energy alone that can turn the most promising seed into a full and precious blessing for himself. It is beneficial only to the extent that it is full of vital power and essentially individual. The highest ideal, therefore, of the co-existence of human beings, seems to me to consist in a union in which each strives to develop himself from his own inmost nature, and for his own sake. The requirements of our physical and moral being would, doubtless, bring men together into communities; and as the conflicts of warfare are more honourable than the fights of the arena, and the struggles of exasperated citizens more glorious than the hired efforts of mercenaries, so the exertions of such spontaneous agents succeed in exciting the highest energies.

. . .

. . . the evil results of a too extensive solicitude on the part of the State, are still more strikingly shown in the suppression of all active energy, and the necessary deterioration of the moral character. This scarcely needs further argument. The man who is often led, easily becomes disposed willingly to sacrifice what remains of his capacity for spontaneous action. He fancies himself released from an anxiety which he sees transferred to other hands, and seems to himself to do enough when he looks to their leadership and follows it. Thus, his notions of merit and guilt become unsettled. The idea of the first no longer inspires him; and the painful consciousness of the last assails him less frequently and forcibly, since he can more easily ascribe his shortcomings to his peculiar position, and leave them to the responsibility of those who have made it what it is. If we add to this, that he may not, possibly, regard the designs of the State as perfectly pure in their objects or execution—that he may suspect that his own advantage only, but along with it some other additional purpose is intended, then, not only the force and energy, but also the purity of his moral nature suffers. He now conceives himself not only completely free from any duty which the State has not expressly imposed upon him, but exonerated at the same time from every personal effort to improve his own condition; and, even fears such an effort, as if it were likely to open out new opportunities, of which the State might take advantage. And as for the laws actually enjoined, he tries as much as possible to escape their operation, considering every such evasion as a positive gain. If we reflect that, among a large part of the nation, its laws and political institutions have the effect of limiting the sphere of morality, it is a melancholy spectacle to see the most sacred duties, and mere trivial and arbitrary enactments, often proclaimed from the same authoritative source, and to see the infraction of both met with the same measure of punishment. Further, the pernicious influence of such a positive policy is no less evident in the behaviour of the citizens to each other. As each individual abandons himself to the solicitous aid of the State, so, and still more, he abandons to it the fate of his fellow-citizens. This weakens sympathy and renders mutual assistance inactive: or, at least, the reciprocal interchange of services and benefits will be most likely to flourish at its liveliest, where the feeling is most acute that such assistance is the only thing to rely upon; and experience teaches us that oppressed classes of the community which are, as it were, overlooked by the government, are always bound together by the closest ties. But wherever the citizen becomes indifferent to his fellows, so will the husband be to his wife, and the father of a family towards the members of his household.

If men were left wholly to themselves in their various undertakings, and were cut off from all external resources, other than those which their own efforts obtained, they would still, whether through their own fault or not, fall frequently into difficulties and misfortune. But the happiness for which man is plainly destined, is no other than that which his own energies procure for him; and the very nature of such a self-reliant position sharpens his intellect and develops his character. Are there no instances of such evils where State agency fetters individual spontaneity by too detailed interference? There are many, doubtless; and the man whom it has accustomed to lean on an external power for support, is thus given up in critical emergencies to a far more hopeless fate. For, just as the very act of struggling against misfortune, and encountering it with vigorous efforts, lightens the calamity; so delusive expectations aggravate its severity tenfold. In short, taking the most favourable view, States like those to which we refer too often resemble the physician, who only retards the death of his patient by nourishing his disease. Before there were physicians, man knew only health and death.

13 James Mill, from 'Government', in *Political Writings* (ed. Terence Ball; Cambridge University Press, 1992), pp. 14–16, 26–7

James Mill (1773–1836) was a political theorist, historian, economist, and journalist. The leading figure in the 'philosophic radicals', who aimed at parliamentary, legislative, and educational reform based upon the principles of Jeremy Bentham's utilitarianism, he was best known in his lifetime for his three-volume *History of British India* (1818).

The chain of inference, in this case, is close and strong, to a most unusual degree. A man desires that the actions of other men shall be instantly and accurately correspondent to his will. He desires that the actions of the greatest possible number shall be so. Terror is the grand instrument. Terror can work only through assurance that evil will follow any want of conformity between the will and the actions willed. Every failure must, therefore, be punished. As there are no bounds to the mind's desire of its pleasure, there are of course no bounds to its desire of perfection in the instruments of that pleasure. There are, therefore, no bounds to its desire of exactness in the conformity between its will and the actions willed; and, by consequence, to the strength of that terror which is its procuring cause. Every, the most minute, failure, must be visited with the heaviest infliction: and, as failure in extreme exactness must frequently happen, the occasions of cruelty must be incessant.

We have thus arrived at several conclusions of the highest possible importance. We have seen, that the very principle of human nature upon which the necessity of Government is founded, the propensity of one man to possess himself of the objects of desire at the cost of another, leads on, by infallible sequence, where power over a community is attained, and nothing checks, not only to that degree of plunder which leaves the members (excepting always the recipients and instruments of the plunder) the bare means of subsistence, but to that degree of cruelty which is necessary to keep in existence the most intense terror.

The world affords some decisive experiments upon human nature, in exact conformity with these conclusions. An English Gentleman may be taken as a favourable specimen of civilization, of knowledge, of humanity, of all the qualities, in short, that make human nature estimable. The degree in which he desires to possess power over his fellow-creatures, and the degree of oppression to which he finds motives for carrying the exercise of that power, will afford a standard from which, assuredly, there can be no appeal. Wherever the same motives exist, the same conduct, as that displayed by the English Gentleman, may be expected to follow, in all men not farther advanced in human excellence than him. In the West Indies, before that vigilant attention of the English nation, which now, for thirty years, has imposed so great a check upon the masters of slaves, there was not a perfect absence of all check upon the dreadful propensities of power. But yet it is true, that these propensities led English Gentlemen, not only to deprive their slaves of property, and to make property of their fellow-creatures, but to treat them with a degree of cruelty, the very description of which froze the blood of their countrymen, who were placed in less unfavourable circumstances. The motives of this deplorable conduct are exactly those which we have described above, as arising out of the universal desire to render the actions of other men exactly conformable to our will. It is of great importance to remark, that not one item in the motives which had led English Gentlemen to make slaves of their fellow-creatures, and to reduce them to the very worst condition in which the negroes have been found in the West Indies, can be shown to be wanting, or to be less strong in the set of motives, which universally operate upon the men who have power over their fellow-creatures. It is proved, therefore, by the closest deduction from the acknowledged laws of human nature, and by direct and decisive experiments, that the ruling One, or the ruling Few, would, if checks did not operate in the way of prevention, reduce the great mass of the people subject to their power, at least to the condition of negroes in the West Indies.

We have thus seen, that of the forms of Government, which have been called the three simple forms, not one is adequate to the ends which Government is appointed to secure; that the community itself, which alone is free from motives opposite to those ends, is incapacitated by its numbers from performing the business of Government; and that whether Government is intrusted to one or a few, they have not only motives opposite to those ends, but motives which will carry them, if unchecked, to inflict the greatest evils.

. . .

We have seen already, that if one man has power over others placed in his hands, he will make use of it for an evil purpose for the purpose of rendering those other men the abject instruments of his will. If we, then, suppose, that one man has the power of choosing the

Representatives of the people, it follows, that he will choose men who will use their power as Representatives for the promotion of this his sinister interest.

We have likewise seen, that when a few men have power given them over others, they will make use of it exactly for the same ends, and to the same extent, as the one man. It equally follows, that, if a small number of men have the choice of the Representatives, such Representatives will be chosen as will promote the interests of that small number, by reducing, if possible, the rest of the community to be the abject and helpless slaves of their will.

In all these cases, it is obvious and indisputable, that all the benefits of the Representative system are lost. The Representative system is, in that case, only an operose and clumsy machinery for doing that which might as well be done without it; reducing the community to subjection, under the One, or the Few.

When we say the Few, it is seen that, in this case, it is of no importance whether we mean a few hundreds, or a few thousands, or even many thousands. The operation of the sinister interest is the same; and the fate is the same of all that part of the community over whom the power is exercised. A numerous Aristocracy has never been found to be less oppressive than an Aristocracy confined to a few.

The general conclusion, therefore, which is evidently established is this; that the benefits of the Representative system are lost, in all cases in which the interests of the choosing body are not the same with those of the community.

It is very evident, that if the community itself were the choosing body, the interest of the community and that of the choosing body would be the same. The question is, whether that of any portion of the community, if erected into the choosing body, would remain the same?

One thing is pretty clear, that all those individuals whose interests are indisputably included in those of other individuals, may be struck off without inconvenience. In this light may be viewed all children, up to a certain age, whose interests are involved in those of their parents. In this light, also, women may be regarded, the interest of almost all of whom is involved either in that of their fathers or in that of their husbands.

Having ascertained that an interest identical with that of the whole community, is to be found in the aggregate males, of an age to be regarded as *sui juris*, who may be regarded as the natural Representatives of the whole population, we have to go on, and inquire, whether this requisite quality may not be found in some less number, some aliquot part of that body.

As degrees of mental qualities are not easily ascertained, outward and visible signs must be taken to distinguish, for this purpose, one part of these males from another. Applicable signs of this description appear to be three; Years, Property, Profession or Mode of Life.

14 Alexis de Tocqueville, from *Democracy in America* (tr. and ed. by Harvey C. Mansfield and Delba Winthrop; Chicago University Press, 2000), pp. 661–5

Scion of a French noble family, Alexis de Tocqueville (1805–1859) as a young man travelled through America, a journey that resulted in the two volumes of *Democracy in America* (1835, 1840). He was a prominent intellectual and deputy in the July monarchy of Louis Phillipe, but retired from political life after the coup of Louis Bonaparte in 1848. His other principal works include *The Old Regime and the Revolution* (1853), a philosophical and sociological essay on the impact of democratic society on the political culture of contemporary France.

During my stay in the United States I had remarked that a democratic social state like that of the Americans could singularly facilitate the establishment of despotism, and I had seen on my return to Europe how most of our princes had already made use of the ideas, sentiments, and needs to which this same social state had given birth to extend the sphere of their power.

That led me to believe that Christian nations would perhaps in the end come under an oppression similar to that which formerly weighed on several of the peoples of antiquity.

A more detailed examination of the subject and five years of new meditations have not diminished my fears, but they have changed their object.

In past centuries, one never saw a sovereign so absolute and so powerful that it undertook to administer all the parts of a great empire by itself without the assistance of secondary powers; there was none who attempted to subjugate all its subjects without distinction to the details of a uniform rule, nor one that descended to the side of each of them to lord it over him and lead him. The idea of such an undertaking had never presented itself to the human mind, and if any man had happened to conceive of it, the insufficiency of enlightenment, the imperfection of administrative proceedings, and above all the natural obstacles that inequality of conditions gave rise to would soon have stopped him in the execution of such a vast design.

One sees that in the time of the greatest power of the Caesars, the different peoples who inhabited the Roman world still preserved diverse customs and mores: although subject to the same monarch, most of the provinces were administered separately; they were filled with powerful and active municipalities, and although all the government of the empire was concentrated in the hands of the emperor alone and he always remained the arbitrator of all things in case of need, the details of social life and of individual existence ordinarily escaped his control.

It is true that the emperors possessed an immense power without counterweight, which permitted them to indulge the outlandishness of their penchants freely and to employ the entire force of the state in satisfying them; they often came to abuse this power so as to deprive a citizen of his goods or life arbitrarily: their tyranny weighed enormously on some, but it did not extend over many; it applied itself to a few great principal objects and neglected the rest; it was violent and restricted.

It seems that if despotism came to be established in the democratic nations of our day, it would have other characteristics: it would be more extensive and milder, and it would degrade men without tormenting them.

I do not doubt that in centuries of enlightenment and equality like ours, sovereigns will come more easily to gather all public powers in their hands alone and to penetrate the sphere of private interests more habitually and more deeply than any of those in antiquity was ever able to do. But the same equality that facilitates despotism tempers it; we have seen how, as men are more alike and more equal, public mores become more humane and milder; when no citizen has either great power or great wealth, tyranny in a way lacks an occasion and a stage. All fortunes being mediocre, passions are naturally contained, imagination bounded, pleasures simple. This universal moderation moderates the sovereign itself and holds the disordered sparks of its desires within certain limits.

Independently of these reasons drawn from the very nature of the social state, I could add many others that I would take from outside my subject, but I want to stay within the bounds I have set for myself.

Democratic governments can become violent and even cruel at certain moments of great excitement and great peril; but these crises will be rare and transient.

When I think of the small passions of men of our day, the softness of their mores, the extent of their enlightenment, the purity of their religion, the mildness of their morality, their laborious and steady habits, the restraint that almost all preserve in vice as in virtue, I do not fear that in their chiefs they will find tyrants, but rather schoolmasters.

I think therefore that the kind of oppression with which democratic peoples are threatened will resemble nothing that has preceded it in the world; our contemporaries would not find its image in their memories. I myself seek in vain an expression that exactly reproduces the idea that I form of it for myself and that contains it; the old words despotism and tyranny are not suitable. The thing is new, therefore I must try to define it, since I cannot name it.

I want to imagine with what new features despotism could be produced in the world: I see an innumerable crowd of like and equal men who revolve on themselves without repose, procuring the small and vulgar pleasures with which they fill their souls. Each of them, withdrawn and apart, is like a stranger to the destiny of all the others: his children and his particular friends form the whole human species for him; as for dwelling with his fellow citizens, he is beside them, but he does not see them; he touches them and does not feel them; he exists only in himself and for himself alone, and if a family still remains for him, one can at least say that he no longer has a native country.

Above these an immense tutelary power is elevated, which alone takes charge of assuring their enjoyments and watching over their fate. It is absolute, detailed, regular, far-seeing, and mild. It would resemble paternal power if, like that, it had for its object to prepare men for manhood; but on the contrary, it seeks only to keep them fixed irrevocably in childhood; it likes citizens to enjoy themselves provided that they think only of enjoying themselves. It willingly works for their happiness; but it wants to be the unique agent and sole arbiter of that; it provides for their security, foresees and secures their needs, facilitates their pleasures, conducts their principal affairs, directs their industry, regulates their estates, divides their inheritances; can it not take away from them entirely the trouble of thinking and the pain of living?

So it is that every day it renders the employment of free will less useful and more rare; it confines the action of the will in a smaller space and little by little steals the very use of it from each citizen. Equality has prepared men for all these things: it has disposed them to tolerate them and often even to regard them as a benefit.

Thus, after taking each individual by turns in its powerful hands and kneading him as it likes, the sovereign extends its arms over society as a whole; it covers its surface with a network of small, complicated, painstaking, uniform rules through which the most original minds and the most vigorous souls cannot clear a way to surpass the crowd; it does not break wills, but it softens them, bends them, and directs them; it rarely forces one to act, but it constantly opposes itself to one's acting; it does not destroy, it prevents things from being born; it does not tyrannize, it hinders, compromises, enervates, extinguishes, dazes, and finally reduces each nation to being nothing more than a herd of timid and industrious animals of which the government is the shepherd.

I have always believed that this sort of regulated, mild, and peaceful servitude, whose picture I have just painted, could be combined better than one imagines with some of the external forms of freedom, and that it would not be impossible for it to be established in the very shadow of the sovereignty of the people.

Our contemporaries are incessantly racked by two inimical passions: they feel the need to be led and the wish to remain free. Not being able to destroy either one of these contrary instincts, they strive to satisfy both at the same time. They imagine a unique power, tutelary, all powerful, but elected by citizens. They combine centralization and the sovereignty of the people. That gives them some respite. They console themselves for being in tutelage by thinking that they themselves have chosen their schoolmasters. Each individual allows himself to be attached because he sees that it is not a man or a class but the people themselves that hold the end of the chain.

In this system citizens leave their dependence for a moment to indicate their master, and then reenter it.

In our day there are many people who accommodate themselves very easily to this kind of compromise between administrative despotism and the sovereignty of the people, and who think they have guaranteed the freedom of individuals well enough when they deliver it to the national power. That does not suffice for me. The nature of the master is much less important to me than the obedience.

Nevertheless I shall not deny that such a constitution is infinitely preferable to one which, after having concentrated all powers, would deposit them in the hands of an irresponsible man or body. Of all the different forms that democratic despotism could take, this would surely be the worst.

When the sovereign is elected or closely overseen by a really elected and independent legislature, the oppression it makes individuals undergo is sometimes greater; but it is always less degrading, because each citizen, while he is hindered and reduced to impotence, can still fancy that in obeying he submits only to himself and that it is to one of his wills that he sacrifices all the others.

I understand as well that when the sovereign represents the nation and depends on it, the strength and rights that are taken away from each citizen serve not only the head of state but profit the state itself, and that particular persons get some fruit from the sacrifice of their independence that they have made to the public.

To create a national representation in a very centralized country is therefore to diminish the evil that extreme centralization can produce, but not to destroy it.

I see very well that in this manner one preserves individual intervention in the most important affairs; but one does not suppress it any less in small and particular ones. One forgets that it is above all in details that it is dangerous to enslave men. For my part, I would be brought to believe freedom less necessary in great things than in lesser ones if I thought that one could ever be assured of the one without possessing the other.

Subjection in small affairs manifests itself every day and makes itself felt without distinction by all citizens. It does not make them desperate; but it constantly thwarts them and brings them to renounce the use of their wills. Thus little by little, it extinguishes their spirits and enervates their souls, whereas obedience, which is due only in a few very grave but very rare circumstances, shows servitude only now and then and makes it weigh only on certain men. In vain will you charge these same citizens, whom you have rendered so dependent on the central power, with choosing the representatives of this power from time to time; that use of their free will, so important but so brief and so rare, will not prevent them from losing little by little the faculty of thinking, feeling, and acting by themselves, and thus from gradually falling below the level of humanity.

I add that they will soon become incapable of exercising the great, unique privilege that remains to them. Democratic peoples who have introduced freedom into the political sphere at the same time that they have increased despotism in the administrative sphere have been led to very strange oddities. If one must conduct small affairs in which simple good sense can suffice, they determine that citizens are incapable of it; if it is a question of the government of the whole state, they entrust immense prerogatives in these citizens; they make them alternatively the playthings of the sovereign and its masters, more than kings and less than men. After exhausting all the different systems of election without finding one that suits them, they are astonished and seek again, as if the evil they notice were not due much more to the constitution of the country than to that of the electoral body.

It is in fact difficult to conceive how men who have entirely renounced the habit of directing themselves could succeed at choosing well those who will lead them; and one will not make anyone believe that a liberal, energetic, and wise government can ever issue from the suffrage of a people of servants.

A constitution that was republican at the head and ultramonarchical in all other parts has always seemed to me to be an ephemeral monster. The vices of those who govern and the imbecility of the governed would not be slow to bring it to ruin; and the people, tired of their representatives and of themselves, would create freer institutions or soon return to lying at the feet of a single master.

15 J. S. Mill, from (a) 'On Liberty', in *On Liberty and Other Essays* (ed. John Gray; Oxford University Press, 1991), pp, 13–17, 62–3, 65–6 and (b) *Chapters on Socialism* in *On Liberty and Other Writings* (ed. Stefan Collini; Cambridge University Press, 1989), pp. 275–9

John Stuart Mill (1806–1873), the son of James Mill, was famously educated from an extremely early age in the classics, philosophy, history, political economy, and the sciences, as he described in his posthumously published *Autobiography* (1873). His early discipleship of Bentham's utilitarianism was significantly modified in the wake of what he described as a 'mental crisis' at the age of twenty, and his philosophy and political thought drew on an eclectic range of sources, including Carlyle, Saint-Simon, Comte, and Tocqueville. He held an administrative post in the East India Company, and, from 1865 to 1868, was the Member of

Parliament for Westminster, during which time he advocated radical reforms such as the enfranchisement of women and proportional representation. As well as *On Liberty* (1859), his major political works included *Utilitarianism* (1861), *Considerations on Representative Government* (1861), and *The Subjection of Women* (1869).

(a) The object of this Essay is to assert one very simple principle, as entitled to govern absolutely the dealings of society with the individual in the way of compulsion and control, whether the means used be physical force in the form of legal penalties, or the moral coercion of public opinion. That principle is, that the sole end for which mankind are warranted, individually or collectively, in interfering with the liberty of action of any of their number, is self-protection. That the only purpose for which power can be rightfully exercised over any member of a civilized community, against his will, is to prevent harm to others. His own good, either physical or moral, is not a sufficient warrant. He cannot rightfully be compelled to do or forbear because it will be better for him to do so, because it will make him happier, because, in the opinions of others, to do so would be wise, or even right. These are good reasons for remonstrating with him, or reasoning with him, or persuading him, or entreating him, but not for compelling him, or visiting him with any evil in case he do otherwise. To justify that, the conduct from which it is desired to deter him, must be calculated to produce evil to some one else. The only part of the conduct of any one, for which he is amenable to society, is that which concerns others. In the part which merely concerns himself, his independence is, of right, absolute. Over himself, over his own body and mind, the individual is sovereign.

It is, perhaps, hardly necessary to say that this doctrine is meant to apply only to human beings in the maturity of their faculties. We are not speaking of children, or of young persons below the age which the law may fix as that of manhood or womanhood. Those who are still in a state to require being taken care of by others, must be protected against their own actions as well as against external injury. For the same reason, we may leave out of consideration those backward states of society in which the race itself may be considered as in its nonage. The early difficulties in the way of spontaneous progress are so great, that there is seldom any choice of means for overcoming them; and a ruler full of the spirit of improvement is warranted in the use of any expedients that will attain an end, perhaps otherwise unattainable. Despotism is a legitimate mode of government in dealing with barbarians, provided the end be their improvement, and the means justified by actually effecting that end. Liberty, as a principle, has no application to any state of things anterior to the time when mankind have become capable of being improved by free and equal discussion. Until then, there is nothing for them but implicit obedience to an Akbar or a Charlemagne, if they are so fortunate as to find one. But as soon as mankind have attained the capacity of being guided to their own improvement by conviction or persuasion (a period long since reached in all nations with whom we need here concern ourselves), compulsion, either in the direct form or in that of pains and penalties for non-compliance, is no longer admissible as a means to their own good, and justifiable only for the security of others.

It is proper to state that I forgo any advantage which could be derived to my argument from the idea of abstract right, as a thing independent of utility. I regard utility as the ultimate appeal on all ethical questions; but it must be utility in the largest sense, grounded on the permanent interests of man as a progressive being. Those interests, I contend, authorize the subjection of individual spontaneity to external control, only in respect to those actions of each, which concern the interest of other people. If any one does an act hurtful to others, there is a prima facie case for punishing him, by law, or, where legal penalties are not safely applicable, by general disapprobation. There are also many positive acts for the benefit of others, which he may rightfully be compelled to perform; such as, to give evidence in a court of justice; to bear his fair share in the common defence, or in any other joint work necessary to the interest of the society of which he enjoys the protection; and to perform certain acts of individual beneficence, such as saving a fellow creature's life, or interposing to protect the defenceless against ill-usage, things which whenever it is obviously a man's duty to do, he may rightfully be made responsible to society for not doing. A person may cause evil to others not only by his actions but by his inaction, and in either case he is justly accountable to them for the injury. The latter case, it is true, requires a much more cautious exercise of compulsion than the former. To make any one answerable for doing evil to others, is the rule; to make him answerable for not preventing evil, is, comparatively speaking, the exception. Yet there are many cases clear enough and grave enough to justify that exception. In all things which regard the external relations of the individual, he is *de jure* amenable to those whose interests are concerned, and if need be, to society as their protector. There are often good reasons for not holding him to the responsibility; but these reasons must arise from the special expediencies of the case: either because it is a kind of case in which he is on the whole likely to act better, when left to his own discretion, than when controlled in any way in which society have it in their power to control him; or because the attempt to exercise control would produce other evils, greater than those which it would prevent. When such reasons as these preclude the enforcement of responsibility, the conscience of the agent himself should step into the vacant judgement-seat, and protect those interests of others which have no external protection; judging himself all the more rigidly, because the case does not admit of his being made accountable to the judgement of his fellow creatures.

But there is a sphere of action in which society, as distinguished from the individual, has, if any, only an indirect interest; comprehending all that portion of a person's life and conduct which affects only himself, or if it also affects others, only with their free, voluntary, and undeceived consent and participation. When I say only himself, I mean directly, and in the first instance: for whatever affects himself, may affect others through himself; and the objection which may be grounded on this contingency will receive consideration in the sequel. This, then, is the appropriate region of human liberty. It comprises, first, the inward domain of consciousness; demanding liberty of conscience, in the most comprehensive sense; liberty of thought and feeling; absolute freedom of opinion and sentiment on all subjects, practical or speculative, scientific, moral, or theological. The liberty of expressing and publishing opinions may seem to fall under a different principle, since it belongs to that part of the conduct of an individual which concerns other people; but, being almost of as much importance as the liberty of thought itself, and resting in great part on the same reasons, is practically inseparable from it. Secondly, the principle requires liberty of tastes and pursuits; of framing the plan of our life to suit our own character; of doing as we like, subject to such consequences as may follow: without impediment from our follow creatures, so long as what we do does not harm them, even though they should think our conduct foolish, perverse, or wrong. Thirdly, from this liberty of each individual, follows the liberty, within the same limits, of combination among individuals; freedom to unite, for any purpose not involving harm to others: the persons combining being supposed to be of full age, and not forced or deceived.

No society in which these liberties are not, on the whole, respected, is free, whatever may be its form of government; and none is completely free in which they do not exist absolute and unqualified. The only freedom which deserves the name, is that of pursuing our own good in our own way, so long as we do not attempt to deprive others of theirs, or impede their efforts to obtain it. Each is the proper guardian of his own health, whether bodily, or mental and spiritual. Mankind are greater gainers by suffering each other to live as seems good to themselves, than by compelling each to live as seems good to the rest.

. . .

Such being the reasons which make it imperative that human beings should be free to form opinions, and to express their opinions without reserve; and such the baneful consequences to the intellectual, and through that to the moral nature of man, unless this liberty is either conceded, or asserted in spite of prohibition; let us next examine whether the same reasons do not require that men should be free to act upon their opinions—to carry these out in their lives, without hindrance, either physical or moral, from their fellow men, so long as it is at their own risk and peril. This last proviso is of course indispensable. No one pretends that actions should be as free as opinions. On the contrary, even opinions lose their immunity, when the circumstances in which they are expressed are such as to constitute their expression a positive instigation to some mischievous act. An opinion that corn-dealers are starvers of the poor, or that private property is robbery, ought to be unmolested when simply circulated through the press, but may justly incur punishment when delivered orally to an excited mob assembled before the house of a corn-dealer, or when handed about among the same mob in the form of a placard. Acts, of whatever kind, which, without justifiable cause, do harm to others, may be, and in the more important cases absolutely require to be, controlled by the unfavourable sentiments, and, when needful, by the active interference of mankind. The liberty of the individual must be thus far limited; he must not make himself a nuisance to other people. But if he refrains from molesting others in what concerns them, and merely acts according to his own inclination and judgement in things which concern himself, the same reasons which show that opinion should be free, prove also that he should be allowed, without molestation, to carry his opinions into practice at his own cost. That mankind are not infallible; that their truths, for the most part, are only half-truths; that unity of opinion, unless resulting from the fullest and freest comparison of opposite opinions, is not desirable, and diversity not an evil, but a good, until mankind are much more capable than at present of recognizing all sides of the truth, are principles applicable to men's modes of action, not less than to their opinions. As it is useful that while mankind are imperfect there should be different opinions, so is it that there should be different experiments of living; that free scope should be given to varieties of character, short of injury to others; and that the worth of different modes of life should be proved practically, when any one thinks fit to try them. It is desirable, in short, that in things which do not primarily concern others, individuality should assert itself. Where, not the person's own character, but the traditions or customs of other people are the rule of conduct, there is wanting one of the principal ingredients of human happiness, and quite the chief ingredient of individual and social progress.

. . .

He who lets the world, or his own portion of it, choose his plan of life for him, has no need of any other faculty than the ape-like one of imitation. He who chooses his plan for himself, employs all his faculties. He must use observation to see, reasoning and judgement to foresee, activity to gather materials for decision, discrimination to decide, and when he has decided, firmness and self-control to hold to his deliberate decision. And these qualities he requires and exercises exactly in proportion as the part of his conduct which he determines according to his own judgement and feelings is a large one. It is possible that he might be guided in some good path, and kept out of harm's way, without any of these things. But what will be his comparative worth as a human being? It really is of importance, not only what men do, but also what manner of men they are that do it. Among the works of man, which human life is rightly employed in perfecting and beautifying, the first in importance surely is man himself. Supposing it were possible to get houses built, corn grown, battles fought, causes tried, and even churches erected and prayers said, by machinery—by automatons in human form—it would be a considerable loss to exchange for these automatons even the men and women who at present inhabit the more civilized parts of the world, and who assuredly are but starved specimens of what nature can and will produce. Human nature is not a machine to be built after a model, and set to do exactly the work prescribed for it, but a tree, which requires to grow and develop itself on all sides, according to the tendency of the inward forces which make it a living thing.

. . .

(b) The preceding considerations appear sufficient to show that an entire renovation of the social fabric, such as is contemplated by Socialism, establishing the economic constitution of society upon an entirely new basis, other than that of private property and competition, however valuable as an ideal, and even as a prophecy of ultimate possibilities, is not available as a present resource, since it requires from those who are to carry on the new order of things qualities both moral and intellectual, which require to be tested in all, and to be created in most; and this cannot be done by an Act of Parliament, but must be, on the most favourable supposition, a work of considerable time. For a long period to come the principle of individual property will be in possession of the field; and even if in any country a popular movement were to place Socialists at the head of a revolutionary government, in however many ways they might violate private property, the institution itself would survive, and would either be accepted by them or brought back by their expulsion, for the plain reason that people will not lose their hold of what is at present their sole reliance for subsistence and security until a substitute for it has been got into working order. Even those, if any, who had shared among themselves what was the property of others would desire to keep what they had acquired, and to give back to property in the new hands the sacredness which they had not recognised in the old.

But though, for these reasons, individual property has presumably a long term before it, if only of provisional existence, we are not, therefore, to conclude that it must exist during that whole term unmodified, or that all the rights now regarded as appertaining to property belong to it inherently, and must endure while it endures. On the contrary, it is both the duty and the interest of those who derive the most direct benefit from the laws of property to give impartial consideration to all proposals for rendering those laws in any way less onerous to the majority. This, which would in any case be an obligation of justice, is an injunction of prudence also, in order to place themselves in the right against the attempts which are sure to be frequent to bring the Socialist forms of society prematurely into operation.

One of the mistakes oftenest committed, and which are the sources of the greatest practical errors in human affairs, is that of supposing that the same name always stands for the same aggregation of ideas. No word has been the subject of more of this kind of misunderstanding than the word property. It denotes in every state of society the largest powers of exclusive use or exclusive control over things (and sometimes, unfortunately, over persons) which the law accords, or which custom, in that state of society, recognises; but these powers of exclusive use and control are very various, and differ greatly in different countries and in different states of society.

For instance, in early states of society, the right of property did not include the right of bequest. The power of disposing of property by will was in most countries of Europe a rather late institution; and long after it was introduced it continued to be limited in favour of what were called natural heirs. Where bequest is not permitted, individual property is only a life interest. And in fact, as has been so well and fully set forth by Sir Henry Maine in his most instructive work on Ancient Law, the primitive idea of property was that it belonged to the family, not the individual. The head of the family had the management and was the person who really exercised the proprietary rights. As in other respects, so in this, he governed the family with nearly despotic power. But he was not free so to exercise his power as to defeat the co-proprietors of the other portions; he could not so dispose of the property as to deprive them of the joint enjoyment or of the succession. By the laws and customs of some nations the property could not be alienated without the consent of the male children; in other cases the child could by law demand a division of the property and the assignment to him of his share, as in the story of the Prodigal Son. If the association kept together after the death of the head, some other member of it, not always his son, but often the eldest of the family, the strongest, or the one selected by the rest, succeeded to the management and to the managing rights, all the others retaining theirs as before. If, on the other hand, the body broke up into separate families, each of these took away with it a part of the property. I say the property, not the inheritance, because the process was a mere continuance of existing rights, not a creation of new; the manager's share alone lapsed to the association.

Then, again, in regard to proprietary rights over immovables (the principal kind of property in a rude age) these rights were of very varying extent and duration. By the Jewish law property in immovables was only a temporary concession; on the Sabbatical year it returned to the common stock to be redistributed; though we may surmise that in the historical times of the Jewish state this rule may have been successfully evaded. In many countries of Asia, before European ideas intervened, nothing existed to which the expression property in land, as we understand the phrase, is strictly applicable. The ownership was broken up among several distinct parties, whose rights were determined rather by custom than by law. The government was part owner, having the right to a heavy rent. Ancient ideas and even ancient laws limited the government share to some particular fraction of the gross produce, but practically there was no fixed limit. The government might make over its share to an individual, who then became possessed of the right of collection and all the other rights of the state, but not those of any private person connected with the soil. These private rights were of various kinds. The actual cultivators, or such of them as had been long settled on the land, had a right to retain possession; it was held unlawful to evict them while they paid the rent—a rent not in general fixed by agreement, but by the custom of the neighbourhood. Between the actual cultivators and the state, or the substitute to whom the state had transferred its rights, there were intermediate persons with rights of various extent. There were officers of government who collected the state's share of the produce, sometimes for large districts, who, though bound to pay over to government all they collected, after deducting a percentage, were often hereditary officers. There were also, in many cases, village communities, consisting of the reputed descendants of the first settlers of a village, who shared among themselves either the land or its produce according to rules established by custom, either cultivating it themselves or employing others to cultivate it for them, and whose rights in the land approached nearer to those of a landed proprietor, as understood in England, than those of any other party concerned. But the proprietary right of the village was not individual, but collective; inalienable (the rights of individual sharers could only be sold or mortgaged with the consent of the community) and governed by fixed rules. In mediæval Europe almost all land was held from the sovereign on tenure of service, either military or agricultural; and in Great Britain even now, when the services as well as all the reserved rights of the sovereign have long since fallen into disuse or been commuted for taxation, the theory of the law does not acknowledge an absolute right of property in land in any individual; the fullest landed proprietor known to the law, the freeholder, is but a 'tenant' of the Crown. In Russia, even when the cultivators of the soil were serfs of the landed proprietor, his proprietary right in the land was limited by rights of theirs belonging to them as a collective body managing its own affairs, and with which he could not interfere. And in most of the countries of continental Europe when serfage was abolished or went out of use, those who had cultivated the land as serfs remained in possession of rights as well as subject to obligations. The great land reforms of Stein and his successors in Prussia consisted in abolishing both the rights and the obligations, and dividing the land bodily between the proprietor and the peasant, instead of leaving each of them with a limited right over the whole. In other cases, as in Tuscany, the *metayer* farmer is virtually co-proprietor with a landlord, since custom, though not law, guarantees to him a permanent possession and half the gross produce, so long as he fulfils the customary conditions of his tenure.

Again, if rights or property over the same things are of different extent in different countries, so also are they exercised over different things. In all countries at a former time, and in some countries still, the right of property extended and extends to the ownership of human beings. There has often been property in public trusts, as in judicial offices, and a vast multitude of others in France before the Revolution; there are still a few patent offices in Great Britain, though I believe they will cease by operation of law on the death of the present holders; and we are only now abolishing property in army rank. Public bodies, constituted and endowed for public purposes, still claim the same inviolable right of property in their estates which individuals have in theirs, and though a sound political morality does not acknowledge this claim, the law supports it. We thus see that the right of property is differently interpreted, and held to be of different extent, in different times and places; that the conception entertained of it is a varying conception, has been frequently revised, and may admit of still further revision. It is also to be noticed that the revisions which it has hitherto undergone in the progress of society have generally been improvements. When, therefore, it is maintained, rightly or wrongly, that some change or modification in the powers exercised over things by the persons legally recognised as their proprietors would be beneficial to the public and conducive to the general improvement, it is no good answer to this merely to say that the proposed change conflicts with the idea of property. The idea of property is not some one thing, identical throughout history and incapable of alteration, but is variable like all other creatures of the human mind; at any given time it is a brief expression denoting the rights over things conferred by the law or custom of some given society at that time; but neither on this point nor on any other has the law and custom of a given time and place a claim to be stereotyped for ever. A proposed reform in laws or customs is not necessarily objectionable because its adoption would imply, not the adaptation of all human affairs to the existing idea of property, but the adaptation of existing ideas of property to the growth and improvement of human affairs. This is said without prejudice to the equitable claim of proprietors to be compensated by the state for such legal rights of a proprietary nature as they may be dispossessed of for the public advantage. That equitable claim, the grounds and the just limits of it, are a subject by itself, and as such will be discussed hereafter. Under this condition, however, society is fully entitled to abrogate or alter any particular right of property which on sufficient consideration it judges to stand in the way of the public good. And assuredly the terrible case which, as we saw in a former chapter, Socialists are able to make out against the present economic order of society, demands a full consideration of all means by which the institution may have a chance of being made to work in a manner more beneficial to that large portion of society which at present enjoys the least share of its direct benefits.

16   T. H. Green, from 'Liberal Legislation and Freedom of Contract', in *Works*, vol. 3 (ed. R. L. Nettleship; Longmans, Green, 1888), pp. 370–7

Thomas Hill Green (1836–1882) taught at Oxford University, and from there exercised a deep influence not only on the philosophical thought of his day but on a generation of social reformers. His students included the philosophers F. H. Bradley and Bernard Bosanquet as well as the future Liberal Prime Minister H. H. Asquith. 'Liberal Legislation and Freedom of

Contract' was one of his few works to appear before his premature death, and the bulk of his philosophical work was collected and edited posthumously by his memoirist, R. L. Nettleship.

We shall probably all agree that freedom, rightly understood, is the greatest of blessings; that its attainment is the true end of all our effort as citizens. But when we thus speak of freedom, we should consider carefully what we mean by it. We do not mean merely freedom from restraint or compulsion. We do not mean merely freedom to do as we like irrespectively of what it is that we like. We do not mean a freedom that can be enjoyed by one man or one set of men at the cost of a loss of freedom to others. When we speak of freedom as something to be so highly prized, we mean a positive power or capacity of doing or enjoying something worth doing or enjoying, and that, too, something that we do or enjoy in common with others. We mean by it a power which each man exercises through the help or security given him by his fellow-men, and which he in turn helps to secure for them. When we measure the progress of a society by its growth in freedom, we measure it by the increasing development and exercise on the whole of those powers of contributing to social good with which we believe the members of the society to be endowed; in short, by the greater power on the part of the citizens as a body to make the most and best of themselves. Thus, though of course there can be no freedom among men who act not willingly but under compulsion, yet on the other hand the mere removal of compulsion, the mere enabling a man to do as he likes, is in itself no contribution to true freedom. In one sense no man is so well able to do as he likes as the wandering savage. He has no master. There is no one to say him nay. Yet we do not count him really free, because the freedom of savagery is not strength, but weakness. The actual powers of the noblest savage do not admit of comparison with those of the humblest citizen of a law-abiding state. He is not the slave of man, but he is the slave of nature. Of compulsion by natural necessity he has plenty of experience, though of restraint by society none at all. Nor can he deliver himself from that compulsion except by submitting to this restraint. So to submit is the first step in true freedom, because the first step towards the full exercise of the faculties with which man is endowed. But we rightly refuse to recognise the highest development on the part of an exceptional individual or exceptional class, as an advance towards the true freedom of man, if it is founded on a refusal of the same opportunity to other men. The powers of the human mind have probably never attained such force and keenness, the proof of what society can do for the individual has never been so strikingly exhibited, as among the small groups of men who possessed civil privileges in the small republics of antiquity. The whole framework of our political ideas, to say nothing of our philosophy, is derived from them. But in them this extraordinary efflorescence of the privileged class was accompanied by the slavery of the multitude. That slavery was the condition on which it depended, and for that reason it was doomed to decay. There is no clearer ordinance of that supreme reason, often dark to us, which governs the course of man's affairs, than that no body of men should in the long run be able to strengthen itself at the cost of others' weakness. The civilisation and freedom of the ancient world were shortlived because they were partial and exceptional. If the ideal of true freedom is the maximum of power for all members of human society alike to make the best of themselves, we are right in refusing to ascribe the glory of freedom to a state in which the apparent elevation of the few is founded on the degradation of the many, and in ranking modern society, founded as it is on free industry, with all its confusion and ignorant licence and waste of effort, above the most splendid of ancient republics.

If I have given a true account of that freedom which forms the goal of social effort, we shall see that freedom of contract, freedom in all the forms of doing what one will with one's own, is valuable only as a means to an end. That end is what I call freedom in the positive sense: in other words, the liberation of the powers of all men equally for contributions to a common good. No one has a right to do what he will with his own in such a way as to contravene this end. It is only through the guarantee which society gives him that he has property at all, or, strictly speaking, any right to his possessions. This guarantee is founded on a sense of common interest. Every one has an interest in securing to every one else the free use and enjoyment and disposal of his possessions, so long as that freedom on the part of one does not interfere with a like freedom on the part of others, because such freedom contributes to that equal development of the faculties of all which is the highest good for all. This is the true and the only justification of rights of property. Rights of property, however, have been and are claimed which cannot be thus justified. We are all now agreed that men cannot rightly be the property of men. The institution of property being only justifiable as a means to the free exercise of the social capabilities of all, there can be no true right to property of a kind which debars one class of men from such free exercise altogether. We condemn slavery no less when it arises out of a voluntary agreement on the part of the enslaved person. A contract by which any one agreed for a certain consideration to become the slave of another we should reckon a void contract. Here, then, is a limitation upon freedom of contract which we all recognise as rightful. No contract is valid in which human persons, willingly or unwillingly, are dealt with as commodities, because such contracts of necessity defeat the end for which alone society enforces contracts at all.

Are there no other contracts which, less obviously perhaps but really, are open to the same objection? In the first place, let us consider contracts affecting labour. Labour, the economist tells us, is a commodity exchangeable like other commodities. This is in a certain sense true, but it is a commodity which attaches in a peculiar manner to the person of man. Hence restrictions may need to be placed on the sale of this commodity which would be unnecessary in other cases, in order to prevent labour from being sold under conditions which make it impossible for the person selling it ever to become a free contributor to social good in any form. This is most plainly the case when a man bargains to work under conditions fatal to health, *e.g.* in an unventilated factory. Every injury to the health of the individual is, so far as it goes, a public injury. It is an impediment to the general freedom; so much deduction from our power, as members of society, to make the best of ourselves. Society is, therefore, plainly within its right when it limits freedom of contract for the sale of labour, so far as is done by our laws for the sanitary regulations of factories, workshops, and mines. It is equally within its right in prohibiting the labour of women and young persons beyond certain hours. If they work beyond those hours, the result is demonstrably physical deterioration; which, as demonstrably, carries with it a lowering of the moral forces of society. For the sake of that general freedom of its members to make the best of themselves, which it is the object of civil society to secure, a prohibition should be put by law, which is the deliberate voice of society, on all such contracts of service as in a general way yield such a result. The purchase or hire of unwholesome dwellings is properly forbidden on the same principle. Its application to compulsory education may not be quite so obvious, but it will appear on a little reflection. Without a command of certain elementary arts and knowledge, the individual in modern society is as effectually crippled as by the loss of a limb or a broken constitution. He is not free to develop his faculties. With a view to securing such freedom among its members it is as certainly within the province of the state to prevent children from growing up in that kind of ignorance which practically excludes them from a free career in life, as it is within its province to require the sort of building and drainage necessary for public health.

Our modern legislation then with reference to labour, and education, and health, involving as it does manifold interference with freedom of contract, is justified on the ground that it is the business of the state, not indeed directly to promote moral goodness, for that, from the very nature of moral goodness, it cannot do, but to maintain the conditions without which a free exercise of the human faculties is impossible. It does not indeed follow that it is advisable for the state to do all which it is justified in doing. We are often warned nowadays against the danger of over-legislation; or, as I heard it put in a speech of the present home secretary in days when he was sowing his political wild oats, of 'grandmotherly government.' There may be good ground for the warning, but at any rate we should be quite clear what we mean by it. The outcry against state interference is often raised by men whose real objection is not to state interference but to centralisation, to the constant aggression of the central executive upon local authorities. As I have already pointed out, compulsion at the discretion of some elected municipal board proceeds just as much from the state as does compulsion exercised by a government office in London. No doubt, much needless friction is avoided, much is gained in the way of elasticity and adjustment to circumstances, by the independent local administration of general laws; and most of us would agree that of late there has been a dangerous tendency to override municipal discretion by the hard and fast rules of London 'departments.' But centralisation is one thing: over-legislation, or the improper exercise of the power of the state, quite another. It is one question whether of late the central government has been unduly trenching on local government, and another question whether the law of the state, either as administered by central or by provincial authorities, has been unduly interfering with the discretion of individuals. We may object most strongly to advancing centralisation, and yet wish that the law should put rather more than less restraint on those liberties of the individual which are a social nuisance. But there are some political speculators whose objection is not merely to centralisation, but to the extended action of law altogether. They think that the individual ought to be left much more to himself than has of late been the case. Might not our people, they ask, have been trusted to learn in time for themselves to eschew unhealthy dwellings, to refuse dangerous and degrading employment, to get their children the schooling necessary for making their way in the world? Would they not for their own comfort, if not from more chivalrous feeling, keep their wives and daughters from overwork? Or, failing this, ought not women, like men, to learn to protect themselves? Might not all the rules, in short, which legislation of the kind we have been discussing is intended to attain, have been attained without it; not so quickly, perhaps, but without tampering so dangerously with the independence and self-reliance of the people?

Now, we shall probably all agree that a society in which the public health was duly protected, and necessary education duly provided for, by the spontaneous action of individuals, was in a higher condition than one in which the compulsion of law was needed to secure these ends. But we must take men as we find them. Until such a condition of society is reached, it is the business of the state to take the best security it can for the young citizens' growing up in such health and with so much knowledge as is necessary for their real freedom. In so doing it need not at all interfere with the independence and self-reliance of those whom it requires to do what they would otherwise do for themselves. The man who, of his own right feeling, saves his wife from overwork and sends his children to school, suffers no moral degradation from a law which, if he did not do this for himself, would seek to make him do it. Such a man does not feel the law as constraint at all. To him it is simply a powerful friend. It gives him security for that being done efficiently which, with the best wishes, he might have much trouble in getting done efficiently if left to himself. No doubt it relieves him from some of the responsibility which would otherwise fall to him as head of a family, but, if he is what we are supposing him to be, in proportion as he is relieved of responsibilities in one direction he will assume them in another. The security which the state gives him for the safe housing and sufficient schooling of his family will only make him the more careful for their well-being in other respects, which he is left to look after for himself. We need have no fear, then, of such legislation having an ill effect on those who, without the law, would have seen to that being done, though probably less efficiently, which the law requires to be done. But it was not their case that the laws we are considering were especially meant to meet. It was the overworked women, the ill-housed and untaught families, for whose benefit they were intended. And the question is whether without these laws the suffering classes could have been delivered quickly or slowly from the condition they were in. Could the enlightened self-interest or benevolence of individuals, working under a system of unlimited freedom of contract, have ever brought them into a state compatible with the free development of the human faculties? No one considering the facts can have any doubt as to the answer to this question. Left to itself, or to the operation of casual benevolence, a degraded population perpetuates and increases itself. Read any of the authorised accounts, given before royal or parliamentary commissions, of the state of the labourers, especially of the women and children, as they were in our great industries before the law was first brought to bear on them, and before freedom of contract was first interfered with in them. Ask yourself what chance there was of a generation, born and bred under such conditions, ever contracting itself out of them. Given a certain standard of moral and material well-being, people may be trusted not to sell their labour, or the labour of their children, on terms which would not allow that standard to be maintained. But with large masses of our population, until the laws we have been considering took effect, there was no such standard. There was nothing on their part, in the way either of self-respect or established demand for comforts, to prevent them from working and living, or from putting their children to work and live, in a way in which no one who is to be a healthy and free citizen can work and live. No doubt there were many high-minded employers who did their best for their workpeople before the days of state-interference, but they could not prevent less scrupulous hirers of labour from hiring it on the cheapest terms. It is true that cheap labour is in the long run dear labour, but it is so only in the long run, and eager traders do not think of the long run. If labour is to be had under conditions incompatible with the health or decent housing or education of the labourer, there will always be plenty of people to buy it under those conditions, careless of the burden in the shape of rates and taxes which they may be laying up for posterity. Either the standard of well-being on the part of the sellers of labour must prevent them from selling their labour under those conditions, or the law must prevent it. With a population such as ours was forty years ago, and still largely is, the law must prevent it and continue the prevention for some generations, before the sellers will be in a state to prevent it for themselves.

As there is practically no danger of a reversal of our factory and school laws, it may seem needless to dwell at such length on their justification. I do so for two reasons; partly to remind the younger generation of citizens of the great blessing which they inherited in those laws, and of the interest which they still have in their completion and extension; but still more in order to obtain some clear principles for our guidance when we approach those difficult questions of the immediate future, the questions of the land law and the liquor law.

17 L. T. Hobhouse, from *Liberalism* (ed. A. P. Grimes; Oxford University Press, 1964), pp. 98–101, 121–3

Leonard Trelawney Hobhouse (1864–1929) was an academic and journalist, the first professor of sociology at the University of London and associate of the Manchester Guardian and other liberal newspapers. His philosophical and political views were particularly influenced by the idealism of Green and Bosanquet, J. S. Mill's utilitarianism, and evolutionary theory. He wrote extensively on the theory of mind, ethics, and society in evolutionary perspective as well as on national and international politics.

There is a social element in value and a social element in production. In modern industry there is very little that the individual can do by his unaided efforts. Labour is minutely divided; and in proportion as it is divided it is forced to be co-operative. Men produce goods to sell, and the rate of exchange, that is, price, is fixed by relations of demand and supply the rates of which are determined by complex social forces. In the methods of production every man makes use, to the best of his ability, of the whole available means of civilization, of the machinery which the brains of other men have devised, of the human apparatus which is the gift of acquired civilization. Society thus provides conditions or opportunities of which one man will make much better use than another, and the use to which they are put is the individual or personal element in production which is the basis of the personal claim to reward. To maintain and stimulate this personal effort is a necessity of good economic organization, and without asking here whether any particular conception of Socialism would or would not meet this need we may lay down with confidence that no form of Socialism which should ignore it could possibly enjoy enduring success. On the other hand, an individualism which ignores the social factor in wealth will deplete the national resources, deprive the community of its just share in the fruits of industry and so result in a one-sided and inequitable distribution of wealth. Economic justice is to render what is due not only to each individual but to each function, social or personal, that is engaged in the performance of useful service, and this due is measured by the amount necessary to stimulate and maintain the efficient exercise of that useful function. This equation between function and sustenance is the true meaning of economic equality.

Now to apply this principle to the adjustment of the claims of the community on the one hand and the producers or inheritors of wealth on the other would involve a discrimination of the factors of production which is not easy to make in all instances. If we take the case of urban land, referred to above, the distinction is tolerably clear. The value of a site in London is something due essentially to London, not to the landlord. More accurately a part of it is due to London, a part to the British empire, a part, perhaps we should say, to Western civilization. But while it would be impossible to disentangle these subsidiary factors, the main point that the entire increment of value is due to one social factor or another is sufficiently clear, and this explains why Liberal opinion has fastened on the conception of site value as being by right communal and not personal property. The monopoly value of licensed premises, which is the direct creation of laws passed for the control of the liquor traffic, is another case in point. The difficulty which society finds in dealing with these cases is that it has allowed these sources of wealth to pass out of its hands, and that property of these kinds has freely passed from one man to another in the market, in the belief that it stood and would stand on the same basis in law as any other. Hence, it is not possible for society to insist on the whole of its claim. It could only resume its full rights at the cost of great hardship to individuals and a shock to the industrial system. What it can do is to shift taxation step by step from the wealth due to individual enterprise to the wealth that depends on its own collective progress, thus by degrees regaining the ownership of the fruits of its own collective work.

Much more difficult in principle is the question of the more general elements of social value which run through production as a whole. We are dealing here with factors so intricately interwoven in their operation that they can only be separated by an indirect process. What this process would be we may best understand by imagining for a moment a thoroughgoing centralized organization of the industrial system endeavouring to carry out the principles of remuneration outlined above. The central authority which we imagine as endowed with such wisdom and justice as to find for every man his right place and to assign to every man his due reward would, if our argument is sound, find it necessary to assign to each producer, whether working with hand or brain, whether directing a department of industry or serving under direction, such remuneration as would stimulate him to put forth his best efforts and would maintain him in the condition necessary for the life-long exercise of his function. If we are right in considering that a great part of the wealth produced from year to year is of social origin, it would follow that, after the assignment of this remuneration, there would remain a surplus, and this would fall to the coffers of the community and be available for public purposes, for national defence, public works, education, charity, and the furtherance of civilized life.

Now, this is merely an imaginary picture, and I need not ask whether such a measure of wisdom on the part of a Government is practically attainable, or whether such a measure of centralization might not carry consequences which would hamper progress in other directions. The picture serves merely to illustrate the principles of equitable distribution by which the State should be guided in dealing with property. It serves to define our conception of economic justice, and therewith the lines on which we should be guided in the adjustment of taxation and the reorganization of industry.

. . .

The cause of democracy is bound up with that of internationalism. The relation is many-sided. It is national pride, resentment, or ambition one day that sweeps the public mind and diverts it from all interest in domestic progress. The next day the same function is performed no less adequately by a scare. The practice of playing on popular emotions has been reduced to a fine art which neither of the great parties is ashamed to employ. Military ideals possess the mind, and military expenditure eats up the public resources. On the other side, the political, economic and social progress of other nations reacts on our own. The backwardness of our commercial rivals in industrial legislation was long made an argument against further advances among ourselves. Conversely, when they go beyond us, as now they often do, we can learn from them. Physically the world is rapidly becoming one, and its unity must ultimately be reflected in political institutions. The old doctrine of absolute sovereignty is dead. The greater States of the day exhibit a complex system of government within government, authority limited by authority, and the world-state of the not impossible future must be based on a free national self-direction as full and satisfying as that enjoyed by Canada or Australia within the British Empire at this moment. National emulation will express itself less in the desire to extend territory or to count up ships and guns, and more in the endeavour to magnify the contribution of our own country to civilized life. Just as in the rebirth of our municipal life we find a civic patriotism which takes interest in the local university, which feels pride in the magnitude of the local industry, which parades the lowest death rate in the country, which is honestly ashamed of a bad record for crime or pauperism, so as Englishmen we shall concern ourselves less with the question whether two of our Dreadnoughts might not be pitted against one German, and more with the question whether we cannot equal Germany in the development of science, of education, and of industrial technique. Perhaps even, recovering from our present artificially induced and radically insincere mood of national self-abasement, we shall learn to take some pride in our own characteristic contributions as a nation to the arts of government, to the thought, the literature, the art, the mechanical inventions which have made and are re-making modern civilization.

Standing by national autonomy and international equality, Liberalism is necessarily in conflict with the Imperial idea as it is ordinarily presented. But this is not to say that it is indifferent to the interests of the Empire as a whole, to the sentiment of unity pervading its white population, to all the possibilities involved in the bare fact that a fourth part of the human race recognizes one flag and one supreme authority. In relation to the self-governing colonies the Liberal of today has to face a change in the situation since Cobden's time not unlike that which we have traced in other departments. The Colonial Empire as it stands is in substance the creation of the older Liberalism. It is founded on self-government, and self-government is the root from which the existing sentiment of unity has sprung. The problem of our time is to devise means for the more concrete and living expression of this sentiment without impairing the rights of self-government on which it depends. Hitherto the "Imperialist" has had matters all his own way and has cleverly exploited Colonial opinion, or an appearance of Colonial opinion, in favour of class ascendancy and reactionary legislation in the mother country. But the colonies include the most democratic communities in the world. Their natural sympathies are not with the Conservatives, but with the most Progressive parties in the United Kingdom. They favour Home Rule, they set the pace in social legislation. There exist accordingly the political conditions of a democratic alliance which it is the business of the British Liberal to turn to account. He may hope to make his country the centre of a group of self-governing, democratic communities, one of which, moreover, serves as a natural link with the other great commonwealth of English-speaking people. The constitutional mechanism of the new unity begins to take shape in the Imperial Council, and its work begins to define itself as the adjustment of interests as between different portions of the Empire and the organization of common defence. Such a union is no menace to the world's peace or to the cause of freedom. On the contrary, as a natural outgrowth of a common sentiment, it is one of the steps towards a wider unity which involves no backstroke against the ideal of self-government. It is a model, and that on no mean scale, of the International State.

Internationalism on the one side, national self-government on the other, are the radical conditions of the growth of a social mind which is the essence, as opposed to the form, of democracy.

18   John Dewey, from 'Liberty and Social Control', in *John Dewey: The Later Works, 1925–1953, vol. 11: 1935–1937* (eds. J. Boydston et al.; Southern Illinois University Press, 1987), pp. 360–3

John Dewey (1859–1952) was born in Vermont and enjoyed a lengthy academic career at the universities of Michigan, Chicago, and Columbia. He was also a journalist, particularly associated with *The New Republic*, and advocate of radical economic, educational, and political reform. He wrote extremely widely, on psychology, metaphysics, logic, education, politics, religion, and art, and was an immensely influential figure for more than one generation of American progressive reformers.

Today there is no word more bandied about than liberty. Every effort at planned control of economic forces is resisted and attacked, by a certain group, in the name of liberty. The slightest observation shows that this group is made up of those who are interested, from causes that are evident, in the preservation of the economic status quo; that is to say, in the maintenance of the customary privileges and legal rights they already possess. When we look at history in the large we find that the demand for liberty and efforts to achieve it have come from those who wanted to *alter* the institutional set-up. This striking contrast is a stimulus to thoughtful inquiry. What does liberty mean anyway? Why should the cause of liberty have been identified in the past with efforts at change of laws and institutions while at the present time a certain group is using all its vast resources to convince the public that change of economic institutions is an attack upon liberty?

Well, in the first place, liberty is not just an idea, an abstract principle. It is power, effective power to do specific things. There is no such thing as liberty in general; liberty, so to speak, at large. If one wants to know what the condition of liberty is at a given time, one has to examine what persons *can* do and what they *cannot* do. The moment one examines the question from the standpoint of effective action, it becomes evident that the demand for liberty is a demand for power, either for possession of powers of action not already possessed or for retention and expansion of powers already possessed. The present ado in behalf of liberty by the managers and beneficiaries of the existing economic system is immediately explicable if one views it as a demand for preservation of the powers they already possess. Since it is the existing system that gives them these powers, liberty is thus inevitably identified with the perpetuation of that system. Translate the present hullaballoo about liberty into struggle to retain powers already possessed, and it has a meaning.

In the second place, the possession of effective power is always a matter of the *distribution* of power that exists at the time. A physical analogy may make clear what I mean. Water runs down hill and electric currents flow because of *difference in potentials*. If the ground is level, water is stagnant. If on the level ocean, there are dashing waves, it is because there is another power operating, that of the winds, occasioned ultimately by a difference in the distribution of temperature at different points. There is no such thing physically as manifestation of energy or effective power by one thing except in relation to the energy manifested by other things. There is no such thing as the liberty or effective power of an individual, group, or class, except in relation to the liberties, the effective powers, of *other* individuals, groups, and classes.

Demand for retention of powers already possessed on the part of a particular group means, therefore, that other individuals and groups shall continue to possess only the capacities in and for activity which *they* already possess. Demand for increased power at one point means demands for change in the distribution of powers, that is, for less power somewhere else. You cannot discuss or measure the liberty of one individual or group of individuals without thereby raising the question of the effect upon the liberty of others, any more than you can measure the energy of a head water at the head without measuring the difference of levels.

In the third place, this relativity of liberty to the existing distribution of powers of action, while meaning that there is no such thing as absolute liberty, also necessarily means that wherever there is liberty at one place there is restraint at some other place. *The system of liberties that exists at any time is always the system of restraints or controls that exists at that time.* No one can *do* anything except in relation to what others can do and cannot do.

These three points are general. But they cannot be dismissed as mere abstractions. For when they are applied either in idea or in action they mean that liberty is always a *social* question, not an individual one. For the liberties that any individual actually has depends upon the distribution of powers or liberties that exists, and this distribution is identical with actual social arrangements, legal and political—and, at the present time, economic, in a peculiarly important way.

Return now to the fact that historically the great movements for human liberation have always been movements to change institutions and not to preserve them intact. It follows from what has been said that there have been movements to bring about a changed distribution of power to do—and power to think and to express thought is a power to do—such that there would be a more balanced, a more equal, even, and equitable system of human liberties.

The present movement for social control of industry, money and credit, is simply a part of this endless human struggle. The present attempt to define liberty in terms of the existing distribution of liberty is an attempt to maintain the existing system of control of power, of social restraints and regimentations. I cannot go here into the nature and consequences of this system. If one is satisfied with it, let him support the conception of liberty put forth by, say, the Liberty League which represents the present economic system. But let him not be fooled into thinking that the issue is liberty versus restraint and regimentation. For the issue is simply that of one system of control of the social forces upon which the distribution of liberties depends, versus some other system of social control which would bring about another distribution of liberties. And let those who are struggling to replace the present economic system by a cooperative one also remember that in struggling for a new system of social restraints and controls they are also struggling for a more equal and equitable balance of powers that will enhance and multiply the effective liberties of the mass of individuals. Let them not be jockeyed into the position of supporting social control at the expense of liberty, when what they want is another method of social control than the one that now exists, one that will increase significant human liberties.

It is nonsense to suppose that we do not have social control *now*. The trouble is that it is exercised by the few who have economic power, at the expense of the liberties of the many and at the cost of increasing disorder, culminating in that chaos of war which the representatives of liberty for the possessive class identify with true discipline.

19 Max Weber, from 'Parliament and Government in Germany', in *Political Writings* (eds. Peter Lassman and Ronald Speirs; Cambridge University Press, 1994), pp. 156–61

Max Weber (1864–1920) was born in Erfurt into a distinguished and cosmopolitan family. He enjoyed a successful academic career as a professor of law, economics, and of politics, but a brief and unsuccessful political career. Prodigiously learned and usually held to be a 'founding father' of sociology, Weber is famous for his writings on religion, authority, bureaucracy, capitalism, and the philosophy of the social sciences. He once declared that the political was his 'secret love' and the future of the state, and in particular the problems and prospects of liberalism in Germany, were a persistent concern for him.

Bureaucracy is, however, distinguished from other historical bearers of the modern, rational way of ordering life by the fact of its far greater *inescapability*. History records no instance of it having disappeared again once it had achieved complete and sole dominance—in China, Egypt, or in a less consistent form in the later Roman Empire and Byzantium, except when the whole culture supporting it also disappeared completely.

Relatively speaking, however, these were still highly irrational forms of bureaucracy; they were 'patrimonial bureaucracies'. Compared with all these older forms, modern bureaucracy is distinguished by a characteristic which makes its inescapability much more absolute than theirs, namely *rational, technical specialisation and training*. The ancient Chinese mandarin was no specialist official; on the contrary, he was a 'gentleman' with a literary–humanist education. The Egyptian, later Roman and Byzantine official was essentially much more of a bureaucrat in our sense of the word. But the tasks of state for which he had responsibility were infinitely more simple and modest than modern ones, his conduct always being bound in part by tradition, and being in part patriarchal, and thus irrational, in its orientation. He was a pure empiricist, just like the practitioner of a trade in the past. As befits the rational technique of modern life, the modern official is always and increasingly a person with professional training and a specialisation. All bureaucracies throughout the world follow this path. The fact that they had not reached the end of this road before the war gave us our superiority over others. Although, for example, the older American official (a creation of party patronage) was a 'connoisseur' of the electoral arena and the practices appropriate to it, he was in no sense an expert with specialist training. It is on this fact, and not on democracy as such (as our littérateurs would have the public believe), that the corruption over there rested, for this is as alien to the university-trained, professional official in die 'civil service' which is only just emerging there as it is to the modern English bureaucracy that is now increasingly taking the place of 'self-government' by notables ('gentlemen'). But wherever the trained, specialist, modern official has once begun to rule, his power is absolutely unbreakable, because the entire organisation of providing even the most basic needs in life then depends on his performance of his duties. In theory one could probably conceive of the progressive elimination of private capitalism—although this is certainly not the trivial matter some littérateurs, who are unfamiliar with it, imagine it to be, and it will quite certainly not be a consequence of this war. But assuming this were to be achieved at some point, what would it mean in practice? Would it perhaps mean that the steel housing (*Gehäuse*) of modern industrial work would break open? No! It would mean rather that the *management* of businesses taken into state ownership or into some form of 'communal economy' would also become bureaucratised. Is there any appreciable *difference* between the lives of the workers and clerks in the Prussian state-run mines and railways and those of people working in large private capitalist enterprises? They are *less free*, because there is *no hope* of winning any battle against the state bureaucracy and because no help can be summoned from any authority with an interest in *opposing* that bureaucracy and its power, whereas this is possible in relation to private capitalism. *That* would be the entire difference. If private capitalism were eliminated, state bureaucracy would rule *alone*. Private and public bureaucracies would then be merged into a single hierarchy, whereas they now operate alongside and, at least potentially, against one another, thus keeping one another in check. The situation would resemble that of ancient Egypt, but in an incomparably more rational and hence more inescapable form.

A lifeless machine is *congealed spirit*. It is *only* this fact that gives the machine the power to force men to serve it and thus to rule and determine their daily working lives, as in fact happens in factories. This same *congealed spirit* is, however, also embodied in that *living machine* which is represented by bureaucratic organisation with its specialisation of trained, technical work, its delimitation of areas of responsibility, its regulations and its graduated hierarchy of relations of obedience. Combined with the dead machine, it is in the process of manufacturing the housing of that future serfdom to which, perhaps, men may have to submit powerlessly, just like the slaves in the ancient state of Egypt, *if they consider that the ultimate and only value by which the conduct of their affairs is to be decided is good administration and provision for their needs by officials (that is 'good' in the purely technical sense of rational administration).* Bureaucracy achieves this, after all, incomparably better than any other structure of rule. This housing, so praised by our naive littérateurs, will be augmented by shackles chaining each individual to his firm (the beginnings of this are to be found in so-called 'welfare arrangements'), to his class (by an increasingly rigid structure of ownership) and perhaps at some time in the future to his occupation (by state provision for needs on a 'liturgical' principle, whereby associations structured along occupational lines carry a burden of state responsibilities). This housing would become even more indestructible if, in the social area, as in those states in the past where enforced labour existed, an organisation of the ruled based on their social and occupational status were to be attached (which in truth means subordinated) to the bureaucracy. An 'organic', that is an Oriental–Egyptian social structure would begin to emerge, but, in contrast to that ancient form, one which would be as strictly rational as a machine. Who would deny that some such *possibility* lies in the womb of the future? Such things have often been said, and a confused, shadowy notion of these possibilities drifts through the products of our littérateurs. Assuming that precisely this possibility were to be an inescapable fate, who could help smiling at the anxiety of our littérateurs lest future social and political developments might bestow on us *too much* 'individualism' or 'democracy' or the like, or that 'true freedom' would not emerge until the present 'anarchy' in our economic production and the 'party machinations' in our parliaments had been *eliminated* in favour of 'social order' and an 'organic structure'—which means in favour of the pacifism of social impotence under the wing of the one quite definitely *inescapable* power, that of the bureaucracy in the state and the economy.

In view of the fundamental fact that the advance of bureaucratisation is unstoppable, there is only one possible set of questions to be asked about future forms of political organisation: (1) How is it *at all possible* to salvage any remnants of 'individual' freedom of movement *in any sense*, given this all-powerful trend towards bureaucratisation? It is, after all, a piece of crude self-deception to think that even the most conservative amongst us could carry on living at all today without these achievements from the age of the 'Rights of Man'. However, let us put this question to one side for now, for there is another which is directly relevant to our present concerns: (2) In view of the growing indispensability and hence increasing power of state officialdom, which is our concern here, how can there be any guarantee that forces exist which can impose limits on the enormous, crushing power of this constantly growing stratum of society and control it effectively? How is democracy even in this restricted sense to be *at all possible?* Yet this too is not the only question of concern to us here, for there is (3) a third question, the most important of all, which arises from any consideration of what is *not* performed by bureaucracy as such. It is clear that its effectiveness has strict internal limits, both in the management of public, political affairs and in the private economic sphere. The *leading* spirit, the 'entrepreneur' in the one case, the 'politician' in the other, is something different from an 'official'. Not necessarily in form, but certainly in substance. The entrepreneur, too, sits in an 'office'. An army commander does the same. The army commander is an officer and thus formally no different from all other officers. If the general manager of a large enterprise is the hired official of a limited company, his legal position is also no different in principle from that of other officials. In the sphere of the state the same applies to the leading politician. The leading minister is *formally* an official with a pensionable salary. The fact that, according to all known constitutions, he can be dismissed at any time and can demand to be discharged distinguishes his position outwardly from that of many, but not all other officials. Yet much more striking is the fact that, unlike other officials, he and he *alone* is not required to demonstrate any kind of *qualification based on training*. This fact indicates that the meaning and purpose (*Sinn*) of his position differs from that of other officials in the same way as the position of the entrepreneur and managing director in a private firm is a special one. Or to be more accurate, he is *meant* to be something different. And this is how it is in fact. If a man in a *leading* position performs his leadership function in the *spirit* of an 'official', even a most able one, if he is a man accustomed to performing his work dutifully and honourably in accordance with regulations and orders, then he is useless, whether he is at the head of a private firm or a state. Unfortunately, we in Germany have seen the proof of this in our own political life.

Only in part does the difference lie in the kind of achievement expected of this type of person. Like 'leaders', 'officials' too are expected to make independent decisions and show organisational ability and initiative, not only in countless individual cases but also on larger issues. It is typical of littérateurs and of a country lacking any insight into the conduct of its own affairs or into the achievements of its officials, even to *imagine* that the work of an official amounts to no more than the subaltern performance of routine duties, while the leader alone is expected to carry out the 'interesting' tasks which make special intellectual demands. This is not so. The difference lies, rather, in the kind of *responsibility* borne by each of them, and this is largely what determines the demands made on their particular abilities. An official who receives an order which, in his view, is wrong can—and should—raise objections. If his superior then insists on the instruction it is not merely the duty of the official, it is also a point of *honour* for him to carry out that instruction as if it corresponded to his own innermost conviction, thereby demonstrating that his sense of duty to his office overrides his individual wilfulness. It is irrelevant whether his superior is a 'public authority' or a 'corporation' or an 'assembly' from which he has an imperative mandate. This is what is demanded by the spirit of *office*. A political *leader* who behaved like this would deserve our *contempt*. He will often be obliged to make compromises, which means sacrificing something of lesser importance to something of greater importance. If, however, he is incapable of saying to his master, whether this be a monarch or the *demos*, 'Either you give me this instruction *or I resign*', he is not a leader but merely what Bismarck called a miserable 'clinger' to office. The official should stand 'above the parties', which in truth means that he must remain outside the *struggle* for power of his own. The struggle for personal power and the acceptance of full *personal responsibility for one's cause (Sache)* which is the consequence of such power—this is the very element in which the politician and the entrepreneur live and breathe.

20 John Maynard Keynes, from 'The End of Laissez-Faire', in *Collected Writings*, vol. 9, *Essays in Persuasion* (Macmillan, 1972), pp. 287–92

John Maynard Keynes (1883–1946) was a student of the great economists Alfred Marshall and Arthur Pigou at the University of Cambridge, and an associate of G. E. Moore and the 'Bloomsbury Group'. He was a civil servant in the India Office and then the Treasury, in which capacity he was involved in the Versailles Peace Conference at the end of the First World War. Disillusionment with this led to his resignation and *Economic Consequences of the Peace* (1919). His main economic work is *The General Theory of Employment, Interest and Money* (1936). He played an important role in the 1944 Bretton Woods agreement that shaped the post-war economy.

Let us clear from the ground the metaphysical or general principles upon which, from time to time, *laissez-faire* has been founded. It is *not* true that individuals possess a pre-scriptive 'natural liberty' in their economic activities. There is *no* 'compact' conferring perpetual rights on those who Have or on those who Acquire. The world is *not* so governed from above that private and social interest always coincide. It is *not* so managed here below that in practice they coincide. It is *not* a correct deduction from the principles of economics that enlightened self-interest always operates in the public interest. Nor is it true that self-interest generally *is* enlightened; more often individuals acting separately to promote their own ends are too ignorant or too weak to attain even these. Experience does *not* show that individuals, when they make up a social unit, are always less clear-sighted than when they act separately.

We cannot therefore settle on abstract grounds, but must handle on its merits in detail what Burke termed 'one of the finest problems in legislation, namely, to determine what the State ought to take upon itself to direct by the public wisdom, and what it ought to leave, with as little interference as possible, to individual exertion'. We have to discriminate between what Bentham, in his forgotten but useful nomenclature, used to term *Agenda* and *Non-Agenda*, and to do this without Bentham's prior presumption that interference is, at the same time, 'generally needless' and 'generally pernicious'. Perhaps the chief task of economists at this hour is to distinguish afresh the *Agenda* of government from the *Non-Agenda*; and the companion task of politics is to devise forms of government within a democracy which shall be capable of accomplishing the *Agenda*. I will illustrate what I have in mind by two examples.

(1) I believe that in many cases the ideal size for the unit of control and organisation lies somewhere between the individual and the modern State. I suggest, therefore, that progress lies in the growth and the recognition of semi-autonomous bodies within the State—bodies whose criterion of action within their own field is solely the public good as they understand it, and from whose deliberations motives of private advantage are excluded, though some place it may still be necessary to leave, until the ambit of men's altruism grows wider, to the separate advantage of particular groups, classes, or faculties—bodies which in the ordinary course of affairs are mainly autonomous within their prescribed limitations, but are subject in the last resort to the sovereignty of the democracy expressed through Parliament.

I propose a return, it may be said, towards medieval conceptions of separate autonomies. But, in England at any rate, corporations are a mode of government which has never ceased to be important and is sympathetic to our institutions. It is easy to give examples, from what already exists, of separate autonomies which have attained or are approaching the mode I designate—the universities, the Bank of England, the Port of London Authority, even perhaps the railway companies. In Germany there are doubtless analogous instances.

But more interesting than these is the trend of joint stock institutions, when they have reached a certain age and size, to approximate to the status of public corporations rather than that of individualistic private enterprise. One of the most interesting and unnoticed developments of recent decades has been the tendency of big enterprise to socialise itself. A point arrives in the growth of a big institution—particularly a big railway or big public utility enterprise, but also a big bank or a big insurance company—at which the owners of the capital, i.e. the shareholders, are almost entirely dissociated from the management, with the result that the direct personal interest of the latter in the making of great profit becomes quite secondary. When this stage is reached, the general stability and reputation of the institution are the more considered by the management than the maximum of profit for the shareholders. The shareholders must be satisfied by conventionally adequate dividends; but once this is secured, the direct interest of the management often consists in avoiding criticism from the public and from the customers of the concern. This is particularly the case if their great size or semi-monopolistic position renders them conspicuous in the public eye and vulnerable to public attack. The extreme instance, perhaps, of this tendency in the case of an institution, theoretically the unrestricted property of private persons, is the Bank of England. It is almost true to say that there is no class of persons in the kingdom of whom the Governor of the Bank of England thinks less when he decides on his policy than of his shareholders. Their rights, in excess of their conventional dividend, have already sunk to the neighbourhood of zero. But the same thing is partly true of many other big institutions. They are, as time goes on, socialising themselves.

Not that this is unmixed gain. The same causes promote conservatism and a waning of enterprise. In fact, we already have in these cases many of the faults as well as the advantages of State Socialism. Nevertheless, we see here, I think, a natural line of evolution. The battle of Socialism against unlimited private profit is being won in detail hour by hour. In these particular fields—it remains acute elsewhere—this is no longer the pressing problem. There is, for instance, no so-called important political question so really unimportant, so irrelevant to the reorganisation of the economic life of Great Britain, as the nationalisation of the railways.

It is true that many big undertakings, particularly public utility enterprises and other business requiring a large fixed capital, still need to be semi-socialised. But we must keep our minds flexible regarding the forms of this semi-socialism. We must take full advantage of the natural tendencies of the day, and we must probably prefer semi-autonomous corporations to organs of the central government for which ministers of State are directly responsible.

I criticise doctrinaire State Socialism, not because it seeks to engage men's altruistic impulses in the service of society, or because it departs from *laissez-faire*, or because it takes away from man's natural liberty to make a million, or because it has courage for bold experiments. All these things I applaud. I criticise it because it misses the significance of what is actually happening; because it is, in fact, little better than a dusty survival of a plan to meet the problems of fifty years ago, based on a misunderstanding of what someone said a hundred years ago. Nineteenth-century State Socialism sprang from Bentham, free competition, etc., and is in some respects a clearer, in some respects a more muddled version of just the same philosophy as underlies nineteenth-century individualism. Both equally laid all their stress on freedom, the one negatively to avoid limitations on existing freedom, the other positively to destroy natural or acquired monopolies. They are different reactions to the same intellectual atmosphere.

(2) I come next to a criterion of *Agenda* which is particularly relevant to what it is urgent and desirable to do in the near future. We must aim at separating those services which are *technically social* from those which are *technically individual*. The most important *Agenda* of the State relate not to those activities which private individuals are already fulfilling, but to those functions which fall outside the sphere of the individual, to those decisions which are made by *no one* if the State does not make them. The important thing for government is not to do things which individuals are doing already, and to do them a little better or a little worse; but to do those things which at present are not done at all.

It is not within the scope of my purpose on this occasion to develop practical policies. I limit myself, therefore, to naming some instances of what I mean from amongst those problems about which I happen to have thought most.

Many of the greatest economic evils of our time are the fruits of risk, uncertainty, and ignorance. It is because particular individuals, fortunate in situation or in abilities, are able to take advantage of uncertainty and ignorance, and also because for the same reason big business is often a lottery, that great inequalities of wealth come about; and these same factors are also the cause of the unemployment of labour, or the disappointment of reasonable business expectations, and of the impairment of efficiency and production. Yet the cure lies outside the operations of individuals; it may even be to the interest of individuals to aggravate the disease. I believe that the cure for these things is partly to be sought in the deliberate control of the currency and of credit by a central institution, and partly in the collection and dissemination on a great scale of data relating to the business situation, including the full publicity, by law if necessary, of all business facts which it is useful to know. These measures would involve society in exercising directive intelligence through some appropriate organ of action over many of the inner intricacies of private business, yet it would leave private initiative and enterprise unhindered. Even if these measures prove insufficient, nevertheless, they will furnish us with better knowledge than we have now for taking the next step.

My second example relates to savings and investment. I believe that some coordinated act of intelligent judgement is required as to the scale on which it is desirable that the community as a whole should save, the scale on which these savings should go abroad in the form of foreign investments, and whether the present organisation of the investment market distributes savings along the most nationally productive channels. I do not think that these matters should be left entirely to the chances of private judgement and private profits, as they are at present.

My third example concerns population. The time has already come when each country needs a considered national policy about what size of population, whether larger or smaller than at present or the same, is most expedient. And having settled this policy, we must take steps to carry it into operation. The time may arrive a little later when the community as a whole must pay attention to the innate quality as well as to the mere numbers of its future members.

21   From the *Universal Declaration of Human Rights*, Adopted and Proclaimed by the United Nations General Assembly, 10 December 1948.

John Peters Humphrey, a Canadian law professor, was the principal drafter of this document, to which French, Chinese, and Americans also contributed. It was proclaimed in the General Assembly of the United Nations in 1948.

PREAMBLE

Whereas recognition of the inherent dignity and of the equal and inalienable rights of all members of the human family is the foundation of freedom, justice and peace in the world,

Whereas disregard and contempt for human rights have resulted in barbarous acts which have outraged the conscience of mankind, and the advent of a world in which human beings shall enjoy freedom of speech and belief and freedom from fear and want has been proclaimed as the highest aspiration of the common people,

Whereas it is essential, if man is not to be compelled to have recourse, as a last resort, to rebellion against tyranny and oppression, that human rights should be protected by the rule of law,

Whereas it is essential to promote the development of friendly relations between nations,

Whereas the peoples of the United Nations have in the Charter reaffirmed their faith in fundamental human rights, in the dignity and worth of the human person and in the equal rights of men and women and have determined to promote social progress and better standards of life in larger freedom,

Whereas Member States have pledged themselves to achieve, in cooperation with the United Nations, the promotion of universal respect for and observance of human rights and fundamental freedoms,

Whereas a common understanding of these rights and freedoms is of the greatest importance for the full realization of this pledge,

Now, Therefore THE GENERAL ASSEMBLY proclaims THIS UNIVERSAL DECLARATION OF HUMAN RIGHTS as a common standard of DECLARATION OF HUMAN RIGHTS as a common standard of achievement for all peoples and all nations, to the end that every individual and every organ of society, keeping this Declaration constantly in mind, shall strive by teaching and education to promote respect for these rights and freedoms and by progressive measures, national and international, to secure their universal and effective recognition and observance, both among the peoples of Member States themselves and among the peoples of territories under their jurisdiction.

ARTICLE 1

All human beings are born free and equal in dignity and rights. They are endowed with reason and conscience and should act towards one another in a spirit of brotherhood.

ARTICLE 2

Everyone is entitled to all the rights and freedoms set forth in this Declaration, without distinction of any kind, such as race, colour, sex, language, religion, political or other opinion, national or social origin, property, birth or other status. Furthermore, no distinction shall be made on the basis of the political, jurisdictional or international status of the country or territory to which a person belongs, whether it be independent, trust, non-self-governing or under any other limitation of sovereignty.

ARTICLE 3

Everyone has the right to life, liberty and security of person.

ARTICLE 4

No one shall be held in slavery or servitude; slavery and the slave trade shall be prohibited in all their forms.

ARTICLE 5

No one shall be subjected to torture or to cruel, inhuman or degrading treatment or punishment.

ARTICLE 6

Everyone has the right to recognition everywhere as a person before the law.

ARTICLE 7

All are equal before the law and are entitled without any discrimination to equal protec-tion of the law. All are entitled to equal protection against any discrimination in violation of this Declaration and against any incitement to such discrimination.

ARTICLE 8

Everyone has the right to an effective remedy by the competent national tribunals for acts violating the fundamental rights granted him by the constitution or by law.

ARTICLE 9

No one shall be subjected to arbitrary arrest, detention or exile.

ARTICLE 10

Everyone is entitled in full equality to a fair and public hearing by an independent and impartial tribunal, in the determination of his rights and obligations and of any criminal charge against him.

ARTICLE 11

(1)   Everyone charged with a penal offence has the right to be presumed innocent until proved guilty according to law in a public trial at which he has had all the guarantees necessary for his defence.

(2)   No one shall be held guilty of any penal offence on account of any act or omission which did not constitute a penal offence, under national or international law, at the time when it was committed. Nor shall a heavier penalty be imposed than the one that was applicable at the time the penal offence was committed.

ARTICLE 12

No one shall be subjected to arbitrary interference with his privacy, family, home or correspondence, nor to attacks upon his honour and reputation. Everyone has the right to the protection of the law against such interference or attacks.

ARTICLE 13

(1)   Everyone has the right to freedom of movement and residence within the borders of each state.

(2)   Everyone has the right to leave any country, including his own, and to return to his country.

ARTICLE 14

(1)   Everyone has the right to seek and to enjoy in other countries asylum from persecution.

(2)   This right may not be invoked in the case of prosecutions genuinely arising from non-political crimes or from acts contrary to the purposes and principles of the United Nations.

ARTICLE 15

(1)   Everyone has the right to a nationality.

(2)   No one shall be arbitrarily deprived of his nationality nor denied the right to change his nationality.

ARTICLE 16

(1)   Men and women of full age, without any limitation due to race, nationality or religion, have the right to marry and to found a family. They are entitled to equal rights as to marriage, during marriage and at its dissolution.

(2)   Marriage shall be entered into only with the free and full consent of the intending spouses.

(3)   The family is the natural and fundamental group unit of society and is entitled to protection by society and the State.

ARTICLE 17

(1)   Everyone has the right to own property alone as well as in association with others.

(2)   No one shall be arbitrarily deprived of his property.

ARTICLE 18

Everyone has the right to freedom of thought, conscience and religion; this right includes freedom to change his religion or belief, and freedom, either alone or in community with others and in public or private, to manifest his religion or belief in teaching, practice, worship and observance.

ARTICLE 19

Everyone has the right to freedom of opinion and expression; this right includes freedom to hold opinions without interference and to seek, receive and impart information and ideas through any media seek, receive and impart information and ideas through any media and regardless of frontiers.

ARTICLE 20

(1)   Everyone has the right to freedom of peaceful assembly and association.

(2)   No one may be compelled to belong to an association.

ARTICLE 21

(1)   Everyone has the right to take part in the government of his country, directly or through freely chosen representatives.

(2)   Everyone has the right of equal access to public service in his country.

(3)   The will of the people shall be the basis of the authority of government; this will shall be expressed in periodic and genuine elections which shall be by universal and equal suffrage and shall be held by secret vote or by equivalent free voting procedures.

ARTICLE 22

Everyone, as a member of society, has the right to social security and is entitled to realization, through national effort and international cooperation and in accordance with the organization and resources of each State, of the economic, social and cultural rights indispensable for his dignity and the free development of his personality.

ARTICLE 23

(1)   Everyone has the right to work, to free choice of employment, to just and favorable conditions of work and to protection against unemployment.

(2)   Everyone, without any discrimination, has the right to equal pay for equal work.

(3) Everyone who works has the right to just and favourable remuneration ensuring for himself and his family an existence worthy of human dignity, and supplemented, if necessary, by other means of social protection.

(4) Everyone has the right to form and to join trade unions for the protection of his interests.

ARTICLE 24

Everyone has the right to rest and leisure, including reasonable limitation of working hours and periodic holidays with pay.

ARTICLE 25

(1) Everyone has the right to a standard of living adequate for the health and well-being of himself and of his family, including food, clothing, housing and medical care and necessary social services, and the right to security in the event of unemployment, sickness, disability, widowhood, old age or other lack of livelihood in circumstances beyond his control.

(2) Motherhood and childhood are entitled to special care and assistance. All children, whether born in or out of wedlock, shall enjoy the same social protection.

ARTICLE 26

(1) Everyone has the right to education. Education shall be free, at least in the elementary and fundamental stages. Elementary education shall be compulsory. Technical and professional education shall be compulsory. Technical and professional education shall be made generally available and higher education shall be equally accessible to all on the basis of merit.

(2) Education shall be directed to the full development of the human personality and to the strengthening of respect for human rights and fundamental freedoms. It shall promote understanding, tolerance and friendship among all nations, racial or religious groups, and shall further the activities of the United Nations for the maintenance of peace.

(3) Parents have a prior right to choose the kind of education that shall be given to their children.

ARTICLE 27

(1) Everyone has the right freely to participate in the cultural life of the community, to enjoy the arts and to share in scientific advancement and its benefits.

(2) Everyone has the right to the protection of the moral and material interests resulting from any scientific, literary or artistic production of which he is the author.

ARTICLE 28

Everyone is entitled to a social and international order in which the rights and freedoms set forth in this Declaration can be fully realized.

ARTICLE 29

(1) Everyone has duties to the community in which alone the free and full development of his personality is possible.

(2) In the exercise of his rights and freedoms, everyone shall be subject only to such limitations as are determined by law solely for the purpose of securing due recognition and respect for the rights and freedoms of others and of meeting the just requirements of morality, public order and the general welfare in a democratic society.

(3) These rights and freedoms may in no case be exercised contrary to the purposes and principles of the United Nations.

ARTICLE 30

Nothing in this Declaration may be interpreted as implying for any State, group or person any right to engage in any activity or to perform any act aimed at the destruction of any of the rights and freedoms set forth herein.

22 Isaiah Berlin, from 'Two Concepts of Liberty', in *Four Essays on Liberty* (Oxford University Press, 1969), pp. 122–5, 124–34

Isaiah Berlin (1909–1997) was born in Riga, then the capital of Livonia, a province in the Russian empire, and moved to London in 1921. Trained in philosophy at the University of Oxford, he was the first Jew elected to All Souls College. A diplomat during the Second World War, he became Chichele Professor of Social and Political Theory at Oxford, and later President of Wolfson College.

THE NOTION OF 'NEGATIVE' FREEDOM

I am normally said to be free to the degree to which no man or body of men interferes with my activity. Political liberty in this sense is simply the area within which a man can act unobstructed by others. If I am prevented by others from doing what I could otherwise do, I am to that degree unfree; and if this area is contracted by other men beyond a certain minimum, I can be described as being coerced, or, it may be, enslaved. Coercion is not, however, a term that covers every form of inability. If I say that I am unable to jump more than ten feet in the air, or cannot read because I am blind, or cannot understand the darker pages of Hegel, it would be eccentric to say that I am to that degree enslaved or coerced. Coercion implies the deliberate interference of other human beings within the area in which I could otherwise act. You lack political liberty or freedom only if you are prevented from attaining a goal by human beings. Mere incapacity to attain a goal is not lack of political freedom. This is brought out by the use of such modern expressions as 'economic freedom' and its counterpart, 'economic slavery'. It is argued, very plausibly, that if a man is too poor to afford something on which there is no legal ban—a loaf of bread, a journey round the world, recourse to the law courts—he is as little free to have it as he would be if it were forbidden him by law. If my poverty were a kind of disease, which prevented me from buying bread, or paying for the journey round the world or getting my case heard, as lameness prevents me from running, this inability would not naturally be described as a lack of freedom, least of all political freedom. It is only because I believe that my inability to get a given thing is due to the fact that other human beings have made arrangements whereby I am, whereas others are not, prevented from having enough money with which to pay for it, that I think myself a victim of coercion or slavery. In other words, this use of the term depends on a particular social and economic theory about the causes of my poverty or weakness. If my lack of material means is due to my lack of mental or physical capacity, then I begin to speak of being deprived of freedom (and not simply about poverty) only if I accept the theory. If, in addition, I believe that I am being kept in want by a specific arrangement which I consider unjust or unfair, I speak of economic slavery or oppression. 'The nature of things does not madden us, only ill will does', said Rousseau. The criterion of oppression is the part that I believe to be played by other human beings, directly or indirectly, with or without the intention of doing so, in frustrating my wishes. By being free in this sense I mean not being interfered with by others. The wider the area of non-interference the wider my freedom.

This is what the classical English political philosophers meant when they used this word. They disagreed about how wide the area could or should be. They supposed that it could not, as things were, be unlimited, because if it were, it would entail a state in which all men could boundlessly interfere with all other men; and this kind of 'natural' freedom would lead to social chaos in which men's minimum needs would not be satisfied; or else the liberties of the weak would be suppressed by the strong. Because they perceived that human purposes and activities do not automatically harmonize with one another, and because (whatever their official doctrines) they put high value on other goals, such as justice, or happiness, or culture, or security, or varying degrees of equality, they were prepared to curtail freedom in the interests of other values and, indeed, of freedom itself. For, without this, it was impossible to create the kind of association that they thought desirable. Consequently, it is assumed by these thinkers that the area of men's free action must be limited by law. But equally it is assumed, especially by such libertarians as Locke and Mill in England, and Constant and Tocqueville in France, that there ought to exist a certain minimum area of personal freedom which must on no account be violated; for if it is overstepped, the individual will find himself in an area too narrow for even that minimum development of his natural faculties which alone makes it possible to pursue, and even to conceive, the various ends which men hold good or right or sacred. It follows that a frontier must be drawn between the area of private life and that of public authority. Where it is to be drawn is a matter of argument, indeed of haggling. Men are largely interdependent, and no man's activity is so completely private as never to obstruct the lives of others in any way. 'Freedom for the pike is death for the minnows'; the liberty of some must depend on the restraint of others. 'Freedom for an Oxford don', others have been known to add, 'is a very different thing from freedom for an Egyptian peasant.'

This proposition derives its force from something that is both true and important, but the phrase itself remains a piece of political claptrap. It is true that to offer political rights, or safeguards against intervention by the state, to men who are half-naked, illiterate, underfed, and diseased is to mock their condition; they need medical help or education before they can understand, or make use of, an increase in their freedom. What is freedom to those who cannot make use of it? Without adequate conditions for the use of freedom, what is the value of freedom? First things come first: there are situations, as a nineteenth-century Russian radical writer declared, in which boots are superior to the works of Shakespeare; individual freedom is not everyone's primary need. For freedom is not the mere absence of frustration of whatever kind; this would inflate the meaning of the word until it meant too much or too little. The Egyptian peasant needs clothes or medicine before, and more than, personal liberty, but the minimum freedom that he needs today, and the greater degree of freedom that he may need tomorrow, is not some species of freedom peculiar to him, but identical with that of professors, artists, and millionaires.

. . .

In the second place, the doctrine is comparatively modern. There seems to be scarcely any discussion of individual liberty as a conscious political ideal (as opposed to its actual existence) in the ancient world. Condorcet had already remarked that the notion of individual rights was absent from the legal conceptions of the Romans and Greeks; this seems to hold equally of the Jewish, Chinese, and all other ancient civilizations that have since come to light. The domination of this ideal has been the exception rather than the rule, even in the recent history of the West. Nor has liberty in this sense often formed a rallying cry for the great masses of mankind. The desire not to be impinged upon, to be left to oneself, has been a mark of high civilization both on the part of individuals and communities. The sense of privacy itself, of the area of personal relationships as something sacred in its own right, derives from a conception of freedom which, for all its religious roots, is scarcely older, in its developed state, than the Renaissance or the Reformation. Yet its decline would mark the death of a civilization, of an entire moral outlook.

The third characteristic of this notion of liberty is of greater importance. It is that liberty in this sense is not incompatible with some kinds of autocracy, or at any rate with the absence of self-government. Liberty in this sense is principally concerned with the area of control, not with its source. Just as a democracy may, in fact, deprive the individual citizen of a great many liberties which he might have in some other form of society, so it is perfectly conceivable that a liberal-minded despot would allow his subjects a large measure of personal freedom. The despot who leaves his subjects a wide area of liberty may be unjust, or encourage the wildest inequalities, care little for order, or virtue, or knowledge; but provided he does not curb their liberty, or at least curbs it less than many other régimes, he meets with Mill's specification. Freedom in this sense is not, at any rate logically, connected with democracy or self-government. Self-government may, on the whole, provide a better guarantee of the preservation of civil liberties than other régimes, and has been defended as such by libertarians. But there is no necessary connexion between individual liberty and democratic rule. The answer to the question 'Who governs me?' is logically distinct from the question 'How far does government interfere with me?' It is in this difference that the great contrast between the two concepts of negative and positive liberty, in the end, consists. For the 'positive' sense of liberty comes to light if we try to answer the question, not 'What am I free to do or be?', but 'By whom am I ruled?' or 'Who is to say what I am, and what I am not, to be or do?' The connexion between democracy and individual liberty is a good deal more tenuous than it seemed to many advocates of both. The desire to be governed by myself, or at any rate to participate in the process by which my life is to be controlled, may be as deep a wish as that of a free area for action, and perhaps historically older. But it is not a desire for the same thing. So different is it, indeed, as to have led in the end to the great clash of ideologies that dominates our world. For it is this—the 'positive' conception of liberty: not freedom from, but freedom to—to lead one prescribed form of life—which the adherents of the 'negative' notion represent as being, at times, no better than a specious disguise for brutal tyranny.

THE NOTION OF POSITIVE FREEDOM

The 'positive' sense of the word 'liberty' derives from the wish on the part of the individual to be his own master. I wish my life and decisions to depend on myself, not on external forces of whatever kind. I wish to be the instrument of my own, not of other men's, acts of will. I wish to be a subject, not an object; to be moved by reasons, by conscious purposes, which are my own, not by causes which affect me, as it were, from outside. I wish to be somebody, not nobody; a doer—deciding, not being decided for, self-directed and not acted upon by external nature or by other men as if I were a thing, or an animal, or a slave incapable of playing a human role, that is, of conceiving goals and policies of my own and realizing them. This is at least part of what I mean when I say that I am rational, and that it is my reason that distinguishes me as a human being from the rest of the world. I wish, above all, to be conscious of myself as a thinking, willing, active being, bearing responsibility for my choices and able to explain them by references to my own ideas and purposes. I feel free to the degree that I believe this to be true, and enslaved to the degree that I am made to realize that it is not.

The freedom which consists in being one's own master, and the freedom which consists in not being prevented from choosing as I do by other men, may, on the face of it, seem concepts at no great logical distance from each other—no more than negative and positive ways of saying much the same thing. Yet the 'positive' and 'negative' notions of freedom historically developed in divergent directions not always by logically reputable steps, until, in the end, they came into direct conflict with each other.

One way of making this clear is in terms of the independent momentum which the, initially perhaps quite harmless, metaphor of self-mastery acquired. 'I am my own master'; 'I am slave to no man'; but may I not (as Platonists or Hegelians tend to say) be a slave to nature? Or to my own 'unbridled' passions? Are these not so many species of the identical genus 'slave'—some political or legal, others moral or spiritual? Have not men had the experience of liberating themselves from spiritual slavery, or slavery to nature, and do they not in the course of it become aware, on the one hand, of a self which dominates, and, on the other, of something in them which is brought to heel? This dominant self is then variously identified with reason, with my 'higher nature', with the self which calculates and aims at what will satisfy it in the long run, with my 'real', or 'ideal', or 'autonomous' self, or with my self 'at its best'; which is then contrasted with irrational impulse, uncontrolled desires, my 'lower' nature, the pursuit of immediate pleasures, my 'empirical' or 'heteronomous' self, swept by every gust of desire and passion, needing to be rigidly disciplined if it is ever to rise to the full height of its 'real' nature. Presently the two selves may be represented as divided by an even larger gap: the real self may be conceived as something wider than the individual (as the term is normally understood), as a social 'whole' of which the individual is an element or aspect: a tribe, a race, a church, a state, the great society of the living and the dead and the yet unborn. This entity is then identified as being the 'true' self which, by imposing its collective, or 'organic', single will upon its recalcitrant 'members', achieves its own, and therefore their, 'higher' freedom. The perils of using organic metaphors to justify the coercion of some men by others in order to raise them to a 'higher' level of freedom have often been pointed out. But what gives such plausibility as it has to this kind of language is that we recognize that it is possible, and at times justifiable, to coerce men in the name of some goal (let us say, justice or public health) which they would, if they were more enlightened, themselves pursue, but do not, because they are blind or ignorant or corrupt. This renders it easy for me to conceive of myself as coercing others for their own sake, in their, not my, interest. I am then claiming that I know what they truly need better than they know it themselves. What, at most, this entails is that they would not resist me if they were rational and as wise as I and understood their interests as I do. But I may go on to claim a good deal more than this. I may declare that they are actually aiming at what in their benighted state they consciously resist, because there exists within them an occult entity—their latent rational will, or their 'true' purpose—and that this entity, although it is belied by all that they overtly feel and do and say, is their 'real' self, of which the poor empirical self in space and time may know nothing or little; and that this inner spirit is the only self that deserves to have its wishes taken into account. Once I take this view, I am in a position to ignore the actual wishes of men or societies, to bully, oppress, torture them in the name, and on behalf, of their 'real' selves, in the secure knowledge that whatever is the true goal of man (happiness, performance of duty, wisdom, a just society, self-fulfilment) must be identical with his freedom—the free choice of his 'true', albeit often submerged and inarticulate, self.

This paradox has been often exposed. It is one thing to say that I know what is good for X, while he himself does not; and even to ignore his wishes for its—and his—sake; and a very different one to say that he has *eo ipso* chosen it, not indeed consciously, not as he seems in everyday life, but in his role as a rational self which his empirical self may not know—the 'real' self which discerns the good, and cannot help choosing it once it is revealed. This monstrous impersonation, which consists in equating what X would choose if he were something he is not, or at least not yet, with what X actually seeks and chooses, is at the heart of all political theories of self-realization. It is one thing to say that I may be coerced for my own good which I am too blind to see: this may, on occasion, be for my benefit; indeed it may enlarge the scope of my liberty. It is another to say that if it is my good, then I am not being coerced, for I have willed it, whether I know this or not, and am free (or 'truly' free) even while my poor earthly body and foolish mind bitterly reject it, and struggle against those who seek however benevolently to impose it, with the greatest desperation.

This magical transformation, or sleight of hand (for which William James so justly mocked the Hegelians), can no doubt be perpetrated just as easily with the 'negative' concept of freedom, where the self that should not be interfered with is no longer the individual with his actual wishes and needs as they are normally conceived, but the 'real' man within, identified with the pursuit of some ideal purpose not dreamed of by his empirical self. And, as in the case of the 'positively' free self, this entity may be inflated into some super-personal entity—a state, a class, a nation, or the march of history itself, regarded as a more 'real' subject of attributes than the empirical self. But the 'positive' conception of freedom as self-mastery, with its suggestion of a man divided against himself, has, in fact, and as a matter of history, of doctrine and of practice, lent itself more easily to this splitting of personality into two: the transcendent, dominant controller, and the empirical bundle of desires and passions to be disciplined and brought to heel. It is this historical fact that has been influential. This demonstrates (if demonstration of so obvious a truth is needed) that conceptions of freedom directly derive from views of what constitutes a self, a person, a man. Enough manipulation with the definition of man, and freedom can be made to mean whatever the manipulator wishes. Recent history has made it only too clear that the issue is not merely academic.

The consequences of distinguishing between two selves will become even clearer if one considers the two major forms which the desire to be self-directed—directed by one's 'true' self—has historically taken: the first, that of self-abnegation in order to attain independence; the second, that of self-realization, or total self-identification with a specific principle or ideal in order to attain the selfsame end.

23   John Rawls, from (a) *A Theory of Justice* (Oxford University Press, 1972), pp. 60–2, 78, 102–5; and (b) 'Justice as Fairness: Political Not Metaphysical', in *Collected Papers* (ed. Samuel Freeman; Harvard University Press, 1999), pp. 393–5

John Rawls (1921–2003) was born in Baltimore, Maryland. He served in the army in the Second World War and for most of his career was a professor at Harvard University, where he was an influential teacher. His immensely important book *A Theory of Justice* (1971, revised edition 1999) is often credited with having revived political philosophy as an academic discipline, and for establishing the centrality of liberalism for the study of political philosophy. His later work focused on the problems of justifying political principles in pluralistic societies and on international justice.

(a) TWO PRINCIPLES OF JUSTICE

I shall now state in a provisional form the two principles of justice that I believe would be chosen in the original position. In this section I wish to make only the most general comments, and therefore the first formulation of these principles is tentative. As we go on I shall run through several formulations and approximate step by step the final statement to be given much later. I believe that doing this allows the exposition to proceed in a natural way.

The first statement of the two principles reads as follows.

First: each person is to have an equal right to the most extensive basic liberty compatible with a similar liberty for others.

Second: social and economic inequalities are to be arranged so that they are both (a) reasonably expected to be to everyone's advantage, and (b) attached to positions and offices open to all. There are two ambiguous phrases in the second principle, namely "everyone's advantage" and "equally open to all." Determining their sense more exactly will lead to a second formulation of the principle in § 13. The final version of the two principles is given in § 45; § 39 considers the rendering of the first principle.

By way of general comment, these principles primarily apply, as I have said, to the basic structure of society. They are to govern the assignment of rights and duties and to regulate the distribution of social and economic advantages. As their formulation suggests, these principles presuppose that the social structure can be divided into two more or less distinct parts, the first principle applying to the one, the second to the other. They distinguish between those aspects of the social system that define and secure the equal liberties of citizenship and those that specify and establish social and economic inequalities. The basic liberties of citizens are, roughly speaking, political liberty (the right to vote and to be eligible for public office) together with freedom of speech and assembly; liberty of conscience and freedom of thought; freedom of the person along with the right to hold (personal) property; and freedom from arbitrary arrest and seizure as defined by the concept of the rule of law. These liberties are all required to be equal by the first principle, since citizens of a just society are to have the same basic rights.

The second principle applies, in the first approximation, to the distribution of income and wealth and to the design of organizations that make use of differences in authority and responsibility, or chains of command. While the distribution of wealth and income need not be equal, it must be to everyone's advantage, and at the same time, positions of authority and offices of command must be accessible to all. One applies the second principle by holding positions open, and then, subject to this constraint, arranges social and economic inequalities so that everyone benefits.

These principles are to be arranged in a serial order with the first principle prior to the second. This ordering means that a departure from the institutions of equal liberty required by the first principle cannot be justified by, or compensated for, by greater social and economic advantages. The distribution of wealth and income, and the hierarchies of authority, must be consistent with both the liberties of equal citizenship and equality of opportunity.

It is clear that these principles are rather specific in their content, and their acceptance rests on certain assumptions that I must eventually try to explain and justify. A theory of justice depends upon a theory of society in ways that will become evident as we proceed. For the present, it should be observed that the two principles (and this holds for all formulations) are a special case of a more general conception of justice that can be expressed as follows:

> All social values—liberty and opportunity, income and wealth, and the bases of self-respect—are to be distributed equally unless an unequal distribution of any, or all, of these values is to everyone's advantage.

Injustice, then, is simply inequalities that are not to the benefit of all. Of course, this conception is extremely vague and requires interpretation.

As a first step, suppose that the basic structure of society distributes certain primary goods, that is, things that every rational man is presumed to want. These goods normally have a use whatever a person's rational plan of life. For simplicity, assume that the chief primary goods at the disposition of society are rights and liberties, powers and opportunities, income and wealth. (Later on in Part Three the primary good of self-respect has a central place.) These are the social primary goods. Other primary goods such as health and vigor, intelligence and imagination, are natural goods; although their possession is influenced by the basic structure, they are not so directly under its control. Imagine, then, a hypothetical initial arrangement in which all the social primary goods are equally distributed: everyone has similar rights and duties, and income and wealth are evenly shared. This state of affairs provides a benchmark for judging improvements. If certain inequalities of wealth and organizational powers would make everyone better off than in this hypothetical starting situation, then they accord with the general conception.

. . .

To illustrate the difference principle, consider the distribution of income among social classes. Let us suppose that the various income groups correlate with representative individuals by reference to whose expectations we can judge the distribution. Now those starting out as members of the entrepreneurial class in property-owning democracy, say, have a better prospect than those who begin in the class of unskilled laborers. It seems likely that this will be true even when the social injustices which now exist are removed. What, then, can possibly justify this kind of initial inequality in life prospects? According to the difference principle, it is justifiable only if the difference in expectation is to the advantage of the representative man who is worse off, in this case the representative unskilled worker. The inequality in expectation is permissible only if lowering it would make the working class even more worse off. Supposedly, given the rider in the second principle concerning open positions, and the principle of liberty generally, the greater expectations allowed to entrepreneurs encourages them to do things which raise the long-term prospects of laboring class. Their better prospects act as incentives so that the economic process is more efficient, innovation proceeds at a faster pace, and so on. Eventually the resulting material benefits spread throughout the system and to the least advantaged. I shall not consider how far these things are true. The point is that something of this kind must be argued if these inequalities are to be just by the difference principle.

. . .

In view of these remarks we may reject the contention that the injustice of institutions is always imperfect because the distribution of natural talents and the contingencies of social circumstance are unjust, and this injustice must inevitably carry over to human arrangements. Occasionally this reflection is offered as an excuse for ignoring injustice, as if the refusal to acquiesce in injustice is on a par with being unable to accept death. The natural distribution is neither just nor unjust; nor is it unjust that men are born into society at some particular position. These are simply natural facts. What is just and unjust is the way that institutions deal with these facts. Aristocratic and caste societies are unjust because they make these contingencies the ascriptive basis for belonging to more or less enclosed and privileged social classes. The basic structure of these societies incorporates the arbitrariness found in nature. But there is no necessity for men to resign themselves to these contingencies. The social system is not an unchangeable order beyond human control but a pattern of human action. In justice as fairness men agree to share one another's fate. In designing institutions they undertake to avail themselves of the accidents of nature and social circumstance only when doing so is for the common benefit. The two principles are a fair way of meeting the arbitrariness of fortune; and while no doubt imperfect in other ways, the institutions which satisfy these principles are just.

A further point is that the difference principle expresses a conception of reciprocity. It is a principle of mutual benefit. We have seen that, at least when chain connection holds, each representative man can accept the basic structure as designed to advance his interests. The social order can be justified to everyone, and in particular to those who are least favored; and in this sense it is egalitarian. But it seems necessary to consider in an intuitive way how the condition of mutual benefit is satisfied. Consider any two representative men A and B, and let B be the one who is less favored. Actually, since we are most interested in the comparison with the least favored man, let us assume that B is this individual. Now B can accept A's being better off since A's advantages have been gained in ways that improve B's prospects. If A were not allowed his better position, B would be even worse off than he is. The difficulty is to show that A has no grounds for complaint. Perhaps he is required to have less than he might since his having more would result in some loss to B. Now what can be said to the more favored man? To begin with, it is clear that the well-being of each depends on a scheme of social cooperation without which no one could have a satisfactory life. Secondly, we can ask for the willing cooperation of everyone only if the terms of the scheme are reasonable. The difference principle, then, seems to be a fair basis on which those better endowed, or more fortunate in their social circumstances, could expect others to collaborate with them when some workable arrangement is a necessary condition of the good of all.

There is a natural inclination to object that those better situated deserve their greater advantages whether or not they are to the benefit of others. At this point it is necessary to be clear about the notion of desert. It is perfectly true that given a just system of cooperation as a scheme of public rules and the expectations set up by it, those who, with the prospect of improving their condition, have done what the system announces that it will reward are entitled to their advantages. In this sense the more fortunate have a claim to their better situation; their claims are legitimate expectations established by social institutions, and the community is obligated to meet them. But this sense of desert presupposes the existence of the cooperative scheme; it is irrelevant to the question whether in the first place the scheme is to be designed in accordance with the difference principle or some other criterion.

Perhaps some will think that the person with greater natural endowments deserves those assets and the superior character that made their development possible. Because he is more worthy in this sense, he deserves the greater advantages that he could achieve with them. This view, however, is surely incorrect. It seems to be one of the fixed points of our considered judgments that no one deserves his place in the distribution of native endowments, any more than one deserves one's initial starting place in society. The assertion that a man deserves the superior character that enables him to make the effort to cultivate his abilities is equally problematic; for his character depends in large part upon fortunate family and social circumstances for which he can claim no credit. The notion of desert seems not to apply to these cases. Thus the more advantaged representative man cannot say that he deserves and therefore has a right to a scheme of cooperation in which he is permitted to acquire benefits in ways that do not contribute to the welfare of others. There is no basis for his making this claim. From the standpoint of common sense, then, the difference principle appears to be acceptable both to the more advantaged and to the less advantaged individual. Of course, none of this is strictly speaking an argument for the principle, since in a contract theory arguments are made from the point of view of the original position. But these intuitive considerations help to clarify the nature of the principle and the sense in which it is egalitarian.

I noted earlier (§ 13) that a society should try to avoid the region where the marginal contributions of those better off to the well-being of the less favored are negative. It should operate only on the upward rising part of the contribution curve (including of course the maximum). One reason for this, we can now see, is that on this segment of the curve the criterion of mutual benefit is always fulfilled. Moreover, there is a natural sense in which the harmony of social interests is achieved; representative men do not gain at one another's expense since only reciprocal advantages are allowed. To be sure, the shape and slope of the contribution curve is determined in part at least by the natural lottery in native assets, and as such it is neither just nor unjust. But suppose we think of the forty-five degree line as representing the ideal of a perfect harmony of interests; it is the contribution curve (a straight line in this case) along which everyone gains equally. Then it seems that the consistent realization of the two principles of justice tends to raise the curve closer to the ideal of a perfect harmony of interests. Once a society goes beyond the maximum it operates along the downward sloping part of the curve and a harmony of interests no longer exists. As the more favored gain the less advantaged lose, and vice versa. The situation is analogous to being on an efficiency frontier. This is far from desirable when the justice of the basic structure is involved. Thus it is to realize the ideal of the harmony of interests on terms that nature has given us, and to meet the criterion of mutual benefit, that we should stay in the region of positive contributions.

A further merit of the difference principle is that it provides an interpretation of the principle of fraternity. In comparison with liberty and equality, the idea of fraternity has had a lesser place in democratic theory. It is thought to be less specifically a political concept, not in itself defining any of the democratic rights but conveying instead certain attitudes of mind and forms of conduct without which we would lose sight of the values expressed by these rights. Or closely related to this, fraternity is held to represent a certain equality of social esteem manifest in various public conventions and in the absence of manners of deference and servility. No doubt fraternity does imply these things, as well as a sense of civic friendship and social solidarity, but so understood it expresses no definite requirement. We have yet to find a principle of justice that matches the underlying idea. The difference principle, however, does seem to correspond to a natural meaning of fraternity: namely, to the idea of not wanting to have greater advantages unless this is to the benefit of others who are less well off. The family, in its ideal conception and often in practice, is one place where the principle of maximizing the sum of advantages is rejected. Members of a family commonly do not wish to gain unless they can do so in ways that further the interests of the rest. Now wanting to act on the difference principle has precisely this consequence. Those better circumstanced are willing to have their greater advantages only under a scheme in which this works out for the benefit of the less fortunate.

. . .

(b) We must now ask: how might political philosophy find a shared basis for settling such a fundamental question as that of the most appropriate institutional forms for liberty and equality? Of course, it is likely that the most that can be done is to narrow the range of public disagreement. Yet even firmly held convictions gradually change: religious toleration is now accepted, and arguments for persecution are no longer openly professed; similarly, slavery is rejected as inherently unjust, and however much the aftermath of slavery may persist in social practices and unavowed attitudes, no one is willing to defend it. We collect such settled convictions as the belief in religious toleration and the rejection of slavery and try to organize the basic ideas and principles implicit in these convictions into a coherent conception of justice. We can regard these convictions as provisional fixed points which any conception of justice must account for if it is to be reasonable for us. We look, then, to our public political culture itself, including its main institutions and the historical traditions of their interpretation, as the shared fund of implicitly recognized basic ideas and principles. The hope is that these ideas and principles can be formulated clearly enough to be combined into a conception of political justice congenial to our most firmly held convictions. We express this by saying that a political conception of justice, to be acceptable, must be in accordance with our considered convictions, at all levels of generality, on due reflection (or in what I have called "reflective equilibrium").

The public political culture may be of two minds even at a very deep level. Indeed, this must be so with such an enduring controversy as that concerning the most appropriate institutional forms to realize the values of liberty and equality. This suggests that if we are to succeed in finding a basis of public agreement, we must find a new way of organizing familiar ideas and principles into a conception of political justice so that the claims in conflict, as previously understood, are seen in another light. A political conception need not be an original creation but may only articulate familiar intuitive ideas and principles so that they can be recognized as fitting together in a somewhat different way than before. Such a conception may, however, go further than this: it may organize these familiar ideas and principles by means of a more fundamental intuitive idea within the complex structure of which the other familiar intuitive ideas are then systematically connected and related. In justice as fairness, as we shall see in the next section, this more fundamental idea is that of society as a system of fair social cooperation between free and equal persons. The concern of this section is how we might find a public basis of political agreement. The point is that a conception of justice will only be able to achieve this aim if it provides a reasonable way of shaping into one coherent view the deeper bases of agreement embedded in the public political culture of a constitutional regime and acceptable to its most firmly held considered convictions.

Now suppose justice as fairness were to achieve its aim and a publicly acceptable political conception of justice is found. Then this conception provides a publicly recognized point of view from which all citizens can examine before one another whether or not their political and social institutions are just. It enables them to do this by citing what are recognized among them as valid and sufficient reasons singled out by that conception itself. Society's main institutions and how they fit together into one scheme of social cooperation can be examined on the same basis by each citizen, whatever that citizen's social position or more particular interests. It should be observed that, on this view, justification is not regarded simply as valid argument from listed premises, even should these premises be true. Rather, justification is addressed to others who disagree with us, and therefore it must always proceed from some consensus, that is, from premises that we and others publicly recognize as true; or better, publicly recognize as acceptable to us for the purpose of establishing a working agreement on the fundamental questions of political justice. It goes without saying that this agreement must be informed and uncoerced, and reached by citizens in ways consistent with their being viewed as free and equal persons.

Thus, the aim of justice as fairness as a political conception is practical, and not metaphysical or epistemological. That is, it presents itself not as a conception of justice that is true, but one that can serve as a basis of informed and willing political agreement between citizens viewed as free and equal persons. This agreement when securely founded in public political and social attitudes sustains the goods of all persons and associations within a just democratic regime. To secure this agreement we try, so far as we can, to avoid disputed philosophical, as well as disputed moral and religious, questions. We do this not because these questions are unimportant or regarded with indifference, but because we think them too important and recognize that there is no way to resolve them politically. The only alternative to a principle of toleration is the autocratic use of state power. Thus, justice as fairness deliberately stays on the surface, philosophically speaking. Given the profound differences in belief and conceptions of the good at least since the Reformation, we must recognize that, just as on questions of religious and moral doctrine, public agreement on the basic questions of philosophy cannot be obtained without the state's infringement of basic liberties. Philosophy as the search for truth about an independent metaphysical and moral order cannot, I believe, provide a workable and shared basis for a political conception of justice in a democratic society.

We try, then, to leave aside philosophical controversies whenever possible, and look for ways to avoid philosophy's longstanding problems. Thus, in what I have called "Kantian constructivism," we try to avoid the problem of truth and the controversy between realism and subjectivism about the status of moral and political values. This form of constructivism neither asserts nor denies these doctrines. Rather, it recasts ideas from the tradition of the social contract to achieve a practicable conception of objectivity and justification founded on public agreement in judgment on due reflection. The aim is free agreement, reconciliation through public reason. And similarly, as we shall see (in Section V), a conception of the person in a political view, for example, the conception of citizens as free and equal persons, need not involve, so I believe, questions of philosophical psychology or a metaphysical doctrine of the nature of the self. No political view that depends on these deep and unresolved matters can serve as a public conception of justice in a constitutional democratic state. As I have said, we must apply the principle of toleration to philosophy itself. The hope is that, by this method of avoidance, as we might call it, existing differences between contending political views can at least be moderated, even if not entirely removed, so that social cooperation on the basis of mutual respect can be maintained. Or if this is expecting too much, this method may enable us to conceive how, given a desire for free and uncoerced agreement, a public understanding could arise consistent with the historical conditions and constraints of our social world. Until we bring ourselves to conceive how this could happen, it can't happen.

3 Conservatism

Introduction

Conservatism enjoys a paradoxical status as a political ideology. Many of its leading exponents regard it as a tradition, rather than a rationally developed system of belief, and they therefore stress its non- or anti-ideological character. Considered in this way, conservatism represents the antithesis of rationalist or utopian ideologies like liberalism and socialism, and is regarded as a distinctive mixture of historical wisdom, customary knowledge, and political pragmatism. A related interpretation suggests that this may be an ideology, but of a positional kind—deriving a malleable set of commitments and convictions from the elements in its ideological rivals to which it is most opposed. Through the extracts presented below, we aim to illustrate the divergent ideas that flowed into political conservatism prior to the establishment of the modern democratic polity, as well as the different forms that this ideology has since taken. While some of the leading proponents of this tradition were, as we shall see, sceptical about the effects of both democracy and modernity, conservatism has swiftly, and often successfully, adapted to the rigours of electoral competition, and the pace and character of social change typical of modern societies.

Many of its critics and interpreters remain dubious about the claim that conservatism is not an ideology. Grounding one's own political preferences upon a particular sense of the value of the past and the merits of the *status quo*, or upon a trenchant, sometimes bleak, account of human nature, might well be regarded as skilful attempts to place cherished conservative values beyond the boundaries of partisan debate. And this is the sort of move that is typical of political ideologies. The political tradition of conservatism has certainly attracted and motivated numerous philosophers, political intellectuals, and groups. Some of these, as we shall see, have been unashamed about using genres of argument, such as practical reason, or the claims of science, that are more familiar to liberals or socialists. Equally, conservatives have often invoked abstract moral ideas, such as the free market or the merits of social authority, when justifying their opposition to other ideologically informed political groups and projects.

Amidst the diversity of conservative thought, a recurrent tension has emerged in the twentieth century between those who emphasize the values of social custom, stable community, and inherited tradition, and regard modern society as increasingly destructive of such values; and those who endorse the principles of the free market, regarding its operation as closely tied to the spread of individual liberty. While this tension is apparent in late twentieth-century conservatism especially, in the wake of the emergence of a so-called 'New Right' in Anglo-American circles, earlier conservatives often regarded these values as complementary rather than opposed. A related tension for proponents of conservative politics concerns the character and role of the state in relation to the market in particular, and civil society more generally.

From the late nineteenth century onwards, conservatives began to develop different perspectives upon the optimal size and role of the modern state, with some advocating various forms of *laissez faire*, and others suggesting that the examples of Disraeli in Britain and Bismarck in Germany pointed towards conservative-dominated mass democracies, and right-wing governments that were prepared to improve the social welfare of citizens on the grounds of national self-interest. This tension re-emerged in conservative politics in the wake of the sharp reaction against the welfare regimes, redistributive aspirations, and the mixed economy of liberal capitalist democracies orchestrated (especially in the United States and Britain) by New Right and neo-conservative thinkers in the 1970s and 1980s.

One reason why the suggestion that conservatism defies or transcends the status of political ideology has been so influential is that this claim was central to some of the earliest manifestations of this tradition: for instance, in the work of the Irish-born writer Edmund Burke. Writing in late eighteenth-century England, he justified his opposition to the principles guiding the French Revolution of 1789 on the basis of a distinctive conception of the merits of a naturally evolving and hierarchically ordered society [Reading 24]. He defended the wisdom of imparting authority to those most capable of exercising the virtues required for political rule. Those trusted with the governance of the state, however, are required to exercise discretion and restraint in the decisions they make, avoiding arbitrary or tyrannical acts that might turn the people against them. This ideal of leadership is contrasted in Burke's writings with the growing influence of novel, democratically inclined political theories. The principal danger of these is that they threaten to cut the ties between the current generation and its predecessors; jettisoning the inherited wisdom and insight gathered during these earlier eras. Once this path is taken, he maintains, dire consequences will follow—not least the demise of a sense of honourable conduct and its associated social values.

Among the new doctrines of popular self-government that Burke opposed, he reserved particular venom for the argument that the relationship between governors and governed is akin to a contract—a social compact which either side can revoke at will. Such a notion dissolves the mystery and reverence with which the people ought to regard their government. Rather than a contract, he likens political relationships to a sacred covenant that extends 'not only between those who are living, but between those who are living, those who are dead, and those who are to be born'. These particular bonds arise within the parameters of the transcendent natural laws that inform the laws and customs of stable political communities. Radical schemes of reform and political re-organization signal the dissolution of these organic ties, and may result in civil strife and social chaos. The chains linking different social groups are, ultimately, sanctioned and legitimated by the authority of God. The public culture of a stable and wise polity continues to remind the people of these connections and values. It also teaches all that a higher social purpose justifies the relative wealth and luxury of some, in comparison to the circumstances of others.

Though he spent much of his political career advocating judicious, piecemeal reforms, Burke's ruminations upon the importance of continuity, community, and hierarchy within a social order provide one of the cornerstones for the subsequent development of conservatism, and have echoed far and wide in the political and intellectual cultures of the Anglo-American world. Other eighteenth-century thinkers keen to preserve the power of monarchs and the authority of the absolutist state developed a different kind of political response to the revolutionary upheaval in France. Writing shortly after the Revolution, Joseph de Maistre stressed the unavoidable character and historical significance of armed hostility between states [Reading 25]. The recurrence and effects of war are akin to a divine authority regularly pruning the tree of mankind. Without warfare, there would be no compensating fruits of human endeavour. It is through armed conflict that a nation locates its soul and finds its greatness. While war may not in itself be desirable, it is best avoided by accepting and restraining the various disorders that give rise to it; not by pursuing dangerous myths of human perfectibility and philosophical Enlightenment. This excerpt finishes with him medi-tating upon the symbolic and moral implications of the epic myth of self-sacrifice. The sacred and human meanings of this ideal are incomprehensible if we approach human society from the presumption of its benevolence and goodness. It is only through disaster and carnage that higher religious truths and noble ideals enter the world.

The emphases upon national history, culture, and mission that inform de Maistre's martial conception of a social order are also apparent in the less dramatic reflections of the German legal theorist, Friedrich von Savigny [Reading 26]. In his *Of the Vocation of Our Age for Legis-lation and Jurisprudence* (1814), he polemicizes against the idea of introducing a uniform code of law. This was occasioned by the prospect of the victorious French armies imposing the Napoleonic Code throughout the whole of Germany (as they had begun to do in some of its constituent states). Savigny considers the merits and history of the case for the imposition of legal uniformity across Germany's various territories. He links this imperative with the rise of various rationalist philosophies since the mid-eighteenth century. These threaten the integrity of the distinctive perspectives and traditions of different communities. Like de Maistre and Burke, he pours scorn on the underlying commitment to the perfectibility of the self that animates eighteenth-century rationalism. He connects such arguments to the mechanical application of abstract juridical principles.

In the present period, however, this drive towards abstract universalism in legal codification has given way, he believes, to a renewed conception of national uniqueness. He approves, in particular, the revival of the idea of 'positive law' in which legislation is regarded as the product of various contingent and customary pressures and forces. Only under particular circumstances, this view holds, is it necessary to shift from the customary conventions enshrined in particular bodies of law. The history of legal development makes sense when considered in relation to a study of the character, language, and customs of different peoples. While in modern society, the power and authority of the law derive in part from its manifestation in written and non-written rules, this characteristic is peculiar to the relatively recent historical past. In early periods, law was instantiated and understood through practices and rituals that now appear outmoded. Yet the passage from ancient to modern justice is not necessarily best understood simply as progress. Against those who understand the law through the formulation of timeless univer-sal principles of justice, he contends that it evolves organically, and is embedded in the historical practices of different peoples. In the modern period, the law becomes 'more artificial and com-plex', assuming both a political character—in relation to the life of a whole community—and a technical one, as elaborated and practised by an increasingly independent and sophisticated judicial profession. Despite hangovers from an earlier age, when legal rules applied variously to different classes in society, there is an increasingly powerful drive, he observes, towards legal uniformity. Against the arguments in favour of the latter, he proposes a model in which the autonomy of cities, corporations, and provinces is balanced against the interests of the German state as a whole.

While much conservative thinking was developed in legal and political discourses in the nineteenth and early twentieth centuries, other intellectual genres also proved fertile terrain for the development of this tradition. William Sumner, an early twentieth-century American sociologist, offered a very different justification of conservative precepts [Reading 27]. He argued that the organization of primitive societies was determined by the imperative to fulfil the most basic needs of their members, and that these give way to the emergence of a set of communal 'folkways'. He uses this term to depict an amalgam of traditionally formed and sanctioned beliefs, myths, and narratives that structure the moral and intellectual life of a community. Steeped in the evolutionary thinking associated with Social Darwinism, he observes the ineliminable importance of group-life to the development of the individual. As societies evolve, their 'folkways' come to play a different role, and no longer sanction the complete avoidance of change. Sumner attempts to show that there is a latent dynamic towards development in any society. He also maintains that the folkways of a community arise prior to the development of the mental and reasoning faculties of the individual. They are more akin to the 'instinctive ways of animals', or 'habits of the heart'. More complex and sophisticated contemporary societies are connected through the evolution of these habitual ways to their more primitive societal predecessors. In the second part of this extract, he describes an inexorable trend in primitive social contexts towards the formation of a sense of collective identity which depends crucially upon the exclusion of various 'others' from one's community, and the emergence of a functionally important form of 'ethnocentrism'. In Sumner's eyes, the establishment of civil peace and the development of law are the results of the hostility that communal insiders show towards outsiders, and their corresponding desire to deepen their own sense of fraternity and reciprocity.

The hostility to rationalistic ideas of morality and human perfectibility, evinced by all of these writers, constitutes one of the major strands running through different brands of Western conservatism. The idea of an ordered society in which a clearly established sovereign authority prevails, constitutes another, inter-linked thread of conservative belief. For writers like the French royalist Charles Maurras, the establishment of democratic institutions contravenes this latter principle [Reading 28]. What worries him particularly is that with the rising power of the legislature, the notion of royal authority being exercised through Ministers selected by the Crown begins to recede. As parliament develops, there emerges a class of parliamentarians corrupted by the very nature of democratic politics. In a bleak, but perhaps prescient, commentary, he observes that in the modern political arena governments rotate continually, parliamentarians become parasitic upon public money, and funds are diverted to projects for electoral purposes. Democratic governance rests upon a hypocritical conceit: those elected to rule are accorded a tremendous authority over citizens' lives, yet it simultaneously maintains that all subjects are equally powerful. The modern electorate is fickle and unreliable; and the interests of powerful parties replace the good of the nation.

Aspects of these different forms of conservative argument survived into the era of mass democratic politics, though the anti-democratic stance of de Maistre and Maurras faded from view in the nineteenth century. The influential philosopher Michael Oakeshott, writing in England during the 1940s, offers a sharp critique of the rise and influence of Enlightenment rationalism in political life [Reading 29]. Rationalists, he maintains, regard their own arguments both as a technique peculiar to, and a manifestation of, reason itself. It is to the truth-basis of a position that they ultimately refer, and hence they seek to subordinate complicated and messy social, political, and legal phenomena before the tribunal of philosophical logic. Through the application of this mode of thinking, the value of tradition is invariably down-played. Echoing Burke, he suggested that a mentality comes to prevail whereby the swift dismantling of familiar practices and the invention of new ones seems the most appropriate mode of political conduct. Reform in the modern rationalist worldview means to create something anew, according to an *a priori* principle, not making reparation or achieving continuity. In relation to political ideas, he asserts, rationalists supplant living, evolving traditions with abstractly formulated ideologies.

For the rationalist, public life is about solving problems, and this mission requires a mentality that is devoid of traditionally based thinking or sentiment. The analogy he offers for this technical approach to politics is that of the engineer. The modern social planner sees problems only in their contemporary manifestation, and assumes that an infinite range of social possibilities is available. As well as these lamentable characteristics, such a figure regrettably believes in the possibility of perfection and uniformity since to his mind no problem is immune to rational solution. This idea sustains a belief in the attainability of social perfection. Moreover, such a mentality encourages a sense of the intrinsic value of uniformly applicable solutions, and the need to conquer contingency and circumstance. Oakeshott then invokes several historical examples to illustrate the futility of such ambitions. The source of the rationalist folly is traced once again to the French Revolution, the Declaration of the Rights of Man in particular, and to the romantic mythology of human self-creation.

Though his writings were largely philosophically inclined, Oakeshott's thinking complemented some of the dominant strands of British Toryism. This tradition has generally regarded the governance of the country in pragmatic vein and cherished the art of state-craft. A tradition of one-nation Toryism stretched back into the nineteenth century and was in the ascendant in the middle years of the twentieth century. It was articulated in the 1950s and 1960s through the language of the 'middle way'. Here, we include an excerpt from Prime Minister Harold Macmillan's statement of this position [Reading 30]. Conservatism is presented as a sensible alternative to unfettered capitalism and socialist planning. It aspires to blend the strengths of both, and to restrict each to appropriate social domains. The 'middle way' stands at the head of an evolving tradition of 'planned capitalism', and signals a broad continuation of, not departure from, distinctively English values. Macmillan's thinking illustrates that mainstream conservative opinion was not uncomfortable with the idea of a welfare state and of the mixed economy that dominated British politics in the 1950s and 1960s.

A marked reaction against the kind of moderate conservatism espoused by Macmillan and others set in during the 1970s, just as a major reconfiguration of rightist thinking was relatedly happening in the United States. An important cause for this trend was a resurgence of nationalist sentiment—in the British case, as a direct product of anxieties about the fortunes of the nation's economy and its declining international standing. These themes are central to the philosophical writing on conservatism of the English writer Roger Scruton [Reading 31]. For him, one of the central conservative values is its recognition of the importance for citizens of their membership of a national community. The ceremonies, cultures, and symbols through which this allegiance is experienced are integral to a subject's identification with, and integration in, their society. Observing the symbolic significance of the head of state, whether elected or not, he detects within this institution the potency of the conservative instinct—the desire to constrain the future in the image of the past.

This argument underpins his discussion of the value of tradition in modern society. Tradition is presented as the performance of a political act, or the fashioning of an argument, using a form of reasoning which invokes 'what has been'. Projecting an analogy between art and politics, he argues that the politically conservative bent of many individual artists can be understood in relation to their shared attempt to give a voice to modern consciousness and common experience: this can only be done by rendering this mentality within a tradition of artistic expression. The re-creation of tradition in different cultural fields is analogous to what occurs in political life. For conservatives, viable traditions are the ones that connect those in the present with something that has flourished; they must engage the allegiances of their bearers, and refer to something long-standing and meaningful for contemporaries. Traditions connect individuals to the wider society, and give various meanings to social practices. Finally, he takes up the difficult question of whether tradition remains significant in societies characterized by rapid economic and social change. Scruton's philosophically grounded conservatism builds upon and departs from earlier Burkean ideas. In his view, the non-contractarian, allegiance-based view of society, and the recognition of authority, are indispensable conditions for any political society and defy historical contingency. One particular social tradition provides an important legitimation of these transcendental values and a powerful analogy for the conservative view of the relationship of the individual subject to wider society—the family.

In political terms, he has argued that it is the mission of conservatives to bolster state power against the overly keen assertion of individual rights. The desire to defend one's culture and society is natural to every social being, he argues. Like earlier thinkers in this tradition, he prefers values rooted in experience to moral abstractions in the political domain. Society works through the continuity of authority and the exercise of power. Conservatives naturally defend institutions that maintain both. The family, in particular, plays a vital role in forming the moral personality of subjects who appreciate the importance of love, and their need for higher social authority.

An even more influential contributor to the important shifts in conservative politics and political thinking apparent in the Anglo-American world from the 1980s onwards was the Austrian economist, Friedrich von Hayek. His writings were picked up with enthusiasm during this period, and provided the basis for a powerful philosophical challenge to the moral and political implications of collectivism in general and the welfare state in particular. Writing in the mid-twentieth century, he too regarded its early decades as a period in which socialism was the leading political force [Reading 32]. By socialism he means the pursuit by state authorities of redistributive goals in order to realize an ideal of social justice. But socialism is now in decline internationally, in part because the logical outcomes of its political economy—inefficiency, declining productivity, greater hierarchy, and the destruction of individual liberty—are increasingly apparent. While this development is broadly to be welcomed, he maintains, one legacy of socialism remains important and damaging—the aspiration to achieve social justice. The continuing hold of such an idea means that socialism is still a likely outcome, if indirectly, of a state and bureaucracy that aspire to pursue a just social order. Hayek connects this argument to the rise and character of the modern welfare state. While it may be legitimate for public authorities to provide means of support and relief to the victims of a market order, and to furnish other public goods such as education, for those concerned with the value of individual liberty, the welfare state is a worrying development. The extension of public interference and social intervention it implies are misrepresented as measures designed to enable and support individuals. In reality, these legitimate an immoral assertion of state monopoly, and an extension of its coercive authority.

Hayek was not alone in raising fundamental moral objections to the trajectory of state development and the mentality pervading democratic politics in the decades after 1945. Other authors developed broadly similar ideas in different intellectual genres. The American writer, Ayn Rand, has authored a number of popular novels in which an even more robust mixture of libertarian and rugged individualism is promoted. In *The Fountainhead*, the novel's 'hero' Roark delivers a courtroom speech in which these ideas are central [Reading 33]. He rehearses a view of historical development in which heroic, misunderstood creators are the catalysts for social improvement and advance. But these heroes become the objects of the fear and resentment of the majority. These entrepreneurs, prophets, and adventurers pursue goals not from an overriding sense of the common interest, but for their own sake. Yet in striving for these ambitions, they create ideas and objects that become vital for the development of mankind. Behind all of these contributions lies the creative capacity of the individual mind, and the key operative condition for this is independence. This perspective is contrasted against the conventional view that altruism is the highest social ideal for the individual, and that one should place others before oneself. This, Roark declares, is the philosophy of dependence. Underpinning it is the mistaken idea that redistribution and sacrifice are ethically superior to creation. The origins of tyranny and corruption in politics lie in the triumph of the creed of the altruist and spurious dogmas about the common good. The excerpt ends with a homage to the virtues of individualism, a value which sustains the vision of a good society in which privacy, not collectivism, reigns supreme.

There are strong echoes of Hayekian ideas, and American individualism, in the career of the British politician Margaret Thatcher, though she was also influenced by more familiar Burkean themes and ideas. From her perspective, Macmillan's 'middle way' represented a capitulation before the rising tide of collectivism that had taken hold of Britain's political elite since the early twentieth century. Thatcher was an unusual Prime Minister in various respects, not least for the self-confidence with which she propounded a critique of the terms of the political consensus that, she believed, had infected British politics. In the speech extracted below [Reading 34], she returns to a tradition of conservative individualism, and locates its highest point in the Victorian ethos of self-reliance and charity. Collectivism—synonomous with 'socialism' for Thatcher—has buried these and other important social values: as state regulation has increased, so moral decline has set in. The 'free society' that she proclaims requires a strong state—one committed to preserving the 'frame which surrounds society'. Britain has stagnated, and indeed declined, she argues, because of the hold of important illusions among its governing class and the people at large. Thus she justifies some of the radical and controversial aspects of her governments' programmes—the monetarist approach to fiscal policy, efforts to cut public expenditures, and the end of state subsidies to failing industries.

Throughout her speeches and interviews, she reiterated the belief that Britain required limited but firm government, and that it needed to be set on a different course from that associated with collectivism. She was hailed and loathed as a conviction politician, eliciting unusually strong reactions from friends and enemies alike; in part because few conservative leaders have shown such evangelical ardour and explicit ideological ambition. The relentless assault that she preached upon Britain's elite, collectivist-orientated institutions, and her championing of free-market solutions and radical privatization programmes, divided conservatives then and since.

Conservative emphases upon tradition, spontaneous social order and the significance of nationally instantiated values have been attacked by a host of ideological currents and social forces throughout the last century. One of the most potent recent challenges arose in the 1960s, when a popular mixture of anti-authoritarianism and social libertarianism spread through many of the cities and university campuses of the Western world. The conflicts unleashed by these developments continue to reverberate in American political culture. In reaction to the new 'permissiveness' (as some conservatives often put it) associated with the 1960s, a reconfigured conservatism—often labelled 'neo-conservatism'—was developed by some important thinkers and public intellectuals in the 1970s. This came to influence aspects of the thinking and politics of the Republican party during the 1980s and beyond.

Allan Bloom was an influential contributor to this current. In the extract reprinted here from his controversial critique of the demise of the American system of higher education, *The Closing of the American Mind*, he presents the 1960s as the moment when the decline of American intellectual culture took hold [Reading 35]. He laments in particular the abandonment of a sense of higher calling among university professors, and their disconnection from a classical tradition of scholarly enquiry and non-partisan critical judgement. The intelligentsia capitulated before the radical myth that intellectual enquiry can be conducted to serve the purpose of whichever values and concerns are currently in vogue. The abandonment of a critical standpoint beyond the horizon of current opinion signals the demise of this higher philosophical calling. He sardonically observes the emergence of various radical political causes on the intellectual agenda of the modern academy. In a powerful, and controversial, analogy, he likens the collapse of this independent standpoint in 1960s America to the failure of the German academy to stand up to the Nazis in Germany during the 1930s. Indeed, there are various shared ideological agendas, he claims, between these disparate currents, united as they are by their unmitigated contempt for bourgeois society.

Conservatism was not only influenced in this period by the 'neo-conservative' intellectual agenda. An important, rival strand of libertarian thinking, which paid homage to Hayek among others, was also apparent during this period. Writing in a more formal, philosophical, genre, Robert Nozick probed and extended the logic of this strand of libertarian conservatism in his influential work, *Anarchy, State, and Utopia* [Reading 36]. Like Hayek, he too attacked the intellectual merits of the idea of social justice, and the philosophical conception of distributive justice favoured by liberal theorists in the 1970s. He countered this position with his own entitlement theory of justice. This relies upon the claim that so long as we can demonstrate that agents are entitled to dispose of the resources they own, then whatever social outcome results from their willing actions is, by definition, a just one. This is so even if society is riddled with inequalities. By contrast, a distributive conception of justice implies a just end-state, in which unjust inequalities are overcome; and such an ideal necessitates continual interference with people's lives and choices by an external authority, since individuals, if left to their own devices, will normally behave in ways that upset any such patterned end-state.

In other respects, Nozick departs from more conservative terrain, or at least fits oddly into its patterns of thinking. He was more utopian and rationalistic in his theoretical reasoning than other proponents of free-market conservatism in this period, such as Hayek. And he was by no means a social conservative in his outlook, regarding his own thinking as a continuation of the classical liberalism of the seventeenth- and eighteenth-centuries. Simultaneously, the individualist libertarianism he espoused connected his thought in some respects with the perspectives of anarchism, as much as conservatism. His opposition to egalitarian conceptions of liberalism was premised upon his own preference for a minimalist, non-distributive state. For Nozick, humans are largely self-interested and rational individuals who, when faced with the threats and challenges of the lawless 'state of nature', hire agencies to protect their property. The interaction of these agencies leads to one of them becoming the dominant agent in a given territory, he surmised. If the original pattern of acquisition in this state of nature is broadly just (Nozick invoked the seventeeth-century theorist John Locke's theory about rightful acquisition to justify this stance), and if successive acquisitions have also happened according to the principle of voluntary transfer, then any property holdings in that sequence are themselves just. The state cannot interfere with an extant distribution or propertied resources on the grounds of justice, or for other purposes, like social utility. Nozick labels this an entitlement theory of distributive justice, and contrasts it (see the extract below) with the 'end-state' or patterned principle favoured by liberals enamoured of the interventionist state. Only unimpeded market exchanges respect people as ends in themselves. Progressive taxation, by contrast, violates the principle that individuals ought to be regarded as ends ('self-owners' in Nozick's terminology), treating them as means to some higher moral goal.

Neo-conservatism has increasingly moved to the fore within American political life since the 1970s. While it was originally an intellectually orientated current, 'neo-cons' now occupy important positions as journalists, TV pundits, opinion-formers and indeed as Republican politicians. They propound an unyielding hostility to the culture of liberalism, an aggressive conception of American foreign policy, and propose conservative schemes for social reform. One of this current's leading contemporary voices, William Kristol, argues that neo-conservatism conjoins two important contemporary moral impulses—a deeply entrenched commitment to individual liberty, on the one hand, and a burgeoning concern for the re-establishment of traditional virtues in society, without the interference of the over mighty state, on the other [Reading 37]. These values are, he acknowledges, sometimes in tension in political life particularly over the question of the crisis of the modern family. Citing one of the right-wing sociologist Charles Murray's (in)famous essays on the growing threat to civil society posed by a feckless underclass, Kristol notes how this particular neo-conservative intervention involves both of these values. Murray stresses the dysfunctions associated with the rising number of births to parents who are not married, but is ambivalent about whether the state is the agency that ought to rectify this problem. Like many 'neo-cons' Murray is sceptical about the motivations and capacities of the federal state, yet he also implies a major role for it in, for instance, establishing a pattern of 'legal discrimination' against illegitimacy or nontraditional family patterns (as opposed to the liberal ideal of legal neutrality in such matters). Kristol concludes that for conservatives, politics must simultaneously address the problem of virtue, as well as liberty; and in social life, where virtue is the preponderant conservative concern, liberty too must be supported. In the neo-conservative view, society and politics are deeply interrelated, and both need to be animated by a common view of what constitutes morality and human nature. A primary concern for advocates of this kind of moralized politics is to turn the tide against those social forces that have, since the 1960s, risen within civil society—such as feminism—and gained the support and legitimacy of political authorities.

FURTHER READING

One of the most impressive and unusual depictions of the character of conservative thought can be found in A. O. Hirschman, *The Rhetoric of Reaction* (Belknap Press of Harvard University, 1991). Other insightful, philosophically orientated treatments can be found in Noël O'Sullivan's *Conservatism* (Dent, 1976), Roger Scruton's *The Meaning of Conservatism* (Penguin, 1980), which offers a bold defence of inequality and authority, and Ted Honderich, *Conservatism* (Hamish Hamilton, 1991). Historical treatments can be located in the essays collected in Roger Eatwell and Noël O'Sullivan (eds.), *The Nature of the Right* (Pinter, 1989), which consider the different national traditions of Conservative thought, including France, Germany, Britain, and America; and Arthur Aughey, Greta Jones, and W. M. Riches, *The Conservative Political Tradition in Britain, and the United States* (Pinter, 1992).

24 Edmund Burke, from *Reflections on the Revolution in France* (ed. C. C. O'Brien; Penguin, 1969), pp. 191–7

Burke (1729–1797) grew up in Ireland, the son of a Protestant father and Catholic mother, and moved to London in 1750 to read law. Abandoning this career soon after, he sought to make a living as a writer. Increasingly drawn to politics, he emerged as a leading spokesman and political mouthpiece for the Parliamentary grouping known as the Whigs. From 1770, he acted as Parliamentary agent for the colony of New York, and in a famous series of speeches and letters tried to persuade the British to moderate their attitude to the colonial rebels. During this portion of his political career, he was associated with several high-profile causes: the reformation of the Crown's finances; the case for Catholic emancipation in Ireland; and the regulation of British rule in India. But it was the events in France of 1789, and his famously critical response to them, that established his contemporary and subsequent fame, notably in his *Reflections on the Revolution in France* (1790).

When the people have emptied themselves of all the lust of selfish will, which without religion it is utterly impossible they ever should, when they are conscious that they exercise, and exercise perhaps in an higher link of the order of delegation, the power, which to be legitimate must be according to that eternal immutable law, in which will and reason are the same, they will be more careful how they place power in base and incapable hands. In their nomination to office, they will not appoint to the exercise of authority, as to a pitiful job, but as to an holy function; not according to their sordid selfish interest, nor to their wanton caprice, nor to their arbitrary will; but they will confer that power (which any man may well tremble to give or to receive) on those only, in whom they may discern that predominant proportion of active virtue and wisdom, taken together and fitted to the charge, such, as in the great and inevitable mixed mass of human imperfections and infirmities, is to be found.

When they are habitually convinced that no evil can be acceptable, either in the act or the permission, to him whose essence is good, they will be better able to extirpate out of the minds of all magistrates, civil, ecclesiastical, or military, any thing that bears the least resemblance to a proud and lawless domination.

But one of the first and most leading principles on which the commonwealth and the laws are consecrated, is lest the temporary possessors and life-renters in it, unmindful of what they have received from their ancestors, or of what is due to their posterity, should act as if they were the entire masters; that they should not think it amongst their rights to cut off the entail, or commit waste on the inheritance, by destroying at their pleasure the whole original fabric of their society; hazarding to leave to those who come after them, a ruin instead of an habitation—and teaching these successors as little to respect their contrivances, as they had themselves respected the institutions of their forefathers. By this unprincipled facility of changing the state as often, and as much, and in as many ways as there are floating fancies or fashions, the whole chain and continuity of the common-wealth would be broken. No one generation could link with the other. Men would become little better than the flies of a summer.

And first of all the science of jurisprudence, the pride of the human intellect, which, with all its defects, redundancies, and errors, is the collected reason of ages, combining the principles of original justice with the infinite variety of human concerns, as a heap of old exploded errors, would be no longer studied. Personal self-sufficiency and arrogance (the certain attendants upon all those who have never experienced a wisdom greater than their own) would usurp the tribunal. Of course, no certain laws, establishing invariably grounds of hope and fear, would keep the actions of men in a certain course, or direct them to a certain end. Nothing stable in the modes of holding property, or exercising function, could form a solid ground on which any parent could speculate in the educa-tion of his offspring, or in a choice for their future establishment in the world. No principles would be early worked into the habits. As soon as the most able instructor had completed his laborious course of institution, instead of sending forth his pupil, accom-plished in a virtuous discipline, fitted to procure him attention and respect, in his place in society, he would find every thing altered; and that he had turned out a poor creature to the contempt and derision of the world, ignorant of the true grounds of estimation. Who would insure a tender and delicate sense of honour to beat almost with the first pulses of the heart, when no man could know what would be the test of honour in a nation, continually varying the standard of its coin? No part of life would retain its acqui-sitions. Barbarism with regard to science and literature, unskilfulness with regard to arts and manufactures, would infallibly succeed to the want of a steady education and settled principle; and thus the commonwealth itself would, in a few generations, crumble away, be disconnected into the dust and powder of individuality, and at length dispersed to all the winds of heaven.

To avoid therefore the evils of inconstancy and versatility, ten thousand times worse than those of obstinacy and the blindest prejudice, we have consecrated the state, that no man should approach to look into its defects or corruptions but with due caution; that he should never dream of beginning its reformation by its subversion; that he should approach to the faults of the state as to the wounds of a father, with pious awe and trembling sollicitude. By this wise prejudice we are taught to look with horror on those children of their country who are prompt rashly to hack that aged parent in pieces, and put him into the kettle of magicians, in hopes that by their poisonous weeds, and wild incantations, they may regenerate the paternal constitution, and renovate their father's life.

Society is indeed a contract. Subordinate contracts for objects of mere occasional interest may be dissolved at pleasure—but the state ought not to be considered as nothing better than a partnership agreement in a trade of pepper and coffee, callico or tobacco, or some other such low concern, to be taken up for a little temporary interest, and to be dissolved by the fancy of the parties. It is to be looked on with other reverence; because it is not a partnership in things subservient only to the gross animal existence of a temporary and perishable nature. It is a partnership in all science; a partnership in all art; a partnership in every virtue, and in all perfection. As the ends of such a partnership cannot be obtained in many generations, it becomes a partnership not only between those who are living, but between those who are living, those who are dead, and those who are to be born. Each contract of each particular state is but a clause in the great primaeval contract of eternal society, linking the lower with the higher natures, connecting the visible and invisible world, according to a fixed compact sanctioned by the inviolable oath which holds all physical and all moral natures, each in their appointed place. This law is not subject to the will of those, who by an obligation above them, and infinitely superior, are bound to submit their will to that law. The municipal corporations of that universal kingdom are not morally at liberty at their pleasure, and on their speculations of a contingent improvement, wholly to separate and tear asunder the bands of their subordinate community, and to dissolve it into an unsocial, uncivil, unconnected chaos of elementary principles. It is the first and supreme necessity only, a necessity that is not chosen but chooses, a necessity paramount to deliberation, that admits no discussion, and demands no evidence, which alone can justify a resort to anarchy. This necessity is no exception to the rule; because this necessity itself is a part too of that moral and physical disposition of things to which man must be obedient by consent or force; but if that which is only submission to necessity should be made the object of choice, the law is broken, nature is disobeyed, and the rebellious are outlawed, cast forth, and exiled, from this world of reason, and order, and peace, and virtue, and fruitful penitence, into the antagonist world of madness, discord, vice, confusion, and unavailing sorrow.

These, my dear Sir, are, were, and I think long will be the sentiments of not the least learned and reflecting part of this kingdom. They who are included in this description, form their opinions on such grounds as such persons ought to form them. The less enquiring receive them from an authority which those whom Providence dooms to live on trust need not be ashamed to rely on. These two sorts of men move in the same direction, tho' in a different place. They both move with the order of the universe. They all know or feel this great antient truth: 'Quod illi principi et praepotenti deo qui omnem hunc mundum regit, nihil eorum quae quidem fiant in terris acceptius quam concilia et caetus hominum jure sociati quae civitates appellantur.' They take this tenet of the head and heart, not from the great name which it immediately bears, nor from the greater from whence it is derived; but from that which alone can give true weight and sanction to any learned opinion, the common nature and common relation of men. Persuaded that all things ought to be done with reference, and referring all to the point of reference to which all should be directed, they think themselves bound, not only as individuals in the sanctuary of the heart, or as congregated in that personal capacity, to renew the memory of their high origin and cast; but also in their corporate character to perform their national homage to the institutor, and author and protector of civil society; without which civil society man could not by any possibility arrive at the perfection of which his nature is capable, nor even make a remote and faint approach to it. They conceive that He who gave our nature to be perfected by our virtue, willed also the necessary means of its perfection—He willed therefore the state— He willed its connexion with the source and original archetype of all perfection. They who are convinced of this his will, which is the law of laws and the sovereign or sovereigns, cannot think it reprehensible, that this our corporate fealty and homage, that this our recognition of a signiory paramount, I had almost said this oblation of the state itself, as a worthy offering on the high altar of universal praise, should be performed as all publick solemn acts are performed, in buildings, in musick, in decoration, in speech, in the dignity of persons, according to the customs of mankind, taught by their nature; that is, with modest splendour, with unassuming state, with mild majesty and sober pomp. For those purposes they think some part of the wealth of the country is as usefully employed as it can be, in fomenting the luxury of individuals. It is the publick ornament. It is the publick consolation. It nourishes the publick hope. The poorest man finds his own importance and dignity in it, whilst the wealth and pride of individuals at every moment makes the man of humble rank and fortune sensible of his inferiority, and degrades and vilifies his condition. It is for the man in humble life, and to raise his nature, and to put him in mind of a state in which the privileges of opulence will cease, when he will be equal by nature, and may be more than equal by virtue, that this portion of the general wealth of his country is employed and sanctified.

25 Joseph de Maistre, from *Considerations on France* (ed. R. A. Lebrun; Cambridge University Press, 1994), pp. 27–31

De Maistre (1753–1821) was born into a devout Catholic family in Savoy, France. Though initially enthused by the Revolution of 1789, he supported the counter-revolutionary forces when the new Republic's army invaded his home state in 1792. He fled, eventually to Sardinia, where he sought to establish himself as a political writer, and authored his most famous work, *Considerations on France*. He subsequently spent several years in Russia, at the behest of the Sardinian Crown, producing a number of widely read essays (for instance *Pope* (1819)). These were all characterized by his unremitting hostility to the Enlightenment, and his assertion of the merits of a reactionary brand of social conservatism.

I will not carry this frightful catalogue any further; our own century and the preceding one are too well known. If you go back to the birth of nations, if you come down to our own day, if you examine peoples in all possible conditions from the state of barbarism to the most advanced civilization, you always find war. From this primary cause, and from all the other connected causes, the effusion of human blood has never ceased in the world. Sometimes blood flows less abundantly over some larger area, sometimes it flows more abundantly in a more restricted area, but the flow remains nearly constant.

But from time to time the flow is augmented prodigiously by such extraordinary events as the Punic Wars, the Triumvirate, the victories of Caesar, the irruption of the barbarians, the Crusades, the wars of religion, the Spanish Succession, the French Revolution, etc. If one had a table of massacres similar to a meteorological table, who knows whether, after centuries of observation, some law might not be discovered? Buffon has proven quite clearly that a large percentage of animals are destined to die a violent death. He could apparently have extended the demonstration to man; but let the facts speak for themselves.

Yet there is room to doubt whether this violent destruction is, in general, such a great evil as is believed; at least, it is one of those evils that enters into an order of things where everything is violent and *against nature*, and that produces compensations. First, when the human soul has lost its strength through laziness, incredulity, and the gangrenous vices that follow an excess of civilization, it can be retempered only in blood. Certainly there is no easy explanation of why war produces different effects in different circumstances. But it can be seen clearly enough that mankind may be considered as a tree which an invisible hand is continually pruning and which often profits from the operation. In truth the tree may perish if the trunk is cut or if the tree is *overpruned*; but who knows the limits of the human tree? What we do know is that excessive carnage is often allied with excessive population, as was seen especially in the ancient Greek republics and in Spain under the Arab domination. Platitudes about war mean nothing. One need not be very clever to know that when more men are killed, fewer remain at the moment, just as it is true that the more branches one cuts off, the fewer remain on the tree. But the results of the operation are what must be considered. Moreover, following the same comparison, we may observe that the skilful gardener directs the pruning less towards lush vegetation than towards the fructification of the tree; he wants fruit, not wood or leaves. Now the real *fruits* of human nature—the arts, sciences, great enterprises, lofty conceptions, manly virtues—are due especially to the state of war. We know that nations have never achieved the highest point of the greatness of which they are capable except after long and bloody wars. Thus, Greece's most brilliant hour was the terrible epoch of the Peloponnesian War; the Age of Augustus followed immediately the civil war and the proscriptions; French genius was hewn by the League and polished by the Fronde; all the great men of the century of Queen Anne were born in the midst of political upheavals. In a word, we can say that blood is the manure of the plant we call *genius*.

I wonder if those who say that *the arts are the friends of peace* really know what they are saying. It would at least be necessary to explain and circumscribe the proposition, for I see nothing less pacific than the centuries of Alexander and Pericles, of Augustus, of Leo X and Francis I, of Louis XIV and Queen Anne.

Could the shedding of human blood possibly not have serious causes and serious effects? Let us reflect; history and fable, the discoveries of modern physiology and antique tradition all unite to furnish material for these meditations. We should not be more ashamed of speculating on this subject than on a thousand others less relevant to man.

In the meantime let us thunder against war and try to teach sovereigns an aversion to it; but let us not give in to the dreams of Condorcet, that *philosophe* so dear to the Revolution, who used his life to prepare the unhappiness of the present generation, graciously willing perfection to posterity. There is only one way of restraining the scourge of war, and that is by restraining the disorders that lead to this terrible purification.

In the Greek tragedy of Orestes, Helen, one of the characters in the play, is taken away by the gods to the just resentment of the Greeks, and placed in the sky beside her two brothers to be a guiding sign to navigators. Apollo appears in order to justify this strange apotheosis. 'Helen's beauty', he says, 'was only an instrument that the gods used to set the Greeks and Trojans against each other to cause their blood to flow, in order to quench on earth the iniquity of men become too numerous.'

Apollo spoke very well. Men gather the clouds, and then they complain of the tempests that follow. 'It is the anger of kings that arms the earth; it is the anger of heaven that arms the kings.'

I know well that in all these considerations we are continually troubled by the wearisome sight of the innocent who perish with the guilty. But without becoming deeply involved in this most profound question, we can consider it solely in the light of the age-old dogma that *the innocent suffer for the benefit of the guilty*.

It was from this dogma, it seems to me, that the ancients derived the custom of sacrifices that was practised everywhere and that was judged useful not only for the living but also for the dead, a typical custom that habit has led us to regard without astonishment, but whose roots are nonetheless difficult to discover.

Self-sacrifices, so famous in antiquity, come from the same dogma. Decius had *faith* that the sacrifice of his life would be accepted by the Divinity and that he could use it to balance all the evils that menaced his country.

Christianity came to consecrate this dogma, which is perfectly natural to man although appearing difficult to arrive at by reason.

Thus, there could have been in the heart of Louis XVI, in that of the saintly Elizabeth, such an impulse, such an acceptance, capable of saving France.

Sometimes it is asked, Of what use are these terrible austerities, which are also self-sacrifices, practised by certain religious orders? It would be precisely the same thing to ask of what use is Christianity, which rests entirely on an enlargement of this same dogma of innocence paying for crime.

The authority that approves these orders chooses certain men and *insulates* them from the world in order to make them *conductors*.

There is nothing but violence in the universe; but we are spoiled by a modern philosophy that tells us *all is good*, whereas evil has tainted everything, and in a very real sense, *all is evil*, since nothing is in its place. The keynote of the system of our creation has been lowered, and following the rules of harmony, all the others have been lowered proportionately. *All creation groans*, and tends with pain and effort towards another order of things.

The spectators of great human calamities, especially, are led to these sad meditations. But let us not lose courage: there is no chastisement that does not purify; there is no disorder that ETERNAL LOVE does not turn against the principle of evil. It is gratifying amid the general upheaval to have a presentiment of the plans of Divinity. We will never see the complete picture during our earthly sojourn, and often we will deceive ourselves; but in all possible sciences, except the exact sciences, are we not reduced to conjecture? And if our conjectures are plausible, if there are analogies for them, if they are based on universally accepted ideas, above all if they are consoling and suited to make us better men, what do they lack? If they are not true, they are good; or rather, since they are good, are they not true?

Having envisaged the French Revolution from a purely moral point of view, I now turn my speculations to politics, without, however, forgetting the primary aim of my work.

26 Friedrich Karl von Savigny, from *Of the Vocation of our Age for Legislation and Jurisprudence*, in J. B. Halsted (ed.), *Romanticism* (Harper & Row, 1969), pp. 200–8

Savigny (1779–1861) held the Chair of Law at the University of Berlin, 1810–1842. He then served as Minister of Justice in Prussia until 1847. He emerged in this period as one of the leading figures in the German historical school of legal theorizing. He established his reputation as a legal scholar through his major study of the history of Roman law, *Right of Possession* (1803). Within his historical studies, he placed considerable emphasis upon the importance and role of institutions. In contrast to the growing influence of rationalist doctrines and abstract moral theorizing upon the juristic thinking of his era, he relied upon an organic understanding of social change, and defended the merits of the evolution of the customary traditions of distinctive communities.

In many countries of Germany, a want, of an adventitious nature, has now raised the question as to the best mode of dealing with the law; and thus a question, which our governments were for a long time enabled to leave unagitated, has grown into a general subject of deliberation amongst statesmen and jurists. But a more honourable motive than the mere want, has contributed to bring about this public deliberation,—the feeling that Germany, on her deliverance from oppression, is imperatively called upon by every living energy, to shew herself not unworthy of the times. It is no mark of presumption therefore, but right and proper, for every man, who has a heart for his vocation, and a clear conception of it, publicly to communicate his views; and jurists should, least of all, be behindhand in this respect. For it is precisely in the law that the difference between the present time and the past is remarkable. Much perversion, in particular instances, may undoubtedly still occur upon the subject, from misconception or bad intention; but we are once again at liberty to ask, what is proper and expedient? The subject may again be viewed without reference to external considerations: rulers may again act according to conviction, and place their honour in the general weal. No one can say as much of the time that is past. When the code broke into Germany, and ate in, further and further, like a cancer, there was no mention of its intrinsic merits, scarcely here and there in empty phrases; extraneous motives, wholly foreign to the proper value of the code, determined every thing,—a state of things flagitious in itself, independently of the consideration that the object in view was the most pernicious of all objects. Until now, therefore, it was fruitless to speak upon the subject. Those who, during this period, did speak upon it, were partly advocates of the bad cause from interested motives; partly, with inconceivable simplicity, stultified by it; most of them merely assisted in the undertaking, as practical men, without adopting an opinion of their own; some few voices, well meriting attention, were raised, rebuking and warning; others, making signs and indicating, but none with any hope of success. That once again a diversity of opinions may exist; that once again the decision can be a subject of dispute, is one of the blessings which God has vouchsafed to us; for only from this diversity can a living and firm unity proceed,—the unity of conviction, for which our nature compels us to struggle in all matters of mind.

But there are two modes of carrying on a controversy; one hostile, and one amicable. We adopt the first when we find the motive and object to be bad; the latter, when we are investigating the means to objects of general good. The former would be applicable, even now when there is no longer any question of the code, should any one maintain that this is the proper time for each particular state of Germany to isolate itself, that the law is a fit instrument for the purpose, and that every government should provide a separate code for itself, in order to remove, even from the law, every thing that might revive a recollection of the common national tie. This view is any thing but imaginary; on the contrary, many a government notoriously inclines to it; but a certain apprehension prevents it from being publicly avowed at present, and I doubt whether it has ever been advanced in any work on the law. Wholly different is it with the plans, which, up to the present time, have been proposed with regard to this law; for with them, even where we do not agree, the amicable mode is possible; and this leads, if not to the unanimity of the disputants, at least to a better understanding on the whole.

Of two opinions as to the establishment of the law, with which I am acquainted, the one inclines to the restoration of the old system, the other to the adoption of a general code for all the states of Germany. To illustrate this second opinion, some observations are necessary here; as it must be considered in a twofold historical connection.

In the first place, it is connected with many plans and experiments of the kind since the middle of the eighteenth century. During this period the whole of Europe was actuated by a blind rage for improvement. All sense and feeling of the greatness by which other times were characterized, as also of the natural development of communities and institutions, all, consequently, that is wholesome and profitable in history, was lost; its place was supplied by the most extravagant anticipations of the present age, which was believed to be destined to be nothing less than to the being a picture of absolute perfection. This impulse manifested itself in all directions; what it has effected in religion and government, is known; and it is also evident how everywhere, by a natural reaction, it could not fail to pave the way for a new and more lively love for what is permanent. The law was likewise affected by it. Men longed for new codes, which, by their completeness, should insure a mechanically precise administration of justice; insomuch that the judge, freed from the exercise of private opinion, should be confined to the mere literal application: and at the same time, they were to be divested of all historical associations, and, in pure abstraction, be equally adapted to all nations and all times. It would be very erroneous to ascribe this impulse, and these applications of it, to any false teachers in particular; it was, with some highly honourable exceptions, the opinion of nations. It was, therefore, not in the power of the governments to ward off all the effects; and, in fact, the mere tempering and controlling of it might often be looked upon as highly meritorious, and as a proof of internal vigour. On comparing the present time with the past, we may be allowed to congratulate ourselves. An historical spirit has been every where awakened, and leaves no room for the shallow self-sufficiency above alluded to. And although young writers often adopt a similar tone, it is no longer the prevailing one. Even in the above-mentioned plans of codes, this pleasing comparison is partially confirmed. Free from those extravagant pretensions, they are directed to a fixed practical object, and the reasonings, also, on which they are founded, are good. The lapse of this period, however, secures to us the great advantage of being able to take counsel by their experience. Those theories have successively given rise to codes for three great countries. These, and, in part, their effects, are before us, and it would be unpardonable to despise the lesson which, in the way of encouragement or warning, they are capable of affording us. In the second place, those plans are connected with a general theory of the origin of all positive law, which was always prevalent with the great majority of German jurists. According to this theory, all law, in its concrete form, is founded upon the express enactments of the supreme power. Jurisprudence has only the contents of the enactments for its object. Accordingly, legislation itself, and jurisprudence as well, are of a wholly accidental and fluctuating nature; and it is very possible that the law of to-morrow may not at all resemble the law of to-day. A complete code is, consequently, of primary importance, and it is only in case of its defectiveness that we can ever be exposed to the lamentable necessity of making shift with customary law as an uncertain kind of supplement. This theory is of much greater antiquity than the theory above-mentioned; both have come into hostile collision on many points, but have far oftener agreed very well. The conviction that there is a practical law of nature or reason, an ideal legislation for all times and all circumstances, which we have only to discover to bring positive law to permanent perfection, often served to reconcile them. Whether there be any real foundation for this theory of the origin of positive law, will be seen in the next chapter.

We first inquire of history, how law has actually developed itself amongst nations of the nobler races; the question—What may be good, or necessary, or, on the contrary, censurable herein,—will be not at all prejudiced by this method of proceeding.

In the earliest times to which authentic history extends, the law will be found to have already attained a fixed character, peculiar to the people, like their language, manners and constitution. Nay, these phenomena have no separate existence, they are but the particular faculties and tendencies of an individual people, inseparably united in nature, and only wearing the semblance of distinct attributes to our view. That which binds them into one whole is the common conviction of the people, the kindred consciousness of an inward necessity, excluding all notion of an accidental and arbitrary origin.

How these peculiar attributes of nations, by which they are first individualized, originated—this is a question which cannot be answered historically. Of late, the prevalent opinion has been that all lived at first a sort of animal life, advancing gradually to a more passable state, until at length the height on which they now stand, was attained. We may leave this theory alone, and confine ourselves to the mere matter of fact of that first authentic condition of the law. We shall endeavour to exhibit certain general traits of this period, in which the law, as well as the language, exists in the consciousness of the people.

This youth of nations is poor in ideas, but enjoys a clear perception of its relations and circumstances, and feels and brings the whole of them into play; whilst we, in our artificial complicated existence, are overwhelmed by our own riches, instead of enjoying and controlling them. This plain natural state is particularly observable in the law; and as, in the case of an individual, his family relations and patrimonial property may possess an additional value in his eyes from the effect of association,—so on the same principle, it is possible for the rules of the law itself to be amongst the objects of popular faith. But these moral faculties require some bodily existence to fix them. Such, for language, is its constant uninterrupted use; such, for the constitution, are palpable and public powers,—but what supplies its place with regard to the law? In our times it is supplied by rules, communicated by writing and word of mouth. This mode of fixation, however, presupposes a high degree of abstraction, and is, therefore, not practicable in the early time alluded to. On the contrary, we then find symbolical acts universally employed where rights and duties were to be created or extinguished: it is their palpableness which externally retains law in a fixed form; and their solemnity and weight correspond with the importance of the legal relations themselves, which have been already mentioned as peculiar to this period. In the general use of such formal acts, the Germanic races agree with the ancient Italic, except that, amongst these last, the forms themselves appear more fixed and regular, which perhaps arose from their city constitutions. These formal acts may be considered as the true grammar of law in this period; and it is important to observe that the principal business of the early Roman jurists consisted in the preservation and accurate application of them. We, in latter times, have often made light of them as the creation of barbarism and superstition, and have prided ourselves on not having them, without considering that we, too, are at every step beset with legal forms, to which, in fact, only the principal advantages of the old forms are wanting,—namely, their palpableness, and the popular prejudice in their favour, whilst ours are felt by all as something arbitrary, and therefore burdensome. In such partial views of early times we resemble the travellers, who remark, with great astonishment, that in France the little children, nay, even the common people, speak French with perfect fluency.

But this organic connection of law with the being and character of the people, is also manifested in the progress of the times; and here, again, it may be compared with language. For law, as for language, there is no moment of absolute cessation; it is subject to the same movement and development as every other popular tendency; and this very development remains under the same law of inward necessity, as in its earliest stages. Law grows with the growth, and strengthens with the strength of the people, and finally dies away as the nation loses its nationality. But this inward progressive tendency, even in highly cultivated times, throws a great difficulty in the way of discussion. It has been maintained above, that the common consciousness of the people is the peculiar seat of law. This, for example, in the Roman law, is easily conceivable of its essential parts, such as the general definition of marriage, of property, &c.&c., but with regard to the endless detail, of which we have only a remnant in the Pandects, every one must regard it as impossible.

This difficulty leads us to a new view of the development of law. With the progress of civilization, national tendencies become more and more distinct, and what otherwise would have remained common, becomes appropriated to particular classes; the jurists now become more and more a distinct class of the kind; law perfects its language, takes a scientific direction, and, as formerly it existed in the consciousness of the community, it now devolves upon the jurists, who thus, in this department, represent the community.

Law is henceforth more artificial and complex, since it has a twofold life; first, as part of the aggregate existence of the community, which it does not cease to be; and, secondly, as a distinct branch of knowledge in the hands of the jurists. All the latter phenomena are explicable by the co-operation of those two principles of existence; and it may now be understood, how even the whole of that immense detail might arise from organic causes, without any exertion of arbitrary will or intention. For the sake of brevity, we call, technically speaking, the connection of law with the general existence of the people—the political element; and the distinct scientific existence of law—the technical element.

At different times, therefore, amongst the same people, law will be natural law (in a different sense from our law of nature), or learned law, as the one or the other principle prevails, between which a precise line of demarcation is obviously impossible. Under a republican constitution, the political principle will be able to preserve an immediate influence longer than in monarchical states; and under the Roman republic in particular, many causes co-operated to keep this influence alive, even during the progress of civilization. But in all times, and under all constitutions, this influence continues to shew itself in particular applications, as where the same constantly-recurring necessity makes a general consciousness of the people at large possible. Thus, in most cities, a separate law for menial servants and house-renting will grow up and continue to exist, equally independent of positive rules and scientific jurisprudence: such laws are the individual remains of the primitive legal formations. Before the great overthrow of almost all institutions, which we have witnessed, cases of this sort were of much more frequent occurrence in the small German states than now, parts of the old Germanic institutions having frequently survived all revolutions whatever. The sum, therefore, of this theory is, that all law is originally formed in the manner, in which, in ordinary but not quite correct language, customary law is said to have been formed: i.e. that it is first developed by custom and popular faith, next by jurisprudence,—everywhere, therefore, by internal silently-operating powers, not by the arbitrary will of a law-giver . . .

The most important argument urged in favour of the uniformity of the law, is, that our love for our common country is enhanced by it, but weakened by a multiplicity of particular laws. If this supposition be well founded, every German of good feeling will wish that Germany may have throughout the same system of law. But this very supposition is now the subject of discussion.

The well-being of every organic being, (consequently of states,) depends on the maintenance of an equipoise between the whole and its parts—on each having its due. For a citizen, a town, a province to forget the state to which they belong, is a very common phenomenon, and every one will regard this as an unnatural and morbid state of things. But for this very reason a lively affection for the whole can only proceed from the thorough participation in all particular relations; and he only who takes good care of his own family, will be a truly good citizen. It is, therefore, an error to suppose that the common weal would gain new life by the annihilation of all individual relations. Were it possible to generate a peculiar corporate spirit in every class, every town, nay, every village, the common weal would gain new strength from this heightened and multiplied individuality. When, therefore, the influence of law on the love of country, is the question, the particular laws of particular provinces and states are not to be regarded as obstacles. In this point of view, the law merits praise, in so far as it falls in, or is adapted to fall in, with the feelings and consciousness of the people; blame, if, like an uncongenial and arbitrary thing, it leaves the people without participation. That, however, will be oftener and more easily the case with the distinct systems of particular districts, although it certainly is not every municipal law that will be truly popular.

Indeed, for this political end, no state of law appears more favourable than that which was formerly general in Germany: great variety and individuality in particulars, but with the common law for the general foundation, constantly reminding all the Germanic nations of their indissoluble unity. The most pernicious, however, in this point of view, is the light and capricious alteration of law; and even were uniformity and fitness attainable by change, the advantage would not be worth naming in comparison with the political disadvantage just alluded to. That which is thus constructed by men's hands before our eyes, will always hold a very different place in popular estimation from that which has not so plain and palpable an origin; and when we, in our praiseworthy zeal, inveigh against this decision as a blind prejudice, we ought not to forget that all faith in, and feeling for, that which is not on a level with us, but more exalted than we, depends upon the same kind of spirit. This consideration might well lead us to doubt of the impropriety of the decision.

27 William Graham Sumner, from *Folkways: A Study of the Sociological Importance of Usages, Manners, Customs, Mores and Morals* (Dover Publications, 1908), pp. 2–4, 11–13

Born in Hartford, Connecticut, Sumner (1840–1910) became a leading Professor of Sociology and well-known commentator upon social and political affairs. He was ordained an Episcopalian Minister, but left this vocation in 1872 to take up a Professorship of Sociology and Anthropology at Yale University. There he emerged as one of the leading American exponents of social Darwinism, a set of doctrines that he harnessed for politically conservative ends. He was involved in the reform of the American University system, successfully advocating a more modern curriculum in favour of its 'divinity-classics' roots. Intellectually, he was an advocate of *laissez-faire* economics and an inveterate opponent of socialism and natural rights thinking, commitments that flowed from his strong Darwinist beliefs and adherence to the Calvinist work ethic (for instance, in his *The Challenge of Facts* (1914)). He was a sharp critic of government intervention in the economy, on the grounds that it would disturb the natural, organic character of market relations.

1. **Definition and mode of origin of the folkways.** If we put together all that we have learned from anthropology and ethnography about primitive men and primitive society, we perceive that the first task of life is to live. Men begin with acts, not with thoughts. Every moment brings necessities which must be satisfied at once. Need was the first experience, and it was followed at once by a blundering effort to satisfy it. It is generally taken for granted that men inherited some guiding instincts from their beast ancestry, and it may be true, although it has never been proved. If there were such inheritances, they controlled and aided the first efforts to satisfy needs. Analogy makes it easy to assume that the

ways of beasts had produced channels of habit and predisposition along which dexterities and other psychophysical activities would run easily. Experiments with newborn animals show that in the absence of any experience of the relation of means to ends, efforts to satisfy needs are clumsy and blundering. The method is that of trial and failure, which produces repeated pain, loss, and disappointments. Nevertheless, it is a method of rude experiment and selection. The earliest efforts of men were of this kind. Need was the impelling force. Pleasure and pain, on the one side and the other, were the rude constraints which defined the line on which efforts must proceed. The ability to distinguish between pleasure and pain is the only psychical power which is to be assumed. Thus ways of doing things were selected, which were expedient. They answered the purpose better than other ways, or with less toil and pain. Along the course on which efforts were compelled to go, habit, routine, and skill were developed. The struggle to maintain existence was carried on, not individually, but in groups. Each profited by the other's experience; hence there was concurrence towards that which proved to be most expedient. All at last adopted the same way for the same purpose; hence the ways turned into customs and became mass phenomena. Instincts were developed in connection with them. In this way folkways arise. The young learn them by tradition, imitation, and authority. The folkways, at a time, provide for all the needs of life then and there. They are uniform, universal in the group, imperative, and invariable. As time goes on, the folkways become more and more arbitrary, positive, and imperative. If asked why they act in a certain way in certain cases, primitive people always answer that it is because they and their ancestors always have done so. A sanction also arises from ghost fear. The ghosts of ancestors would be angry if the living should change the ancient folkways (see sec. 6).

2. **The folkways are a societal force**. The operation by which folkways are produced consists in the frequent repetition of petty acts, often by great numbers acting in concert or, at least, acting in the same way when face to face with the same need. The immediate motive is interest. It produces habit in the individual and custom in the group. It is, therefore, in the highest degree original and primitive. By habit and custom it exerts a strain on every individual within its range; therefore it rises to a societal force to which great classes of societal phenomena are due. Its earliest stages, its course, and laws may be studied; also its influence on individuals and their reaction on it. It is our present purpose so to study it. We have to recognize it as one of the chief forces by which a society is made to be what it is. Out of the unconscious experiment which every repetition of the ways includes, there issues pleasure or pain, and then, so far as the men are capable of reflection, convictions that the ways are conducive to societal welfare. These two experiences are not the same. The most uncivilized men, both in the food quest and in war, do things which are painful, but which have been found to be expedient. Perhaps these cases teach the sense of social welfare better than those which are pleasurable and favorable to welfare. The former cases call for some intelligent reflection on experience. When this conviction as to the relation to welfare is added to the folkways they are converted into mores, and, by virtue of the philosophical and ethical element added to them, they win utility and importance and become the source of the science and the art of living.

3. **Folkways are made unconsciously**. It is of the first importance to notice that, from the first acts by which men try to satisfy needs, each act stands by itself, and looks no

further than the immediate satisfaction. From recurrent needs arise habits for the individual and customs for the group, but these results are consequences which were never conscious, and never foreseen or intended. They are not noticed until they have long existed, and it is still longer before they are appreciated. Another long time must pass, and a higher stage of mental development must be reached, before they can be used as a basis from which to deduce rules for meeting, in the future, problems whose pressure can be foreseen. The folkways, therefore, are not creations of human purpose and wit. They are like products of natural forces which men unconsciously set in operation, or they are like the instinctive ways of animals, which are developed out of experience, which reach a final form of maximum adaptation to an interest, which are handed down by tradition and admit of no exception or variation, yet change to meet new conditions, still within the same limited methods, and without rational reflection or purpose. From this it results that all the life of human beings, in all ages and stages of culture, is primarily controlled by a vast mass of folkways handed down from the earliest existence of the race, having the nature of the ways of other animals, only the topmost layers of which are subject to change and control, and have been somewhat modified by human philosophy, ethics, and religion, or by other acts of intelligent reflection. We are told of savages that "It is difficult to exhaust the customs and small ceremonial usages of a savage people. Custom regulates the whole of a man's actions,—his bathing, washing, cutting his hair, eating, drinking, and fasting. From his cradle to his grave he is the slave of ancient usage. In his life there is nothing free, nothing original, nothing spontaneous, no progress towards a higher and better life, and no attempt to improve his condition, mentally, morally, or spiritually." All men act in this way with only a little wider margin of voluntary variation.

. . .

12. Tradition and its restraints. It is evident that the "ways" of the older and more experienced members of a society deserve great authority in any primitive group. We find that this rational authority leads to customs of deference and to etiquette in favor of the old. The old in turn cling stubbornly to tradition and to the example of their own predecessors. Thus tradition and custom become intertwined and are a strong coercion which directs the society upon fixed lines, and strangles liberty. Children see their parents always yield to the same custom and obey the same persons. They see that the elders are allowed to do all the talking, and that if an outsider enters, he is saluted by those who are at home according to rank and in fixed order. All this becomes rule for children, and helps to give to all primitive customs their stereotyped formality. "The fixed ways of looking at things which are inculcated by education and tribal discipline, are the precipitate of an old cultural development, and in their continued operation they are the moral anchor of the Indian, although they are also the fetters which restrain his individual will."

13. The concept of "primitive society"; we-group and others-group. The conception of "primitive society" which we ought to form is that of small groups scattered over a territory. The size of the groups is determined by the conditions of the struggle for existence. The internal organization of each group corresponds to its size. A group of groups may have some relation to each other (kin, neighborhood, alliance, connubium and commercium) which draws them together and differentiates them from others. Thus a differentiation arises between ourselves, the we-group, or in-group, and everybody else, or the others-groups, out-groups. The insiders in a we-group are in a relation of peace, order, law, government, and industry, to each other. Their relation to all outsiders, or others-groups, is one of war and plunder, except so far as agreements have modified it. If a group is exogamic, the women in it were born abroad somewhere. Other foreigners who might be found in it are adopted persons, guest friends, and slaves.

14. **Sentiments in the in-group and towards the out-group**. The relation of comradeship and peace in the we-group and that of hostility and war towards others-groups are correlative to each other. The exigencies of war with outsiders are what make peace inside, lest internal discord should weaken the we-group for war. These exigencies also make government and law in the in-group, in order to prevent quarrels and enforce discipline. Thus war and peace have reacted on each other and developed each other, one within the group, the other in the intergroup relation. The closer the neighbors, and the stronger they are, the intenser is the warfare, and then the intenser is the internal organization and discipline of each. Sentiments are produced to correspond. Loyalty to the group, sacrifice for it, hatred and contempt for outsiders, brotherhood within, warlikeness without,—all grow together, common products of the same situation. These relations and sentiments constitute a social philosophy. It is sanctified by connection with religion. Men of an others-group are outsiders with whose ancestors the ancestors of the we-group waged war. The ghosts of the latter will see with pleasure their descendants keep up the fight, and will help them. Virtue consists in killing, plundering, and enslaving outsiders.

15. **Ethnocentrism** is the technical name for this view of things in which one's own group is the center of everything, and all others are scaled and rated with reference to it. Folkways correspond to it to cover both the inner and the outer relation. Each group nourishes its own pride and vanity, boasts itself superior, exalts its own divinities, and looks with contempt on outsiders. Each group thinks its own folkways the only right ones, and if it observes that other groups have other folkways, these excite its scorn. Opprobrious epithets are derived from these differences. "Pig-eater," "cow-eater," "uncircumcised," "jabberers," are epithets of contempt and abomination. The Tupis called the Portuguese by a derisive epithet descriptive of birds which have feathers around their feet, on account of trousers. For our present purpose the most important fact is that ethnocentrism leads a people to exaggerate and intensify everything in their own folkways which is peculiar and which differentiates them from others. It therefore strengthens the folkways.

28   Charles Maurras, from *Les Oeuvres Capitales*, in J. S. McClelland (ed.), *The French Right* (Jonathan Cape, 1970), pp. 220–6

Born in the South of France, Maurras (1868–1952) was a writer of both poetic and philosophical ambitions who subsequently turned to politics. His major political legacy arises from his role as one of the founders of the ultra-nationalist movement *Action Française*. Though small numerically, it exercised considerable political influence within Europe, providing an important influence upon and foretaste of the fascist movements that would arise between the First and Second World Wars. Maurras was elected to the *Academie Francaise* in 1939, and emerged as the leading intellectual defender of the Vichy regime following the Nazi invasion. He propounded an increasingly virulent brand of anti-semitism in this period and justified the racial laws introduced by the French administration. He was given a life sentence for his collaboration with the Germans following the liberation of France by the Allies.

The French state, which meddles in everything today, even in schooling and the sale of matches, and which, as a result, does everything infinitely badly, distributing non-inflammable matches and hare-brained education, is powerless to fulfil its true function as a state. It has been handed over lock, stock and barrel to the representatives of the legislative. Ministers are nothing but clerks and servants to the senators and deputies and devote themselves exclusively to obeying these their masters in order to preserve the portfolios. As a forceful aphorism has it: 'The elector begs favours from the deputy, the deputy begs favours from the minister, the minister begs votes from the deputy, the deputy begs votes from the elector.' A class of citizens, heartily despised by the entire country, makes its living by a trade in influence and intrigue; senators, deputies, vote-jobbers—it is only by chance that one finds one single independent character in a thousand such individuals in that profession. Those of their number who pass for having clean hands merely testify to their own stupidity. On the very day of the Loubet election, one of our masters could write that the future representative in congress was distinguished above all by his intellectual inadequacy.

Invariably ignorant and limited, often impoverished and corrupt, these are the masters of France. We are told they can be changed. A change of personnel serves no purpose. A parliament, composed by some chance of enlightened men, would of necessity be very quickly replaced, like the Assembly of 1871, by a horde of agitators, catchers of the popular vote. If these newcomers are honest on their arrival, they will soon be corrupted by the working of the regime. The Count of Paris has rightly observed: 'These institutions corrupt their men, whoever they may be.'

What then is such a government? A shadow, a juxtaposition of meaningless syllables! One set of leaders is too much like another for any to stand out or prevail for long. Ten, twenty or thirty months is as long as the victory of any of their ministerial groups can endure: a republican cabinet, charged with the task of providing for the grave political and economic necessities of the nation, is incapable of lasting any longer. What department store or corner shop, what vegetable stall or shoeshine stand would survive this continual and systematic change of management? What industry would not be ruined if the board of directors was overthrown every ten, twenty or thirty months?

No minister has the time to study the services he is supposed to direct. It is only by good luck if he knows what they are. And so the poor fellow leaves his head civil servants to decide everything. From time to time, upon the command of some parliamentary group, he pushes them around with ignorant and violent passion. Thus we pass from routine to revolution with no possible happy medium. Neither genuine, stable and personal control, nor dependable tradition. Neither does our administration make any progress: it is only too happy to avoid its own downfall.

For this unstable ministerial direction is, furthermore, divided against itself to the point of madness. You do not even achieve unity of view in one minister. He has his political friends to satisfy, his adversaries to placate. Thus parliamentary manœuvre clashes with his general policy aims; the latter is totally subordinated to the former. As most ministers are drawn from the shameful class which lives on public funds, just as they exist only by courtesy of the class of their own vote-gathering pimps, the resources of the nations are put to the sack. Useless expenditure, electorally inspired, increases daily and the revenue declines for the same reasons. National defence, the industrial and commercial life of the nation, everything is sacrificed to the petty interests of the vote manufacturers. If a port is built, it is for them. It is for them that roads are laid. It is for them that railways are constructed. The general interest has but a miserable share in it. Our financial power is dissipated to satisfy the electoral clientele of influential deputies and senators just as our political power is frittered away in cementing the foundations of influence and in defending it with tenacity. Powerless to act in the public good, the regime, when it supposes itself to be in a position of strength, lavishes its fiscal resources and its powers of control upon the task of establishing its own supporters or consolidating the anarchy which reigns at their side.

This wastefulness and the lack of competent and continuous direction causes industry and commerce to dwindle, despite the artless illusion created by the 1900 Exhibition. Agriculture cannot sell its produce or only at low prices, and the political prestige of France follows the same curve of depression as her economic power. A power, without force to sustain it, which feebly administers rather than commands the army, has allowed itself to be flouted for two years now. This power, having at a diplomatic level and not without incoherence committed itself to the Fashoda venture, has been unable to extract itself from the mire except at the price of our collective shame. The Russian alliance has even ceased to figure in the vocabulary of Europe's conversations.

Bismarck undoubtedly foresaw many of our present misfortunes when he did all he could to dedicate us to the republican system. Bismarck was not ignorant of the fact that the strength of a state presupposes unity of view and the spirit of continuity, cohesion and organization. As a republican regime is synonymous with the absence of a master will and continuity of thought at the centre of power, he sensed the extent to which such a regime divides and condemns to perpetual upheaval any people that abandons itself to its tender mercies.

We are told by the parliamentary republicans as well as by the proponents of plebiscite, that this unstable and feeble power rests upon a solid base. The base they find so solid is the national will, as expressed by parliamentary elections or referenda.

From the national will springs, since in the national will resides, government authority. The very people who refuse the citizen the right to deal with the matters he knows best and to look after his own closest interests, the very people who refuse the municipal elector the right to change a public fountain or lay a path without state permission, are the ones who accord to the same citizen, the same elector, by the most astonishing of constitutional fictions, absolute power to make a judicious choice, to express a valid opinion on the most remote, the most profound, the most complex questions of general policy. This elector and citizen, whose competence to make the humblest decision was but a moment ago regarded as suspect, is suddenly supposed to possess all the intellectual powers of the Académie Française for he is called upon to choose between radical policy and opportunism, between authoritarian and liberal, between socialism and capitalism, and to acknowledge his right, by his choice and by his vote, to guide the direction of legislation, supreme justice, diplomacy, and the military and naval organization of the whole nation!

So staggering an illusion could never be fulfilled with integrity. Instead of complaining about it, we must recognize that it is unattainable and assert clearly that however independent, however honest, however intelligent the elector may be, he can never be competent to decide the majority of the questions put to him. This disability makes him either violent and blind or hesitant and fickle, or all simultaneously.

The French elector spends his time giving blank cheques to men he does not know, with no other guarantee than the fine shades of meaning written into the election posters upon which candidates publish their intentions. This system is an incentive, a stimulant, an imperative to the opposition parties (even the honest ones though it applies much more forcibly to the less honest) to provoke the greatest possible number of scandals and disasters in order to bring about as many changes as possible at each new election. In this way party interest replaces the public interest. In this way France sinks into decay.

What becomes of the state in all this? It becomes a slave. The slave of parliament. The slave of the parliamentary parties, of electoral deals. The slave of unforeseen events even, events which under such a regime unleash both panic and opinion changes, hence ministerial changes, changes of direction, events which are precisely those requiring for the public good the maximum possible of firmness, stability and self-control. At the very moment when it is most necessary to stand firm, the system compels the foundations to be shaken; Varron is kicked out at the very moment when, however incompetent or unworthy he may be, he should have received from the state an overwhelming demonstration of confidence. Subject to these multiple forms of slavery within, the French state finds itself similarly enslaved in its external relations. Other states tolerate its apparent independence solely for the purpose of giving it the maximum opportunity to decline, to degenerate and to disintegrate on its own.

29 Michael Oakeshott, from *Rationalism in Politics and Other Essays* (Methuen, 1962), pp. 3–7

Oakeshott (1901–1990) was one of the best known and most influential British political philosophers of the twentieth century. He was appointed to the Chair of Political Science at the London School of Economics in 1951. In 1933 he published *Experience and its Modes*, in which he sought to delineate the abiding characteristics of the main ways of interpreting human experience. Oakeshott turned to explicitly political matters following his wartime experiences in the early 1940s. He penned an Introduction to Hobbes's *Leviathan* (1946), and a number of other influential essays in this period. Several of these were subsequently collected in his *Rationalism in Politics and Other Essays*.

Now, of all worlds, the world of politics might seem the least amenable to rationalist treatment—politics, always so deeply veined with both the traditional, the circumstantial and the transitory. And, indeed, some convinced Rationalists have admitted defeat here: Clemenceau, intellectually a child of the modern Rationalist tradition (in his treatment of morals and religion, for example), was anything but a Rationalist in politics. But not all have admitted defeat. If we except religion, the greatest apparent victories of Rationalism have been in politics: it is not to be expected that whoever is prepared to carry his rationalism into the conduct of life will hesitate to carry it into the conduct of public affairs.

But what is important to observe in such a man (for it is characteristic) is not the decisions and actions he is inspired to make, but the source of his inspiration, his idea (and with him it will be a deliberate and conscious idea) of political activity. He believes, of course, in the open mind, the mind free from prejudice and its relic, habit. He believes that the unhindered human 'reason' (if only it can be brought to bear) is an infallible guide in political activity. Further, he believes in argument as the technique and operation of 'reason'; the truth of an opinion and the 'rational' ground (not the use) of an institution is all that matters to him. Consequently, much of his political activity consists in bringing the social, political, legal and institutional inheritance of his society before the tribunal of his intellect; and the rest is rational administration, 'reason' exercising an uncontrolled jurisdiction over the circumstances of the case. To the Rationalist, nothing is of value merely because it exists (and certainly not because it has existed for many generations), familiarity has no worth, and nothing is to be left standing for want of scrutiny. And his disposition makes both destruction and creation easier for him to understand and engage in, than acceptance or reform. To patch up, to repair (that is, to do anything which requires a patient knowledge of the material), he regards as waste of time; and he always prefers the invention of a new device to making use of a current and well-tried expedient. He does not recognize change unless it is a self-consciously induced change, and consequently he falls easily into the error of identifying the customary and the traditional with the changeless. This is aptly illustrated by the rationalist attitude towards a tradition of ideas. There is, of course, no question either of retaining or improving such a tradition, for both these involve an attitude of submission. It must be destroyed. And to fill its place the Rationalist puts something of his own making—an ideology, the formalized abridgment of the supposed substratum of rational truth contained in the tradition.

The conduct of affairs, for the Rationalist, is a matter of solving problems, and in this no man can hope to be successful whose reason has become inflexible by surrender to habit or is clouded by the fumes of tradition. In this activity the character which the Rationalist claims for himself is the character of the engineer, whose mind (it is supposed) is controlled throughout by the appropriate technique and whose first step is to dismiss from his attention everything not directly related to his specific intentions. This assimilation of politics to engineering is, indeed, what may be called the myth of rationalist politics. And it is, of course, a recurring theme in the literature of Rationalism. The politics it inspires may be called the politics of the felt need; for the Rationalist, politics are always charged with the feeling of the moment. He waits upon circumstance to provide him with his problems, but rejects its aid in their solution. That anything should be allowed to stand between a society and the satisfaction of the felt needs of each moment in its history must appear to the Rationalist a piece of mysticism and nonsense. And his politics are, in fact, the rational solution of those practical conundrums which the recognition of the sovereignty of the felt need perpetually creates in the life of a society. Thus, political life is resolved into a succession of crises, each to be surmounted by the application of 'reason'. Each generation, indeed, each administration, should see unrolled before it the blank sheet of infinite possibility. And if by chance this *tabula rasa* has been defaced by the irrational scribblings of tradition-ridden ancestors, then the first task of the Rationalist must be to scrub it clean; as Voltaire remarked, the only way to have good laws is to burn all existing laws and to start afresh.

Two other general characteristics of rationalist politics may be observed. They are the politics of perfection, and they are the politics of uniformity; either of these characteristics without the other denotes a different style of politics, the essence of rationalism is their combination. The evanescence of imperfection may be said to be the first item of the creed of the Rationalist. He is not devoid of humility; he can imagine a problem which would remain impervious to the onslaught of his own reason. But what he cannot imagine is politics which do not consist in solving problems, or a political problem of which there is no 'rational' solution at all. Such a problem must be counterfeit. And the 'rational' solution of any problem is, in its nature, the perfect solution. There is no place in his scheme for a 'best in the circumstances', only a place for 'the best'; because the function of reason is precisely to surmount circumstances. Of course, the Rationalist is not always a perfectionist in general, his mind governed in each occasion by a comprehensive Utopia; but invariably he is a perfectionist in detail. And from this politics of perfection springs the politics of uniformity; a scheme which does not recognize circumstance can have no place for variety. 'There must in the nature of things be one best form of government which all intellects, sufficiently roused from the slumber of savage ignorance, will be irresistibly incited to approve,' writes Godwin. This intrepid Rationalist states in general what a more modest believer might prefer to assert only in detail; but the principle holds—there may not be one universal remedy for all political ills, but the remedy for any particular ill is as universal in its application as it is rational in its conception. If the rational solution for one of the problems of a society has been determined, to permit any relevant part of the society to escape from the solution is, *ex hypothesi*, to countenance irrationality. There can be no place for preference that is not rational preference, and all rational preferences necessarily coincide. Political activity is recognized as the imposition of a uniform condition of perfection upon human conduct.

The modern history of Europe is littered with the projects of the politics of Rationalism. The most sublime of these is, perhaps, that of Robert Owen for 'a world convention to emancipate the human race from ignorance, poverty, division sin and misery'—so sublime that even a Rationalist (but without much justification) might think it eccentric. But not less characteristic are the diligent search of the present generation for an innocuous power which may safely be made so great as to be able to control all other powers in the human world, and the common disposition to believe that political machinery can take the place of moral and political education. The notion of founding a society, whether of individuals or of States, upon a Declaration of the Rights of Man is a creature of the rationalist brain, so also are 'national' or racial self-determination when elevated into universal principles. The project of the so-called Re-union of the Christian Churches, of open diplomacy, of a single tax, of a civil service whose members 'have no qualifications other than their personal abilities', of a self-consciously planned society, the Beveridge Report, the Education Act of 1944, Federalism, Nationalism, Votes for Women, the Catering Wages Act, the destruction of the Austro-Hungarian Empire, the World State (of H. G. Wells or anyone else), and the revival of Gaelic as the official language of Eire, are alike the progeny of Rationalism. The odd generation of rationalism in politics is by sovereign power out of romanticism.

30 Harold Macmillan, from *The Middle Way: A Study of the Problem of Economic and Social Progress in a Free and Democratic Society*, in *English Conservatism since the Restoration* (ed. R. Eccleshall; Unwin Hyman, 1990), pp. 192–4

Born into a prosperous Scottish family, Maurice Harold Macmillan (First Earl of Stockton: 1894–1986) entered political life after serving in the First World War. He was deeply influenced by the Disraelian brand of one-nation conservatism. He entered government in 1940 and provided its liaison with the Gaullist anti-Nazi forces based in North Africa. He became Minister of Housing and Local Government in the 1951 Conservative government, and subsequently took over as Minister for Defence. After the party's victory in 1955, he served briefly as Foreign Secretary and then became Chancellor of the Exchequer. As the Prime Minister, Anthony Eden, fell ill in the wake of the disastrous Suez crisis of 1956, Macmillan emerged as his successor. Under his leadership, the Conservative party won a large majority at the 1959 election.

This book is offered as a contribution towards the clearer formulation of the new ideas of society that have been slowly emerging since the political crisis of 1931. I hope it will be given sympathetic consideration by men and women of all parties who recognise that some new theory of social evolution must be conceived if we are to retain our heritage of political, intellectual, and cultural freedom while, at the same time, opening up the way to higher standards of social welfare and economic security . . .

I want to argue, therefore, for the deliberate preservation of private enterprise in a field lying outside the range of minimum human needs. I support it for the purely economic reasons that it ensures initiative, the adoption of new methods, the exploration of the market possibilities of new products, and speculative experimentation with new scientific discoveries. But, more than that, I mean to submit that freedom of individual initiative and enterprise in these fields is essential to the preservation of liberty, to the freedom of each person to live his life in his own way, and to provide for that diversity which is characteristic of the human mind.

But I do not propose to employ this defence of private enterprise in the fields for which it is best suited in order to condone or excuse the poverty and insecurity in the basic necessities of life, which we have today as a legacy of unrestrained competition and uneconomic waste and redundancy. I shall advocate all the more passionately on grounds of morality, of social responsibility, as well as of economic wisdom, a wide extension of social enterprise and control in the sphere of minimum human needs. The satisfaction of those needs is a duty which society owes to its citizens. In carrying out that responsibility it should adopt the most economical methods of large-scale co-operative enterprise. The volume of the supply of these necessities, the prices at which they are sold, and the power of the consumer to buy them should not be left to the determination of the push and pull of competitive effort. We have to evolve a new system by which the supply of those articles which we have classified as being of common need and more or less standardised in character, would be absorbed into an amplified conception of the social services . . .

The argument in favour of planning is not . . . some new and unheard-of principle. It is merely an extension of that principle of interference and regulation which has been common to the political thought of England since the first Factory Act was passed. But, if we are to become masters of our fate instead of slaves of circumstance, the principle must now be extended, and applied to a much wider field, because this has become essential in the changed conditions of today . . .

For as far ahead as we can see, it is both possible and desirable to find a solution of our economic difficulties in a mixed system which combines State ownership, regulation or control of certain aspects of economic activity with the drive and initiative of private enterprise in those realms of origination and expansion for which it is, by general admission, so admirably suited.

I realise, of course, that it is contended both by Socialist Planners and by Anti-Planners that this mixed system—this half-way house between a Free Capitalism and complete State Socialist planning—is an impossibility. They unite in claiming that we must be whole-hoggers or nothing; that we must, as it were, either leap forward into the twenty-first century or retreat into the nineteenth. I profoundly disagree with that view. Britain has been moving along the road towards economic planning for many years now in accordance with the traditional English principles of compromise and adjustment. Unless we can continue this peaceful evolution from a free capitalism to a planned capitalism, or, it may be, a new synthesis of Capitalist and Socialist theory, there will be little hope of preserving the civil, democratic, and cultural freedom which, limited as it may be at the moment by economic inefficiency, is a valuable heritage. It is only by the adoption of this middle course that we can avoid resorting to measures of political discipline and dictatorship. Such methods, whether exercised by the 'right' or by the 'left', are the very opposite of that liberation and freedom which mankind should be striving to achieve . . .

An adequate policy must therefore provide for—

(a) A form of industrial organisation which curbs unwise speculative over-expansion of any industry and assists by an intelligent system of market anticipation in guiding capital investment into the correct channels and in the correct proportions, to maintain a balance in the quantities of separate goods which, if stability is to be preserved, must exchange for one another.

(b) A method of ensuring that financial policy is conducted in such a way as to keep the factors of production at the highest possible degree of permanent employment.

(c) A method of insuring the consumer against a loss of purchasing power arising from unforeseen fluctuations, and which, by maintaining his standard of life at an irreducible minimum by means of social provisions, would check in its early stages any tendency towards depression that might still arise.

31 Roger Scruton, from *The Meaning of Conservatism* (Macmillan, 1981), pp. 38–45

Scruton (1944–) is one of England's most prominent contemporary political intellectuals. He was formerly Professor at Birkbeck College, London and at Boston University, Massachusetts. He has now established his position as a leading philosopher in tandem with the roles of novelist and composer. He has published extensively in the fields of political philosophy, aesthetics, and conservative thought. As one of the founders of the Conservative Philosophy Group, he helped gather together some of the most significant thinkers and commentators on the political right, who in turn influenced the climate of opinion and debate in the 1980s. And he served as editor of the important magazine *Salisbury Review* from 1982 until 2000. He is currently well-known for his public defence of the practice of fox-hunting and the value of rural traditions.

PATRIOTISM

We now begin to see the relevance of our second conservative axiom—the axiom that politics deals with the surface of social consciousness. A full understanding of the idea of allegiance will require in its turn an understanding of tradition, custom and ceremony—of the totality of practices through which the citizen is able to perceive his allegiance as an *end*. For the liberal, allegiance to society is a means: 'stick to this arrangement and on the whole you'll be left to yourself'. But the conservative cannot see it as a means to an end, since there is no description of the end in question that does not refer back to the values—and hence to the customs, institutions and allegiances—of those who pursue it. It follows that while the forms of patriotism will be many and varied, they will seek always to translate themselves into *symbolic* acts, acts which resist translation as 'means to an end'.

Consider the Englishman's allegiance to the Crown, as he envisages and enacts it. Monarchy is an institution, with a complex constitutional background, that elevates the person of the monarch above the realm of individual character and endows him or her with the dignity and, so to speak, the objectivity of office. It is not the personal qualities of the Queen that draw the Englishman to her nor is it any considered knowledge of the function and history of the Crown. It is rather a sense of the monarch as a symbol of nationhood, as an incarnation of the historical entity of which he is a part. His loyalty to the monarch requires ceremonial enactment, customary usage, an established code of deference: for this is the style of all symbolic gestures in which society and individual are merged.

Now a conservative is likely to value the institution of monarchy, and the kind of patriotism that it engenders. For the legitimacy of monarchical rule arises 'transcendentally', in the manner of the duties and obligations of family life. The monarch is not chosen for his personal attributes, nor does he have obligations and expectations which are the subject-matter of any 'social contract'. He is simply the representation of sovereignty, and its ceremonial presence. His will as monarch is not his individual will, but the will of state. The monarch forms part of that surface of concepts and symbols whereby the citizen can perceive his social identity, and perceive society not as a means to an end, but as an end in itself. Attachment to the monarch is therefore patriotism in a pure form, a form that could not be translated into attachment to a policy, or to a choice of means.

As a matter of fact, even when the titular head of state is 'chosen'—where there is an elected president, say, who offers 'promises' to the people—the choice is not in fact a choice of policy. The aims of politics, as they arise from day to day, are beyond the voter's competence, the ideals of social policy largely beyond his care. Usually, therefore, the president is chosen not as a means to an end, but as a peculiar kind of end in himself—as a 'figure of state'. Once again, he is a symbol. In a world of mass communication this means that a president will be chosen for his 'style', where style carries an implication of inward identity between president and nation, an identity that derives from no common end to which they might both be moving. This attachment to style represents an attempt to escape from the burden of democratic election, to escape from the 'contractual' element of the choice, to escape most of all from the sense of the state as constantly remade at each election, like a machine that has become outclassed. It is an expression of the conservative instinct, the instinct to make a future in the image of the past.

But just as the past constrains the future, so does the future commandeer the past. The past enacted by the citizen is the past *directed* to the future. Continuity is a selective aim; it looks both backwards and forwards with a measure of distrust. But we must remember the distinctive place of the past in our practical understanding: unlike the future, the past is *known*. How then should it enter our political calculations?

TRADITION

That question brings us to the final concept that will be necessary in giving articulate voice to the conservative instinct towards society, the concept of tradition. Under this concept I include all manner of custom, ceremony, and participation in institutional life, where what is done is done, not mechanically, but for a reason, and where the reason lies, not in what will be, but in what *has* been. It does not matter if the reason cannot be voiced by the man who obeys it: traditions are enacted and not designed, and none the less conscious for the lack of speech.

The power of tradition is twofold. First, it makes history into reason, and therefore the past into a present aim (as the whole history of the nation is enacted in the ceremony of coronation). Secondly, tradition arises from every organization in society, and is no mere trapping of the exercise of power. Traditions arise and command respect wherever the individual seeks to relate himself to something transcendent. They arise in clubs and societies, in local life, in religion and family custom, in education, and in every institution where man is brought into contact with his kind. Later, in considering questions of politics, we must show how the state can bring authority, allegiance, and tradition together, in order to define the citizen as *subject*.

I am aware that any reference to tradition will cause scepticism among those who believe themselves free from its charm. And there is no doubt that, while the concept may be essential to conservative dogma, it will also (like the 'equality', 'freedom' and 'social justice' which rival it) have to bear more weight of political argument than any single conception can sustain. But we must do our best for it. Whatever difficulties may attend the enterprise of defending tradition, the fight concerns no fiction but a genuine reality. Now it is salutary at this juncture to compare the realms of politics and art. Both activities are imbued with significance and purposefulness, and yet neither (on the conservative view) has any real external purpose. Art shows in microcosm the great architectural problem of politics as we are beginning to envisage it. And the comparison enables us to see why we should consider again the complaint that conservatism holds no prospect for the 'modern man': that it is far from being the impulse of life in death, but rather the will for death in life. For in art too we have felt the cravings, the disorientation, the overwhelming estrangement of 'modern' man, and in art too it has seemed necessary to present as self-conscious what was previously felt as nature, instinct and life.

But in the very sphere where the embattled consciousness of 'modern man' has most displayed itself, so too has the conservative principle been repeatedly affirmed. By this I do not mean that the artists who brought about the major aesthetic achievements of our century were, politically, of a conservative cast. If this is true, then it is only an instance of a more general truth—swallowed with some difficulty by critics of the New Left—that significant artists can be, and very often are, that way. (It is interesting to note the frequency with which it has been assumed, since the Romantic movement, that art must necessarily be a revolutionary force, simply because it has revolutionized *itself*. The assumption looks very odd when set beside the varieties of social conservatism expressed and advocated by James, Conrad, Yeats, Pound, Eliot, Joyce, Waugh and Lawrence—to name only the greatest of those who created our modern literature.)

What does it mean, then, to say that the conservative principle has been repeatedly reaffirmed in contemporary art? Partly this: that for most significant artists—for Eliot, Pound and Joyce, for Schoenberg and Stravinsky, for Braque and Moore—the problem of giving articulate voice to the modern consciousness was conceived as the problem of making that consciousness part of a *tradition* of artistic expression, and so bringing it back, by whatever complicated route, to the point where it might be understood. For Schoenberg the tradition of German music was what principally mattered: the problem was to re-create it, through self-conscious understanding of its inner life. The 'live tradition' that Pound hoped to 'gather from the air' was conceived in equally self-conscious terms. Eliot went so far as to represent tradition as an individual artifact: to belong to a tradition is also to make that tradition; to be part of history is to have created history. However, this process, which begins in loss and in conscious exploration, ends too in genuine discovery, the discovery that 'History is now and England'. In that discovery is a restoration of the whole of things.

It would be interesting to digress further into the transformation of the idea of tradition in the mind of alienated man. But let us simply draw the obvious conclusion from our parallel. Just as tradition circumscribes the possibilities of artistic expression, and so must be constantly re-created in artistic change, so too does it lay down the forms of political life, and must be re-created in every conscious political act. Now it is both difficult and yet (it seems) at the same time necessary for the modern consciousness to create tradition, setting itself in the centre of tradition as it sets tradition in the centre of itself. It may require an act of imagination, insight and will for a politician, in the midst of confusion, to reassert the identity of the society that he seeks to govern, even when, in their most secret innervations, it is just such an adventure that the people require from him. His route back to that place he started from will not find the place unchanged, and the way will be hard and uncertain. He will need exceptional qualities—the qualities of a De Gaulle or a Disraeli—if he is to reaffirm as a statesman the reality which he knows as a man. Yet, if he has the will to live, and the will to govern, nothing short of that can satisfy him.

As one writer has suggested, there is no general explanation of *how* men re-create and accept traditions. Nor is it easy to draw the line between genuine re-creation and the establishment of new and divergent social forms. But in all attempts to restore, re-create and assimilate tradition, the feature of continuity remains. When a man acts from tradition he sees what he *now* does as belonging to a pattern that transcends the focus of his present interest, binding it to what has previously been done, and done successfully. (This is obvious from the case of artistic creation.) Naturally there are rival traditions, and it would be vain to pretend that there is reason to belong to *all* of them. There are traditions of torture, crime and revolution. The traditions which the conservative fosters and upholds must therefore satisfy independent criteria. First, they must have the weight of a *successful* history—which is to say that they must be the palpable remainder of something that has flourished, and not the latest in a series of abortive starts. Secondly, they must engage the loyalty of their participants, in the deep sense of moulding their idea of what they are and should be. (Contrast the traditions of family life with those of torture.) Finally, they must point to something durable, something which survives and gives meaning to the acts that emerge from it.

But what does this tradition concretely amount to? No simple answer to this question can prove satisfactory: the task of dogma is to bridge the gap between philosophy and practice, and it is only in practice that the sum of our traditions can be understood. Nevertheless, it still belongs to dogma to delineate the *kind* of thing that is intended, and to present some partial exposition of its instances. Tradition, then, must include all those practices which serve to define the individual's 'being in society'. It constitutes his image of himself as a fragment of the greater social organism, and at the same time as the whole of that organism implicit in this individual part. The institution of the family, as it has variously developed, provides a clear example. No man who participates in that institution can remain unaffected in his conception of himself. He can no longer regard the fact of fatherhood, for example, as a biological accident. In seeing himself as father he finds himself entangled in a social bond, a bond of responsibility. And the reason for this bond and for the actions which express it, lies in the fact that this is how things are. Moreover, they are like this because they have been like this. The idea of 'family', through which his responsibilities, aims and preoccupations are from day to day defined, is one inherited without thought from his own participation in the arrangement which it designates. This is what is 'given'. Had he not conceived his activities as exemplifying the historical pattern contained in that concept, then he would nevertheless have needed some adequate replacement, some rival conception in terms of which to define his ends. And if this conception does not belong to tradition it will make way for the dangerous thought: 'Perhaps I do this, not for its own sake, not for what it *is*, but as a means to an end. Where then is the end? Where is the profit?' This thought signifies the emergence of the individual from social life, and the first glimpse of the empty solipsism that waits outside. Tradition restores the individual to the present act: it shows the reason *in* the act, and stills the desire for a justifying aim.

The family is of course an obvious example. But there are others, such as the customs which surround the momentous occasions of birth, coupling and death, the customs of hospitality, rivalry and class allegiance, of manners, dress and common courtesy. There are also the institutions of religion, in which man's desire for an identity greater than his nature provides reaches out of history altogether, to what is outside time and change. Only some of these institutions, it might be thought, are truly political. But to take such a view is to take too narrow a view of politics. Every tradition of any importance in the life of the citizen will tend to become part of the establishment of a state. This principle—which we might call the law of establishment and which I shall illustrate in Chapter 8—is part of the natural history of politics, and shows the continuing necessity for political action to extend beyond the bounds of economic management. It is illustrated not only by the explicit establishment of the Church and, through the operation of law, of the family and private property, but by the implicit establishment of class rule in parliamentary institutions, by the more recent establishment of the traditions of organized labour in the trade-union movement, and by the extension of law (less automatic in America than in England, but manifest even there) to protect every aspect of social life, just so soon as it seems to be of more than individual concern.

A NOTE OF SCEPTICISM

What of the conservative attitude to social transformation? What 'tradition' has force, in comparison with the violence of industrial expansion and of over-population, with the spread of irreligion, and the growth of the urban working-class? Is there not an element of make-believe in the view that allegiance, authority and custom might have survived these historical convulsions, so as still to provide the bond from which politics derives its inspiration and appeal?

If this scepticism is the prelude to a rival politics, then it calls for only one reply: what other bond are you imagining? And how will you bring it about? But usually it takes a more unsettling form, the form, as one might put it, of the 'broad historical perspective'. It makes no recommendations, espouses no policies, and stands above the particular beliefs of the communities which it seeks to observe. The historical perspective looks down on the world of men from a height where their activity is seen only as the movement of impersonal forces, which propel the politician precisely when he most believes that he is guiding them. Withdrawing to this height, it may for the moment seem as though the task of discovering and asserting continuity is a hopeless one, that all things have changed utterly, and that in nothing is there a lasting principle of government.

I shall try to answer certain common forms of this historian's doubt. But two things should be said at once in reply to it. First, some of the items of dogma that I have considered have a philosophical basis which places them beyond the reach of historical criticism. The view of society as requiring forms of allegiance, and a recognition of authority, both of which transcend the operation of any contractual bond, is a view not of this or that community, but of the essence of civil life. It is this transcendent bond that constitutes society, and which is misrepresented by the liberal theories of contract and consent. Moreover, one particular tradition, which both embodies a transcendent bond, and also reinforces social allegiance, has survived all the upheavals of recent history. This is the tradition of family life. Even a 'revolutionary state' will find itself dependent upon it, and placed under the necessity to create (usually through the old expedient of belligerent foreign policy) the corresponding bond of social unity.

Secondly, it may be true that particular bonds of allegiance have decayed or fallen apart. But if some people *think* (in their vociferous part) that the bond of British citizenship has been loosened or undone, this does not show that their thought corresponds either to reality or to the true political sentiments which guide them. Much is disturbed; old allegiances have gone under and new ones risen in their place. But through all this, I shall argue, the conservative can find and uphold a genuine continuity. And his reason for doing so will be apparent in the attempt.

Concluding Remarks

I have surveyed the great 'datum' of civil society. What, then, are the dogmas to which that survey gives support? There are two principles so basic as to constitute axioms of conservative thinking. First, the principle that there is no general politics of conservatism. The forms of conservatism will be as varied as the forms of social order. Second, the principle that conservatism engages with the surface of things, with the motives, reasons, traditions and values of the society from which it draws its life. There are further dogmas, abstract in their origin, but specific in their implications. Society exists through authority, and the recognition of this authority requires the allegiance to a bond that is not contractual but transcendent, in the manner of the family tie. Such allegiance requires tradition and custom through which to find enactment. But tradition is no static thing. It is the active achievement of continuity; it can be restored, rescued and amended as grace and opportunity allow.

Having discovered the allegiance of society, the conservative seeks to lend to it the support of a constituted state. It is therefore to the political implications of social life, and the constitution of the order in which it is lived, that we now must turn.

32   Friedrich August von Hayek, from *The Constitution of Liberty* (Routledge & Kegan Paul, 1960), pp. 253–8

Born in Vienna, Hayek (1899–1992) was a talented student in the fields of economics, philosophy, and psychology who was originally drawn towards socialist ideas. He was later a key member of the leading 'Austrian school' of economics which invoked the tenets of economic liberalism against its socialist opponents. He proved an adept contributor on a number of technical problems, notably business cycle theory. In 1931 he took up the post of Professor at the London School of Economics where he began a lengthy and famous exchange with John Maynard Keynes over monetary theory. From the early 1940s, he broadened his intellectual agenda and began to address questions of political philosophy and epistemology, as well as economics. He was Professor at the University of Chicago, 1950–1962, and received the Nobel Prize for Economics in 1974.

THE DECLINE OF SOCIALISM AND THE RISE OF THE WELFARE STATE

Experience should teach us to be most on our guard to protect liberty when the Government's purposes are beneficent. Men born to freedom are naturally alert to repel invasion of their liberty by evil-minded rulers. The greatest dangers to liberty lurk in insidious encroachment by men of zeal, well meaning but without understanding.

L. BRANDEIS

1. Efforts toward social reform, for something like a century, have been inspired mainly by the ideals of socialism—during part of this period even in countries like the United States which never has had a socialist party of importance. Over the course of these hundred years socialism captured a large part of the intellectual leaders and came to be widely regarded as the ultimate goal toward which society was inevitably moving. This development reached its peak after the second World War, when Britain plunged into her socialist experiment. This seems to have marked the high tide of the socialist advance. Future historians will probably regard the period from the revolution of 1848 to about 1948 as the century of European socialism.

During this period socialism had a fairly precise meaning and a definite program. The common aim of all socialist movements was the nationalization of the "means of production, distribution, and exchange," so that all economic activity might be directed according to a comprehensive plan toward some ideal of social justice. The various socialist schools differed mainly in the political methods by which they intended to bring about the reorganization of society. Marxism and Fabianism differed in that the former was revolutionary and the latter gradualist; but their conceptions of the new society they hoped to create were basically the same. Socialism meant the common ownership of the means of production and their "employment for use, not for profit."

The great change that has occurred during the last decade is that socialism in this strict sense of a particular method of achieving social justice has collapsed. It has not merely lost its intellectual appeal; it has also been abandoned by the masses so unmistakably that socialist parties everywhere are searching for a new program that will insure the active support of their followers. They have not abandoned their ultimate aim, their ideal of social justice. But the methods by which they had hoped to achieve this and for which the name "socialism" had been coined have been discredited. No doubt the name will be transferred to whatever new program the existing socialist parties will adopt. But socialism in the old definite sense is now dead in the Western world.

Though such a sweeping statement will still cause some surprise, a survey of the stream of disillusionist literature from socialist sources in all countries and the discussions inside the socialist parties amply confirm it. To those who watch merely the developments inside a single country, the decline of socialism may still seem no more than a temporary setback, the reaction to political defeat. But the international character and the similarity of the developments in the different countries leave no doubt that it is more than that. If, fifteen years ago, doctrinaire socialism appeared as the main danger to liberty, today it would be tilting at windmills to direct one's argument against it. Most of the arguments that were directed at socialism proper can now be heard from within the socialist movements as arguments for a change of program.

2.   The reasons for this change are manifold. So far as the socialist school which at one time was most influential is concerned, the example of the "greatest social experiment" of our time was decisive: Marxism was killed in the Western world by the example of Russia. But for a long time comparatively few intellectuals comprehended that what had happened in Russia was the necessary outcome of the systematic application of the traditional socialist program. Today, however, it is an effective argument, even within socialist circles, to ask: "If you want one hundred per cent socialism, what's wrong with the Soviet Union?" But the experience of that country has in general discredited only the Marxist brand of socialism. The widespread disillusionment with the basic methods of socialism is due to more direct experiences.

The chief factors contributing to the disillusionment were probably three: the increasing recognition that a socialist organization of production would be not more but much less productive than private enterprise; an even clearer recognition that, instead of leading to what had been conceived as greater social justice, it would mean a new arbitrary and more inescapable order of rank than ever before; and the realization that, instead of the promised greater freedom, it would mean the appearance of a new despotism.

The first to be disappointed were those labor unions which found that, when they had to deal with the state instead of a private employer, their power was greatly reduced. But the individuals also soon discovered that to be confronted everywhere by the authority of the state was no improvement upon their position in a competitive society. This happened at a time when the general rise in the standard of living of the working class (especially of the manual workers) destroyed the conception of a distinct proletarian class and, with it, the class-consciousness of the workers—creating in most of Europe a situation similar to that which in the United States had always prevented the growth of an organized socialist movement. In the countries that had experienced a totalitarian regime there also took place a strong individualist reaction among the younger generation, who became deeply distrustful of all collective activities and suspicious of all authority.

Perhaps the most important factor in the disillusionment of socialist intellectuals has been the growing apprehension among them that socialism would mean the extinction of individual liberty. Though the contention that socialism and individual liberty were mutually exclusive had been indignantly rejected by them when advanced by an opponent, it made a deep impression when stated in powerful literary form by one from their own midst. More recently the situation has been very frankly described by one of the leading intellectuals of the British Labour Party. Mr. R. H. S. Crossman, in a pamphlet entitled *Socialism and the New Despotism*, records how "more and more serious-minded people are having second thoughts about what once seemed to them the obvious advantages of central planning and the extension of State ownership"; and he continues to explain that "the discovery that the Labour Government's 'Socialism' meant the establishment of vast bureaucratic corporations," of "a vast centralized State bureaucracy [which] constitutes a grave potential threat to democracy," had created a situation in which "the main task of socialists today is to convince the nation that its liberties are threatened by this new feudalism."

3. But, though the characteristic methods of collectivist socialism have few defenders left in the West, its ultimate aims have lost little of their attraction. While the socialists no longer have a clear-cut plan as to how their goals are to be achieved, they still wish to manipulate the economy so that the distribution of incomes will be made to conform to their conception of social justice. The most important outcome of the socialist epoch, however, has been the destruction of the traditional limitations upon the powers of the state. So long as socialism aimed at a complete reorganization of society on new principles, it treated the principles of the existing system as mere encumbrances to be swept away. But now that it no longer has any distinctive principles of its own, it can only present its new ambitions without any clear picture of the means. As a result, we approach the new tasks set by the ambition of modern man as un-principled, in the original meaning of this word, as never before.

What is significant is that, in consequence, though socialism has been generally abandoned as a goal to be deliberately striven for, it is by no means certain that we shall not still establish it, albeit unintentionally. The reformers who confine themselves to whatever methods appear to be the most effective for their particular purposes and pay no attention to what is necessary to preserve an effective market mechanism are likely to be led to impose more and more central control over economic decisions (though private property may be preserved in name) until we get that very system of central planning which few now consciously wish to see established. Furthermore, many of the old socialists have discovered that we have already drifted so far in the direction of a redistributive state that it now appears much easier to push further in that direction than to press for the somewhat discredited socialization of the means of production. They seem to have recognized that by increasing governmental control of what nominally remains private industry, they can more easily achieve that redistribution of incomes that had been the real aim of the more spectacular policy of expropriation.

It is sometimes regarded as unfair, as blind conservative prejudice, to criticize those socialist leaders who have so frankly abandoned the more obviously totalitarian forms of "hot" socialism, for having now turned to a "cold" socialism which in effect may not be very different from the former. We are in danger, however, unless we succeed in distinguishing those of the new ambitions which can be achieved in a free society from those which require for their realization the methods of totalitarian collectivism.

4. Unlike socialism, the conception of the welfare state has no precise meaning. The phrase is sometimes used to describe any state that "concerns" itself in any manner with problems other than those of the maintenance of law and order. But, though a few theorists have demanded that the activities of government should be limited to the maintenance of law and order, such a stand cannot be justified by the principle of liberty. Only the coercive measures of government need be strictly limited. We have already seen [in chap. xv] that there is undeniably a wide field for non-coercive activities of government and that there is a clear need for financing them by taxation.

Indeed, no government in modern times has ever confined itself to the "individualist minimum" which has occasionally been described, nor has such confinement of governmental activity been advocated by the "orthodox" classical economists. All modern governments have made provision for the indigent, unfortunate, and disabled and have concerned themselves with questions of health and the dissemination of knowledge. There is no reason why the volume of these pure service activities should not increase with the general growth of wealth. There are common needs that can be satisfied only by collective action and which can be thus provided for without restricting individual liberty. It can hardly be denied that, as we grow richer, that minimum of sustenance which the community has always provided for those not able to look after themselves, and which can be provided outside the market, will gradually rise, or that government may, usefully and without doing any harm, assist or even lead in such endeavors. There is little reason why the government should not also play some role, or even take the initiative, in such areas as social insurance and education, or temporarily subsidize certain experimental developments. Our problem here is not so much the aims as the methods of government action.

References are often made to those modest and innocent aims of governmental activity to show how unreasonable is any opposition to the welfare state as such. But, once the rigid position that government should not concern itself at all with such matters is abandoned—a position which is defensible but has little to do with freedom—the defenders of liberty commonly discover that the program of the welfare state comprises a great deal more that is represented as equally legitimate and unobjectionable. If, for instance, they admit that they have no objection to pure-food laws, this is taken to imply that they should not object to any government activity directed toward a desirable end. Those who attempt to delimit the functions of government in terms of aims rather than methods thus regularly find themselves in the position of having to oppose state action which appears to have only desirable consequences or of having to admit that they have no general rule on which to base their objections to measures which, though effective for particular purposes, would in their aggregate effect destroy a free society. Though the position that the state should have nothing to do with matters not related to the maintenance of law and order may seem logical so long as we think of the state solely as a coercive apparatus, we must recognize that, as a service agency, it may assist without harm in the achievement of desirable aims which perhaps could not be achieved otherwise. The reason why many of the new welfare activities of government are a threat to freedom, then, is that, though they are presented as mere service activities, they really constitute an exercise of the coercive powers of government and rest on its claiming exclusive rights in certain fields.

33 Ayn Rand, from *The Fountainhead* (Grafton, 1972), pp. 663–9

Rand (1905–1982) was born in St. Petersburg in Russia. Deeply alienated by the Bolshevik revolution, she moved to Los Angeles, aged twenty-one, and became a Hollywood screenwriter. In her various writings she was a vigorous proponent of the virtue of selfishness.

She sought to propound a moral case for free enterprise, the only economic system based on what she labelled 'objective reason'. In her various novels, an archetypal hero emerges—a (male) figure who celebrates the virtues of self-interest against opponents who promulgate socialism. This pattern is followed in her most famous work, *The Fountainhead* (see the extract below) which tells the story of an architect, Howard Roark, whose plan for the redesign of a public housing complex is frustrated by the state. Rand was one of the first intellectuals to make an unapologetic public case for supply-side economics. She was an important influence too upon the fledgling Libertarian Party of the 1970s, and remains a cult figure among right-wing American students.

The judge looked at Roark.

"Proceed," he said. His voice was gentle.

Roark got up "Your Honour, I shall call no witnesses. This will be my testimony and my summation."

"Take the oath."

Roark took the oath. He stood by the steps of the witness-stand. The audience looked at him. They felt he had no chance. They could drop the nameless resentment, the sense of insecurity which he aroused in most people. And so, for the first time, they could see him as he was: a man totally innocent of fear.

The fear of which they thought was not the normal kind, not a response to a tangible danger, but the chronic, unconfessed fear in which they all lived. They remembered the misery of the moments when, in loneliness, a man thinks of the bright words he could have said, but had not found and hates those who robbed him of his courage. The misery of knowing how strong and able one is in one's own mind, the radiant picture never to be made real. Dreams? Self-delusion? Or a murdered reality, unborn, killed by that corroding emotion without name—fear—need—dependence—hatred?

Roark stood before them as each man stands in the innocence of his own mind. But Roark stood like that before a hostile crowd—and they knew suddenly that no hatred was possible to him. For the flash of an instant, they grasped the manner of his consciousness. Each asked himself: Do I need anyone's approval?—does it matter?—am I tied? And for that instant, each man was free—free enough to feel benevolence for every other man in the room.

It was only a moment; the moment of silence when Roark was about to speak.

"Thousands of years ago, the first man discovered how to make fire. He was probably burned at the stake he had taught his brothers to light. He was considered an evildoer who had dealt with a demon mankind dreaded. But thereafter men had fire to keep them warm, to cook their food, to light their caves. He had left them a gift they had not conceived and he had lifted darkness off the earth. Centuries later, the first man invented the wheel. He was probably torn on the rack he had taught his brothers to build. He was considered a transgressor who ventured into forbidden territory. But thereafter, men could travel past any horizon. He had left them a gift they had not conceived and he had opened the roads of the world.

"That man, the unsubmissive and first, stands in the opening chapter of every legend mankind has recorded about its beginning. Prometheus was chained to a rock and torn by vultures—because he had stolen the fire of the gods. Adam was condemned to suffer—because he had eaten the fruit of the tree of knowledge. Whatever the legend, somewhere in the shadows of its memory mankind knew that its glory began with one, and that that one paid for his courage.

"Throughout the centuries there were men who took first steps down new roads armed with nothing but their own vision. Their goals differed, but they all had this in common: that the step was first, the road new, the vision unborrowed, and the response they received—hatred. The great creators—the thinkers, the artists, the scientists, the inventors—stood alone against the men of their time. Every great new thought was opposed. Every great new invention was denounced. The first motor was considered foolish. The aeroplane was considered impossible. The power loom was considered vicious. Anaesthesia was considered sinful. But the men of unborrowed vision went ahead. They fought, they suffered and they paid. But they won.

"No creator was prompted by a desire to serve his brothers, for his brothers rejected the gift he offered and that gift destroyed the slothful routine of their lives. His truth was his only motive. His own truth, and his own work to achieve it in his own way. A symphony, a book, an engine, a philosophy, an aeroplane or a building—that was his goal and his life. Not those who heard, read, operated, believed, flew or inhabited the thing he had created. The creation, not its users. The creation, not the benefits others derived from it. The creation which gave form to his truth. He held his truth above all things and against all men.

"His vision, his strength, his courage came from his own spirit. A man's spirit, however, is his self. That entity which is his consciousness. To think, to feel, to judge, to act are functions of the ego.

"The creators were not selfless. It is the whole secret of their power—that it was self-sufficient, self-motivated, self-generated. A first cause, a fount of energy, a life force, a Prime Mover. The creator served nothing and no one. He lived for himself.

"And only by living for himself was he able to achieve the thing which are the glory of mankind. Such is the nature of achievement.

"Man cannot survive except through his mind. He comes on earth unarmed. His brain is his only weapon. Animals obtain food by force. Man had no claws, no fangs, no horns, no great strength of muscle. He must plant his food or hunt it. To plant, he needs a process of thought. To hunt, he needs weapons, and to make weapons—a process of thought. From this simplest necessity to the highest religious abstraction, from the wheel to the skyscraper, everything we are and everything we have comes from a single attribute of man—the function of his reasoning mind.

"But the mind is an attribute of the individual. There is no such thing as a collective brain. There is no such thing as a collective thought. An agreement reached by a group of men is only a compromise or an average drawn upon many individual thoughts. It is a secondary consequence. The primary act—the process of reason—must be performed by each man alone. We can divide a meal among many men. We cannot digest it in a collective stomach. No man can use his lungs to breathe for another man. No man can use his brain to think for another. All the functions of body and spirit are private. They cannot be shared or transferred.

"We inherit the products of the thought of other men. We inherit the wheel. We make a cart. The cart becomes an automobile. The automobile becomes an aeroplane. But all through the process what we receive from others is only the end product of their thinking. The moving force is the creative faculty which takes this product as material, uses it and originates the next step. This creative faculty cannot be given or received, shared or borrowed. It belongs to single, individual men. That which it creates is the property of the creator. Men learn from one another. But all learning is only the exchange of material. No man can give another the capacity to think. Yet that capacity is our only means of survival.

"Nothing is given to man on earth. Everything he needs has to be produced. And here man faces his basic alternative: he can survive in only one of two ways—by the independent work of his own mind or as a parasite fed by the minds of others. The creator originates. The parasite borrows. The creator faces nature alone. The parasite faces nature through an intermediary.

"The creator's concern is the conquest of nature. The parasite's concern is the conquest of men.

"The creator lives for his work. He needs no other men. His primary goal is within himself. The parasite lives second-hand. He needs other. Others become his prime motive.

"The basic need of the creator is independence. The reasoning mind cannot work under any form of compulsion. It cannot be curbed, sacrificed or subordinated to any consideration whatsoever. It demands total independence in function and in motive. To a creator, all relations with men are secondary.

"The basic need of the second-hander is to secure his ties with men in order to be fed. He declares relations first. He declares that man exists in order to serve others. He preaches altruism.

"Altruism is the doctrine which demands that man live for others and place others above self.

"No man can live for another. He cannot share his spirit just as he cannot share his body. But the second-hander has used altruism as a weapon of exploitation and reversed the base of mankind's moral principles. Men have been taught every precept that destroys the creator. Men have been taught dependence as a virtue.

"The man who attempts to live for others is a dependant. He is a parasite in motive and makes parasites of those he serves. The relationship produces nothing but mutual corruption. It is impossible in concept. The nearest approach to it in reality—the man who lives to serve others—is the slave. If physical slavery is repulsive, how much more repulsive is the concept of servility of the spirit? The conquered slave has a vestige of honour. He has the merit of having resisted and of considering his condition evil. But the man who enslaves himself voluntarily in the name of love is the basest of creatures. He degrades the dignity of man and he degrades the conception of love. But this is the essence of altruism.

"Men have been taught that the highest virtue is not to achieve, but to give. Yet one cannot give that which has not been created. Creation comes before distribution—or there will be nothing to distribute. The need of the creator comes before the need of any possible beneficiary. Yet we are taught to admire the second-hander who dispenses gifts he has not produced above the man who made the gifts possible. We praise an act of charity. We shrug at an act of achievement.

"Men have been taught that their first concern is to relieve the suffering of others. But suffering is a disease. Should one come upon it, one tries to give relief and assistance.

To make that the highest test of virtue is to make suffering the most important part of life. Then man must wish to see others suffer—in order that he may be virtuous. Such is the nature of altruism. The creator is not concerned with disease, but with life. Yet the work of the creators has eliminated one form of disease after another, in man's body and spirit, and brought more relief from suffering than any altruist could ever conceive.

"Men have been taught that it is a virtue to agree with others. But the creator is the man who disagrees. Men have been taught that it is a virtue to swim with the current. But the creator is the the man who goes against the current. Men have been taught that it is a virtue to stand together. But the creator is the man who stands alone.

"Men have been taught that the ego is the synonym of evil, and selflessness the ideal of virtue. But the creator is the egotist in the absolute sense, and the selfless man is the one who does not think, feel, judge, or act. These are functions of the self.

"Here the basic reversal is most deadly. The issue has been perverted and man has been left no alternative—and no freedom. As poles of good and evil, he was offered two conceptions: egotism and altruism. Egotism was held to mean the sacrifice of others to self. Altruism—the sacrifice of self to others. This tied man irrevocably to other men and left him nothing but a choice of pain: his own pain borne for the sake of others or pain inflicted upon others for the sake of self. When it was added that man must find joy in self-immolation, the trap was closed. Man was forced to accept masochism as his ideal—under the threat that sadism was his only alternative. This was the greatest fraud ever perpetrated on mankind.

"This was the device by which dependence and suffering were perpetuated as fundamentals of life.

"The choice is not self-sacrifice or domination. The choice is independence or dependence. The code of the creator or the code of the second-hander. This is the basic issue. It rests upon the alternative of life or death. The code of the creator is built on the needs of the reasoning mind which allows man to survive. The code of the second-hander is built on the needs of a mind incapable of survival. All that which proceeds from man's independent ego is good. All that which proceeds from man's dependence upon men is evil.

"The egotist in the absolute sense is not the man who sacrifices others. He is the man who stands above the need of using others in any manner. He does not function through them. He is not concerned with them in any primary matter. Not in his aim, not in his motive, not in his thinking, not in his desires, not in the source of his energy. He does not exist for any other man—and he asks no other man to exist for him. This is the only form of brotherhood and mutual respect possible between men.

"Degrees of ability vary, but the basic principle remains the same: the degree of a man's independence, initiative and personal love for his work determines his talent as a worker and his worth as a man. Independence is the only gauge of human virtue and value. What a man is and makes of himself; not what he has or hasn't done for others. There is no substitute for personal dignity. There is no standard of personal dignity except independence.

"In all proper relationships there is no sacrifice of anyone to anyone. An architect needs clients, but he does not subordinate his work to their wishes. They need him, but they do not order a house just to give him a commission. Men exchange their work by free, mutual consent to mutual advantage when their personal interests agree and they both desire the exchange. If they do not desire it, they are not forced to deal with each other. They seek further. This is the only possible form of relationship between equals. Anything else is a relation of slave to master, or victim to executioner.

"No work is ever done collectively, by a majority decision. Every creative job is achieved under the guidance of a single individual thought. An architect requires a great many men to erect his building. But he does not ask them to vote on his design. They work together by free agreement and each is free in his proper function. An architect uses steel, glass, concrete, produced by others. But the materials remain just so much steel, glass and concrete until he touches them. What he does with them is his individual product and his individual property. This is the only pattern for proper co-operation among men.

"The first right on earth is the right of the ego. Man's first duty is to himself. His moral law is never to place his prime goal within the persons of others. His moral obligation is to do what he wishes, provided his wish does not depend *primarily* upon other men. This includes the whole sphere of his creative faculty, his thinking, his work. But it does not include the sphere of the gangster, the altruist and the dictator.

"A man thinks and works alone. A man cannot rob, exploit or rule—alone. Robbery, exploitation and ruling presuppose victims. They imply dependence. They are the province of the second-hander.

"Rulers of men are not egotists. They create nothing. They exist entirely through the persons of others. Their goal is in their subjects in the activity of enslaving. They are as dependent as the beggar, the social worker and the bandit. The form of dependence does not matter.

"But men were taught to regard second-handers—tyrants, emperors, dictators—as exponents of egotism. By this fraud they were made to destroy the ego, themselves and others. The purpose of the fraud was to destroy the creators. Or to harness them. Which is a synonym.

"From the beginning of history, the two antagonists have stood face to face: the creator and the second-hander. When the first creator invented the wheel, the first second-hander responded. He invented altruism.

"The creator—denied, opposed, persecuted, exploited—went on, moved forward and carried all humanity along on his energy. The second-hander contributed nothing to the process except the impediments. The contest has another name: the individual against the collective.

"The 'common good' of a collective—a race, a class, a state—was the claim and justification of every tyranny ever established over men. Every major horror of history was committed in the name of an altruistic motive. Has any act of selfishness ever equalled the carnage perpetrated by disciples of altruism? Does the fault lie in men's hypocrisy or in the nature of the principle? The most dreadful butchers were the most sincere. They believed in the perfect society reached through the guillotine and the firing squad. Nobody questioned their right to murder since they were murdering for an altruistic purpose. It was accepted that man must be sacrificed for other men. Actors change, but the course of the tragedy remains the same. A humanitarian who starts with declarations of love for mankind and ends with a sea of blood. It goes on and will go on so long as men believe that an action is good if it is unselfish. That permits the altruist to act and forces his victims to bear it. The leaders of collectivist movements ask nothing for themselves. But observe the results.

"The only good which men can do to one another and the only statement of their proper relationship is—Hands off!

"Now observe the results of a society built on the principle of individualism. This, our country. The noblest country in the history of men. The country of greatest achievement, greatest prosperity, greatest freedom. This country was not based on selfless service, sacrifice, renunciation or any precept of altruism. It was based on a man's right to the pursuit of happiness. His own happiness. Not anyone else's. A private, personal, selfish motive. Look at the results. Look into your own conscience.

"It is an ancient conflict. Men have come close to the truth, but it was destroyed each time and one civilization fell after another. Civilization is the progress towards a society of privacy. The savage's whole existence is public, ruled by the laws of his tribe. Civilization is the process of setting man free from men.

"Now, in our age, collectivism, the rule of the second-hander and second-rater, the ancient monster, has broken loose and is running amuck. It has brought men to a level of intellectual indecency never equalled on earth. It has reached a scale of horror without precedent. It has poisoned every mind. It has swallowed most of Europe. It is engulfing our country.

"I am an architect. I know what is to come by the principle on which it is built. We are approaching a world in which I cannot permit myself to live.

"Now you know why I dynamited Cortlandt.

"I designed Cortlandt. I gave it to you. I destroyed it.

"I destroyed it because I did not choose to let it exist. It was a double monster. In form and in implication. I had to blast both. The form was mutilated by two second-handers who assumed the right to improve upon that which they had not made and could not equal. They were permitted to do it by the general implication that the altruistic purpose of the building superseded all rights and that I had no claim to stand against it.

34   Margaret Thatcher, from *In Defence of Freedom: Speeches on Britain's Relation with the World, 1976–1986*, in *English Conservatism since the Restoration* (ed. R. Eccleshall; Unwin Hyman, 1990), pp. 242–4

Margaret Thatcher (1925–) was the first female Prime Minister in Britain, and the first in the twentieth century to give her name to a quasi-ideology—Thatcherism. She was born into a lower middle-class family in Lincolnshire and was deeply influenced by her father's Methodist convictions. After graduating from Oxford with a degree in Chemistry, she tried and failed to win a parliamentary constituency for the Conservatives in 1951. Having secured the prize seat of Finchley in 1958, she quickly became a Junior Opposition Minister, and eventually Shadow Minister for Education. From 1970, she was the Secretary of State for Education and Science; a competent, reliable, and relatively uncontroversial figure. She emerged as leader in the fall-out of the party elite's decision to ditch its leader Edward Heath, after his successive defeats at the polls in 1974. A 'New Right' agenda was being assiduously promoted by sympathetic think-tanks at this time, and by figures such as Keith Joseph within the party. This involved emphasis upon the virtues of an authoritarian brand of moral individualism, a deep contempt for collectivist orthodoxy, and a marked preference for the free market. These ideas constituted an important backdrop to the three different administrations that Thatcher oversaw from 1979 to 1990, informing her boldly enunciated public discourse and many of the policy developments of this period.

I have reason to believe that the tide is beginning to turn against collectivism, Socialism, statism, dirigism, whatever you call it. And this turn is rooted in a revulsion against the sour fruit of Socialist experience . . .

In our philosophy the purpose of the life of the individual is not to be the servant of the state and its objectives, but to make the best of his talents and qualities. The sense of being self-reliant, of playing a role within the family, of owning one's own property, of paying one's way, are all part of the spiritual ballast which maintains responsible citizenship, and provides the solid foundation from which people look around to see what more they might do, for others and for themselves.

That is what we mean by a moral society; not a society where the state is responsible for everything, and no one is responsible for the state . . .

[T]he better moral philosophy of the free society underlies its economic performance. In turn the material success of the free society enables people to show a degree of generosity to the less fortunate unmatched in any other society. It is noteworthy that the Victorian era—the heyday of free enterprise in Britain—was also the era of the rise of selflessness and benefaction . . .

Experience has shown that Socialism corrodes the moral values which form part of a free society. Traditional values are also threatened by increasing state regulation. The more the state seeks to impose its authority, the less respect that authority receives. The more living standards are squeezed by taxation, the greater is the temptation to evade that taxation. The more pay and prices are controlled, the more those controls are avoided.

In short, where the state is too powerful, efficiency suffers and morality is threatened . . .

In our party we do not ask for a feeble state. On the contrary, we need a strong state to preserve both liberty and order, to prevent liberty from crumbling and to keep order from hardening into despotism.

The state has, let us not forget, certain duties which are incontrovertibly its own: for example, to uphold and maintain the law; to defend the nation against attack from without; to safeguard the currency; to guarantee essential services.

We have frequently argued that the state should be more strongly concerned with those matters than it has been . . .

What we need is a strong state determined to maintain in good repair the frame which surrounds society. But the frame should not be so heavy or so elaborate as to dominate the whole picture. Ordinary men and women who are neither poor nor suffering should not look to the state as a universal provider.

We should remind ourselves of President Kennedy's great injunction: 'Ask not what your country can do for you, but what you can do for your country.' We should not expect the state to appear in the guise of an extravagant good fairy at every christening, a loquacious and tedious companion at every stage of life's journey, the unknown mourner at every funeral.

The relationship between state and people is crucial to our economic approach. Our understanding of economics, our economic philosophy is an extension of our general philosophy . . .

[I]f, during recent years, we have in Britain done so much less well than we might have done, it is not because we are bad or incompetent, but because a layer of illusion has smothered our moral sense. Let me list a few of the illusions which have blinded us.

The illusion that government can be a universal provider, and yet society still stay free and prosperous;

the illusion that government can print money, and yet the nation still have sound money;

the illusion that every loss can be covered by a subsidy;

the illusion that we can break the link between reward and effort, and still get the reward;

the illusion that basic economic laws can somehow be suspended because we are British.

For years some people have harboured these illusions which have prevented us from facing the realities of the world in which we live. It is time we abandoned them so that we can tackle our problems.

Government and people both have a part to play. For government, facing our national problems entails, above all, keeping the growth in the amount of money in line with the growth in the amount of goods and services. After years of printing too much money, to which the economy has become addicted, this will take time: but it must be done.

But it is not only the total amount of money that matters. It is how that money is distributed between on the one hand the public sector, which produces little real wealth, and on the other hand industry and commerce, the mainstays of our economy.

At present too much is spent on the public sector. It follows that the government's second most important task is to reduce state spending, so that more resources can be put to investment in industry and commerce. This too takes time but it must be done.

Too much money spent by government has gone to support industries which have made and are continuing to make heavy losses. The future requires that industry adapt to produce goods that will sell in tomorrow's world. Older industries that cannot change must be slimmed down and their skills transferred to new products if they are to serve the nation. This too takes time but it must be done.

Economics means harnessing change instead of being dominated by it. But government cannot do it alone. These policies are a necessary but not a sufficient condition for recovery. The British economy is the British people at work—their efforts and their attitudes. Success will only be achieved in so far as people relate the rewards they receive to the efforts they make, and in so far as managers, freed from restrictions imposed by previous governments, respond to their new-found freedom to manage.

35 **Allan Bloom, from *The Closing of the American Mind*
(Simon and Schuster, 1987), pp. 313–15**

Born in Indianapolis, Bloom (1930–1992) was a student in Paris and Heidelberg in the 1950s,
and later taught at several leading American Universities, as well as in Toronto, Paris, and Tel
Aviv. His major post was as Professor in the Committee on Social Thought at the University of
Chicago. A noted translator of Plato's *Republic* and Rousseau's *Émile*, Bloom published
widely in the fields of moral thought and literature. In his best-selling polemic against current
trends in American University education—*The Closing of the American Mind* (1987) (see the
extract below), he blamed technology, the sexual revolution and European theoretical fashions for an intellectual culture that produced overly specialized students entirely lacking in
wisdom and insight. After his death, his name became attached to yet further controversy
when he appeared, thinly disguised, in his friend Saul Bellow's novel *Ravelstein*.

"You don't have to intimidate us," said the famous professor of philosophy in April 1969,
to ten thousand triumphant students supporting a group of black students who had just
persuaded "us," the faculty of Cornell University, to do their will by threatening the use of
firearms as well as threatening the lives of individual professors. A member of the ample
press corps newly specialized in reporting the hottest item of the day, the university, mut-
tered, "You said it, brother." The reporter had learned a proper contempt for the moral
and intellectual qualities of professors. Servility, vanity and lack of conviction are not
difficult to discern.

The professors, the repositories of our best traditions and highest intellectual aspirations, were fawning over what was nothing better than a rabble; publicly confessing their
guilt and apologizing for not having understood the most important moral issues, the
proper response to which they were learning from the mob; expressing their willingness
to change the university's goals and the content of what they taught. As I surveyed this
spectacle, Marx's overused dictum kept coming to my mind against my will: History
always repeats itself, the first time as tragedy, the second as farce. The American university in the sixties was experiencing the same dismantling of the structure of rational
inquiry as had the German university in the thirties. No longer believing in their higher
vocation, both gave way to a highly ideologized student populace. And the content of the
ideology was the same—value commitment. The university had abandoned all claim to
study or inform about value—undermining the sense of the value of what it taught, while
turning over the *decision* about values to the folk, the *Zeitgeist*, the relevant. Whether it be
Nuremberg or Woodstock, the principle is the same. As Hegel was said to have died in
Germany in 1933, Enlightenment in America came close to breathing its last during the
sixties. The fact that the universities are no longer in convulsions does not mean that they
have regained their health. As in Germany, the value crisis in philosophy made the university prey to whatever intense passion moved the masses. It went comfortably along
until there was a popular fit of moralism, and then became aware that it had nothing to
contribute and was persuaded by a guilty sense that its distance from the world made it
immoral. Hardly any element in the university believed seriously that its distance was
based on something true and necessary, the self-confident possession of the kinds of

standpoint outside of public opinion that made it easy for Socrates to resist the pious fanaticism of the Athenian people who put their victorious generals to death after Arginusae, or to refuse to collaborate with the Athenian tyrants. Socrates thought it more important to discuss justice, to try to know what it is, than to engage himself in implementing whatever partial perspective on it happened to be exciting the passions of the day, causing the contemplative to be called unjust and impious.

Of course anyone who is a professional contemplative holding down a prestigious and well-paying job, and who also believes there is nothing to contemplate, finds himself in a difficult position with respect to himself and to the community. The imperative to promote equality, stamp out racism, sexism and elitism (the peculiar crimes of our democratic society), as well as war, is overriding for a man who can define no other interest worthy of defending. The fact that in Germany the politics were of the Right and in the United States of the Left should not mislead us. In both places the universities gave way under the pressure of mass movements, and did so in large measure because they thought those movements possessed a moral truth superior to any the university could provide. Commitment was understood to be profounder than science, passion than reason, history than nature, the young than the old. In fact, as I have argued, the thought was really the same. The New Left in America was a Nietzscheanized-Heideggerianized Left. The unthinking hatred of "bourgeois society" was exactly the same in both places. A distinguished professor of political science proved this when he read to his radical students some speeches about what was to be done. They were enthusiastic until he informed them that the speeches were by Mussolini. Heidegger himself, late in his life, made overtures to the New Left. The most sinister formula in his Rectoral Address of 1933 was, with only the slightest of alterations, the slogan of the American professors who collaborated with the student movements of the sixties: "The time for decision is past. The decision has already been made by the youngest part of the German nation."

At Cornell and elsewhere in the United States, it was farce because—whatever the long-range future of our polity—the mass of the country (there really was no mass but a citizenry) was at that moment unusually respectful of the universities, regarded them as resources for the improvement of Americans, and accepted the notion that scholarship should be left undisturbed and was likely to produce a great range of views that should be treated seriously and with tolerance. The nation was not ready for great changes and believed about universities the things professors professed to believe about them. A few students discovered that pompous teachers who catechized them about academic freedom could, with a little shove, be made into dancing bears. Children tend to be rather better observers of adults' characters than adults are of children's, because children are so dependent on adults that it is very much in their interest to discover the weaknesses of their elders. These students discerned that their teachers did not really believe that freedom of thought was necessarily a good and useful thing, that they suspected all this was ideology protecting the injustices of our "system," and that they could be pressured into benevolence toward violent attempts to change the ideology. Heidegger was fully aware that the theoretical foundations of academic freedom had been weakened and, as I have said, treated the mass movement he faced with a certain irony. The American professors were not aware of what they no longer believed, and they took ever so seriously the movements they were entangled with.

36   Robert Nozick, from *Anarchy, State, and Utopia* (Basic Books, 1974), pp. 160–4

Nozick (1938–2002) was born in Brooklyn, his father being a Jewish entrepreneur of Russian descent. He studied at Columbia in the 1950s where he joined the Socialist Party and, sub-sequently, the Student League for Industrial Democracy. Nozick broke with socialism soon afterwards, while a graduate student at Princeton. Aged thirty, he was appointed a full Professor at Harvard in 1969, where he remained for the remainder of his career. Political philosophy constituted only one of the concerns of his writings that ranged also over questions such as the nature of philosophical reasoning, freedom of the will and the nature of con-sciousness. Nozick gained a degree of political notoriety and philosophical salience with the publication in 1974 of his *Anarchy, State and Utopia*. Though Nozick's argument was primarily with Rawls's philosophical defence of social justice, his ideas contributed to a rising tide of libertarian, anti-state thinking that gripped parts of the Republican right in the United States in the 1970s and 1980s.

HOW LIBERTY UPSETS PATTERNS

It is not clear how those holding alternative conceptions of distributive justice can reject the entitlement conception of justice in holdings. For suppose a distribution favored by one of these non-entitlement conceptions is realized. Let us suppose it is your favorite one and let us call this distribution D_1; perhaps everyone has an equal share, perhaps shares vary in accordance with some dimension you treasure. Now suppose that Wilt Chamberlain is greatly in demand by basketball teams, being a great gate attraction. (Also suppose contracts run only for a year, with players being free agents.) He signs the fol-lowing sort of contract with a team: In each home game, twenty-five cents from the price of each ticket of admission goes to him. (We ignore the question of whether he is "goug-ing" the owners, letting them look out for themselves.) The season starts, and people cheerfully attend his team's games; they buy their tickets, each time dropping a separate twenty-five cents of their admission price into a special box with Chamberlain's name on it. They are excited about seeing him play; it is worth the total admission price to them. Let us suppose that in one season one million persons attend his home games, and Wilt Chamberlain winds up with $250, 000, a much larger sum than the average income and larger even than anyone else has. Is he entitled to this income? Is this new distribution D_2 unjust? If so, why? There is *no* question about whether each of the people was entitled to the control over the resources they held in D_1; because that was the distribution (your favorite) that (for the purposes of argument) we assumed was acceptable. Each of these persons *chose* to give twenty-five cents of their money to Chamberlain. They could have spent it on going to the movies, or on candy bars, or on copies of *Dissent* magazine, or of *Monthly Review*. But they all, at least one million of them, converged on giving it to Wilt Chamberlain in exchange for watching him play basketball. If D_1 was a just distribution, and people voluntarily moved from it to D_2, transferring parts of their shares they were given under D_1 (what was it for if not to do something with?), isn't D_2 also just? If the people were entitled to dispose of the resources to which they were entitled (under D_1), didn't this include their being entitled to give it to, or exchange it with, Wilt Chamberlain? Can anyone else complain on grounds of justice? Each other person already has his legitimate share under D_1. Under D_1, there is nothing that anyone has that anyone else has a claim of justice against. After someone transfers something to Wilt Chamberlain, third parties *still* have their legitimate shares; *their* shares are not changed. By what process could such a transfer among two persons give rise to a legitimate claim of distributive justice on a portion of what was transferred, by a third party who had no claim of justice on any holding of the others *before* the transfer? To cut off objections irrelevant here, we might imagine the exchanges occurring in a socialist society, after hours. After playing whatever basketball he does in his daily work, or doing whatever other daily work he does, Wilt Chamberlain decides to put in *overtime* to earn additional money. (First his work quota is set; he works time over that.) Or imagine it is a skilled juggler people like to see, who puts on shows after hours.

Why might someone work overtime in a society in which it is assumed their needs are satisfied? Perhaps because they care about things other than needs. I like to write in books that I read, and to have easy access to books for browsing at odd hours. It would be very pleasant and convenient to have the resources of Widener Library in my back yard. No society, I assume, will provide such resources close to each person who would like them as part of his regular allotment (under D_1). Thus, persons either must do without some extra things that they want, or be allowed to do something extra to get some of these things. On what basis could the inequalities that would eventuate be forbidden? Notice also that small factories would spring up in a socialist society, unless forbidden. I melt down some of my personal possessions (under D_1) and build a machine out of the material. I offer you, and others, a philosophy lecture once a week in exchange for your cranking the handle on my machine, whose products I exchange for yet other things, and so on. (The raw materials used by the machine are given to me by others who possess them under D_1, in exchange for hearing lectures.) Each person might participate to gain things over and above their allotment under D_1. Some persons even might want to leave their job in socialist industry and work full time in this private sector. I shall say something more about these issues in the next chapter. Here I wish merely to note how private property even in means of production would occur in a socialist society that did not forbid people to use as they wished some of the resources they are given under the socialist distribution D_1. The socialist society would have to forbid capitalist acts between consenting adults.

The general point illustrated by the Wilt Chamberlain example and the example of the entrepreneur in a socialist society is that no end-state principle or distributional patterned principle of justice can be continuously realized without continuous interference with people's lives. Any favored pattern would be transformed into one unfavored by the principle, by people choosing to act in various ways; for example, by people exchanging goods and services with other people, or giving things to other people, things the transferrers are entitled to under the favored distributional pattern. To maintain a pattern one must either continually interfere to stop people from transferring resources as they wish to, or continually (or periodically) interfere to take from some persons resources that others for some reason chose to transfer to them. (But if some time limit is to be set on how long people may keep resources others voluntarily transfer to them, why let them keep these resources for *any* period of time? Why not have immediate confiscation?) It might be objected that all persons voluntarily will choose to refrain from actions which would upset the pattern. This presupposes unrealistically (1) that all will most want to maintain the pattern (are those who don't, to be "reeducated" or forced to undergo "self-criticism"?), (2) that each can gather enough information about his own actions and the ongoing activities of others to discover which of his actions will upset the pattern, and (3) that diverse and far-flung persons can coordinate their actions to dovetail into the pattern. Compare the manner in which the market is neutral among persons' desires, as it reflects and transmits widely scattered information via prices, and coordinates persons' activities.

It puts things perhaps a bit too strongly to say that every patterned (or end-state) principle is liable to be thwarted by the voluntary actions of the individual parties transferring some of their shares they receive under the principle. For perhaps some *very* weak patterns are not so thwarted. Any distributional pattern with any egalitarian component is over-turnable by the voluntary actions of individual persons over time; as is every patterned condition with sufficient content so as actually to have been proposed as presenting the central core of distributive justice. Still, given the possibility that some weak conditions or patterns may not be unstable in this way, it would be better to formulate an explicit description of the kind of interesting and contentful patterns under discussion, and to prove a theorem about their instability. Since the weaker the patterning, the more likely it is that the entitlement system itself satisfies it, a plausible conjecture is that any patterning either is unstable or is satisfied by the entitlement system.

37   William Kristol, from 'The Politics of Liberty, the Sociology of Virtue', in *The Essential Neoconservative Reader* (ed. M. Gerson; Addison-Wesley Publishing Company, 1996), pp. 441–3

Kristol (1964–) is the son of the leading conservative thinkers Gertrude Himmelfarb and Irving Kristol (the inventor of the term 'neo-conservative'). He was born in Manhattan in New York and educated at Harvard. He worked originally for the anti-Communist Democratic politicians, Daniel Patrick Moynihan and Hubert Humphrey, and then switched in 1976 to the Republicans. He taught briefly at the Universities of Pennsylvania and Harvard, and then served in the Reagan and Bush administrations as the chief of staff to Secretary of Education William Bennett and then Vice President Dan Quayle. In 1994, he persuaded the media mogul Rupert Murdoch to underwrite a new conservative magazine, *The Weekly Standard*, which he edits. He is a well-known TV pundit and print journalist who remains closely connected to some of the leading figures within the Republican party.

LIBERTY, VIRTUE, AND THE FAMILY

The politics of liberty and the sociology of virtue might be said to be the twin tracks for a postprogressive American politics. They are, on the whole, consistent and complementary tracks—and they influence each other. A politics of liberty can allow for new kinds of common pursuits in the space cleared by the retrenchment of government. Thus these tracks run parallel to one another for a considerable distance, allowing libertarians to limit government and social conservatives to attend to the sociology of virtue.

But the two tracks cannot be kept forever parallel; the two efforts—though basically complementary—do come into some tension, especially around a core set of issues involving the family. Here the politics of liberty runs up against the impossibility of neutrality about the fundamental arrangements of society; and the sociology of virtue runs up against the limits of what can be achieved in the civil sphere without some legal or policy support.

This can perhaps be made clear by reflecting briefly on Charles Murray's famous October 1993 *Wall Street Journal* article, "The Coming White Underclass." Murray argued that the problems of crime, illiteracy, welfare, homelessness, drugs, and poverty all stem from a core problem, which is illegitimacy. Illegitimacy is therefore "the single most important social problem of our time." Doing something about it is not just one more item on the American political and social agenda; it should be at the top of the agenda. The broad and deep response to Murray's article suggests that it struck a chord—and, in fact, it has implications for both the politics of liberty and sociology of virtue.

Murray argues that we need a politics of liberty. We do not need additional progressive social engineering to solve a problem such engineering has in part created; we need the state to stop interfering with the social forces that kept the overwhelming majority of births within marriage for millennia. While Murray is pessimistic about how much government can do (except for getting out of the way), he is optimistic about how little it needs to do. Perhaps government could make the tax code friendlier to families with children; otherwise, a politics of liberty, presumably supplemented by a private-sector sociology of virtue, would seem to be Murray's recommendation.

But near the end of his article Murray adds this: "A more abstract but ultimately crucial step is to make marriage once again the sole legal institution through which parental rights and responsibilities are defined and exercised." Indeed, "a marriage certificate should establish that a man and woman have entered into a unique legal relationship. The changes that have blurred the distinctiveness of marriage are subtly but importantly destructive."

Murray's suggestion that we reverse these changes goes beyond a mere "politics of liberty." It implies legal "discrimination" against illegitimacy or nontraditional family arrangements. In other words, a pure politics of liberty seems insufficient to Murray to combat "the single most important social problem of our time." State welfare policies, for example, cannot today discriminate against illegitimate children. Part of this problem could be solved by undoing welfare as we know it. But if it is essential that the law explicitly support marriage and the family—if we can't depend on civil society in a climate of legal neutrality simply to produce healthy families and to see to it that children are mostly born into intact families—then we come to the point where the politics of liberty and the sociology of virtue intersect. At this intersection, the politics of liberty would have to accommodate the special status of the family, and the sociology of virtue would have to acknowledge its need for political support for the family as a social institution. In other words, the political sphere, whose primary goal is liberty, cannot be entirely inattentive to the claims of virtue; and the social sphere, whose focus is virtue, requires some political support. For the two spheres to accommodate one another, a common view of what is right and just must ultimately underlie and inform both our politics and our society.

To support the family, one must hold a certain view of human nature and possibilities, a view different from that animating the sexual revolution, whose effects Murray laments. Murray thinks that our public policy should lean against the sexual revolution. But Murray also alludes to the (differing) expectations we need to have for "little boys" and "little girls"; he would seem to want our public policy to lean as well against the other powerful revolution of our time, the feminist revolution. For Murray emphasizes that the burden of preserving the family inevitably must fall primarily on women, and he believes public policy has to recognize this fact.

The sexual and feminist revolutions sprang up in civil society, so to speak. Politicians did not invent them. But the policy helped them along by legitimizing them and delegitimizing those who tried to resist them. No politics can simply be neutral between the sexual revolution and those who would resist it, or between radical feminism and those who would resist it. So even though our new American politics should be overwhelmingly a politics of liberty, and the pursuit of virtue should be primarily a "sociological" matter, at the intersection of politics and society—especially at the family—some judgments will have to be made. These judgments will always be more problematic than the relatively clear and mostly separate agendas of the politics of liberty and the sociology of virtue; but they cannot be avoided. We can pursue the politics of liberty and the sociology of virtue for quite a distance before we reach their intersection, but they do come together at a point at which neither our politics nor our sociology can be neutral as to the content of "the laws of Nature and Nature's God." Ultimately, the return to nature, an ascent from the progressive view of history, underlies both the politics of liberty and the sociology of virtue.

4   Socialism

Introduction

The readings we have selected reflect some of the main preoccupations of the various thinkers, revolutionaries, and politicians who have shaped socialist thinking. We have sought to highlight some of the principal disagreements and fundamental differences of moral belief and political outlook that this ideology has spawned, not least the divergence of emphasis (though not total incompatibility) between those figures who have stressed the ethical claims and character of socialist politics, and those who have developed its precepts within a stringent and specialist economic discourse. Much of the latter is associated with the writings of Karl Marx, and those theoreticians and revolutionaries whom he influenced (though Marx's own writings are by no means devoid of ethical commitments).

Some interpreters regard Marxism as a special sub-set of, and perhaps even a rival to, the various brands of socialism. Certainly, his emphasis upon the methodology of historical materialism, the political commitment to revolution, and the contempt for 'bourgeois ethics' that Marx enunciated do appear to place him outside the main circles of socialist thinking. But while there are good reasons to treat Marxism as a 'special case' in relation to socialism, we have left it open to readers to decide whether Marx and the Marxists constitute an entirely separate tradition. Against such an idea, it is worth remembering that Marx influenced many other non-Marxist socialist thinkers, and that he was in turn in dialogue (usually of an argumentative sort) with other socialist currents. Most importantly of all, however, understanding social democracy, one of the leading strands of socialist politics and thinking in the twentieth century, requires consideration of how leading German Marxists developed an 'internal' critique of his ideas, and began to chart a very different political trajectory for the political left. There are therefore good reasons for considering Marxism as a special, if rancorous, member of the socialist family.

In historical terms, early socialist ideas and experiments were for the most part associated with radical groups and intellectuals in France, Germany, and Britain. The revolution in Russia engineered by the Bolsheviks in 1917 changed this geographical bias. Not only did the newly formed Soviet Union lay claim to be the first achieved socialist state, but leftist theory was refined in highly significant and influential ways following this seismic political event. In its wake, Marxist-Leninism was exported and transformed by various revolutionary movements and governing parties in other, non-western regions.

We have tended to stress the importance of disagreement and the differential interpretation of core values for all of the ideologies presented in this book. In the case of socialism, this feature needs particular emphasis. Doctrinal differences have provided the basis for profound disagreements—particularly between ethical and economic socialists, reformists, and revolutionaries, and between statists and communitarians. These have sometimes remained in the realm of theory, but they have also spilled into the world of politics, and have shaped the history of all those parties, governments, and movements that have developed under the aegis of socialism.

We present, first, three nineteenth-century thinkers who were among the first to articulate themes that later became staple elements of socialist thinking. Henri Saint-Simon's [Reading 38] writings appear quirky and unusual by later socialist standards, yet he contributed to some of the thinking that made up this current in the nineteenth century. He sought to trace the emergence of a distinctively new socio-economic order—the 'industrial system'. Rather than bemoaning the advent of this new world, he laments the incapacity of social and political elites to adapt to its potential. Socialism, in his eyes, is associated with a distinctly modern political attitude, one needed to appreciate and encourage the various processes associated with the 'march of civilisation'. The emergent industrial order requires a mental and intellectual shift, a reconfiguration signalled in this extract by his criticism of the anachronistic character of the legal and philosophical thinking of his day.

As his various writings make clear, Saint-Simon was among the first social theorists to grapple with the generic features of, and cultural preconditions for, an industrialized society, and to consider the corrosive effects of moral individualism. Industrialism signals more than change in the technological and economic domains. It ushers in the emergence of a new societal order in which scientists, engineers, and artists form a leading social stratum, as well as entrepreneurs, industrialists, and producers. He also advocated the merits of rule by technocratic experts in a broadly capitalist economic system, in which some forms of collective provision were undertaken by the state.

The industrial revolution, and its various consequences, were central themes too in the life and writings of the British 'utopian' socialist Robert Owen [Reading 39]. In this, one of his major writings, he outlined the social and moral effects of the new system of manufacture upon those labouring within it. Anticipating later, more developed socialist attacks upon the impact and nature of market relationships, Owen bemoans the decline of communal relations and familial order. In the age of the modern factory, hours are long, conditions unhealthy, labour is all-consuming, and work itself inescapably instrumental. He reserved particular condemnation for the immorality of the practice of child labour.

Both in the design of his utopian community at New Lanark, and in his various writings, Owen expounded his hostility to the modern factory system, which, he believed, encouraged a lack of social responsibility and destructive forms of competitiveness. He eulogized the pre-industrial world, and propounded his firm convictions about the effects that a social environment exercises upon human character. While he broadly shared the utilitarian philosophers' conception of a 'good' social order as one that maximized the happiness of the majority, he did not believe that a free market system represented the best way of achieving this end, preferring instead the methods of co-operation and enlightened planning. These themes figured prominently in his widely read *A New View of Society*. In his later writings, in the 1830s especially, he gave greater emphasis to the prospects of the dawn of a new millennium. This he defined as a kind of social utopia freed of poverty, social misery, and inequality. Increasingly, he viewed education as the main way of advancing towards such a society.

For the French radical Pierre-Joseph Proudhon [Reading 40] the major socio-economic and cultural obstacle to the kind of egalitarian society he supported was private property.

Challenging the main theoretical justifications for this institution offered by the leading political economists of the day, he argued that both the ownership of land, and the rents charged to tenants, enjoy no persuasive independent justification. Instead, he proposes a moral distinction between the possession of goods and the idea that these represent the just entitlements of those who happen to own them. In this extract, he proceeds to outline his theory of how unjust rents lead to economic hardship and immiseration, as well as the gradual reduction of the size of the peasantry.

As suggested above, the shadow of Karl Marx looms over the history of socialist thought and politics. The importance and impact of his thinking are undeniable, and his influence stretched through several generations of the European intelligentsia, and into the fledgling labour and socialist groups of the mid-late nineteenth century. Below we present extracts from two of his many writings. In the first [Reading 41], which is taken from the different pieces collected together in his *Paris Manuscripts*, he offers an early indication of his root-and-branch rejection of prevailing understandings of the laws and nature of commercial society (the perspectives of 'political economy'). Market society, he argues, is distinguished both by its subjugation of individuals through the processes of commodity production, and by its unavoidable drive towards social polarization—between the proletariat and the capitalist. He pinpoints the alienation of the labourer—from the products upon which she expends her creative energies and, indeed, from her authentic being—as integral to commercial society. Political economy neglects and mystifies the main relationships of this social order, which arise in relation to the world of production. Commodity production seeks to exploit and dominate both the natural world and humanity's own nature.

Marx's ideas were developed in these writings from within the traditions and language of German philosophy. Towards the end of the same decade, a different tone, and more programmatic political outlook were apparent in his writings, not least because of the influence of his collaborator Friedrich Engels. The second extract from their work [also Reading 41] is taken from their jointly authored *Communist Manifesto*, perhaps their most famous and widely cited text. In this they pronounced, with some exaggeration, upon the significance of Communism in the political crises affecting several of Europe's monarchies around 1848. They also provided a synopsis of the Marxist account of historical development, in which modern bourgeois society emerges as the successor to other, now departed, societal orders. In the contemporary world, an increasingly apparent class polarity pervades all other relationships. An important consequence of the capitalist order is the emergence of an international market. The bourgeoisie is presented as the source of a relentless and subversive dynamism. Its mission is to spread the values and practices of market exchange across social domains and territorial locations. For all its current ascendancy, however, the bourgeoisie is also doomed. The laws of historical development point to the likelihood that the capitalist order will one day cease to be an agent of human progress and dynamism, and will then hold back the tides of further productive development. At that point, there will step onto the stage of history the unified forces of the proletariat—the one social class capable of acting as the agent of humanity's emancipation. This showdown is anticipated and hastened by the many different particular battles and struggles between workers and various bourgeois interests.

Marx was by no means the only socialist intellectual to advocate revolutionary action. In France, Georges Sorel [Reading 42] asserted that a social order maintains itself through the propagation of influential mythologies, not through rationally derived norms. In the current context, he argues, some powerful extant myths were in decline, and the opportunity for a process of creative social destruction and reconstruction had emerged. Socialism heralded the propagation of a new foundational myth—the ideal of the general strike. This represented an expression of a collective will to act decisively against the prevailing order. Those on the left who sought either the reform of the system, or who floated idealized schemes (utopias) as an alternative to capitalism, were faint-hearts whom socialists should ignore. The form of revolutionary activity which he advocated, involved both the liberation of the capacities of the free individual, and presaged a fundamental reconstruction of the system of industrial production and the wider social order.

Sorel is widely known for his discussion of mythologies, an unusual concern for a socialist in this period. Myths generate a mode of consciousness that encourage workers to reject philosophical rationalism and the elitism of intellectuals. Closely related to this view is his commitment to violence as both a source of moral energy and a political tool. Violent actions represent the legitimate revolutionary denial of the existing social order and was to be exercised against the 'force' at the behest of social elites. His immediate preoccupation in *Reflections* was the value of the myth of the general strike in relation to the consciousness of the working class. His writings sought to establish the instrumental and integral importance of ideological struggle in socialist politics, especially since he sensed that bourgeois values were slowly taking hold of sections of the working class. He evinced a marked suspicion of the influence upon the left of the nineteenth-century notions of ineluctable progress and inevitable socialist advance. These ideas encouraged an undesirable passivity and acquiescence among workers.

Other socialist thinkers remained more 'orthodox' in their adherence to Marxism, though they began to refine his understanding of left-wing politics in crucial respects. The German socialist party intellectual, Eduard Bernstein [Reading 43] asserted the indispensability of democracy to the socialist aim of removing class distinctions and pervasive social inequalities. In contrast to the Bolsheviks' hostility to the system of parliamentary democracy established in Central and Western Europe, Bernstein asserted the importance of universal suffrage for socialist advance and inveighed against such ideas as the dictatorship of the proletariat. His argument helped pave the way for the development of the many different left-wing parliamentary parties, and indeed governments, that emerged in the twentieth century.

Bernstein was not the only major German theoretician to justify a different kind of socialist politics on the basis of an 'internal' critique of Marx's ideas. Thus, Karl Kautsky [Reading 44], writing towards the end of the First World War, suggested that the achievement of a socialist society required that a particular state reach a sufficient level of industrial development, experience associated social trends such as urbanization, and contain a sufficiently self-conscious and politically capable working-class movement. The proletariat must emancipate itself, a process that is best undertaken using democratic methods. Warning the left of the dangers of emulating the revolutionary tactics of the Bolsheviks, he argued that a major step towards socialism involved the cultivation of a degree of maturity and independence among the masses.

In other respects, however, Kautsky remained a fairly devout Marxist, though he was equally influenced by Darwinist thinking. His brand of socialism was both deterministic and gradualist in character: he argued that the increasingly powerful position of monopolies and cartels signalled the onset of the final stages of capitalism, and also stressed the immiseration of the middle classes. And he remained convinced of the unavoidability of class conflict and the imminence of capitalist collapse. Compromise between the classes was impossible, as Marx had explained. Like his mentor, he placed great emphasis on the role of the intelligentsia in disseminating the principles of scientific socialism.

The reaction against Marxist thinking and the continuing influence of nineteenth-century socialist thought in the early twentieth century are illustrated by the influence of the authors Beatrice and Sidney Webb, writing in Britain, and the wider Fabian circle in which they participated. Host to a galaxy of political figures and intellectuals, the Fabian Society became associated with an influential strand of moderate socialist thinking. This cohered around such themes as: the importance of trained experts in the management of public affairs; a hostility to revolutionary socialism; rational persuasion in political life; and the value of efficiency in public affairs. The gradualism and reformism preached by the Fabians in Britain were, however, in stark contrast to the insurrectionary ethos and radical ambitions of other parts of the European left in the same period.

In this extract [Reading 45] the Webbs reflect upon the character and limitations of the struggles of trades unions. Arguing against a defensively orientated unionism, designed to protect the historic privileges and practices of particular groups of craft workers and skilled labourers, they also criticize the tendency for unions to focus upon bargaining over wages at the expense of equally important social demands about the character and length of the working-day. A narrowing focus upon wages is also self-defeating because it neglects the wider political and social implications of industrial disputes, as well as the drift towards lower wages associated with sweatshop production. The process of voluntary collective bargaining, on a trade-by-trade basis, is unlikely to survive the advent of democracy. The Webbs therefore propose that the union movement adopt the goal of achieving a living minimum wage (a demand that was subsequently taken up by various unions but not implemented in Britain until the end of the twentieth century).

In direct opposition to this and other brands of parliamentary socialism, Lenin threw himself into the life and mind-set of the revolutionary agitator. A keen disciple of Marx's writings, and a capable, if dogmatic, theoretician himself, Lenin became the political figure-head of the small sect, the Bolsheviks, that led the political putsch of 1917 in Russia, which resulted in the first nominally socialist republic. One of the main (perhaps fateful) strands of the strategic thinking he elaborated during the years of isolation and frustration he experienced before 1917, concerned the need for a revolutionary party to exercise decisive leadership. In his famous *What is to be Done?* [Reading 46] he polemicized against the strategic vision of rival leftist groups. In particular, he sought to distil and defend the 'correct' Marxist approach to the growth of trades unions in Russia. While he commends the various manifestations of unionization, these are to be understood as insufficient for the task of achieving socialism. The duty of revolutionary intellectuals is to develop the appropriate kind of political consciousness in the working class. Again and again, Lenin hammered home the difference between *merely* trade union activities and the political vision and leadership required of revolutionary leaders.

In his later writings, he became preoccupied by the changing character of early twentieth-century capitalism, and launched himself into debates with other European Marxists about this issue. Accepting that capitalism had changed significantly, he argued that it now typically relied upon the export of capital and needed to commit far more resources to the military defence of its possessions. Monopoly now replaced competition in national economies, and the large banks and other financial interests increasingly dominated both industrial capital and the state. The system of finance capitalism and its accompanying commitment to imperialism together represented the final, decrepit form of the capitalist system.

Another major figure in the Revolution, whose reputation and influence, like Lenin's, remain the subject of controversy, is Leon Trotsky. Having served in the Bolshevik government established after the Revolution, he found himself at odds with the murderous regime overseen by Joseph Stalin after Lenin's death. In exile, Trotsky set himself to re-examine the historical character of the Revolution and projected the significance, and betrayal, of his own ideas in relation to it. He drew particular attention to the singularity of the Russian situation prior to 1917—its economic 'backwardness' and its pre-industrial social structure [Reading 47]. In his influential *The Revolution Betrayed* (1940) he highlighted the importance of economic scarcity and social and cultural backwardness as the contexts facing the Revolutionary Government of 1917. He remained adamant that the Bolsheviks had established a 'workers, state' that had degenerated and ossified due to the triumph of an encompassing bureaucracy under Stalin's opportunist leadership. And he dismissed the argument (favoured by some later Trotskyists) that the Revolution had merely established a new kind of (state) capitalist social order.

In the passage below, he reiterates one of his major theoretical insights—the theory of 'permanent revolution'. A revolutionary break was required, first, to force Russia towards the model of a bourgeois democracy, and then without cessation, towards socialism. A central element in this strategic vision was the justification of a transitional period of coercive rule by a left government—a phase he labelled the 'dictatorship of the proletariat'. Trotsky, like Lenin, presented this as consonant with Marx's own writings. He was the first thinker in Russian socialist circles to argue confidently that the revolutionary rupture anticipated by Marx could take place in the relatively 'backward' context of Tsarist Russia. Underpinning this argument was his conception of the 'law of combined and uneven development'. This suggested that capitalism develops in an inherently uneven fashion. This results in the interpenetration of different modes of production, and the co-existence of different technologies and social forms in a single economy. In Russia, this explained the emergence in a predominantly pre-modern society of a tiny, modern industrial economy, a small, but concentrated working class, and an intelligentsia open to Western influences. This social mixture was not, he argued, conducive to parliamentary democracy. The bourgeoisie was insufficiently confident to lead the radical democratic revolution. This was to be the role of the proletariat, in alliance with the peasantry. But its revolutionary dynamism would not end there, and in the teeth of the resistance of the factory-owners and large landowners, the proletariat would inevitably press on towards its maximalist ambitions. As is clear from the extract reprinted here, this argument was combined with a commitment to the necessarily international character of socialist advance.

While most of the major disputes that shaped socialist thinking and politics in the twentieth century took place in Europe, vital developments of this ideology took place outside the West. A number of revolutionary movements and parties in the 'third world' were inspired by Marxist doctrines, though these were often blended with other indigenous cultural traditions. One of the most significant examples of this process occurred in China in the first half of the twentieth century, and culminated in the Chinese revolution of 1949. The leader of this insurrectionary movement, Mao Tse-Tung [Reading 48] reflected upon the 'special nature of Chinese society' and the imminence of Communist revolution in terms drawn from Western Marxism. The unfolding revolutionary situation, he maintained, was 'bourgeois-democratic' in character, and would result first in the removal of the shackles of the colonial rule of the Japanese. Unlike in Europe, however, this situation would rapidly give way to the transition to socialism. The democratic republic would be introduced by an alliance of different classes—a strategic necessity in a largely agrarian society in which only a tiny proletariat was in existence. Mao's debt to the political framework of Bolshevism is apparent throughout this extract; not least when he argues for the historic singularity of the Communist party—the only force, he maintains, capable of performing the twin roles of leading the democratic revolution and ushering in its socialist successor.

Mao's major theoretical contribution arose from his recurrent claim that revolution in China would comprise two distinct stages—a democratic one when the existing state structures would be smashed, and a dictatorship of the proletariat and its allies would be established; and a socialist phase that would prepare the transition to Communism. A key theme in his writings was the strategic implication of seizing state power in the first of these stages. The peasantry should be organized to establish 'red bases' in the countryside to surround hostile cities. From the early 1960s, his thoughts were increasingly directed towards rectification of the Stalinist 'error' whereby socialism was interpreted as a historical stage from which class distinction and struggle were absent. Under this guise, Mao came to declaim the effects of a revisionist elite arguing for a resumption of the 'capitalist road' for China.

Other thinkers have debated the adequacy of socialist ideas for societies and states that are both capitalist and governed as parliamentary democracies. In western Europe over the last sixty years, the establishment of state welfare regimes, the call to defend democracy against the Nazi threat, the economic expansion of the years after 1945, and the influence of a hegemonic liberalism, all combined to encourage a profound rethinking of socialist values and approaches to capitalism. An important example and source of this 'revisionism' in British political life was the Labour MP and writer, Anthony Crosland. In the passage taken from his best-selling *The Future of Socialism* [Reading 49], he reflects upon the heterogeneity of the family of socialist thought and draws attention to the importance of its members' disagreements about means and methods, as well as over its main ethical goals. He argues, in particular, against the orthodoxy current in the British Labour party, which suggested that taking private industry into public ownership is the main redistributive strategy to pursue. He questioned too the adequacy of a number of other policies and methods associated with nineteenth-century socialism. These arguments rested upon his assertion that the British economy was no longer run in the interests of those who owned the means of production. Ownership, he declared, was less important than management. He emphasized too the transformations engendered by the welfare state, the advent of virtually full employment, and the effects of the post-war Labour government's nationalization programme.

Underpinning this argument was Crosland's deep concern with equality. Social equality was at the heart of the socialist case, and this required much more than the establishment of bare equality of opportunity. A more egalitarian society, he maintained, was one that would realize various other important goals, notably: economic efficiency; the establishment of a more community-orientated social culture; and the achievement of a fairer society in which talents and abilities over which individuals have limited responsibilities count for less. Crosland combined this staunch egalitarianism with a deep commitment to a more culturally dynamic and ethically diverse society—unusual commitments for a socialist intellectual in this period.

Since the high tide signalled by the Chinese and other revolutionary movements in the 1960s, the global prospects of socialism have receded dramatically. This retreat has been precipitated by the collapse of a number of 'state socialist' regimes in Eastern Europe after 1989. Elsewhere too, the apparent failure of left-wing parties to effect fundamental transformations of their states and societies resulted in a sustained process of the re-examination of core values by socialist-inclined intellectuals, and accentuated the tendency of socialists to blame each other for the ideology's lack of success. These themes are central to the writings of the leading Italian theorist, Noberto Bobbio [Reading 50]. In his widely read book *Left and Right*, he offers a bold defence of the continued relevance of the idea that political allegiances take shape along a left-right dimension. In his analytical discussion of the continuing validity of this dichotomy, he explores the different values over which this distinction continues to take shape. One of these is equality. In the extract below, Bobbio considers the deeply rooted association in socialist thinking between the ideal of equality and a visceral opposition to private property. One of the major mistakes made by socialists, he argues, has been its adherents' efforts to convert the vision of a property-less egalitarian utopia into reality. This mistake does not however vitiate the left's concern to do something about inequality, which remains as relevant and serious a problem as ever. As awareness of internationally rooted inequities has grown, the socialist quest to re-order the world in the image of the egalitarian ideal remains as relevant, and as hard to achieve, as ever. In his earlier writings, Bobbio focused particularly upon socialists' damaging impatience with democratic procedures, not least their suspicion of regimes that are both capitalist and democratic. This kind of argument helped inform a much wider process of debate and rethinking by social democratic intellectuals in the 1980s and 1990s.

Not all left-wing thinkers go along with this kind of self-critical and revisionist impulse. Marxism has, in its different guises, survived the downturn of the fortunes of left-wing parties and the implosion of the Communist regimes in Eastern Europe after 1989. The British writer Alex Callinicos, has emerged as a leading critic of the abandonment of socialist principle by many 'radical' intellectuals, and an uncompromising advocate of the relevance of Marxism for the analysis of contemporary capitalism [Reading 51]. In the Afterword to his essay on *Equality*, he recaps some of the core commitments animating his, and other socialists', opposition to global capitalism. Like Bobbio, he regards social and economic inequalities as endemic features of contemporary society, yet Callinicos offers a much more critical account of liberalism's failure to address these problems. Turning to some of the most significant debates that have gripped liberal philosophers, he sides with those egalitarian theorists who interpret equality in fairly expansive terms—as the 'successful pursuit of goals that are both valuable and freely chosen'. But liberal political thinking is hamstrung, he maintains, by its unwillingness to challenge the framework of capitalism. A capitalist system is simply incompatible with real equality. The paucity of real-world societies that embody this assertion means that the left needs to revive its utopian heritage, and teach people to dream of such a possibility.

FURTHER READING

Informative introductions to the history of socialist thought can be found in: Robert Berki, *Socialism* (Dent, 1959), Charles Landauer, *European Socialism: a History of Ideas and Movements* (University of Calif. Press, 1979), Leszek Kolakowski, *Main Currents of Marxism: Volumes 1–3* (Clarendon Press, 1978), and the anthology of writings collected in: Anthony Wright (ed.), *British Socialism: Socialist Thought from the 1880s to the 1960s* (Longman, 1983). Leading socialist writers have provided important accounts of the development of socialism, for instance: G. D. H. Cole, *A History of Socialist Thought* (7 vols) (Macmillan, 1953–60), and George Lichtheim, *A Short History of Socialism* (Weidenfeld & Nicolson, 1970). On the evolution of Marxist thought, see D. McLellan, *Marxism after Marx: an Introduction* (Macmillan, 1970). A major recent overview of the socialist tradition can be found in Donald Sassoon, *One Hundred Years of Socialism: the West European Left in the Twentieth Century* (Fontana, 1997).

38 Claude-Henri Saint-Simon, from 'On the Industrial System', in *The Political Thought of Saint-Simon* (ed. G. Ionescu; Oxford University Press, 1976), pp. 153–9

Born into an aristocratic French family, Saint-Simon (1760–1825) proceeded to become a major influence on the evolution of European socialist thought. He experienced at first hand the upheavals of the American and French revolutions of the late eighteenth century, narrowly avoiding the guillotine in France. From an early age, he produced a number of unusual studies of social behaviour and urged various measures of reform. He shifted from a broadly liberal understanding towards a firm embrace of the theory of 'industrialism'. In his later writings he decried the inegalitarian character of Christian theology, and advocated the generation of a new religion that would be Christian in spirit but shaped by an intellectual elite. Unlike other, later socialists, he did not foresee the achievement of a classless society, but presumed that social divisions would reflect various functional social imperatives.

The root cause of the crisis in which the body politic has been involved for the last thirty years is the complete change in the social system, which is taking place today in the most advanced countries as the final outcome of all the successive modifications undergone by the old political order up to now. More accurately, the crisis consists essentially in the passage from a feudal ecclesiastical system to an industrial and scientific one. Inevitably, it will last until the new system is fully operative.

These fundamental truths have been ignored to date, and still are being ignored by both the governors and the governed; or rather they have been and they still are felt only in a vague and incomplete way, which is utterly inadequate. The nineteenth century is still dominated by the critical spirit of the eighteenth; it still has not adopted the organizational character which really belongs to it. This is the real, primary cause of the frightening prolongation of the crisis, and of the terrible storms which have accompanied it up to now. But, of necessity, the crisis will come to an end, or at least will change into a simple moral movement, as soon as we can bring ourselves to fill the eminent rôle assigned to us by the march of civilization, as soon as the temporal and spiritual forces which must come into play have emerged from their inertia.

The general aim of the philosophical work, of which I am presenting a fragment to the public today, will be to develop and prove the important propositions which I have just stated briefly; it will be to fix the general attention as forcibly as possible on the true character of the great social re-organization reserved for the nineteenth century; to show that this re-organization, gradually prepared for by all the advances which civilization has made up to the present, has reached its full maturity today, and that it cannot be postponed without serious setbacks; to indicate clearly and accurately the way to bring this about, calmly, safely and quickly, in spite of the real difficulties; in a word, to co-operate, as far as lies in the power of philosophy, in the moulding of the industrial and scientific system, the establishment of which, alone, can bring to an end the present social turmoil.

I boldly put forward the idea that the industrial doctrine would spread without difficulty and would be accepted without much effort, if the majority of people were in a position to grasp it and to judge it. Unfortunately, this is not so. Bad and deeply ingrained attitudes of mind prevent most people from grasping how intelligent this doctrine is. Bacon's *tabula rasa* is infinitely more necessary for political ideas than for any others and, for this reason if for no other, it must encounter many more difficulties as regards this area of ideas.

The problem faced by the scientists when they tried to instil the true meaning of astronomy and chemistry into minds which until then had been accustomed to look at these sciences in the manner of astrologers and alchemists, can be seen today in relation to politics, in which a similar kind of change must be made, i.e. the transition from the conjectural to the positive, from the metaphysical to the physical.

Forced to combat obstinate and widely held attitudes, I think that it will be useful to by-pass these and to anticipate a small part of my work, by explaining here in a general, brief way, the influence which vague and metaphysical doctrines have had and still retain on politics, the mistaken way in which they were taken for true politics, and lastly the necessity of abandoning them today.

The industrial and scientific system arose and developed under the domination of the feudal and ecclesiastical system. Now, this simple comparison is enough to show that between two systems so utterly opposed, there must have existed a kind of vague, intermediary system, uniquely destined to modify the old system in such a way that the new system could develop and, later, bring about the transition. This is the universal historical fact most easily predicted from the data I have put forward. Any change, temporal or spiritual, can only take place gradually. Here, the change was so great and, on the other hand, the feudal and ecclesiastical system was so totally opposed by its very nature to any modifications that, for these modifications to take place, it was necessary for special action to be carried on for several centuries by particular classes derived from, but also distinct from, the *ancien régime* and independent of it up to a point, and which, in consequence, must have constituted, by the sole fact of their political existence, what

I call by abstraction an intermediary and transitional system in the heart of society. These classes were, in the temporal sphere, the jurists, and in the spiritual one, the metaphysicians, who are closely linked in their political action, like feudalism and theology, or industry and the observational sciences.

This universal truth is of the highest importance. It is one of the fundamental facts which should serve as a basis for the positive theory of politics. This is what it is most important to stress today because the vagueness and obscurity which have surrounded it up to now are what most complicate political ideas today and cause nearly all the digressions.

It would be completely unphilosophical not to recognize the useful and distinguished influence exercised by the jurists and metaphysicians in modifying the feudal and ecclesiastical system, and in preventing it from stifling the industrial and scientific system in its earliest stages. The abolition of the feudal courts, the establishment of a less oppressive and fairer system of justice were the efforts of the jurists. How often in France the action of the parliaments has served to safeguard industry against feudalism! To blame these bodies for their ambition is to blame the inevitable results of a cause which is useful, reasonable and necessary. It is to beg the question. As for the metaphysicians, it is to them that we owe the Reformation of the sixteenth century and the establishment of the principle of freedom of conscience, which undermined ecclesiastical power.

I should overstep the bounds of a preface, were I to insist further upon remarks which every unbiased mind can easily develop from the preceding points. As for myself, I declare that I cannot see how the old system could have been modified and the new developed, without the intervention of the jurists and metaphysicians.

On the other hand, if it is foolish to deny the particular usefulness of the part played by the jurists and metaphysicians in the advance of civilization, it is very dangerous to exaggerate this usefulness or to misconstrue its true nature. By the very fact of the end it had in view, the political influence of the jurists and metaphysicians was limited to an ephemeral existence, because it was of necessity modificatory and transitional and not in any way organizational. It had fulfilled its whole natural function at the moment when the old system had lost the greater part of its power, and the forces of the new had become really powerful in society, both temporally and spiritually. Up to that point, which was reached in the middle of the last century, the political career of the jurists and metaphysicians was still honourable and useful, whereas it has now in fact become positively harmful because it has outlived its natural limit.

When the French Revolution broke out, there was no longer any question of modifying the feudal and ecclesiastical system, which has already lost nearly all its real strength. It was a question of organizing the industrial and scientific system, which was called for in that phase of civilization to replace it. Consequently, the industrialists and scientists were the ones who should have taken the political stage, each in their natural rôles. Instead, the jurists put themselves at the head of the Revolution and conducted it according to the doctrines of the metaphysicians. It is superfluous to recall the strange twists and turns which followed and the evils which resulted from these digressions. But it must be carefully noted that, in spite of this terrible experience, the jurists and metaphysicians have remained consistently at the head of affairs and it is they alone who today direct all political discussions.

This experience, however costly it may have been and however decisive it really was, will not bear fruit because of its complexity, until a direct analysis has proved the absolute necessity of removing the universal political influence which is granted to the jurists and the metaphysicians which stems only from the assumption that their doctrines are pre-eminent. But it is very easy to prove that the doctrines of the jurists and metaphysicians are, today, by their very nature, quite unfitted to guide the political action of either the governors or the governed properly. This obstacle is so great that it outweighs the advantages which might be presented by individual abilities, no matter how brilliant they are.

Today, more enlightened minds recognize clearly the necessity for a complete recasting of the social system; this need has become so immediately pressing that it must be met. But the biggest mistake which is generally made in this respect is to believe that the new system should be built upon the doctrines of the jurists and metaphysicians. This mistake only persists because we do not climb high enough in the scale of political observations, because general theories are not examined carefully enough, or because political thinking is not yet based upon historical facts. Were this not so, the mistake would not be made of taking a modification of the social system—a modification which has exhausted its effect and which has no further part to play—for a genuine change in the system itself.

The jurists and metaphysicians are prone to take the form for the substance and words for things. Leading from that comes the generally accepted idea of political systems of almost infinite multiplicity. But, in fact, there are and can only be two really distinct systems of social organization, the feudal or military system and the industrial system; and in the spiritual realm, a system of beliefs and a system of positive demonstrations. The entire history of civilized mankind is inevitably divided between these two great systems of society. For a nation, as for an individual, there are in effect only two ends, conquest or work, to which correspond spiritually either blind faith or scientific demonstration, that is to say, demonstrations founded upon positive observations. Now, the end of universal activity must be changed, if the social system is genuinely to be changed. All other improvements, no matter how important they may be, are only modifications, that is to say, changes in the form and not in the system. Only metaphysics can make this seem otherwise, through its unfortunate talent for confounding what should be separate and separating what should be confounded.

Society was organized in a precise and characteristic manner so long as the feudal or military system was flourishing, because it then had a clear, predetermined objective, which was to wage war, an end to which all parts of the body politic were co-ordinated. Today, too, it tends to organize itself in a more perfect manner, a manner no less precise and characteristic, but directed towards an industrial objective, towards which all social forces will converge. But from the decline of the feudal or military system until the present, society has not really been organized because the two goals having been pursued simultaneously, the political order of necessity has showed nothing but a mixed character. Now what was useful and even necessary in a transitional and preparatory state of affairs, clearly becomes absurd as a permanent system today, when the transition has really taken place in all major respects. It is to this state, nevertheless, that the doctrines of the jurists and metaphysicians lead.

It cannot be too often repeated that a society needs an active goal, for without this there would be no political system. Now to legislate is not an end in itself; it can only be a means.

Would it not be odd if, as a result of all the progress of civilization, mankind today had succeeded in associating in societies merely to pass laws for each other? This would surely be the purest humbug. Would this not mean that men met solemnly in order to draw up new rules for the pawns, imagining them to be the players? Such an obvious absurdity is nevertheless natural and, as such, excusable among jurists whose judgement is usually vitiated by the habit of only looking at the forms. But among the industrialists accustomed, on the contrary, to consider only fundamentals, the prolongation of such an error is utterly inexcusable . . .

39   Robert Owen, from 'Observations on the Effect of the Manufacturing System', in *A New View of Society, and other Writings* (Dent/Everyman, 1963), pp. 120–6

Owen (1771–1858) was a pioneering figure in the co-operative movement that emerged in the early-middle years of the nineteenth century. Through the utopian, co-operative communities he helped establish, as well as his writings, he helped shape the intellectual and political outlook of subsequent generations of British socialists. His name is above all associated with the utopian community that he founded at the cotton mills of New Lanark in Scotland; and which he jointly owned and managed. He sought to design both a workplace and a miniature society in which the twin goals of profit and social co-operation might be combined. This model community involved the construction of good quality housing for its (mainly imported) workers, as well as the public provision of a school, a day-nursery, a playground, and evening classes for adults. Social harmony was to be achieved by the promotion of an overarching set of rules for the community. Owen tried unsuccessfully to establish a similar community in America in the 1820s, founding 'New Harmony' in Indiana. Thereafter he returned to England and spent the remainder of his life involved in the fledgling labour movement.

Those who were engaged in the trade, manufactures, and commerce of this country thirty or forty years ago formed but a very insignificant portion of the knowledge, wealth, influence, or population of the Empire.

Prior to that period, Britain was essentially agricultural. But, from that time to the present, the home and foreign trade have increased in a manner so rapid and extraordinary as to have raised commerce to an importance, which it never previously attained in any country possessing so much political power and influence.

(By the returns to the Population Act in 1811, it appears that in England, Scotland and Wales there are 895,998 families chiefly employed in agriculture—1,129,049 families chiefly employed in trade and manufactures—640,500 individuals in the army and navy—and 519,168 families not engaged in any of these employments. It follows that nearly half as many more persons are engaged in trade as in agriculture—and that of the whole population the agriculturists are about 1 to 3.)

This change has been owing chiefly to the mechanical inventions which introduced the cotton trade into this country, and to the cultivation of the cotton tree in America.

The wants which this trade created for the various materials requisite to forward its multiplied operations, caused an extraordinary demand for almost all the manufactures previously established, and, of course, for human labour. The numerous fanciful and useful fabrics manufactured from cotton soon became objects of desire in Europe and America: and the consequent extension of the British foreign trade was such as to astonish and confound the most enlightened statesmen both at home and abroad.

The immediate effects of this manufacturing phenomenon were a rapid increase of the wealth, industry, population, and political influence of the British Empire; and by the aid of which it has been enabled to contend for five-and-twenty years against the most formidable military and *immoral* power that the world perhaps ever contained.

These important results, however, great as they really are, have not been obtained without accompanying evils of such a magnitude as to raise a doubt whether the latter do not preponderate over the former.

Hitherto, legislators have appeared to regard manufactures only in one point of view, as a source of national wealth.

The other mighty consequences which proceed from extended manufactures *when left to their natural progress*, have never yet engaged the attention of any legislature. Yet the political and moral effects to which we allude, well deserve to occupy the best faculties of the greatest and the wisest statesmen.

The general diffusion of manufactures throughout a country generates a new character in its inhabitants; and as this character is formed upon a principle quite unfavourable to individual or general happiness, it will produce the most lamentable and permanent evils, unless its tendency be counteracted by legislative interference and direction.

The manufacturing system has already so far extended its influence over the British Empire, as to effect an essential change in the general character of the mass of the people. This alteration is still in rapid progress; and ere long, the comparatively happy simplicity of the agricultural peasant will be wholly lost amongst us. It is even now scarcely anywhere to be found without a mixture of those habits which are the offspring of trade, manufactures, and commerce.

The acquisition of wealth, and the desire which it naturally creates for a continued increase, have introduced a fondness for essentially injurious luxuries among a numerous class of individuals who formerly never thought of them, and they have also generated a disposition which strongly impels its possessors to sacrifice the best feelings of human nature to this love of accumulation. To succeed in this career, the industry of the lower orders, from whose labour this wealth is now drawn, has been carried by new competitors striving against those of longer standing, to a point of real oppression, reducing them by successive changes, as the spirit of competition increased and the ease of acquiring wealth diminished, to a state more wretched than can be imagined by those who have not attentively observed the changes as they have gradually occurred. In consequence, they are at present in a situation infinitely more degraded and miserable than they were before the introduction of these manufactories, upon the success of which their bare subsistence now depends.

To support the additional population which this increased demand for labour has produced, it now becomes necessary to maintain the present extent of our foreign trade, or, under the existing circumstances of our population, it will become a serious and alarming evil.

It is highly probable, however, that the export trade of this country has attained its utmost height, and that by the competition of other states, possessing equal or greater local advantages, it will now gradually diminish.

The direct effect of the Corn Bill lately passed will be to hasten this decline and prematurely to destroy that trade. In this view it is deeply to be regretted that the Bill passed into a law; and I am persuaded its promoters will ere long discover the absolute necessity for its repeal, to prevent the misery which must ensue to the great mass of the people.

The inhabitants of every country are trained and formed by its great leading existing circumstances, and the character of the lower orders in Britain is now formed chiefly by circumstances arising from trade, manufactures, and commerce; and the governing principle of trade, manufactures, and commerce is immediate pecuniary gain, to which on the great scale every other is made to give way. All are sedulously trained to buy cheap and to sell dear; and to succeed in this art, the parties must be taught to acquire strong powers of deception; and thus a spirit is generated through every class of traders, destructive of that open, honest sincerity, without which man cannot make others happy, nor enjoy happiness himself.

Strictly speaking, however, this defect of character ought not to be attributed to the individuals possessing it, but to the overwhelming effect of the system under which they have been trained.

But the effects of this principle of gain, unrestrained, are still more lamentable on the working classes, those who are employed in the operative parts of the manufactures; for most of these branches are more or less unfavourable to the health and morals of adults. Yet parents do not hesitate to sacrifice the well-being of their children by putting them to occupations by which the constitution of their minds and bodies is rendered greatly inferior to what it might and ought to be under a system of common foresight and humanity.

Not more than thirty years since, the poorest parents thought the age of fourteen sufficiently early for their children to commence regular labour: and they judged well; for by that period of their lives they had acquired by play and exercise in the open air, the foundation of a sound robust constitution; and if they were not all initiated in book learning, they had been taught the far more useful knowledge of domestic life, which could not but be familiar to them at the age of fourteen, and which, as they grew up and became heads of families, was of more value to them (as it taught them economy in the expenditure of their earnings) than one half of their wages under the present circumstances.

It should be remembered also that twelve hours per day, including the time for regular rest and meals, were then thought sufficient to extract all the working strength of the most robust adult; when it may be remarked local holidays were much more frequent than at present in most parts of the kingdom.

At this period, too, they were generally trained by the example of some landed proprietor, and in such habits as created a mutual interest between the parties, by which means even the lowest peasant was generally considered as belonging to, and forming somewhat of a member of, a respectable family. Under these circumstances the lower orders experienced not only a considerable degree of comfort, but they had also frequent opportunities of enjoying healthy rational sports and amusements; and in consequence they became strongly attached to those on whom they depended; their services were willingly performed; and mutual good offices bound the parties by the strongest ties of human nature to consider each other as friends in somewhat different situations; the servant indeed often enjoying more solid comfort and ease than his master.

Contrast this state of matters with that of the lower orders of the present day;—with human nature trained as it now is, under the new manufacturing system.

In the manufacturing districts it is common for parents to send their children of both sexes at seven or eight years of age, in winter as well as summer, at six o'clock in the morning, sometimes of course in the dark, and occasionally amidst frost and snow, to enter the manufactories, which are often heated to a high temperature, and contain an atmosphere far from being the most favourable to human life, and in which all those employed in them very frequently continue until twelve o'clock at noon, when an hour is allowed for dinner, after which they return to remain, in a majority of cases, till eight o'clock at night.

The children now find they must labour incessantly for their bare subsistence: they have not been used to innocent, healthy, and rational amusements; they are not permitted the requisite time, if they had been previously accustomed to enjoy them. They know not what relaxation means, except by the actual cessation from labour. They are surrounded by others similarly circumstanced with themselves; and thus passing on from childhood to youth, they become gradually initiated, the young men in particular, but often the young females also, in the seductive pleasures of the pot-house and inebriation: for which their daily hard labour, want of better habits, and the general vacuity of their minds, tend to prepare them.

Such a system of training cannot be expected to produce any other than a population weak in bodily and mental faculties, and with habits generally destructive of their own comforts, of the well-being of those around them, and strongly calculated to subdue all the social affections. Man so circumstanced sees all around him hurrying forward, at a mail-coach speed, to acquire individual wealth, regardless of him, his comforts, his wants, or even his sufferings, except by way of a *degrading parish charity*, fitted only to steel the heart of man against his fellows, or to form the tyrant and the slave. To-day he labours for one master, to-morrow for a second, then for a third, and a fourth, until all ties between employers and employed are frittered down to the consideration of what immediate gain each can derive from the other.

The employer regards the employed as mere instruments of gain, while these acquire a gross ferocity of character, which, if legislative measures shall not be judiciously devised to prevent its increase, and ameliorate the condition of this class, will sooner or later plunge the country into a formidable and perhaps inextricable state of danger.

The direct object of these observations is to effect the amelioration and avert the danger. The only mode by which these objects can be accomplished is to obtain an Act of Parliament—

First,—To limit the regular hours of labour in mills of machinery to twelve per day, including one hour and a half for meals.

Second,—To prevent children from being employed in mills of machinery until they shall be ten years old, or that they shall not be employed more than six hours per day until they shall be twelve years old.

Third,—That children of either sex shall not be admitted into any manufactory,— after a time to be named,—until they can read and write in an useful manner, understand the first four rules of arithmetic, and the girls be likewise competent to sew their common garments of clothing.

These measures, when influenced by no party feelings or narrow mistaken notions of immediate self-interest, but considered solely in a national view, will be found to be beneficial to the child, to the parent, to the employer, and to the country. Yet, as we are now trained, many individuals cannot detach general subjects from party considerations, while others can see them only through the medium of present pecuniary gain. It may thence be concluded, that individuals of various descriptions will disapprove of some or all of these measures. I will therefore endeavour to anticipate their objections, and reply to them.

The child cannot be supposed to make any objection to the plans proposed: he may easily be taught to consider them, as they will prove to be by experience, essentially beneficial to him in childhood, youth, manhood, and old age.

Parents who have grown up in ignorance and bad habits, and who consequently are in poverty, may say "We cannot afford to maintain our children until they shall be twelve years of age, without putting them to employment by which they may earn wages, and we therefore object to that part of the plan which precludes us from sending them to manufactories until they shall be of that age."

If the poorest and most miserable of the people formerly supported their children without regular employment until they were fourteen, why may they not now support them until they shall be twelve years old? If parents who decline this duty had not been ignorant and trained in bad habits which render their mental faculties inferior to the instinct of many animals, they would understand that by forcing their children to labour in such situations at a premature age, they place their offspring in circumstances calculated to retard their growth, and make them peculiarly liable to bodily disease and mental injury, while they debar them the chance of acquiring that sound robust constitution which otherwise they would possess, and without which they cannot enjoy much happiness, but must become a burthen to themselves, their friends, and their country. Parents by so acting also deprive their children of the opportunity of acquiring the habits of domestic life, without a knowledge of which high nominal wages can procure them but few comforts, and without which among the working classes very little domestic happiness can be enjoyed.

Children thus prematurely employed are prevented from acquiring any of the common rudiments of book learning; but in lieu of this useful and valuable knowledge, they are likely to acquire the most injurious habits by continually associating with those as ignorant and as ill instructed as themselves. And thus it may be truly said, that for every penny gained by parents from the premature labour of their offspring, they sacrifice not only future pounds, but also the future health, comfort, and good conduct of their children; and unless this pernicious system shall be arrested by the introduction of a better, the evil is likely to extend, and to become worse through every succeeding generation.

40   Pierre-Joseph Proudhon, from *What is Property?* (ed. and trans. by D. R. Kelley and B. G. Smith; Cambridge University Press, 1994), pp. 122–9, 140–6

Proudhon (1809–1865) was intimately involved in the revolutionary insurrection that erupted in Paris in 1848. By then he had already published his most celebrated work, *What is Property?* His main theoretical contribution arose from the case he advanced against government of all kinds, and his argument for a mutualist society in which social co-operation would be achieved without state regulation. Dismissed by Karl Marx as a *petit bourgeois* apologist, Proudhon's thinking played an important role in the European socialist milieu of the mid-nineteenth century, both for his attack upon the bourgeois state and its political institutions, and for his unmitigated assault upon the ethical implications of a system of private property.

FIRST PROPOSITION

Property is impossible because it demands something from nothing

The investigation of this proposition is the same as that of the origin of farm-rent, which is so much debated by economists. When I read the writings of most of these men, I cannot avoid a feeling of contempt mixed with anger, in view of this mass of nonsense, in which the detestable competes with the absurd. It would amount to repeating the story of the elephant in the moon, were it not for the atrocity of the consequences. To seek a rational and legitimate origin of what is and must always be only theft, extortion, and plunder would be the height of the proprietor's folly, the last degree of delusion into which otherwise enlightened minds can be thrown by the perversity of selfishness.

As [J.-B.] Say says,

> A farmer is a wheat manufacturer who, among other tools which serve him in modifying the material from which he makes the wheat, employs one great tool, which we call a field. If he is not the proprietor of the field, if he is only a tenant, he pays the proprietor for the productive service of this tool. The tenant is reimbursed by the purchaser, the latter by another, until the product reaches the consumer, who reimburses the first payment and all the others by means of which the product has finally come to him.

Let us lay aside the subsequent payments by which the product reaches the consumer and for now attend only to the first rent, that paid to the proprietor by the tenant. The question is, on what ground is the proprietor entitled to this rent?

According to [David] Ricardo, [J. R.] MacCulloch, and [James] Mill, farm-rent, properly speaking, is simply the excess of the produce of the most fertile land over that of inferior land, so that farm-rent is not demanded for the former until the increase of population makes necessary the cultivation of the latter.

It is difficult to see any sense in this. How can different qualities of land result in a right to the land? How can varieties of soil engender a principle of legislation and politics? To me this metaphysics is either so subtle or so stupid that the more I think of it, the more at a loss I become. Assume two pieces of land of equal extent, one of them, A, capable of supporting 10,000 inhabitants, and the other, B, only 9,000: when, through an increase in their number, the inhabitants of A are forced to cultivate B, the landed proprietors of A will exact from their tenants in A a rent in proportion of 10 to 9. I think this is what Ricardo, MacCulloch, and Mill say. But if A supports as many inhabitants as it can maintain, that is, if the inhabitants have, accroding to their numbers, just enough land to keep them alive, how can they pay farm-rent?

If they had said merely that the difference in land was the occasion instead of the cause of the farm-rent, this simple observation would have taught us a valuable lesson, which is that farm-rent arose from a desire for equality. Indeed, if all men have an equal right to the possession of good land, no one can be forced to cultivate bad land without indemnification. Farm-rent, according to Ricardo, MacCulloch, and Mill would then have been a compensation for loss of profit and effort. This system of practical equality is a bad one, we must agree, but it was well-intended. What consequence can Ricardo, MacCulloch, and Mill deduce from this in favour of property? Their theory turns against them and strangles them.

Malthus thinks that farm-rent has its source in the power of land to produce more subsistence than is necessary to support the men who cultivate it. I would ask [Thomas] Malthus why successful labour should give the idle a right to participate in the products?

But the Seigneur Malthus is mistaken about his facts. Yes, land has the power of producing more than is needed by those who cultivate it, if by "cultivators" is meant only tenants. The tailor also makes more clothes than he wears, and the cabinet-maker more furniture than he uses. But since the various professions imply and sustain one another, the result is that not only the farmer but the members of all the arts and trades, even the doctor and the schoolteacher, are and ought to be regarded as cultivators of the land. Malthus bases farm-rent on the principle of commerce. Now, since the fundamental law of commerce is equivalence of the products exchanged, anything that destroys this equivalence violates the law. It is the error in the evaluation which needs to be corrected.

[David] Buchanan, a commentator on [Adam] Smith, regarded farm-rent as the result of a monopoly and claimed that labour alone is productive. Consequently, he thought that without this monopoly products would rise in price, and he found no basis for farm-rent except in the civil law. This opinion is a corollary of that which makes the civil law the basis of property. But why has the civil law, which is supposed to be "written reason," authorized this monopoly? Whoever says monopoly, necessarily excludes justice; now, to say that farm-rent is a monopoly sanctioned by the law is to say that injustice is based on justice, which is a contradiction.

Say responds to Buchanan that the proprietor is not a monopolist because a monopolist "is one who in no way adds to the utility of a product."

How much utility do the products of the farmer receive from the proprietor? Has he plowed, sowed, reaped, mowed, winnowed, weeded? These are the processes by which the tenant and his helpers increase the utility of the material which they consume for purposes of reproduction.

> The landed proprietor increases the utility of products by means of his instrument, the land. This instrument receives the materials of which wheat is composed in one state and returns it in another. The action of the land is a chemical process which modifies the material in such a way that it multiplies it by destroying it. The soil is thus a producer of utility, and when it (the soil?) requires its pay in the form of profit, or farm-rent, for its proprietor, this is not done without giving something to the consumer in exchange for whatever the consumer pays it. It gives him a produced utility, and it is the production of this utility that makes the land as well as labour productive.

Let us clarify this.

The blacksmith who makes farming equipment for the farmer, the wheelwright who makes him a cart, the mason who builds his barn, the carpenter, the basket-maker, etc., all of whom contribute to agricultural production by the tools they provide, are producers of utility; and to this extent they have a right to a part of the products.

"Without any doubt," Say says, "but the land is also an instrument whose service must be paid for, and so . . . "

I agree that the land is an instrument, but who made it? The proprietor? Did he, by the efficacious virtue of the right of property, by this moral quality infused into the soil, endow it with vigour and fertility? The monopoly of the proprietor lies just in the fact that, though he did not make the implement, he requires payment for its use. When the Creator presents himself and claims farm-rent, we will be accountable to him, even when the proprietor, his pretended representative, shall show us his power of attorney?

"I admit that the proprietor's service is easy," adds Say—a frank confession.

"But we cannot disregard it. Without property, one farmer would contend with another to cultivate any field without a proprietor, and the field would lie fallow . . . ."

The role of the proprietor is thus to reconcile farmers by robbing them. O reason! O justice! O marvelous wisdom of the economists! According to them, the proprietor is like Perrin-Dandin who, when summoned by two travellers to settle a dispute about an oyster, opened it, devoured it, and said to them: "The Court awards you each a shell." Could anything worse be said of property?

Will Say tell us why the same farmers who, if there were no proprietors, would fight with each other for possession of the soil, do not fight with the proprietors for this possession today? Obviously, because they think them legitimate possessors and because their respect for even an imaginary right exceeds their cupidity. I proved in chapter II that possession, without property, is enough to maintain social order. Would it be more difficult, then, to reconcile possessors without masters than tenants controlled by proprietors? Would working men who, to their own cost, respect the pretended rights of the idler, violate the natural rights of the producer and the manufacturer? What! If the cultivator forfeited his right to the land as soon as he ceased to occupy it, would he become more grasping? Would the impossibility of demanding increase, of imposing a tax on the labour of another, be a source of quarrels and law suits? The logic of the economists is curious, but we are not yet through. Let us admit that the proprietor is the legitimate master of the land. "The land is an instrument of production," they say, and this is true. But when, changing the noun into an adjective, they alter the phrase to say "The land is a productive instrument," they make a damnable mistake.

According to [François] Quesnay and the early economists, all production comes from the land; Smith, Ricardo, and [Destutt] de Tracy, on the contrary, locate production in labour. Say and most of his successors teach that both labour and capital are productive, which is a sort of Eclecticism in political economy. The truth is that neither land nor labour nor capital is productive. Production results from the combination of all three of these equally necessary elements, which, taken separately, are equally sterile.

Political economy indeed treats of the production, distribution, and consumption of wealth or values; but of what values? Of the values produced by human industry, that is, of the changes made in matter in order to appropriate it for man's own use and not at all the spontaneous productions of nature. Man's labour consists in a simple manual operation, and it has no value until he has taken this trouble. Until then the salt of the sea, the water of the springs, the grass of the fields, and the trees of the forest are to him as if they did not exist. Without the fisherman and his line the sea provides no fish; without the wood-cutter and his axe the forest furnishes neither fuel nor timber; without the mower the field yields neither a first nor a second growth of hay. Nature is a great mass of material for exploitation and production, but nature produces nothing for itself: in an economic sense its products, in their relation to man, are not yet products.

Capital, tools, and machines are likewise unproductive. The hammer and the anvil, without the blacksmith and the iron, do not forge; the mill, without the miller and the grain, does not grind, etc. Put together tools and raw material; place a plough and some seed on fertile soil; enter a smithy, light the fire, and close the shop, and you will produce nothing. The following remark was made by an economist with more good sense than most of his colleagues. "Say gives to capital a larger role than it deserves by nature; left to itself, it is an inert instrument" (J. Droz, *Economie politique*).

Finally, labour and capital together, but poorly combined, produce nothing. Plough a sandy desert, beat the water of the rivers, pass type through a sieve, and you will get neither wheat, nor fish, nor books. Your trouble will be as unproductive as the great labour of the army of Xerxes, who, according to Herodotus, had his three million soldiers flog the Hellespont for twenty-four hours as a punishment for having broken and scattered the pontoon bridge which the great king had constructed.

Tools and capital, land and labour, considered individually and abstractly, are productive only in a metaphorical sense. The proprietor who asks to be rewarded for the use of a tool or for the productive power of his land makes a fundamentally false assumption, namely, that capital by itself produces something and that, in being paid for this imaginary product, he receives literally something for nothing.

Objection. But if the blacksmith, wheelwright, and in short all manufacturers have a right to the products in return for the implements which they furnish; and if land is an instrument of production, why does this instrument not give its proprietor, real or imaginary, a right to a portion of the products, as in the case of the manufacturers of ploughs and wagons?

Reply. This is the heart of the question, the mystery of property, which we must clarify if we would understand anything of the strange effects of the right of increase.

The worker who manufactures or repairs farm tools receives the price once, either at the time of delivery or in several payments; and once this price is paid to the manufacturer, the tools which he has delivered belong to him no more. Never can he claim double payment for the same tool or the same job of repairs. If each year he shares in the products of the farmer, this is because each year he does something for the farmer.

The proprietor, on the contrary, does not yield his instrument; he is paid for it eternally and keeps it eternally.

In fact the rent received by the proprietor is not intended to cover the expense of maintaining and repairing the instrument; this expense is charged to the renter and concerns the proprietor only to the extent that he is interested in the preservation of the article. If he takes it upon himself to attend to this, he sees to it that the money which he expends for this purpose is repaid.

This rent no longer represents the product of the instrument because by itself the instrument produces nothing; we have just seen this and shall see it even more clearly by its consequences.

Finally, this rent does not represent the participation of the proprietor in production, since this participation could only consist, like that of the blacksmith and the wheelwright, in the surrender of the whole or a part of his instrument, in which case he would cease to be its proprietor, which would contradict the idea of property.

Thus, between the proprietor and his tenant there is no exchange either of values or services; thus, as our axiom says, farm-rent is real increase, an extortion based solely on fraud and violence on the one hand and weakness and ignorance on the other. Products, say economists, are only bought by products. This maxim is the condemnation of property. The proprietor, producing neither by himself nor by his instrument and receiving products in return for nothing, is either a parasite or a thief. Thus, if property can exist only as a right, it is impossible.

Corollaries. 1. The republican constitution of 1793, which defined property as "the right to enjoy the fruit of one's labour," is grossly mistaken. It should have said, "Property is the right to enjoy and dispose of at will the goods of another, the fruit of his industry and labour of another."

2. Every possessor of lands, houses, furniture, machinery, tools, money, etc., who lends a thing for a price exceeding the cost of repairs, which repairs are charged to the lender, and representing products which he exchanges for other products, is fraudulent and guilty of swindling and extortion. In short, all rent received, not as damages but as payment for a loan, is an act of property—of theft.

Historical Commentary. The tribute which a victorious nation imposes on a conquered nation is actually farm-rent. The seigneurial rights abolished by the Revolution of 1789—tithes, mortmain, statue-labour, etc.—were different forms of the rights of property; and they who under the titles of nobles, seigneurs, prebendaries, beneficiaries, etc. enjoyed these rights, were nothing else than proprietors. To defend property today is to condemn the Revolution.

. . .

FIFTH PROPOSITION

Property is impossible because with it society devours itself

When the mule is too heavily loaded, it lies down, but man always advances. On this well-known courage the proprietor bases the hopes for his speculation. The free labourer produces 10, thinks the proprietor; for me he will produce 12.

Indeed, before consenting to the confiscation of his fields, before bidding farewell to the paternal roof, the peasant whose story we have just told makes a desperate effort and leases new land; he will sow a third more; and since half of this new product belongs to him, he will harvest an additional sixth and thereby pay his rent. What an evil! To add a sixth to his production the farmer must add not one but two sixths to his labour. At such a price, he pays a farm-rent which in the eyes of God he does not owe.

What the tenant did the manufacturer does in his turn. The former tills more land and dispossesses his neighbours; the latter lowers the price of his merchandise and tries to monopolize its manufacture and sale and to crush his competitors. To satisfy property, the labourer must first produce beyond his needs; then he must produce beyond his strength; for by the withdrawal of labourers who become proprietors, the one results from the other. But producing beyond his strength and needs means that he takes over the production of another and consequently diminishes the number of producers. Thus the proprietor, after having decreased production by moving outside it, decreases it still further by encouraging the monopoly of labour. Let us calculate this.

The deficit of the labourer after paying his rent being, as we have seen, one tenth, he tries to increase his production by this amount. He sees no other way of doing this except by increasing his labour, and this he also does. The discontent of proprietors who have not received the full amount of their rent, the advantageous offers and promises made to them by other farmers, whom they suppose more diligent, more industrious, and more reliable, the secret plots and intrigues—all these give rise to a movement for the redivision of labour and the elimination of a certain number of producers. Out of 900, 90 will be expelled in order to add a tenth to the production of the others. But will the total product be increased? Not at all: there will be 810 labourers producing as 900, although they need to produce as 1000. Now, since farm-rent has been shown to be proportionate to the landed capital, not to labour, and never to diminish, the debts must continue as in the past, although efforts have increased. Here, then, we have a society which is continually decimating itself and which would be destroyed if it were not that failures, bankruptcies, and political and economic catastrophes periodically reestablish equilibrium and distract attention from the real causes of the universal distress.

From the monopoly of land and capital come economic processes that also result in the elimination of labourers from production. Since interest follows the farmer and the manufacturer everywhere, each of them say, "I would have the means to pay my rent and interest if I did not have to pay so many hands." Then those admirable inventions, designed to make labour easy and rapid, become so many infernal machines which kill labourers by the thousands.

"A few years ago, the Countess of Strafford ejected from her estate 15,000 persons, who as tenants increased its value. This act of private administration was repeated in 1820 by another great Scottish proprietor, towards 600 tenants and their families" (Tissot, *On Suicide and Revolt*).

The author whom I quote and who has written eloquent pages about the spirit of revolt that agitates modern societies does not say whether he would have disapproved of a revolt on the part of these exiles. For myself, I declare boldly that in my eyes it would have been the first of rights and most sacred of duties; and all I desire today is that my profession of faith be understood.

Society devours itself: (1) by the violent and periodic sacrifice of labourers, as we have just seen and shall see again, and (2) by the elimination of the producer's consumption caused by property. These two modes of suicide are at first simultaneous, but soon the first is intensified by the second, famine joining with usury to render labour at once more necessary and more scarce.

According to the principles of commerce and political economy, for an industrial enterprise to be successful its product must be equal to (1) the interest on the capital, (2) the preservation of this capital, and (3) the wages of all the workers and contractors; and furthermore, as large a profit as possible must be realised.

Let us acknowledge the financial shrewdness and rapacity of property. For every name that increase takes, the proprietor makes a claim on it: (1) in the form of interest and (2) in the form of profit. For, he says, the interest on capital is part of the income derived from manufacture. If 100,000 francs are invested in a manufacturing enterprise and if in a year's time 5,000 francs have been received from it in addition to expenses, there has been no profit but only interest on the capital. Now, the proprietor is not a man to labour for nothing: like the lion in the fable, he gets paid in each of his capacities, so that after he has been served, nothing is left for his associates.

> *Ego primum tollo, nominor quia leo:*
> *Secundum quia sum fortis tribuetis mihi:*
> *Tum quia plus valco, me sequetur tertia:*
> *Malo adficietur, si quis quartam tetigerit.*

I know nothing prettier than this fable.

> I am the contractor, I take the first share:
> I am the labourer, I take the second:
> I am the capitalist, I take the third:
> I am the proprietor, I take the whole.

In four lines Phaedrus has summed up all the forms of property.

I say that this interest, even more than this profit, is impossible.

What are labourers in relation to each other? They are members of a great industrial society, each one charged with a certain part of the general production according to the principle of the division of labour and functions. Suppose, first, that this society is composed of but three individuals, a cattle-raiser, a tanner, and a shoemaker. The social industry, then, is shoe-making. If I should ask what should be each producer's share of the social product, any schoolboy would answer, by a rule of commerce and association, that it should be a third of the production. But it is not a question here of balancing the rights of labourers conventionally associated; it is necessary to prove that, whether associated or not, our three workers are obliged to act as if they were and that, whether they want to or not, they are associated by the force of things and by mathematical necessity.

Three processes are required in the manufacture of shoes, the rearing of cattle, the preparation of their hides, and the processes of cutting and sewing. If the hide on leaving the farmers's stable is worth I, it is worth 2 on leaving the tanner's pit, and 3 on leaving the shoemaker's shop. Each labourer has produced part of the utility, so that by adding together these parts, we arrive at the value of this article, each producer must therefore pay first for his own labour, and second for the labour of the other producers. Thus, shoes corresponding to 10 hides, the farmer will give 30 raw hides, and the tanner 20 tanned hides. For the shoes made from 10 hides are worth 30 raw hides because of the two extra operations performed on them, just as 20 tanned hides are worth 30 hides because of the tanner's labour. But if the shoemaker demands 33 of the farmer's product, or 22 of the tanner's for 10 of his own, there will be no exchange; for otherwise, the farmer and the tanner, after paying the shoemaker 10 for his labour, would have to pay 11 for that which they had themselves sold for 10, which is impossible.

Well, this is just what happens whenever a benefit of any kind—whether called revenue, farm-rent, interest, or profit—is realised by a manufacturer. In the little community which we are considering, if the shoemaker, in order to procure tools, buy his material, and support himself until he receives a return on his investment, borrows money at interest, it is clear that to pay this interest he will have to make a profit from the tanner and the farmer. But since this profit is impossible without fraud, the interest will fall back on the unfortunate shoemaker and ruin him.

I take my example from a case of unnatural simplicity, for there is no human society reduced to merely three functions. The least civilized society assumes numerous industries; today the number of industrial functions (that is, all useful functions) may total more than a thousand. But however numerous the occupations, the economic law remains the same: *For the producer to survive, his wages must be enough to repurchase his product.*

Economists cannot be ignorant of this rudimentary principle of their so-called science. Why, then, do they so obstinately defend property, the inequality of wages, the legitimacy of usury, and the honesty of profit, which all contradict economic law and make exchange impossible? A contractor pays 100,000 francs for raw material and 50,000 francs in wages, and then wants to receive a product worth 200,000 francs—that is, wants to make a profit on both the material and the labour of his workers; but if the one who furnished the material and those who work on it cannot, with their combined wages, repurchase what they have produced for the contractor, how can they live? I shall develop my question, for here details become necessary.

If a worker receives for his labour an average of 3 francs per day, the bourgeois who employs him (in order to gain anything beyond his own salary, if only interest on his capital) must sell the day's labour of his employee in the form of merchandise, for more than 3 francs. The worker cannot, then, repurchase that which he has produced for his master. And so it is with all trades without exception. The tailor, the hatter, the cabinet-maker, the blacksmith, the tanner, the mason, the jeweller, the printer, the clerk, etc., etc., even to the farmer and wine-grower, cannot repurchase their products; for since they produce for a master who in one form or another makes a profit, they must pay more for their own labour than they get for it.

In France 20 million labourers, engaged in all the branches of science, art, and industry, produce everything which is useful to man. Hypothetically, their annual wages amount to

20 billion; but because of the right of property and the many forms of increase, premiums, tithes, interests, fines, profits, farm-rents, house-rents, revenues, and benefits of every kind and color, their products are estimated by the proprietors and employers at 25 billion. What does this mean? That the labourers, who are obliged to repurchase these products to survive, must either pay 5 for that which they produced for 4, or else fast one out five days.

If there is an economist in France able to show that this calculation is false, I ask him to appear, and I promise to retract all that is erroneous and wicked in my attacks on property.

Let us now look at the results of this profit.

If the wages of the workers in all trades were the same, the deficit caused by the proprietor's tax would be felt equally everywhere, but the cause of the evil would also be so apparent that it would soon be perceived and suppressed. But since among wage-earners (from that of street-sweepers to that of the minister of state) there is the same inequality of wages as there is among proprietors, robbery continually rebounds from the stronger to the weaker, so that the labourer experiences more deprivation the further down he is in the social scale, and the lowest class of people are literally stripped naked and eaten alive by the others.

Laboring people cannot buy the cloth they weave, the furniture they manufacture, the metal they forge, the jewels they cut, or the prints they engrave, nor procure the wheat they plant, the wine they produce, or the flesh of the animals they raise. They are not allowed to dwell in the houses they build, to attend the plays their labour supports, or to enjoy the rest their body requires. Why is this? Because the right of increase does not permit these things to be sold at the cost-price, which is all that labourers can afford to pay. On the signs of the magnificent warehouses which he in his poverty admires the worker reads in large letters: THIS IS YOUR WORK; YOU SHALL NOT HAVE IT: *Sic vos no vobis!*

Every manufacturer who employs 1,000 labourers and gains one sou per day from each of them is a man who is bringing distress to 1,000 workers; every profiteer has a pact with famine. Nor do the people even have the labour by which they are being starved by property. Why is this? Because the inadequacy of wages forces workers to monopolize their labour and, before being destroyed by scarcity, to destroy each other by competition. Let's pursue this truth no further.

If the worker's wages will not purchase his product, it follows that the product is not made for the producer. For whom, then, is it meant? For the richer consumer, that is, for only a fraction of society. But when the whole society labours, it produces for the whole society; and so if only a part of society consumes, sooner or later a part of society will be idle. Now, idleness is death for the worker as well for the proprietor: this conclusion is inescapable.

The most distressing spectacle imaginable is to see producers resisting and struggling against this mathematical necessity, this power of numbers which their prejudices prevent them from seeing.

If 10,000 thousand printers can furnish reading matter enough for 34 million men and if the price of books is within the reach of only a third of that number, it is evident that these 100,000 printers will produce three times as much as the book-sellers can sell. So that the products of the labourers will never exceed the demands of the consumers, the labourers must either rest two days out of three or, separating into three groups, relieve each other three times a week, month, or quarter—which is to say that for two thirds of their lives they must not live. But industry, under the influence of property, does not proceed with this regularity. Its nature is to produce much in a short time, because the greater the amount and the shorter the time of production, the less each item will cost. At the first sign of a shortage, the factories fill up and everybody returns to work. Then business is good, and both governors and governed are happy. But the more they work today, the more idle they will be afterwards; the more they laugh now, the more they will weep later. Under the regime of property, the flowers of industry serve only as funeral wreaths, and by his labour the worker digs his own grave.

The factory may stop running, but the interest on capital does not. The manufacturer then tries to continue production by lessening expenses. Next comes the lowering of wages, the introduction of machinery, the employment of women and children to do the work of men, decline in skill, and poor quality work. They still produce because the decreased cost creates a larger market, but they do not produce for long because cheapness is the result of the quantity and rapidity of production, and so the productive power tends more than ever to surpass consumption. It is when production is carried on by labourers whose wages are bare enough to support them from day to day that the consequences of the principle of property become most frightful. They cannot economise, make savings, or accumulate capital to support them even one day more. Today the factory is closed; tomorrow the people starve in the streets; the day after tomorrow they will either die in the hospital or eat in the jail.

Then new misfortunes come to complicate this terrible situation. Because of the glut of merchandise and the sharp fall in prices, the manufacturer finds it impossible to pay the interest on his borrowed capital, so that his alarmed creditors hasten to withdraw their funds, production is suspended, and labour comes to a standstill. Then people are astonished to see capital desert commerce and transfer to the stock market; and I once heard Monsieur Blanqui bitterly lamenting the ignorance and irrationality of capitalists. The cause of this movement of capital is very simple; but for that reason an economist could not perceive it, or rather must not explain it. This cause lies entirely in competition.

By competition I mean not only the rivalry between two businesses of the same kind but the general and simultaneous effort of all kinds of business to get ahead of each other. This effort is today so strong, that the price of merchandise hardly covers the cost of production and distribution, so that, since the wages of all labourers are deducted, nothing remains, not even profit for the capitalists.

The primary cause of commercial and industrial stagnations is thus interest on capital, that interest which all earlier generations agreed in naming *usury* (whenever it was paid for the use of money) but which they did not dare to condemn in the forms of house-rent, farm-rent, or profit—as if the nature of the thing lent could ever justify a charge for the lending, which is theft.

Whatever the increase received by the capitalist is, such will be the frequency and intensity of commercial crises: once the first is given, we always can determine the two others and vice versa. Do you want to know the regulator of a society? Find the amount of active capital, that is, capital bearing interest, and the legal rate of this interest. The course of events will be a series of collapses, whose number and violence will be proportionate to the activity of capital.

In 1839 the number of failures in Paris alone was 1,064. This rate was maintained in the early months of 1840; and as I write these lines, the crisis is not yet ended. It is said, moreover, that the number of houses which have been liquidated is greater than the number of declared failures. By this flood we may judge the power of the waterspout.

The decimation of society is sometimes imperceptible and permanent, sometimes periodic and violent; it depends on the diverse movements of property. In a country of divided holdings and small business, the rights and claims of each being balanced by those of others, the invasive power [of property] is destroyed. There, it may be truly said, property does not exist, since the right of increase is hardly exercised at all. The condition of the labourers in terms of security of life is almost the same as if absolute equality prevailed among them. They are deprived of all the advantages of full and free association, but their existence is not endangered in the least. Aside from a few isolated victims of the right of property, of this misfortune whose primary cause no one perceives, society seems to rest calmly in the bosom of this sort of equality. But be careful; it is balanced on the edge of a sword, and at the slightest shock it will fall and be cut to death.

Ordinarily, the turbulence of properly is localized. On the one hand, farm-rent stops at a certain point; on the other, because of competition and overproduction, the price of manufactured goods does not rise, so that the condition of the peasant remains the same, depending mainly on the seasons. It is thus on business that the devouring action of property is based, and from this arise what we commonly call "commercial crises" rather than "agricultural crises," because while the farmer is slowly being eaten up by the right of increase, the manufacturer is swallowed at a single mouthful. From this come the closing of factories, the destruction of fortunes, and the inactivity of the working class, a part of which regularly dies on the highways, and in the hospitals, prisons, and galleys.

To sum up this proposition: Property sells products to the labourer for more than it pays him for them; therefore it is impossible.

41   Karl Marx, from (a) 'The Paris Manuscripts', Karl Marx and Friedrich Engels, (b) 'The Communist Manifesto', both in *Selected Writings* (ed. D. McLellan; Oxford University Press, 1977), pp. 77–87, 221–31

For biographical information, see Chapter 1, Reading 1.

(a) We started from the presuppositions of political economy. We accepted its vocabulary and its laws. We presupposed private property, the separation of labour, capital, and land, and likewise of wages, profit, and ground rent; also division of labour; competition; the concept of exchange value, etc. Using the very words of political economy we have demonstrated that the worker is degraded to the most miserable sort of commodity; that the misery of the worker is in inverse proportion to the power and size of his production; that the necessary result of competition is the accumulation of capital in a few hands, and thus a more terrible restoration of monopoly; and that finally the distinction between capitalist and landlord, and that between peasant and industrial worker disappears and the whole of society must fall apart into the two classes of the property owners and the propertyless workers.

Political economy starts with the fact of private property, it does not explain it to us. It conceives of the material process that private property goes through in reality in general abstract formulas which then have for it a value of laws. It does not understand these laws, i.e. it does not demonstrate how they arise from the nature of private property. Political economy does not afford us any explanation of the reason for the separation of labour and capital, of capital and land. When, for example, political economy defines the relationship of wages to profit from capital, the interest of the capitalist is the ultimate court of appeal, that is, it presupposes what should be its result. In the same way competition enters the argument everywhere. It is explained by exterior circumstances. But political economy tells us nothing about how far these exterior, apparently fortuitous circumstances are merely the expression of a necessary development. We have seen how it regards exchange itself as something fortuitous. The only wheels that political economy sets in motion are greed and war among the greedy, competition.

It is just because political economy has not grasped the connections in the movement that new contradictions have arisen in its doctrines, for example, between that of monopoly and that of competition, freedom of craft and corporations, division of landed property and large estates. For competition, free trade, and the division of landed property were only seen as fortuitous circumstances created by will and force, not developed and comprehended as necessary, inevitable, and natural results of monopoly, corporations, and feudal property.

So what we have to understand now is the essential connection of private property, selfishness, the separation of labour, capital, and landed property, of exchange and competition, of the value and degradation of man, of monopoly and competition, etc.—the connection of all this alienation with the money system.

Let us not be like the political economist who, when he wishes to explain something, puts himself in an imaginary original state of affairs. Such an original stage of affairs explains nothing. He simply pushes the question back into a grey and nebulous distance. He presupposes as a fact and an event what he ought to be deducing, namely the necessary connection between the two things, for example, between the division of labour and exchange. Similarly, the theologian explains the origin of evil through the fall, i.e. he presupposes as an historical fact what he should be explaining.

We start with a contemporary fact of political economy:

The worker becomes poorer the richer is his production, the more it increases in power and scope. The worker becomes a commodity that is all the cheaper the more commodities he creates. The depreciation of the human world progresses in direct proportion to the increase in value of the world of things. Labour does not only produce commodities; it produces itself and the labourer as a commodity and that to the extent to which it produces commodities in general.

What this fact expresses is merely this: the object that labour produces, its product, confronts it as an alien being, as a power independent of the producer. The product of labour is labour that has solidified itself into an object, made itself into a thing, the objectification of labour. The realization of labour is its objectification. In political economy this realization of labour appears as a loss of reality for the worker, objectification as a loss of the object or slavery to it, and appropriation as alienation, as externalization.

The realization of labour appears as a loss of reality to an extent that the worker loses his reality by dying of starvation. Objectification appears as a loss of the object to such an extent that the worker is robbed not only of the objects necessary for his life but also of the objects of his work. Indeed, labour itself becomes an object he can only have in his power with the greatest of efforts and at irregular intervals. The appropriation of the object appears as alienation to such an extent that the more objects the worker produces, the less he can possess and the more he falls under the domination of his product, capital.

All these consequences follow from the fact that the worker relates to the product of his labour as to an alien object. For it is evident from this presupposition that the more the worker externalizes himself in his work, the more powerful becomes the alien, objective world that he creates opposite himself, the poorer he becomes himself in his inner life and the less he can call his own. It is just the same in religion. The more man puts into God, the less he retains in himself. The worker puts his life into the object and this means that it no longer belongs to him but to the object. So the greater this activity, the more the worker is without an object. What the product of his labour is, that he is not. So the greater this product the less he is himself. The externalization of the worker in his product implies not only that his labour becomes an object, an exterior existence but also that it exists outside him, independent and alien, and becomes a self-sufficient power opposite him, that the life that he has lent to the object affronts him, hostile and alien.

Let us now deal in more detail with objectification, the production of the worker, and the alienation, the loss of the object, his product, which is involved in it.

The worker can create nothing without nature, the sensuous exterior world. It is the matter in which his labour realizes itself, in which it is active, out of which and through which it produces.

But as nature affords the means of life for labour in the sense that labour cannot live without objects on which it exercises itself, so it affords a means of life in the narrower sense, namely the means for the physical subsistence of the worker himself.

Thus the more the worker appropriates the exterior world of sensuous nature by his labour, the more he doubly deprives himself of the means of subsistence, firstly since the exterior sensuous world increasingly ceases to be an object belonging to his work, a means of subsistence for his labour; secondly, since it increasingly ceases to be a means of subsistence in the direct sense, a means for the physical subsistence of the worker.

Thus in these two ways the worker becomes a slave to his object: firstly he receives an object of labour, that is he receives labour, and secondly, he receives the means of subsistence. Thus it is his object that permits him to exist first as a worker and secondly as a physical subject. The climax of this slavery is that only as a worker can he maintain himself as a physical subject and it is only as a physical subject that he is a worker.

(According to the laws of political economy the alienation of the worker in his object is expressed as follows: the more the worker produces the less he has to consume, the more values he creates the more valueless and worthless he becomes, the more formed the product the more deformed the worker, the more civilized the product, the more barbaric the worker, the more powerful the work the more powerless becomes the worker, the more cultured the work the more philistine the worker becomes and more of a slave to nature.)

Political economy hides the alienation in the essence of labour by not considering the immediate relationship between the worker (labour) and production. Labour produces works of wonder for the rich, but nakedness for the worker. It produces palaces, but only hovels for the worker; it produces beauty, but cripples the worker; it replaces labour by machines but throws a part of the workers back to a barbaric labour and turns the other part into machines. It produces culture, but also imbecility and cretinism for the worker.

The immediate relationship of labour to its products is the relationship of the worker to the objects of his production. The relationship of the man of means to the objects of production and to production itself is only a consequence of this first relationship. And it confirms it. We shall examine this other aspect later.

So when we ask the question: what relationship is essential to labour, we are asking about the relationship of the worker to production.

Up to now we have considered only one aspect of the alienation or externalization of the worker, his relationship to the products of his labour. But alienation shows itself not only in the result, but also in the act of production, inside productive activity itself. How would the worker be able to affront the product of his work as an alien being if he did not alienate himself in the act of production itself? For the product is merely the summary of the activity of production. So if the product of labour is externalization, production itself must be active externalization, the externalization of activity, the activity of externalization. The alienation of the object of labour is only the resume of the alienation, the externalization in the activity of labour itself.

What does the externalization of labour consist of then?

Firstly, that labour is exterior to the worker, that is, it does not belong to his essence. Therefore he does not confirm himself in his work, he denies himself, feels miserable instead of happy, deploys no free physical and intellectual energy, but mortifies his body and ruins his mind. Thus the worker only feels a stranger. He is at home when he is not working and when he works he is not at home. His labour is therefore not voluntary but compulsory, forced labour. It is therefore not the satisfaction of a need but only a means to satisfy needs outside itself. How alien it really is is very evident from the fact that when there is no physical or other compulsion, labour is avoided like the plague. External labour, labour in which man externalizes himself, is a labour of self-sacrifice and mortification. Finally, the external character of labour for the worker shows itself in the fact that it is not his own but someone else's, that it does not belong to him, that he does not belong to himself in his labour but to someone else. As in religion the human imagination's own activity, the activity of man's head and his heart, reacts independently on the individual as an alien activity of gods or devils, so the activity of the worker is not his own spontaneous activity. It belongs to another and is the loss of himself.

The result we arrive at then is that man (the worker) only feels himself freely active in his animal functions of eating, drinking, and procreating, at most also in his dwelling and dress, and feels himself an animal in his human functions.

Eating, drinking, procreating, etc. are indeed truly human functions. But in the abstraction that separates them from the other round of human activity and makes them into final and exclusive ends they become animal.

We have treated the act of alienation of practical human activity, labour, from two aspects. (1) The relationship of the worker to the product of his labour as an alien object that has power over him. This relationship is at the same time the relationship to the sensuous exterior world and to natural objects as to an alien and hostile world opposed to him. (2) The relationship of labour to the act of production inside labour. This relationship is the relationship of the worker to his own activity as something that is alien and does not belong to him; it is activity that is passivity, power that is weakness, procreation that is castration, the worker's own physical and intellectual energy, his personal life (for what is life except activity?) as an activity directed against himself, independent of him and not belonging to him. It is self-alienation, as above it was the alienation of the object.

We now have to draw a third characteristic of alienated labour from the two previous ones.

Man is a species-being not only in that practically and theoretically he makes both his own and other species into his objects, but also, and this is only another way of putting the same thing, he relates to himself as to the present, living species, in that he relates to himself as to a universal and therefore free being.

Both with man and with animals the species-life consists physically in the fact that man (like animals) lives from inorganic nature, and the more universal man is than animals the more universal is the area of inorganic nature from which he lives. From the theoretical point of view, plants, animals, stones, air, light, etc. form part of human consciousness, partly as objects of natural science, partly as objects of art; they are his intellectual inorganic nature, his intellectual means of subsistence, which he must first prepare before he can enjoy and assimilate them. From the practical point of view, too, they form a part of human life and activity. Physically man lives solely from these products of nature, whether they appear as food, heating, clothing, habitation, etc. The universality of man appears in practice precisely in the universality that makes the whole of nature into his inorganic body in that it is both (i) his immediate means of subsistence and also (ii) the material object and tool of his vital activity. Nature is the inorganic body of a man, that is, in so far as it is not itself a human body. That man lives from nature means that nature is his body with which he must maintain a constant interchange so as not to die. That man's physical and intellectual life depends on nature merely means that nature depends on itself, for man is a part of nature.

While alienated labour alienates (1) nature from man, and (2) man from himself, his own active function, his vital activity, it also alienates the species from man; it turns his species-life into a means towards his individual life. Firstly it alienates species-life and individual life, and secondly in its abstraction it makes the latter into the aim of the former which is also conceived of in its abstract and alien form. For firstly, work, vital activity, and productive life itself appear to man only as a means to the satisfaction of a need, the need to preserve his physical existence. But productive life is species-life. It is life producing life. The whole character of a species, its generic character, is contained in its manner of vital activity, and free conscious activity is the species-characteristic of man. Life itself appears merely as a means to life.

The animal is immediately one with its vital activity. It is not distinct from it. They are identical. Man makes his vital activity itself into an object of his will and consciousness. He has a conscious vital activity. He is not immediately identical to any of his characterizations. Conscious vital activity differentiates man immediately from animal vital activity. It is this and this alone that makes man a species-being. He is only a conscious being, that is, his own life is an object to him, precisely because he is a species-being. This is the only reason for his activity being free activity. Alienated labour reverses the relationship so that, just because he is a conscious being, man makes his vital activity and essence a mere means to his existence.

The practical creation of an objective world, the working-over of inorganic nature, is the confirmation of man as a conscious species-being, that is, as a being that relates to the species as to himself and to himself as to the species. It is true that the animal, too, produces. It builds itself a nest, a dwelling, like the bee, the beaver, the ant, etc. But it only produces what it needs immediately for itself or its offspring; it produces one-sidedly whereas man produces universally; it produces only under the pressure of immediate physical need, whereas man produces freely from physical need and only truly produces when he is thus free; it produces only itself whereas man reproduces the whole of nature. Its product belongs immediately to its physical body whereas man can freely separate himself from his product. The animal only fashions things according to the standards and needs of the species it belongs to, whereas man knows how to produce according to the measure of every species and knows everywhere how to apply its inherent standard to the object; thus man also fashions things according to the laws of beauty.

Thus it is in the working over of the objective world that man first really affirms himself as a species-being. This production is his active species-life. Through it nature appears as his work and his reality. The object of work is therefore the objectification of the species-life of man; for he duplicates himself not only intellectually, in his mind, but also actively in reality and thus can look at his image in a world he has created. Therefore when alienated labour tears from man the object of his production, it also tears from him his species-life, the real objectivity of his species and turns the advantage he has over animals into a disadvantage in that his inorganic body, nature, is torn from him.

Similarly, in that alienated labour degrades man's own free activity to a means, it turns the species-life of man into a means for his physical existence.

Thus consciousness, which man derives from his species, changes itself through alienation so that species-life becomes a means for him.

Therefore alienated labour:

(3) makes the species-being of man, both nature and the intellectual faculties of his species, into a being that is alien to him, into a means for his individual existence. It alienates from man his own body, nature exterior to him, and his intellectual being, his human essence.

(4) An immediate consequence of man's alienation from the product of his work, his vital activity and his species-being, is the alienation of man from man. When man is opposed to himself, it is another man that is opposed to him. What is valid for the relationship of a man to his work, of the product of his work and himself, is also valid for the relationship of man to other men and of their labour and the objects of their labour.

In general, the statement that man is alienated from his species-being, means that one man is alienated from another as each of them is alienated from the human essence.

The alienation of man and in general of every relationship in which man stands to himself is first realized and expressed in the relationship with which man stands to other men.

Thus in the situation of alienated labour each man measures his relationship to other men by the relationship in which he finds himself placed as a worker.

We began with a fact of political economy, the alienation of the worker and his production. We have expressed this fact in conceptual terms: alienated, externalized labour. We have analysed this concept and thus analysed a purely economic fact.

Let us now see further how the concept of alienated, externalized labour must express and represent itself in reality.

If the product of work is alien to me, opposes me as an alien power, whom does it belong to then?

If my own activity does not belong to me and is an alien, forced activity to whom does it belong then?

To another being than myself.

Who is this being?

The gods? Of course in the beginning of history the chief production, as for example, the building of temples etc. in Egypt, India, and Mexico was both in the service of the gods and also belonged to them. But the gods alone were never the masters of the work. And nature just as little. And what a paradox it would be if, the more man mastered nature through his work and the more the miracles of the gods were rendered superfluous by the miracles of industry, the more man had to give up his pleasure in producing and the enjoyment in his product for the sake of these powers.

The alien being to whom the labour and the product of the labour belongs, whom the labour serves and who enjoys its product, can only be man himself. If the product of labour does not belong to the worker but stands over against him as an alien power, this is only possible in that it belongs to another man apart from the worker.

If his activity torments him it must be a joy and a pleasure to someone else. This alien power above man can be neither the gods nor nature, only man himself.

Consider further the above sentence that the relationship of man to himself first becomes objective and real to him through his relationship to other men. So if he relates to the product of his labour, his objectified labour, as to an object that is alien, hostile, powerful, and independent of him, this relationship implies that another man is the alien, hostile, powerful, and independent master of this object. If he relates to his own activity as to something unfree, it is a relationship to an activity that is under the domination, oppression, and yoke of another man.

Every self-alienation of man from himself and nature appears in the relationship in which he places himself and nature to other men distinct from himself. Therefore religious self-alienation necessarily appears in the relationship of layman to priest, or, because here we are dealing with a spiritual world, to a mediator, etc. In the practical, real world, the self-alienation can only appear through the practical, real relationship to other men. The means through which alienation makes progress are themselves practical. Through alienated labour, then, man creates not only his relationship to the object and act of production as to alien and hostile men; he creates too the relationship in which other men stand to his production and his product and the relationship in which he stands to these other men. Just as he turns his production into his own loss of reality and punishment and his own product into a loss, a product that does not belong to him, so he creates the domination of the man who does not produce over the production and the product. As he alienates his activity from himself, so he hands over to an alien person an activity that does not belong to him.

Up till now we have considered the relationship only from the side of the worker and we will later consider it from the side of the non-worker.

Thus through alienated, externalized labour the worker creates the relationship to this labour of a man who is alien to it and remains exterior to it. The relationship of the worker to his labour creates the relationship to it of the capitalist, or whatever else one wishes to call the master of the labour. Private property is thus the product, result, and necessary consequence of externalized labour, of the exterior relationship of the worker to nature and to himself.

Thus private property is the result of the analysis of the concept of externalized labour, i.e. externalized man, alienated work, alienated life, alienated man.

We have, of course, obtained the concept of externalized labour (externalized life) from political economy as the result of the movement of private property. But it is evident from the analysis of this concept that, although private property appears to be the ground and reason for externalized labour, it is rather a consequence of it, just as the gods are originally not the cause but the effect of the aberration of the human mind, although later this relationship reverses itself.

It is only in the final culmination of the development of private property that these hidden characteristics come once more to the fore, in that firstly it is the product of externalized labour and secondly it is the means through which labour externalizes itself, the realization of this externalization.

This development sheds light at the same time on several previously unresolved contradictions.

1. Political economy starts from labour as the veritable soul of production, and yet it attributes nothing to labour and everything to private property. Proudhon has drawn a conclusion from this contradiction that is favourable to labour and against private property. But we can see that this apparent contradiction is the contradiction of alienated labour with itself and that political economy has only expressed the laws of alienated labour.

We can therefore also see that wages and private property are identical: for wages, in which the product, the object of the labour, remunerates the labour itself, are just a necessary consequence of the alienation of labour. In the wage system the labour does not appear as the final aim but only as the servant of the wages. We will develop this later and for the moment only draw a few consequences.

An enforced raising of wages (quite apart from other difficulties, apart from the fact that, being an anomaly, it could only be maintained by force) would only mean a better payment of slaves and would not give this human meaning and worth either to the worker or to his labour.

Indeed, even the equality of wages that Proudhon demands only changes the relationship of the contemporary worker to his labour into that of all men to labour. Society is then conceived of as an abstract capitalist.

Wages are an immediate consequence of alienated labour and alienated labour is the immediate cause of private property. Thus the disappearance of one entails also the disappearance of the other.

2. It is a further consequence of the relationship of alienated labour to private property that the emancipation of society from private property, etc., from slavery, is expressed in its political form by the emancipation of the workers. This is not because only their emancipation is at stake but because general human emancipation is contained in their emancipation. It is contained within it because the whole of human slavery is involved in the relationship of the worker to his product and all slave relationships are only modifications and consequences of this relationship.

Just as we have discovered the concept of private property through an analysis of the concept of alienated, externalized labour, so all categories of political economy can be deduced with the help of these two factors. We shall recognize in each category of market, competition, capital, money, only a particular and developed expression of these first two fundamental elements.

However, before we consider this structure let us try to solve two problems:

1. To determine the general essence of private property as it appears as a result of alienated labour in its relationship to truly human and social property.

2. We have taken the alienation and externalization of labour as a fact and analysed this fact. We now ask, how does man come to externalize, to alienate his labour? How is this alienation grounded in human development? We have already obtained much material for the solution of this problem, in that we have turned the question of the origin of private property into the question of the relationship of externalized labour to the development of human history. For when we speak of private property we think we are dealing with something that is exterior to man. When we speak of labour, then we are dealing directly with man. This new formulation of the problem already implies its solution.

To take point 1, the general nature of private property and its relationship to truly human property.

Externalized labour has been broken down into two component parts that determine each other or are only different expressions of one and the same relationship. Appropriation appears as alienation, as externalization, and externalization as appropriation, and alienation as true enfranchisement. We have dealt with one aspect, alienated labour as regards the worker himself, that is, the relationship of externalized labour to itself. As a product and necessary result of this relationship we have discovered the property relationship of the non-worker to the worker and his labour.

As the material and summary expression of alienated labour, private property embraces both relationships, both that of the worker to his labour, the product of his labour and the non-worker, and that of the non-worker to the worker and the product of his labour.

We have already seen that for the worker who appropriates nature through his work, this appropriation appears as alienation, his own activity as activity for and of someone else, his vitality as sacrifice of his life, production of objects as their loss to an alien power, an alien man: let us now consider the relationship that this man, who is alien to labour and the worker, has to the worker, to labour and its object.

The first remark to make is that everything that appears in the case of the worker to be an activity of externalization, of alienation, appears in the case of the non-worker to be a state of externalization, of alienation.

Secondly, the real, practical behaviour of the worker in production and towards his product (as a state of mind) appears in the case of the non-worker opposed to him as theoretical behaviour. Thirdly, the non-worker does everything against the worker that the worker does against himself but he does not do against himself what he does against the worker.

Let us consider these three relationships in more detail . . . . [The manuscript breaks off unfinished here.]

. . .

(b) A spectre is haunting Europe—the spectre of Communism. All the Powers of old Europe have entered into a holy alliance to exorcise this spectre: Pope and Tsar, Metternich and Guizot, French Radicals and German police-spies.

Where is the party in opposition that has not been decried as Communistic by its opponents in power? Where the Opposition that has not hurled back the branding reproach of Communism, against the more advanced opposition parties, as well as against its reactionary adversaries?

Two things result from this fact.

I. Communism is already acknowledged by all European Powers to be itself a Power.

II. It is high time that Communists should openly, in the face of the whole world, publish their views, their aims, their tendencies, and meet this nursery tale of the Spectre of Communism with a Manifesto of the party itself.

To this end, Communists of various nationalities have assembled in London, and sketched the following Manifesto, to be published in the English, French, German, Italian, Flemish, and Danish languages.

BOURGEOIS AND PROLETARIANS

The history of all hitherto existing society is the history of class struggles.

Freeman and slave, patrician and plebeian, lord and serf, guild-master and journeyman—in a word, oppressor and oppressed, stood in constant opposition to one another, carried on an uninterrupted, now hidden, now open fight, a fight that each time ended either in a revolutionary re-constitution of society at large or in the common ruin of the contending classes.

In the earlier epochs of history, we find almost everywhere a complicated arrangement of society into various orders, a manifold gradation of social rank. In ancient Rome we have patricians, knights, plebeians, slaves; in the Middle Ages, feudal lords, vassals, guild-masters, journeymen, apprentices, serfs; in almost all of these classes, again, subordinate gradations.

The modern bourgeois society that has sprouted from the ruins of feudal society has not done away with class antagonisms. It has but established new classes, new conditions of oppression, new forms of struggle in place of the old ones.

Our epoch, the epoch of the bourgeoisie, possesses, however, this distinctive feature: it has simplified the class antagonisms. Society as a whole is more and more splitting up into two great hostile camps, into two great classes directly facing each other: Bourgeoisie and Proletariat.

From the serfs of the Middle Ages sprang the chartered burghers of the earliest towns. From these burgesses the first elements of the bourgeoisie were developed.

The discovery of America, the rounding of the Cape, opened up fresh ground for the rising bourgeoisie. The East Indian and Chinese markets, the colonization of America, trade with the colonies, the increase in the means of exchange and in commodities generally, gave to commerce, to navigation, to industry, an impulse never before known, and thereby, to the revolutionary element in the tottering feudal society, a rapid development.

The feudal system of industry, under which industrial production was monopolized by closed guilds, now no longer sufficed for the growing wants of the new markets. The manufacturing system took its place. The guild-masters were pushed on one side by the manufacturing middle class; division of labour between the different corporate guilds vanished in the face of division of labour in each single workshop.

Meantime the markets kept ever growing, the demand ever rising. Even manufacture no longer sufficed. Thereupon, steam and machinery revolutionized industrial production. The place of manufacture was taken by the giant, Modern Industry, the place of the industrial middle class, by industrial millionaires, the leaders of whole industrial armies, the modern bourgeois.

Modern industry has established the world-market, for which the discovery of America paved the way. This market has given an immense development to commerce, to navigation, to communication by land. This development has, in its turn, reacted on the extension of industry; and in proportion as industry, commerce, navigation, railways extended, in the same proportion the bourgeoisie developed, increased its capital, and pushed into the background every class handed down from the Middle Ages.

We see, therefore, how the modern bourgeoisie is itself the product of a long course of development, of a series of revolutions in the modes of production and of exchange.

Each step in the development of the bourgeoisie was accompanied by a corresponding political advance of that class. An oppressed class under the sway of the feudal nobility, an armed and self-governing association in the medieval commune; here independent urban republic (as in Italy and Germany), there taxable 'third estate' of the monarchy (as in France), afterwards, in the period of manufacture proper, serving either the semi-feudal or the absolute monarchy as a counterpoise against the nobility, and, in fact, corner-stone of the great monarchies in general, the bourgeoisie has at last, since the establishment of Modern Industry and of the world-market, conquered for itself, in the modern representative State, exclusive political sway. The executive of the modern State is but a committee for managing the common affairs of the whole bourgeoisie.

The bourgeoisie, historically, has played a most revolutionary part.

The bourgeoisie, wherever it has got the upper hand, has put an end to all feudal, patri-archal, idyllic relations. It has pitilessly torn asunder the motley feudal ties that bound man to his 'natural superiors', and has left remaining no other nexus between man and man than naked self-interest, than callous 'cash payment'. It has drowned the most heav-enly ecstasies of religious fervour, of chivalrous enthusiasm, of philistine sentimentalism, in the icy water of egotistical calculation. It has resolved personal worth into exchange value, and in place of the numberless indefeasible chartered freedoms, has set up that single, unconscionable freedom—Free Trade. In one word, for exploitation, veiled by religious and political illusions, it has substituted naked, shameless, direct, brutal exploitation.

The bourgeoisie has stripped of its halo every occupation hitherto honoured and looked up to with reverent awe. It has converted the physician, the lawyer, the priest, the poet, the man of science into its paid wage-labourers.

The bourgeoisie has torn away from the family its sentimental veil, and has reduced the family relation to a mere money relation.

The bourgeoisie has disclosed how it came to pass that the brutal display of vigour in the Middle Ages, which Reactionists so much admire, found its fitting complement in the most slothful indolence. It has been the first to show what man's activity can bring about. It has accomplished wonders far surpassing Egyptian pyramids, Roman aqueducts, and Gothic cathedrals; it has conducted expeditions that put in the shade all former Exoduses of nations and crusades.

The bourgeoisie cannot exist without constantly revolutionizing the instruments of production, and thereby the relations of production, and with them the whole relations of society. Conservation of the old modes of production in unaltered form, was, on the contrary, the first condition of existence for all earlier industrial classes. Constant revolu-tionizing of production, uninterrupted disturbance of all social conditions, everlasting uncertainty and agitation distinguish the bourgeois epoch from all earlier ones. All fixed, fast-frozen relations, with their train of ancient and venerable prejudices and opinions, are swept away, all new-formed ones become antiquated before they can ossify. All that is solid melts into air, all that is holy is profaned, and man is at last compelled to face with sober senses, his real conditions of life, and his relations with his kind.

The need of a constantly expanding market for its products chases the bourgeoisie over the whole surface of the globe. It must nestle everywhere, settle everywhere, establish connections everywhere.

The bourgeoisie has through its exploitation of the world-market given a cosmopol-itan character to production and consumption in every country. To the great chagrin of Reactionists, it has drawn from under the feet of industry the national ground on which it stood. All old-established national industries have been destroyed or are daily being destroyed. They are dislodged by new industries, whose introduction becomes a life-and-death question for all civilized nations, by industries that no longer work up indigenous raw material, but raw material drawn from the remotest zones; industries whose products are consumed, not only at home, but in every quarter of the globe. In place of the old wants, satisfied by the productions of the country, we find new wants, requiring for their satisfaction the products of distant lands and climes. In place of the old local and national seclusion and self-sufficiency, we have intercourse in every direction, universal interdependence of nations. And as in material, so also in intellectual production. The intellectual creations of individual nations become common property. National one-sidedness and narrow-mindedness become more and more impossible, and from the numerous national and local literatures, there arises a world literature.

The bourgeoisie, by the rapid improvement of all instruments of production, by the immensely facilitated means of communication, draws all, even the most barbarian, nations into civilization. The cheap prices of its commodities are the heavy artillery with which it batters down all Chinese walls, with which it forces the barbarians' intensely obstinate hatred of foreigners to capitulate. It compels all nations, on pain of extinction, to adopt the bourgeois mode of production; it compels them to introduce what it calls civilization into their midst, i.e., to become bourgeois themselves. In one word, it creates a world after its own image.

The bourgeoisie has subjected the country to the rule of the towns. It has created enormous cities, has greatly increased the urban population as compared with the rural, and has thus rescued a considerable part of the population from the idiocy of rural life. Just as it has made the country dependent on the towns, so it has made barbarian and semi-barbarian countries dependent on the civilized ones, nations of peasants on nations of bourgeois, the East on the West.

The bourgeoisie keeps more and more doing away with the scattered state of the population, of the means of production, and of property. It has agglomerated population, centralized means of production, and has concentrated property in a few hands. The necessary consequence of this was political centralization. Independent or but loosely connected provinces, with separate interests, laws, governments, and systems of taxation, became lumped together into one nation, with one government, one code of laws, one national class-interest, one frontier, and one customs-tariff.

The bourgeoisie, during its rule of scarcely one hundred years, has created more massive and more colossal productive forces than have all preceding generations together. Subjection of Nature's forces to man, machinery, application of chemistry to industry and agriculture, steam-navigation, railways, electric telegraphs, clearing of whole continents for cultivation, canalization of rivers, whole populations conjured out of the ground—what earlier century had even a presentiment that such productive forces slumbered in the lap of social labour?

We see then that the means of production and of exchange, on whose foundation the bourgeoisie built itself up, were generated in feudal society. At a certain stage in the development of these means of production and of exchange, the conditions under which feudal society produced and exchanged, the feudal organization of agriculture and manufacturing industry, in one word, the feudal relations of property become no longer compatible with the already developed productive forces; they became so many fetters. They had to be burst asunder; they were burst asunder.

Into their place stepped free competition, accompanied by a social and political constitution adapted to it, and by the economical and political sway of the bourgeois class.

A similar movement is going on before our own eyes. Modern bourgeois society with its relations of production, of exchange and of property, a society that has conjured up such gigantic means of production and of exchange, is like the sorcerer, who is no longer able to control the powers of the nether world which he has called up by his spells. The history of industry and commerce for many a decade past is but the history of the revolt of modern productive forces against modern conditions of production, against the property relations that are the conditions for the existence of the bourgeoisie and of its rule. It is enough to mention the commercial crises that by their periodical return put on trial, each time more threateningly, the existence of the entire bourgeois society. In these crises a great part not only of the existing products, but also of the previously created productive forces, are periodically destroyed. In these crises there breaks out an epidemic that, in all earlier epochs, would have seemed an absurdity—the epidemic of over-production. Society suddenly finds itself put back into a state of momentary barbarism; it appears as if a famine, a universal war of devastation, has cut off the supply of every means of subsistence; industry and commerce seem to be destroyed; and why? Because there is too much civilization, too much means of subsistence, too much industry, too much commerce. The productive forces at the disposal of society no longer tend to further the development of the conditions of bourgeois property; on the contrary, they have become too powerful for these conditions, by which they are fettered, and so soon as they overcome these fetters, they bring disorder into the whole of bourgeois society, endanger the existence of bourgeois property. The conditions of bourgeois society are too narrow to comprise the wealth created by them. And how does the bourgeoisie get over these crises? On the one hand by enforced destruction of a mass of productive forces; on the other, by the conquest of new markets, and by the more thorough exploitation of the old ones. That is to say, by paving the way for more extensive and more destructive crises, and by diminishing the means whereby crises are prevented.

The weapons with which the bourgeoisie felled feudalism to the ground are now turned against the bourgeoisie itself.

But not only has the bourgeoisie forged the weapons that bring death to itself; it has also called into existence the men who are to wield those weapons—the modern working class—the proletarians.

In proportion as the bourgeoisie, i.e., capital, is developed, in the same proportion is the proletariat, the modern working class, developed—a class of labourers, who live only so long as they find work, and who find work only so long as their labour increases capital. These labourers, who must sell themselves piecemeal, are a commodity, like every other article of commerce, and are consequently exposed to all the vicissitudes of competition, to all the fluctuations of the market.

Owing to the extensive use of machinery and to division of labour, the work of the proletarians has lost all individual character, and, consequently, all charm for the workman. He becomes an appendage of the machine, and it is only the most simple, most monotonous, and most easily acquired knack, that is required of him. Hence, the cost of production of a workman is restricted, almost entirely, to the means of subsistence that he requires for his maintenance, and for the propagation of his race. But the price of a commodity, and therefore also of labour, is equal to its cost of production. In proportion, therefore, as the repulsiveness of the work increases, the wage decreases. Nay more, in proportion as the use of machinery and division of labour increases, in the same proportion the burden of toil also increases, whether by prolongation of the working hours, by increase of the work exacted in a given time or by increased speed of the machinery, etc.

Modern industry has converted the little workshop of the patriarchal master into the great factory of the industrial capitalist. Masses of labourers, crowded into the factory, are organized like soldiers. As privates of the industrial army they are placed under the command of a perfect hierarchy of officers and sergeants. Not only are they slaves of the bourgeois class, and of the bourgeois State; they are daily and hourly enslaved by the machine, by the overlooker, and, above all, by the individual bourgeois manufacturer himself. The more openly this despotism proclaims gain to be its end and aim, the more petty, the more hateful, and the more embittering it is.

The less the skill and exertion of strength implied in manual labour, in other words, the more modern industry becomes developed, the more is the labour of men superseded by that of women. Differences of age and sex have no longer any distinctive social validity for the working class. All are instruments of labour, more or less expensive to use, according to their age and sex.

No sooner is the exploitation of the labourer by the manufacturer, so far, at an end, and he receives his wages in cash, than he is set upon by the other portions of the bourgeoisie, the landlord, the shopkeeper, the pawnbroker, etc.

The lower strata of the middle class—the small tradespeople, shopkeepers, and retired tradesmen generally, the handicraftsmen and peasants—all these sink gradually into the proletariat, partly because their diminutive capital does not suffice for the scale on which Modern Industry is carried on, and is swamped in the competition with the large capitalists, partly because their specialized skill is rendered worthless by new methods of production. Thus the proletariat is recruited from all classes of the population.

The proletariat goes through various stages of development. With its birth begins its struggle with the bourgeoisie. At first the contest is carried on by individual labourers, then by the workpeople of a factory, then by the operatives of one trade, in one locality, against the individual bourgeois who directly exploits them. They direct their attacks not against the bourgeois conditions of production, but against the instruments of production themselves; they destroy imported wares that compete with their labour, they smash to pieces machinery, they set factories ablaze, they seek to restore by force the vanished status of the workman of the Middle Ages.

At this stage the labourers still form an incoherent mass scattered over the whole country, and broken up by their mutual competition. If anywhere they unite to form more compact bodies, this is not yet the consequence of their own active union, but of the union of the bourgeoisie, which class, in order to attain its own political ends, is compelled to set the whole proletariat in motion, and is moreover yet, for a time, able to do so. At this stage, therefore, the proletarians do not fight their enemies, but the enemies of their enemies, the remnants of absolute monarchy, the landowners, the non-industrial bourgeois, the petty bourgeoisie. Thus the whole historical movement is concentrated in the hands of the bourgeoisie; every victory so obtained is a victory for the bourgeoisie.

But with the development of industry the proletariat not only increases in number; it becomes concentrated in greater masses, its strength grows, and it feels that strength more. The various interests and conditions of life within the ranks of the proletariat are more and more equalized, in proportion as machinery obliterates all distinctions of labour, and nearly everywhere reduces wages to the same low level. The growing competition among the bourgeois, and the resulting commercial crises; make the wages of the workers ever more fluctuating. The unceasing improvement of machinery, ever more rapidly developing, makes their livelihood more and more precarious; the collisions between individual workmen and individual bourgeois take more and more the character of collisions between two classes. Thereupon the workers begin to form combinations (Trades' Unions) against the bourgeois; they club together in order to keep up the rate of wages; they found permanent associations in order to make provision beforehand for these occasional revolts. Here and there the contest breaks out into riots.

Now and then the workers are victorious, but only for a time. The real fruit of their battles lies, not in the immediate result, but in the ever-expanding union of the workers. This union is helped on by the improved means of communication that are created by modern industry and that place the workers of different localities in contact with one another. It was just this contact that was needed to centralize the numerous local struggles, all of the same character, into one national struggle between classes. But every class struggle is a political struggle. And that union, to attain which the burghers of the Middle Ages, with their miserable highways, required centuries, the modern proletarians, thanks to railways, achieve in a few years.

This organization of the proletarians into a class, and consequently into a political party, is continually being upset again by the competition between the workers themselves. But it ever rises up again, stronger, firmer, mightier. It compels legislative recognition of particular interests of the workers, by taking advantage of the divisions among the bourgeoisie itself. Thus the ten-hours' bill in England was carried.

Altogether, collisions between the classes of the old society further in many ways the course of development of the proletariat. The bourgeoisie finds itself involved in a constant battle. At first with the aristocracy; later on, with those portions of the bourgeoisie itself whose interests have become antagonistic to the progress of industry; at all times, with the bourgeoisie of foreign countries. In all these battles it sees itself compelled to appeal to the proletariat, to ask for its help, and thus to drag it into the political arena. The bourgeoisie itself, therefore, supplies the proletariat with its own elements of political and general education, in other words, it furnishes the proletariat with weapons for fighting the bourgeoisie.

Further, as we have already seen, entire sections of the ruling classes are, by the advance of industry, precipitated into the proletariat, or are at least threatened in their conditions of existence. These also supply the proletariat with fresh elements of enlightenment and progress.

Finally, in times when the class struggle nears the decisive hour, the process of dissolution going on within the ruling class, in fact within the whole range of old society, assumes such a violent, glaring character, that a small section of the ruling class cuts itself adrift, and joins the revolutionary class, the class that holds the future in its hands. Just as, therefore, at an earlier period, a section of the nobility went over to the bourgeoisie, so now a portion of the bourgeoisie goes over to the proletariat, and in particular, a portion of the bourgeois ideologists, who have raised themselves to the level of comprehending theoretically the historical movement as a whole.

Of all the classes that stand face to face with the bourgeoisie today, the proletariat alone is a really revolutionary class. The other classes decay and finally disappear in the face of Modern Industry; the proletariat is its special and essential product.

The lower middle class, the small manufacturer, the shopkeeper, the artisan, the peasant, all these fight against the bourgeoisie, to save from extinction their existence as fractions of the middle class. They are therefore not revolutionary, but conservative. Nay more, they are reactionary, for they try to roll back the wheel of history. If by chance they are revolutionary, they are so only in view of their impending transfer into the proletariat; they thus defend not their present, but their future interests, they desert their own standpoint to place themselves at that of the proletariat.

The 'dangerous class', the social scum, that passively rotting mass thrown off by the lowest layers of old society, may, here and there, be swept into the movement by a proletarian revolution; its conditions of life, however, prepare it far more for the part of a bribed tool of reactionary intrigue.

In the conditions of the proletariat, those of old society at large are already virtually swamped. The proletarian is without property; his relation to his wife and children has no longer anything in common with the bourgeois family relations; modern industrial labour, modern subjection to capital, the same in England as in France, in America as in Germany, has stripped him of every trace of national character. Law, morality, religion are to him so many bourgeois prejudices, behind which lurk in ambush just as many bourgeois interests.

All the preceding classes that got the upper hand, sought to fortify their already acquired status by subjecting society at large to their conditions of appropriation. The proletarians cannot become masters of the productive forces of society, except by abolishing their own previous mode of appropriation, and thereby also every other previous mode of appropriation. They have nothing of their own to secure and to fortify; their mission is to destroy all previous securities for, and insurances of, individual property.

All previous historical movements were movements of minorities, or in the interests of minorities. The proletarian movement is the self-conscious, independent movement of the immense majority, in the interests of the immense majority. The proletariat, the lowest stratum of our present society, cannot stir, cannot raise itself up, without the whole superincumbent strata of official society being sprung into the air.

Though not in substance, yet in form, the struggle of the proletariat with the bourgeoisie is at first a national struggle. The proletariat of each country must, of course, first of all settle matters with its own bourgeoisie.

In depicting the most general phases of the development of the proletariat, we traced the more or less veiled civil war, raging within existing society, up to the point where that war breaks out into open revolution, and where the violent overthrow of the bourgeoisie lays the foundation for the sway of the proletariat.

Hitherto, every form of society has been based, as we have already seen, on the antagonism of oppressing and oppressed classes. But in order to oppress a class, certain conditions must be assured to it under which it can, at least, continue its slavish existence. The serf, in the period of serfdom, raised himself to membership in the commune, just as the petty bourgeois, under the yoke of feudal absolutism, managed to develop into a bourgeois. The modern labourer, on the contrary, instead of rising with the progress of industry, sinks deeper and deeper below the conditions of existence of his own class. He becomes a pauper, and pauperism develops more rapidly than population and wealth. And here it becomes evident, that the bourgeoisie is unfit any longer to be the ruling class in society, and to impose its conditions of existence upon society as an overriding law. It is unfit to rule because it is incompetent to assure an existence to its slave within his slavery, because it cannot help letting him sink into such a state, that it has to feed him, instead of being fed by him. Society can no longer live under this bourgeoisie, in other words, its existence is no longer compatible with society.

The essential condition for the existence, and for the sway of the bourgeois class, is the formation and augmentation of capital; the condition for capital is wage-labour. Wage-labour rests exclusively on competition between the labourers. The advance of industry, whose involuntary promoter is the bourgeoisie, replaces the isolation of the labourers, due to competition, by their revolutionary combination, due to association. The development of Modern Industry, therefore, cuts from under its feet the very foundation on which the bourgeoisie produces and appropriates products. What the bourgeoisie, therefore, produces, above all, is its own grave-diggers. Its fall and the victory of the proletariat are equally inevitable.

42   Georges Sorel, from *Reflections on Violence* (ed. J. Jennings; Cambridge University Press, 1999), pp. 24–31

Sorel (1847–1922) trained originally as an engineer in Paris, but retired early from this occupation, in 1892. He then devoted his energies to political writing. Scathing about the merits of 'electoralism' and parliamentary politics, he remained an unmitigated critic of the mediocrity and decadence of the bourgeois order. In intellectual terms, he tried to blend Marxism with the 'direct action' tactics celebrated by the burgeoning syndicalist movement. Syndicalism grew out of trade union bodies that held the utopian vision of capturing key industries and the state. In the wake of a number of defeats and setbacks for syndicalist organizations from 1908 onwards, Sorel became increasingly pessimistic about the prospects of revolution. For a while he flirted with royalism as the only political force which, he believed, was capable of inspiring moral renewal and social change. After 1918, he made some ambiguous remarks about the merits of Mussolini (which have encouraged fascists, erroneously, to claim him for their cause). Yet his political sympathies were most engaged in this period by the Bolshevik revolution in Russia.

The mind of man is so constituted that it cannot remain content with the mere observation of facts but wishes to understand the inner reason of things; I therefore ask myself whether it might not be desirable to study this theory of myths more thoroughly, utilizing the insights we owe to the philosophy of Bergson. The attempt that I am about to submit to you is doubtless very imperfect, but I think that it has been conceived in accordance with the method that must be followed to throw light on the problem.

Firstly, we should notice that moralists rarely ever discuss what is truly fundamental about our individuality; as a rule they try to appraise our already completed acts with the aid of judgements formulated in advance by society for different types of action most common in contemporary life. They say that in this way they are determining motives; but these motives are of the same nature as those of which jurists take account in criminal law: they are social evaluations of facts known to everybody. Many philosophers, especially those of antiquity, have believed it possible to reduce everything to a question of utility; and if any social evaluation does exist it is surely utility;—theologians estimate transgressions by the place they occupy on the road which, according to average human experience, leads to mortal sin; they are thus able to ascertain the degree of malice represented by sexual desire and therefore the appropriate punishment;—the moderns teach that we judge our will before acting, comparing our projected conduct with general principles which are, to a certain extent, analogous to declarations of the rights of man; and this theory is, very probably, inspired by the admiration engendered by the *Bills of Rights* placed at the head of each American constitution.

We are all so extremely concerned to know what the world thinks of us that, sooner or later, considerations analogous to those moralists speak do pass through our mind; as a result of this the latter have been able to imagine that they have really made an appeal to experience so as to discover what exists at the bottom of the creative conscience, when, as a matter of fact, all they have done is to consider already accomplished acts from the point of view of their social effects.

Bergson, on the contrary, invites us to consider the inner depths of the mind and what happens during a creative moment: 'There are', he says, 'two different selves, one of which is, as it were, the external projection of the other, its spatial and, so to speak, social representation. We reach the former by deep introspection, which leads us to grasp our inner states as living things, constantly in a process of becoming, as states not amenable to measure . . . But *the moments when we grasp ourselves are rare*, and this is why we are rarely free. The greater part of the time we live outside ourselves; we perceive only a colourless shadow . . . We live for the external world rather than ourselves; we speak more than we think; we are *acted upon* rather than act ourselves. To act freely is to recover possession of oneself, and to get back into pure duration.'

In order to acquire a real understanding of this psychology we must 'carry ourselves back in thought to those moments of our life when we made some serious decision, moments unique of their kind, which will not be repeated any more than the past phases of the history of a people will come back again'. It is very evident that we enjoy this liberty most of all when we are making an effort to create a new individuality within ourselves, thus endeavouring to break the bonds of habit which enclose us. It might at first be supposed that it would be sufficient to say that, at such moments, we are dominated by an overwhelming emotion; but everybody now recognizes that movement is the essence of emotional life and it is then in terms of movement that we must speak of creative consciousness.

Here is how it seems to me the psychology of the deeper life must be represented. We should abandon the idea that the soul can be compared to something moving, which, obeying a more or less mechanical law, is impelled in the direction of certain given motive forces. When we act we are creating a completely artificial world placed ahead of the present world and composed of movements which depend entirely on us. In this way our freedom becomes perfectly intelligible. Starting from these constructions, which cover everything that interests us, several philosophers, inspired by Bergsonian doctrines, have been led to formulate a rather startling theory. For example, Edouard Le Roy says: 'Our real body is the entire universe as far as it is experienced by us. And what common sense more strictly calls our body is only the region of least unconsciousness and greatest free activity, the part which we most directly control and by means of which we are able to act on the rest.' We must not, as this subtle philosopher constantly does, confuse a passing state of our willing activity with the stable affirmations of science.

These artificial worlds generally disappear from our minds without leaving any trace in our memory; but when the masses are deeply moved it then becomes possible to describe a picture which constitutes a social myth.

The belief in glory, which Renan praised so much, quickly fades away into rhapsodies when it has not been supported by myths, which have themselves varied greatly in different epochs: the citizen of the Greek republics, the Roman legionary, the soldier of the wars of Liberty, and the artist of the Renaissance did not picture their conception of glory through the same set of images. Renan complained that 'faith in glory is compromised by the *limited historical outlook* that tends to be prevalent in our day'. 'Very few people', he wrote, 'act with eternity in mind . . . Everyone wants to enjoy his own glory; they eat the unripened seed in their lifetime; and do not gather it in sheaves after death.' In my opinion, this limited historical outlook is not a cause but a consequence; it results from the weakening of the heroic myths which enjoyed such great popularity at the beginning of the nineteenth century; the belief in glory perished and the limited historical outlook became predominant at the same time that these myths vanished.

As long as there are no myths accepted by the masses, one may go on talking of revolts indefinitely without ever provoking any revolutionary movement; this is what gives such importance to the general strike and renders it so odious to socialists who are afraid of revolution; they do all they can to shake the confidence felt by the workers in the preparations they are making for the revolution; and in order to succeed in this they cast ridicule on the idea of the general strike, which alone has a value as a motive force. One of the chief means employed by them is to represent it as a utopia; this is easy enough, as there are very few myths which are perfectly free from any utopian element.

The revolutionary myths which exist at the present time are almost pure; they allow us to understand the activity, the sentiments and the ideas of the masses as they prepare themselves to enter on a decisive struggle; they are not descriptions of things but expressions of a will to act. A utopia is, on the contrary, an intellectual product; it is the work of theorists who, after observing and discussing the facts, seek to establish a model to which they can compare existing societies in order to estimate the amount of good and evil they contain; it is a combination of imaginary institutions having sufficient analogies to real institutions for the jurist to be able to reason about them; it is a construction which can be broken into parts and of which certain pieces have been shaped in such a way that they can (with a few alterations) be fitted into future legislation.—Whilst contemporary myths lead men to prepare themselves for a combat which will destroy the existing state of things, the effect of utopias has always been to direct men's minds towards reforms which can be brought about by patching up the system; it is not surprising then that so many believers in utopias were able to develop into able statesmen when they had acquired greater experience of political life.—A myth cannot be refuted since it is, at bottom, identical to the convictions of a group, being the expression of these convictions in the language of movement; and it is, in consequence, unanalysable into parts which could be placed on the plane of historical descriptions. A utopia, on the other hand, can be discussed like any other social constitution; the spontaneous movements it presupposes can be compared with those actually observed in the course of history, and we can in this way evaluate their verisimilitude; it is possible to refute it by showing that the economic system on which it has been made to rest is incompatible with the necessary conditions of modern production.

Liberal political economy is one of the best examples of a utopia that could be given. A society was imagined where everything could be reduced to types produced by commerce and operating under the law of the fullest competition; it is recognized today that this kind of ideal society would be as difficult to realize as that of Plato; but several great statesmen of modern times have owed their fame to the efforts they made to introduce something of this ideal of commercial liberty into industrial legislation.

We have here a utopia free from any element of myth; the history of French democracy, however, offers us a very remarkable combination of utopias and myths. The theories that inspired the authors of our first constitutions are today regarded as extremely fanciful; indeed, often people are loath to concede them the value which they have been so long recognized to possess: that of an ideal on which legislators, magistrates and administrators should constantly fix their eyes in order to secure for men an element of justice. With these utopias were mixed myths which represented the struggle against the *ancien régime*; as long as the myths survived, all the refutations of liberal utopias could produce no effect; the myth safe-guarded the utopia with which it was mixed.

For a long time socialism was scarcely anything but a utopia; and the Marxists were right in claiming for their master the honour of having changed the situation: socialism has now become the preparation of the masses employed in large-scale industry who wish to do away with the State and with property; it is no longer necessary therefore to discuss how men must organize themselves in order to enjoy future happiness; everything is reduced to the *revolutionary apprenticeship* of the proletariat. Unfortunately, Marx was not acquainted with the facts which have now become familiar to us; we know better than he did what strikes are, because we have been able to observe economic conflicts of considerable extent and duration: the myth of the general strike has now become popular and is now firmly established in the minds of the workers; we have ideas about violence that it would have been difficult for him to form; we can therefore complete his doctrine, instead of making commentaries on his texts as his unfortunate disciples have done for so long.

In this way utopianism tends to disappear completely from socialism; the latter has no longer any need to concern itself with the organization of industry since capitalism does this. I think, moreover, that I have shown that a general strike corresponds to sentiments which are closely related to those that are necessary to promote production in a very progressive form of industry, that a revolutionary apprenticeship may also be an apprenticeship as a producer.

People who are living in this world of myths are secure from all refutation; something which has led many to assert that socialism is a kind of religion. For a long time people have been struck by the fact that religious convictions are unaffected by criticism; and from this they have concluded that everything which claims to be beyond science must be a religion. It has also been observed that in our day Christianity tends to be less a system of dogmas than a Christian life, that is, a moral reform penetrating to the roots of one's being; consequently, a new analogy has been discovered between religion and a revolutionary socialism which aims at the apprenticeship, preparation and even reconstruction of the individual which takes place with this gigantic task in mind. But Bergson has taught us that it is not only religion which occupies the profounder region of our mental life; revolutionary myths have their place there equally with religion. The arguments which Yves Guyoto puts forward against socialism on the ground that it is a religion therefore seem to me to be founded on an imperfect knowledge of the new psychology.

Renan was very surprised to discover that socialists were beyond discouragement: 'After each abortive experience they begin again; the solution has not been found, we will find it. The idea that no solution exists never occurs to them, and there lies their strength.' The explanation given by Renan is superficial; it sees socialism as a utopia, as a thing comparable to observed realities; we can hardly understand how confidence can thus survive so many failures. But, by the side of utopias, there have always existed myths capable of leading the workers on to revolt. For a long time these myths were founded on the legends of the Revolution, and they preserved all of their value as long as these legends remained unshaken. Today the confidence of the socialists is much greater than it was in the past, now that the myth of the general strike dominates the true working-class movement in its entirety. No failure proves anything against socialism, as it has become a work of preparation; if it fails, it merely proves that the apprenticeship has been insufficient; they must set to work again with more courage, persistence and confidence than before; the experience of labour has taught the workers that it is by means of patient apprenticeship that one can become a true comrade at work; and it is also the only way of becoming a true revolutionary.

43   Eduard Bernstein, from *Evolutionary Socialism: A Criticism and Affirmation* (Schocken Books, 1967), pp. 141–7

Bernstein (1850–1932) joined the Social Democratic Workers' Party at the age of twenty-two, and was present, two years later, at the historic meeting that formed the German Social Democratic Party. His orthodox Marxist beliefs, and collaboration with Engels, ensured that he was regarded as one of the major German theorists of the left. During the 1890s, Bernstein began to rethink some of the major tenets of Marx's analysis of capitalism. He rejected the idea that the demise of the capitalist order was imminent, and other associated doctrines, such as the immiseration of the proletariat and the inevitability of class conflict. Socialism, he came to believe, might well be accomplished through the ballot-box. He put these views forward in a controversial series of articles that he authored, in the late 1890s, for *Die Neue Zeit*, and then in his *Evolutionary Socialism*. While his ideas were officially defeated in these years, his influence grew within the party. He was among the deputies in the *Reichstag* who voted in favour of Germany's participation in the conflict of 1914, yet changed his mind in the years that followed. He rejoined the SPD in 1918 and served briefly in government in 1919. His political influence waned considerably in the final years of his political life.

What is the principle of democracy?

The answer to this appears very simple. At first one would think it settled by the definition "government by the people." But even a little consideration tells us that by that only quite a superficial, purely formal definition is given, whilst nearly all who use the word democracy to-day understand by it more than a mere form of government. We shall come much nearer to the definition if we express ourselves negatively, and define democracy as an absence of class government, as the indication of a social condition where a political privilege belongs to no one class as opposed to the whole community. By that the explanation is already given as to why a monopolist corporation is in principle anti-democratic. This negative definition has, besides, the advantage that it gives less room than the phrase "government by the people" to the idea of the oppression of the individual by the majority which is absolutely repugnant to the modern mind. To-day we find the oppression of the minority by the majority " undemocratic," although it was originally held to be quite consistent with government by the people. The idea of democracy includes, in the conception of the present day, a notion of justice—an equality of rights for all members of the community, and in that principle the rule of the majority, to which in every concrete case the rule of the people extends, finds its limits. The more it is adopted and governs the general consciousness, the more will democracy be equal in meaning to the highest possible degree of freedom for all.

Democracy is in principle the suppression of class government, though it is not yet the actual suppression of classes. They speak of the conservative character of the democracy, and to a certain degree rightly. Absolutism, or semi-absolutism, deceives its supporters as well as its opponents as to the extent of their power. Therefore in countries where it obtains, or where its traditions still exist, we have flitting plans, exaggerated language, zigzag politics, fear of revolution, hope in oppression. In a democracy the parties, and the classes standing behind them, soon learn to know the limits of their power, and to undertake each time only as much as they can reasonably hope to carry through under the existing circumstances. Even if they make their demands rather higher than they seriously mean in order to give way in the unavoidable compromise—and democracy is the high school of compromise—they must still be moderate. The right to vote in a democracy makes its members virtually partners in the community, and this virtual partnership must in the end lead to real partnership. With a working class undeveloped in numbers and culture the general right to vote may long appear as the right to choose "the butcher"; with the growing number and knowledge of the workers it is changed,

however, into the implement by which to transform the representatives of the people
from masters into real servants of the people.

Universal suffrage in Germany could serve Bismarck temporarily as a tool, but finally
it compelled Bismarck to serve it as a tool. It could be of use for a time to the squires of
the East Elbe district, but it has long been the terror of these same squires. In 1878 it
could bring Bismarck into a position to forge the weapon of socialistic law, but through
it this weapon became blunt and broken, until by the help of it Bismarck was thoroughly beaten. Had Bismarck in 1878, with his then majority, created a politically
exceptional law, instead of a police one, a law which would have placed the worker outside the franchise, he would for a time have hit social democracy more sharply than
with the former. It is true, he would then have hit other people also. Universal franchise
is, from two sides, the alternative to a violent revolution. But universal suffrage is only
a part of democracy, although a part which in time must draw the other parts after it as
the magnet attracts to itself the scattered portions of iron. It certainly proceeds more
slowly than many would wish, but in spite of that it is at work. And social democracy
cannot further this work better than by taking its stand unreservedly on the theory of
democracy—on the ground of universal suffrage with all the consequences resulting
therefrom to its tactics.

In practice—that is, in its actions—it has in Germany always done so. But in their
explanations its literary advocates have often acted otherwise, and still often do so to-day.
Phrases which were composed in a time when the political privilege of property ruled
all over Europe, and which under these circumstances were explanatory, and to a certain
degree also justified, but which to-day are only a dead weight, are treated with such
reverence as though the progress of the movement depended on them and not on
the understanding of what can be done, and what should be done. Is there any sense, for
example, in maintaining the phrase of the "dictatorship of the proletariat" at a time
when in all possible places representatives of social democracy have placed themselves
practically in the arena of Parliamentary work, have declared for the proportional
representation of the people, and for direct legislation—all of which is inconsistent with
a dictatorship.

The phrase is to-day so antiquated that it is only to be reconciled with reality by
stripping the word dictatorship of its actual meaning and attaching to it some kind of
weakened interpretation. The whole practical activity of social democracy is directed
towards creating circumstances and conditions which shall render possible and secure a
transition (free from convulsive outbursts) of the modern social order into a higher one.
From the consciousness of being the pioneers of a higher civilisation, its adherents are
ever creating fresh inspiration and zeal. In this rests also, finally, the moral justification of
the socialist expropriation towards which they aspire. But the "dictatorship of the classes"
belongs to a lower civilisation, and apart from the question of the expediency and
practicability of the thing, it is only to be looked upon as a reversion, as political atavism.
If the thought is aroused that the transition from a capitalist to a socialist society must
necessarily be accomplished by means of the development of forms of an age which did
not know at all, or only in quite an imperfect form, the present methods of the initiating
and carrying of laws, and which was without the organs fit for the purpose, reaction will
set in.

44 Karl Kautsky, from *The Dictatorship of the Proletariat* (National Labour Press Ltd, ILP Library, 1918), pp. 12–22

Kautsky (1854–1938) was one of the major socialist theoreticians of the mid-late nineteenth century. He was first involved in social democratic politics, in Austria, in 1874 and worked as a journalist with the German Workers' Party from 1879. He came to political prominence as editor of *Die Neue Zeit*, the journal of the Social Democratic Party (SPD) which he had founded. He was influential upon the party's *Erfurt Program* in 1891, which committed the German Social Democratic Party to an evolutionary form of Marxism. With the onset of the First World War, Kautsky sided with the party's left who opposed German involvement in it. Following the short-lived German socialist revolution of 1918–19 he briefly acted as Assistant Secretary of State for Foreign Affairs. Though he did join the reunited SPD in Germany in 1922, following the collapse of the revolution, he was never again such an influential figure within it.

Socialism postulates special historical conditions, which render it possible and necessary. This is pretty generally recognised. Yet there is by no means unanimity amongst us as regards the conditions which must be fulfilled in order to make modern Socialism possible, should a country be ripe for it. This divergence on such an important question is not a calamity, and so far as it causes us to be occupied with the problem at the present time is a matter for rejoicing. We are obliged to consider this matter because, for most of us, Socialism has ceased to be something that must be expected in hundreds of years, as we were assured by many at the time of the outbreak of war. Socialism has become a practical question on the order of the day.

What, then, are the pre-requisites for the establishment of Socialism?

Every conscious human action presupposes a will. The Will to Socialism is the first condition for its accomplishment.

This Will is created by the great industry. Where small production is uppermost in a society, the masses of the people are possessors of the means of production. He who happens to be without property conceives his ideal to be the acquirement of a small possession. This desire may, in some circumstances, assume a revolutionary form, but such a social revolution would not have a Socialist character—it would only redistribute the existing wealth in such a manner that everyone would receive a share. Small production always creates the Will to uphold or to obtain private property in the means of production which are in vogue, not the will to social property, to Socialism. This Will first appears amongst the masses when large scale industry is already much developed, and its superiority over small production is unquestioned; when it would be a retrograde step, if it were possible, to break up large scale industry when the workers engaged in the large industry cannot obtain a share in the means of production unless they take on a social form; when small production, so far as it exists, steadily deteriorates, so that the small producers can no longer support themselves thereby. In this way the Will to Socialism grows.

At the same time, the material possibilities of its achievement increase with the growth of the large industry. The larger the number of producers, and the more independent of each other they are, the more difficult it is to organise them socially. This difficulty disappears in the measure in which the number of producers decreases, and the relations between them become more close and uniform. Finally, alongside of the will to Socialism, and its material conditions—the raw material of Socialism—the strength to realise it must also exist. Those who want Socialism must become stronger than those who do not want it.

This factor, too, is created by the development of the large industry, which causes an increase in the number of proletarians—those who have an interest in Socialism—and a decrease in the number of capitalists, that is a decrease as compared with the number of proletarians. In comparison with the non-proletarian classes, the small peasants and lower middle classes, the number of capitalists may increase for some time. But the proletariat increases more rapidly than any other class in the State.

These factors are the direct outcome of the economic development. They do not arise of themselves, without human co-operation, but they arise without proletarian co-operation, solely through the operations of the capitalists, who have an interest in the growth of their large industry. This development is in the first place industrial, and confined to the towns. The agrarian development is only a weak echo of it. Socialism will come from the towns and from industry, but not from agriculture. For its realisation yet another—a fourth—factor is needful besides those already mentioned. The proletariat must not only have an interest in the establishment of Socialism, it must not merely have the material conditions for Socialism ready to hand, and possess the strength to make use of them; it must also have the capacity to retain its hold of them, and properly to employ them. Only then can Socialism be realised as a permanent method of production.

To the ripening of the conditions, the necessary level of the industrial development, must be added the maturity of the proletariat, in order to make Socialism possible. This factor will not, however, be created by the efforts of the capitalist to obtain rent, interest and profit, without the co-operation of the proletariat. It must, on the contrary, be obtained by the exertions of the proletariat in opposition to the capitalist.

Under the system of small production those without property fall into two sections. For one of them, viz., apprentices and peasants' sons, their lack of property is only a temporary condition. The members of this class expect one day to become possessors and have an interest in private property. The other section of the class without property are the vagabonds, who are unnecessary and even harmful parasites on society, without education, without self-consciousness, without cohesion. When a chance offers itself, they are quite ready to expropriate the possessors, but they neither want nor are able to construct a new social order.

The capitalist method of production makes use of this propertyless class of vagabonds, whose numbers assume large proportions in the beginning of the capitalist system. Out of superfluous, even dangerous parasites, they are transformed into the indispensable economic foundations of production, and therefore of society. Capitalism increases their numbers and multiplies their strength, but it exploits their ignorance, rawness and incapacity. It even seeks to depress the working classes to their level. By overwork, monotony and dulness of toil, labour of women and children, capitalism even presses the working classes below the level of the former vagabond class. The impoverishment of the proletariat increases in an alarming degree.

From it, however, the first striving towards Socialism appears as an effort to make an end of the growing poverty of the masses. It seemed, however, that this poverty must render the proletariat for ever incapable of emancipating itself. Middle-class sympathy must save it, and bring Socialism about.

It is soon apparent that nothing can be expected from this sympathy. Sufficient strength to accomplish Socialism can only be expected from those whose interests lie that way, that is the proletarians. But were not they perishing without hope?

Not all, in fact. There were particular sections which had shown strength and courage to fight against poverty. This small fraction would do what the Utopians were not capable of doing.

By a sudden stroke it would capture the powers of the State, and bring Socialism to the people. This was the conception of Blanqui and Weitling. The proletariat, which was too ignorant and demoralised to organise and rule itself, should be organised and ruled by a government comprised of its educated elite, something like the Jesuits in Paraguay who had organised and governed the Indians.

Weitling foresaw the dictatorship of a single person, who would carry through Socialism at the head of a victorious revolutionary army. He called him a Messiah.

"I see a new Messiah coming with the sword, to carry into effect the teachings of the first. By his courage he will be placed at the head of the revolutionary army, and with its help he will crumble the decayed structure of the old social order, and drown the sources of tears in the ocean of forgetfulness, and transform the earth into a paradise."—(Guarantees of Harmony and Freedom.)

A generous and enthusiastic anticipation. It is based, however, solely upon the expectation that the revolutionary army will find the right man. But suppose one is not disposed to accept this belief in a coming Messiah, and holds the conviction that unless the proletariat can free itself Socialism must remain an Utopia?

In view of the fact that the proletariat has not attained to the capacity for self-government in any of the organisations with which it is concerned, is not the hopelessness of Socialism, in face of the impoverishment of the workers by capitalism, thereby demonstrated?

So it would appear. Yet practice and theory soon showed a way out. In England the industrial proletariat first became a mass movement, there it found some instalment of democratic rights, some possibilities of organisation and of propaganda, and was stirred into motion by being summoned to the aid of the middle class in the struggle with the nobles for the franchise.

Among the Trade Unions and the Chartists the beginnings of the Labour movement first arose, with the resistance offered by the proletariat to its impoverishment and disfranchisement. It commenced its strikes, and its great fight for the suffrage and the normal working day.

Marx and Engels early recognised the significance of this movement. It was not the "theory of impoverishment" which characterised Marx and Engels. They held this in common with other Socialists, but were superior to them by not only recognising the capitalist tendency towards impoverishment, but also the proletarian counter tendency, and in this, in the class struggle, they recognised the great factor which would uplift the proletariat, and give it the capacity which it needs if it is not merely to grasp political power by the luck of an accident, but is to be in a position to make itself master of that power, and to use it.

The proletarian class struggle, as a struggle of the masses, presupposes democracy. If not absolute and pure democracy, yet so much of democracy as is necessary to organise masses, and give them uniform enlightenment. This cannot be adequately done by secret methods. A few fly sheets cannot be a substitute for an extensive daily Press. Masses cannot be organised secretly, and, above all, a secret organisation cannot be a democratic one. It always leads to the dictatorship of a single man, or of a small knot of leaders. The ordinary members can only become instruments for carrying out orders. Such a method may be rendered necessary for an oppressed class in the absence of democracy, but it would not promote the self-government and independence of the masses. Rather would it further the Messiah-consciousness of leaders, and their dictatorial habits.

The same Weitling, who gave such prominence to the function of a Messiah, spoke most contemptuously of democracy.

"Communists are still pretty undecided about the choice of their form of government. A large part of those in France incline to a dictatorship, because they well know that the sovereignty of the people, as understood by republicans and politicians, is not suited for the period of transition from the old to a completely new organisation. Owen, the chief of the English Communists, would have the performance of specified duties allotted to men according to age, and the chief leaders of a government would be the oldest members of it. All Socialists with the exception of the followers of Fourier, to whom all forms of government are the same, are agreed that the form of government which is called the sovereignty of the people is a very unsuitable, and even dangerous, sheet anchor for the young principle of Communism about to be realised."

Weitling goes further. He will have nothing of democracy, even in a Socialist community.

"If the idea of the sovereignty of the people is to be applied, all must rule. This can never be the case, and it is, therefore, not the sovereignty of the people, but the chance sovereignty of some of the people."

Weitling wanted the greatest geniuses to govern. They would be selected in a competition by scientific assemblies.

I have quoted Weitling in detail in order to show that the contempt for democracy, which is now recommended to us as the highest wisdom, is quite an old conception, and corresponds to a primitive stage in the working-class movement. At the same time that Weitling poured scorn on Universal Suffrage and freedom of the Press, the workers of England were fighting for these rights, and Marx and Engels ranged themselves by their side.

Since then the working classes of the whole of Europe, in numerous—often bloody—struggles, have conquered one instalment of democracy after the other, and by their endeavours to win, maintain and extend democracy, and by constantly making use of each instalment for organisation, for propaganda, and for wresting social reforms, have they grown in maturity from year to year, and from the lowest have become the highest placed section of the masses of the people.

45   Sidney and Beatrice Webb, from *Industrial Democracy* (Longman, Green & Co., 1902), pp. 809–17

Sidney (1859–1947) and Beatrice (1858–1943) Webb were two of the central intellectual figures in the Fabian Society, founded in 1884. Within this grouping there gathered a heterogenous mixture of intellectuals and aspirant politicians. The Society was committed to the importance of empirically based investigation and, through its many pamphlets, disseminated influential arguments on a variety of social issues. One of the main sources of these publications was Sidney Webb. In 1892 he married Beatrice Potter and they formed a remarkably productive and famous intellectual partnership. Prior to meeting Sidney, she had been an investigator on Charles Booth's study of London's poor, and had also authored a book on consumer co-operation. The minority report she wrote as a member of the Royal Commission on the Poor Law from 1906 to 1908 anticipated many aspects of the welfare state established after 1945. Despite their unease with the kinds of socialism that were included within the newly formed British Labour Party, they exercised considerable influence over its political ambitions and strategic thinking. Sidney was nominated to its National Executive Committee by the Fabians and drafted the party's new constitution and its 1918 election manifesto. He held office, as President of the Board of Trade, in the minority Labour Government elected in 1924, and was Colonial Secretary in its successor in 1929.

We see at once that the complete acceptance of democracy, with its acute consciousness of the interests of the community as a whole, and its insistence on equality of opportunity for all citizens, will necessitate a reconsideration by the Trade Unionists of their three Doctrines—the abandonment of one, the modification of another, and the far-reaching extension and development of the third. To begin with the Doctrine of Vested Interests, we may infer that, whatever respect may be paid to the "established expectations" of any class, this will not be allowed to take the form of a resistance to inventions, or of any obstruction of improvements in industrial processes. Equitable consideration of the interests of existing workers will no doubt be more and more expected, and popular governments may even adopt Mill's suggestion of making some provision for operatives displaced by a new machine. But this consideration and this provision will certainly not take the form of restricting the entrance to a trade, or of recognising any exclusive right to a particular occupation or service. Hence the old Trade Union conception of a vested interest in an occupation must be entirely given up—a change of front will be the more easy in that, as we have seen, no union is now able to embody this conception in a practical policy.

Coming now to the Doctrine of Supply and Demand, we see that any attempt to better the strategic position of a particular section by the Device of Restriction of Numbers will be unreservedly condemned. Not only is this Device inconsistent with the democratic instinct in favor of opening up the widest possible opportunity for every citizen, but it is hostile to the welfare of the community as a whole, and especially to the manual workers, in that it tends to distribute the capital, brains, and labor of the nation less productively than would otherwise be the case. Trade Unionism has, therefore, absolutely to abandon one of its two Devices. This throwing off of the old Adam of monopoly will be facilitated by the fact that the mobility of modern industry has, in all but a few occupations, already made any effective use of Restriction of Numbers quite impracticable. Even if, in particular cases, the old Device should again become feasible, those Trade Unions which practised it would be placing themselves directly in antagonism to the conscious interests of the remainder of their own class, and of the community as a whole. And in so far as industry passes from the hands of private capitalists into the control of representatives of the consumers, whether in the form of voluntary co-operative societies, or in that of the municipality or the central government, any interference with freedom to choose the best man or woman for every vacancy, more and more consciously condemned by public opinion, will certainly not be tolerated.

But the manipulation of the labor market to the advantage of particular sections does not always take the form of a limitation of apprenticeship, or any Restriction of Numbers. Among the Cotton-spinners the piecers, and among the Cotton-weavers the tenters, are engaged and paid by the operatives themselves, whose earnings are accordingly partly made up of the profit on this juvenile labor. It therefore suits the interest of the adult workers, no less than that of the capitalist manufacturers, that there should be as little restriction as possible on the age or numbers of these subordinate learners: the Cotton-spinners, in fact, as we have more than once mentioned, go so far as to insist on there being always ten times as many of them as would suffice to recruit the trade. In this parasitic use of child-labor, the Cotton Operatives are sharing with the manufacturers what is virtually a subsidy from the community as a whole. The enforcement of a National Minimum would, as we have seen, involve such a raising of the minimum age, both for half and whole time employment, as would put a stop to this particular expression of corporate self-help.

Thus, the Doctrine of Supply and Demand will have to manifest itself exclusively in the persistent attempts of each trade to specialise its particular grade of skill, by progressively raising the level of its own Common Rules. In so far as this results in a corresponding increase in efficiency it will, as we have shown, not only benefit the trade itself, but also cause the capital, brains, and labor of the community to be distributed in the most productive way. And the demands of each grade will, in the absence of any Restriction of Numbers or resistance to innovations, be automatically checked by the liberty of the customer to resort to an alternative product and the absolute freedom of the directors of industry to adopt an alternative process, or to select another grade of labor. Thus, the permanent bias of the manual worker towards higher wages and shorter hours of labor is perpetually being counteracted by another—his equally strong desire for continuity of employment. If the Common Rule in any industry at any time is pressed upward further or more quickly than is compensated for by an equivalent advance in the efficiency of the industry, the cost of production, and, therefore, the price, will be raised, and the consumers' demand for that particular commodity will, in the vast majority of cases, be thereby restricted. The rise of wages will, in such a case, have been purchased at the cost of throwing some men out of work. And though the working-class official cannot, any more than the capitalist or the economist, predict the effect on demand of any particular rise of wages, even the most aggressive members of a Trade Union discover, in an increase of the percentage of unemployed colleagues whom they have to maintain, an unmistakable and imperative check upon any repetition of an excessive claim. How constantly and effectively this check operates on the mind of the Trade Union officials can be realised only by those who have heard their private discussions, or who have watched the silent postponement of cherished aims by particular unions. It is not fear of the employers' strength, or lack of desire for shorter hours that is (1897) preventing the Cotton Operatives from using their power to obtain an eight hours' day or a rise in their piecework rates, but the ever-present dread, quickened by the sight of unemployed spinners and weavers on short-time, of driving away some of the trade of Lancashire. Paradoxical as it may seem, the sins of the Trade Unions in this respect would tend to be those of omission rather than those of commission. Whether with regard to sanitation, hours, or wages, each Trade Union would, in its fear of encouraging new inventions, be apt to stop short in its claims at an earlier point than the fullest efficiency demanded, rather than push ever onward the specialisation of its craft, at the cost of seeing some part of it, to the common advantage, superseded by another process.

So far democracy may be expected to look on complacently at the fixing, by mutual agreement between the directors of industry and the manual workers, of special rates of wages for special classes. But this use of the Method of Collective Bargaining for the advantage of particular sections—this "freedom of contract" between capitalists and wage-earners—will become increasingly subject to the fundamental condition that the business of the community must not be interfered with. When in the course of bargaining there ensues a deadlock—when the workmen strike, or the employers lock out—many other interests are affected than those of the parties concerned. We may accordingly expect that, whenever an industrial dispute reaches a certain magnitude, a democratic state will, in the interests of the community as a whole, not scruple to intervene, and settle the points at issue by an authoritative fiat. The growing impatience with industrial dislocation will, in fact, where Collective Bargaining breaks down, lead to its supersession by some form of compulsory arbitration; that is to say, by Legal Enactment. And when the fixing of the conditions on which any industry is to be carried on, is thus taken out of the hands of employers and workmen, the settlement will no longer depend exclusively on the strategic position of the parties, or of the industry, but will be largely influenced by the doctrine of a living wage. The Trade Union official would then have to prove that the claims of his clients were warranted by the greater intensity of their effort, or by the rareness of their skill in comparison with those of the lowest grade of labor receiving only the National Minimum; whilst the case of the associated employers would have to rest on a demonstration, both that the conditions demanded were unnecessary, if not prejudicial, to the workmen's efficiency, and that equally competent recruits could be obtained in sufficient numbers without the particular "rent of ability," demanded by the Trade Union over and above the National Minimum.

It is accordingly on the side of the Doctrine of a Living Wage that the present policy of Trade Unionism will require most extension. Democratic public opinion will expect each trade to use its strategic position to secure the conditions necessary for the fulfilment of its particular social function in the best possible way—to obtain, that is to say, not what will be immediately most enjoyed by the "average sensual man," but what, in the long run, will most conduce to his efficiency as a professional, a parent, and a citizen. This will involve some modification of Trade Union policy. Powerful Trade Unions show no backwardness in exacting the highest money wages that they know how to obtain; but even the best organised trades will at present consent, as a part of their bargain with the employer, to work for excessive and irregular hours, and to put up with unsafe, insanitary, indecent, and hideous surroundings. In all the better-paid crafts in the England of to-day, shorter and more regular hours, greater healthfulness, comfort, and refinement in the conditions of work, and the definite provision of periodical holidays for recreation and travel, are, in the interests of industrial and civic efficiency, more urgently required than a rise in the Standard Rate. Such an application of the Doctrine of a Living Wage will involve, not only a growth of deliberate foresight and self-control among the rank and file, but also a development of capacity in the Civil Service of the Trade Union movement. To haggle over an advance in wages is within the capacity of any labor leader; to suggest to the employer and the legislature the "special rules" calculated to ensure the maximum comfort to the operatives, and cause the minimum cost and inconvenience to the industry, demands a higher degree of technical expertness.

Nor is it enough for each trade to maintain and raise its own Standard of Life. Unless the better-paid occupations are to be insidiously handicapped in the competition for the home and foreign market, it is, as we have demonstrated, essential that no one of the national industries should be permitted to become parasitic by the use of subsidised or deteriorating labor. Hence the organised trades are vitally concerned in the abolition of "sweating" in all occupations whatsoever, whether these compete with them for custom by manufacturing for the same demand, or for the means of production by diverting the organising capacity and capital of the nation. And this self-interest of the better-paid trades coincides, as we have seen, with the welfare of the community, dependent as this is on securing the utmost development of health, intelligence, and character in the weaker as well as in the stronger sections. Thus we arrive at the characteristic device of the Doctrine of a Living Wage, which we have termed the National Minimum—the deliberate enforcement, by an elaborate Labor Code, of a definite quota of education, sanitation, leisure, and wages for every grade of workers in every industry. This National Minimum the public opinion of the democratic state will not only support, but positively insist on for the common weal. But public opinion alone will not suffice. To get the principle of a National Minimum unreservedly adopted; to embody it in successive Acts of Parliament of the requisite technical detail; to see that this legislation is properly enforced; to cause the regulations to be promptly and intelligently adapted to changes in the national industry, requires persistent effort and specialised skill. For this task no section of the community is so directly interested and so well-equipped as the organised trades, with their prolonged experience of industrial regulation and their trained official staff. It is accordingly upon the Trade Unions that the democratic state must mainly rely for the stimulus, expert counsel, and persistent watchfulness, without which a National Minimum can neither be obtained nor enforced.

46   Vladimir Illich Ulyanov (Lenin), from *What is to be Done?* (Clarendon Press, 1963), pp. 98–100, 100–3

Lenin (1870–1924) led the first successful revolution, in Russia, in the name of Marxist ideas, and became the effective head of the fledgling socialist state established thereafter. He was drawn into revolutionary agitation following the hanging of his brother for his involvement in a plot to assassinate the Tsar. By his mid-twenties, he had established himself as the spokesman for the most prominent group of Marxists in Russia, and became a key figure in radical workers' circles in St. Petersburg. He laid down a set of guidelines for a revolutionary party operating in a hostile political environment. By 1914 he had come to the view that the era of socialism was at hand. He led the Bolshevik party during the heady events of 1917 in Russia. After ill-health forced him to relax his leadership of the government in 1922, Lenin began to reflect more critically upon the revolution, arguing for the reorganization of the Soviet state and doubting the prospects for socialism in an, internationally isolated country.

Our 'Economists', including *The Workers' Cause*, were successful because they pandered to simple workers. But a worker Social-Democrat, a worker revolutionary (and the number of such workers is constantly growing) will indignantly reject all these disquisitions about fighting for demands 'that promise tangible results', &c., because he will understand that they are merely variants of the old song about adding a kopeck to a rouble. Such a worker will say to his counsellors from *Workers' Thought* and *The Workers' Cause*: you are busying yourselves for nothing, gentlemen, when you interfere too zealously in a job that we are managing ourselves and at the same time neglect your real obligations. It is really completely stupid of you to say that the task of Social-Democrats is to lend the economic struggle itself a political character; this is only the beginning, and the main task of Social-Democrats does not lie in this because throughout the world, including Russia, it *not infrequently happens that the police themselves begin to lend* the economic struggle a political character, and the workers themselves are learning to understand on whose side the government is. Indeed, that 'economic struggle of the workers against the employers and the government', about which you fuss as if you had discovered America, is being carried on in countless Russian backwoods by workers themselves who have heard about strikes but probably have not heard anything about Socialism. Indeed, that 'activity' among us workers which all of you want to support by putting forward concrete demands which promise tangible results already exists, and we ourselves in our petty everyday trade-union work are putting forward these concrete demands, frequently without any help from intellectuals. But *such* activity is not enough for us; we are not children to be fed with sops of 'Economist' politics alone; we want to know everything that others know, we want to acquaint ourselves in detail with *all* sides of political life and to participate *actively* in every political event. For this, it is necessary that the intellectuals should talk to us less about what we know ourselves and give us more of what we do not yet know, what we ourselves can never learn from our factory and 'economic' experience, namely: political knowledge. You intellectuals can acquire this knowledge, and it is your *duty* to convey it to us a hundred and a thousand times more than you have done so far, and to convey it not only in the shape of disquisitions, brochures, and articles (which are often—excuse my frankness—somewhat boring) but, without fail, in the form of living *arraignments* of what at this very time our government and our ruling classes are doing in all spheres of life. Fulfil this duty of yours with greater zeal and *talk less about 'raising the activity of the working mass'*. There is far more activity with us than you think and we are able to support, by fighting openly in the streets, even demands that do not promise any 'tangible results'! And it is not for you to 'raise' our activity, because *activity is just the very thing that you yourselves are lacking in*. Worship spontaneity a bit less, and think a bit more about raising *your own* activity, gentlemen!

. . .

THE WORKING CLASS AS THE VANGUARD FIGHTER FOR DEMOCRACY

We have seen that the carrying on of the broadest political agitation, and therefore also the organizing of all-embracing political arraignments, is an absolutely necessary, an *overridingly* necessary, task for a truly Social-Democratic activity. But we came to this conclusion starting *only* from the most pressing need of the working class for political knowledge and political education. Yet such a presentation of the question would by itself be too narrow, it would ignore the general democratic tasks of any Social-Democracy and of contemporary Russian Social-Democracy especially. In order to explain this proposition as concretely as possible, let us try to approach the problem from the side that is 'nearest' for an 'Economist', namely from the practical side. 'Everyone agrees' that it is necessary to develop the political consciousness of the working class. The question is *how* it is to be done, and what is needed in order to get it done. The economic struggle brings the workers 'up against' only the questions relating to the attitude of the government towards the working class, and therefore *however much we might labour* at the task of 'lending the economic struggle itself a political character' *we shall never be able* to develop the political consciousness of the workers (to the degree of Social-Democratic political consciousness) within the framework of this task because *this framework itself is too narrow*. Martynov's formula is valuable for us not at all because it illustrates Martynov's ability to confuse, but because it clearly expresses the fundamental mistake of all 'Economists', namely the conviction that it is possible to develop the class political consciousness of the workers *from within*, so to speak, their economic struggle—that is, starting only (or at least chiefly) from this struggle, basing oneself only (or at least chiefly) on this struggle. Such a view is radically mistaken—and precisely because the 'Economists', angry with us for our polemics against them, are unwilling to have a good think about the sources of our differences. The result is that we literally do not understand each other: we speak different languages.

Class political consciousness can be brought to the worker *only from without*, that is, from outside the economic struggle, outside the sphere of the relations between the workers and the employers. The only field from which it is possible to extract this knowledge is the field of relations of *all* classes and strata to the state and government, the field of interrelationships between *all* classes. Therefore, to the question 'what to do in order to bring to the workers political knowledge?', one cannot give only the answer which in the majority of cases satisfies the practical party workers, not to speak of those among them who are inclined towards 'Economism'—namely, the answer 'to go to the workers'. In order to bring the *workers* political knowledge, Social-Democrats must *go into all classes of the population*, must send out units of their army *in all directions*.

We deliberately choose such an awkward formula, we deliberately express ourselves with simplified sharpness, not in the least from a desire to indulge in paradoxes, but in order properly to bring the 'Economists' face to face with those tasks which they unforgivably neglect, face to face with the distinction between trade-unionist and Social-Democratic politics which they do not want to understand. And therefore, we ask the reader not to get excited but to listen to us attentively until the end.

Take the type of Social-Democratic circle most common in recent years and watch its work. It has 'contacts with the workers' and is satisfied with this, publishing leaflets in which factory abuses, the government's partiality towards capitalists, and the violence of the police are strongly condemned; at meetings with the workers the conversation does not usually go, or rarely goes, beyond the limits of these themes; talks and discussions on the history of the revolutionary movement, on questions of the internal and foreign policy of our government, on questions of the economic evolution of Russia and Europe, and the position in contemporary society of the various classes, &c., are the greatest rarity, while no one even thinks of systematically acquiring and widening contacts in the other classes of society. Essentially, the ideal of a leader—as he is pictured by the members of such circles in the majority of cases—is something more resembling a trade-union secretary than a Socialist political leader. For the secretary of, for example, any English trade union always helps the workers to carry on the economic struggle, organizes factory arraignments, explains the injustice of the laws and of measures which hamper the freedom to strike and the freedom to picket (i.e. to warn everyone that there is a strike at a given works), explains the partiality of an arbitration court judge who belongs to the bourgeois classes of the people, &c., &c. In a word, every secretary of a trade union carries on and helps to carry on 'the economic struggle with the employers and government'. And it is impossible to insist sufficiently strongly that *this is not yet* Social-Democratism, that the ideal of a Social-Democrat should be not a trade-union secretary but a *popular tribune* who knows how to react to all and sundry expressions of arbitrariness and oppression wherever they occur, whichever stratum or class they affect; who knows how to generalize all these expressions into one picture of police violence and capitalist exploitation, who knows how to utilize every little thing in order to expound *before all men* his Socialist convictions and his democratic demands, to explain to *each* and everyone the universal historical significance of the liberating struggle of the proletariat.

47   Leon Trotsky, from 'Stalin', in *The Basic Writings of Trotsky* (ed. I. Howe; Secker & Warburg, 1964), pp. 133–41

Trotsky (1879–1940) was involved in revolutionary politics from a young age and experienced imprisonment and exile on two separate occasions as a result. He became a prominent activist in the community of revolutionary exiles based in Europe in the early years of the twentieth century. He was closely involved in the failed uprising of 1905, an experience that shaped his ideas about permanent revolution. He was subsequently a key figure in the events of 1917 and in the post-revolutionary government. As Commissar of Foreign Affairs he negoti-ated the treaty of Brest-Litovsk between the Soviet Union and the advancing German army, and then, as Commissar of War, led the Red Army during the tumultuous battles of the Civil War. After Lenin's death, he emerged as the chief opponent of Joseph Stalin's growing control over the state and was outspoken in his criticism of the tendency towards bureaucratization. In 1929 he was exiled by Stalin and wrote an important historical review of the Russian revolution (*The History of the Russian Revolution* (1932); see the extract below). He was murdered by one of Stalin's agents in 1940.

Such were the divergent positions of the two main factions of the Russian social democracy. But alongside them, as early as the dawn of the First Revolution, a third position was formulated, which met with practically no recognition in those days, but which we must explain—not only because it was confirmed by the events of 1917, but particularly because seven years after the revolution, after being turned upside down, it began to play an utterly unforeseen role in the political evolution of Stalin and of the entire Soviet bureaucracy.

Early in 1905 I published in Geneva a pamphlet which analyzed the political situation as it existed around the winter of 1904. I came to the conclusion that the independent campaign of liberal petitions and banquets had exhausted its possibilities; that the radical intellectuals, who had shifted their hopes to the liberals, had found themselves in a blind alley together with the latter; that the peasant movement was creating conditions favorable for victory yet incapable of assuring it; that the showdown could be brought about only through an armed insurrection of the proletariat; that the very next stage along that way must be the general strike. This pamphlet, called "Until the Ninth of January," had been written prior to the Bloody Sunday in Petersburg. The powerful wave of strikes which began that day, together with the first armed clashes that supplemented it, was an unequivocal confirmation of the pamphlet's strategic prognosis.

The preface to my work was written by Parvus, a Russian émigré, who had already become by then a prominent German writer. Parvus was an extraordinarily creative personality, capable of becoming infected with the ideas of others as well as enriching others with his ideas. He lacked the inward balance and application necessary to contribute anything worthy of his talents as a thinker and writer to the labor movement. There is no doubt that he exerted considerable influence on my personal development, especially with respect to the social-revolutionary understanding of our epoch. A few years before our first meeting Parvus passionately defended the idea of a general strike in Germany; but the country was passing through prolonged industrial prosperity, the Social Democracy was adjusting itself to the Hohenzollern regime, and foreigners' revolutionary propaganda met nothing but ironical indifference. Having read my pamphlet in manuscript, the very next day after the bloody events in Petersburg, Parvus was overwhelmed with the thought of the exceptional role which the proletariat of backward Russia was called upon to play. Several days spent jointly in Munich were filled with conversations that clarified much to both of us and brought us personally close together. The preface Parvus then wrote to the pamphlet entered permanently into the history of the Russian Revolution. In a few pages he shed light on those social peculiarities of backward Russia which, true enough, were already well known, but from which no one before him had drawn all the necessary inferences:

Political radicalism throughout western Europe [wrote Parvus], as everybody knows, depended primarily on the petty bourgeoisie. These were artisans and generally all of that part of the bourgeoisie which was caught up by the industrial development but which at the same time was superseded by the class of capitalists . . . . In Russia of the pre-capitalist period, cities developed on the Chinese rather than on the European model. These were administrative centers, purely official and bureaucratic in character, devoid of any political significance, while in the economic sense they were trade bazaars for the landlord and peasant milieu of its environs. Their development was still rather inconsiderable, when it was terminated by the capitalist process, which began to establish large cities in its own image, that is, factory towns and centers of world trade . . . That which had hindered the development of petty bourgeois democracy came to benefit the class consciousness of the proletariat in Russia—the weak development of the artisan form of production. The proletariat was immediately concentrated in the factories . . . .

Greater and greater masses of peasants will be drawn into the movement. But all they can do is to aggravate the political anarchy rampant in the country and thus weaken the government; they cannot become a compact revolutionary army. Hence, as the revolution develops, an even greater portion of political work will fall to the lot of the proletariat. At the same time its political awareness will be enhanced and its political energy will grow apace . . . .

The Social Democracy will be confronted with this dilemma: to assume responsibility for the provisional government or to stand aloof from the labor movement. The workers will regard that government as their own, no matter what the attitude of the Social Democracy. . . . In Russia only workers can accomplish a revolutionary insurrection. In Russia the revolutionary provisional government will be a government of the *workers' democracy.* That government will be social democratic, should the Social Democracy be at the head of the revolutionary movement of the Russian proletariat. . . .

The Social Democratic provisional government cannot accomplish a socialist insurrection in Russia, but the very process of liquidating the autocracy and establishing a democratic republic will provide it with fertile ground for political activity.

In the heyday of revolutionary events in the autumn of 1905, I met Parvus again, this time in Petersburg. Remaining organizationally independent of both factions, we jointly edited *Russkoye Slovo* (The Russian World), a newspaper for the working class masses, and, in coalition with the Mensheviks, the important political newspaper *Nachalo* (The Beginning). The theory of permanent revolution was usually associated with the names of "Parvus and Trotsky." That was only partially correct. Parvus attained revolutionary maturity at the end of the preceding century, when he marched at the head of the forces that fought so-called Revisionism, i.e., the opportunistic distortions of Marx's theory. But his optimism was undermined by the failure of all his efforts to push the German Social Democracy in the direction of a more resolute policy. Parvus grew increasingly more reserved about the perspectives of a socialist revolution in the West. At the same time he felt that "the Social-Democratic provisional government cannot accomplish a socialist insurrection in Russia." Hence, his prognosis indicated, instead of the transformation of the democratic into the socialist revolution, merely the establishment in Russia of a regime of workers' democracy, more or less as in Australia, where the first labor government, resting on a farmerist foundation, did not venture beyond the limits of the bourgeois regime.

I did not share that conclusion. Australian democracy, maturing organically on the virgin soil of a new continent, immediately assumed a conservative character and dominated the youthul yet rather privileged proletariat. Russian democracy, on the contrary, could come about only in consequence of a large-scale revolutionary insurrection, the dynamics of which would never permit the labor government to maintain itself within the framework of bourgeois democracy. Our differences of opinion, which began soon after the Revolution of 1905, led to a complete break at the beginning of the war, when Parvus, in whom the skeptic had completely killed the revolutionist, proved to be on the side of German imperialism and subsequently became the counselor and inspirer of the first President of the German Republic, Ebert.

After writing my pamphlet, "Until the Ninth of January," I repeatedly returned to the development and the grounding of the theory of permanent revolution. In view of the significance it subsequently acquired in the intellectual evolution of the hero of this biography, it is necessary to present it here in the from of exact quotations from my works of the years 1905 and 1906.

> The nucleus of population in a contemporary city—at least, in a city of economic and political significance—is the sharply differentiated class of hired labor. It is this class, essentially unknown to the Great French Revolution, which is fated to play the decisive role in our revolution. . . . In an economically more backward country the proletariat may come to power sooner than in a country more advanced capitalistically. The conception of a kind of automatic dependence of the proletarian dictatorship on a country's technical forces and means is a prejudice of extremely simplified "economic" materialism. Such a view has nothing in common with Marxism. . . . Notwithstanding the fact that the productive forces of United States industry are ten times greater than ours, the political role of the Russian proletariat, its influence on the politics of its own country and the possibility that it may soon influence world politics are incomparably greater than the role of significance of the American proletariat. . . .
>
> It seems to me that the Russian Revolution will create such conditions that the power may (in the event of victory, *must*) pass into the hands of the proletariat before the politicians of bourgeois liberalism will find it possible fully to unfold their genius for statecraft. . . . The Russian bourgeoisie will surrender all the revolutionary positions to the proletariat. It will also have to surrender revolutionary hegemony over the peasantry. The proletariat in power will come to the peasantry as the class liberator. . . . The proletariat, leaning on the peasantry, will bring into motion all the forces for raising the cultural level of the village and for developing political consciousness in the peasantry. . . .
>
> But will not perhaps the peasantry itself drive the proletariat away and supersede it? That is impossible. All historic experience repudiates that supposition. It shows that the peasantry is utterly incapable of an *independent* political role . . . From the aforesaid it is clear how I look upon the idea of the "dictatorship of the proletariat and the peasantry." The point is not whether I deem it admissible in principle, whether I "want" or "do not want" such a form of political co-operation. I deem it unrealizable—at least, in the direct and immediate sense.

The foregoing already shows how incorrect is the assertion that the conception here expounded "jumped over the bourgeois revolution," as has been subsequently reiterated without end. "The struggle for the democratic renovation of Russia . . ." I wrote at the same time, "is in its entirety derived from capitalism, is being conducted by forces formed on the basis of capitalism, and *immediately, in the first place*, is directed against the feudal and vassal obstacles that stand in the way of developing a capitalist society." But the substance of the question was with what forces and by which methods these obstacles could be overcome.

> The framework of all the questions of the revolution may be limited by the assertion that our revolution is *bourgeois* in its objective goals and consequently, in all its inevitable results, and it is possible at the same time to close one's eyes to the fact that the principal active force of that bourgeois revolution is the proletariat, which is pushing itself toward power with all the impact of the revolution. . . . One may comfort himself with the thought that Russia's social conditions have not yet ripened for a socialist economy—and at the same time overlook the thought that, upon coming to power, the proletariat would inevitably, with all the logic of its situation, push itself toward the management of the economy at the expense of the state. . . . Coming into the government not as helpless hostages but as the leading force, the representatives of the proletariat will by virtue of that alone smash the demarcation between the minimal and maximal program, i.e., *place collectivism on the order of the day*. At what point in that tendency the proletariat would be stopped will depend on the interrelation of forces, but certainly not on the initial intentions of the proletariat's party. . . .
>
> But we may already ask ourselves: must the dictatorship of the proletariat inevitably smash itself against the framework of the bourgeois revolution or can it, on the basis of the existing historical situation of the *world*, look forward to the perspective of victory, after smashing this limiting framework? . . . One thing may be said with certainty: without the direct governmental support of the European proletariat, the working class of Russia will not be able to maintain itself in power and transform its temporary reign into an enduring socialist dictatorship.

But this does not necessarily lead to a pessimistic prognosis:

> The political liberation, led by the working class of Russia, will raise the leader to a height unprecedented in history, transmit to him colossal forces and means, and make him the initiator of the world-wide liquidation of capitalism, for which history has created all the objective prerequisites.

As to the extent to which international Social Democracy will prove capable of fulfilling its revolutionary task, I wrote in 1906:

> The European socialist parties—and in the first place, the mightiest of them, the German party—have developed their conservatism, which grows stronger in proportion to the size of the masses embraced by socialism and the effectiveness of the organization and the discipline of these masses. Because of that, the Social Democracy, as the organization that embodies the political experience of the proletariat, may at a given moment become the immediate obstacle on the path of an open clash between the workers and the bourgeois reaction.

Yet I concluded my analysis by expressing the assurance that

> the Eastern revolution will infect the Western proletariat with revolutionary idealism and arouse in it the desire to start talking "Russian" with its enemy . . .

To sum up. Populism, like Slavophilism, proceeded from illusions that Russia's course of development would be utterly unique, escaping capitalism and the bourgeois republic. Plekhanov's Marxism concentrated on proving the identity in principle of Russia's historical course with that of the West. The program that grew out of that ignored the very real and far from mystical peculiarities of Russia's social structure and revolutionary development. The Menshevik view of the revolution, purged of its episodic stratifications and individual deviations, was tantamount to the following: the victory of the Russian bourgeois revolution was possible only under the leadership of the liberal bourgeoisie and must put the latter in power. Later the democratic regime would let the Russian proletariat, with incomparably greater success than heretofore, catch up with its elder Western brothers on the road of the struggle for socialism.

Lenin's perspective may be briefly expressed in the following words: the backward Russian bourgeoisie is incapable of completing its own revolution! The complete victory of the revolution, through the intermediacy of the "democratic dictatorship of the proletariat and the peasantry," would purge the land of medievalism, invest the development of Russian capitalism with American tempo, strengthen the proletariat in city and village, and make really possible the struggle for socialism. On the other hand, the victory of the Russian Revolution would give tremendous impetus to the socialist revolution in the West, while the latter would not only protect Russia from the dangers of restoration but would also enable the Russian proletariat to come to the conquest of power in a comparatively brief historical period.

The perspective of permanent revolution may be summarized in the following way: the complete victory of the democratic revolution in Russia is conceivable only in the form of the dictatorship of the proletariat, leaning on the peasantry. The dictatorship of the proletariat, which would inevitably place on the order of the day not only democratic but socialistic tasks as well, would at the same time give a powerful impetus to the international socialist revolution. Only the victory of the proletariat in the West could protect Russia from bourgeois restoration and assure it the possibility of rounding out the establishment of socialism.

That compact formula discloses with equal distinctness the similarity of the latter two concepts in their irreconcilable differentiation from the liberal Menshevik perspective as well as their extremely essential distinction from each other on the question of the social character and the tasks of the "dictatorship" which must grow out of the revolution. The not infrequent complaint in the writings of the present Moscow theoreticians that the program of the dictatorship of the proletariat was "premature" in 1905 is beside the point. In an empirical sense the program of the democratic dictatorship of the proletariat and the peasantry proved equally "premature." The unfavorable combination of forces at the time of the First Revolution did not so much preclude the dictatorship of the proletariat as the victory of the revolution in general. Yet all the revolutionary groups were based on the hope of complete victory; the supreme revolutionary struggle would have been impossible without such a hope. The differences of opinion dealt with the general perspective of the revolution and the strategy arising from that. The perspective of Menshevism was false to the core: it pointed out the wrong road to the proletariat. The perspective of Bolshevism was not complete: it correctly pointed out the general direction of the struggle, but characterized its stages incorrectly. The insufficiency in the perspective of Bolshevism did not become apparent in 1905 only because the revolution itself did not undergo further development. But then at the beginning of 1917 Lenin was obliged to alter his perspective, in direct conflict with the old cadres of his party.

No political prognosis can pretend to be mathematically exact; suffice it if it correctly indicates the general line of development and helps to orient the actual course of events, which inevitably bends the main line right and left. In that sense it is impossible not to see that the concept of permanent revolution has completely passed the test of history. During the initial years of the Soviet regime no one denied that; on the contrary, that fact found acknowledgment in a number of official publications. But when the bureaucratic reaction against October opened up in the calmed and cooled upper crust of Soviet society, it was at once directed against the theory which reflected the first proletarian revolution more completely than anything else while at the same time openly exposing its unfinished, limited, and partial character. Thus, by way of repulsion, originated the theory of socialism in a separate country, the basic dogma of Stalinism.

48   Mao Tse-Tung, from 'The Chinese Revolution and the Chinese Communist Party', *The Selected Works of Mao Tse-Tung* in Volume II (Foreign Languages Press, 1967), pp. 326–31

One of the founders of the Chinese Communist Party, Mao (1893–1976) was impressed by the Bolshevik revolution and absorbed its major principles. In 1927, he led peasant rebellions in Hunan and Jiangxi. In theoretical terms, he began to identify the class struggle of the peasantry with that of the proletariat. Following the defeat of the uprisings of 1927–8, and the Soviet-influenced politics that was influential within the CCP in this period, Mao's heterodox brand of 'peasant Marxism' came to the fore. In response to the campaigns of 'encirclement' of the CCP's Red Army pursued by the Chang Kai-Shek's Kuomintang Government in the early 1930s, Mao led 85,000 troops and 15,000 party officials on the epic 'Long March' to Yunan in the North-West. In January 1935 he became undisputed leader of the CCP. Following the defeat of the Japanese, he led the Peoples' Liberation Army against its nationalist rivals and became head of the newly established People's Republic in 1949. Throughout these years, Mao's grip upon the CCP and intolerance of dissent were near total. He wrote extensively on politics and questions of military strategy.

We have now gained an understanding of the nature of Chinese society, *i.e.*, of the specific conditions in China; this understanding is the essential prerequisite for solving all China's revolutionary problems. We are also clear about the targets, the tasks and the motive forces of the Chinese revolution; these are basic issues at the present stage of the revolution and arise from the special nature of Chinese society, *i.e.*, from China's specific conditions. Understanding all this, we can now understand another basic issue of the revolution at the present stage, *i.e.*, the character of the Chinese revolution.

What, indeed, is the character of the Chinese revolution at the present stage? Is it a bourgeois-democratic or a proletarian-socialist revolution? Obviously, it is not the latter but the former.

Since Chinese society is colonial, semi-colonial and semi-feudal, since the principal enemies of the Chinese revolution are imperialism and feudalism, since the tasks of the revolution are to overthrow these two enemies by means of a national and democratic revolution in which the bourgeoisie sometimes takes part, and since the edge of the revolution is directed against imperialism and feudalism and not against capitalism and capitalist private property in general even if the big bourgeoisie betrays the revolution and becomes its enemy—since all this is true, the character of the Chinese revolution at the present stage is not proletarian-socialist but bourgeois-democratic.

However, in present-day China the bourgeois-democratic revolution is no longer of the old general type, which is now obsolete, but one of a new special type. We call this type the new-democratic revolution and it is developing in all other colonial and semi-colonial countries as well as in China. The new-democratic revolution is part of the world proletarian-socialist revolution, for it resolutely opposes imperialism, i.e., international capitalism. Politically, it strives for the joint dictatorship of the revolutionary classes over the imperialists, traitors and reactionaries, and opposes the transformation of Chinese society into a society under bourgeois dictatorship. Economically, it aims at the nationalization of all the big enterprises and capital of the imperialists, traitors and reactionaries, and the distribution among the peasants of the land held by the landlords, while preserving private capitalist enterprise in general and not eliminating the rich-peasant economy. Thus, the new type of democratic revolution clears the way for capitalism on the one hand and creates the prerequisites for socialism on the other. The present stage of the Chinese revolution is a stage of transition between the abolition of the colonial, semi-colonial and semi-feudal society and the establishment of a socialist society, i.e., it is a process of new-democratic revolution. This process, begun only after the First World War and the Russian October Revolution, started in China with the May 4th Movement of 1919. A new-democratic revolution is an anti-imperialist and anti-feudal revolution of the broad masses of the people under the leadership of the proletariat. Chinese society can advance to socialism only through such a revolution; there is no other way.

The new-democratic revolution is vastly different from the democratic revolutions of Europe and America in that it results not in a dictatorship of the bourgeoisie but in a dictatorship of the united front of all the revolutionary classes under the leadership of the proletariat. In the present War of Resistance, the anti-Japanese democratic political power established in the base areas which are under the leadership of the Communist Party is the political power of the Anti-Japanese National United Front; this is neither a bourgeois nor a proletarian one-class dictatorship, but a joint dictatorship of the revolutionary classes under the leadership of the proletariat. All who stand for resistance to Japan and for democracy are entitled to share in this political power, regardless of their party affiliation.

The new-democratic revolution also differs from a socialist revolution in that it overthrows the rule of the imperialists, traitors and reactionaries in China but does not destroy any section of capitalism which is capable of contributing to the anti-imperialist, anti-feudal struggle.

The new-democratic revolution is basically in line with the revolution envisaged in the Three People's Principles as advocated by Dr. Sun Yat-sen in 1924. In the Manifesto of the First National Congress of the Kuomintang issued in that year, Dr. Sun stated:

> The so-called democratic system in modern states is usually monopolized by the bourgeoisie and has become simply an instrument for oppressing the common people. On the other hand, the Kuomintang's Principle of Democracy means a democratic system shared by all the common people and not privately owned by the few.

He added:

> Enterprises, such as banks, railways and airlines, whether Chinese-owned or foreign-owned, which arc either monopolistic in character or too big for private management, shall be operated and administrated by the state, so that private capital cannot dominate the livelihood of the people: this is the main principle of the regulation of capital.

And again in his Testament, Dr. Sun pointed out the fundamental principle for domestic and foreign policy: "We must arouse the masses of the people and unite in a common struggle with those nations of the world which treat us as equals." The Three People's Principles of the old democracy, which were adapted to the old international and domestic conditions, were thus reshaped into the Three People's Principles of New Democracy, which are adapted to the new international and domestic conditions. The Communist Party of China was referring to the latter kind of Three People's Principles and to no other when, in its Manifesto of September 22, 1937, it declared that "the Three People's Principles being what China needs today, our Party is ready to fight for their complete realization". These Three People's Principles embody Dr. Sun Yat-sen's Three Great Policies—alliance with Russia, co-operation with the Communist Party and assistance to the peasants and workers. In the new international and domestic conditions, any kind of Three People's Principles which departs from the Three Great Policies is not revolutionary. (Here we shall not deal with the fact that, while communism and the Three People's Principles agree on the basic political programme for the democratic revolution, they differ in all other respects.)

Thus, the role of the proletariat, the peasantry and the other sections of the petty bourgeoisie in China's bourgeois-democratic revolution cannot be ignored, either in the alignment of forces for the struggle (that is, in the united front) or in the organization of state power. Anyone who tries to bypass these classes will certainly be unable to solve the problem of the destiny of the Chinese nation or indeed any of China's problems. The Chinese revolution at the present stage must strive to create a democratic republic in which the workers, the peasants and the other sections of the petty bourgeoisie all occupy a definite position and play a definite role. In other words, it must be a democratic republic based on a revolutionary alliance of the workers, peasants, urban petty bourgeoisie and all others who are against imperialism and feudalism. Only under the leadership of the proletariat can such a republic be completely realized.

THE PERSPECTIVES OF THE CHINESE REVOLUTION

Now that the basic issues—the nature of Chinese society and the targets, tasks, motive forces and character of the Chinese revolution at the present stage—have been clarified, it is easy to see its perspectives, that is, to understand the relation between the bourgeois-democratic and the proletarian-socialist revolution, or between the present and future stages of the Chinese revolution.

There can be no doubt that the ultimate perspective of the Chinese revolution is not capitalism but socialism and communism, since China's bourgeois-democratic revolution at the present stage is not of the old general type but is a democratic revolution of a new special type—a new-democratic revolution—and since it is taking place in the new international environment of the Nineteen Thirties and Forties characterized by the rise of socialism and the decline of capitalism, in the period of the Second World War and the era of revolution.

However, it is not at all surprising but entirely to be expected that a capitalist economy will develop to a certain extent within Chinese society with the sweeping away of the obstacles to the development of capitalism after the victory of the revolution, since the purpose of the Chinese revolution at the present stage is to change the existing colonial, semi-colonial and semi-feudal state of society, *i.e.,* to strive for the completion of the new-democratic revolution. A certain degree of capitalist development will be an inevitable result of the victory of the democratic revolution in economically backward China. But that will be only one aspect of the outcome of the Chinese revolution and not the whole picture. The whole picture will show the development of socialist as well as capitalist factors. What will the socialist factors be? The increasing relative importance of the proletariat and the Communist Party among the political forces in the country; leadership by the proletariat and the Communist Party which the peasantry, intelligentsia and the urban petty bourgeoisie already accept or arc likely to accept; and the state sector of the economy owned by the democratic republic, and the co-operative sector of the economy owned by the working people. All these will be socialist factors. With the addition of a favourable international environment, these factors render it highly probable that China's bourgeois-democratic revolution will ultimately avoid a capitalist future and enjoy a socialist future.

THE TWOFOLD TASK OF THE CHINESE REVOLUTION
AND THE CHINESE COMMUNIST PARTY

Summing up the foregoing sections of this chapter, we can see that the Chinese revolution taken as a whole involves a twofold task. That is to say, it embraces both the bourgeois-democratic revolution (the new-democratic revolution) and the proletarian-socialist revolution, *i.e.,* both the present and future stages of the revolution. The leadership in this twofold revolutionary task devolves on the Chinese Communist Party, the party of the proletariat, without whose leadership no revolution can succeed.

To complete China's bourgeois-democratic revolution (the new-democratic revolution) and to transform it into a socialist revolution when all the necessary conditions are ripe—such is the sum total of the great and glorious revolutionary task of the Chinese Communist Party. Every Party member must strive for its accomplishment and must under no circumstances give up halfway. Some immature Communists think that our task is confined to the present democratic revolution and does not include the future socialist revolution, or that the present revolution or the Agrarian Revolution is actually a socialist revolution. It must be emphatically pointed out that these views are wrong. Every Communist ought to know that, taken as a whole, the Chinese revolutionary movement led by the Communist Party embraces the two stages, *i.e.,* the democratic and the socialist revolutions, which are two essentially different revolutionary processes, and that the second process can be carried through only after the first has been completed. The democratic revolution is the necessary preparation for the socialist revolution, and the socialist revolution is the inevitable sequel to the democratic revolution. The ultimate aim for which all communists strive is to bring about a socialist and communist society. A clear understanding of both the differences and the interconnections between the democratic and the socialist revolutions is indispensable to correct leadership in the Chinese revolution.

Except for the Communist Party, no political party (bourgeois or petty-bourgeois) is equal to the task of leading China's two great revolutions, the democratic and the socialist revolutions, to complete fulfilment. From the very day of its birth, the Communist Party has taken this twofold task on its own shoulders and for eighteen years has fought strenuously for its accomplishment.

It is a task at once glorious and arduous. And it cannot be accomplished without a bolshevized Chinese Communist Party which is national in scale and has a broad mass character, a party fully consolidated ideologically, politically and organizationally. Therefore every Communist has the duty of playing an active part in building up such a Communist Party.

49   Anthony Crosland, from *The Future of Socialism* (Jonathan Cape, 1967), pp. 51–7

Crosland (1918–1977) served as a Member of Parliament in Britain from the 1950s to the 1970s, and was a senior Minister in the Labour governments of 1964–70 and 1974–77. In the several major books he authored during these decades, he attacked the Labour party's continuing commitment to nationalization, as expressed in Clause Four of its Constitution. This was becoming far less useful as an egalitarian strategy in contemporary society. Instead he focused upon the merits of a system of comprehensive state education, in opposition to the grammar and public school systems.

It is obvious enough that socialist thought varies through time, and that different doctrines prevail at different periods. This is as it should be. It is not even surprising that different doctrines should be supported at the same time—Owenism and Chartism, Marxism and Christian Socialism, Fabianism and Guild Socialism; there must always be divergent views on the right emphasis and order of priorities, and these will prevent a uniformity of thought. The trouble is that some of the divergences are not a matter simply of emphasis or the right priorities. They are fundamental, and the doctrines mutually inconsistent.

Thus Fabian collectivism and Welfare Statism require a view of the State diametrically opposed to the Marxist view. The syndicalist tradition is anti-collectivist. The Marxist tradition is anti-reformist. Owenism differs fundamentally from Marxism and syndicalism on the class-war. Morrisite communes and Socialist Guilds are incompatible with nationalisation: and so on.

How then to decide which is the correct scripture? It is, of course, impossible. All we can do is to pick out certain recurrent themes (whether mutually consistent or not) which have exercised a predominant influence, and which are common to more than one school of thought: and ask whether they are applicable in Britain to-day. In so doing, we need to distinguish in each case between the objective, the means and policies chosen to carry out the objective, and the ideologies or theories by which the objectives and the choice of means are justified.

Five predominant themes can be distinguished (though they often overlap): the appropriation of property incomes, co-operation, workers' control, social welfare, and full employment.

(1) The objective of the appropriation by society of the rewards of capital (rent, interest, profits) by means of the abolition of private property, and the substitution for it either of communal co-operative ownership (the land reformers, Owen, Morris) or collectivist state ownership (Marx, the Fabians, the modern Labour Party), the collectivist view naturally gaining ground with the growth of large-scale units.

The theoretical justification has varied through time, but the constant element has been the theory of a surplus product, due to the effort of labour, but impounded by the owners of property. This theme, of the exploitation of the worker, runs through all the natural law doctrines, the deductions from Ricardo's theory of value, the Marxist theory of surplus value, the Mill-George theory of rent, and the generalised Fabian theory of unearned increment.

Few of these justifications have stood the test of time. Not many people to-day accept the doctrine of *ius naturale*, or the Ricardo-Marx labour theory of value, or the theories of Henry George. This, however, is of no great importance, since a desire to diminish extravagant property incomes can be quite soundly based on a normative judgment about equality, such as Robert Owen made when he argued that inequality created social discontent, or on a moral objection to large unearned incomes.

But, more serious, the means chosen to carry out the objective are not, in contemporary Britain, necessarily the most appropriate ones. The Labour Party having decided, rightly, to pay full compensation, the transfer of industries to state ownership does not have any large or immediate effect on the distribution of income. Over the long run there is, of course, a connection; but even in the long run other methods of redistribution are now seen to be simpler and more effective. As a determinant of relative shares in total income, the ownership of industrial property is less important than the level of employment, the behaviour of prices, government controls (e.g. over rent or dividends), and above all taxation policy; and a determined government can restrict property incomes more easily than by the collectivisation of industry with full compensation. In addition, nationalisation has thrown up certain stubborn and largely unexpected problems which, so long as they remain unsolved, in any case make it impracticable to rely on public ownership as the main method of raising wages at the expense of property incomes.

In fact the other methods have already gone some way to fulfilling the desired objective. There has been an important transfer from property-incomes to wages since 1939; and the distribution of wealth is now much more egalitarian. Certainly much remains to be done; but fiscal policies offer a simpler and quicker way of doing it than wholesale collectivisation.

This does not mean that nationalisation may not be justified on other grounds, nor that over the long period it has no influence of any kind on income-distribution, nor that the egalitarian objective to which it was directed has lost its relevance. It simply means that the ownership of the means of production, as the last chapter has already shown, is no longer the *essential* determinant of the distribution of incomes; private ownership is compatible with a high degree of equality, while state ownership, as the Russian experience has demonstrated, may be used to support a high degree of inequality.

(2) The objective of substituting for unrestricted competition and the motive of personal profit some more social organisation and set of motives, by means either of co-operative undertakings or state ownership. (R. H. Tawney, a magisterial authority in these matters, considers this objective to be the basic element in socialism.) It has two sources of inspiration.

(a) The first is ethical, and springs from a desire to replace competitive social relations by fellowship and social solidarity, and the motive of personal profit by a more altruistic and other-regarding motive. The combination of competition and the profit motive was equally offensive to Robert Owen (because it militated against human happiness), the Christian Socialists (because it ran counter to Christian ethics), Ruskin and Morris (because it bred ugliness and commercialism, and debased the quality of labour), and the pioneers of the I.L.P. (because it denied the brotherhood of man).

Few will quarrel with this ethical aspiration towards a more fraternal and co-operative society—indeed, it is remarkable how it anticipates the writings of many contemporary sociologists. The difficulty is to find the framework within which it can be fulfilled. So far as social organisation is concerned, it will clearly not be fulfilled simply by eliminating industrial competition, since this constitutes only a small (and diminishing) part of the sum total of competition in modern society. We are now more vividly aware of the wide extent, in any country having pretensions to equal opportunity, of feelings of emulation, rivalry, and competitive envy; indeed, the more successful the Left is in equalising opportunities, the more all-pervasive must competition (for jobs, promotion, social prestige) become—whether or not the organisation of industry is formally competitive.

Industry itself, moreover, has become a great deal less competitive since these doctrines were in their prime, so much so that it is now an applauded object of government policy to make the private sector rather *more* competitive. There is little risk, in view of the mild and refined character of the British businessman's competitive instinct, that this will set citizens too violently at one another's throats; and this reinforces the point that there are now more pressing causes of antagonism to be attended to than competition between capitalists.

In addition, most people would now feel doubts about Robert Owen's view of the relation between social organisation and individual character. On the one hand, we know enough to perceive that the simple act of replacing individual by group or collective relationships does not necessarily make people more contented, or fraternal, or amiable; while on the other hand, we know too little to dogmatise about how groups can or should be organised in such a way as to achieve these desired results. And the traditional means are either wholly inappropriate, or not sufficient in themselves: small-scale co-operative units are not practicable under modern conditions, while state ownership, as at present conceived in terms of nationalised public boards, does not self-evidently induce a co-operative spirit or sense of social solidarity—at the very least the point remains unproven.

When we turn to the question of personal motives, we find again that developments over the last century have served to complicate the issue. Those socialists who think it immoral and degrading that men should work for money, and not for loving-kindness or social duty, cannot now fasten on profit as the only object of their obloquy; for profits are no different in kind as an incentive from piecework earnings, bonus systems, or even the incentive of a rise in salary. And the steady spread of incentive payments has extended the system of differential rewards for differential effort over so large a part of the population that merely to abolish industrial competition or private ownership would do little to alter matters—the money incentive is just as pervasive under monopoly or public ownership. Even assuming, moreover, that people would work better and be happier, or that the moral tone of society would be improved, if they no longer worked for personal gain, it is increasingly hard, in view of the growth of large-scale production, to see the institutional framework within which a change in motives could be effected. Again the traditional means do not provide a sufficient answer; guilds and communes are ruled out on technical grounds, and state ownership has not produced the hoped-for change. Although, therefore, the aspiration has clearly not been fulfilled, the method of attaining a more co-operative society must be re-appraised in the light of technical changes and greater knowledge.

(b) The second objection to private profit and competition was economic, and related to the actual material results of classical capitalism. Poverty, slums, malnutrition—these were ascribed to the fact that production was carried on for profit and not for use, and was directed to satisfying the demands of the rich before the needs of the poor. Only public ownership would ensure a more equitable and socially desirable allocation of resources.

Now it is quite true that production for profit, conducted within a framework of very unequal incomes, must give a distribution of resources highly distasteful to socialists, because it takes no account of needs, however urgent, but only of monetary demand. It is further true that the means chosen (state ownership) could in principle fulfil the objective of a different and more equitable distribution of resources.

But the objective can also be achieved by other means, and has been largely so achieved to-day. The statement that production for profit gives a bad distribution of resources (caviar for the rich before milk for the poor) is only a shorthand. What is meant is that production is undertaken for profit: that the distribution of purchasing power determines what is profitable: and that if this is very unequal, then the wants of the rich will be met before the needs of the poor. But if purchasing power is distributed more equally, it becomes more profitable to produce necessities, and less profitable to produce luxuries. The objection is thus fundamentally not to the role of profit, which is merely to reflect and communicate the distribution of demand, but to the distribution of demand itself—to the fact that the rich had so much money to spend on caviar, and the poor so little to spend on milk.

But to-day the redistribution of incomes, and the rise in working-class purchasing power, have banished the worst effects of production for profit by calling forth a quite different pattern of output. It is now highly profitable to produce articles, whether necessities or luxuries, for mass working-class consumption; indeed, by far the greater part of production for the home market takes this form. Moreover, a further weapon is at hand—fiscal and physical controls—which can also be used, and was widely used by the Labour Government, to enforce a pattern of output even on privately-owned industry different from that which the price-system, left to itself, would call forth. These influences now give an allocation of resources much nearer to what most people would consider desirable; that is, far more resources than previously are devoted to satisfying the wants of 90% of the population, and far fewer to satisfying those of the richest 10%. And if a further move towards an 'ideal' distribution is desired, this can be easily accomplished without an extension of state ownership.

Thus the historic anti-competitive theme, in both its aspects, provides a second case where so much has changed that the traditional doctrine now seems over-simplified, and new ways of fulfilling the aspiration either have been, or can be, or must be found.

50 Noberto Bobbio, from *Left and Right: the Significance of a Political Distinction* (trans. by A. Cameron; Polity Press, 1996), pp. 80–2

Bobbio (1909–) remains one of Italy's most influential and best-known post-war political thinkers. He studied political philosophy and jurisprudence as a student, and was imprisoned twice under Mussolini's fascist regime in the 1930s. He has served, since 1984, as a senator in the Italian parliament and has been one of the country's leading public intellectuals in this period. Bobbio is a prolific and wide-ranging political thinker and writer, who has been especially drawn to areas of overlap between liberal and socialist ideas. The principal target of much of his political writings was the Italian Communist Party, and the political left more generally, who tended to undervalue the importance of democracy. Democracy, he maintained, ought to be the central, and defining, value of socialism.

1 'Left' and 'right' are two antithetical terms which for more than two centuries have been used habitually to signify the contrast between the ideologies and movements which divide the world of political thought and action. As antithetical terms, they are mutually exclusive, and together they are exhaustive within that eminently conflict-riven universe.

They are exclusive in the sense that no doctrine or movement can be both left-wing and right-wing at the same time. They are exhaustive in the sense that a doctrine or movement can only be either left-wing or right-wing, at least as far as the more rigid application of the twin definition is concerned, as we shall see later.

The antithetical pair, left and right, can be put to descriptive, axiological or historical use, as I have often said of what I call the 'great dichotomies' which divide up every field of knowledge. They are descriptive in that they can summarize two sides of a conflict, evaluative in that they can express a positive or negative value-judgement of one side or the other, and historical in that they can indicate the passage from one phase to another in the political life of a nation. Their historical use can, in turn, be either descriptive or evaluative.

The opposition between left and right represents a typically dyadic way of thinking, which has been variously explained in psychological, sociological, historical and even biological terms. There are examples in all fields of thought; the all-inclusive distinction or dyad dominates every discipline. In sociology it is society/community, in economics market/planned, in law public/private, in aesthetics classical/romantic, and in philosophy transcendent/immanent. Left/right is not the only distinction in the political sphere, but it is encountered everywhere.

There are distinctions in which the two constituent terms are antithetical, and others in which they are complementary. The former interpret a universe as a composition of divergent entities which oppose each other, whereas the latter interpret a harmonious universe composed of convergent entities which tend to fuse into a superior whole. The left/right pair belongs to the first type. Given that triadic thought is often generated from dyadic thought or represents, as it were, a development from it, the transition from one to the other will differ according to whether the dyad one starts from consists of antithetical or complementary terms. In the first case the transition occurs through a dialectical synthesis or negation of the negation, in the second case through composition.

The following reflections arise from the assertion that there is no longer any relevance to the distinction between left and right which, over the two centuries since the French Revolution, has been used to divide the political universe into opposing camps, an assertion which has been made repeatedly in recent years, to the point of becoming a cliché. It is now *de rigueur* to quote Sartre who, it appears, was one of the first to argue that left and right were empty vessels. They are no longer supposed to have any heuristic or classificatory value, and emphatically no evaluative application. Often they are referred to with a certain irritation, as though they represent one of the many linguistic traps which political debate can fall into.

2 There are various reasons for this opinion which is gaining increasing currency, and countless examples could be produced every day. Let us look at a few.

The first doubts about whether the distinction had disappeared, or at least ceased to have the same descriptive force, arose from the so-called crisis of ideology, and therefore the pointlessness of contrasting the ideologies involved. The objection which can easily be raised is that ideologies have not disappeared at all, but are still very much with us. The ideologies of the past have merely been replaced by others which are new or claim to be new. The ideological tree is always green. Besides, it has been shown repeatedly that there is nothing more ideological than declaring the demise of ideologies. Then again 'left' and 'right' are not just ideologies. To reduce them to purely ideological expressions would be an unjustifiable simplification: they indicate opposing programmes in relation to many problems whose solution is part of everyday political activity. These contrasts concern not only ideas, but also interests and judgements on which direction society should be moving in; they exist in all societies, and it is not apparent how they could disappear. Naturally, one could reply that such contrasting positions exist, but they are not the same as those encountered when the distinction was created, and during the period of its success these positions have changed so much as to make the old names anachronistic and therefore misleading.

Recently it has been argued that, since the concept of a left wing has been so drastically emptied of its descriptive powers as to be one of the least informative expressions in political usage, the time has come to replace the old pair of terms with a more appropriate one: that of progressives and conservatives. But some have taken a more radical stance, rejecting any residual dichotomy in their vision, and arguing that this last dichotomy is one of those 'follies' of political jargon, which we must free ourselves from in order to form new groupings, based not on positions, but on problems.

3 Secondly, it is argued that the division into two distinct and opposing political camps has become inappropriate, and the resulting political spectrum insufficient, in the increasingly complex political world of large-scale societies, particularly large-scale democratic societies which tolerate and indeed presuppose the existence of a multitude of pressure groups and interest groups which compete with each other (and which on occasion oppose each other, and on other occasions make common cause with each other; they converge on some points and diverge on others, like dancers joining together and then turning their backs in an elaborate choreography). Basically, the objection is that in a multi-faceted democratic society, in which many forces are at play, which agree on some points and not on others, and permit a great variety of alliances, problems cannot be posed in antithetical form as one thing or another: either left or right, and if it is not left-wing, it must be right-wing, or vice versa.

This objection strikes home, but it is not decisive. The distinction between left and right does not at all preclude, even in everyday language, the existence of a continuous spectrum which joins the left and the right, or of intermediate positions where the left meets the right. These positions make up a central area between the extremes which is well known as the 'centre'. If one wanted to flirt a little with the terminology of logic, one could say that while the dyadic concept of politics can be defined as the excluded middle, according to which politics is divided into just two parts, which are mutually exclusive, with nothing in between them, a triadic concept can be defined as the 'included middle', according to which there is an intermediate space between the left and the right which is neither one nor the other. In the first case, the two terms, which have an 'either . . . or . . .' relationship, are contradictory; whereas in the second case, in which the intermediate area can be expressed as 'neither . . . nor . . .', they are opposites. No problem then: black and white are divided by grey, and day and night are divided by dusk. Grey takes nothing away from the distinction between black and white, and dusk takes nothing away from the distinction between day and night.

4 The fact that in many democratic systems with high levels of pluralism the 'included middle' can become so all-embracing as to relegate the left and the right to the extreme margins of the political system does not in any way invalidate the original antithesis. As the centre is defined as neither left-wing nor right-wing and cannot be defined in any other way, its very existence and *raison d'être* are based on this antithesis. The duration of dusk varies according to the season and the latitude, but its duration in no way affects the fact that its definition depends on the definition of day and night.

Identification of this intermediate space allows for a more graduated interpretation of the political system, as the centre which is closer to the left, the centre-left, can be distinguished from the centre which is closer to the right, the centre-right. Equally, on the left, one can distinguish between a moderate left which tends towards the centre and an extreme left which is opposed to the centre, and on the right, a right wing which is attracted towards the centre and a right wing which distances itself so much from the centre as to be equally opposed to the centre as to the left. If it is then considered that whatever way the centre is divided up there is still a centre which remains intact and could be defined as the centre of the centre, a spectrum emerges with a range of positions.

It need hardly be said that fragmentation of the political system is assisted by the adoption of proportional representation. This fragmentation can be clearly seen in a chamber of deputies shaped like an amphitheatre, in which the various positions are represented, moving from the extreme right to the extreme left. However, the distinction which divides the elected representatives in each sector is still between left and right. While in the British parliament, one has to sit either on the left or on the right, reflecting the great left/right antithesis, representatives in a parliament like the Italian Montecitorio are graded from right to left (or vice versa). However, the nostalgia for a first-past-the-post electoral system (whether based on one or two ballots) which has arisen in recent years and has led to repeated attempts at reform and a referendum, reflects a desire to return to a bipolar political system. This campaign, which has finally achieved success through an act of parliament, is proof enough that a dichotomous interpretation of politics persists even in a fragmented system, whatever views might be expressed, and leaving aside all doctrinal arguments. Besides, what better proof could there be of the persistence of this dichotomy than the presence, even where there is pluralism, of a left wing which tends to perceive the centre as the right wing in disguise and a right wing which tends to perceive the same centre as a cover for the left which does not wish to show its true colours.

. . .

6 A third reason for rejecting the traditional opposition between left and right and claiming its demise is the view that it has lost a great deal of its descriptive value, because the continuous development of society and the creation of new political problems (political in the sense that they require solutions through the traditional instruments of political activity—that is to say, activity aimed at collective decisions which, once they are taken, become binding on the entire community) have produced movements which cannot be categorized in terms of the traditional opposition between left and right, as claimed by the movements themselves. The most interesting current example is that of

the Greens. Are the Greens on the left or the right? If we use the criteria usually adopted for making this distinction, it appears that sometimes they are on the left and sometimes on the right, or that they are neither left-wing nor right-wing. The Greens could be defined as a *transversal* movement, which has become a political buzz-word, albeit a pejorative used in another context. This is because green issues run through all the enemy camps, and pass effortlessly from one camp to another, thus proving that in practice there is a third way of subverting the dyad, in addition to being in the *middle* (the centre) and going *beyond* (synthesis). This moving *through* the spectrum entails a reduction in the authority of the dyad, rather than its rejection or obsolescence.

The best proof of the ubiquity of the green movement is the fact that all parties have adopted the ecological theme without changing any of their traditional political baggage. They have perhaps merely added to it. No one today would dare to challenge the rights of nature, which are perhaps an unconscious anthropomorphization of the natural world. These are the rights which nature should expect of humanity, and this relationship implies duties which humanity must accord to nature (without entering into the argument of whether a right precedes an obligation, or vice versa). There are various explanations for this radical shift in attitude to nature (particularly in the West) from a perception of nature as something purely to be dominated and as a passive instrument of human needs to the idea of nature (even inanimate nature) as a subject, or at least an object which should not be used arbitrarily, but within the dictates of reason. According to a somewhat metaphysical or religious interpretation, nature belongs to the world not created by man, and, like man, is a free agent within it, acting alongside other free agents. A more pragmatic and utilitarian point of view asserts that since man is obliged to live in a finite universe whose available resources for survival are limited, these resources should be used with due consideration to their eventual exhaustion. Given these different philosophies based on opposing value systems and concepts of the world, it is quite possible that the spread of ecological movements will not make the traditional left/right split anachronistic, but that, instead, this split will be reproduced within the various ecological movements, which are already troubled by internal divisions, despite their recent appearance. It is a question of whether human beings have a duty to other beings besides themselves, or to other human beings, in particular to future generations; or, in other words, whether these restrictions are imposed on humanity from outside or are imposed by humanity on itself. This question will introduce a distinction between right-wing greens and left-wing greens, and has in part already done so.

51 Alex Callinicos, from *Equality* (Polity Press, 2000), pp. 130–3

Callinicos (1950–) is Professor of Politics at the University of York in the UK. He has been a leading figure within the Trotskyist Socialist Workers Party for a number of years, and remains one of its most prominent theoreticians. He has written widely in the fields of social and political theory, specifically on Marxism and Trotskyism, and on the character of the contemporary global anti-capitalist movement.

It may be helpful, in conclusion, to state the argument of this book in the shape of four theses:

1 Social and economic inequality is a chronic feature of the contemporary world. The available evidence suggests that, in the era of capitalist triumphalism ushered in during the 1980s by the victories of the New Right in the United States and Britain and by the collapse of the Eastern bloc, the gap between rich and poor has steadily grown, both on a world scale and within individual countries. Of course, there is nothing new about such inequalities, but they represent a standing reproach to modern liberal societies that, since the American and French Revolutions, have guaranteed their citizens equal respect. The promise of what Etienne Balibar calls *égaliberté*—of equality and liberty conceived as principles that can only be realized jointly—seems indeed to be a constitutive feature of modernity, and one that it is far from fulfilling. The pressure that this failure places on politicians—even at a time when much trouble has been taken to expunge large-scale ideological conflicts from mainstream discourse—is reflected in the considerable efforts by the New Labour government in Britain to demonstrate that it is pursuing a strategy aimed at significantly diminishing inequality. The fact that, as I have tried to show, this strategy stands very little chance of succeeding hardly diminishes the urgency of the issue.

2 Egalitarian liberalism has, since the appearance of John Rawls's *A Theory of Justice* nearly a generation ago, greatly improved our philosophical understanding of the nature of distributive justice. The difference principle offers a criterion by which to judge whether unequal distributions are to be tolerated, namely only when they are to the advantage of the worst-off. The debate over the currency of egalitarian justice has also, despite the arcane by-roads into which it has sometimes strayed, also produced greater clarity. Both G.A. Cohen's equal access to advantage and Amartya Sen's equality of capabilities suggest that what we should be seeking to equalize is individuals' ability to engage in as wide a range as possible of activities and states (what Sen calls 'functionings') that they have reason to value. Sen's capabilities approach has the further merit of indicating that egalitarianism is driven not merely by the justified desire to eliminate the harmful consequences of brute luck, but by the objective of ensuring that all have equal access to well-being, where well-being involves the successful pursuit of goals that are both valuable and freely chosen. The fact that well-being cannot be reduced to the satisfaction of individual preference is important because it rules out the more subjectivist versions of luck egalitarianism that hold individuals responsible for the consequences of all the choices they make once access to welfare or resources has been equalized. Often circumstances so confine choices that individual preferences adapt to this constrained situation. To treat the decisions reflecting these preferences as the outcome of free choice would be to do the individuals concerned a grave injustice.

3 The greatest weakness of egalitarian liberalism is, however, its assumption that justice can be done within the framework of a capitalist market economy. This is a premiss that it shares with the ideologists of the Third Way. It is reflected in egalitarian liberals' tendency to neglect the role of exploitation—the extraction of surplus labour from wage-labourers—in creating and sustaining the existing structures of inequality (Cohen is an exception: his concern with exploitation reflects a continuing socialist commitment). They focus on differences in natural talent as the main source of inequality—a view that

completely fails to address the entrenched structures of privilege and power on a world scale. The inherent conflict between capitalism and equality is suggested by the direct connection between the various measures taken to revive profitability over the past two decades—deregulation, corporate downsizing, tax cuts for the better off, reductions in social provision—and the growing gap between rich and poor. More abstract reflection suggests that the measures that egalitarians recommend to improve the condition of the worst-off would, above all by undermining the incentive to take part in the labour-market on terms favourable to capital, severely disrupt the profitable functioning of the capitalist economy. Egalitarian justice can be achieved only *against* capitalism.

4 This conclusion, of course, poses the greatest political difficulty: since the collapse of the Soviet Union, few believe that there is a viable and attractive socio-economic alternative to capitalism. The idea of market socialism offers a half-way house, seeking to combine collective ownership of the means of production with the market's supposed superiority to other forms in the efficient allocation of resources. Even if this combination were stable (which seems doubtful), it would leave unremedied the injustices arising from differences in individual ability and need. But a non-market alternative to capitalism seems quite outside the bounds of contemporary common sense. To change this state of affairs will require, among other things, a revival in Utopian imagination—that is, in our capacity to anticipate, at least in outline, an efficient and democratic non-market form of economic co-ordination. Our current inability to do so is a consequence both of disappointed hopes and of the imaginative dominance that a particular type of capitalism—the Anglo-American *laissez-faire* model—has acquired for various contingent reasons. What the French call *la pensée unique*—a narrow set of neo-liberal dogmas and recipes—currently exerts an almost totalitarian hold on policy debate. But this will pass. Already we can see the signs of a developing popular reaction to the effects of this consensus. From the movements that are currently emerging against neo-liberalism will develop new visions of how to run the world better. Here lies our best hope of forcing modernity finally to fulfil its promise of equality and liberty.

5   Nationalism

Introduction

Few topics excite disagreement with the intensity evoked by nationalism. For writers such as the political theorist John Dunn, nationalism is 'the starkest political shame of the twentieth century, the deepest, most intractable and yet most unanticipated blot on the political history of the world since the year 1900'. For others, of course, including the authors excerpted in this chapter, it is an indispensable and commendable part of political life—at least, when it is understood in the right way. But precisely how the concepts of nationalism and the nation are to be understood is a hotly contested topic. At its core, nationalism invokes a sense of belonging to and serving a national community, a pride in culture and traditions, and a sense that this community is entitled to form a state and to promote its own interests. But this core concept can be fleshed out in many different ways, leading some commentators to see nationalism as Janus-faced: a sense of common nationality is necessary for stability of a political community, and for resistance to domination by foreign states (as social cement, or the engine of social mobilization) but can spill over into xenophobia, racism, and militaristic self-aggrandisement. Even nationalism's harshest critics accept that it has become a potent global ideology, visible in the politics of every region in the world and possessing immense power to mobilize populations and to legitimize, and subvert, states.

Etymologically, the word 'nation' has its Origins in the Latin *natio*, meaning something born. In Rome, the word was used in a derogatory sense to refer to foreigners coming from a particular region, whose status was below that of Roman citizens. In medieval church councils, it came to refer to communities of opinion and differing elite groups. By the early sixteenth century, the term came to be used in something like its modern sense, to refer to a population. Etymology gives us little guidance on the important analytical and conceptual questions, and historians and sociologists of national identity differ deeply over how primordial or modern the phenomenon of nationhood should be considered to be. While some find signs of a nascent national consciousness in England and the Netherlands in the sixteenth and seventeenth centuries, there is rather more consensus that nationalism as a self-conscious ideology emerges in the same period as the 'classical' ideological traditions, liberalism and socialism. Particularly important in understanding the emergence of this ideology was the shaking of absolutist monarchies of Prussia, Russia, and Austria by the French Revolution and the Napoleonic Wars.

The text from Jean-Jacques Rousseau, with which we start, is often taken to be important in marking the emergence of a distinctive national ideology and way of thinking from an older tradition of republican patriotism [Reading 52]. For republican patriots, such as the Roman Cicero and the Renaissance Florentine Machiavelli, political loyalty to the *patria* or fatherland was loyalty to a political concept of the republic. Love of country, which every true republican has drunk along with his mother's milk, is identified with 'love of law and liberty', as Rousseau puts it elsewhere in his *Considerations on the Government of Poland*. We need loyalty to our political community in order to follow its laws, participate in their enactment, guard against political corruption, and, when necessary, to fight to preserve the community against foreign domination.

In the *Government of Poland*, Rousseau argues that intensifying and concentrating love of a nation as a particular cultural unity is necessary to preserve the sense of political loyalty that citizens of a free republic require. Rousseau inveighs against a bland European cosmopolitanism, which he views as replacing a citizen's sense of duty to a fatherland with a materialistic egoism. Poland has weak political institutions, a small population, and is constantly exposed to the greater military power of neighbours such as Prussia and Russia. Since the polity is vulnerable, it is all the more important to foster and, if necessary, invent particular national traditions and customs in order to prevent the absorption of the Poles' identity into that of their neighbours, particularly Russia. In the absence of a robust and free political community, in other words, the Poles need to celebrate their distinctive national culture, for example, through adopting a national dress and public games and ceremonies. This emphasis on the cultural and spiritual unity of a people is an important nationalist theme. But it is worth noting that Rousseau here is unsentimental in his view of national tradition: national customs should be valued primarily because they help to promote loyalty to the political fatherland, not as themselves intrinsically valuable. In other words, his nationalist proposals can be viewed as growing out of his republican patriotic belief in the need to encourage citizens' loyalty to their particular political institutions and society.

The Prussian J. G. Herder more explicitly finds the foundation for a sense of common political identity not in a common polity but in a shared culture, particularly a language. For Herder, political institutions are external and artificial, and a political theory that places too much importance on them is dissociated from the vital sources of authentic human life and action. By contrast, a person's particular culture is the expression of a natural inner awareness that one is part of a social whole. Herder calls this spiritual unity grounded in a common culture or language *Volk* or nation. Furthermore, as he puts it in his *Ideas for a Philosophy of the History of Mankind*, the 'most natural state is *one* nationality with one national character'. His nationalism sprang from a deep dissatisfaction with the absolutist states of the late eighteenth century, such as Prussia, Russia, and Austria, which held together peoples belonging to diverse cultures through political force and a centralized bureaucracy. Ideas of cultural cosmopolitanism served only to mask these imperial forms of rule, which mechanically imposed an artificial and external order on the natural and organic processes of human social growth and development.

The reading here is from the satirically entitled *Yet Another History of Philosophy of History* [Reading 53], an attack on the view held by many Enlightenment authors such as Voltaire and Hume that there exists a common and immutable human nature. Like Rousseau, Herder was sceptical of the claims of enlightened European cosmopolitanism to represent the highest stage of historical progress. Instead, he argues, there is no such single standard of value: nature places the inclination toward diversity in our heart, and Herder defends the particularity that results against any single standard of cultural worth. At the same time, he resists the sceptical idea that acknowledgement of this diversity robs the claim that there exists historical progress of all meaning. Instead, progress consists in each element of divine creation in fulfilling its particular purpose, a formulation that allows Herder to combine universalism with pluralism. Accordingly, Herder's nationalism stresses the equal value of all nations, and emphasizes the possibility of peaceful coexistence rather than mutual competition and war.

The following two readings reflect the patriotic and nationalist ferment in Europe of the early and mid-nineteenth century. The French Revolution and Napoleonic Wars had damaged the great European empires and nationalists sought to achieve self-government for their peoples. Adam Mickiewicz offers an intense and romantic statement of Polish nationalism [Reading 54]. His view of Poland emphasizes a virtuous peasantry in its traditional and unsullied rural habitat. This is combined with suspicion of Russian imperialism and distaste for Western materialism and egoism. These sentiments are overlaid with an exile's nostalgia—often an important emotion for nationalists who necessarily had to flee or were expelled from their countries. The evocation of the particularities of place and tradition and nostalgia for a pre-modern innocence were important themes for the romantic strand of nineteenth and twentieth century nationalism.

John Stuart Mill also writes against the background of small European nations under the dominance of, or threatened by, the Austro-Hungarian and Russian empires [Reading 55]. He sees nationality as consisting of a specific sentiment, a shared sense among a group of people that they belong together, rather than as consisting in any shared objective characteristics, such as language, culture, religion, or geography, although the latter may contribute to and reinforce the sense of shared identity. For, as he points out, a shared sentiment of nationality may exist even in the absence of shared race, religion, or culture (as in Switzerland), or fail to exist even where many of these objective characteristics appear, as in Sicily's estrangement from Naples. For Mill, where there exists a common sentiment of nationality, there is a *prima facie* case for shared government. In part, this derives from a belief in individuals' freedom to associate with whomever they choose. But he also makes the point (which echoes the excerpt from Rousseau above) that a sense of common sympathy, together with a shared language, are vital for the flourishing of the institutions of representative government. Mill represents here an important strand of liberal nationalism, which was concerned with the liberation of minority nations from the yoke of imperial rule. In this vein, later in the nineteenth century George Bernard Shaw remarked that 'a liberal is a man who has three duties: a duty to Ireland, a duty to Finland, and a duty to Macedonia'. Each of these countries was under imperial rule at the time, respectively the British, Russian, and Austro-Hungarian.

At the same time, a shared sentiment of nationality makes only a prima facie case for common institutions of government. Mill noted elsewhere that the sentiment of nationality could be mobilized to crush the spirit of liberty. In this excerpt, he makes two further significant caveats. Where populations are intermingled, as in Hungary and elsewhere in central and eastern Europe, 'there is no course open to them but to make a virtue of necessity, and reconcile themselves to living together under equal rights and laws'. His other 'moral and social' qualification less comfortably comports with contemporary liberal thinking. Inferior and backward national minorities, such as the Bretons and Basques in France and the Welsh and Highland Scots in Britain, would undoubtedly benefit from absorption into the great nationalities available to them. These great nations are viewed as the carriers of human progress, in contrast to the stagnant and parochial minorities. Yet for Mill the great nation may benefit too from a judicious mixing with minority nationalities, at least under the right circumstances: like a crossed breed of animal, the result may hope to inherit the strengths of all its progenitors.

The excerpts from Heinrich Von Treitschke, the German historian, offer a robust conservative retort to liberals who invoke freedom of association as a basis for common political institutions [Reading 56]. Alsace Lorraine was taken by the Prussians in the Franco-Prussian War of 1871. Here Treitschke makes clear that the wishes of the inhabitants one way or the other, as invoked by liberals such as Mill and the French author Ernest Renan, had nothing to do with the strength of the national claim to this territory. When the delegates from the border region of Alsace Lorraine declared in the French National Assembly, which agreed to peace with Prussia, that they had an immutable will to remain French, Treitschke mordantly commented 'against their will we shall restore them to their true selves'. The nationalist claim to territory is also the subject of the second part of this excerpt. While some states such as Russia may be ungovernably large, Treitschke argues, others need to expand in order to fulfil their 'historical task'. The second excerpt brings out the anti-semitism (by no means originating with or unique to German nationalism, of course) accompanying an emphasis on the historic mission of the German people or *Volk*. Membership of the nation is not merely legal but cultural and spiritual, and involves repelling foreign influences: waves of anti-semitism are, then, an admirable by-product of a healthy national consciousness. It is worth noting that Treitschke here, unlike racial ideologues (see the readings from Hitler and Rosenberg in chapter 9 [Readings 86 and 87]), does not preclude the successful assimilation of Jews through submersion of Jewish identity into particular European national identities.

In the excerpt from Max Weber's 'Nation-State and Economic Policy' [Reading 57], his inaugural lecture at the University of Freiburg in 1895, a different sort of nationalist struggle is emphasized. This is the economic battle for national paramountcy. Where the earlier Herder and the Anglo-American liberal nationalists such as Mill emphasized that nationalism is compatible with harmony among nations, Weber views struggle and *Machtpolitik* as inexpugnable features of the political landscape. While as an explanatory and analytic science political economy is international, as he puts it, as soon as we make value judgements about which policies to pursue we must fall back on specifically national criteria. The torpidity of the German state and society, as he sees it, results from a failure to pursue this insight with sufficient vigour.

The subsequent readings focus on extra-European expressions of nationalism. In the excerpt from Gandhi's *Hind Swaraj*, which is set out in dialogue form, a number of important themes in Gandhi's thoughts emerge [Reading 58]. The context is a debate on the character of Indian national identity, and Gandhi's argument that India is a *praja* or nation. Famously, Gandhi resisted both the constitutionalism of moderates in the struggle against British colonial rule over India and the violent tactics of extremists. Instead, he endorsed strategies of passive resistance and civil disobedience, *satyagraha* (roughly translated as the way of truth or pursuit of truth). In the excerpt here, Gandhi emphasizes that sectarianism in both Hindu and Muslim forms is an obstacle to Indian liberation, and that nationality should not be identified with sect. He was a vehement opponent of partition, which separated a Muslim-dominated Pakistan from a Hindu-dominated India, and spent the day of Indian independence mourning partition. Two other strands of Gandhi's brand of nationalism that emerge from the excerpts are worth drawing attention to here. The first is the need for Indians to overcome postures of blame and insecurity in relation to the British: real home-rule is a spiritual condition, from which political home-rule derives. The other theme to note is Gandhi's support of traditional Indian civilization through espousing anti-industrialism, famously embodied in his wearing of home-spun clothes.

A very different but roughly contemporaneous movement of non-European national liberation is the subject of the next excerpt. Marcus Garvey was a political activist who became the foremost exponent of black nationalism among the peoples of the African diaspora. His statement 'The Future as I See It' was made in 1919, which marked the period of greatest success for Garvey and his organization the Universal Negro Improvement Association, and sets out some characteristic themes [Reading 59]. Only through relying on themselves, spurning aid from whites, and building independent social and economic institutions can blacks be liberated from oppression. Crucial to this programme is the liberation of Africa from colonialism as a homeland for the global African diaspora. Where necessary, this liberation project needs to take the form of armed struggle, a position that led Garvey's newspapers to be banned by French and British colonial authorities, and Garvey himself to be investigated by J. Edgar Hoover's Federal Bureau of Investigation.

The following extract is from the Kenyan nationalist and political leader Jomo Kenyatta's work *Facing Mount Kenya: The Tribal Life of the Gikuyu*, which he completed in London in 1938 [Reading 60]. In one sense, this is a work of academic ethnography and the product of Kenyatta's study with the eminent anthropologist Bronislaw Malinowski. Yet it mobilizes its ethnographic study for political ends, attacking the colonial government of what was then British East Africa and the European encroachment more generally. Kenyatta particularly focuses on the seizure of land, since much of the Kikuyu way of life depended on traditional patterns of land use. By taking away the 'material symbol' that holds together family and tribe, the colonist 'cuts away the foundation from the whole of Gikuyu life, social, moral and economic'. Only through eliminating external rule and returning power to the original inhabitants of this land can these destructive consequences be reversed. While Kenyatta allows that some progressive ideas may have emanated from the Europeans, he inveighs against the 'civilising mission', which operates in practice through 'the gas bomb and armed police'. We will encounter some of the themes of this extract—the importance of land and the widespread destructive consequences of its colonial appropriation, the hypocrisy, and the sham of European treaties and legality—in considering the movement for the rights of indigenous and aboriginal peoples in chapter 10 below [Reading 95].

In *The Wretched of the Earth*, Frantz Fanon argues for the necessity of violence as a response to the Manichean world of colonization [Reading 61]. Imperialism creates a divided world in which the black or colonized are identified with every negative value and the white or colonizers with every positive value, a schism which creates profound social and psychological scars in the populations subject to them. Only total revolution or absolute violence can liberate colonized societies from the past, purifying the society and eliminating the social division drawn across society between black and white. Elsewhere in the same work, he cautions against viewing national culture as 'a folklore' or 'abstract populism that believes that it can discover the people's true nature'. But he does not wish to abandon the notion, since it promises a form of solidarity or unity that may help a people struggling to free itself from oppression.

FURTHER READING

There is an immense literature on nationalism among historians, sociologists, political scientists, and others. For useful selections from this, see John Hutchinson and Anthony Smith (eds.), *Nationalism* (Oxford University Press, 1995), Gopal Balakrishnan (ed.), *Mapping the Nation* (Verso, 1996), and Geoff Eley and Ronald Gregor Suny (eds.), *Becoming National: A Reader* (Oxford University Press, 1996). Influential books include Hans Kohn, *The Idea of Nationalism: A Study in Its Origins and Background* (MacMillan, 1944), Ernest Gellner, *Nations and Nationalism* (Blackwell, 1983), Anthony Smith, *Theories of Nationalism* (Duckworth, 1983), Benedict Anderson, *Imagined Communities* (rev edn., Verso, 1991), Liah Greenfeld, *Nationalism: Five Roads to Modernity* (Harvard University Press, 1992), Elie Kedourie, *Nationalism* (4th edn., Blackwell, 1993), Partha Chatterjee, *The Nation and Its Fragments: Colonial and Post-Colonial Histories* (Princeton University Press, 1993), and Maurizio Viroli, *For Love of Country: An Essay on Patriotism and Nationalism* (Oxford: Oxford University Press, 1995). Influential recent philosophical discussions include Yael Tamir, *Liberal Nationalism* (Princeton University Press, 1993), and David Miller, *On Nationality* (Oxford University Press, 1995).

52 J. J. Rousseau, from *Considerations on the Government of Poland*, in *The Social Contract and Other Later Political Writings* (ed. Victor Gourevitch; Cambridge University Press, 1997), pp. 182–6

Jean-Jacques Rousseau (1712–1774) was born in the city-state of Geneva and moved to France in 1742. A novelist, composer, and autobiographer, he wrote on the arts, science, education, literature, and philosophy, as well as political theory. He was a close associate of many of the key figures of the French Enlightenment, but a ferocious critic of their belief in human progress. His principal political writings include *The Discourse on Inequality* (1755) and *The Social Contract* (1762). The latter work, as well as his novel *Émile*, published in the same year, led to his denunciation in France and Geneva for his unorthodox view of religion, and he spent the rest of his life leading a nomadic existence. *Considerations on the Government of Poland* was completed in 1772, in response to an approach from Count Wielhorski, a member of the Confederation of Bar (mentioned in the excerpt here), a body dedicated to the defence of Poland against absorption into the Russian empire. This work was probably only ever intended for circulation among members of the Confederation.

[1] Poland is a large State surrounded by even larger States which, because of their despotism and military discipline, possess great offensive force. It, by contrast, being weak because of its anarchy, is, in spite of Polish valor, the butt of all their offenses. It has no fortifications to stop their incursions. Its depopulation renders it almost completely incapable of defending itself. No economic organization, few troops or none at all, no

military discipline, no order, no subordination; ever divided within; ever threatened from without, it is without stability of its own, and dependent on its neighbors' whim. In the present state of things I see only one way of giving it the stability it lacks: to infuse, so to speak, the soul of its confederates into the entire nation, to establish the Republic in the hearts of the Poles so thoroughly that it endures there in spite of all of its oppressors' efforts. That, it seems to me, is the only refuge where force can neither reach nor destroy it. We have just witnessed a forever memorable proof of this. Poland was in the Russian's chains, but the Poles remained free. A great example which shows you how you can defy your neighbors' power and ambitions. You may not be able to keep them from swallowing you, do at least see to it that they cannot digest you. No matter what is done, Poland will have been overwhelmed by its enemies a hundred times before it can be given everything it needs in order to be in a position to resist them. The virtue of Citizens, their patriotic zeal, the distinctive form which its national institutions may give their soul, this is the only rampart that will stand ever ready to defend it, and which no army could subdue by force. If you see to it that a Pole can never become a Russian, I assure you that Russia will never subjugate Poland.

[2] It is national institutions which form the genius, the character, the tastes, and the morals of a people, which make it be itself and not another, which inspire in it that ardent love of fatherland founded on habits impossible to uproot, which cause it to die of boredom among other peoples in the midst of delights of which it is deprived in its own. Remember the Spartan, gorged with the voluptuous pleasures at the Court of the Great King, who was chided for missing his black broth. Ah! he said, sighing, to the satrap, I know your pleasures, but you do not know ours.

[3] There are no more Frenchmen, Germans, Spaniards, even Englishmen, nowadays, regardless of what people may say; there are only Europeans. All have the same tastes, the same passions, the same morals, because none has been given a national form by a distinctive institution. All will do the same things under the same circumstances; all will declare themselves disinterested and be cheats; all will speak of the public good and think only of themselves; all will praise moderation and wish to be Croesuses; they have no other ambition than for luxury, no other passion than for gold. Confident that with it they will have whatever tempts them, all will sell themselves to the first man willing to pay them. What do they care what master they obey, the laws of what State they follow? Provided they find money to steal and women to corrupt, they are at home in any country.

[4] Give a different bent to the Poles' passions, and you will give their souls a national physiognomy which will set them apart from all other peoples, which will keep them from merging, from feeling at ease, from inter-marrying with them, you will give them a vigor which will take the place of deceptive appeals to empty precepts, which will make them do by preference and passion the things one never does well enough when one does them only by duty or interest. It is upon souls such as these that an appropriate legislation will take hold. They will obey the laws and not elude them because they will suit them and will have the inward assent of their wills. Loving their fatherland, they will serve it out of zeal and with all their heart. With this sentiment alone, legislation, even if it were bad, would make good Citizens; and only good Citizens ever make for the force and prosperity of the State.

[5] I shall discuss below the administrative regime which, while leaving the foundation of your laws virtually untouched, seems to me suited to raise patriotism and the virtues inseparable from it to their highest possible pitch. But whether or not you adopt this regime, always begin by giving the Poles a great opinion of themselves and their fatherland: in view of the account they have just given of themselves, it will not be a false opinion. You must seize the occasion of the latest event to raise their souls to the level of the souls of the ancients. Certain it is that the Confederation of Bar saved the dying fatherland. You must engrave this great epoch in sacred characters in every Polish heart. I should wish to see a monument erected to its memory, and the names of all the Confederates inscribed on it, even of those who may subsequently have betrayed the common cause; so great a deed ought to erase the faults of an entire lifetime; I should wish to have a regular solemn occasion to celebrate it every ten years with a pomp not brilliant and frivolous, but plain, proud, and republican; to have the worthy Citizens who had the honor of suffering for the fatherland in the enemy's chains be eulogized with dignity, but without ostentation, even to have their families granted some honorific privilege which would forever recall this fair memory to the eyes of the public. However, I should not wish anyone to take the liberty of inveighing against the Russians or even of mentioning them. It would be doing them too much honor. This silence, the memory of their barbarity, and the eulogy of those who resisted them, will say all that needs to be said about them: you ought to despise them too much to hate them.

[6] I should wish all the patriotic virtues to be given luster by attaching to them honors and public rewards, the Citizens to be kept constantly occupied with the fatherland, for it to be made their principal business, for it to be continuously kept before their eyes. I admit that this way they would have less opportunity and time to grow rich, but they would also have less desire or need to do so: their hearts would get to know a happiness other than fortune, and therein lies the art of ennobling souls and turning them into an instrument more powerful than gold.

[7] The brief account of Polish morals which M. de Wielhorski kindly conveyed to me is not sufficient to instruct me of their civil and domestic practices. Yet a great nation which has never mingled much with its neighbors must have many practices that are distinctively its own, and are perhaps being daily bastardized by the general European tendency to adopt the tastes and morals of the French. These ancient practices ought to be preserved, restored, and suitable new ones introduced that are distinctively the Poles' own. These practices, even if they are indifferent, even if they are in some respects bad, provided they are not essentially so, will still have the advantage of making the Poles fond of their country and give them a natural revulsion to mingling with foreigners. I deem it fortunate that they have a distinctive mode of dress. Preserve this asset. Take care to do precisely the opposite of what this widely praised Tsar did. Let not the King, nor the Senators, nor any public figure ever wear any but the national dress, and let no Pole dare show himself at Court dressed in the French fashion.

[8] [Let there be] many public games where the good mother country delights in seeing her children at play. Let her frequently attend to them so that they always attend to her. The usual courtly entertainments must be eliminated, even at Court, because of the example it sets: gambling, theaters, comedies, opera; all that makes men effeminate, all that distracts them, isolates them, makes them forget their fatherland and their duty; all

that makes them be comfortable anywhere at all so long as they are entertained; games must be devised, festivals, solemn occasions so distinctive of this particular Court that they are found at none other. People should feel entertained in Poland more than in other countries, but not in the same way. In a word, the execrable proverb must be reversed, and every Pole be made to say in his inmost heart: *Ubi patria, ibi bene.*

[9] Nothing, if possible, exclusively for the Great and the rich. Many spectacles in the open, where ranks are carefully distinguished but the entire people participates equally, as among the ancients, and where, on certain occasions, young nobles display force and skill. The contribution of bullfights in maintaining a certain vigor in the Spanish nation is not negligible. The amphitheaters in which the youth of Poland used formerly to exercise should be carefully restored; they should be turned into theaters of honor and emulation for these youths. Nothing could be easier than to replace the fights that formerly took place in these amphitheaters by exercises less cruel but nevertheless requiring force and skill, and with honors and rewards for the victors as in the past. Horsemanship, for example, is an exercise well suited to Poles and it readily makes for dazzling spectacle.

53   J. G. Herder, from *Yet Another Philosophy of History*, in *Herder on Social and Political Culture* (ed. F. M. Barnard; Cambridge University Press, 1969), pp. 185–8

Johann Gottfried Herder (1744–1803) was a central figure in the flowering of German intellectual life in the late eighteenth century. Born in East Prussia, he spent most of his life as a Lutheran pastor in the cities of Riga, Bueckeberg, and Weimar. He was a student of Kant and Hamann, and many commentators have seen his philosophy as an attempt to marry the Enlightenment rationalism of the first to the passionate romanticism of the second. His principal intellectual legacy is in the fields of the philosophy of language, culture, and political theory. His writings include *On the Origin of Language* (1770), *Yet Another Philosophy of History* (1774), and his most ambitious work *Ideas for a Philosophy of the History of Humanity* (1784–1791).

A learned society of our time proposed, doubtless with the best of intentions, the following question: 'Which was the happiest people in history?' If I understand the question aright, and if it does not lie beyond the horizon of a human response, I can only say that at a certain time and in certain circumstances, *each* people met with such a moment or else there never was one. Indeed, human nature is not the vessel of an absolute, unchanging and independent happiness, as defined by the philosopher; everywhere it attracts that measure of happiness of which it is capable: it is a pliant clay which assumes a different shape under different needs and circumstances. Even the image of happiness changes with each condition and climate. (What is it then, if not the sum of 'satisfaction of desires, realization of ends and a quiet surmounting of needs', which everyone interprets according to the land, the time and the place?) Basically, therefore, all comparison is unprofitable. When the inner sense of happiness has altered, this or that attitude has changed; when the external circumstances and needs fashion and fortify this new sentiment: who can then compare the different forms of satisfaction perceived by different senses in different worlds? Who can compare the shepherd and the Oriental patriarch, the ploughman and the artist, the sailor, the runner, the conqueror of the world? Happiness lies not in the laurel wreath or in the sight of the blessed herd, in the cargo ship or in the captured field-trophy, but in the soul which needs this, aspires to that, has attained this and claims no more—each nation has its centre of happiness within itself, just as every sphere has its centre of gravity.

Mother Nature has taken good care of this. She placed in men's hearts inclinations towards diversity, but made each of them so little pressing in itself that if only some of them are satisfied the soul soon makes a concert out of the awakened notes and only senses the unawakened ones as if they mutely and obscurely supported the sounding melody. She has put tendencies towards diversity in our hearts; she has placed part of the diversity in a close circle around us; she has restricted man's view so that by force of habit the circle became a horizon, beyond which he could not see nor scarcely speculate. All that is akin to my nature, all that can be assimilated by it, I hanker and strive after, and adopt; beyond that, kind nature has armed me with insensibility, coldness and blindness, which can even turn into contempt and disgust. Her aim is only to force me back on myself so that I find satisfaction in my own centre. The Greek adopts as much of the Roman, the Roman of the Greek, as he needs for himself; he is satisfied, the rest falls to the earth and he no longer strives for it. If, in this development of particular national tendencies towards particular forms of national happiness, the distance between the nations grows too great, we find prejudices arising. The Egyptian detests the shepherd and the nomad and despises the frivolous Greek. Similarly prejudices, mob judgment and narrow nationalism arise when the dispositions and spheres of happiness of two nations collide. But prejudice is good, in its time and place, for happiness may spring from it. It urges nations to converge upon their centre, attaches them more firmly to their roots, causes them to flourish after their kind, and makes them more ardent and therefore happier in their inclinations and purposes. The most ignorant, most prejudiced nation is often superior in this respect. The moment men start dwelling in wishful dreams of foreign lands from whence they seek hope and salvation they reveal the first symptoms of disease, of flatulence of unhealthy opulence, of approaching death!

The general, philosophical, philanthropical tone of our century wishes to extend 'our own ideal' of virtue and happiness to each distant nation, to even the remotest age in history. But can one such single ideal act as an arbiter praising or condemning other nations or periods, their customs and laws; can it remake them after its own image? Is good not dispersed over the earth? Since one form of mankind and one region could not encompass it, it has been distributed in a thousand forms, changing shape like an eternal Proteus throughout continents and centuries. And even if it does not strive, as it keeps on changing, towards the greater virtue and happiness of the individual—for man remains forever man—nonetheless a plan of progressive endeavour becomes evident. This is my great theme.

Those who have so far undertaken to explain the progress of the centuries have mostly cherished the idea that such progress must lead towards greater virtue and individual happiness. In support of this idea they have embellished or invented facts, minimized or suppressed contrary facts; covered whole pages; taken words for works, enlightenment for happiness, greater sophistication for virtue, and in this way invented the fiction of the 'general, progressive amelioration of the world' which few believed, least of all the true student of history and the human heart.

Others, who saw the harmfulness of this dream without knowing a better one, saw vices and virtues alternating like climates, perfections sprouting and dying like spring leaves, human customs and preferences strewn about like leaves of fate. No plan! No progress, but an endless revolution! Weaving and unravelling like Penelope! They fell into a whirlpool of scepticism about all virtue, about all happiness and the destiny of man, and introduced into history, religion and ethics the latest fad of recent philosophy (especially that of France): doubt. Doubt in a hundred forms, but almost invariably sporting the dazzling title 'history of the world'! We founder on contradictions as on the waves of the sea; and either we miscarry completely, or the modicum of morality and philosophy that we save from the wreck is not worth talking about.

Does this mean that there can be no manifest progress and development, in some higher sense than we usually think? Do you see this river flowing on, how it springs from a tiny source, swells, divides, joins up again, winds in and out and cuts farther and deeper but, whatever the intricacies of its course, still remains water. A river! A drop of water! Nothing but a drop of water, until it plunges into the sea! Might it not be the same with human kind? Or do you see that tree growing there, or that striving man? He must pass through different ages of life, between which are apparent resting-places, revolutions, changes, and each of which obviously constitutes a form of progress from the one before. Each age is different, but each has the centre of its happiness within itself. The youth is not happier than the innocent, contented child; nor is the peaceful old man unhappier than the energetic man in his prime. The force of the pendulum is the same whether it swings quickly through its widest arc or slowly as it approaches a state of rest. And yet the striving never ceases. No one lives in his own period only; he builds on what has gone before and lays a foundation for what comes after. Thus speaks the analogy of nature, the pattern of God eloquent in all His works; obviously mankind must be similar. The Egyptian could not have existed without the Oriental, nor the Greek without the Egyptian; the Roman carried on his back the whole world. This indeed is genuine progress, continuous development, however little it may prosper the individual! Becoming on a grand scale! History may not manifestly be revealed as the theatre of a directing purpose on earth—of which our shallow histories boast so much—for we may not be able to espy its final end. But it may conceivably offer us glimpses of a divine theatre through the openings and ruins of individual scenes . . .

54 Adam Mickiewicz, from *Pan Tadeusz, or The Last Foray into Lithuania* (trans. by Kenneth McKenzie; Dent, 1966), pp. 283–6

Adam Mickiewicz (1798–1855) was born in Zaosie, in the former grand duchy of Lithuania (now in Belarus) into an impoverished family of Polonized nobility. In 1823 he joined the Philomaths, a secret patriotic society, and was imprisoned and then exiled to Russia. Allowed to leave in 1829, he eventually settled in Paris, where he held a chair of Slav literature at the Collège de France. His writings blend romantic nationalism, influenced by Byron and Schiller, with Catholic Christianity. He died during a cholera epidemic in Constantinople, trying to raise Polish armies in Turkey in order to fight the Russians in the Crimean War.

To think of such things in a Paris street,
Where on my ears the city's noises beat
With lies and curses, and with plans ill-fated,
And fiendish quarrels and regrets belated!

Alas for us who fled in times of pest
And, timid souls, took refuge in the west!
Terror pursued wherever we might go,
In every neighbour we discerned a foe;
At last they bound us up in fetters tight,
And bade us die as quickly as we might.

But if the world will not regard their woe,
If every moment fresh news strikes a blow,
Sounding from Poland like a funeral bell,
If gaolers wish them to an early hell,
And foes like hangmen offer them the rope,
If even in high heaven they see no hope—
No wonder that they hate the world, mankind,
Themselves, and by their torments reft of mind
They spit upon themselves, each other bite.

* * * * *

I longed to fly, a bird of feeble flight,
Beyond the thunder and the stormy zone,
And seek the sunshine and the shade alone,
The homely plot and endless childhood days . . .

One happiness remains: when evening greys,
You sit with a few friends and lock the door,
And by the fireside shut out Europe's roar,
Escape in thought to happier time and tide,
And muse and dream of your own countryside . . .

But of those wounds that run so fresh with blood,
And of the tears that over Poland flood,
And of the glory that does yet resound,
The heart to think of these we never found . . .
For in such torments even Valour stands
And gazes, and can only wring her hands.

Those generations black with mourning clothes,
That air so pregnant with so many oaths,
Our thought dared not to wing its passage there,
Where e'en the birds of thunder fear to fare.

O Mother Poland, thou that in this hour
Art laid within the grave—what man hath power
To speak of thee today? Whose lips would dare
To boast that they will find that word so rare
That it shall melt marmoreal despair,
And lift the gravestone from the hearts of men,
And unlock eyes that brim with tears again,
And shall release the frozen tide of tears?
Those lips shall not be found in many years.

Sometime when lions of vengeance cease to roar,
And trumpets hush and armies are no more,
When the last enemy shall make his dying cry,
Be dumb and to the world give liberty,
And when our eagles in their lightning flight
On Brave Boleslaw's boundaries shall light,
And eat their fill of flesh, and drunk with gore
Shall fold their wings to rest for evermore,
Then, then our knights with oak leaves shall be crowned,
And fling aside their swords, and sit around

Unarmed ! the world shall envy them at last,
And when they hear us singing of the past,
Then they shall weep upon their fathers' pain,
And on their cheeks the tears shall leave no stain.
For us unbidden guests in every clime
From the beginning to the end of time
There is but one place in this planet whole
Where happiness may be for every Pole—
The land of childhood ! that shall aye endure
As holy as a first love and as pure,
Unshattered by the memory of mistake,
That no deceitful hopes can ever shake,
Nor can the changing tide of life unmake.
How gladly I would greet in thought those lands,
Where I would seldom weep nor wring my hands,
The lands of childhood; everywhere we roved
As in a meadow, and the flowers we loved
Were sweet and fair; the harmful weed
We flung aside, nor would the useful heed.

That happy country, happy, poor and small!
The world is God's but that was ours—ours all.
And all belonged to us that lay around.
How we remember everything we found,
The linden with her crown magnificent,
That to the village children shadow lent,
And every little rivulet and stone.
How every corner of the place was known,
And far as the next house was all our own!

And only those who were its denizens
Remain my sure allies, my faithful friends.
And who were they? My mother, brothers, all
My kin and neighbours. And when one did fall,
How often was the name of him still spoken!
How many memories, what grief unbroken—
That land where servants more for masters care
Than wives do for their husbands otherwhere,
And where a soldier mourns his weapons more
Than sons their fathers here; and where they pour
More tears, and grief is longer, more sincere,
For a dead dog than for a hero here.

And in those days my friends would oft afford
Help for my song, and threw me word on word;
As on the desert isle those cranes once heard,
When o'er the fairy palace they were flying,
From the enchanted boy a mournful crying,
And each one threw a single feather down,
And he made wings and flew back to his own.

Would I might live to see the happy day
When under the thatched roofs these books shall stray,
Where country girls with nimble fingers rove
The spinning wheel and sing the songs they love
About that girl, whom music so did please
That through her fiddling she lost all her geese,
Or of that orphan, fair as morning light,
Who went to fetch her geese at fall of night—
Would that some happy chance to them might bring
These books as simple as the songs they sing.

So at their country pleasures in my time
They sometimes read aloud beneath the lime
Justina's ballad or Wieslaw's fable.

Meanwhile the bailiff dozing at the table,
The steward or the landlord deigned to hear,
And to the young folk made the hard things clear,
And praised the beauties and the faults would blame.

And young men envied then the singer's fame,
Which echoes in their woods and forests still.
To whom the laurel crown on Jove's high hill
Is less dear than the wreaths of cornflower blue,
Twined by the hands of village girls with rue.

55 J. S. Mill, from *Considerations on Representative Government*, in *On Liberty and Other Essays* (ed. John Gray; Oxford University Press, 1991), pp. 427–32

For biographical information, see Chapter 2, Reading 15.

A portion of mankind may be said to constitute a Nationality, if they are united among themselves by common sympathies, which do not exist between them and any others—which make them co-operate with each other more willingly than with other people, desire to be under the same government, and desire that it should be government by themselves or a portion of themselves, exclusively. This feeling of nationality may have been generated by various causes. Sometimes it is the effect of identity of race and descent. Community of language, and community of religion, greatly contribute to it. Geographical limits are one of its causes. But the strongest of all is identity of political antecedents; the possession of a national history, and consequent community of recollections; collective pride and humiliation, pleasure and regret, connected with the same incidents in the past. None of these circumstances however are either indispensable, or necessarily sufficient by themselves. Switzerland has a strong sentiment of nationality, though the cantons are of different races, different languages, and different religions. Sicily has, throughout history, felt itself quite distinct in nationality from Naples, notwithstanding identity of religion, almost identity of language, and a considerable amount of common historical antecedents. The Flemish and the Walloon provinces of Belgium, notwithstanding diversity of race and language, have a much greater feeling of common nationality, than the former have with Holland, or the latter with France. Yet in general the national feeling is proportionally weakened by the failure of any of the causes which contribute to it. Identity of language, literature, and, to some extent, of race and recollections, have maintained the feeling of nationality in considerable strength among the different portions of the German name, though they have at no time been really united under the same government; but the feeling has never reached to making the separate States desire to get rid of their autonomy. Among Italians an identity far from complete, of language and literature, combined with a geographical position which separates them by a distinct line from other countries, and, perhaps more than everything else, the possession of a common name, which makes them all glory in the past achievements in arts, arms, politics, religious primacy, science, and literature, of any who share the same designation, give rise to an amount of national feeling in the population, which, though still imperfect, has been sufficient to produce the great events now passing before us, notwithstanding a great mixture of races, and although they have never, in either ancient or modern history, been under the same government, except while that government extended or was extending itself over the greater part of the known world.

Where the sentiment of nationality exists in any force, there is a prima facie case for uniting all the members of the nationality under the same government, and a government to themselves apart. This is merely saying that the question of government ought to be decided by the governed. One hardly knows what any division of the human race should be free to do, if not to determine, with which of the various collective bodies of human beings they choose to associate themselves. But, when a people are ripe for free institutions, there is a still more vital consideration. Free institutions are next to impossible in a country made up of different nationalities. Among a people without fellow-feeling, especially if they read and speak different languages, the united public opinion, necessary to the working of representative government, cannot exist. The influences which form opinions and decide political acts, are different in the different sections of the country. An altogether different set of leaders have the confidence of one part of the country and of another. The same books, newspapers, pamphlets, speeches, do not reach them. One section does not know what opinions, or what instigations, are circulating in another. The same incidents, the same acts, the same system of government, affect them in different ways; and each fears more injury to itself from the other nationalities, than from the common arbiter, the State. Their mutual antipathies are generally much stronger than jealousy of the government. That any one of them feels aggrieved by the policy of the common ruler, is sufficient to determine another to support that policy. Even if all are aggrieved, none feel that they can rely on the others for fidelity in a joint resistance; the strength of none is sufficient to resist alone, and each may reasonably think that it consults its own advantage most by bidding for the favour of the government against the rest. Above all, the grand and only effectual security in the last resort against the despotism of the government, is in that case wanting: the sympathy of the army with the people. The military are the part of every community in whom, from the nature of the case, the distinction between their fellow countrymen and foreigners is the deepest and strongest. To the rest of the people, foreigners are merely strangers; to the soldier, they are men against whom he may be called, at a week's notice, to fight for life or death. The difference to him is that between friends and foes—we may almost say between fellow men and another kind of animals: for as respects the enemy, the only law is that of force, and the only mitigation, the same as in the case of other animals—that of simple humanity. Soldiers to whose feelings half or three-fourths of the subjects of the same government are foreigners, will have no more scruple in mowing them down, and no more desire to ask the reason why, than they would have in doing the same thing against declared enemies. An army composed of various nationalities has no other patriotism than devotion to the flag. Such armies have been the executioners of liberty through the whole duration of modern history. The sole bond which holds them together is their officers, and the government which they serve; and their only idea, if they have any, of public duty, is obedience to orders. A government thus supported, by keeping its Hungarian regiments in Italy and its Italian in Hungary, can long continue to rule in both places with the iron rod of foreign conquerors.

If it be said that so broadly marked a distinction between what is due to a fellow countryman and what is due merely to a human creature, is more worthy of savages than of civilized beings, and ought, with the utmost energy, to be contended against, no one holds that opinion more strongly than myself. But this object, one of the worthiest to which human endeavour can be directed, can never, in the present state of civilization, be promoted by keeping different nationalities of anything like equivalent strength, under the same government. In a barbarous state of society, the case is sometimes different. The government may then be interested in softening the antipathies of the races, that peace may be preserved, and the country more easily governed. But when there are either free institutions, or a desire for them, in any of the peoples artificially tied together, the interest of the government lies in an exactly opposite direction. It is then interested in keeping up and envenoming their antipathies; that they may be prevented from coalescing, and it may be enabled to use some of them as tools for the enslavement of others. The Austrian Court has now for a whole generation made these tactics its principal means of government; with what fatal success, at the time of the Vienna insurrection and the Hungarian contest, the world knows too well. Happily there are now signs that improvement is too far advanced, to permit this policy to be any longer successful.

For the preceding reasons, it is in general a necessary condition of free institutions, that the boundaries of governments should coincide in the main with those of nationalities. But several considerations are liable to conflict in practice with this general principle. In the first place, its application is often precluded by geographical hindrances. There are parts even of Europe, in which different nationalities are so locally intermingled, that it is not practicable for them to be under separate governments. The population of Hungary is composed of Magyars, Slovacks, Croats, Serbs, Roumans, and in some districts, Germans, so mixed up as to be incapable of local separation; and there is no course open to them but to make a virtue of necessity, and reconcile themselves to living together under equal rights and laws. Their community of servitude, which dates only from the destruction of Hungarian independence in 1849, seems to be ripening and disposing them for such an equal union. The German colony of East Prussia is cut off from Germany by part of the ancient Poland, and being too weak to maintain separate independence, must, if geographical continuity is to be maintained, be either under a non-German government, or the intervening Polish territory must be under a German one. Another considerable region in which the dominant element of the population is German, the provinces of Courland, Esthonia, and Livonia, is condemned by its local situation to form part of a Slavonian state. In Eastern Germany itself there is a large Slavonic population: Bohemia is principally Slavonic, Silesia and other districts partially so. The most united country in Europe, France, is far from being homogeneous: independently of the fragments of foreign nationalities at its remote extremities, it consists, as language and history prove, of two portions, one occupied almost exclusively by a Gallo-Roman population, while in the other the Frankish, Burgundian, and other Teutonic races form a considerable ingredient.

When proper allowance has been made for geographical exigencies, another more purely moral and social consideration offers itself. Experience proves, that it is possible for one nationality to merge and be absorbed in another: and when it was originally an inferior and more backward portion of the human race, the absorption is greatly to its advantage. Nobody can suppose that it is not more beneficial to a Breton, or a Basque of French Navarre, to be brought into the current of the ideas and feelings of a highly civilized and cultivated people—to be a member of the French nationality, admitted on equal terms to all the privileges of French citizenship, sharing the advantages of French protection, and the dignity and prestige of French power—than to sulk on his own rocks, the half-savage relic of past times, revolving in his own little mental orbit, without participation or interest in the general movement of the world. The same remark applies to the Welshman or the Scottish Highlander, as members of the British nation.

Whatever really tends to the admixture of nationalities, and the blending of their attributes and peculiarities in a common union, is a benefit to the human race. Not by extinguishing types, of which, in these cases, sufficient examples are sure to remain, but by softening their extreme forms, and filling up the intervals between them. The united people, like a crossed breed of animals (but in a still greater degree, because the influences in operation are moral as well as physical), inherits the special aptitudes and excellences of all its progenitors, protected by the admixture from being exaggerated into the neighbouring vices. But to render this admixture possible, there must be peculiar conditions. The combinations of circumstances which occur, and which affect the result, are various.

56   H. von Treitschke, from *Politics* (trans. by Blanche Dugdale and Torben de Bille; Constable & Co., 1916), pp. 202–3, 221–2, 300–2

Heinrich von Treitschke (1834–1896) was born in Saxony, and began his intellectual career as a liberal constitutionalist. He became an increasingly nationalistic admirer of Prussia, in 1874 was appointed successor to Leopold von Ranke as professor of History at the Humboldt University, Berlin, and in 1886 became the official Prussian state historian. He was also a member of the Reichstag. He was an influential exponent of state expansionism, admirer of Bismarck and the Hohenzollerns, and an anti-socialist and anti-semitic controversialist. His principal works include *History of Germany in the Nineteenth Century*, *Politics*, and *Origins of Prussianism*.

In the days of a preponderatingly economic life, men clung so fast to their own soil that they even found it bearable to change their Fatherland. But even as we speak opinions on this matter begin to alter. The feeling of national honour has become so keen and sensitive that we have clearly entered upon a new stage in the public consciousness regarding it. The idea of becoming Frenchmen is so terrible to us that we would sooner forfeit our material existence. This was already recognized in 1871 by the giving of an option to the individual inhabitants of Alsace and Lorraine. This very instance has shown us the danger of granting this right, and how true it is that, in political life, no man can serve two masters. We were far too good-natured, and the choice should never have been given.

We see, then, that sentiments change on this point, but it remains unalterably true that the opinion of the surrendered province itself should not be asked by the State as a whole when it takes the decision. If the dominions of a State are indivisible in law, save by the deliberate action of the supreme Government, then it follows that no single portion of the realm may raise its voice against that decree. No town is consulted as to whether it shall be made into a fortress, and it must be equally acquiescent if, by legal decision, it is torn away from its parent State. Terrible and hard as it may be for those who suffer by it, there is no alternative. Suppose that we had taken a referendum of the people in Alsace-Lorraine in 1871. If the Alsatians had declared against annexation we could not have agreed to their refusal, and *in saecula saeculorum* we should have had to go on fighting. That is where the modern doctrine of the philanthropic pacifist prigs would have landed us. There can be no end to a war until the hard fact is faced that the part must be obedient to the whole.

. . .

A great expansion of the territory of the State is desirable in itself on grounds of national economy as well as for military reasons. Pestilence, floods, or a failure of crops would not be likely to befall every part of a large country at the same time, so that in this way also an equalization becomes possible. It is evident that a certain extent of territory is valuable for military defence, it is in itself a guarantee of security, but it is quite possible for a State to be too large, especially in relation to its population. This is the unnatural position of Russia, where the proverb runs, "Russia is wide and the Czar is far away." Uniformity of administration is much hampered and the military establishment is also made more difficult, since the size of the Army is dependent upon the number of the population.

Some States, on the other hand, have not yet attained their full growth, nor become possessed of the whole extent of territory which they must eventually claim. This sometimes gives rise to very complicated conditions. The United States of America could never have rested until they reached the western coast, and their geographical position justifies their present claim to possess the whole of North America. But these desires bring elements of immaturity, unrest, and fermentation into a State.

Lastly, a State may be too small for its historical task, as was Prussia under Frederick the Great, and up till the year 1866. Then the word went round that Prussia must grow if she was to live, and the results have proved that it was true.

. . .

Presently, however, the Jews ceased to be indispensable, for the Aryan races learnt how to manage their own finance themselves. It then became apparent what a dangerous disintegrating force lurked in this people who were able to assume the mask of any other nationality. Fair-minded Jews must themselves admit that after a nation has become conscious of its own personality there is no place left for the cosmopolitanism of the Semites; we can find no use for an international Judaism in the world to-day. We must speak plainly upon this point, undeterred by the abuse which the Jewish press pours upon what is a simple historical truth. It is indisputable that the Jews can only continue to hold a place if they will make up their minds to become Englishmen, Frenchmen, or Germans, as the case may be, and provisionally consent to merge their old memories into those of the nation to which they belong politically. This is the perfectly just and reasonable demand which we Western races must make of them; no people can concede a double nationality to the Jews.

The considerations in this matter are extremely complicated, because we have no certain standard by which we can ascertain the extent to which the Jews have spread themselves among the alien nationality. Baptism alone is no guide. There are unbaptized Jews who are good Germans—I have known some myself—and there are others who are not, although they have been baptized; the legal aspect of the question is therefore a difficult one. If legislation were to treat the Jews simply as sojourners in the country, allowing them to ply civil trades, but withholding political and magisterial rights, it would be an injustice because it would not fulfil the purpose for which it was designed. A baptized Christian cannot be legally regarded as a Jew. I can see only one means by which the end can be attained, and that is to arouse an energy of national pride, so real that it becomes a second nature to repel involuntarily everything which is foreign to the Germanic nature. This principle must be carried into everything; it must apply to our visits to the theatre and to the music-hall as much as to the reading of the newspapers. Whenever he finds his life sullied by the filth of Judaism the German must turn from it, and learn to speak the truth boldly about it. The party of compromise must bear the blame for any unsavoury wave of anti-Semitism which may arise.

57 Max Weber, from 'The Nation-State and Economic Policy', in *Political Writings* (ed. Peter Lassman and Ronald Speirs; Cambridge University Press, 1994), pp. 14–17, 20–1

For biographical information, see Chapter 2, Reading 19.

As we have seen, the economic struggle (*Kampf*) between the nationalities runs its course even under the semblance of 'peace'. The German peasants and day-labourers in the east are not being driven off the soil by politically superior enemies in open conflict. Rather they are coming off worse in a silent and bleak struggle for everyday economic existence in competition with an inferior race; they are leaving their homeland and are about to submerge themselves in a dark future. In the economic struggle for life, too, there is no peace to be had. Only if one takes the semblance of peace for its reality can one believe that the future holds peace and a happy life for our descendants. As we know, the vulgar conception of political economy is that it consists in devising recipes for universal happiness; in this view, adding to the 'balance of pleasure' in human existence is the only comprehensible purpose our work has. Yet the sombre gravity of the population problem alone is enough to prevent us from being eudaemonists, from imagining that peace and happiness lie waiting in the womb of the future, and from believing that anything other than the hard struggle of man with man can create any elbow-room in this earthly life.

Certainly, only on the basis of altruism is any work in political economy possible. Overwhelmingly, what is produced by the economic, social and political endeavours of the present benefits future generations rather than the present one. If our work is to have any meaning, it lies, and can only lie, in providing for the *future*, for our *descendants*. But there can also be no work in political economy on the basis of optimistic hopes of happiness. As far as the dream of peace and human happiness is concerned, the words written over the portal into the unknown future of human history are: 'lasciate ogni speranza'.

The question which stirs us as we think beyond the grave of our own generation is not the *well-being* human beings will enjoy in the future but what kind of people they will *be*, and it is this same question which underlies all work in political economy. We do not want to breed well-being in people, but rather those characteristics which we think of as constituting the human greatness and nobility of our nature.

The criteria of value which political economists have naively identified or given prominence to have alternated between the technical economic problem of the production of goods and the problem of their distribution ('social justice'). Yet, again and again both these criteria have been overshadowed by the recognition, in part unconscious, but nevertheless all-dominating, that a science (*Wissenschaft*) concerned with *human beings*—and that is what political economy is—is concerned above all else with the *quality of the human beings* reared under those economic and social conditions of existence. Here we should be on our guard against one particular illusion.

As an explanatory and analytic science, political economy is *international*, but as soon as it makes *value judgements* it is tied to the particular strain of humankind (*Menschentum*) we find within our own nature. Often these ties are strongest precisely when we think we have escaped our personal limitations most completely. If—to use a somewhat fanciful image—we could arise from the grave thousands of years hence, it would be the distant traces of our own nature that we would search for in the countenance of that future race. Even our highest, our ultimate ideals in this life change and pass away. It cannot be our ambition to impose them on the future. But we *can* want the future to recognise the character *of its own ancestors* in us. Through our work and our nature we want to be the forerunners of that future race.

The economic policy of a German state, and, equally, the criterion of value used by a German economic theorist, can therefore only be a German policy or criterion.

Have things perhaps become different in this regard since economic development began to extend beyond national frontiers, creating an all-embracing economic community of nations? Is the 'nationalistic' criterion of evaluation to be thrown on the scrapheap along with 'national egoism' in economic policy? Has indeed the struggle for one's own economic interests, for one's own wife and children, become a thing of the past, now that the family has been divested of its original functions as a productive community and become woven into the circle of the national economic community? We know that this is not the case. The struggle has assumed *other forms*, and it is an open question whether these new forms can be said to have mitigated the severity of the struggle or internalised and exacerbated it. Equally, the expanded economic community is just another form of the struggle of the nations with each other, one which has not eased the struggle to defend one's own culture but made it more *difficult*, because this enlarged economic community summons material interests within the body of the nation to ally themselves with it in the fight *against* the future of the nation.

We do not have peace and human happiness to hand down to our descendants, but rather the *eternal struggle* to preserve and raise the quality of our national species. Nor should we indulge in the optimistic expectation that we shall have completed our task once we have made our economic culture as advanced as it can be, and that the process of selection through free and 'peaceful' economic competition will then automatically bring victory to the more highly developed type.

Our successors will hold us answerable to history not primarily for the kind of economic organisation we hand down to them, but for the amount of elbow-room in the world which we conquer and bequeath to them. In the final analysis, processes of economic development are *power* struggles too, and the ultimate and decisive interests which economic policy must serve are the interests of national *power*, whenever these interests are in question. The science of political economy is a *political* science. It is a servant of politics, not the day-to-day politics of the persons and classes who happen to be ruling at any given time, but the enduring power-political interests of the nation. For us the *nation state* is not something vague which, as some believe, is elevated ever higher, the more its nature is shrouded in mystical obscurity. Rather, it is the worldly organisation of the nation's power. In this nation state the ultimate criterion for economic policy, as for all others, is in our view '*reason of state*'. By this we do not mean, as some strange misunderstanding would have it, 'help from the state' rather than 'self-help', state regulation of economic life rather than the free play of economic forces. In using this slogan of 'reason of state' we wish to present the demand that the economic and political power-interests of our nation and their bearer, the German nation-state, should have the final and decisive say in all questions of German economic policy, including the questions of whether, and how far, the state should intervene in economic life, or of whether and when it is better for it to free the economic forces of the nation from their fetters and to tear down the barriers in the way of their autonomous development.

. . .

We economic nationalists measure the classes who lead the nation or aspire to do so with the one *political criterion* we regard as sovereign. What concerns us is their *political maturity*, which is to say their grasp of the nation's enduring economic and political *power* interests and their ability, in any given situation, to place these interests above all other considerations. A nation is favoured by fate if naive identification of the interests of one's own class with the general interest also corresponds to the enduring interests of national power. On the other hand, it is one of the delusions which arise from the modern over-estimation of the 'economic' in the usual sense of the word when people assert that feelings of political community would be stretched beyond breaking point by temporary divergences of economic interest, indeed that such feelings *merely* reflect the economic base underlying that shifting constellation of interests. Only at times when the structure of society is changing fundamentally is this approximately accurate. One thing is certainly true: where nations are not reminded daily of the dependence of their economic success on their position of political power (as happens in England), the instinct for these specifically political interests does *not*, or at least not as a rule, dwell in the broad *masses* of the nation as they struggle with daily necessity, nor would it be fair to expect it of them. At great moments, in time of war, for example, their souls too become aware of the significance of national power, and at such times it becomes evident that the nation state rests on deeply rooted psychological foundations in the broad, economically subordinate strata of the nation as well, and that it is far from being a mere 'superstructure', the organisation of the ruling economic classes. It is just that in normal times this political instinct sinks below the level of consciousness amongst the masses. Then it is the specific function of the leading economic and political strata to be the bearers of the nation's sense of political purpose (*Sinn*). In fact this is the *only* political justification for their existence.

58 M. K. Gandhi, from *Hind Swaraj*, in *Hind Swaraj and Other Writings* (ed. Anthony J. Parel; Cambridge University Press, 1997), pp. 52–4, 116–19

Mohandas Karamchand Gandhi (1869–1948) was born in Gujarat in India, and trained as a lawyer in London. From 1893 until the outbreak of the First World War, he practised law in South Africa, where he was arrested for leading a march of Indian miners. On his return to India, he became involved with the Indian National Congress and the movement for independence. He was repeatedly imprisoned by the British authorities for his campaigns of civil disobedience. Resolutely anti-sectarian, he was deeply opposed to the partition that led to the creation of a Hindu-dominated India and a Muslim-dominated Pakistan. Assassinated by a Hindu radical, he remains an immensely revered figure in India.

EDITOR: India cannot cease to be one nation because people belonging to different religions live in it. The introduction of foreigners does not necessarily destroy the nation, they merge in it. A country is one nation only when such a condition obtains in it. That country must have a faculty for assimilation. India has ever been such a country. In reality, there are as many religions as there are individuals, but those who are conscious of the spirit of nationality do not interfere with one another's religion. If they do, they are not fit to be considered a nation. If the Hindus believe that India should be peopled only by Hindus, they are living in dreamland. The Hindus, the Mahomedans, the Parsees and the Christians who have made India their country are fellow countrymen, and they will have to live in unity if only for their own interest. In no part of the world are one nationality and one religion synonymous terms: nor has it ever been so in India.

READER: But what about the inborn enmity between Hindus and Mahomedans?

EDITOR: That phrase has been invented by our mutual enemy. When the Hindus and Mahomedans fought against one another, they certainly spoke in that strain. They have long since ceased to fight. How, then, can there be any inborn enmity? Pray remember this too, that we did not cease to fight only after British occupation. The Hindus flourished under Moslem sovereigns, and Moslems under the Hindu. Each party recognised that mutual fighting was suicidal, and that neither party would abandon its religion by force of arms. Both parties, therefore, decided to live in peace. With the English advent the quarrels recommenced.

The proverbs you have quoted were coined when both were fighting; to quote them now is obviously harmful. Should we not remember that many Hindus and Mahomedans own the same ancestors, and the same blood runs through their veins? Do people become enemies because they change their religion? Is the God of the Mahomedan different from the God of the Hindu? Religions are different roads converging to the same point. What does it matter that we take different roads, so long as we reach the same goal? Wherein is the cause for quarrelling?

Moreover, there are deadly proverbs as between the followers of Shiva and those of Vishnu, yet nobody suggests that these two do not belong to the same nation. It is said that the Vedic religion is different from Jainism, but the followers of the respective faiths are not different nations. The fact is that we have become enslaved, and, therefore, quarrel and like to have our quarrels decided by a third party. There are Hindu iconoclasts as there are Mahomedan. The more we advance in true knowledge, the better we shall understand that we need not be at war with those whose religion we may not follow.

. . .

It is only those Indians who are imbued with real love who will be able to speak to the English in the above strain without being frightened, and those only can be said to be so imbued who conscientiously believe that Indian civilisation is the best, and that European is a nine days' wonder. Such ephemeral civilisations have often come and gone, and will continue to do so. Those only can be considered to be so imbued, who, having experienced the force of the soul within themselves, will not cower before brute force, and will not, on any account, desire to use brute force. Those only can be considered to have been so imbued who are intensely dissatisfied with the present pitiable condition, having already drunk the cup of poison.

If there be only one such Indian, he will speak as above to the English, and the English will have to listen to him.

These demands are not demands, but they show our mental state. We will get nothing by asking; we shall have to take what we want, and we need the requisite strength for the effort, and that strength will be available to him only who

1   will only on rare occasions make use of the English language;
2   if a lawyer, will give up his profession, and take up a hand-loom;
3   if a lawyer, will devote his knowledge to enlightening both his people and the English;
4   if a lawyer, will not meddle with the quarrels between parties, but will give up the courts and from his experience induce the people to do likewise;
5   if a lawyer, will refuse to be a judge, as he will give up his profession;
6   if a doctor, will give up medicine, and understand that, rather than mending bodies, he should mend souls;

281

7 if a doctor, he will understand that, no matter to what religion he belong, it is better that bodies remain diseased rather than that they are cured through the instrumentality of the diabolical vivisection that is practised in European schools of medicine;

8 although a doctor, will take up a hand-loom, and, if any patients come to him, will tell them the cause of their diseases, and will advise them to remove the cause rather than pamper them by giving useless drugs; he will understand that, if by not taking drugs, perchance the patient dies, the world will not come to grief, and that he will have been really merciful to him;

9 although a wealthy man, regardless of his wealth, will speak out his mind and fear no one;

10 if a wealthy man, will devote his money to establishing hand-looms, and encourage others to use hand-made goods by wearing them himself;

11 like every other Indian, will know that this is a time for repentance, expiation and mourning;

12 like every other Indian, will know that to blame the English is useless, that they came because of us, and remain also for the same reason, and that they will either go or change their nature only when we reform ourselves;

13 like others, will understand that, at a time of mourning, there can be no indulgence, and that, whilst we are in a fallen state, to be in gaol or in banishment is much the best;

14 like others, will know that it is superstition to imagine it necessary that we should guard against being imprisoned in order that we may deal with the people;

15 like others, will know that action is much better than speech; that it is our duty to say exactly what we think and face the consequences, and that it will be only then that we shall be able to impress anybody with our speech;

16 like others, will understand that we will become free only through suffering;

17 like others, will understand that deportation for life to the Andamans is not enough expiation for the sin of encouraging European civilisation;

18 like others, will know that no nation has risen without suffering; that, even in physical warfare, the true test is suffering and not the killing of others, much more so in the warfare of passive resistance;

19 like others, will know that it is an idle excuse to say that we will do a thing when the others also do it; that we should do what we know to be right, and that others will do it when they see the way; that, when I fancy a particular delicacy, I do not wait till others taste it; that to make a national effort and to suffer are in the nature of delicacies; and that to suffer under pressure is no suffering.

READER: This is a large order. When will all carry it out?

EDITOR: You make a mistake. You and I have nothing to do with the others. Let each do his duty. If I do my duty, that is, serve myself, I shall be able to serve others. Before I leave you, I will take the liberty of repeating:

1 Real home-rule is self-rule or self-control.

2 The way to it is passive resistance: that is soul-force or love-force.

3   In order to exert this force, Swadeshi in every sense is necessary.

4   What we want to do should be done, not because we object to the English or that we want to retaliate, but because it is our duty to do so. Thus, supposing that the English remove the salt-tax, restore our money, give the highest posts to Indians, withdraw the English troops, we shall certainly not use their machine-made goods, nor use the English language, nor many of their industries. It is worth noting that these things are, in their nature, harmful; hence we do not want them. I bear no enmity towards the English, but I do towards their civilisation.

In my opinion, we have used the term 'Swaraj' without understanding its real significance. I have endeavoured to explain it as I understand it, and my conscience testifies that my life henceforth is dedicated to its attainment.

59   Marcus Garvey, from 'The Future As I See It', in *The Philosophy and Opinions of Marcus Garvey* (comp. by Amy Jacques Garvey; Frank Cass, 1967), pp. 54–8

Marcus Garvey (1887–1940), a political activist and publisher, was born in Jamaica, then part of the British Empire. After leading a printers' strike in 1907, he was forced to leave and travelled in the West Indies and Central America, and met members of the black nationalist movement in London. On his return to Jamaica in 1914, he founded the United Negro Improvement Association, an organization which flourished after his move to the United States in 1916, although he enjoyed often acrimonious relations with other black leaders. He was deported in 1927 from the USA after conviction of mail fraud, but continued his activities from Jamaica and London.

It comes to the individual, the race, the nation, once in a life time to decide upon the course to be pursued as a career. The hour has now struck for the individual Negro as well as the entire race to decide the course that will be pursued in the interest of our own liberty.

We who make up the Universal Negro Improvement Association have decided that we shall go forward, upward and onward toward the great goal of human liberty. We have determined among ourselves that all barriers placed in the way of our progress must be removed, must be cleared away for we desire to see the light of a brighter day.

The Negro is Ready

The Universal Negro Improvement Association for five years has been proclaiming to the world the readiness of the Negro to carve out a pathway for himself in the course of life. Men of other races and nations have become alarmed at this attitude of the Negro in his desire to do things for himself and by himself. This alarm has become so universal that organizations have been brought into being here, there and everywhere for the purpose of deterring and obstructing this forward move of our race. Propaganda has been waged here, there and everywhere for the purpose of misinterpreting the intention of this organization; some have said that this organization seeks to create discord and discontent among the races; some say we are organized for the purpose of hating other people. Every sensible, sane and honest-minded person knows that the Universal Negro Improvement Association has no such intention. We are organized for the absolute purpose of bettering our condition, industrially, commercially, socially, religiously and politically. We are organized not to hate other men, but to lift ourselves, and to demand respect of all humanity. We have a program that we believe to be righteous; we believe it to be just, and we have made up our minds to lay down ourselves on the altar of sacrifice for the realization of this great hope of ours, based upon the foundation of righteousness. We declare to the world that Africa must be free, that the entire Negro race must be emancipated from industrial bondage, peonage and serfdom; we make no compromise, we make no apology in this our declaration. We do not desire to create offense on the part of other races, but we are determined that we shall be heard, that we shall be given the rights to which we are entitled.

The Propaganda Of Our Enemies

For the purpose of creating doubts about the work of the Universal Negro Improvement Association, many attempts have been made to cast shadow and gloom over our work. They have even written the most uncharitable things about our organization; they have spoken so unkindly of our effort, but what do we care? They spoke unkindly and uncharitably about all the reform movements that have helped in the betterment of humanity. They maligned the great movement of the Christian religion; they maligned the great liberation movements of America, of France, of England, of Russia; can we expect, then, to escape being maligned in this, our desire for the liberation of Africa and the freedom of four hundred million Negroes of the world?

We have unscrupulous men and organizations working in opposition to us. Some trying to capitalize the new spirit that has come to the Negro to make profit out of it to their own selfish benefit; some are trying to set back the Negro from seeing the hope of his own liberty, and thereby poisoning our people's mind against the motives of our organization; but every sensible far-seeing Negro in this enlightened age knows what propaganda means. It is the medium of discrediting that which you are opposed to, so that the propaganda of our enemies will be of little avail as soon as we are rendered able to carry to our peoples scattered throughout the world the true message of our great organization.

"Crocodiles" As Friends

Men of the Negro race, let me say to you that a greater future is in store for us; we have no cause to lose hope, to become faint-hearted. We must realize that upon ourselves depend our destiny, our future; we must carve out that future, that destiny, and we who make up the Universal Negro Improvement Association have pledged ourselves that nothing in the world shall stand in our way, nothing in the world shall discourage us, but opposition shall make us work harder, shall bring us closer together so that as one man the millions of us will march on toward that goal that we have set for ourselves. The new Negro shall not be deceived. The new Negro refuses to take advice from anyone who has not felt with him, and suffered with him. We have suffered for three hundred years, therefore we feel that the time has come when only those who have suffered with us can interpret our feelings and our spirit. It takes the slave to interpret the feelings of the slave; it takes the unfortunate man to interpret the spirit of his unfortunate brother; and so it takes the suffering Negro to interpret the spirit of his comrade. It is strange that so many people are interested in the Negro now, willing to advise him how to act, and what organizations he should join, yet nobody was interested in the Negro to the extent of not making him a slave for two hundred and fifty years, reducing him to industrial peonage and serfdom after he was freed; it is strange that the same people can be so interested in the Negro now, as to tell him what organization he should follow and what leader he should support.

Whilst we are bordering on a future of brighter things, we are also at our danger period, when we must either accept the right philosophy, or go down by following deceptive propaganda which has hemmed us in for many centuries.

Deceiving The People

There is many a leader of our race who tells us that everything is well, and that all things will work out themselves and that a better day is coming. Yes, all of us know that a better day is coming; we all know that one day we will go home to Paradise, but whilst we are hoping by our Christian virtues to have an entry into Paradise we also realize that we are living on earth, and that the things that are practised in Paradise are not practised here. You have to treat this world as the world treats you; we are living in a temporal, material age, an age of activity, an age of racial, national selfishness. What else can you expect but to give back to the world what the world gives to you, and we are calling upon the four hundred million Negroes of the world to take a decided stand, a determined stand, that we shall occupy a firm position; that position shall be an emancipated race and a free nation of our own. We are determined that we shall have a free country; we are determined that we shall have a flag; we are determined that we shall have a government second to none in the world.

An Eye For An Eye

Men may spurn the idea, they may scoff at it; the metropolitan press of this country may deride us; yes, white men may laugh at the idea of Negroes talking about government; but let me tell you there is going to be a government, and let me say to you also that whatsoever you give, in like measure it shall be returned to you. The world is sinful, and therefore man believes in the doctrine of an eye for an eye, a tooth for a tooth. Everybody believes that revenge is God's, but at the same time we are men, and revenge sometimes springs up, even in the most Christian heart.

Why should man write down a history that will react against him? Why should man perpetrate deeds of wickedness upon his brother which will return to him in like measure? Yes, the Germans maltreated the French in the Franco-Prussian war of 1870, but the French got even with the Germans in 1918. It is history, and history will repeat itself. Beat the Negro, brutalize the Negro, kill the Negro, burn the Negro, imprison the Negro, scoff at the Negro, deride the Negro, it may come back to you one of these fine days, because the supreme destiny of man is in the hands of God. God is no respector of persons, whether that person be white, yellow or black. Today the one race is up, tomorrow it has fallen; today the Negro seems to be the footstool of the other races and nations of the world; tomorrow the Negro may occupy the highest rung of the great human ladder.

But when we come to consider the history of man, was not the Negro a power, was he not great once? Yes, honest students of history can recall the day when Egypt, Ethiopia and Timbuctoo towered in their civilizations, towered above Europe, towered above Asia. When Europe was inhabited by a race of cannibals, a race of savages, naked men, heathens and pagans, Africa was peopled with a race of cultured black men, who were masters in art, science and literature; men who were cultured and refined; men who, it was said, were like the gods. Even the great poets of old sang in beautiful sonnets of the delight it afforded the gods to be in companionship with the Ethiopians. Why, then, should we lose hope? Black men, you were once great; you shall be great again. Lose not courage, lose not faith, go forward. The thing to do is to get organized; keep separated and you will be exploited, you will be robbed, you will be killed. Get organized, and you will compel the world to respect you. If the world fails to give you consideration, because you are black men, because you are Negroes, four hundred millions of you shall, through organization, shake the pillars of the universe and bring down creation, even as Samson brought down the temple upon his head and upon the heads of the Philistines.

An Inspiring Vision

So Negroes, I say, through the Universal Negro Improvement Association, that there is much to live for. I have a vision of the future, and I see before me a picture of a redeemed Africa, with her dotted cities, with her beautiful civilization, with her millions of happy children, going to and fro. Why should I lose hope, why should I give up and take a back place in this age of progress? Remember that you are men, that God created you Lords of this creation. Lift up yourselves, men, take yourselves out of the mire and hitch your hopes to the stars; yes, rise as high as the very stars themselves. Let no man pull you down, let no man destroy your ambition, because man is but your companion, your equal; man is your brother; he is not your lord; he is not your sovereign master.

We of the Universal Negro Improvement Association feel happy; we are cheerful. Let them connive to destroy us; let them organize to destroy us; we shall fight the more. Ask me personally the cause of my success, and I say opposition; oppose me, and I fight the more, and if you want to find out the sterling worth of the Negro, oppose him, and under the leadership of the Universal Negro Improvement Association he shall fight his way to victory, and in the days to come, and I believe not far distant, Africa shall reflect a spendid demonstration of the worth of the Negro, of the determination of the Negro, to set himself free and to establish a government of his own.

60   Jomo Kenyatta, from *Facing Mount Kenya* (Heinemann Educational Books, 1979), pp. 47–52

Jomo Kenyatta (1889?–1978) was born in British East Africa, now Kenya. He spent much of the nineteen-thirties in Moscow and England, where he studied anthropology under Bronislaw Malinowski. In 1946, he founded the Pan-African Congress with the Ghanaian political leader

Kwame Nkrumah, and in 1952 was sentenced to seven years' imprisonment by the British colonial authorities for supposed Mau Mau pro-independence activities. In 1961 he became President of the political party the Kenyan African National Union, and, after Kenyan independence, first prime minister and then president of the state. He was re-elected to the presidency in 1966 and 1974. He pursued a non-aligned foreign policy and provided internal stability, which his critics ascribed to authoritarianism and the dominance of the Kikuyu-led KANU party.

The relation between the Gikuyu and the Europeans can well be illustrated by a Gikuyu story which says: That once upon a time an elephant made a friendship with a man. One day a heavy thunderstorm broke out, the elephant went to his friend, who had a little hut at the edge of the forest, and said to him: "My dear good man, will you please let me put my trunk inside your hut to keep it out of this torrential rain?" The man, seeing what situation his friend was in, replied: "My dear good elephant, my hut is very small, but there is room for your trunk and myself. Please put your trunk in gently." The elephant thanked his friend, saying: "You have done me a good deed and one day I shall return your kindness." But what followed? As soon as the elephant put his trunk inside the hut, slowly he pushed his head inside, and finally flung the man out in the rain, and then lay down comfortably inside his friend's hut, saying: "My dear good friend, your skin is harder than mine, and as there is not enough room for both of us, you can afford to remain in the rain while I am protecting my delicate skin from the hailstorm."

The man, seeing what his friend had done to him, started to grumble, the animals in the nearby forest heard the noise and came to see what was the matter. All stood around listening to the heated argument between the man and his friend the elephant. In this turmoil the lion came along roaring, and said in a loud voice: "Don't you all know that I am the King of the Jungle! How dare anyone disturb the peace of my kingdom?" On hearing this the elephant, who was one of the high ministers in the jungle kingdom, replied in a soothing voice, and said: "My Lord, there is no disturbance of the peace in your kingdom. I have only been having a little discussion with my friend here as to the possession of this little hut which your lordship sees me occupying." The lion, who wanted to have "peace and tranquillity" in his kingdom, replied in a noble voice, saying: "I command my ministers to appoint a Commission of Enquiry to go thoroughly into this matter and report accordingly." He then turned to the man and said: "You have done well by establishing friendship with my people, especially with the elephant who is one of my honourable ministers of state. Do not grumble any more, your hut is not lost to you. Wait until the sitting of my Imperial Commission, and there you will be given plenty of opportunity to state your case. I am sure that you will be pleased with the findings of the Commission." The man was very pleased by these sweet words from the King of the Jungle, and innocently waited for his opportunity, in the belief, that naturally, the hut would be returned to him.

The elephant, obeying the command of his master, got busy with other ministers to appoint the Commission of Enquiry. The following elders of the jungle were appointed to sit in the Commission: (1) Mr. Rhinoceros; (2) Mr. Buffalo; (3) Mr. Alligator; (4) The Rt. Hon. Mr. Fox to act as chairman; and (5) Mr. Leopard to act as Secretary to the

Commission. On seeing the personnel, the man protested and asked if it was not necessary to include in this Commission a member from his side. But he was told that it was impossible, since no one from his side was well enough educated to understand the intricacy of jungle law. Further, that there was nothing to fear, for the members of the Commission were all men of repute for their impartiality in justice, and as they were gentlemen chosen by God to look after the interests of races less adequately endowed with teeth and claws, he might rest assured that they would investigate the matter with the greatest care and report impartially.

The Commission sat to take the evidence. The Rt. Hon. Mr. Elephant was first called. He came along with a superior air, brushing his tusks with a sapling which Mrs. Elephant had provided, and in an authoritative voice said: "Gentlemen of the Jungle, there is no need for me to waste your valuable time in relating a story which I am sure you all know. I have always regarded it as my duty to protect the interests of my friends, and this appears to have caused the misunderstanding between myself and my friend here. He invited me to save his hut from being blown away by a hurricane. As the hurricane had gained access owing to the unoccupied space in the hut, I considered it necessary, in my friend's own interests, to turn the undeveloped space to a more economic use by sitting in it myself; a duty which any of you would undoubtedly have performed with equal readiness in similar circumstances."

After hearing the Rt. Hon. Mr. Elephant's conclusive evidence, the Commission called Mr. Hyena and other elders of the jungle, who all supported what Mr. Elephant had said. They then called the man, who began to give his own account of the dispute. But the Commission cut him short, saying: "My good man, please confine yourself to relevant issues. We have already heard the circumstances from various unbiased sources; all we wish you to tell us is whether the undeveloped space in your hut was occupied by anyone else before Mr. Elephant assumed his position?" The man began to say: "No, but—" But at this point the Commission declared that they had heard sufficient evidence from both sides and retired to consider their decision. After enjoying a delicious meal at the expense of the Rt. Hon. Mr. Elephant, they reached their verdict, called the man, and declared as follows: "In our opinion this dispute has arisen through a regrettable misunderstanding due to the backwardness of your ideas. We consider that Mr. Elephant has fulfilled his sacred duty of protecting your interests. As it is clearly for your good that the space should be put to its most economic use, and as you yourself have not yet reached the stage of expansion which would enable you to fill it, we consider it necessary to arrange a compromise to suit both parties. Mr. Elephant shall continue his occupation of your hut, but we give you permission to look for a site where you can build another hut more suited to your needs, and we will see that you are well protected."

The man, having no alternative, and fearing that his refusal might expose him to the teeth and claws of members of the Commission, did as they suggested. But no sooner had he built another hut than Mr. Rhinoceros charged in with his horn lowered and ordered the man to quit. A Royal Commission was again appointed to look into the matter, and the same finding was given. This procedure was repeated until Mr. Buffalo, Mr. Leopard, Mr. Hyena and the rest were all accommodated with new huts. Then the man decided that he must adopt an effective method of protection, since Commissions of Enquiry did not seem to be of any use to him. He sat down and said: "*Ng'enda thi ndeagaga motegi,*" which literally means "there is nothing that treads on the earth that cannot be trapped," or in other words, you can fool people for a time, but not for ever.

Early one morning, when the huts already occupied by the jungle lords were all beginning to decay and fall to pieces, he went out and built a bigger and better hut a little distance away. No sooner had Mr. Rhinoceros seen it than he came rushing in, only to find that Mr. Elephant was already inside, sound asleep. Mr. Leopard next came in at the window, Mr. Lion, Mr. Fox, and Mr. Buffalo entered the doors, while Mr. Hyena howled for a place in the shade and Mr. Alligator basked on the roof. Presently they all began disputing about their rights of penetration, and from disputing they came to fighting, and while they were all embroiled together the man set the hut on fire and burnt it to the ground, jungle lords and all. Then he went home, saying: "Peace is costly, but it's worth the expense," and lived happily ever after.

61 F. Fanon, from *The Wretched of the Earth* (trans. by Constance Farrington; Penguin, 1990), pp. 27–33

Franz Fanon (1925–1961) was born to a middle-class family in the French colony of Martinique. He left in 1943, joining the Free French in the Second World War. He remained in France after the war to study psychiatry and in 1953 became Head of the Psychiatry Department at Blida-Joinville Hospital in Algeria. During his tenure there, the Algerian War of independence broke out, and in 1956 he resigned his post to join the Algerian cause. He served as Ambassador to Ghana for the Provisional Algerian Government. His principal works were *Black Skin, White Masks* (1952), and *The Wretched of the Earth* (1961), completed in the year of his premature death from leukaemia. He remains an important figure for post-colonial studies.

National liberation, national renaissance, the restoration of nationhood to the people, commonwealth: whatever may be the headings used or the new formulas introduced, decolonization is always a violent phenomenon. At whatever level we study it—relationships between individuals, new names for sports clubs, the human admixture at cocktail parties, in the police, on the directing boards of national or private banks—decolonization is quite simply the replacing of a certain 'species' of men by another 'species' of men. Without any period of transition, there is a total, complete and absolute substitution. It is true that we could equally well stress the rise of a new nation, the setting up of a new state, its diplomatic relations, and its economic and political trends. But we have precisely chosen to speak of that kind of *tabula rasa* which characterizes at the outset all decolonization. Its unusual importance is that it constitutes, from the very first day, the minimum demands of the colonized. To tell the truth, the proof of success lies in a whole social structure being changed from the bottom up. The extraordinary importance of this change is that it is willed, called for, demanded. The need for this change exists in its crude state, impetuous and compelling, in the consciousness and in the lives of the men and women who are colonized. But the possibility of this change is equally experienced in the form of a terrifying future in the consciousness of another 'species' of men and women: the colonizers.

Decolonization, which sets out to change the order of the world, is, obviously, a programme of complete disorder. But it cannot come as a result of magical practices, nor of a natural shock, nor of a friendly understanding. Decolonization, as we know, is a historical process: that is to say that it cannot be understood, it cannot become intelligible nor clear to itself except in the exact measure that we can discern the movements which give it historical form and content. Decolonization is the meeting of two forces, opposed to each other by their very nature, which in fact owe their originality to that sort of substantification which results from and is nourished by the situation in the colonies. Their first encounter was marked by violence and their existence together—that is to say the exploitation of the native by the settler—was carried on by dint of a great array of bayonets and cannon. The settler and the native are old acquaintances. In fact, the settler is right when he speaks of knowing 'them' well. For it is the settler who has brought the native into existence and who perpetuates his existence. The settler owes the fact of his very existence, that is to say his property, to the colonial system.

Decolonization never takes place unnoticed, for it influences individuals and modifies them fundamentally. It transforms spectators crushed with their inessentiality into privileged actors, with the grandiose glare of history's floodlights upon them. It brings a natural rhythm into existence, introduced by new men, and with it a new language and a new humanity. Decolonization is the veritable creation of new men. But this creation owes nothing of its legitimacy to any supernatural power; the 'thing' which has been colonized becomes man during the same process by which it frees itself.

In decolonization, there is therefore the need of a complete calling in question of the colonial situation. If we wish to describe it precisely, we might find it in the well-known words: 'The last shall be first and the first last.' Decolonization is the putting into practice of this sentence. That is why, if we try to describe it, all decolonization is successful.

The naked truth of decolonization evokes for us the searing bullets and bloodstained knives which emanate from it. For if the last shall be first, this will only come to pass after a murderous and decisive struggle between the two protagonists. That affirmed intention to place the last at the head of things, and to make them climb at a pace (too quickly, some say) the well-known steps which characterize an organized society, can only triumph if we use all means to turn the scale, including, of course, that of violence.

You do not turn any society, however primitive it may be, upside-down with such a programme if you are not decided from the very beginning, that is to say from the actual formulation of that programme, to overcome all the obstacles that you will come across in so doing. The native who decides to put the programme into practice, and to become its moving force, is ready for violence at all times. From birth it is clear to him that this narrow world, strewn with prohibitions, can only be called in question by absolute violence.

The colonial world is a world divided into compartments. It is probably unnecessary to recall the existence of native quarters and European quarters, of schools for natives and schools for Europeans; in the same way we need not recall Apartheid in South Africa. Yet, if we examine closely this system of compartments, we will at least be able to reveal the lines of force it implies. This approach to the colonial world, its ordering and its geographical lay-out will allow us to mark out the lines on which a decolonized society will be reorganized.

The colonial world is a world cut in two. The dividing line, the frontiers are shown by barracks and police stations. In the colonies it is the policeman and the soldier who are the official, instituted go-betweens, the spokesmen of the settler and his rule of oppression. In capitalist societies the educational system, whether lay or clerical, the structure of moral reflexes handed down from father to son, the exemplary honesty of workers who are given a medal after fifty years of good and loyal service, and the affection which springs from harmonious relations and good behaviour—all these aesthetic expressions of respect for the established order serve to create around the exploited person an atmosphere of submission and of inhibition which lightens the task of policing considerably. In the capitalist countries a multitude of moral teachers, counsellors and 'bewilderers' separate the exploited from those in power. In the colonial countries, on the contrary, the policeman and the soldier, by their immediate presence and their frequent and direct action maintain contact with the native and advise him by means of rifle-butts and napalm not to budge. It is obvious here that the agents of government speak the language of pure force. The intermediary does not lighten the oppression, nor seek to hide the domination; he shows them up and puts them into practice with the clear conscience of an upholder of the peace; yet he is the bringer of violence into the home and into the mind of the native.

The zone where the natives live is not complementary to the zone inhabited by the settlers. The two zones are opposed, but not in the service of a higher unity. Obedient to the rules of pure Aristotelian logic, they both follow the principle of reciprocal exclusivity. No conciliation is possible, for of the two terms, one is superfluous. The settler's town is a strongly-built town, all made of stone and steel. It is a brightly-lit town; the streets are covered with asphalt, and the garbage-cans swallow all the leavings, unseen, unknown and hardly thought about. The settler's feet are never visible, except perhaps in the sea; but there you're never close enough to see them. His feet are protected by strong shoes although the streets of his town are clean and even, with no holes or stones. The settler's town is a well-fed town, an easy-going town; its belly is always full of good things. The settler's town is a town of white people, of foreigners.

The town belonging to the colonized people, or at least the native town, the Negro village, the medina, the reservation, is a place of ill fame, peopled by men of evil repute. They are born there, it matters little where or how; they die there, it matters not where, nor how. It is a world without spaciousness; men live there on top of each other, and their huts are built one on top of the other. The native town is a hungry town, starved of bread, of meat, of shoes, of coal, of light. The native town is a crouching village, a town on its knees, a town wallowing in the mire. It is a town of niggers and dirty arabs. The look that the native turns on the settler's town is a look of lust, a look of envy; it expresses his dreams of possession—all manner of possession: to sit at the settler's table, to sleep in the settler's bed, with his wife if possible. The colonized man is an envious man. And this the settler knows very well; when their glances meet he ascertains bitterly, always on the defensive 'They want to take our place'. It is true, for there is no native who does not dream at least once a day of setting himself up in the settler's place.

This world divided into compartments, this world cut in two is inhabited by two different species. The originality of the colonial context is that economic reality, inequality and the immense difference of ways of life never come to mask the human realities. When you examine at close quarters the colonial context, it is evident that what parcels out the world is to begin with the fact of belonging to or not belonging to a given race, a given species. In the colonies the economic substructure is also a superstructure. The cause is the consequence; you are rich because you are white, you are white because you are rich. This is why Marxist analysis should always be slightly stretched every time we have to do with the colonial problem.

Everything up to and including the very nature of pre-capitalist society, so well explained by Marx, must here be thought out again. The serf is in essence different from the knight, but a reference to divine right is necessary to legitimize this statutory difference. In the colonies, the foreigner coming from another country imposed his rule by means of guns and machines. In defiance of his successful transplantation, in spite of his appropriation, the settler still remains a foreigner. It is neither the act of owning factories, nor estates, nor a bank balance which distinguishes the governing classes. The governing race is first and foremost those who come from elsewhere, those who are unlike the original inhabitants, 'the others'.

The violence which has ruled over the ordering of the colonial world, which has ceaselessly drummed the rhythm for the destruction of native social forms and broken up without reserve the systems of reference of the economy, the customs of dress and external life, that same violence will be claimed and taken over by the native at the moment when, deciding to embody history in his own person, he surges into the forbidden quarters. To wreck the colonial world is henceforward a mental picture of action which is very clear, very easy to understand and which may be assumed by each one of the individuals which constitute the colonized people. To break up the colonial world does not mean that after the frontiers have been abolished lines of communication will be set up between the two zones. The destruction of the colonial world is no more and no less than the abolition of one zone, its burial in the depths of the earth or its expulsion from the country.

The natives' challenge to the colonial world is not a rational confrontation of points of view. It is not a treatise on the universal, but the untidy affirmation of an original idea propounded as an absolute. The colonial world is a Manichaean world. It is not enough for the settler to delimit physically, that is to say with the help of the army and the police force, the place of the native. As if to show the totalitarian character of colonial exploitation the settler paints the native as a sort of quintessence of evil. Native society is not simply described as a society lacking in values. It is not enough for the colonist to affirm that those values have disappeared from, or still better never existed in, the colonial world. The native is declared insensible to ethics; he represents not only the absence of values, but also the negation of values. He is, let us dare to admit, the enemy of values, and in this sense he is the absolute evil. He is the corrosive element, destroying all that comes near him; he is the deforming element, disfiguring all that has to do with beauty or morality; he is the depository of maleficent powers, the unconscious and irretrievable instrument of blind forces. Monsieur Meyer could thus state seriously in the French National Assembly that the Republic must not be prostituted by allowing the Algerian people to become part of it. All values, in fact, are irrevocably poisoned and diseased as soon as they are allowed in contact with the colonized race. The customs of the colonized people, their traditions, their myths—above all, their myths—are the very sign of that poverty of spirit and of their constitutional depravity. That is why we must put the D.D.T.

which destroys parasites, the bearers of disease, on the same level as the Christian religion which wages war on embryonic heresies and instincts, and on evil as yet unborn. The recession of yellow fever and the advance of evangelization form part of the same balance-sheet. But the triumphant *communiqués* from the missions are in fact a source of information concerning the implantation of foreign influences in the core of the colonized people. I speak of the Christian religion, and no one need be astonished. The Church in the colonies is the white people's Church, the foreigner's Church. She does not call the native to God's ways but to the ways of the white man, of the master, of the oppressor. And as we know, in this matter many are called but few chosen.

At times this Manichaeism goes to its logical conclusion and dehumanizes the native, or to speak plainly it turns him into an animal. In fact, the terms the settler uses when he mentions the native are zoological terms. He speaks of the yellow man's reptilian motions, of the stink of the native quarter, of breeding swarms, of foulness, of spawn, of gesticulations. When the settler seeks to describe the native fully in exact terms he constantly refers to the bestiary. The European rarely hits on a picturesque style; but the native, who knows what is in the mind of the settler, guesses at once what he is thinking of. Those hordes of vital statistics, those hysterical masses, those faces bereft of all humanity, those distended bodies which are like nothing on earth, that mob without beginning or end, those children who seem to belong to nobody, that laziness stretched out in the sun, that vegetative rhythm of life—all this forms part of the colonial vocabulary. General de Gaulle speaks of 'the yellow multitudes' and François Mauriac of the black, brown and yellow masses which soon will be unleashed. The native knows all this, and laughs to himself every time he spots an allusion to the animal world in the other's words. For he knows that he is not an animal; and it is precisely at the moment he realizes his humanity that he begins to sharpen the weapons with which he will secure its victory.

6   Feminism

Introduction

Feminism exploded in the political consciousness of Western democracies in the 1970s. But, as many of its chroniclers and proponents have observed, this was not the first occasion on which elements of this ideological perspective had been publicly aired. Some present the arrival, recession, and re-appearance of proto-feminist ideas as a succession of 'waves' that appeared on the political shore from the mid-late nineteenth century onwards. Scholars have accordingly sought to rescue the work of a litany of overlooked female political writers and, more generally, emphasized how some of the major categories and concepts of western political thought are loaded with normative assumptions about gender. Historians illustrate the variety of cultural and intellectual sources upon which feminist-inclined authors drew from the nineteenth century onwards. And, more recently, there has emerged a body of theorizing committed to examining political and social life from an independent feminist perspective. This latter enterprise is marked by its internal diversity and some strong disagreements—both of philosophical stance and political vision.

Our selection of authors begins with an extract from one of the most influential arguments for women's equality to have emerged in modern Anglo-American political discourse—Mary Wollstonecraft's *A Vindication of the Rights of Woman* [Reading 62]. Deeply influenced by her encounter with political radicals in the late eighteenth century, she proclaims the centrality of the value of individual independence, and makes plain her ambition to extend the Enlightenment principles to which she subscribes to the position of women (an issue ignored by her fellow male radicals). Central to her understanding of how some of the debilitating cultural differences afflicting women should be overcome, is a commitment to the role of education. This enables the development of the autonomy of individual women, a vital prerequisite if they are to appreciate the Enlightenment values of truth and progress. Women need to be educated so that they can grasp the significance of the duties allotted to them by their female natures: above all, to act as guardians and educators of the next generation of citizens. Her argument also anticipates the concerns of later generations of campaigners for womens' equality: the prevailing idolization of female beauty lays traps for women, she maintains, undermining an appreciation of their intellectual faculties and capacity for reason. On what moral grounds, she demands, can men pursue the value of freedom, and simultaneously subjugate the interests of the other half of the population? A social order that confines women to the domestic realm infantilizes women, making them more of a menace when they do engage in public affairs, because they have not been schooled in the demands of reason. Such a situation, she argues, tends to undermine the standards of public morality. It gives women little appreciation of ethical values and civic duty, and encourages men to relate to women purely through physical relations, rather than respect and friendship.

Not all proponents of female equality before the twentieth century were women. One famous and influential convert to this cause was the nineteenth-century philosopher and politician, John Stuart Mill. His relationship with the writer Harriet Taylor was a key influence on his thinking in this respect. In this extract from his book, *The Subjection of Women*, he undermines the conventional argument that the preponderance of male-dominated societies reflects a timeless moral truth [Reading 63]. This state of affairs is actually an obstacle in the path of social progress and antithetical to the spirit of modern society, in which the freedom of the individual to determine her own life-plan has become the defining principle. Modern societies, he argues, tend to remove legal regulations that protect the hold of particular social groups over certain professions. This 'general principle of social and economic science' reflects widespread acceptance of the idea that individuals are the best judges of 'their capabilities and vocation'. It is immoral in such a society that a person's position and chances in life are determined by arbitrary characteristics such as their skin colour, social class, or gender. By denying to its highest ranks persons of talent with these backgrounds, a society does itself more harm than if it provides opportunities for all, including those not capable of using them properly. The disadvantages faced by women are, in certain respects, uniquely unfair, surpassing even those facing men of the lower orders: no male is banned by law from particular occupations and social opportunities.

Both Wollstonecraft's assertion of womens' capacity for autonomy and Mill's critique of the injustices associated with the arbitrary distribution of experiences and opportunities associated with gender, had their echoes beyond Britain. Other nineteenth-century authors developed important, related arguments about the public roles denied to women. The American social campaigner Jane Addams highlighted the growing interdependency of mothers and various kinds of public authority peculiar to modern urban societies. Women have a vested interest in the provision of high-quality public education as well as various kinds of legal protection. The qualities of female insight and experience are linked, in this argument, with her sense of the importance of education as a vehicle for the integration of the different national minorities that co-exist in the United States. Addams observes the coincidence of the growing scope of education beyond the household with the industrialization of various traditional forms of female labour, which have resulted in a narrowing of womens' interests in the home [Reading 64]. In such a context, she suggests that a widening of women's sense of obligation, beyond the domestic sphere, is inevitable. This she connects with the demand that women be given their own vote as independent citizens; not regarded merely as sources of influence upon male members of their families. Like Mill, she undergirds the case for female political equality with an argument for the merits of pluralism and tolerance for a political community committed to progress. She brings to this argument a distinctive and intriguing element—the suggestion that aspects of the governance of cities are more likely to be addressed if women are involved in public life.

These different positions were influential upon a wave of campaigning and activism concerned with winning the vote for women around the turn of the nineteenth- and twentieth-centuries. Later activists absorbed these arguments and brought distinctive new elements to bear in their more self-conscious elaboration of a political outlook grounded in women's subordinate position. Perhaps the key figure whose work signals the transition between these various feminist 'waves' is that of the French philosopher and social critic Simone de Beauvoir. In her highly influential study, *The Second Sex*, she contrasts the egalitarian promise of the Soviet revolution in relation to the positions of men and women with western capitalism [Reading 65]. She then proceeds to isolate influential cultural and intellectual perceptions of the respective characters of men and women as among the causes of gender based inequality. For de Beauvoir and many other feminists of the 1960s, the very notion that there is such a thing as a natural identity available to men or women is mistaken. Ideas about what it is to be a woman are socially produced, and typically rely upon entrenched cultural assumptions about womens' bodies. This claim leads her to emphasize the possibility of altering female identities and the need to tackle the economic conditions and imperatives that shape gender-based inequality. Women are caught uneasily between two paradigms: the model of femininity associated with the patriarchal past, and the prospect of achieving a new ideal of womanhood. The aspiration to equality does not mean persuading women to be like men, but would guide a society in which each individual expresses her or his own individuality beyond the 'cages' associated with gendered identity. Only in such a social context will the self-esteem and expectations of girls match that of their male counterparts.

The impact of this position can be traced throughout the feminist political upsurge of the late 1960s and early 1970s in different Western societies. Later thinkers, such as Kate Millet, developed de Beauvoir's characterization of the history and social processes whereby restrictive images and understandings of womanhood were generated [Reading 66]. In Millet's influential characterization of the nature of gendered inequality and womens' struggles against subordination, central place is given to the claim that a new 'sexual politics' has come into being. Through this term, she challenges conventional understandings of politics that restrict its application to the world of institutions and public life. Such a view ignores (and tacitly approves) the oppressive relationships that pertain in what is typically regarded as the *private* domains of social life. The major remaining oppressive relation within modern democracy is that between men and women. Without a transformed, expanded sense of the political, we fail to appreciate that conventional politics inhibits women from mobilizing to advance their interests and challenge the roles allotted to them. The power men wield over women is simultaneously pervasive and invisible: it stretches across all of the institutional domains of society and is rarely open to challenge because its exclusion from conventional political debate means that it is rarely apparent. The source and nature of this domination she labels 'patriarchy'. While its character varies between different types of society, her deployment of this term shapes her discussion of the socialization of men and women into prevalent 'sex roles'. Questioning justifications of patriarchy that invoke dubious theories about the inherently superior strength and physique of men, she raises the possibility that patriarchy may have been preceded by a societal model in which a different relationship between men and women prevailed. This excerpt finishes with Millet establishing a significant analytical distinction between the biologically determinist idea that we are members of a 'sex' and the culturally suggestive notion that our identities are profoundly shaped by the 'genders' into which we are socialized.

A sense that feminism needs to be re-evaluated, and that earlier advances have stalled, became apparent in feminist circles at the end of the 1970s. The British writer Lynne Segal critically observes recent developments in feminist culture in this period [Reading 67]. She reminds her readers that second-wave feminism regarded conventional female roles and pursuits as offering important, yet limited, kinds of consolation for many women. These provide ways of dealing with feelings of powerlessness. Detecting a sea-change in current feminist consciousness, however, she notes the rise of a discourse that proclaims the special, unique natures of women. This she labels 'cultural feminism', and, in her view, this reproduces, rather than challenges, traditional aspects of gender ideology. Cultural feminists provide an uncanny echo of the assertions made about women by conservatives. They celebrate as 'authentic' aspects of women's experience that stem form insubordination and male power.

The influence of feminism has spread far and wide throughout democratic debate. For theorists of the political, this new politics has brought a fresh set of critical insights, and some formidable challenges to prevalent understandings. Susan Moller Okin argues that the shift within American political philosophy towards the question of social justice, from the 1970s onwards, has overlooked the realities of gendered inequality [Reading 68]. Not only is it inadequate to ignore gender related injustice, but serious attention to the value of equality of opportunity (dear to many liberals) requires their consideration. Only if the principles of morality are brought to bear upon the institution of the family, can a truly coherent understanding of social justice be achieved. The usage of gender-neutral language by political philosophy is therefore hypocritical: its favoured conceptions of justice apply only to male members of the political community. She finishes by rejecting the argument that such concepts as rights and justice are anathema to feminist ways of thinking.

It is exactly this last claim, however, that is at the heart of Carol Gilligan's psychological interpretation of the moral character of women [Reading 69]. For Gilligan, the vocabulary of justice and rights ignores the prevalence of an ethical discourse in which care is central, and a more context-specific and particularistic kind of moral reasoning takes shape. Women, she claims, tend to orientate towards the latter, because they develop a fundamentally different moral psychology to their male counterparts.

Rather different concerns and concepts are associated with feminists outside the Anglo-American orbit. French intellectuals have, in particular, had a major impact upon the development of this ideology both in developing particular philosophical ideas and in relation to the women's movement in France. Here, we include an extract from the work of one of the major French-based feminist thinkers—Julia Kristeva [Reading 70]. She argues that in its earliest incarnations, the women's movement pursued the goal of equality by accepting the philosophical and epistemological terms set by Enlightenment rationality. Even while achieving some ideological difference from this broadly liberal mainstream, feminism was initially guilty of accepting the underlying, anti-female logic sustaining egalitarian thought. The various struggles and campaigns for women's equality that gathered under the banner of the pursuit of universal equality for women have been augmented, since the late 1960s, by a different intellectual current. This is embedded within the experiences of a younger generation of women, for whom the struggle for female recognition points away from such conventional political goals. In an echo of Gilligan's position, she suggests that this feminist impulse is more interested in re-valuing those bodily, aesthetic and psychological aspects of womanhood that are unique to women and regarded as underpinning womens' differences to men. It has helped shape what she terms a different 'temporality' to that associated with liberalism—a highly particular conception of identity and being.

Her stress upon the fluidity and singularity of women's identities is informed by an appreciation that the experiences and identities conferred by gender are also overlain with other sources of inequity and identification, such as race. How these relations should be understood in philosophical and political terms has emerged as a major issue for feminism over the last few decades. The question of whether the politics of gender supersedes ethnicity, or *vice versa*, has been especially contentious in the American women's movement. The well-known writer and campaigner bell hooks (her name is deliberately non-capitalized) argues that the women's movement perpetuated a denial of the realities of racial inequality and implicitly sidelined the needs of black women [Reading 71]. When second-wave feminism began, racial integration was still relatively rare, and black women were unable to challenge the priorities and culture of the women's movement. This was less the case for African-American women of her generation, and hooks suggests that the resultant dialogue about 'difference' that has developed among feminists is both unique and beneficial. She remains sceptical, however, about whether these theoretical insights have translated into political practice.

FURTHER READING

Useful studies of the development of feminist thinking include: Rosemarie Tong, *Feminist Thought: A More Comprehensive Introduction* (Westview Press, 1998); Valerie Bryson, *Feminist Political Theory: An Introduction* (Macmillan, 1992); and Chris Corrin, *Feminist Perspectives on Politics* (Longman, 1999). Some of the most important debates animating contemporary feminist theorists can be found in: Juliet Mitchell and Ann Oakley (eds.) *What is Feminism?* (Blackwell, 1986); Toril Moi (ed.) *French Feminist Thought: a Reader* (Basil Blackwell, 1987); and Terry Lovell (ed.) *British Feminist Thought: A Reader* (Blackwell, 1990). Important studies of the ways in which women have been represented in Western political thought are offered by: Carole Pateman, *The Sexual Contract* (Polity, 1988); Susan Moller Okin, *Women in Western Political Thought* (Princeton University Press, 1992); and Diana Coole, *Women in Political Theory: from Ancient Mysogny to Contemporary Feminism* (Harvester Wheatsheaf, 1993).

62   Mary Wollstonecraft, from *A Vindication of the Rights of Women* (Dent/Dutton, 1965), pp. 9–13

Wollstonecraft (1759–1797) was born in Spitalfields in London. In 1784 she was involved in founding a school in Newington Green. After meeting Richard Price, a minister at a nearby Dissenting Chapel, she was introduced to the ideas and personalities of late eighteenth-century political radicalism. She expressed her support for the ideals of the French Revolution in her *Vindication of the Rights of Man*, a reply to Edmund Burke that brought her to the attention of a wide political audience. In 1792 she published her most famous work, *Vindication of the Rights of Women* (see the extract below), in which she attacked the educational restraints that infantilized women and fixed their dependence upon men. In the face of the climate of reaction engendered by the largely conservative political response to the revolution of the 1790s, Wollstonecraft moved to France in 1793, but returned to London two years later. She married the celebrated radical writer William Godwin in 1797, and died as a result of childbirth in the same year.

To

M. Talleyrand-Périgord,

*Late Bishop Of Autun**

Sir,

Having read with great pleasure a pamphlet which you have lately published*, I dedicate this volume to you; to induce you to reconsider the subject, and maturely weigh what I have advanced respecting the rights of woman and national education: and I call with the firm tone of humanity; for my arguments, Sir, are dictated by a disinterested spirit— I plead for my sex—not for myself. Independence I have long considered as the grand blessing of life, the basis of every virtue—and independence I will ever secure by contracting my wants, though I were to live on a barren heath.

It is then an affection for the whole human race that makes my pen dart rapidly along to support what I believe to be the cause of virtue: and the same motive leads me earnestly to wish to see woman placed in a station in which she would advance, instead of retarding, the progress of those glorious principles that give a substance to morality. My opinion, indeed, respecting the rights and duties of woman, seems to flow so naturally from these simple principles, that I think it scarcely possible, but that some of the enlarged minds who formed your admirable constitution, will coincide with me.

In France there is undoubtedly a more general diffusion of knowledge than in any part of the European world, and I attribute it, in a great measure, to the social intercourse which has long subsisted between the sexes. It is true, I utter my sentiments with freedom, that in France the very essence of sensuality has been extracted to regale the voluptuary, and a kind of sentimental lust has prevailed, which, together with the system of duplicity that the whole tenour of their political and civil government taught, have given a sinister sort of sagacity to the French character, properly termed finesse: from which naturally flow a polish of manners that injures the substance, by hunting sincerity out of society.— And, modesty, the fairest garb of virtue! has been more grossly insulted in France than even in England, till their women have treated as *prudish* that attention to decency, which brutes instinctively observe.

Manners and morals are so nearly allied that they have often been confounded; but, though the former should only be the natural reflection of the latter, yet, when various causes have produced factitious and corrupt manners, which are very early caught, morality becomes an empty name. The personal reserve, and sacred respect for cleanliness and delicacy in domestic life, which French women almost despise, are the graceful pillars of modesty; but, far from despising them, if the pure flame of patriotism have reached their bosoms, they should labour to improve the morals of their fellow-citizens, by teaching men, not only to respect modesty in women, but to acquire it themselves, as the only way to merit their esteem.

Contending for the rights of woman, my main argument is built on this simple principle, that if she be not prepared by education to become the companion of man, she will stop the progress of knowledge and virtue; for truth must be common to all, or it will be inefficacious with respect to its influence on general practice. And how can woman be expected to co-operate unless she know why she ought to be virtuous? unless freedom strengthen her reason till she comprehend her duty, and see in what manner it is connected with her real good? If children are to be educated to understand the true principle of patriotism, their mother must be a patriot; and the love of mankind, from which an orderly train of virtues spring, can only be produced by considering the moral and civil interest of mankind; but the education and situation of woman, at present, shuts her out from such investigations.

In this work I have produced many arguments, which to me were conclusive, to prove that the prevailing notion respecting a sexual character was subversive of morality, and I have contended, that to render the human body and mind more perfect, chastity must more universally prevail, and that chastity will never be respected in the male world till the person of a woman is not, as it were, idolized, when little virtue or sense embellish it with the grand traces of mental beauty, or the interesting simplicity of affection.

Consider, Sir, dispassionately, these observations—for a glimpse of this truth seemed to open before you when you observed, 'that to see one half of the human race excluded by the other from all participation of government, was a political phenomenon that, according to abstract principles, it was impossible to explain'. If so, on what does your constitution rest? If the abstract rights of man will bear discussion and explanation, those of woman, by a parity of reasoning, will not shrink from the same test: though a different opinion prevails in this country, built on the very arguments which you use to justify the oppression of woman—prescription.

Consider, I address you as a legislator, whether, when men contend for their freedom, and to be allowed to judge for themselves respecting their own happiness, it be not inconsistent and unjust to subjugate women, even though you firmly believe that you are acting in the manner best calculated to promote their happiness? Who made man the exclusive judge, if woman partake with him the gift of reason?

In this style, argue tyrants of every denomination, from the weak king to the weak father of a family; they are all eager to crush reason; yet always assert that they usurp its throne only to be useful. Do you not act a similar part, when you *force* all women, by denying them civil and political rights, to remain immured in their families groping in the dark? for surely, Sir, you will not assert, that a duty can be binding which is not founded on reason? If indeed this be their destination, arguments may be drawn from reason: and thus augustly supported, the more understanding women acquire, the more they will be attached to their duty—comprehending it—for unless they comprehend it, unless their morals be fixed on the same immutable principle as those of man, no author-ity can make them discharge it in a virtuous manner. They may be convenient slaves, but slavery will have its constant effect, degrading the master and the abject dependent.

But, if women are to be excluded, without having a voice, from a participation of the natural rights of mankind, prove first, to ward off the charge of injustice and inconsistency, that they want reason—else this flaw in your NEW CONSTITUTION will ever shew that man must, in some shape, act like a tyrant, and tyranny, in whatever part of society it rears its brazen front, will ever undermine morality.

I have repeatedly asserted, and produced what appeared to me irrefragable arguments drawn from matters of fact, to prove my assertion, that women cannot, by force, be con-fined to domestic concerns; for they will, however ignorant, intermeddle with more weighty affairs, neglecting private duties only to disturb, by cunning tricks, the orderly plans of reason which rise above their comprehension.

Besides, whilst they are only made to acquire personal accomplishments, men will seek for pleasure in variety, and faithless husbands will make faithless wives; such ignorant beings, indeed, will be very excusable when, not taught to respect public good, nor allowed any civil rights, they attempt to do themselves justice by retaliation.

The box of mischief thus opened in society, what is to preserve private virtue, the only security of public freedom and universal happiness?

Let there be then no coercion *established* in society, and the common law of gravity prevailing, the sexes will fall into their proper places. And, now that more equitable, laws are forming your citizens, marriage may become more sacred: your young men may choose wives from motives of affection, and your maidens allow love to root out vanity.

The father of a family will not then weaken his constitution and debase his sentiments, by visiting the harlot, nor forget, in obeying the call of appetite, the purpose for which it was implanted. And, the mother will not neglect her children to practise the arts of coquetry, when sense and modesty secure her the friendship of her husband.

But, till men become attentive to the duty of a father, it is vain to expect women to spend that time in their nursery which they, 'wise in their generation', choose to spend at their glass; for this exertion of cunning is only an instinct of nature to enable them to obtain indirectly a little of that power of which they are unjustly denied a share: for, if women are not permitted to enjoy legitimate rights, they will render both men and themselves vicious, to obtain illicit privileges.

I wish, Sir, to set some investigations of this kind afloat in France; and should they lead to a confirmation of my principles, when your constitution is revised the Rights of Woman may be respected, if it be fully proved that reason calls for this respect, and loudly demands JUSTICE for one half of the human race.

I am, SIR,
Yours respectfully,
M. W.

63 John Stuart Mill, from *The Subjection of Women* in *On Liberty and Other Essays* (ed. by John Gray; Oxford University Press, 1991), p. 487–91

For biographical details, see Chapter 2, Reading 15.

The preceding considerations are amply sufficient to show that custom, however universal it may be, affords in this case no presumption, and ought not to create any prejudice, in favour of the arrangements which place women in social and political subjection to men. But I may go farther, and maintain that the course of history, and the tendencies of progressive human society, afford not only no presumption in favour of this system of inequality of rights, but a strong one against it; and that, so far as the whole course of human improvement up to this time, the whole stream of modern tendencies, warrants any inference on the subject, it is, that this relic of the past is discordant with the future, and must necessarily disappear.

For what is the peculiar character of the modern world—the difference which chiefly distinguishes modern institutions, modern social ideas, modern life itself, from those of times long past? It is, that human beings are no longer born to their place in life, and chained down by an inexorable bond to the place they are born to, but are free to employ their faculties, and such favourable chances as offer, to achieve the lot which may appear to them most desirable. Human society of old was constituted on a very different principle. All were born to a fixed social position, and were mostly kept in it by law, or interdicted from any means by which they could emerge from it. As some men are born white and others black, so some were born slaves and others freemen and citizens; some were born patricians, others plebeians; some were born feudal nobles, others commoners and *roturiers*. A slave or serf could never make himself free, nor, except by the will of his master, become so. In most European countries it was not till towards the close of the Middle Ages, and as a consequence of the growth of regal power, that commoners could be enobled. Even among nobles, the eldest son was born the exclusive heir to the paternal possessions, and a long time elapsed before it was fully established that the father could disinherit him. Among the industrious classes, only those who were born members of a guild, or were admitted into it by its members, could lawfully practice their calling within its local limits; and nobody could practise any calling deemed important, in any but the legal manner—by processes authoritatively prescribed. Manufacturers have stood in the pillory for presuming to carry on their business by new and improved methods. In modern Europe, and most in those parts of it which have participated most largely in all other modern improvements, diametrically opposite doctrines now prevail. Law and government do not undertake to prescribe by whom any social or industrial operation shall or shall not be conducted, or what modes of conducting them shall be lawful. These things are left to the unfettered choice of individuals. Even the laws which required that workmen should serve an apprenticeship, have in this country been repealed: there being ample assurance that in all cases in which an apprenticeship is necessary, its necessity will suffice to enforce it. The old theory was, that the least possible should be left to the choice of the of the individual agent; that all he had to do should, as far as practicable, be laid down for him by superior wisdom. Left to himself he was sure to go wrong. The modern conviction, the fruit of a thousand years of experience, is, that things in which the individual is the person directly interested, never go right but as they are left to his own discretion; and that any regulation of them by authority, except to protect the rights of others, is sure to be mischievous. This conclusion, slowly arrived at, and not adopted until almost every possible application of the contrary theory had been made with disastrous result, now (in the industrial department) prevails universally in the most advanced countries, almost universally in all that have pretensions to any sort of advancement. It is not that all processes are supposed to be equally good, or all persons to be equally qualified for everything; but that freedom of individual choice is now known to be the only thing which procures the adoption of the best processes, and throws each operation into the hands of those who are best qualified for it. Nobody thinks it necessary to make a law that only a strongarmed man shall be a blacksmith. Freedom and competition suffice to make blacksmiths strong-armed men, because the weak-armed can earn more by engaging in occupations for which they are more fit. In consonance with this doctrine, it is felt to be an overstepping of the proper bounds of authority to fix beforehand, on some general presumption, that certain persons are not fit to do certain things. It is now thoroughly known and admitted that if some such presumptions exist, no such presumption is infallible. Even if it be well grounded in a majority of cases, which it is very likely not to be, there will be a minority of exceptional cases in which it does not hold: and in those it is both an injustice to the individuals, and a detriment to society, to place barriers in the way of their using their faculties for their own benefit and for that of others. In the cases, on the other hand, in which the unfitness is real, the ordinary motives of human conduct will on the whole suffice to prevent the incompetent person from making, or from persisting in, the attempt.

If this general principle of social and economical science is not true; if individuals, with such help as they can derive from the opinion of those who know them, are not better judges that the law and the government, of their own capabilities and vocation; the world cannot too soon abandon this principle, and return to the old system of regulations and disabilities. But if the principle is true, we ought to act as if we believed it, and not to ordain that to be born a girl instead of a boy, any more than to be born black instead of white, or a commoner instead of a nobleman, shall decide the person's position through all life—shall interdict people from all the more elevated social positions, and from all, except a few, respectable occupations. Even were we to admit the utmost that is ever pretended as to the superior fitness of men for all the functions now reserved to them, the same argument applies which forbids a legal qualification for members of Parliament. If only once in a dozen years the conditions of eligibility exclude a fit person, there is a real loss, while the exclusion of thousands of unfit persons is no gain; for if the constitution of the electoral body disposes them to choose unfit persons, there are always plenty of such persons to choose from. In all things of any difficulty and importance, those who can do them well are fewer than the need, even with the most unrestricted latitude of choice: and any limitation of the field of selection deprives society of some chances of being served by the competent, without ever saving it from the incompetent.

At present, in the more improved countries, the disabilities of women are the only case, save one, in which laws and institutions take persons at their birth, and ordain that they shall never in all their lives be allowed to compete for certain things. The one exception is that of royalty. Persons still are born to the throne; no one, not of the reigning family, can ever occupy it, and no one even of that family can, by any means but the course of hereditary succession, attain it. All other dignities and social advantages are open to the whole male sex: many indeed are only attainable by wealth, but wealth may be striven for by any one, and is actually obtained by many men of the very humblest origin. The difficulties, to the majority, are indeed insuperable without the aid of fortunate accidents; but no male human being is under any legal ban: neither law nor opinion superadd artificial obstacles to the natural ones. Royalty, as I have said, is excepted; but in this case every one feels it to be an exception—an anomaly in the modern world, in marked opposition to its customs and principles, and to be justified only by extraordinary special expediencies, which though individuals and nations differ in estimating their weight, unquestionable do in fact exist. But in this exceptional case, in which a high social function is, for important reasons, bestowed on birth instead of being put up to competition, all free nations contrive to adhere in substance to the principle from which they nominally derogate; for they circumscribe this high function by conditions avowedly intended to prevent the person to whom it ostensibly belongs from really performing it; while the person by whom it is performed, the responsible minister, does obtain the post by a competition from which no full-grown citizen of the male sex is legally excluded. The disabilities, therefore, to which women are subject from the mere fact of their birth, are the solitary examples of the kind in modern legislation. In no instance except this, which comprehends half the human race, are the higher social functions closed against any one by a fatality of birth which no exertions, and no change of circumstances, can overcome; for even religious disabilities (besides that in England and in Europe they have practically almost ceased to exist) do not close any career to the disqualified person in case of conversion.

64   Jane Addams, from 'Why Women Should Have the Vote', in *The Social Thought of Jane Addams* (ed. by C. Lasch; Bobbs-Merrill, 1965), pp. 44–51

Addams (1860–1935) was born in Cedarville, Illinois. Following a visit to Toynbee Hall in the East End of London, she was instrumental in founding an equivalent institution in Chicago, which provided a range of services for the families of recent immigrants and proved a magnet for American social reformers. Addams was involved in a range of progressive causes: she was a founder member of the National Association for the Advancement of Colored People and one of the founders of the Woman's Peace Party formed during the First World War. In protest against the post-war crackdown on socialists occasioned by the Russian Revolution of 1917, she was involved in the founding of the American Civil Liberties Union. She was recognized with the award of the Nobel Peace Prize in 1931.

For many generations it has been believed that woman's place is within the walls of her own home, and it is indeed impossible to imagine the time when her duty there shall be ended or to forecast any social change which shall release her from that paramount obligation.

This paper is an attempt to show that many women today are failing to discharge their duties to their own households properly simply because they do not perceive that as society grows more complicated it is necessary that woman shall extend her sense of responsibility to many things outside of her own home if she would continue to preserve the home in its entirety. One could illustrate in many ways. A woman's simplest duty, one would say, is to keep her house clean and wholesome and to feed her children properly. Yet if she lives in a tenement house, as so many of my neighbors do, she cannot fulfill these simple obligations by her own efforts because she is utterly dependent upon the city administration for the conditions which render decent living possible. Her basement will not be dry, her stairways will not be fireproof, her house will not be provided with sufficient windows to give light and air, nor will it be equipped with sanitary plumbing, unless the Public Works Department sends inspectors who constantly insist that these elementary decencies be provided. Women who live in the country sweep their own dooryards and may either feed the refuse of the table to a flock of chickens or allow it innocently to decay in the open air and sunshine. In a crowded city quarter, however, if the street is not cleaned by the city authorities no amount of private sweeping will keep the tenement free from grime; if the garbage is not properly collected and destroyed a tenement-house mother may see her children sicken and die of diseases from which she alone is powerless to shield them, although her tenderness and devotion are unbounded. She cannot even secure untainted meat for her household, she cannot provide fresh fruit, unless the meat has been inspected by city officials and [unless] the decayed fruit, which is so often placed upon sale in the tenement districts, has been destroyed in the interests of public health. In short, if woman would keep on with her old business of caring for her house and rearing her children she will have to have some conscience in regard to public affairs lying quite outside of her immediate household. The individual conscience and devotion are no longer effective . . . .

. . . If women follow only the lines of their traditional activities here are certain primary duties which belong to even the most conservative women, and which no one woman or group of women can adequately discharge unless they join the more general movements looking toward social amelioration through legal enactment.

The first of these, of which this article has already treated, is woman's responsibility for the members of her own household that they may be properly fed and clothed and surrounded by hygienic conditions. The second is a responsibility for the education of children: (a) that they may be provided with good schools; (b) that they may be kept free from vicious influences on the street; (c) that when working they may be protected by adequate child-labor legislation.

(a) The duty of a woman toward the schools which her children attend is so obvious that it is not necessary to dwell upon it. But even this simple obligation cannot be effectively carried out without some form of social organization as the mothers' school clubs and mothers' congresses testify, and to which the most conservative women belong because they feel the need of wider reading and discussion concerning the many problems of childhood. It is, therefore, perhaps natural that the public should have been more willing to accord a vote to women in school matters than in any other, and yet women have never been members of a Board of Education in sufficient numbers to influence largely actual school curriculi. If they had been kindergartens, domestic science courses and school playgrounds would be far more numerous than they are. More than once woman has been convinced of the need of the ballot by the futility of her efforts in persuading a business man that young children need nurture in something besides the three r's. Perhaps, too, only women realize the influence which the school might exert upon the home if a proper adaptation to actual needs were considered. An Italian girl who has had lessons in cooking at the public school will help her mother to connect the entire family with American food and household habits. That the mother has never baked bread in Italy—only mixed it in her own house and then taken it out to the village oven—makes it all the more necessary that her daughter should understand the complications of a cooking-stove. The same thing is true of the girl who learns to sew in the public school, and more than anything else, perhaps, of the girl who receives the first simple instruction in the care of little children, that skillful care which every tenement-house baby requires if he is to be pulled through his second summer. The only time, to my knowledge, that lessons in the care of children were given in the public schools of Chicago was one summer when the vacation schools were being managed by a volunteer body of women. The instruction was eagerly received by the Italian girls, who had been "little mothers" to younger children ever since they could remember.

As a result of this teaching I recall a young girl who carefully explained to her Italian mother that the reason the babies in Italy were so healthy and the babies in Chicago were so sickly was not, as her mother had always firmly insisted, because her babies in Italy had goat's milk and her babies in America had cow's milk, but because the milk in Italy was clean and the milk in Chicago was dirty. She said that when you milked your own goat before the door you knew that the milk was clean, but when you bought milk from the grocery store after it had been carried for many miles in the country "you couldn't tell whether or not it was fit for the baby to drink until the men from the City Hall, who had watched it all the way, said that it was all right." She also informed her mother that the "City Hall wanted to fix up the milk so that it couldn't make the baby sick, but that they hadn't quite enough votes for it yet." The Italian mother believed what her child had been taught in the big school; it seemed to her quite as natural that the city should be concerned in providing pure milk for her younger children as that it should provide big schools and teachers for her older children. She reached this naïve conclusion because she had never heard those arguments which make it seem reasonable that a woman should be given the school franchise, but no other.

(b) But women are also beginning to realize that children need attention outside of school hours; that much of the petty vice in cities is merely the love of pleasure gone wrong, the overrestrained boy or girl seeking improper recreation and excitement. It is obvious that a little study of the needs of children, a sympathetic understanding of the conditions under which they go astray, might save hundreds of them. Women traditionally have had an opportunity to observe the plays of children and the needs of youth, and yet in Chicago, at least, they had done singularly little in this vexed problem of juvenile delinquency until they helped to inaugurate the Juvenile Court movement a dozen years ago. The Juvenile Court Committee, made up largely of women, paid the salaries of the probation officers connected with the court for the first six years of its existence, and after the salaries were cared for by the county the same organization turned itself into a Juvenile Protective League, and through a score of paid officers are doing valiant service in minimizing some of the dangers of city life which boys and girls encounter . . . .

. . . *(c)* As the education of her children has been more and more transferred to the school, so that even children four years old go to the kindergarten, the woman has been left in a household of constantly-narrowing interests, not only because the children are away, but also because one industry after another is slipping from the household into the factory. Ever since steam power has been applied to the processes of weaving and spinning woman's traditional work has been carried on largely outside of the home. The clothing and household linen are not only spun and woven, but also usually sewed, by machinery; the preparation of many foods has also passed into the factory and necessarily a certain number of women have been obliged to followed their work there, although it is doubtful, in spite of the large number of factory girls, whether women now are doing as large a proportion of the world's work as they used to do. Because many thousands of those working in factories and shops are girls between the ages of fourteen and twenty-two there is a necessity that older women should be interested in the conditions of industry. The very fact that these girls are not going to remain in industry permanently makes it more important that some one should see to it that they shall not be incapacitated for their future family life because they work for exhausting hours and under insanitary conditions.

If woman's sense of obligation had enlarged as the industrial conditions changed she might naturally and almost imperceptibly have inaugurated the movements for social amelioration in the line of factory legislation and shop sanitation. That she has not done so is doubtless due to the fact that her conscience is slow to recognize any obligation outside of her own family circle, and because she was so absorbed in her own household that she failed to see what the conditions outside actually were. It would be interesting to know how far the consciousness that she had no vote and could not change matters operated in this direction. After all, we see only those things to which our attention has been drawn, we feel responsibility for those things which are brought to us as matters of responsibility. If conscientious women were convinced that it was a civic duty to be informed in regard to these grave industrial affairs, and then to express the conclusions which they had reached by depositing a piece of paper in a ballot-box, one cannot imagine that they would shirk simply because the action ran counter to old traditions.

To those of my readers who would admit that although woman has no right to shirk her old obligations, that all of these measures could be secured more easily through her influence upon the men of her family than through the direct use of the ballot, I should like to tell a little story. I have a friend in Chicago who is the mother of four sons and the grandmother of twelve grandsons who are voters. She is a woman of wealth, of secured social position, of sterling character and clear intelligence, and may, therefore, quite fairly be cited as a "woman of influence." Upon one of her recent birthdays, when she was asked how she had kept so young, she promptly replied: "Because I have always advocated at least one unpopular cause." It may have been in pursuance of this policy that for many years she has been an ardent advocate of free silver, although her manufacturing family are all Republicans! I happened to call at her house on the day that Mr. McKinley was elected President against Mr. Bryan for the first time. I found my friend much disturbed. She said somewhat bitterly that she had at last discovered what the much-vaunted influence of woman was worth; that she had implored each one of her sons and grandsons, had entered into endless arguments and moral appeals to induce one of them to represent her convictions by voting for Bryan! That, although sincerely devoted to her, each one had assured her that his convictions forced him to vote the Republican ticket. She said that all she had been able to secure was the promise from one of the grandsons, for whom she had an especial tenderness because he bore her husband's name, that he would not vote at all. He could not vote for Bryan, but out of respect for her feeling he would refrain from voting for McKinley. My friend said that for many years she had suspected that women could influence men only in regard to those things in which men were not deeply concerned, but when it came to persuading a man to a woman's view in affairs of politics or business it was absolutely useless. I contended that a woman had no right to persuade a man to vote against his own convictions; that I respected the men of her family for following their own judgment regardless of the appeal which the honored head of the house had made to their chivalric devotion. To this she replied that she would agree with that point of view when a woman had the same opportunity as a man to register her convictions by vote. I believed then as I do now, that nothing is gained when independence of judgment is assailed by "influence," sentimental or otherwise, and that we test advancing civilization somewhat by our power to respect differences and by our tolerance of another's honest conviction . . . .

. . . In a complex community like the modern city all points of view need to be represented; the resultants of diverse experiences need to be pooled if the community would make for sane and balanced progress. If it would meet fairly each problem as it arises, whether it be connected with a freight tunnel having to do largely with business men, or with the increasing death rate among children under five years of age, a problem in which women are vitally concerned, or with the question of more adequate street-car transfers, in which both men and women might be said to be equally interested, it must not ignore the judgments of its entire adult population.

To turn the administration of our civic affairs wholly over to men may mean that the American city will continue to push forward in its commercial and industrial development, and continue to lag behind in those things which make a city healthful and beautiful. After all, woman's traditional function has been to make her dwelling-place both clean and fair. Is that dreariness in city life, that lack of domesticity which the humblest farm dwelling presents, due to a withdrawal of one of the naturally coöperating forces? If women have in any sense been responsible for the gentler side of life which softens and blurs some of its harsher conditions, may they not have a duty to perform in our American cities?

In closing, may I recapitulate that if woman would fulfill her traditional responsibility to her own children; if she would educate and protect from danger factory children who must find their recreation on the street; if she would bring the cultural forces to bear upon our materialistic civilization; and if she would do it all with the dignity and directness fitting one who carries on her immemorial duties, then she must bring herself to the use of the ballot—that latest implement for self-government. May we not fairly say that American women need this implement in order to preserve the home?

65 Simone de Beauvoir, from *The Second Sex* (Pan Books, 1988), pp. 733–5

Born in Paris, de Beauvoir (1908–1986) was among the first women to be allowed to complete a programme of study at the *École normale supérieure*. She was an outstanding student of philosophy at the Sorbonne, graduating just behind Jean Paul Sartre, her long-time companion and intellectual collaborator. After leaving a teaching post, she moved to Paris and was involved in the clandestine newspaper *Combat*. She became a prolific novelist and a key philosophical influence in post-war France. Her major book, *The Second Sex*, was published in 1949 (see extract below). In it she traced the development of male oppression through historical, literary, and mythical sources. This earned her the reputation of the 'mother' of second-wave feminism, though she was sometimes out of sympathy with other feminist thinkers. She did, however, publicly identify with the women's movement and its various constituent campaigns.

A world where men and women would be equal is easy to visualize, for that precisely is what the Soviet Revolution *promised*: women reared and trained exactly like men were to work under the same conditions and for the same wages. Erotic liberty was to be recognized by custom, but the sexual act was not to be considered a 'service' to be paid for; woman was to be *obliged* to provide herself with other ways of earning a living; marriage was to be based on a free agreement that the contracting parties could break at will; maternity was to be voluntary, which meant that contraception and abortion were to be authorized and that, on the other hand, all mothers and their children were to have exactly the same rights, in or out of marriage; pregnancy leaves were to be paid for by the State, which would assume charge of the children, signifying not that they would be *taken away* from their parents, but that they would not be *abandoned* to them.

But is it enough to change laws, institutions, customs, public opinion, and the whole social context, for men and women to become truly equal? 'Women will always be women,' say the sceptics. Other seers prophesy that in casting off their femininity they will not succeed in changing themselves into men and they will become monsters. This would be to admit that the woman of today is a creation of nature; it must be repeated once more that in human society nothing is natural and that woman, like much else, is a product elaborated by civilization. The intervention of others in her destiny is fundamental: if this action took a different direction, it would produce a quite different result. Woman is determined not by her hormones or by mysterious instincts, but by the manner in which her body and her relation to the world are modified through the action of others than herself. The abyss that separates the adolescent boy and girl has been deliberately widened between them since earliest childhood; later on, woman could not be other than what she *was made*,and that past was bound to shadow her for life. If we appreciate its influence, we see clearly that her destiny is not predetermined for all eternity.

We must not believe, certainly, that a change in woman's economic condition alone is enough to transform her, though this factor has been and remains the basic factor in her evolution; but until it has brought about the moral, social, cultural, and other consequences that it promises and requires, the new woman cannot appear. At this moment they have been realized nowhere, in Russia no more than in France or the United States; and this explains why the woman of today is torn between the past and the future. She appears most often as a 'true woman' disguised as a man, and she feels herself as ill at ease in her flesh as in her masculine garb. She must shed her old skin and cut her own new clothes. This she could do only through a social evolution. No single educator could fashion a *female human being* today who would be the exact homologue of the *male human being*; if she is brought up like a boy, the young girl feels she is an oddity and thereby she is given a new kind of sex specification. Stendhal understood this when he said: 'The forest must be planted all at once.' But if we imagine, on the contrary, a society in which the equality of the sexes would be concretely realized, this equality would find new expression in each individual.

If the little girl were brought up from the first with the same demands and rewards, the same severity and the same freedom, as her brothers, taking part in the same studies, the same games, promised the same future, surrounded with women and men who seemed to her undoubted equals, the meanings of the castration complex and of the Oedipus complex would be profoundly modified. Assuming on the same basis as the father the material and moral responsibility of the couple, the mother would enjoy the same lasting prestige; the child would perceive around her an androgynous world and not a masculine world. Were she emotionally more attracted to her father—which is not even sure—her love for him would be tinged with a will to emulation and not a feeling of powerlessness; she would not be oriented towards passivity. Authorized to test her powers in work and sports, competing actively with the boys, she would not find the absence of the penis—compensated by the promise of a child—enough to give rise to an inferiority complex; correlatively the boy would not have a superiority complex if it were not instilled into him and if he looked up to women with as much respect as to men. The little girl would not seek sterile compensation in narcissism and dreaming, she would not take her fate for granted; she would be interested in what she was *doing*, she would throw herself without reserve into undertakings.

66   Kate Millett, from *Sexual Politics* (Granada Publishing, 1971), pp. 24–30

Millett (1934–) was born in St. Paul in Minnesota. She was educated at the University of Minnesota, at St. Hilda's College in Oxford, and then at Columbia University. Though she later became a well-known feminist campaigner and author, she was by training a sculptor and artist. She became a Distinguished Visiting Professor at Sacramento State College in 1973, and has been a member of the Congress of Racial Enquiry since 1965.

The following sketch, which might be described as "notes toward a theory of patriarchy," will attempt to prove that sex is a status category with political implications. Something of a pioneering effort, it must perforce be both tentative and imperfect. Because the intention is to provide an overall description, statements must be generalized, exceptions neglected, and subheadings overlapping and, to some degree, arbitrary as well.

The word "politics" is enlisted here when speaking of the sexes primarily because such a word is eminently useful in outlining the real nature of their relative status, historically and at the present. It is opportune, perhaps today even mandatory, that we develop a more relevant psychology and philosophy of power relationships beyond the simple conceptual framework provided by our traditional formal politics. Indeed, it may be imperative that we give some attention to defining a theory of politics which treats of power relationships on grounds less conventional than those to which we are accustomed. I have therefore found it pertinent to define them on grounds of personal contact and interaction between members of well-defined and coherent groups: races, castes, classes, and sexes. For it is precisely because certain groups have no representation in a number of recognized political structures that their position tends to be so stable, their oppression so continuous.

In America, recent events have forced us to acknowledge at last that the relationship between the races is indeed a political one which involves the general control of one collectivity, defined by birth, over another collectivity, also defined by birth. Groups who rule by birthright are fast disappearing, yet there remains one ancient and universal scheme for the domination of one birth group by another—the scheme that prevails in the area of sex. The study of racism has convinced us that a truly political state of affairs operates between the races to perpetuate a series of oppressive circumstances. The subordinated group has inadequate redress through existing political institutions, and is deterred thereby from organizing into conventional political struggle and opposition.

Quite in the same manner, a disinterested examination of our system of sexual relationship must point out that the situation between the sexes now, and throughout history, is a case of that phenomenon Max Weber defined as *herrschaft*, a relationship of dominance and subordinance. What goes largely unexamined, often even unacknow-ledged (yet is institutionalized nonetheless) in our social order, is the birthright priority whereby males rule females. Through this system a most ingenious form of "interior colonization" has been achieved. It is one which tends moreover to be sturdier than any form of segregation, and more rigorous than class stratification, more uniform, certainly more enduring. However muted its present appearance may be, sexual dominion obtains nevertheless as perhaps the most pervasive ideology of our culture and provides its most fundamental concept of power.

This is so because our society, like all other historical civilizations, is a patriarchy. The fact is evident at once if one recalls that the military, industry, technology, universities, science, political office, and finance—in short, every avenue of power within the society, including the coercive force of the police, is entirely in male hands. As the essence of politics is power, such realization cannot fail to carry impact. What lingers of supernatural authority, the Deity, "His" ministry, together with the ethics and values, the philosophy and art of our culture—its very civilization—as T. S. Eliot once observed, is of male manufacture.

If one takes patriarchal government to be the institution whereby that half of the populace which is female is controlled by that half which is male, the principles of patriarchy appear to be two fold: male shall dominate female, elder male shall dominate younger. However, just as with any human institution, there is frequently a distance between the real and the ideal; contradictions and exceptions do exist within the system. While patriarchy as an institution is a social constant so deeply entrenched as to run through all other political, social, or economic forms, whether of caste or class, feudality or bureaucracy, just as it pervades all major religions, it also exhibits great variety in history and locale. In democracies, for example, females have often held no office or do so (as now) in such minuscule numbers as to be below even token representation. Aristocracy, on the other hand, with its emphasis upon the magic and dynastic properties of blood, may at times permit women to hold power. The principle of rule by elder males is violated even more frequently. Bearing in mind the variation and degree in patriarchy—as say between Saudi Arabia and Sweden, Indonesia and Red China—we also recognize our own form in the U.S. and Europe to be much altered and attenuated by the reforms described in the next chapter.

I IDEOLOGICAL

Hannah Arendt has observed that government is upheld by power supported either through consent or imposed through violence. Conditioning to an ideology amounts to the former. Sexual politics obtains consent through the "socialization" of both sexes to basic patriarchal polities with regard to temperament, role, and status. As to status, a pervasive assent to the prejudice of male superiority guarantees superior status in the male, inferior in the female. The first item, temperament, involves the formation of human personality along stereotyped lines of sex category ("masculine" and "feminine"), based on the needs and values of the dominant group and dictated by what its members cherish in themselves and find convenient in subordinates: aggression, intelligence, force, and efficacy in the male; passivity, ignorance, docility, "virtue," and ineffectuality in the female. This is complemented by a second factor, sex role, which decrees a consonant and highly elaborate code of conduct, gesture and attitude for each sex. In terms of activity, sex role assigns domestic service and attendance upon infants to the female, the rest of human achievement, interest, and ambition to the male. The limited role allotted the female tends to arrest her at the level of biological experience. Therefore, nearly all that can be described as distinctly human rather than animal activity (in their own way animals also give birth and care for their young) is largely reserved for the male. Of course, status again follows from such an assignment. Were one to analyze the three categories one might designate status as the political component, role as the sociological, and temperament as the psychological—yet their interdependence is unquestionable and they form a chain. Those awarded higher status tend to adopt roles of mastery, largely because they are first encouraged to develop temperaments of dominance. That this is true of caste and class as well is self-evident.

II BIOLOGICAL

Patriarchal religion, popular attitude, and to some degree, science as well assumes these psycho-social distinctions to rest upon biological differences between the sexes, so that where culture is acknowledged as shaping behavior, it is said to do no more than cooperate with nature. Yet the temperamental distinctions created in patriarchy ("masculine" and "feminine" personality traits) do not appear to originate in human nature, those of role and status still less.

The heavier musculature of the male, a secondary sexual characteristic and common among mammals, is biological in origin but is also culturally encouraged through breeding, diet and exercise. Yet it is hardly an adequate category on which to base political relations *within civilization*. Male supremacy, like other political creeds, does not finally reside in physical strength but in the acceptance of a value system which is not biological. Superior physical strength is not a factor in political relations—vide those of race and class. Civilization has always been able to substitute other methods (technic, weaponry, knowledge) for those of physical strength, and contemporary civilization has no further need of it. At present, as in the past, physical exertion is very generally a class factor, those at the bottom performing the most strenuous tasks, whether they be strong or not.

It is often assumed that patriarchy is endemic in human social life, explicable or even inevitable on the grounds of human physiology. Such a theory grants patriarchy logical as well as historical origin. Yet if as some anthropologists believe, patriarchy is not of primeval origin, but was preceded by some other social form we shall call pre-patriarchal, then the argument of physical strength as a theory of patriarchal *origins* would hardly constitute a sufficient explanation—unless the male's superior physical strength was released in accompaniment with some change in orientation through new values or new knowledge. Conjecture about origins is always frustrated by lack of certain evidence. Speculation about prehistory, which of necessity is what this must be, remains nothing but speculation. Were one to indulge in it, one might argue the likelihood of a hypothetical period preceding patriarchy. What would be crucial to such a premise would be a state of mind in which the primary principle would be regarded as fertility or vitalist processes. In a primitive condition, before it developed civilization or any but the crudest technic, humanity would perhaps find the most impressive evidence of creative force in the visible birth of children, something of a miraculous event and linked analogically with the growth of the earth's vegetation.

It is possible that the circumstance which might drastically redirect such attitudes would be the discovery of paternity. There is some evidence that fertility cults in ancient society at some point took a turn toward patriarchy, displacing and downgrading female function in procreation and attributing the power of life to the phallus alone. Patriarchal religion could consolidate this position by the creation of a male God or gods, demoting, discrediting, or eliminating goddesses and constructing a theology whose basic postulates are male supremacist, and one of whose central functions is to uphold and validate the patriarchal structure.

So much for the evanescent delights afforded by the game of origins. The question of the historical origins of patriarchy—whether patriarchy originated primordially in the male's superior strength, or upon a later mobilization of such strength under certain circumstances—appears at the moment to be unanswerable. It is also probably irrelevant to contemporary patriarchy, where we are left with the realities of sexual politics, still grounded, we are often assured, on nature. Unfortunately, as the psycho-social distinctions made between the two sex groups which are said to justify their present political relationship are not the clear, specific, measurable and neutral ones of the physical sciences, but are instead of an entirely different character—vague, amorphous, often even quasi-religious in phrasing—it must be admitted that many of the generally understood distinctions between the sexes in the more significant areas of role and temperament, not to mention status, have in fact, essentially cultural, rather than biological, bases. Attempts to prove that temperamental dominance is inherent in the male (which for its advocates, would be tantamount to validating, logically as well as historically, the patriarchal situation regarding role and status) have been notably unsuccessful. Sources in the field are in hopeless disagreement about the nature of sexual differences, but the most reasonable among them have despaired of the ambition of any definite equation between temperament and biological nature. It appears that we are not soon to be enlightened as to the existence of any significant inherent differences between male and female beyond the bio-genital ones we already know. Endocrinology and genetics afford no definite evidence of determining mental-emotional differences.

Not only is there insufficient evidence for the thesis that the present social distinctions of patriarchy (status, role, temperament) are physical in origin, but we are hardly in a position to assess the existing differentiations, since distinctions which we know to be culturally induced at present so outweigh them. Whatever the "real" differences between the sexes may be, we are not likely to know them until the sexes are treated differently, that is alike. And this is very far from being the case at present. Important new research not only suggests that the possibilities of innate temperamental differences seem more remote than ever, but even raises questions as to the validity and permanence of psycho-sexual identity. In doing so it gives fairly concrete positive evidence of the overwhelmingly *cultural* character of gender, i.e. personality structure in terms of sexual category.

What Stoller and other experts define as "core gender identity" is now thought to be established in the young by the age of eighteen months. This is how Stoller differentiates between sex and gender:

Dictionaries stress that the major connotation of *sex* is a biological one, as for example, in the phrases *sexual relations* or *the male sex*. In agreement with this, the word *sex*, in this work will refer to the male or female sex and the component biological parts that determine whether one is a male or a female; the word *sexual* will have connotations of anatomy and physiology. This obviously leaves tremendous areas of behavior, feelings, thoughts and fantasies that are related to the sexes and yet do not have primarily biological connotations. It is for some of these psychological phenomena that the term gender will be used: one can speak of the male sex or the female sex, but one can also talk about masculinity and feminity and not necessarily be implying anything about anatomy or physiology. Thus, while *sex* and *gender* seem to common sense inextricably bound together, one purpose this study will be to confirm the fact that the two realms (sex and gender) are not inevitably bound in anything like a one-to-one relationship, but each may go into quite independent ways.

In cases of genital malformation and consequent erroneous gender assignment at birth, studied at the California Gender Identity Center, the discovery was made that it is easier to change the sex of an adolescent male, whose biological identity turns out to be contrary to his gender assignment and conditioning—through surgery—than to undo the educational consequences of years, which have succeeded in making the subject temperamentally feminine in gesture, sense of self, personality and interests. Studies done in California under Stoller's direction offer proof that gender identity (I am a girl, I am a boy) is the primary identity any human being holds—the first as well as the most permanent and far-reaching. Stoller later makes emphatic the distinction that sex is biological, gender psychological, and therefore cultural: "*Gender* is a term that has psychological or cultural rather than biological connotations. If the proper terms for sex are "male" and "female," the corresponding terms for gender are "masculine" and "feminine"; these latter may be quite independent of (biological) sex." Indeed, so arbitrary is gender, that it may even be contrary to physiology: ". . . although the external genitalia (penis, testes, scrotum) contribute to the sense of maleness, no one of them is essential for it, not even all of them together. In the absence of complete evidence, I agree in general with Money, and the Hampsons who show in their large series of intersexed patients that gender role is determined by postnatal forces, regardless of the anatomy and physiology of the external genitalia."

67 Lynne Segal, from *Is the Future Female? Troubled Thoughts on Contemporary Feminism* (Virago, 1987), pp. 1–6.

Born in Sydney, Australia, Segal (1943–) came to London in 1970, having completed a doctorate on the theories and practices of experimental psychology. She was an active participant in both the women's movement and left politcs during the 1970s, and was instrumental in the establishment of a variety of resource centres, campaigns and cultural activities in Islington, London. She was a key member of the collective that edited the journal *Feminist Review*. She taught psychology at Middlesex Polytechnic and was later appointed Professor of Gender Studies, (also at Middlesex). More recently she was appointed Professor of Psychology and Gender Studies at Birkbeck College at the University of London.

1. COMPENSATIONS OF THE POWERLESS: THE THEMES OF POPULAR FEMINISM

> To cast out and incorporate in a person of the opposite sex all we miss in ourselves and desire in the universe and detest in humanity is a deep and universal instinct on the part of both men and women. But though it affords relief, it does not lead to understanding. Rochester is as great a travesty of the truth about men as Cordelia is of the truth about women.
>
> Virginia Woolf

> Feminists have their own version of the Tower of Babel story, They feel that men have undermined women by confounding their language, the language of their bodies, their unconscious, their desire or their experience. In order to act together an authentic language of women must be forged. If there is no common language there can be no true collective action.
>
> Deborah Cameron

I have often sought power in devious ways but I have never been content to be powerless, unnoticed or simply passive. Nor has any other woman I have known. But women's sense of their own power is usually hard to sustain. Most women know only too well the feelings of being trapped, confined and devalued. Subordination to some man's authority regularly threatens to smother the strength and autonomy most of us experience at least at some point in our lives. However, the material disadvantages and cultural devaluation of women compared to men exist alongside an affirmation of 'female' values, virtues and traits. Women can and do find comfort and strength in the confirming consolations of their relative powerlessness, in the existing ideas and ideals of 'men' and 'women'.

Some of these consolations, like the genuine pleasures of motherhood and of running a home, do give women power. Mother dragons may frighten or entrance the kids and may even threaten Father, at least within the confines of home, however much their real domestic lives may be based on financial dependence and social subservience. Other confirming compensations, like the glamour and pleasures of fashion, (now increasingly sought by young men) or the fantasies of romantic fiction, can enable women, if only vicariously, to experience themselves as the fiercely desired objects of those with greater power and status. Out at work, the secretary in her office may be proudly aware that a department could not function without her and that her boss depends on her knowledge of all aspects of his business. She lacks only his authority, money and prestige.

'Feminists', however, are seen as women who scorn such compensatory trappings. This perception certainly did initially apply to the second wave of organised feminism. We did want real power, in every sphere. By power we meant not the means to control and dominate others—at least that is not what most of us thought we wanted—but rather the freedom and space to express our own desires, creativity and potential: to flourish and to find 'our place in the sun'. We sought to build the collective power of all women. We wanted power to participate in the making of a new world which would be free from all forms of domination. These goals were summed up, if rather inelegantly, in the manifesto prepared for the first British Women's Liberation Conference in Oxford in 1970:

> We want eventually to be, and to help other women to be, in charge of our own lives . . . We come together as groups and as individuals to further our part in the struggle for social change and the transformation of society.

Today, the public face of feminism has changed. At any feminist gathering you are far more likely to hear assertions about the special nature of women and their values, with references to the separate and special 'world of women'. It may seem ironic that radical ideas and strategies should rely on conventional assumptions of 'masculinity' and 'femininity', but it is this *traditional* gender ideology which has become the *new* 'common sense' of feminism.

After two decades of feminist research, it is now easier to see that men globally have greater wealth, power and privilege than women. However, it is harder for feminists to agree on the theories or the strategies to explain this or to challenge it. We do know that everywhere, despite the liberal aspirations of the 'decade of women' (the 'invisible decade', as it has been called), women remain considerably poorer and less educated than men, and are largely absent from positions of power in *all* political, economic, religious, cultural and judicial institutions. Ironically, the very popularity and acceptability of many aspects of feminist thought here in Britain across political perspectives, including the conservative, makes the continuing power of men all the harder to understand. Some men, as well as women, applaud much that feminists are saying. Some men shed tears over their own beastliness. But men's power seems all the more invincible as recognition and resistance *appear* to leave it unchanged and immutable. Is feminism itself falling back upon the traditional consolations of the powerless? Certain developments suggest to me that it is.

THE VIRTUES OF WOMEN

The feminist writing which is now most popular in this country, which is always listed among the bestsellers in progressive literary magazines, is a new form of radical feminism.

Mostly from North America, where it is known as 'cultural feminism', it celebrates women's superior virtue and spirituality and decries 'male' violence and technology. Such celebration of the 'female' and denunciation of the 'male', however, arouses fear and suspicion in feminists who, like me, recall that we joined the women's movement to challenge the myths of women's special nature.

Some of us also recall, from the history feminists have revealed, how thoroughly the attempt to revalue women's special virtues and motherhood in the 1920s and 1930s overtook and eventually crushed more confident and rebellious feminisms. Back in 1913, a very young Rebecca West was warning feminists of the 'sin of self-sacrifice', which could turn a movement 'from a march towards freedom to a romp towards voluptuous servitude. Yet today, like any Victorian gentleman, Robin Morgan, Adrienne Rich, Susan Griffin, Judith Arcana, Mary Daly, Dale Spender and their many followers, take for granted and celebrate women's greater humanism, pacifism, nurturance and spiritual development. Robin Morgan tells us that only women can guarantee the future of life on earth. Ronald Reagan and the New Right in the US and anti-feminist conservatives here in Britain tell us much the same thing. Women can save the world from the nightmares of nuclear weaponry, which represents the untamed force of 'male drives and male sexuality', through the power of the feminine mentality and the force of maternal concerns. For the right, this would not of course be achieved by those they have characterised as 'the screaming destructive witches of Greenham', but rather by a return to the traditional values of Victorian family life, where women may continue, in the words of Tory philosopher Roger Scruton, 'to quieten' the 'unbridled ambition of the phallus'.

Feminist thought has always confronted intractable dilemmas in its own appraisal of women. Not only must it fight to end the subjection of women, and to eradicate the existing gender ideologies which endorse and maintain it, but it must fight to protect and respect women in their existing vulnerability and weakness. This means rejecting the cultural disparagement and insidiously false veneration of all that is 'female'. Asserting women's strength and value sits awkwardly beside an awareness that many of women's most distinctive experiences and perceptions are products of subordination.

There is, of course, nothing surprising about the observation that dignity and strength may emerge through subordination and weakness—along with inequality and diminished lives and possibilities. One of the first public declarations of British feminism, Mary Wollstonecraft's manifesto *A Vindication of The Rights of Woman*, published in 1792, portrayed women as emotionally and intellectually stunted by their lives as women and by the prevailing conceptions of true womanhood. But many suffragettes just over a century later elaborated similar conceptions of 'female nature' to insist upon the benefits of enfranchising the 'mothers' of the nation. Tactically, at least, it is clear that women can push for reforms, perhaps even most successfully, without any fundamental challenge to existing gender arrangements (that is, to the social relations between women and men) and the beliefs which maintain them. But the excitement of the feminism I once knew was precisely its promise that we *could* transform our own ideas of ourselves as women, hopefully keeping what was good in what we had learned from subordination, to create quite new relations between women and men, and between women and the world. We did not want to be like men; we wanted to be something new, and better.

Such talk of transformation and change is not found in the new idealised image of women in much contemporary feminism. Here is Susan Griffin:

> We [women] can read bodies with our hands, read the earth, find water, trace gravity's path. We know what grows and how to balance one thing against another . . . and even if over our bodies they [men] have transformed this earth, we say, the truth is, to this day, women still dream.

It is true, of course, if we generalise, that women are in many situations warmer, more sensitive and more caring of others than men; women usually seem less aggressive and competitive than men. And men have always told us that we are. Renowned misogynists like Kingsley Amis find security and comfort in their patronising belief that 'women are really much nicer than men. No wonder we like them.' The image and reality of women's 'niceness', we can all agree, is connected with women's primary involvement with mothering and caring for others. But it is women's mothering and nurturing activities, and the social beliefs which support them, which are crucial to the maintenance of women's general subordination and economic dependence. While the virtues of maternal loving and caring are obvious, they have never been materially valued but instead applauded only with the hypocrisy of cheap sentiment. Might it not be, as some feminists once forcefully argued, that the reason men do not rear children in our society is not to do with any essential incapacity but because it provides little social prestige and little power?

Moreover, the virtues of maternal love can also be problematic. In our intensely individualistic, competitive, capitalist society, love and concern for others become inappropriate outside our very own small family groupings. Class privilege and racist exclusion are most frequently justified, by both women and men, in terms of the interests of one's own children. Narrowly focused on what often seems the threatened and precarious wellbeing of each individual child, maternal behaviour can be over-anxious and controlling, clinging and possessive. Children do become the self-enhancing surrogates for their parents' abandoned dreams. Within the context of male dominance, children may be the only reparation for a woman's more general frustrations and sense of powerlessness. Women's maternal selflessness can easily become a type of unconscious maternal selfishness, and an inability to allow children to develop caring relations with others.

The weight of responsibility for one's own children can mean a contraction of social vision, an envy and resentment of the welfare of others. So, for instance, while it may be true that women are more concerned about peace and a better world for their children (and, certainly, some women are organising for peace at Greenham and in nuclear disarmament groups) this does not necessarily mean that women are any less nationalistic, racist or committed to class privilege than men. Women, in this sense, participate in the social world they share with men, however subordinate they are to men in their own group. An awareness of these contradictions was central to the feminist writing of the early seventies, when, for example, Juliet Mitchell assessed the effects of women's oppression within the family like this:

> It produces a tendency to small-mindedness, petty jealousy, irrational emotionality and random violence, dependency, competitive selfishness and possessiveness, passivity, a lack of vision and conservatism.

The suggestion that any such weaknesses are bound up with the objective conditions of women's mothering is disappearing from the contemporary celebration of female virtues and values.

68 Susan Moller Okin, from *Justice, Gender, and the Family* (Basic Books, 1989), pp. 7–8, 14–15

Born in New Zealand, Okin (1947–2004) read History at the University of Auckland. She continued her studies first in Oxford and then gained her doctorate at Harvard. From 1970 to 1985 she taught at Brandeis University, Massachusetts, and was Professor of Ethics in Society and Political Science at Stanford University after 1990. She is best known for her books *Women in Western Political Thought* (1979) and *Justice, Gender and the Family* (1989). In the first of these volumes, she argued that gender issues are central to modern political thinking, despite being conventionally overlooked or marginalized. More recently, she offered a controversial intervention in liberal debates about multiculturalism, stressing the incompatibility between gender equality and the case for granting group rights to non-liberal cultural traditions and communities. Towards the end of her life she turned her attention to models of economic development and their implications for women's rights.

THEORIES OF JUSTICE AND THE NEGLECT OF GENDER

During these same two decades, there has been a great resurgence of theories of social justice. Political theory, which had been sparse for a period before the late 1960s except as an important branch of intellectual history, has become a flourishing field, with social justice as its central concern. Yet, remarkably, major contemporary theorists of justice have almost without exception ignored the situation I have just described. They have displayed little interest in or knowledge of the findings of feminism. They have largely bypassed the fact that the society to which their theories are supposed to pertain is heavily and deeply affected by gender, and faces difficult issues of justice stemming from its gendered past and present assumptions. Since theories of justice are centrally concerned with whether, how, and why persons should be treated differently from one another, this neglect seems inexplicable. These theories are *about* which initial or acquired characteristics or positions in society legitimize differential treatment of persons by social institutions, laws, and customs. They are *about* how and whether and to what extent beginnings should affect outcomes. The division of humanity into two sexes seems to provide an obvious subject for such inquiries. But, as we shall see, this does not strike most contemporary theorists of justice, and their theories suffer in both coherence and relevance because of it. This book is about this remarkable case of neglect. It is also an attempt to rectify it, to point the way toward a more fully humanist theory of justice by confronting the question, "How just is gender?"

Why is it that when we turn to contemporary theories of justice, we do not find illuminating and positive contributions to this question? How can theories of justice that are ostensibly about people in general neglect women, gender, and all the inequalities between the sexes? One reason is that most theorists *assume*, though they do not discuss, the traditional, gender-structured family. Another is that they often employ gender-neutral language in a false, hollow way. Let us examine these two points.

. . .

GENDER AS AN ISSUE OF JUSTICE

For three major reasons, this state of affairs is unacceptable. The first is the obvious point that women must be fully included in any satisfactory theory of justice. The second is that equality of opportunity, not only for women but for children of both sexes, is seriously undermined by the current gender injustices of our society. And the third reason is that, as has already been suggested, the family—currently the linchpin of the gender structure—must be just if we are to have a just society, since it is within the family that we first come to have that sense of ourselves and our relations with others that is at the root of moral development.

Counting Women In

When we turn to the great tradition of Western political thought with questions about the justice of the treatment of the sexes in mind, it is to little avail. Bold feminists like Mary Astell, Mary Wollstonecraft, William Thompson, Harriet Taylor, and George Bernard Shaw have occasionally challenged the tradition, often using its own premises and arguments to overturn its explicit or implicit justification of the inequality of women. But John Stuart Mill is a rare exception to the rule that those who hold central positions in the tradition almost never question the justice of the subordination of women. This phenomenon is undoubtedly due in part to the fact that Aristotle, whose theory of justice has been so influential, relegated women to a sphere of "household justice"—populated by persons who are not fundamentally equal to the free men who participate in political justice, but inferiors whose natural function is to serve those who are more fully human. The liberal tradition, despite its supposed foundation of individual rights and human equality, is more Aristotelian in this respect than is generally acknowledged. In one way or another, almost all liberal theorists have assumed that the "individual" who is the basic subject of the theories is the male head of a patriarchal household. Thus they have not usually considered applying the principles of justice to women or to relations between the sexes.

When we turn to contemporary theories of justice, however, we expect to find more illuminating and positive contributions to the subject of gender and justice. As the omission of the family and the falseness of their gender-neutral language suggest, however, mainstream contemporary theories of justice do not address the subject any better than those of the past. Theories of justice that apply to only half of us simply won't do; the inclusiveness falsely implied by the current use of gender-neutral terms must become real. Theories of justice must apply to all of us, and to all of human life, instead of *assuming* silently that half of us take care of whole areas of life that are considered outside the scope of social justice. In a just society, the structure and practices of families must afford women the same opportunities as men to develop their capacities, to participate in political power, to influence social choices, and to be economically as well as physically secure.

Unfortunately, much feminist intellectual energy in the 1980s has gone into the claim that "justice" and "rights" are masculinist ways of thinking about morality that feminists should eschew or radically revise, advocating a morality of care. The emphasis is misplaced, I think, for several reasons. First, what is by now a vast literature on the subject shows that the evidence for differences in women's and men's ways of thinking about moral issues is not (at least yet) very clear; neither is the evidence about the source of whatever differences there might be. It may well turn out that any differences can be readily explained in terms of roles, including female primary parenting, that are socially determined and therefore alterable. There is certainly no evidence—nor could there be, in such a gender-structured society—for concluding that women are somehow naturally more inclined toward contextuality and away from universalism in their moral thinking, a false concept that unfortunately reinforces the old stereotypes that justify separate spheres. The capacity of reactionary forces to capitalize on the "different moralities" strain in feminism is particularly evident in Pope John Paul II's recent Apostolic Letter, "On the Dignity of Women," in which he refers to women's special capacity to care for others in arguing for confining them to motherhood or celibacy.

Second, as I shall explain in chapter 5, I think the distinction between an ethic of justice and an ethic of care has been overdrawn. The best theorizing about justice, I argue, has integral to it the notions of care and empathy, of thinking of the interests and well-being of others who may be very different from ourselves. It is, therefore, misleading to draw a dichotomy as though they were two contrasting ethics. The best theorizing about justice is not some abstract "view from nowhere," but results from the carefully attentive consideration of *everyone's* point of view. This means, of course, that the best theorizing about justice is not good enough if it does not, or cannot readily be adapted to, include women and their points of view as fully as men and their points of view.

69 Carol Gilligan, from *In a Different Voice: Psychological Theory and Women's Development* (Harvard University Press, 1993), pp. 100–1

Gilligan (1936–) was a student of the eminent psychological theorist Lawrence Kohlberg. It is his account of moral reasoning, with its emphasis upon the achievement of a position of impartiality by a reasoning subject, that is the primary object of her critical thinking. Based upon her interviews with women about their responses to various moral dilemmas, she argued that their thinking did not fit with Kohlberg's or other conventional models in her major work, *In a Different Voice* (1982). She has held high-profile posts at the Universities of Harvard and Rutgers in the United States, and Cambridge in the UK.

The moral imperative that emerges repeatedly in interviews with women is an injunction to care, a responsibility to discern and alleviate the "real and recognizable trouble" of this world. For men, the moral imperative appears rather as an injunction to respect the rights of others and thus to protect from interference the rights to life and self-fulfillment.

Women's insistence on care is at first self-critical rather than self-protective, while men initially conceive obligation to others negatively in terms of noninterference. Development for both sexes would therefore seem to entail an integration of rights and responsibilities through the discovery of the complementarity of these disparate views. For women, the integration of rights and responsibilities takes place through an understanding of the psychological logic of relationships. This understanding tempers the self-destructive potential of a self-critical morality by asserting the need of all persons for care. For men, recognition through experience of the need for more active responsibility in taking care corrects the potential indifference of a morality of noninterference and turns attention from the logic to the consequences of choice (Gilligan and Murphy, 1979; Gilligan, 1981). In the development of a postconventional ethical understanding, women come to see the violence inherent in inequality, while men come to see the limitations of a conception of justice blinded to the differences in human life.

Hypothetical dilemmas, in the abstraction of their presentation, divest moral actors from the history and psychology of their individual lives and separate the moral problem from the social contingencies of its possible occurrence. In doing so, these dilemmas are useful for the distillation and refinement of objective principles of justice and for measuring the formal logic of equality and reciprocity. However, the reconstruction of the dilemma in its contextual particularity allows the understanding of cause and consequence which engages the compassion and tolerance repeatedly noted to distinguish the moral judgments of women. Only when substance is given to the skeletal lives of hypothetical people is it possible to consider the social injustice that their moral problems may reflect and to imagine the individual suffering their occurrence may signify or their resolution engender.

The proclivity of women to reconstruct hypothetical dilemmas in terms of the real, to request or to supply missing information about the nature of the people and the places where they live, shifts their judgment away from the hierarchical ordering of principles and the formal procedures of decision making. This insistence on the particular signifies an orientation to the dilemma and to moral problems in general that differs from any current developmental stage descriptions. Consequently, though several of the women in the abortion study clearly articulate a postconventional metaethical position, none of them are considered principled in their normative moral judgments of Kohlberg's hypothetical dilemmas. Instead, the women's judgments point toward an identification of the violence inherent in the dilemma itself, which is seen to compromise the justice of any of its possible resolutions. This construction of the dilemma leads the women to recast the moral judgment from a consideration of the good to a choice between evils.

70   **Julia Kristeva, from 'Women's Time', in *The Kristeva Reader* (ed. Toril Moi; Blackwell, 1989), pp. 193–5**

Born in Bulgaria, Kristeva (1941–) arrived in Paris in 1966 and studied with Lucien Goldmann and Roland Barthes. Over the next ten years she made an important contribution to psycho-analytic theorizing in relation to literature and language. She has written widely on political questions, developing her argument that the unconscious is a source of resistance to social order (she has practised as a psychoanalyst since 1979). More recently, as she has turned away from Marxism and familiar forms of left politics, she has urged the merits of the *avant-garde* ethos of critical dissent and lamented the failures of mass movements and conventional politics. These ideas were informed by her participation in the community of critics and thinkers who collaborated under the name of *Tel Quel* in the 1970s and 1980s. Kristeva's significance for feminism lies particularly in her assessment of how Western culture and thought has repressed the value of the 'maternal'.

In its beginnings, the women's movement, as the struggle of suffragists and of existential feminists, aspired to gain a place in linear time as the time of project and history. In this sense, the movement, while immediately universalist, is also deeply rooted in the socio-political life of nations. The political demands of women; the struggles for equal pay for equal work, for taking power in social institutions on an equal footing with men; the rejection, when necessary, of the attributes traditionally considered feminine or maternal in so far as they are deemed incompatible with insertion in that history—all are part of the *logic of identification* with certain values: not with the ideological (these are combated, and rightly so, as reactionary) but, rather, with the logical and ontological values of a rationality dominant in the nation-state. Here it is unnecessary to enumerate the benefits which this logic of identification and the ensuing struggle have achieved and continue to achieve for women (abortion, contraception, equal pay, professional recognition, etc.); these have already had or will soon have effects even more important than those of the Industrial Revolution. Universalist in its approach, this current in feminism *globalizes* the problems of women of different milieux, ages, civilizations or simply of varying psychic structures, under the label 'Universal Woman'. A consideration of *generations* of women can only be conceived of in this global way as a succession, as a progression in the accomplishment of the initial programme mapped out by its founders.

In a second phase, linked, on the one hand, to the younger women who came to feminism after May 1968 and, on the other, to women who had an aesthetic or psychoanalytic experience, linear temporality has been almost totally refused, and as a consequence there has arisen an exacerbated distrust of the entire political dimension. If it is true that this more recent current of feminism refers to its predecessors and that the struggle for socio-cultural recognition of women is necessarily its main concern, this current seems to think of itself as belonging to another generation—qualitatively different from the first one— in its conception of its own identity and, consequently, of temporality as such. Essentially interested in the specificity of female psychology and its symbolic realizations, these women seek to give a language to the intrasubjective and corporeal experiences left mute by culture in the past. Either as artists or writers, they have undertaken a veritable exploration of the *dynamic of signs*, an exploration which relates this tendency, at least at the level of its aspirations, to all major projects of aesthetic and religious upheaval. Ascribing this experience to a new generation does not only mean that other, more subtle problems have been added to the demands for socio-political identification made in the beginning. It also means that, by demanding recognition of an irreducible identity, without equal in the opposite sex arid, as such, exploded, plural, fluid, in a certain way non-identical, this feminism situates itself outside the linear time of identities which communicate through projection and revindication. Such a feminism rejoins, on the one hand, the archaic (mythical) memory and, on the other, the cyclical or monumental temporality of marginal movements. It is certainly not by chance that the European and trans-European problematic has been poised as such at the same time as this new phase of feminism.

Finally, it is the mixture of the two attitudes—*insertion* into history and the radical *refusal* of the subjective limitations imposed by this history's time on an experiment carried out in the name of the irreducible difference—that seems to have broken loose over the past few years in European feminist movements, particularly in France and in Italy.

If we accept this meaning of the expression 'a new generation of women', two kinds of questions might then be posed. What sociopolitical processes or events have provoked this mutation? What are its problems: its contributions as well as dangers?

71   bell hooks, from *Feminism is for Everybody: Passionate Politics* (Pluto, 2000), pp. 55–60

Throughout her published writings and political career, hooks (1955–) has insisted on approaching feminism through the lenses of gender, race, and class. She has also developed a powerful critique of the implicit racism of the white women's movement. A well-known cultural critic, feminist and writer, she was appointed to a Professorship of African-American Studies at Yale University in the 1980s, and is currently Distinguished Professor of English at the City University of New York. Among the best-known of her many books is her *Ain't I a Woman*, and her widely read account of the personae of unconventional women writers, *Remembered Rapture*.

No intervention changed the face of American feminism more than the demand that feminist thinkers acknowledge the reality of race and racism. All white women in this nation know that their status is different from that of black women/women of color. They know this from the time they are little girls watching television and seeing only their images, and looking at magazines and seeing only their images. They know that the only reason nonwhites are absent/invisible is because they are not white. All white women in this nation know that whiteness is a privileged category. The fact that white females may choose to repress or deny this knowledge does not mean they are ignorant: it means that they are in denial.

No group of white women understood the differences in their status and that of black women more than the group of politically conscious white females who were active in civil rights struggle. Diaries and memoirs of this period in American history written by white women document this knowledge. Yet many of these individuals moved from civil rights into women's liberation and spearheaded a feminist movement where they suppressed and denied the awareness of difference they had seen and heard articulated firsthand in civil rights struggle. Just because they participated in anti-racist struggle did not mean that they had divested of white supremacy, of notions that they were superior to black females, more informed, better educated, more suited to "lead" a movement.

In many ways they were following in the footsteps of their abolitionist ancestors who had demanded that everyone (white women and black people) be given the right to vote, but, when faced with the possibility that black males might gain the right to vote while they were denied it on the basis of gender, they chose to ally themselves with men, uniting under the rubric of white supremacy. Contemporary white females witnessing the militant demand for more rights for black people chose that moment to demand more rights for themselves. Some of these individuals claim that it was working on behalf of civil rights that made them aware of sexism and sexist oppression. Yet if this was the whole picture one might think their newfound political awareness of difference would have carried over into the way they theorized contemporary feminist movement.

They entered the movement erasing and denying difference, not playing race alongside gender, but eliminating race from the picture. Foregrounding gender meant that white women could be take center stage, could claim the movement as theirs, even as they called on all women to join. The utopian vision of sisterhood evoked in a feminist movement that initially did not take racial difference or anti-racist struggle seriously did not capture the imagination of most black women/women of color. Individual black women who were active in the movement from its inception for the most part stayed in their place. When the feminist movement began racial integration was still rare. Many black people were learning how to interact with whites on the basis of being peers for the first time in their lives. No wonder individual black women choosing feminism were reluctant to introduce their awareness of race. It must have felt so awesome to have white women evoke sisterhood in a world where they had mainly experienced white women as exploiters and oppressors.

A younger generation of black females/women of color in the late '70s and early '80s challenged white female racism. Unlike our older black women allies we had for the most part been educated in predominately white settings. Most of us had never been in a subordinated position in relation to a white female. Most of had not been in the workforce. We had never been in our place. We were better positioned to critique racism and white supremacy within the women's movement. Individual white women who had attempted to organize the movement around the banner of common oppression evoking the notion that women constituted a sexual class/caste were the most reluctant to acknowledge differences among women, differences that overshadowed all the common experiences female shared. Race was the most obvious difference.

In the '70s I wrote the first draft of *Ain't I a Woman: Black Women and Feminism*. I was 19 years old. I had never worked a full-time job. I had come from a racially segregated small town in the south to Stanford University. While I had grown up resisting patriarchal thinking, college was the place where I embraced feminist politics. It was there as the only black female present in feminist classrooms, in consciousness-raising, that I began to engage race and gender theoretically. It was there that I began to demand recognition of the way in which racist biases were shaping feminist thinking and call for change. At other locations individual black women/women of color were making the same critique.

In those days white women who were unwilling to face the reality of racism and racial difference accused us of being traitors by introducing race. Wrongly they saw us as deflecting away from gender. In reality, we were demanding that we look as the status of females realistically, and that realistic understanding serve as the foundation for a real feminist politic. Our intent was not to diminish the vision of sisterhood. We sought to put in place a concrete politics of solidarity that would make genuine sisterhood possible. We knew that there could no real sisterhood between white women and women of color if they were not able to divest of white supremacy, if feminist movement were not fundamentally anti-racist.

Critical interventions around race did not destroy the women's movement; it became stronger. Breaking through denial about race helped women face the reality of difference on all levels. And we were finally putting in place a movement that did not place the class interests of privileged women, especially white women, over that of all other women. We put in place a vision of sisterhood where all our realities could be spoken. There has been no contemporary movement for social justice where individual participants engaged in the dialectical exchange that occurred among feminist thinkers about race which led to the re-thinking of much feminist theory and practice. The fact that participants in the feminist movement could face critique and challenge while still remaining wholeheartedly committed to a vision of justice, of liberation, is a testament to the movement's strength and power. It shows us that no matter how misguided feminist thinkers have been in the past, the will to change, the will to create the context for struggle and liberation, remains stronger than the need to hold on to wrong beliefs and assumptions.

For years I witnessed the reluctance of white feminist thinkers to acknowledge the importance of race. I witnessed their refusal to divest of white supremacy, their unwillingness to acknowledge that an anti-racist feminist movement was the only political foundation that would make sisterhood be a reality. And I witnessed the revolution in consciousness that occurred as individual women began to break free of denial, to break free of white supremacist thinking. These awesome changes restore my faith in feminist movement and strengthen the solidarity I feel towards all women.

Overall feminist thinking and feminist theory has benefited from all critical interventions on the issue of race. The only problematic arena has been that of translating theory into practice. While individual white women have incorporated an analysis of race into much feminist scholarship, these insights have not had as much impact on the day to day relations between white women and women of color. Anti-racist interactions between women are difficult in a society that remains racially segregated. Despite diverse work settings a vast majority of folks still socialized only with people of their own group. Racism and sexism combined create harmful barriers between women. So far feminist strategies to change this have not been very useful.

Individual white women and women of color who have worked through difficulties to make the space where bonds of love and political solidarity can emerge need to share the methods and strategies that we have successfully employed. Almost no attention is given the relationship between girls of different races. Biased feminist scholarship which attempts to show that white girls are somehow more vulnerable to sexist conditioning than girls of color simply perpetuate the white supremacist assumption that white females require and deserve more attention to their concerns and ills than other groups. Indeed while girls of color may express different behavior than their white counterparts they are not only internalizing sexist conditioning, they are far more likely to be victimized by sexism in ways that are irreparable.

Feminist movement, especially the work of visionary black activists, paved the way for a reconsideration of race and racism that has had positive impact on our society as a whole. Rarely do mainstream social critiques acknowledge this fact. As a feminist theorist who has written extensively about the issue of race and racism within feminist movement, I know that there remains much that needs to be challenged and changed, but it is equally important to celebrate the enormous changes that have occurred. That celebration, understanding our triumphs and using them as models, means that they can become the sound foundation for the building of a mass-based anti-racist feminist movement.

7 Ecologism

Introduction

Ecologism is one of the most recent ideologies to emerge within Western political life. Commentators have rightly observed the various antecedents for, and influences upon, this perspective, stretching back to the nineteenth century and beyond. But as a distinctive, inter-locking web of philosophical, moral, and political ideas linked with particular kinds of policy programme, a green political ideology remains relatively novel. Its representative voices tend to divide into different camps—along axes defined by philosophy and political strategy. The desire to constitute a rival philosophical outlook or system to that associated with the discredited materialism and industrialism of western modernity has generated an interest in the possibility of an 'ecocentric' (or deep green) philosophic standpoint. In its different manifestations, this claims to provide a perspective upon the different forms of life within the biosphere which transcends the narrow interests of humans, and questions the ideals of happiness and want associated with consumerist materialism. Not all greens, however, subscribe to such a demanding ethic, with many happy to extend liberal, socialist, and even conservative ideas in the direction of environmentalist goals. Differences over strategy and over the appropriate attitude to strike towards parliamentary politics, have also shaped green political thinking. While some, so-called, 'deep' greens argue for an uncompromising stance towards conventional politics and the values of western society, Green parties have tended to eschew such fundamentalism in their efforts to maximize their electoral base and gain a foothold in democratic political life. Despite these tensions, during the 1970s environ-mentalist concerns coalesced into a recognizable pattern of green thinking about politics.

The first extract that we introduce here is taken from one of the major texts that prompted this awareness. The naturalist writer Rachel Carson reached, and shocked, a wide section of the American reading public with her best-selling account of the malign impact of pesticides upon the food-chain, *Silent Spring* [Reading 72]. She discusses the widespread usage of powerful toxic agents and the dangers attendant upon their dissemination into the atmo-sphere through agricultural spraying. Mixing moral outrage and scientific understanding, she describes the increasing deployment of dangerous chemicals within American agriculture. These not only present menaces to the human population, but generate a number of unforeseen and unpredictable environmental consequences. She followed the trail of these toxins as they passed through the food chain, showing the different malign consequences they exerted upon insects, birds, fish, plant life, and humans.

More generally, environmentalist concerns were brought to public attention by a host of campaigns, activist groups, and concerned intellectuals in the 1970s. One of the most import-ant contributions of the generally marginal green campaigners was to question the moral basis of the materialism that underpinned all the major political traditions of modern democratic politics. This perspective is central to the arguments developed by the respected economist Ernst Schumacher, in his widely read *Small is Beautiful* [Reading 73]. He contrasts the assumptions and complacency of the materialist philosophies informing conventional economic thinking with the critical imperatives of what he calls 'Buddhist economics'. This book also contains his important critique of the assumptions and implications of mainstream economics, an argument that has exerted an important influence upon greens' advocacy of an alternative political economy. Economic thought, he argues, has lost contact with any meaningful value system and has become unthinkingly attached to the ideal of never-ending economic growth. The ignorance of natural processes and limits exhibited by economics is helping propel the world towards environmental disaster.

Schumacher's argument anticipates both the deliberate appropriation of non-western traditions of thought typical of some parts of the later green political movement, and the centrality to ecologism of an attack upon the precepts of modern political economy. In this passage, he seeks to undermine some of the central categories of mainstream economics—particularly the utilitarian idea that greater consumption leads to increased personal well-being. He proclaims the irrationality of western consumerism from this alternative ethical perspective, anticipating the emergence towards the end of the 1980s of much greater awareness of the consequences of affluent Western lifestyles. He trains his fire upon the economists' assumption that consumption constitutes the primary end of economic activity, while land, labour, and capital merely represent various means of realizing it.

Schumacher links his argument for an ethics of simplicity and restraint in matters of consumption to the ideal of non-violence. One of the bridges between these ideas is the notion of the self-sufficient community committed to production from local resources for local needs. This has the advantageous consequence of minimizing dependence upon exports from elsewhere. Anticipating the massive growth in public concern about the environmental consequences of the global food industry, he points to the linkages between unchecked personal consumption, rising dependence upon fuel sources, and the depletion of natural resources. Adopting a moral vantage point outside a recognizably western frame of reference, he highlights the connection between the lifestyles of affluent consumers and the destruction of forests. Because modern economics quantifies everything in terms of a single scale of monetary value, it cannot make the vital distinction between the use of resources that are renewable and those that are not. From the 'eastern' perspective that he celebrates, the lifestyle of the affluent consumer is both shallow and doomed.

These, and other related, concerns began to percolate into the political mainstreams of various democratic societies during the late 1970s and 1980s. One of the most important manifestations of this process concerned a project entitled *Limits to Growth*, an ambitious computer-generated assessment of the impact of rising population levels and natural resource depletion funded by an international group of industrialists (the Club of Rome). In Reading 74, some of the authors of the report that emanated from this project reflect, nearly two decades later, upon their findings. Donella and Dennis Meadows, and Jorgen Randers describe their original remit, and the computer model they developed to aid their calculations—World3. Their controversial report was intended as a warning, though it was widely regarded as a doom-laden prophecy. Not only had they highlighted the potential for impending ecological disaster, but they anticipated the emergence, in the 1990s and beyond, of an alternative environmental imperative—sustainable development. In the twenty years since their findings were first published, they note a host of policy initiatives and agreements that have begun to address some of the problems they diagnosed. Yet, returning to these issues in the early 1990s, they argue that in different respects resource depletion and pollution flows have already begun to exceed their sustainable boundaries: the 'human world is beyond its limits'. The one beacon of hope in their analysis concerns technological and institutional developments that generate the possibility that socio-economic trends might be steered down more sustainable paths. For such options to be taken, they suggest, a break from the cultural and psychic mind-set of modern industrial culture is needed.

The broadly reformist and technocratic approach to ecological crisis suggested by this approach is rejected by other members of the political coalition that makes up the contemporary environmentalist movement. More radical ideas, experiments in living, and political campaigns have been influenced by the generation, since the early 1970s, of various forms of non-compromising green philosophies. Among the thinkers associated with the development of these ideas is the Norwegian writer and campaigner, Arne Naess [Reading 75]. He argues for the merits of an ethical imperative that he labels 'the universal right to self-unfolding'. This is justified in relation to his intersubjective understanding of identity. This stipulates that there is no 'I' without a larger environment, both organic and inorganic, in which 'I' operate. To distance myself from the natural world is, then, to be cut off from an integral part of that which has made me who I am. A self that moves towards self-realization enjoys a healthy and positive relation with its human and inorganic surroundings. What distinguishes Naess's discussion ('Ecosophy T') from other similar teleological philosophies is his attempt to extend this principle to non-human entities. Plants and animals, he maintains, also possess a right to self-realization. Humans ought to respect this right, and also come to understand that when we damage our natural environment, we are in important respects harming ourselves. He proceeds to argue that an appreciation of the nature of life itself helps us understand the significance and longevity of natural entities much larger and long-lasting than ourselves. Equally, humanity's distinguishing biological feature—our lack of a restraining natural habitat—endows us with the ability to understand the unique potential of the variety of living beings in the world.

The right to self-unfolding that he wishes to allot to all life forms is not like other more familiar social and political rights. It constitutes rather a generalized guideline by which we can evaluate our conduct towards the potentiality of other beings. Naess contrasts this norm with arguments that suggest a moral ranking among living beings depending on their degree of evolution. Though we may rightly behave differently towards different species—distinguishing between apes and viruses for instance, he counters the suggestion that this differentiation relies upon the argument that one is more valuable than another. In the final portion of this extract, he extrapolates from the norms of interdependence and the potential of living beings to justify the principle of 'ecospheric belonging'. This ethic describes the highest interest that humanity as a collective subject (or Self) enjoys, and is vitiated by the divisive and exploitative circumstances in which humanity currently lives.

Naess is one of the most influential eco-philosophical voices, and his work has particularly influenced radical sections of the green movement. This kind of 'deep' ecological thinking is not universally shared or admired in this coalition, however. A forceful critique of the 'deep' green road to environmental salvation has emerged from thinkers who give greater emphasis to human suffering and inequality, as well as to environmentalist problems. Thus, the

American writer and activist, Murray Bookchin, argues that we can only understand humanity's exploitative relationship with the natural environment by considering, first, the ways in which humans dominate each other [Reading 76]. He points to the dissolution of the ties of community in the face of marketization as a prime cause of current woes. Capitalism not only generates intra-human competition and exploitation, but inherently leads to the exploitation and commodification of the natural world. Social and ecological progress, he argues, require a conceptual shift: from seeing the planet as a clump of mineral resources, to the earth as a complex web of life. For human patterns of development, particularly through the creation of vast urban spaces, represent a dangerous imposition of synthetic norms and needs upon the natural world. Such developments are intrinsically linked, Bookchin asserts, with the demise of the civic culture and the rise of the faceless bureaucrat in democratic society. These societal trends deny the merits of a more complex, contingent, and pluralistic pattern of social and ecological development.

Bookchin's alternative vision to 'deep' green thinking, which he termed 'social ecology', reflected both upon his uncompromising critique of different kinds of hierarchy and his advocacy of the merits of participatory, egalitarian communities which would act as partners with, not overlords towards, the natural world. In essays authored in the 1960s and early 1970s (collected in *Post-Scarcity Anarchism*, and *Toward an Ecological Society*), he began to link the domination by some humans of others with humanity's exploitation of the natural world. Hierarchy, he argues, is a malign human invention that banished the prospects of interdependent and egalitarian communities. He associates its appearance with the establishment of patriarchal and statist social orders. In philosophical terms, he proposes a revised version of the philosopher Hegel's dialectical system of logic, which he labels dialectical naturalism (outlined in his *The Philosophy of Social Ecology*).

A notable feature of Bookchin's often combative writings is his readiness to critique the political left as well as industrial society and its representatives; for instance in his *Listen, Marxist!* (1969). He perceives in Marxist groups, New Left organizations and green movements continuing examples of the principle of hierarchy. Critical of the 'old left's' faith in the proletariat, he celebrates the potential of those at the margins of social life—students, women, artists, and so forth—who possess the imaginative potential to develop a new kind of liberatory movement. In political terms, he defends the model of libertarian municipalism, a new politics based upon the recovery of the tradition of face-to-face democratic self-governance. This is combined with an argument for a civic confederalism of these different communities. In moral terms, he claims that a truly emancipatory social alternative needs to expunge all traces of hierarchy in itself. Only with the creation of communities in which social unity is combined with a respect for human individuality, and *vice versa*, can the journey towards the social ecological future begin.

Both Naess and Bookchin are well-known writers and thinkers in western environmentalist circles. Yet there is evidence that as the Green movement has developed since the 1980s, and gained a foothold within the legislatures of various democratic states, these apocalyptic and revolutionary ideas have waned in appeal. Among the activist groups, campaigns, political parties, and discussion forums sponsored by the environmentalist movement, a more hard-headed and strategic approach to politics has taken shape over the last two decades. This is illustrated by the ideas of a figure such as Jonathan Porritt, once a leading light in the UK Green Party and subsequently a high-profile public commentator and campaigner on environmental issues [Reading 77]. He offers a defence of the notion that Green ideology pursues a unique trajectory, one that cuts across familiar partisan political divisions between 'left' and 'right'. Greens, he maintains, attack the underlying commitment to industrialism that sustains the rival ideologies of socialism and conservatism. Both are implicitly convinced of the merits of economic growth, the importance of materialism as a solution to social problems, and the necessity of unimpeded technological advance. They are also prone to generate centralized and hierarchical forms of political control. And each perpetuates the view that nature needs to be tamed and conquered.

As it has developed over the last twenty years, ecologism as an ideology has been extremely open to influence by, and dialogue with, neighbouring ideological paradigms. Various theorists and activists see a natural alliance between feminist and Green emphases, for example. Equally, the western Green movement has become one of the most important venues where concerns about globally entrenched inequalities—between North and South— are publicly aired and opposed. Moreover, ecologism has developed some distinctive national variants, as green concerns are readily blended with local traditions, concerns and perspectives. All of these processes are apparent in the work of the Indian naturalist and public intellectual, Vandana Shiva. She argues [Reading 78] that the export of a western norm of 'development' to non-western countries is underpinned by the assumption that there is only one way in which modernity and progress can be achieved by any state. The specific concerns and concepts of western societies have been accorded the status of universal ideals. Development of this kind is tantamount to a continuation of colonisation: it reinforces massive inequality between men and women, between different cultures, and between humanity and nature. She observes the particular emergence of an ethos of resistance among women to the totalizing, and patriarchal, logic of economic modernization even though it is now national elites, not colonial powers, who oversee today's development plans. She is especially critical of development projects that impact most heavily upon women, 'by removing land, water and forests from their management and control'. This process is paralleled, she asserts, by the despoliation of the natural environment. The link between them is supplied by the justification of development strategies in a patriarchal language that positions women and nature as passive objects of male agency, and classifies traditional cultures as 'unproductive'. Only when a river or a forest are subject to 'development', this mind-set suggests, can they be deemed to constitute productive assets. She is particularly critical of the imposition by development agencies of normative ideas about 'productivity' and 'economic activity'. Throughout her writings, she emphasizes the close relation between women and traditional forms of agricultural labour, and stresses how both are often regarded as hindrances to economic modernity. Though women are the primary food producers and processors in the global economy, female labour, she maintains, is rendered invisible and dismissed as unprofitable in the global capitalist order.

FURTHER READING

Valuable discussion of the history and normative character of green ideology can be found in: Brian Baxter, *Ecologism: an Introduction* (Edinburgh University Press, 1999); Tim Hayward, *Ecological Thought: an Introduction* (Polity, 1995); and Andrew Dobson, *Green Political Thought* (Routledge, 1990; 1995). Important philosophically informed critiques and refinements of ecological thinking can be found in: Robert Goodin, *Green Political Theory* (Polity, 1992) and Robyn Eckersley, *Environmentalism and Political Theory: Toward an Ecocentric Approach* (UCL Press, 1992). Selections from the writings of many Green figures and theorists can be found in Andrew Dobson (ed.) *The Green Reader* (Deutsch, 1991).

72 Rachel Carson, from *Silent Spring* (Penguin Books, 1962), pp. 21–2, 23–7

Born into a poor rural family in Springdale, Pennsylvania, Carson (1907–1964) studied at Pennsylvania University for Women and Johns Hopkins University. Abandoning an academic career, she became a popular writer on scientific and environmental topics, authoring the best-selling *The Sea Around Us* (1951). Carson became increasingly interested in the effects of a wide variety of pesticides and wrote *Silent Spring*, one of the highest-selling non-fiction books of its day (which was subsequently garlanded with a host of awards). In it, she marshalled evidence showing that long-lasting pesticides, such as DDT, had been destructive for different kinds of living beings, including humans. The book generated considerable controversy, and a hostile reaction from the chemical industry and scientific community. But in the wake of its publication, President Kennedy set up a commission to study the effects of pesticides.

As long ago as the mid-1930s a special group of hydrocarbons, the chlorinated naphthalenes, was found to cause hepatitis, and also a rare and almost invariably fatal liver disease in persons subjected to occupational exposure. They have led to illness and death of workers in electrical industries; and more recently, in agriculture, they have been considered a cause of a mysterious and usually fatal disease of cattle. In view of these antecedents, it is not surprising that three of the insecticides that belong to this group are among the most violently poisonous of all the hydrocarbons. These are dieldrin, aldrin, and endrin.

Dieldrin, named after a German chemist, Diels, is about five times as toxic as DDT when swallowed but forty times as toxic when absorbed through the skin in solution. It is notorious for striking quickly and with terrible effect at the nervous system, sending the victims into convulsions. Persons thus poisoned recover so slowly as to indicate chronic effects. As with other chlorinated hydrocarbons, these long-term effects include severe damage to the liver. The long duration of its residues and the effective insecticidal action make dieldrin one of the most used insecticides today, despite the appalling destruction of wildlife that has followed its use. As tested on quail and pheasants, it has proved to be about forty or fifty times as toxic as DDT.

There are vast gaps in our knowledge of how dieldrin is stored or distributed in the body, or excreted, for the chemists' ingenuity in devising insecticides has long ago outrun biological knowledge of the way these poisons affect the living organism. However, there is every indication of long storage in the human body, where deposits may lie dormant like a slumbering volcano, only to flare up in periods of physiological stress when the body draws upon its fat reserves. Much of what we do know has been learned through hard experience in the anti-malarial campaigns carried out by the World Health Organization. As soon as dieldrin was substituted for DDT in malaria-control work (because the malaria mosquitoes had become resistant to DDT), cases of poisoning among the spraymen began to occur. The seizures were severe—from half to all (varying in the different programmes) of the men affected went into convulsions and several died. Some had convulsions as long as *four months* after the last exposure.

Aldrin is a somewhat mysterious substance, for although it exists as a separate entity it bears the relation of alter ego to dieldrin. When carrots are taken from a bed treated with aldrin they are found to contain residues of dieldrin. This change occurs in living tissues and also in soil. Such alchemistic transformations have led to many erroneous reports, for if a chemist, knowing aldrin has been applied, tests for it he will be deceived into thinking all residues have been dissipated. The residues are there, but they are dieldrin and this requires a different test.

Like dieldrin, aldrin is extremely toxic. It produces degenerative changes in the liver and kidneys. A quantity the size of an aspirin tablet is enough to kill more than four hundred quail. Many cases of human poisonings are on record, most of them in connection with industrial handling.

. . .

The second major group of insecticides, the alkyl or organic phosphates, are among the most poisonous chemicals in the world. The chief and most obvious hazard attending their use is that of acute poisoning of people applying the sprays or accidentally coming in contact with drifting spray, with vegetation coated by it, or with a discarded container. In Florida, two children found an empty bag and used it to repair a swing. Shortly thereafter both of them died and three of their playmates became ill. The bag had once contained an insecticide called parathion, one of the organic phosphates; tests established death by parathion poisoning. On another occasion two small boys in Wisconsin, cousins, died on the same night. One had been playing in his yard when spray drifted in from an adjoining field where his father was spraying potatoes with parathion; the other had run playfully into the barn after his father and had put his hand on the nozzle of the spray equipment.

The origin of these insecticides has a certain ironic significance. Although some of the chemicals themselves—organic esters of phosphoric acid—had been known for many years, their insecticidal properties remained to be discovered by a German chemist, Gerhard Schrader, in the late 1930s. Almost immediately the German government recognized the value of these same chemicals as new and devastating weapons in man's war against his own kind, and the work on them was declared secret. Some became the deadly nerve gases. Others, of closely allied structure, became insecticides.

The organic phosphorus insecticides act on the living organism in a peculiar way. They have the ability to destroy enzymes—enzymes that perform necessary functions in the body. Their target is the nervous system, whether the victim is an insect or a warm-blooded animal. Under normal conditions, an impulse passes from nerve to nerve with the aid of a 'chemical transmitter' called acetylcholine, a substance that performs an essential function and then disappears. Indeed, its existence is so ephemeral that medical researchers are unable, without special procedures, to sample it before the body has destroyed it. This transient nature of the transmitting chemical is necessary to the normal functioning of the body. If the acetylcholine is not destroyed as soon as a nerve impulse has passed, impulses continue to flash across the bridge from nerve to nerve, as the chemical exerts its effects in an ever more intensified manner. The movements of the whole body become unco-ordinated: tremors, muscular spasms, convulsions, and death quickly result.

This contingency has been provided for by the body. A protective enzyme called cholinesterase is at hand to destroy the transmitting chemical once it is no longer needed. By this means a precise balance is struck and the body never builds up a dangerous amount of acetylcholine. But on contact with the organic phosphorus insecticides, the protective enzyme is destroyed, and as the quantity of the enzyme is reduced that of the transmitting chemical builds up. In this effect, the organic phosphorus compounds resemble the alkaloid poison muscarine, found in a poisonous mushroom, the fly amanita.

Repeated exposures may lower the cholinesterase level until an individual reaches the brink of acute poisoning, a brink over which he may be pushed by a very small additional exposure. For this reason it is considered important to make periodic examinations of the blood of spray operators and others regularly exposed.

Parathion is one of the most widely used of the organic phosphates. It is also one of the most powerful and dangerous. Honey bees become 'wildly agitated and bellicose' on con-tact with it, perform frantic cleaning movements, and are near death within half an hour. A chemist, thinking to learn by the most direct possible means the dose acutely toxic to human beings, swallowed a minute amount, equivalent to about .00424 ounce. Paralysis followed so instantaneously that he could not reach the antidotes he had prepared at hand, and so he died. Parathion is now said to be a favourite instrument of suicide in Finland. In recent years the State of California has reported an average of more than two hundred cases of accidental parathion poisoning annually. In many parts of the world the fatality rate from parathion is startling: 100 fatal cases in India and 67 in Syria in 1958, and an average of 336 deaths per year in Japan.

Yet some 7,000,000 pounds of parathion are now applied to fields and orchards of the United States—by hand-sprayers, motorized blowers and dusters, and by aeroplane. The amount used on California farms alone could, according to one medical authority, 'provide a lethal dose for five to ten times the whole world's population.'

One of the few circumstances that save us from extinction by this means is the fact that parathion and other chemicals of this group are decomposed rather rapidly. Their residues on the crops to which they are applied are therefore relatively short-lived com-pared with the chlorinated hydrocarbons. However, they last long enough to create hazards and produce consequences that range from the merely serious to the fatal. In Riverside, California, eleven out of thirty men picking oranges became violently ill and all but one had to be hospitalized. Their symptoms were typical of parathion poisoning. The grove had been sprayed with parathion some two and a half weeks earlier; the residues that reduced them to retching, half-blind, semiconscious misery were sixteen to nineteen days old. And this is not by any means a record for persistence. Similar mishaps have occurred in groves sprayed a month earlier, and residues have been found in the peel of oranges six months after treatment with standard dosages.

The danger to all workers applying the organic phosphorus insecticides in fields, orchards, and vineyards, is so extreme that some states using these chemicals have established laboratories where physicians may obtain aid in diagnosis and treatment. Even the physicians themselves may be in some danger, unless they wear rubber gloves in handling the victims of poisoning. So may a laundress washing the clothing of such victims, which may have absorbed enough parathion to affect her.

Malathion, another of the organic phosphates, is almost as familiar to the public as DDT, being widely used by gardeners, in household insecticides, in mosquito spraying, and in such blanket attacks on insects as the spraying of nearly a million acres of Florida communities for the Mediterranean fruit fly. It is considered the least toxic of this group of chemicals and many people assume they may use it freely and without fear of harm. Commercial advertising encourages this comfortable attitude.

The alleged 'safety' of malathion rests on rather precarious ground, although—as often happens—this was not discovered until the chemical had been in use for several years. Malathion is 'safe' only because the mammalian liver, an organ with extraordinary protective powers, renders it relatively harmless. The detoxification is accomplished by one of the enzymes of the liver. If, however, something destroys this enzyme or interferes with its action, the person exposed to malathion receives the full force of the poison.

Unfortunately for all of us, opportunities for this sort of thing to happen are legion. A few years ago a team of Food and Drug Administration scientists discovered that when malathion and certain other organic phosphates are administered simultaneously a massive poisoning results—up to fifty times as severe as would be predicted on the basis of adding together the toxicities of the two. In other words, one-hundredth of the lethal dose of each compound may be fatal when the two are combined.

73   Ernst Schumacher, from *Small is Beautiful* (Abacus, 1974), pp. 52–5

Born in Germany, Schumacher (1911–1977) won a Rhodes scholarship to Oxford during the 1930s, and returned to England shortly before the Second World War. Despite his anti-Nazi politics, he was interned as an enemy alien in the English countryside during the war. After 1945, he worked as an economic adviser to the British Control Commission charged with rebuilding the German economy, and was appointed chief editorial writer on economics for *The Times*. From 1950 to 1970 he was Chief Economic Adviser to the British Coal Board. In 1955 Schumacher travelled as a consultant to Burma, and during this trip began to develop the principles of what he labelled 'Buddhist economics'. His thinking was laid out in his widely read book *Small is Beautiful* (1973).

While the materialist is mainly interested in goods, the Buddhist is mainly interested in liberation. But Buddhism is 'The Middle Way' and therefore in no way antagonistic to physical well-being. It is not wealth that stands in the way of liberation but the attachment to wealth; not the enjoyment of pleasurable things but the craving for them. The keynote of Buddhist economics, therefore, is simplicity and non-violence. From an economist's point of view, the marvel of the Buddhist way of life is the utter rationality of its pattern—amazingly small means leading to extraordinarily satisfactory results.

For the modern economist this is very difficult to understand. He is used to measuring the 'standard of living' by the amount of annual consumption, assuming all the time that a man who consumes more is 'better off' than a man who consumes less. A Buddhist economist would consider this approach excessively irrational: since consumption is merely a means to human well-being, the aim should be to obtain the maximum of well-being with the minimum of consumption. Thus, if the purpose of clothing is a certain amount of temperature comfort and an attractive appearance, the task is to attain this purpose with the smallest possible effort, that is, with the smallest annual destruction of cloth and with the help of designs that involve the smallest possible input of toil. The less toil there is, the more time and strength is left for artistic creativity. It would be highly uneconomic, for instance, to go in for complicated tailoring, like the modern west, when a much more beautiful effect can be achieved by the skilful draping of uncut material. It would be the height of folly to make material so that it should wear out quickly and the height of barbarity to make anything ugly, shabby or mean. What has just been said about clothing applies equally to all other human requirements. The ownership and the consumption of goods is a means to an end, and Buddhist economics is the systematic study of how to attain given ends with the minimum means.

Modern economics, on the other hand, considers consumption to be the sole end and purpose of all economic activity, taking the factors of production—land, labour, and capital—as the means. The former, in short, tries to maximise human satisfactions by the optimal pattern of consumption, while the latter tries to maximise consumption by the optimal pattern of productive effort. It is easy to see that the effort needed to sustain a way of life which seeks to attain the optimal pattern of consumption is likely to be much smaller than the effort needed to sustain a drive for maximum consumption. We need not be surprised, therefore, that the pressure and strain of living is very much less in, say, Burma than it is in the United States, in spite of the fact that the amount of labour-saving machinery used in the former country is only a minute fraction of the amount used in the latter.

Simplicity and non-violence are obviously closely related. The optimal pattern of consumption, producing a high degree of human satisfaction by means of a relatively low rate of consumption, allows people to live without great pressure and strain and to fulfil the primary injunction of Buddhist teaching: 'Cease to do evil; try to do good.' As physical resources are everywhere limited, people satisfying their needs by means of a modest use of resources are obviously less likely to be at each other's throats than people depending upon a high rate of use. Equally, people who live in highly self-sufficient local communities are less likely to get involved in large-scale violence than people whose existence depends on world-wide systems of trade.

From the point of view of Buddhist economics, therefore, production from local resources for local needs is the most rational way of economic life, while dependence on imports from afar and the consequent need to produce for export to unknown and distant peoples is highly uneconomic and justifiable only in exceptional cases and on a small scale. Just as the modern economist would admit that a high rate of consumption of transport services between a man's home and his place of work signifies a misfortune and not a high standard of life, so the Buddhist economist would hold that to satisfy human wants from faraway sources rather than from sources nearby signifies failure rather than success. The former tends to take statistics showing an increase in the number of ton/miles per head of the population carried by a country's transport system as proof of economic progress, while to the latter—the Buddhist economist—the same statistics would indicate a highly undesirable deterioration in the *pattern* of consumption.

Another striking difference between modern economics and Buddhist economics arises over the use of natural resources. Bertrand de Jouvenel, the eminent French political philosopher, has characterised 'western man' in words which may be taken as a fair description of the modern economist:

"He tends to count nothing as an expenditure, other than human effort; he does not seem to mind how much mineral matter he wastes and, far worse, how much living matter he destroys. He does not seem to realise at all that human life is a dependent part of an ecosystem of many different forms of life. As the world is ruled from towns where men are cut off from any form of life other than human, the feeling of belonging to an ecosystem is not revived. This results in a harsh and improvident treatment of things upon which we ultimately depend, such as water and trees."

The teaching of the Buddha, on the other hand, enjoins a reverent and non-violent attitude not only to all sentient beings but also, with great emphasis, to trees. Every follower of the Buddha ought to plant a tree every few years and look after it until it is safely established, and the Buddhist economist can demonstrate without difficulty that the universal observation of this rule would result in a high rate of genuine economic development independent of any foreign aid. Much of the economic decay of south-east Asia (as of many other parts of the world) is undoubtedly due to a heedless and shameful neglect of trees.

Modern economics does not distinguish between renewable and non-renewable materials, as its very method is to equalise and quantify everything by means of a money price. Thus, taking various alternative fuels, like coal, oil, wood, or water-power: the only difference between them recognised by modern economics is relative cost per equivalent unit. The cheapest is automatically the one to be preferred, as to do otherwise would be irrational and 'uneconomic'. From a Buddhist point of view, of course, this will not do; the essential difference between non-renewable fuels like coal and oil on the one hand and renewable fuels like wood and water-power on the other cannot be simply over-looked. Non-renewable goods must be used only if they are indispensable, and then only with the greatest care and the most meticulous concern for conservation. To use them heedlessly or extravagantly is an act of violence, and while complete non-violence may not be attainable on this earth, there is nonetheless an ineluctable duty on man to aim at the ideal of non-violence in all he does.

Just as a modern European economist would not consider it a great economic achievement if all European art treasures were sold to America at attractive prices, so the Buddhist economist would insist that a population basing its economic life on non-renewable fuels is living parasitically, on capital instead of income. Such a way of life could have no permanence and could therefore be justified only as a purely temporary expedient. As the world's resources of non-renewable fuels—coal, oil and natural gas—are exceedingly unevenly distributed over the globe and undoubt-edly limited in quantity, it is clear that their exploitation at an ever-increasing rate is an act of violence against nature which must almost inevitably lead to violence between men.

74 **Donella Meadows, Dennis Meadows, and Jorgen Randers, from** *Beyond the Limits: Global Collapse or a Sustainable Future* **(Earthscan, 1992), pp. xii–xvii**

Donella Meadows (1942–2001) gained a B.A in Chemistry from Carleton College in Canada, and a Ph.D in biophysics from Harvard University in 1968. A highly respected environmental scientist and writer, she was the lead author of the best-selling report, *Limits to Growth* (1972). The bulk of her working life was spent as Professor of Environmental Studies at Dartmouth College in New Hampshire. She combined this post with authorship of an influential syndicated weekly column, 'The Global Citizen', which was nominated for the Pulitzer Prize in 1991. With her husband, Dennis Meadows, she founded the International Network of Resource Information Centers in 1981, and in 1997 became Director of the Sustainability Institute in Hartland, Vermont. Jorgen Randers is currently Deputy Director General of WWF International.

Twenty years ago we wrote a book called *The Limits to Growth*. It described the prospects for growth in the human population and the global economy during the coming century. In it we raised questions such as: What will happen if growth in the world's population continues unchecked? What will be the environmental consequences if economic growth continues at its current pace? What can be done to ensure a human economy that provides sufficiently for all and that also fits within the physical limits of the Earth?

We had been commissioned to examine these questions by The Club of Rome, an international group of distinguished businessmen, statesmen, and scientists. They asked us to undertake a two-year study at the Massachusetts Institute of Technology to investigate the longterm causes and consequences of growth in population, industrial capital, food production, resource consumption, and pollution. To keep track of these interacting entities and to project their possible paths into the future we created a computer model called World3.

The results of our study were described for the general public in *The Limits to Growth*. That book created a furor. The combination of the computer, MIT, and The Club of Rome pronouncing upon humanity's future had an irresistible dramatic appeal. Newspaper headlines announced:

A COMPUTER LOOKS AHEAD AND SHUDDERS
STUDY SEES DISASTER BY YEAR 2100
SCIENTISTS WARN OF GLOBAL CATASTROPHE.

Our book was debated by parliaments and scientific societies. One major oil company sponsored a series of advertisements criticizing it; another set up an annual prize for the best studies expanding upon it. *The Limits to Growth* inspired some high praise, many thoughtful reviews, and a flurry of attacks from the left, the right, and the middle of mainstream economics.

The book was interpreted by many as a prediction of doom, but it was not a prediction at all. It was not about a preordained future. It was about a choice. It contained a warning, to be sure, but also a message of promise. Here are the three summary conclusions we wrote in 1972. The second of them is the promise, a very optimistic one, but our analysis justified it then and still justifies it now. Perhaps we should have listed it first.

1. If the present growth trends in world population, industrialization, pollution, food production, and resource depletion continue unchanged, the limits to growth on this planet will be reached sometime within the next 100 years. The most probable result will be a sudden and uncontrollable decline in both population and industrial capacity.

2. It is possible to alter these growth trends and to establish a condition of ecological and economic stability that is sustainable far into the future. The state of global equilibrium could be designed so that the basic material needs of each person on earth are satisfied and each person has an equal opportunity to realize his or her individual human potential.

3. If the world's people decide to strive for this second outcome rather than the first, the sooner they begin working to attain it, the greater will be their chances of success.

To us those conclusions spelled out not doom but challenge—how to bring about a society that is materially sufficient, socially equitable, and ecologically sustainable, and one that is more satisfying in human terms than the growth-obsessed society of today.

In one way and another, we've been working on that challenge ever since. Millions of other people have been working on it too. They've been exploring energy efficiency and new materials, nonviolent conflict resolution and grassroots community development, pollution prevention in factories and recycling in towns, ecological agriculture and international protocols to protect the ozone layer. Much has happened in twenty years to bring about technologies, concepts, and institutions that can create a sustainable future. And much has happened to perpetuate the desperate poverty, the waste of resources, the accumulation of toxins, and the destruction of nature that are tearing down the support capacity of the earth.

When we began working on the present book, we simply intended to document those countervailing trends in order to update *The Limits to Growth* for its reissue on its twentieth anniversary. We soon discovered that we had to do more than that. As we compiled the numbers, reran the computer model, and reflected on what we had learned over two decades, we realized that the passage of time and the continuation of many growth trends had brought the human society to a new position relative to its limits.

In 1971 we concluded that the physical limits to human use of materials and energy were somewhere decades ahead. In 1991, when we looked again at the data, the computer model, and our own experience of the world, we realized that in spite of the world's improved technologies, the greater awareness, the stronger environment policies, many resource source and pollution flows had grown beyond their sustainable limits.

That conclusion came as a surprise to us, and yet not really a surprise. In a way we had known it all along. We had seen for ourselves the leveled forests, the gullies in the croplands, the rivers brown with silt. We knew the chemistry of the ozone layer and the greenhouse effect. The media had chronicled the statistics of global fisheries, groundwater drawdowns, and the extinction of species. We discovered, as we began to talk to colleagues about the world being "beyond the limits," that they did not question that conclusion. We found many places in the literature of the past twenty years where authors had suggested that resource and pollution flows had grown too far, some of which we have quoted in this book.

But until we started updating *The Limits to Growth* we had not let our minds fully absorb the message. The human world is beyond its limits. The present way of doing things is unsustainable. The future, to be viable at all, must be one of drawing back, easing down, healing. Poverty cannot be ended by indefinite material growth; it will have to be addressed while the material human economy contracts. Like everyone else, we didn't really want to come to these conclusions.

But the more we compiled the numbers, the more they gave us that message, loud and clear. With some trepidation we turned to World3, the computer model that had helped us twenty years before to integrate the global data and to work through their long-term implications. We were afraid that we would no longer be able to find in the model any possibility of a believable, sufficient, sustainable future for all the world's people.

But, as it turned out, we could. World3 showed us that in twenty years some options for sustainability have narrowed, but others have opened up. Given some of the technologies and institutions invented over those twenty years, there are real possibilities for reducing the streams of resources consumed and pollutants generated by the human economy while increasing the quality of human life. It is even possible, we concluded, to eliminate poverty while accommodating the population growth already implicit in present population age structures—but not if population growth goes on indefinitely, not if it goes on for long, and not without rapid improvements in the efficiency of material and energy use and in the equity of material and energy distribution.

As far as we can tell from the global data, from the World3 model, and from all we have learned in the past twenty years, the three conclusions we drew in *The Limits to Growth* are still valid, but they need to be strengthened. Now we would write them this way:

1. Human use of many essential resources and generation of many kinds of pollutants have already surpassed rates that are physically sustainable. Without significant reductions in material and energy flows, there will be in the coming decades an uncontrolled decline in per capita food output, energy use, and industrial production.

2. This decline is not inevitable. To avoid it two changes are necessary. The first is a comprehensive revision of policies and practices that perpetuate growth in material consumption and in population. The second is a rapid, drastic increase in the efficiency with which materials and energy are used.

3. A sustainable society is still technically and economically possible. It could be much more desirable than a society that tries to solve its problems by constant expansion. The transition to a sustainable society requires a careful balance between long-term and short-term goals and an emphasis on sufficiency, equity, and quality of life rather than on quantity of output. It requires more than productivity and more than technology; it also requires maturity, compassion, and wisdom.

These conclusions constitute a conditional warning, not a dire prediction. They offer a living choice, not a death sentence. The choice isn't necessarily a gloomy one. It does not mean that the poor must be frozen in their poverty or that the rich must become poor. It could actually mean achieving at last the goals that humanity has been pursuing in continuous attempts to maintain physical growth.

We hope the world will make a choice for sustainability. That is why we are writing this book. But we do not minimize the gravity or the difficulty of that choice. We think a transition to a sustainable world is technically and economically possible, maybe even easy, but we also know it is psychologically and politically daunting. So much hope, so many personal identities, so much of modern industrial culture has been built upon the premise of perpetual material growth.

A perceptive teacher, watching his students react to the idea that there are limits, once wrote:

> When most of us are presented with the ultimata of potential disaster, when we hear that we "must" choose some form of planned stability, when we face the "necessity" of a designed sustainable state, we are being bereaved, whether or not we fully realize it. When cast upon our own resources in this way we feel, we intuit, a kind of cosmic loneliness that we could not have foreseen. We become orphans. We no longer see ourselves as children of a cosmic order or the beneficiaries of the historical process. Limits to growth denies all that. It tell us, perhaps for the first time in our experience, that the only plan must be our own. With one stroke it strips us of the assurance offered by past forms of Providence and progress and with another it thrusts into our reluctant hands the responsibility for the future.

We went through that entire emotional sequence—grief, loneliness, reluctant responsibility—when we worked on The Club of Rome project twenty years ago. Many other people, through many other kinds of formative events, have gone through a similar sequence. It can be survived. It can even open up new horizons and suggest exciting futures. Those futures will never come to be, however, until the world as a whole turns to face them. The ideas of limits, sustainability, sufficiency, equity, and efficiency are not barriers, not obstacles, not threats. They are guides to a new world. Sustainability, not better weapons or struggles for power or material accumulation, is the ultimate challenge to the energy and creativity of the human race.

We think the human race is up to the challenge. We think that a better world is possible, and that the acceptance of physical limits is the first step toward getting there. We see "easing down" from unsustainability not as a sacrifice, but as an opportunity to stop battering against the earth's limits and to start transcending self-imposed and unnecessary limits in human institutions, mindsets, beliefs, and ethics. That is why we finally decided not just to update and reissue *The Limits to Growth*, but to rewrite it completely and to call it *Beyond the Limits*.

75 Arne Naess, from *Ecology, Community and Lifestyle: Outline of an Ecosophy* (Cambridge University Press, 1989), pp. 164–9

Born in Norway, Naess (1912–) studied in Oslo, Paris, and Vienna, and became the first full Professor of Philosophy at the University of Oslo at the age of twenty-eight. Influenced principally by the thinking of Spinoza and Gandhi, he supplemented his philosophical

writings with a deep commitment to environmental activism and protest. From 1970, he operated as a free-lance writer, naturalist, and campaigner. A skilled mountaineer, his experience
of wilderness and solitude in the mountains of central Norway has been a formative influence
upon his work. His campaigning apart, Naess has been important in green political circles for
his justification of a key philosophical distinction between those aspiring towards a 'deep
ecology', as opposed to those content with a 'shallow' alternative, an idea expressed in a
famous paper he delivered at the Third World Futures Conference in 1972.

THE UNIVERSAL RIGHT TO SELF-UNFOLDING AND THE CORRELATIVE INTRINSIC VALUE OF EVERY LIFE FORM

(a) Ecosophy ties together all life and all nature

'To have a home', 'to belong', 'to live' and many other similar expressions suggest fundamental milieu factors involved in the shaping of an individual's sense of self and self-respect. The
identity of the individual, 'that I am something', is developed through interaction with a
broad manifold, organic and inorganic. There is no completely isolatable I, no isolatable
social unit.

To distance oneself from nature and the 'natural' is to distance oneself from a part of
that which the 'I' is built up of. Its 'identity', 'what the individual I is', and thereby sense of
self and self-respect, are broken down. Some milieu factors, e.g. mother, father, family,
one's first companions, play a central role in the development of an I, but so do home and
the surroundings of home.

Ecological and psychological research furnish overwhelming evidence of the connection our unfolding self has with an unsurveyable variety and richness of natural
phenomena, predominantly with the life in the ecosphere, but also with non-organic
nature. The tiny infant gradually distinguishes its mother from the rest of its surroundings, and it concentrates positive feelings around the relations, the context, with her. The
'grown-up child', the naturalist, extends this positive feeling to all of nature through the
insight that everything is interconnected.

This vaguely outlined development can naturally be destroyed by severe tragedy—
such as loss of mother and later repeated losses and self-denials. Self-realisation receives
a blow which can contribute to a hostile attitude towards a great deal, even to everything:
a destructive urge addressed to the whole world and existence as such. There are many
examples of this, but the essential point is that such development is not a necessary
progression. Favourable conditions for Self-realisation extend the radiation of good
feelings to more and more nature.

In this chapter a basic positive attitude to nature is articulated in philosophical form.
It is not done to win compliance, but to offer some of the many who are at home in such
a philosophy new opportunities to express it in words. This is necessary so that society
and politics will give consideration to the kind of lifestyle which is a natural consequence
of such a philosophy.

(b) 'The unfolding of potentialities is a right'

That one order is just and another is unjust is an old thought, and it has never been
restricted in application only to humanity. One exercises justice or injustice to plants and

animals as well. In the newer so-called tradition of the 'rights of nature', we find these thoughts expressed philosophically. Through countless ages, they have been expressed religiously and mystically. Plants and animals also have a right to unfolding and self-realisation. They have the *right to live*.

What is the *right* to live? A definition is often arbitrary, and it leaves out the mythic component. A good definition, by definition, lacks a mythic function. But sentences with mythic function are still required today. The scientific and philosophical turns of phrase can easily come to overlook important sources of meaningfulness and general appeal. 'All living creatures are fundamentally one' is a good example of a sentence which has a mythic function, but which may also be precised in the direction of a testable hypothesis or norm. While it has cognitive usage, it is also associated at the same time with the more or less mythic conception of a just or injust order in the world. In the beginning of the 60s, Rachel Carson incited opposition to the poisoning of nature, using both scientific and 'mythic' forms of expression. She felt that mankind did not have *the right* to devastate nature and found it unjustifiable that we, mere 'drops in the stream of life', should permit ourselves to do whatever we please with 'the work of God'.

We are not outside the rest of nature and therefore cannot do with it as we please without changing ourselves. We must begin to see what we do to ourselves when we say 'only change external nature'. We are a part of the ecosphere just as intimately as we are a part of our own society. But the expression 'drops in the stream of life' may be misleading if it implies that individuality of the drops is lost in the stream. Here is a difficult ridge to walk: To the left we have the ocean of organic and mystic views, to the right the abyss of atomic individualism.

(c) Life as a vast historical process

The geological history of our globe tells of tremendous changes: the uplifting of mountain chains, the unceasing work of erosion, the slow movements of the continents. Among these enormous processes in time and space, one is nearest to us: *the unfolding of life*. Human beings who wish to attain a maximum perspective in the comprehension of their cosmic condition can scarcely refrain from a proud feeling of genuine participation in something immensely greater than their individual and social career. Palaeontology reveals the various phases in the development: the extension of the boundaries for where life can thrive, the establishment of ever more potentialities for life in the inorganic environment, the development of a nervous system culminating in the brain of the mammals.

The entire study leaves the impression that the development of life on earth is *an integrated process*, despite the steadily increasing diversity and complexity. The nature and limitation of this unity can be debated. Still, this is something basic. 'Life is fundamentally one.'

Homo sapiens is singularly well equipped to comprehend this unity in the light of human extreme lack of biological specialisation. Our hand is just as 'primitive', i.e. unspecialised, as that of the lizard, and much more primitive than horse hooves or eagle claws. The *cortex cerebri* is the decisive factor. It takes over more and more instinctual activities, and allows us to approach the unspecialised state of a clump of protoplasm. Our lack of a definite biological place to call home allows us to feel at home everywhere. We can sympathise with *all* the more specialised life forms. The educational value of palaeontology in its fullness is not yet appreciated, but will in the future be seen as greater than mere attention to evolution and some spectacular dinosaurs.

The traditional way of expressing what is common to all species of life, and more generally to all forms of life, is to point to a basic striving, that of self-preservation. This term is misleading, however, in so far as it does not account for the dynamics of expansion and modification. There is a tendency to realise *every* possibility for development, to explore all possibilities of change within the framework of the species and even to transgress its limits. Palaeontology tells of the 'conquest' of, or 'expansion' from sea to, land and air, and the development of mutual aid.

In view of the defensive passivity suggested by the term self-preservation, I favour Self-realisation or Self-unfolding. Historically I trace the conception back to Spinoza's *perseverare in suo esse*, to persevere in one's own (way of) being, not mere keeping alive. Ecosophy T concentrates especially upon the aspect of general unfolding *in suo esse*. For life in general it implies the 'creative evolution' (Bergson), the steady extension of the biosphere, from the comfortable lukewarm, shallow seas to arctic oceans and steaming hot-water springs. The emergence of human ecological consciousness is a philosophically important idea: a life form has developed on Earth which is capable of understanding and appreciating its relations with all other life forms and to the Earth as a whole.

(d) The universal right to live and blossom

The right of all the forms to live is a universal right which cannot be quantified. No single species of living being has more of this particular right to live and unfold than any other species. Perhaps it is *not* the best way of expressing this to say that there is a right—the *equal* right for all life forms—to unfold its specific capacities. 'Equality' suggests a sort of quantification that is misleading.

From the point of view of analytical philosophy the term 'right', like many other terms used in daily life— 'fact', 'verification' ('shown to be the case'), 'duty', 'value in itself'—is rather suspicious. Does it have any meaning that can be clarified? Is it just a question of coercive power when somebody says that we have no right to do so and so? I do not think so. As I use the term I do not pretend that it has a clearly formulatable meaning, but that it is the best expression I have so far found of an intuition which I am unable to reject in all seriousness. But I completely accept that some environmental philosophers avoid the term and advise others to do the same.

When we attempt to live out our relationships with other living beings in accordance with such *a principle of equal rights* of all fellow beings, difficult questions naturally arise. (This always happens when a normative idea in the central reaches of a norm system is practised.) It suggests a guideline for our behaviour, but it does not tell anything about behaviour. Additional norms and hypotheses are, for instance, necessary as premises in order to derive a norm that killing violates the right. It is not some kind of unconditional *isolatable* norm to treat everything the same way. It is only a fragment of a total view. Our apprehension of the actual conditions under which we live our own lives—that is, certain 'hypotheses' high up in the systematised total view—make it crystal clear that we have to injure and kill, in other words actively hinder the self-unfolding of other living beings. Equal right to unfold potentials as a principle is not a practical norm about equal conduct towards all life forms. It suggests a guideline limiting killing, and more generally limiting obstruction of the unfolding of potentialities in others.

Many contend that living beings can be ranked according to their *relative intrinsic value*. The claims of rankable value are usually based upon one or more of the following contentions.

(1) If a being has an eternal soul, this being is of greater intrinsic value than one which has a time-limited or no soul.

(2) If a being can reason, it has greater value than one which does not have reason or is unreasonable.

(3) If a being is conscious of itself and of its possibilities to choose, it is of greater value than one which lacks such consciousness.

(4) If a being is a higher animal in an evolutionary sense, it is of greater value than those which are farther down on the evolutionary scale.

None of these standpoints, so far as I can see, have been substantially justified. They may appear to be reasonable at first glance, but they fade after reflection and confrontation with the basic intuitions of the unity of life and the right to live and blossom.

The contention that one life form has a higher value than another sometimes leads to the argument that the more valuable being has the right to kill and injure the less valuable. A different approach is to specify under which circumstances it is justifiable to hunt or kill other living beings. We might agree upon rules such as will imply different behaviour towards different kinds of living beings without negating that there is a value inherent in living beings which is *the same value* for all. But it is against my intuition of unity to say 'I can kill you because I am more valuable' but not against the intuition to say 'I will kill you because I am hungry'. In the latter case, there would be an implicit regret: 'Sorry, I am now going to kill you because I am hungry'. In short, I find obviously right, but often difficult to justify, different sorts of behaviour with different sorts of living beings. But this does not imply that we classify some as intrinsically more valuable than others.

Modern ecology has emphasised a high degree of *symbiosis* as a common feature in mature ecosystems, an interdependence for the benefit of all. It has thereby provided *a cognitive basis for a sense of belonging* which was not possible earlier. Family belonging, the tie of kinship, has a material basis in perceived togetherness and cooperation. Through the extension of our understanding of the ecological context, it will ultimately be possible to develop a sense of belonging with a more expansive perspective: *ecospheric belonging*.

'The task is to find a form of togetherness with nature which is to our own greatest benefit. Any other definition is hypocritical.' If such a statement is accepted, 'our own benefit' must then mean 'that which serves the great Self', not merely the individual ego or human societies. If a lesser self is implied, the sentences are misleading. One can desire well-being for an animal or a plant just as naturally as one can for a person. For some dog owners, their dog's well-being is more important to them than that of their neighbour. The identification is stronger, and empathy is greater. One can, without hypocrisy, *desire something which is for the benefit of other living beings*—and one normally obtains great, rich satisfaction from it.

The technical development together with our insight into mutual, symbiotic relationships makes it possible for human beings to allow *cooperation and togetherness* to colour our work days and leisure life much more than before. Unfortunately this is at the moment primarily a theoretical possibility. The coming decades will probably see certain dichotomies between human societies play themselves out (e.g. the North–South conflict), as well as between mankind and other living beings (the destruction of habitats of other species).

Let us examine a rather provoking thought experiment. *Homo sapiens* may be capable, in suitable circumstances, and upon the basis of a wide perspective, of *recommending its own withdrawal* as the dominant living being on earth. By such an act humans would confirm (just as we do in many other actions) that mankind is not bound to the values 'useful for human beings' or 'suitable to human self-preservation' when 'utility' and 'self' are taken in a *narrow* sense. If the terms are understood very broadly, we are bound to our Self, but then as the circle is bound to π (3.14159 . . .). To the great Self of mankind, it may be useful to transfer some power over others to a more sensible and sensitive species.

It is realistic to ask how we would behave faced with living beings from distant planets which look like *Homo sapiens*, so that identification would be easy. Would we as human beings subject ourselves freely to the political will of an alien species which had more or less the same characteristics as us, but which lacked our tendency to torture, torment and exploit one another? The decision would perhaps take a few centuries, but I believe it would be positive. We would abdicate, if we were sure of them.

This thought experiment makes assumptions which cannot be said to be probable. Members of *Homo sapiens* are not genetically or in any other way *bound* to torture, torment and exploit one another for all eternity. The possibility that future research will indicate such a dismal conclusion about human nature can presumably be characterised as extremely unlikely. But the thought experiment intimates that human drive for Self-realisation requires us to give way for the more perfect. Human beings would lose something of their own essential nature if they refrained from abdication.

76 Murray Bookchin, from *Post-Scarcity Anarchism* (Black Rose Books, 1986), pp. 63–6

Bookchin (1921–) was involved in the American Communist youth movement from the early 1930s. Dismayed both by the Stalin–Hitler pact and its bureaucratic and hierarchical organizational style, he was expelled in 1939. After returning from active service in the Second World War, he was deeply involved with the United Auto Workers and participated in the General Motors strike of 1948. From the mid-1940s, he moved away from socialist politics, and engaged more deeply with anarchist and libertarian writings. In 1974 he co-founded and directed the Institute for Social Ecology in Plainfield, Vermont. He has authored many books on anarchist thinking, the social character of technology, and the limitations of socialist politics.

The notion that man must dominate nature emerges directly from the domination of man by man. The patriarchal family planted the seed of domination in the nuclear relations of humanity; the classical split in the ancient world between spirit and reality— indeed, between mind and labor—nourished it; the anti-naturalist bias of Christianity tended to its growth. But it was not until organic community relations, feudal or peasant in form, dissolved into market relationships that the planet itself was reduced to a resource for exploitation. This centuries-long tendency finds its most exacerbating development in modern capitalism. Owing to its inherently competitive nature, bourgeois society not only pits humans against each other, it also pits the mass of humanity against the natural world. Just as men are converted into commodities, so every aspect of nature is converted into a commodity, a resource to be manufactured and merchandised wantonly. The liberal euphemisms for the processes involved are "growth," "industrial society" and "urban blight." By whatever language they are described, the phenomena have their roots in the domination of man by man.

The phrase "consumer society" complements the description of the present social order as an "industrial society." Needs are tailored by the mass media to create a public demand for utterly useless commodities, each carefully engineered to deteriorate after a predetermined period of time. The plundering of the human spirit by the marketplace is paralleled by the plundering of the earth by capital. (The liberal identification is a metaphor that neutralizes the social thrust of the ecological crisis.)

Despite the current clamor about population growth, the strategic ratios in the ecological crisis are not the population growth rates of India but the production rates of the United States, a country that produces more than half of the world's goods. Here, too, liberal euphemisms like "affluence" conceal the critical thrust of a blunt word like "waste." With a ninth of its industrial capacity committed to war production, the U.S. is literally trampling upon the earth and shredding ecological links that are vital to human survival. If current industrial projections prove to be accurate, the remaining thirty years of the century will witness a fivefold increase in electric power production, based mostly on nuclear fuels and coal. The colossal burden in radioactive wastes and other effluents that this increase will place on the natural ecology of the earth hardly needs description.

In shorter perspective, the problem is no less disquieting. Within the next five years, lumber production may increase an overall twenty percent; the output of paper, five percent annually; folding boxes, three percent annually; plastics (which currently form one to two percent of municipal wastes), seven percent annually. Collectively, these industries account for the most serious pollutants in the environment. The utterly senseless nature of modern industrial activity is perhaps best illustrated by the decline in returnable (and reusable) beer bottles from 54 billion bottles in 1960 to 26 billion today. Their place has been taken over by "one-way" bottles (a rise from 8 to 21 billion in the same period) and cans (an increase from 38 to 53 billion). The "one-way" bottles and the cans, of course, pose tremendous problems in solid waste disposal.

The planet, conceived of as a lump of minerals, can support these mindless increases in the output of trash. The earth, conceived of as a complex web of life, certainly cannot. The only question is whether the earth can survive its looting long enough for man to replace the current destructive social system with a humanistic, ecologically oriented society.

Ecologists are often asked, rather tauntingly, to locate with scientific exactness the ecological breaking point of nature—the point at which the natural world will cave in on man. This is equivalent to asking a psychiatrist for the precise moment when a neurotic will become a nonfunctional psychotic. No such answer is ever likely to be available. But the ecologist can supply a strategic insight into the directions man seems to be following as a result of his split with the natural world.

From the standpoint of ecology, man is dangerously oversimplifying his environment. The modern city represents a regressive encroachment of the synthetic on the natural, of the inorganic (concrete, metals, and glass) on the organic, of crude, elemental stimuli on variegated, wide-ranging ones. The vast urban belts now developing in industrialized areas of the world are not only grossly offensive to the eye and the ear, they are chronically smogridden, noisy, and virtually immobilized by congestion.

The process of simplifying man's environment and rendering it increasingly elemental and crude has a cultural as well as a physical dimension. The need to manipulate immense urban populations—to transport, feed, employ, educate and somehow enter-tain millions of densely concentrated people—leads to a crucial decline in civic and social standards. A mass concept of human relations—totalitarian, centralistic and regimented in orientation—tends to dominate the more individuated concepts of the past. Bureau-cratic techniques of social management tend to replace humanistic approaches. All that is spontaneous, creative and individuated is circumscribed by the standardized, the regulated and the massified. The space of the individual is steadily narrowed by restric-tions imposed upon him by a faceless, impersonal social apparatus. Any recognition of unique personal qualities is increasingly surrendered to the manipulation of the lowest common denominator of the mass. A quantitative, statistical approach, a beehive manner of dealing with man, tends to triumph over the precious individualized and qualitative approach which places the strongest emphasis on personal uniqueness, free expression and cultural complexity.

77 Jonathan Porritt, from *Seeing Green: the Politics of Ecology explained* (Blackwell, 1984), pp. 43–4

After studying at Cambridge University, Porritt (1950–) taught drama and English Literature in London. He has since become a well-known writer, broadcaster, and commentator on envi-ronmental issues and sustainable development. He was Directory of the Friends of the Earth from 1984 to 1990, and co-chair of the Green Party from 1980 to 1983. In 2000 he was appointed Chairman of the new UK Sustainable Development Commission, and is co-director of the Prince of Wales' Business and Environment Programme. Porritt remains a controversial figure within UK environmental circles, because of his outspoken criticisms of the Green Party, his extensive contacts with the private sector, and his role as informal adviser to Charles, Prince of Wales.

The claim made by green politics that it's 'neither right, nor left, nor in the centre' has understandably caused a lot of confusion! For people who are accustomed to thinking of politics exclusively in terms of the left/right polarity, green politics has to fit in somewhere. And if it doesn't, then it must be made to.

But it's really not that difficult. We profoundly disagree with the politics of the right and its underlying ideology of capitalism; we profoundly disagree with the politics of the left and its adherence, in varying degrees, to the ideology of communism. That leaves us little choice but to disagree, perhaps less profoundly, with the politics of the centre and its ideological potpourri of socialized capitalism. The politics of the Industrial Age, left, right and centre, is like a three-lane motorway, with different vehicles in different lanes, but *all* heading in the same direction. Greens feel it is the very direction that is wrong, rather than the choice of any one lane in preference to the others. It is our perception that the motorway of industrialism inevitably leads to the abyss—hence our decision to get off it, and seek an entirely different direction.

Yet it's built into our understanding of politics today that capitalism and communism represent the two extremes of a political spectrum. The two poles are apparently separated by such irreconcilable differences that there is no chance of them ever coming together. According to such a view, the history of the world from now on (however long or short a time-span that may be) is predicated upon the separateness of these two ideologies.

There are, indeed, many differences; in social and political organization; in democratic or totalitarian responses; in economic theory and practice. But for the moment, let's not dwell on these. Let us consider the *similarities* rather than the differences. Both are dedicated to industrial growth, to the expansion of the means of production, to a materialist ethic as the best means of meeting people's needs, and to unimpeded technological development. Both rely on increasing centralization and large-scale bureaucratic control and co-ordination. From a viewpoint of narrow scientific rationalism, both insist that the planet is there to be conquered, that big is self-evidently beautiful, and that what cannot be measured is of no importance. Economics dominates; art, morals and social values are all relegated to a dependent status.

I shall be arguing two things in this chapter: first, that the similarities between these two dominant ideologies are of greater significance than their differences, and that the dialectic between them is therefore largely superficial. If this is the case, it may be claimed that they are united in one, all-embracing 'super-ideology', which, for the sake of convenience, I intend to call industrialism. Secondly, that this super-ideology, in that it is conditioned to thrive on the ruthless exploitation of both people and planet, is *itself* the greatest threat we face. As Roszak puts it: 'The two ideological camps of the world go at one another; but, like antagonists in a nightmare, their embattled forms fuse into one monstrous shape, a single force of destruction threatening every assertion of personal rights that falls across the path of their struggle.'

If that is so, there must be something with which we can replace it; not another super-ideology (for ideologies are themselves part of the problem), *but a different world view*. That is the not unambitious role that green politics is in the process of carving out for itself.

78   Vandana Shiva, from *Staying Alive: Women, Ecology and Development* (Zed Books, 1989), pp. 1–5

Born in Dehradun in India, Shiva (1952–) became an activist in the Chipko movement of the 1970s, a coalition of women activists seeking to oppose logging and deforestation. She holds a Masters degree in particle physics and a Ph.D in the philosophy of science. In 1981, the Ministry of Defence in India invited her to report upon the effects of mining in the Doon valley. In the wake of this experience she founded the Research Foundation for Science, Technology and Ecology in 1982, which campaigns for sustainable agriculture and development. Shiva has combined academic research with involvement in a variety of grassroots environmental-ist, feminist, and development campaigns, and has emerged as a leading voice within the movement against global free trade and the Western food industry. In 1991, she founded Navdanya, an organic farming community in India, and, latterly, Bija Bidyapeeth, a 'seed university' that aims to promote the ideals of holistic living.

'Development' was to have been a post-colonial project, a choice for accepting a model of progress in which the entire world remade itself on the model of the colonising modern west, without having to undergo the subjugation and exploitation that colonialism entailed. The assumption was that western style progress was possible for all. Develop-ment, as the improved well-being of all, was thus equated with the westernisation of eco-nomic categories—of needs, of productivity, of growth. Concepts and categories about economic development and natural resource utilisation that had emerged in the specific context of industrialisation and capitalist growth in a centre of colonial power, were raised to the level of universal assumptions and applicability in the entirely different con-text of basic needs satisfaction for the people of the newly independent Third World countries. Yet, as Rosa Luxemberg has pointed out, early industrial development in western Europe necessitated the permanent occupation of the colonies by the colonial powers and the destruction of the local 'natural economy'. According to her, colonialism is a constant necessary condition for capitalist growth: without colonies, capital accumu-lation would grind to a halt. 'Development' as capital accumulation and the commercial-isation of the economy for the generation of 'surplus' and profits thus involved the reproduction not merely of a particular form of creation of wealth, but also of the asso-ciated creation of povety and dispossession. A replication of economic development based on commercialisation of resource use for commodity production in the newly independent countries created the internal colonies. Development was thus reduced to a continuation of the process of colonisation; it became an extension of the project of wealth creation in modern western patriarchy's economic vision, which was based on the exploitation or exclusion of women (of the west and non-west), on the exploitation and degradation of nature, and on the exploitation and erosion of other cultures. 'Development' could not but entail destruction for women, nature and subjugated cultures, which is why, throughout the Third World, women, peasants and tribals are struggling for liberation from 'development' just as they earlier struggled for liberation from colonialism.

The UN Decade for Women was based on the assumption that the improvement of women's economic position would automatically flow from an expansion and diffusion of the development process. Yet, by the end of the Decade, it was becoming clear that development itself was the problem. Insufficient and inadequate 'participation' in 'development' was not the cause for women's increasing under-development; it was rather, their enforced but asymmetric participation in it, by which they bore the costs but were excluded from the benefits, that was responsible. Development exclusivity and dispossession aggravated and deepened the colonial processes of ecological degradation and the loss of political control over nature's sustenance base. Economic growth was a new colonialism, draining resources away from those who needed them most. The discontinuity lay in the fact that it was now new national elites, not colonial powers, that masterminded the exploitation on grounds of 'national interest' and growing GNPs, and it was accomplished with more powerful technologies of appropriation and destruction.

Ester Boserup has documented how women's impoverishment increased during colonial rule; those rulers who had spent a few centuries in subjugating and crippling their own women into de-skilled, de-intellectualised appendages, disfavoured the women of the colonies on matters of access to land, technology and employment. The economic and political processes of colonial under-development bore the clear mark of modern western patriarchy, and while large numbers of women and men were impoverished by these processes, women tended to lose more. The privatisation of land for revenue generation displaced women more critically, eroding their traditional land use rights. The expansion of cash crops undermined food production, and women were often left with meagre resources to feed and care for children, the aged and the infirm, when men migrated or were conscripted into forced labour by the colonisers. As a collective document by women activists, organisers and researchers stated at the end of the UN Decade for Women, 'The almost uniform conclusion of the Decade's research is that with a few exceptions, women's relative access to economic resources, incomes and employment has worsened, their burden of work has increased, and their relative and even absolute health, nutritional and educational status has declined.'

The displacement of women from productive activity by the expansion of development was rooted largely in the manner in which development projects appropriated or destroyed the natural resource base for the production of sustenance and survival. It destroyed women's productivity both by removing land, water and forests from their management and control, as well as through the ecological destruction of soil, water and vegetation systems so that nature's productivity and renewability were impaired. While gender subordination and patriarchy are the oldest of oppressions, they have taken on new and more violent forms through the project of development. Patriarchal categories which understand destruction as 'production' and regeneration of life as 'passivity' have generated a crisis of survival. Passivity, as an assumed category of the 'nature' of nature and of women, denies the activity of nature and life. Fragmentation and uniformity as assumed categories of progress and development destroy the living forces which arise from relationships within the 'web of life' and the diversity in the elements and patterns of these relationships.

The economic biases and values against nature, women and indigenous peoples are captured in this typical analysis of the 'unproductiveness' of traditional natural societies:

> Production is achieved through human and animal, rather than mechanical, power. Most agriculture is unproductive; human or animal manure may be used but chemical fertilisers and pesticides are unknown . . . . For the masses, these conditions mean poverty.

The assumptions are evident: nature is unproductive; organic agriculture based on nature's cycles of renewability spells poverty; women and tribal and peasant societies embedded in nature are similarly unproductive, not because it has been demonstrated that in cooperation they produce *less* goods and services for needs, but because it is assumed that 'production' takes place only when mediated by technologies for commodity production, even when such technologies destroy life. A stable and clean river is not a productive resource in this view: it needs to be 'developed' with dams in order to become so. Women, sharing the river as a commons to satisfy the water needs of their families and society are not involved in productive labour: when substituted by the engineering man, water management and water use become productive activities. Natural forests remain unproductive till they are developed into monoculture plantations of commercial species. Development thus, is equivalent to maldevelopment, a development bereft of the feminine, the conservation, the ecological principle. The neglect of nature's work in renewing herself, and women's work in producing sustenance in the form of basic, vital needs is an essential part of the paradigm of maldevelopment, which sees all work that does not produce profits and capital as non or unproductive work. As Maria Mies has pointed out, this concept of surplus has a patriarchal bias because, from the point of view of nature and women, it is not based on material surplus produced *over and above* the requirements of the community: it is stolen and appropriated through violent modes from nature (who needs a share of her produce to reproduce herself) and from women (who need a share of nature's produce to produce sustenance and ensure survival).

From the perspective of Third World women, productivity is a measure of producing life and sustenance; that this kind of productivity has been rendered invisible does not reduce its centrality to survival—it merely reflects the domination of modern patriarchal economic categories which see only profits, not life.

8 Anarchism

Introduction

The character and contents of the ideology of anarchism have been sources of considerable disagreement among its interpreters. One view regards anarchism as a natural member of the broad church of left-wing politics. Yet for others, anarchist commitments to the merits of unplanned social evolution and the capacity for spontaneous order, beyond the reach of the state, suggest an affinity between this tradition and conservatism. More helpfully, commentators have identified a latent tension between those anarchists who stress the co-operative characteristics of humans and the significance of free communities for individual liberation, on the one hand, and trenchant proponents of self-reliant individualism and libertarian values, on the other. Attempts to read anarchism as simply left- or right-wing, or indeed to divide anarchists into the co-operative or libertarian camps, neglect the independent and distinctive web of conceptual commitments that its theoreticians have woven since the nineteenth century. Within this, a number of rival conceptions of self, community, and state figure prominently, ideas that have informed the distinctive political movements, struggles, and programmes associated with political anarchy.

Like the other ideologies considered in this text, anarchism resembles a family with different, occasionally squabbling, members. Like its political rivals, it has also drawn upon some of the long-standing, familiar intellectual and cultural traditions from the different polities in which it has exercised an impact. This characteristic is often overlooked by those who assume that its normative commitments make it an alien and essentially marginal presence within democratic society.

One of the main sources for latter-day anarchism are the controversial, and idiosyncratic, ideas of the early nineteeth-century philosopher Max Stirner [Reading 79]. His celebration of the value of egotism, in opposition to other kinds of moral philosophy, has proved both important and troubling for later anarchists: important because of his depiction of the struggle for freedom by the individual as the central politico-ethical dynamic of modern politics; and troubling because he cast this struggle in such militantly individualistic and instrumentalized terms. For Stirner, too many religions and other social philosophies strove to teach individuals to find their real interests or true being in movements, goals, or values that lay outside themselves. Religion, in particular, he despised because it harnesses one aspect of our natures—our desire to achieve 'good'—and misleads us into believing that this particular need is superior to all the others that we possess. Freedom can only be secured by the individual's attempt to act in accordance with her full, unique individuality. No moral codes or external authority can determine how I will engage with the world, and it is more important to be governed by my internal desires than to act in ways that are conventionally deemed good or proper.

Like later anarchists he viewed the impulse to resist the claims of external and supposedly higher authorities as intrinsic to human society. The rebellious few, heroes who stand against the claims of such bodies, are in the end the sources of the decline of unjustified forms of religious and secular authority. What individuals possess that socially organized collectivities do not, is the capacity to exercise what he terms 'might'—immediate, effective power. Offering a powerful contrast between 'self-liberation' and 'emancipation', he suggests that real freedom follows from the exercise of this capacity by individuals, not the granting of constitutional protections and rights to them. Only those who have thrown off the psychic yoke of forces like religion can be considered truly free.

One of the political implications of this argument was a deep suspicion of the claims that individuals owe obligation to the sovereign state. While it is claimed that states are associations forged for the interests of all within it, this idea masks the reality that individuals are in fact setting the collective interest above their own particular needs and interests. Indeed, the ideals of popular sovereignty and of association in a state are malign myths. The very existence of the state rests upon the denial of the independence and individuality of individuals. The propensity to allocate to nations and states the status of sovereign wills follows upon similar projections onto religions and nature itself. The self-assertion and achievement of individuality by human subjects represents the negation of these earlier constructions and promises a new stage in human history.

The centralizing and hierarchical properties of the modern state were a target for other nineteenth-century anarchists as well, and shaped the major contributions to this tradition of a variety of Russian authors in particular. For Michael Bakunin, representative democracy is a sham, masking the growing power of the state and the subordination of the people to the political elite [Reading 80]. The deployment of coercion and its military capacity are integral aspects of the modern state, and play an important role, he maintains, in shaping the logic of centralization. In the second part of the extract, Bakunin turns to the prospect of revolution. In a retort to the claims of Marxists, he argues that the aspiration to revolt against the political class cannot be inculcated among workers and peasants from outside their ranks. The ideal of social change arises spontaneously from within the experiences and consciousness of the exploited, not from the minds of intellectuals.

A different, equally influential strand of nineteenth-century anarchism was more sceptical about the revolutionary outlook proposed by Bakunin. For Peter Kropotkin, anarchism builds upon the guiding principle of 'mutual aid'—the ethos of association that he observes as integral to both animals and humans [Reading 81]. Combining this ideal with a Darwinian understanding of social development, he offers a distinctive account of the stages of societal evolution. This culminates with his assertion that while the modern state has sought to supplant associations for mutual aid, it has been unable to do so. Kropotkin's narrative of social development reveals a highly ambivalent attitude to the 'progress' associated with the modern industrial economy. The competitiveness and egotism engendered by the latter required the destruction of a medieval order in which mutual aid flourished through many different guilds, associations, and groups. Even greater economic and material advances, he claims, would have arisen had co-operation and trust been guiding principles of social development, not relentless competition. And in the realm of morality, he argues, co-operation not conflict has been the crucible of ethical development.

In the writings of the Russian revolutionary and radical intellectual Emma Goldman, these apparently divergent strands are drawn together in a distinctive and original argument

[Reading 82]. Anarchy, she suggests, implies the unrestricted liberty of the individual and the recognition that the modern state is defined by its capacity for violence. It comprises a distinctive philosophy that seeks to disentangle the individual from false idols such as God, property, and Government. It does so by reconciling the value of individual self-assertion with social co-operation. None of these false deities can sustain a life that is worthwhile in either material or moral terms. Only in a society where humans exercise control over the work they perform, and that unleashes the creative energies of individuals within it, will true freedom prevail. The political correlation of such a vision, she maintains, is a society formed through the democratic inter-relations of decentralized communities.

Other cultures and different kinds of voice have also contributed much to anarchist thought. The ideas of the English intellectual Herbert Read reveal his debt to Kropotkin's conception of mutual aid, but also invoke some local commitments, notably those of the early twentieth-century pluralists [Reading 83]. Read contrasts anarchists' recognition of the indissoluble uniqueness and difference of every human personality, with conceptions of politics founded upon the presumption that human nature is fixed and uniform. This vision finds political expression, he maintains, in the anarchist sympathy for a society in which a myriad of groups balance one another, and all fulfil some important social function. Against the argument that only a state can provide various basic public goods and remedy social ills, he argues that some societal dysfunctions are in fact the products of such respectable institutions as private property and state authority. Other goods can be provided by the community at large, but in a variety of more intimate social forms, rather than through impersonal state provision. Anarchy is here presented as guided by the principle of decentralization, though Read is clear that this ought not to be regarded as implying a nostalgic return to a medieval golden age. Finally he charges the state with the crime of whipping up artificial and dangerous kinds of nationalist sentiment.

Anarchism is often regarded as an intellectual artefact of the nineteenth century, and—as a political force—an anomaly of the political cultures of Spain and Italy in the twentieth. Both assumptions are mistaken. Anarchism plays an important intellectual and political role in Anglo-American political culture throughout this period, and currently still informs various radical forms of social protest, philosophical undertaking, and political programme. One of the major conduits for anarchist ideas in the English-speaking world in the second half of the twentieth century is the social theorist and critic Paul Goodman [Reading 84]. In his definition, anarchism is founded upon a recognition that individuals and groups are able to respond freely to the circumstances and conditions they inhabit. This understanding of the human potential and capacity for self-direction undergirds the anarchist rejection of the exercise of centralized authority. Anarchism on his view is a diverse family, linked by this one genetic principle; and can find expression in either co-operative, communalist forms, or in more indivdualistic and naturalistic modes of argument. Turning on its head the criticism that anarchism is a speculative and fanciful dream, he connects it with two of the central impulses of western modernity—the rise of the twin ideas of individual liberty and the defeat of hierarchy and conformity.

In the second extract, he focuses upon the notion of freedom, and develops a distinctive reading of this value as rooted in the necessity of its continual practice. Presenting the social field as divided into an on-going struggle between 'those in power' and 'ordinary people', he maintains that freedoms always exist in a state of tension—subject to the interest of the former in limiting and restricting their scope, and pressures from below for their continual extension and realization. While the reigning powers in the modern state possess a host of advantages and resources denied to the people at large, the dynamics of popular protests in the name of freedom are themselves highly potent and hard to control. In the final paragraph, he notes one of the major sources of disagreement within this political tradition—ideas about the social settings in which freedom flourishes and about which social subjects are most likely to carry forward the anarchist struggle.

Perhaps the most celebrated contemporary exponent of anarchism is the radical American intellectual, Noam Chomsky. In this extract [Reading 85], he offers some intriguing autobiographical ruminations upon the place of anarchism within his intellectual make-up. He locates the roots of anarchist thinking in two overlapping contexts—the philosophies of the Enlightenment and the development of a distinctive form of pre-industrial liberalism. He points to the malign consequences of the hegemony within modern democratic states of large-scale institutions and corporate powers. And he follows Thomas Jefferson in pointing to the damaging social impact of the unchecked growth of banking interests and finance capital. He counter opposes to these oligarchical trends the survival of an anarchic anti-authoritarianism that demands a persuasive justification for the involvement of state and corporate institutions in various social arenas.

FURTHER READING

One of the first serious treatments of anarchist thinking is George Woodcock's *Anarchism* (Penguin, 1963). Important subsequent studies include David Miller's blend of conceptual and historical analysis, in his *Anarchism* (Dent, 1984), and Peter Marshall's invaluable reference work, *Demanding the Impossible: A History of Anarchism* (Fontana Press, 1993). One of the most useful collections of anarchist writings can be found in Leonard I. Krimerman and Lewis Perry (eds.) *Patterns of Anarchy: A Collection of Writings on The Anarchist Tradition* (Anchor Books, 1966).

79   Max Stirner, from *The Ego and Its Own* (ed. David Leopold; Cambridge University Press, 1995), pp. 149–52, 198–9

Born in Bavaria, Stirner (1806–1856) studied theology and philosophy in Berlin in the 1820s, being taught by leading figures such as Hegel and Schleiermacher. He acted as a teacher and private scholar, but was forced to turn his hand to journalism for financial reasons. Throughout these years he was a familiar figure within Berlin's intellectual society and on the fringes of the political events shaking the city. His work is best known for its radical individualism, and his commitment to the ineradicability and ethical significance of the individual ego. Deeply hostile to the church and other oppressive social institutions, he denounced many of his philosophical contemporaries for their failure to break with religious modes of thinking.

This position was expressed most fully in his *The Ego and its Own*, a book that influenced, among others, Karl Marx, later anarchists, and more recent thinkers on the political right.

Thousands of years of civilization have obscured to you what you are, have made you believe you are not egoists but are *called* to be idealists ('good men'). Shake that off! Do not seek for freedom, which does precisely deprive you of yourselves, in 'self-denial'; but seek for *yourselves*, become egoists, become each of you an *almighty ego*. Or, more clearly: Just recognize yourselves again, just recognize what you really are, and let go your hypocritical endeavours, your foolish mania to be something else than you are. Hypocritical I call them because you have yet remained egoists all these thousands of years, but sleeping, self-deceiving, crazy egoists, you *heautontimorumenoses*, you self-tormentors. Never yet has a religion been able to dispense with 'promises', whether they referred us to the other world or to this ('long life', etc.); for man is *mercenary* and does nothing 'gratis'. But how about that 'doing the good for the good's sake' without prospect of reward? As if here too the pay was not contained in the satisfaction that it is to afford. Even religion, therefore, is founded on our egoism and—exploits it; calculated for our *desires*, it stifles many others for the sake of one. This then gives the phenomenon of *cheated* egoism, where I satisfy, not myself, but one of my desires, such as the impulse toward blessedness. Religion promises me the—'supreme good'; to gain this I no longer regard any other of my desires, and do not slake them.—All your doings are *unconfessed*, secret, covert, and concealed egoism. But because they are egoism that you are unwilling to confess to yourselves, that you keep secret from yourselves, hence not manifest and public egoism, consequently unconscious egoism, therefore they are *not egoism*, but thraldom, service, self-renunciation; you are egoists, and you are not, since you renounce egoism. Where you seem most to be such, you have drawn upon the word 'egoist'—loathing and contempt.

I secure my freedom with regard to the world in the degree that I make the world my own, 'gain it and take possession of it' for myself, by whatever might, by that of persuasion, of petition, of categorical demand, yes, even by hypocrisy, cheating, etc.; for the means that I use for it are determined by what I am. If I am weak, I have only weak means, like the aforesaid, which yet are good enough for a considerable part of the world. Besides, cheating, hypocrisy, lying, look worse than they are. Who has not cheated the police, the law? Who has not quickly taken on an air of honourable loyalty before the sheriff's officer who meets him, in order to conceal an illegality that may have been committed? He who has not done it has simply let violence be done to him; he was a *weakling* from—conscience. I know that my freedom is diminished even by not being able to carry out my will on another object, be this other something without will, like a rock, or something with will, like a government, an individual; I deny my ownness when—in presence of another—I give myself up, give way, desist, submit; therefore by *loyalty, submission*. For it is one thing when I give up my previous course because it does not lead to the goal, and therefore turn out of a wrong road; it is another when I yield myself a prisoner. I get around a rock that stands in my way, until I have powder enough to blast it; I get around the laws of a people, until I have gathered strength to overthrow them. Because I cannot grasp the moon, is it therefore to be 'sacred' to me, an Astarte? If I only could grasp you, I surely would, and, if I only find a means to get up to you, you shall not frighten me! You inapprehensible one, you shall remain inapprehensible to me only until I have acquired the might for apprehension and call you my *own*; I do not give myself up before you, but only bide my time. Even if for the present I put up with my inability to touch you, I yet remember it against you.

Vigorous men have always done so. When the 'loyal' had exalted an unsubdued power to be their master and had adored it, when they had demanded adoration from all, then there came some such son of nature who would not loyally submit, and drove the adored power from its inaccessible Olympus. He cried his 'stand still' to the rolling sun, and made the earth go round; the loyal had to make the best of it; he laid his axe to the sacred oaks, and the 'loyal' were astonished that no heavenly fire consumed him; he threw the Pope off Peter's chair, and the 'loyal' had no way to hinder it; he is tearing down the divine-right business, and the 'loyal' croak in vain, and at last are silent.

My freedom becomes complete only when it is my—*might;* but by this I cease to be a merely free man, and become an own man. Why is the freedom of the peoples a 'hollow word'? Because the peoples have no might! With a breath of the living ego I blow peoples over, be it the breath of a Nero, a Chinese emperor, or a poor writer. Why is it that the G— legislatures pine in vain for freedom, and are lectured for it by the cabinet ministers? Because they are not of the 'mighty'! Might is a fine thing, and useful for many purposes; for 'one goes further with a handful of might than with a bagful of right'. You long for freedom? You fools! If you took might, freedom would come of itself. See, he who has might 'stands above the law'. How does this prospect taste to you, you 'law-abiding' people? But you have no taste!

The cry for 'freedom' rings loudly all around. But is it felt and known what a donated or chartered freedom must mean? It is not recognized in the full amplitude of the word that all freedom is essentially—self-liberation—that I can have only so much freedom as I procure for myself by my ownness. Of what use is it to sheep that no one abridges their freedom of speech? They stick to bleating. Give one who is inwardly a Moslem, a Jew, or a Christian, permission to speak what he likes: he will yet utter only narrow-minded stuff. If, on the contrary, certain others rob you of the freedom of speaking and hearing, they know quite rightly wherein lies their temporary advantage, as you would perhaps be able to say and hear something whereby those 'certain' persons would lose their credit.

If they nevertheless give you freedom, they are simply rogues who give more than they have. For then they give you nothing of their own, but stolen wares: they give you your own freedom, the freedom that you must take for yourselves; and they *give* it to you only that you may not take it and call the thieves and cheats to an account to boot. In their slyness they know well that given (chartered) freedom is no freedom, since only the freedom one *takes* for himself, therefore the egoist's freedom, rides with full sails. Donated freedom strikes its sails as soon as there comes a storm—or calm; it requires always a—gentle and moderate breeze.

Here lies the difference between self-liberation and emancipation (manumission, setting free). Those who today 'stand in the opposition' are thirsting and screaming to be 'set free'. The princes are to 'declare their peoples of age', that is, emancipate them! Behave as if you were of age, and you are so without any declaration of majority; if you do not behave accordingly, you are not worthy of it, and would never be of age even by a declaration of majority. When the Greeks were of age, they drove out their tyrants, and, when the son is of age, he makes himself independent of his father. If the Greeks had waited until their tyrants graciously allowed them their majority, they might have waited long. A sensible father throws out a son who will not come of age, and keeps the house to himself; it serves the simpleton right.

The man who is set free is nothing but a freed man, a *libertinus*, a dog dragging a piece of chain with him: he is an unfree man in the garment of freedom, like the ass in the lion's skin. Emancipated Jews are nothing bettered in themselves, but only relieved as Jews, although he who relieves their condition is certainly more than a churchly Christian, as the latter cannot do this without inconsistency. But, emancipated or not emancipated, Jew remains Jew; he who is not self-freed is merely an—emancipated man. The Protestant state can certainly set free (emancipate) the Catholics; but, because they do not make themselves free, they remain simply—Catholics.

. . .

What is called a state is a tissue and plexus of dependence and adherence; it is a *belonging together* [*Zusammengehörigkeit*], a holding together, in which those who are placed together fit themselves to each other, or, in short, mutually depend on each other: it is the *order* of this *dependence* [*Abhängigkeit*]. Suppose the king, whose authority lends authority to all down to the beadle, should vanish: still all in whom the will for order was awake would keep order erect against the disorders of bestiality. If disorder were victorious, the state would be at an end.

But is this thought of love, to fit ourselves to each other, to adhere to each other and depend on each other, really capable of winning us? According to this the state should be *love* realized, the being for each other and living for each other of all. Is not self-will being lost while we attend to the will for order? Will people not be satisfied when order is cared for by authority, when authority sees to it that no one 'gets in the way of' another; when, then, the *herd* is judiciously distributed or ordered? Why, then everything is in 'the best order', and it is this best order that is called—state!

Our societies and states *are* without our *making* them, are united without our uniting, are predestined and established, or have an independent *standing* [*Bestand*] of their own, are the indissolubly established against us egoists. The fight of the world today is, as it is said, directed against the 'established [*Bestehende*]'. Yet people are wont to misunderstand this as if it were only that what is now established was to be exchanged for another, a better, established system. But war might rather be declared against establishment itself, the *state*, not a particular state, not any such thing as the mere condition of the state at the time; it is not another state (such as a 'people's state') that men aim at, but their *union*, uniting, this ever-fluid uniting of everything standing.—A state exists even without my co-operation: I am born in it, brought up in it, under obligations to it, and must 'do it homage [*huldigen*]'. It takes me up into its 'favour [*Huld*]', and I live by its 'grace'. Thus the independent establishment of the state founds my lack of independence; its condition as a 'natural growth', its organism, demands that my nature not grow freely, but be cut to fit it. That *it* may be able to unfold in natural growth, it applies to me the shears of 'civilization'; it gives me an education and culture adapted to it, not to me, and teaches me to respect the laws, to refrain from injury to state property (that is, private property), to reverence divine and earthly highness, etc.; in short, it teaches me to be—*unpunishable*, 'sacrificing' my ownness to 'sacredness' (everything possible is sacred; property, others' life, etc.). In this consists the sort of civilization and culture that the state is able to give me: it brings me up to be a 'serviceable instrument', a 'serviceable member of society'.

This every state must do, the people's state as well as the absolute or constitutional one. It must do so as long as we rest in the error that it is an *I*, as which it then applies to itself the name of a 'moral, mystical, or political person'. I, who really am I, must pull off this lion-skin of the I from the strutting thistle-eater. What manifold robbery have I not put up with in the history of the world! There I let sun, moon, and stars, cats and crocodiles, receive the honour of ranking as I; there Jehovah, Allah, and Our Father came and were invested with the I; there families, tribes, peoples, and at last actually mankind, came and were honoured as I's; there the church, the state, came with the pretension to be I—and I gazed calmly on all. What wonder if then there was always a real I too that joined the company and affirmed in my face that it was not my *you* but my real *I*. Why, *the* Son of Man *par excellence* had done the like; why should not *a* son of man do it too? So I saw my I always above me and outside me, and could never really come to myself.

80 Michael Bakunin, from *Statism and Anarchy* (ed. by Marshall S. Shatz; Cambridge University Press, 1990), pp. 13–14, 203–5

Born in Premukhino in Russia, Bakunin (1814–1876) entered the Imperial Russian Artillery School, joined the army soon after, and resigned his commission after being sent to the Polish frontier. Increasingly interested in philosophy and politics, he left Russia in 1842 and threw himself into the popular democratic movement sweeping through Europe in these years. He was arrested and imprisoned in several different European countries. In 1851 he was passed on to the Russian government which imprisoned him for six years and then exiled him to Siberia. He managed to escape in 1861, and continued to live the life of a European revolutionary throughout the 1860s. Famous for the complex political intrigues in which he engaged, Bakunin was a central figure within the First International, a federation of radical political parties committed to the overthrow of capitalism; but fell out with its other luminaries, notably Karl Marx. In 1872 he was expelled from the International for his anarchism, an event that propelled him to write his major political work, *Statism and Anarchy*.

To achieve their fullest development, modern capitalist production and bank speculation require enormous centralized states, which alone are capable of subjecting the many millions of laborers to their exploitation. A federal organization, from below upward, of workers' associations, groups, communes, districts, and, ultimately, regions and nations—the sole condition for real as opposed to fictitious freedom—is as contrary to their essence as any kind of economic autonomy is incompatible with them. They get along very nicely, though, with so-called *representative democracy*. This latest form of the state, based on the pseudo-sovereignty of a sham popular will, supposedly expressed by pseudo-representatives of the people in sham popular assemblies, combines the two main conditions necessary for their success: state centralization, and the actual subordination of the sovereign people to the intellectual minority that governs them, supposedly representing them but invariably exploiting them.

When we come to speak of the social and political program of the Marxists, the Lassalleans, and the German social democrats in general, we will have occasion to examine this factual truth more closely and to elucidate it. Let us turn our attention now to another side of the question.

Any exploitation of the people's labor is a bitter pill for them, whatever the political forms of sham popular sovereignty and sham popular freedom that may gild it. Therefore no people will readily submit to it, however docile they may be by nature and however accustomed they may have grown to obeying authority. It requires constant coercion and compulsion, meaning police surveillance and military force.

The modern state, in its essence and objectives, is necessarily a military state, and a military state necessarily becomes an aggressive state. If it does not conquer others it will itself be conquered, for the simple reason that wherever force exists, it absolutely must be displayed or put into action. From this again it follows that the modern state must without fail be huge and powerful; that is the indispensable condition for its preservation.

The modern state is analogous to capitalist production and bank speculation (which ultimately swallows up even capitalist production). For fear of bankruptcy, the latter must constantly broaden their scope at the expense of the small-scale production and speculation which they swallow up; they must strive to become unique, universal, world-wide. In just the same way the modern state, of necessity a military state, bears within itself the inevitable ambition to become a world-wide state. But a world-wide state, which obviously is unrealizable, could in any event exist only in the singular; two such states, side by side, are a logical impossibility.

Hegemony is only a modest, possible display of this unrealizable ambition inherent in every state. But the primary condition for hegemony is the relative impotence and subordination of at least all surrounding states. Thus the hegemony of France, as long as it existed, was conditional upon the impotence of Spain, Italy, and Germany. To this day French statesmen—and foremost among them, of course, Thiers—cannot forgive Napoleon III for having allowed Italy and Germany to unify and consolidate themselves.

. . .

The two primary elements we would point to as the necessary preconditions for social revolution exist on the broadest scale among the Russian people. They can boast of inordinate poverty and of exemplary servitude. Their sufferings are without number, and they bear them not with patience but with profound and passionate desperation which has already found expression twice in history, in two terrible outbursts—the Stenka Razin and Pugachev uprisings—and to this day has not ceased to manifest itself in an uninterrupted series of local peasant insurrections.

What prevents them from carrying out a fully victorious revolution? Do they lack a common ideal capable of giving meaning to a popular revolution, of giving it a well-defined objective, and without which, as we said above, a simultaneous and universal uprising of the entire people, and, consequently, the success of the revolution itself, is impossible? But it would scarcely be correct to say that the Russian people have not yet developed such an ideal.

If such an ideal did not exist in the people's consciousness, at least in its main outlines, one would have to give up all hope of a Russian revolution, because such an ideal arises from the very depths of popular life. It is the product of the people's historical experiences, of their strivings, sufferings, protests, and struggle, and at the same time it is a graphic expression, as it were, always simple and comprehensible to all, of their real demands and hopes.

If the people do not develop this ideal themselves, of course, no one can give it to them. In general, it must be noted that nobody—neither an individual, a society, nor a people—can be given what does not already exist within him, not just in embryonic form but at a certain level of development. Take the individual. If an idea does not already exist within him as a vital instinct, and as a more or less clear concept which serves, as it were, as the first reflection of that instinct, you will never explain it to him or get him to understand it. Look at a bourgeois who is satisfied with his fate. Can you ever hope to explain to him the proletarian's right to full human development and equal participation in all the enjoyments, satisfactions, and blessings of social life, or prove to him the legitimacy and salutary necessity of social revolution? No, unless you have taken leave of your senses you will not even attempt it. And why not? Because you will be convinced that even if this bourgeois were by nature good, intelligent, noble, magnanimous, and disposed to justice—you see what concessions I am making, but in fact there are not many such bourgeois on earth—even if he were educated, even learned, he still would not understand you and would not become a social revolutionary. And why not? For the simple reason that his life has not generated within him instinctive strivings that would correspond to your social-revolutionary idea. On the other hand, if those strivings did exist within him, even in embryonic form or as the most absurd sorts of concepts, then however much his social position might please his sensibilities and satisfy his vanity, he could not rest content with himself.

On the other hand, take the least educated and most ridiculous fellow: if you can only find within him instincts and honest, though vague, aspirations that correspond to the social-revolutionary idea, however primitive his actual conceptions may be, do not shy away, but occupy yourself with him seriously, with love, and you will see how broadly and passionately he will embrace and assimilate your idea—or, rather, his own idea, for it is nothing other than the clear, full, and logical expression of his own instinct. In essence, you have not given him anything, you have not brought him anything new, but merely clarified for him what existed in him long before he encountered you. That is why I say that no one can give anyone anything.

But if this is true in regard to the individual, it is all the more true in regard to an entire people. One would have to be a complete idiot or an incurable doctrinaire to imagine that one can give anything to the people, that one can bestow upon them any kind of material blessing or a new intellectual or moral outlook, a new truth, and arbitrarily give their lives a new direction, or, as the late Chaadaev put it thirty-six years ago, speaking specifically of the Russian people, write on them what you will, as though they were a blank sheet of paper.

Among the greatest geniuses to date, few have actually done anything for the people. A nation's geniuses are highly aristocratic, and everything they have done up to now has served only to educate, strengthen, and enrich the exploiting minority. The poor masses, forsaken and abused by everyone, have had to break their own martyr's path to freedom and light by means of an infinite number of obscure and fruitless efforts. The greatest geniuses did not and could not bring society a new content. Created by society themselves, they continued and developed the work of many centuries, bringing only new forms to a content which is continually born anew and broadened by the movement of social life itself.

But, I repeat, the most renowned geniuses have done nothing, or very little, specifically for the people, for the many millions of laboring proletarians. Popular life, popular development, popular progress belong exclusively to the people themselves. That progress is achieved, of course, not by book learning but by the natural accumulation of experience and thought, transmitted from generation to generation and necessarily broadening and deepening its content and perfecting itself and assuming its forms very slowly. An infinite number of severe and bitter historical experiences have finally brought the masses in all countries, or at least in all the European countries, to the realization that they can expect nothing from the privileged classes and contemporary states or from political revolutions in general, and that they can liberate themselves only by their own efforts, by means of social revolution. That is what defines the universal ideal that lives within them and acts upon them today.

81   Peter Kropotkin, from *Mutual Aid*, in *The Conquest of Bread and Other Writings* (ed. by Marshall S. Satz; Cambridge University Press, 1995), pp. 31–2, 36–9

Born in Moscow, Kropotkin (1842–1921) entered the aristocratic Corps des Pages of St. Petersburg aged fifteen, and four years later became personal page to Alexander II. Increasingly interested in radical politics, he was arrested and imprisoned in Russia and then in France. During his years in prison, he published his major writings on anarchism. He continued to write following his release and move to England, including an important and widely discussed attack on the place of competition within Darwin's evolutionary theory. He returned to his homeland following the revolution of 1917 but was subsequently critical of the Bolshevik regime. In his most famous work, *Mutual Aid*, he turned his fire upon those who tried to appropriate Darwinist thinking to defend liberalism and capitalism. Co-operation, he maintained, was the basis for more mature states of human evolution.

If we take now the teachings which can be borrowed from the analysis of modern society, in connection with the body of evidence relative to the importance of mutual aid in the evolution of the animal world and of mankind, we may sum up our inquiry as follows.

In the animal world we have seen that the vast majority of species live in societies, and that they find in association the best arms for the struggle for life: understood, of course, in its wide Darwinian sense—not as a struggle for the sheer means of existence, but as a struggle against all natural conditions unfavourable to the species. The animal species in which individual struggle has been reduced to its narrowest limits, and the practice of mutual aid has attained the greatest development are invariably the most numerous, the most prosperous and the most open to further progress. The mutual protection which is obtained in this case, the possibility of attaining old age and of accumulating experience, the higher intellectual development, and the further growth of sociable habits, secure the maintenance of the species, its extension, and its further progressive evolution. The unsociable species, on the contrary, are doomed to decay.

Going next over to man, we found him living in clans and tribes at the very dawn of the stone age; we saw a wide series of social institutions developed already in the lower savage stage, in the clan and the tribe; and we found that the earliest tribal customs and habits gave to mankind the embryo of all the institutions which made later on the leading aspects of further progress. Out of the savage tribe grew up the barbarian village community; and a new, still wider, circle of social customs, habits and institutions, numbers of which are still alive among ourselves, was developed under the principles of common possession of a given territory and common defence of it, under the jurisdiction of the village folkmote, and in the federation of villages belonging, or supposed to belong, to one stem. And when new requirements induced men to make a new start, they made it in the city, which represented a double network of territorial units (village communities), connected with guilds—these latter arising out of the common prosecution of a given art or craft, or for mutual support and defence.

And finally, in the last two chapters facts were produced to show that, although the growth of the State on the pattern of Imperial Rome had put a violent end to all medieval institutions for mutual support, this new aspect of civilization could not last. The State, based upon loose aggregations of individuals and undertaking to be their only bond of union, did not answer its purpose. The mutual-aid tendency finally broke down its iron rules; it reappeared and reasserted itself in an infinity of associations which now tend to embrace all aspects of life and to take possession of all that is required by man for life and for reproducing the waste occasioned by life.

It will probably be remarked that mutual aid, even though it may represent one of the factors of evolution, covers nevertheless one aspect only of human relations; that by the side of this current, powerful though it may be, there is, and always has been, the other current—the self-assertion of the individual, not only in its efforts to attain personal or caste superiority, economical, political and spiritual, but also in its much more important although less evident function of breaking through the bonds, always prone to become crystallized, which the tribe, the village community, the city, and the State impose upon the individual. In other words, there is the self-assertion of the individual taken as a progressive element.

It is evident that no review of evolution can be complete, unless these two dominant currents are analysed. However, the self-assertion of the individual or of groups of individuals, their struggles for superiority, and the conflicts which resulted therefrom, have already been analysed, described, and glorified from time immemorial. In fact, up to the present time, this current alone has received attention from the epical poet, the annalist, the historian and the sociologist. History, such as it has hitherto been written, is almost entirely a description of the ways and means by which theocracy, military power, autocracy and, later on, the richer classes' rule have been promoted, established and maintained. The struggles between these forces make, in fact, the substance of history. We may thus take the knowledge of the individual factor in human history as granted—even though there is full room for a new study of the subject on the lines just alluded to; while, on the other side, the mutual-aid factor has been hitherto totally lost sight of; it was simply denied, or even scoffed at, by the writers of the present and past generation. It was therefore necessary to show, first of all, the immense part which this factor plays in the evolution of both the animal world and human societies. Only after this has been fully recognized will it be possible to proceed to a comparison between the two factors.

To make even a rough estimate of their relative importance by any method more or less statistical, is evidently impossible. One single war—we all know—may be productive of more evil, immediate and subsequent, than hundreds of years of the unchecked action of the mutual-aid principle may be productive of good. But when we see that in the animal world, progressive development and mutual aid go hand in hand, while the inner struggle within the species is concomitant with retrogressive development; when we notice that with man, even success in struggle and war is proportionate to the development of mutual aid in each of the two conflicting nations, cities, parties, or tribes, and that in the process of evolution war itself (so far as it can go this way) has been made subservient to the ends of progress in mutual aid within the nation, the city or the clan—we already obtain a perception of the dominating influence of the mutual-aid factor as an element of progress. But we see also that the practice of mutual aid and its successive developments have created the very conditions of society life in which man was enabled to develop his arts, knowledge and intelligence; and that the periods when institutions based on the mutual-aid tendency took their greatest development were also the periods of the greatest progress in arts, industry, and science. In fact, the study of the inner life of the medieval city and of the ancient Greek cities reveals the fact that the combination of mutual aid, as it was practised within the guild and the Greek clan, with a large initiative which was left to the individual and the group by means of the federative principle, gave to mankind the two greatest periods of its history—the ancient Greek city and the medieval city periods; while the ruin of the above institutions during the State periods of history which followed corresponded in both cases to a rapid decay.

As to the sudden industrial progress which has been achieved during our own century, and which is usually ascribed to the triumph of individualism and competition, it certainly has a much deeper origin than that. Once the great discoveries of the fifteenth century were made, especially that of the pressure of the atmosphere, supported by a series of advances in natural philosophy—and they were made under the medieval city organization—once these discoveries were made, the invention of the steam-motor, and all the revolution which the conquest of a new power implied, had necessarily to follow. If the medieval cities had lived to bring their discoveries to that point, the ethical consequences of the revolution effected by steam might have been different; but the same revolution in techniques and science would have inevitably taken place. It remains, indeed, an open question whether the general decay of industries which followed the ruin of the free cities, and was especially noticeable in the first part of the eighteenth century, did not considerably retard the appearance of the steam-engine as well as the consequent revolution in arts. When we consider the astounding rapidity of industrial progress from the twelfth to the fifteenth centuries—in weaving, working of metals, architecture and navigation, and ponder over the scientific discoveries which that industrial progress led to at the end of the fifteenth century—we must ask ourselves whether mankind was not delayed in its taking full advantage of these conquests when a general depression of arts and industries took place in Europe after the decay of medieval civilization. Surely it was not the disappearance of the artist-artisan, nor the ruin of large cities and the extinction of intercourse between them, which could favour the industrial revolution; and we know indeed that James Watt spent twenty or more years of his life in order to render his invention serviceable, because he could not find in the last century what he would have readily found in medieval Florence or Brügge, that is, the artisans capable of realizing his devices in metal, and of giving them the artistic finish and precision which the steam-engine requires.

To attribute, therefore, the industrial progress of our century to the war of each against all which it has proclaimed, is to reason like the man who, knowing not the causes of rain, attributes it to the victim he has immolated before his clay idol. For industrial progress, as for each other conquest over nature, mutual aid and close intercourse certainly are, as they have been, much more advantageous than mutual struggle.

However, it is especially in the domain of ethics that the dominating importance of the mutual-aid principle appears in full. That mutual aid is the real foundation of our ethical conceptions seems evident enough. But whatever the opinions as to the first origin of the mutual-aid feeling or instinct may be—whether a biological or a supernatural cause is ascribed to it—we must trace its existence as far back as to the lowest stages of the animal world; and from these stages we can follow its uninterrupted evolution, in opposition to a number of contrary agencies, through all degrees of human development, up to the present times. Even the new religions which were born from time to time—always at epochs when the mutual-aid principle was falling into decay in the theocracies and despotic States of the East, or at the decline of the Roman Empire—even the new religions have only reaffirmed that same principle. They found their first supporters among the humble, in the lowest, downtrodden layers of society, where the mutual-aid principle is the necessary foundation of everyday life; and the new forms of union which were introduced in the earliest Buddhist and Christian communities, in the Moravian brotherhoods and so on, took the character of a return to the best aspects of mutual aid in early tribal life.

Each time, however, that an attempt to return to this old principle was made, its fundamental idea itself was widened. From the clan it was extended to the stem, to the federation of stems, to the nation, and finally—in ideal, at least—to the whole of mankind. It was also refined at the same time. In primitive Buddhism, in primitive Christianity, in the writings of some of the Mussulman teachers, in the early movements of the Reform, and especially in the ethical and philosophical movements of the last century and of our own times, the total abandonment of the idea of revenge, or of 'due reward'—of good for good and evil for evil—is affirmed more and more vigorously. The higher conception of 'no revenge for wrongs', and of freely giving more than one expects to receive from his neighbours, is proclaimed as being the real principle of morality—a principle superior to mere equivalence, equity, or justice, and more conducive to happiness. And man is appealed to to be guided in his acts, not merely by love, which is always personal, or at the best tribal, but by the perception of his oneness with each human being. In the practice of mutual aid, which we can retrace to the earliest beginnings of evolution, we thus find the positive and undoubted origin of our ethical conceptions; and we can affirm that in the ethical progress of man, mutual support—not mutual struggle—has had the leading part. In its wide extension, even at the present time, we also see the best guarantee of a still loftier evolution of our race.

82   Emma Goldman, from 'Anarchism', *in Anarchism and Other Essays* (Kennikat Press, 1910), pp. 56–62

Goldman (1869–1940) grew up in a petit-bourgeois Jewish family in the Baltic region of Russia. She emigrated to the United States aged sixteen, and worked in a clothing factory in Rochester before moving to New York in 1889. There she became involved in the anarchist movement, aiding a plot to assassinate the industrialist Henry Clay Frick. Goldman came to reject the methods of terrorism in favour of political organization. She was a tireless campaigner for free speech and other civil liberties, and was involved in campaigns for women's suffrage and for birth control information. She was targeted by the American government for her activities, and was deported to Russia after the First World War. She fled the Soviet Union after two years there, deeply disillusioned with the authoritarian state that was emerging.

Anarchism urges man to think, to investigate, to analyze every proposition; but that the brain capacity of the average reader be not taxed too much, I also shall begin with a definition, and then elaborate on the latter.

ANARCHISM:—The philosophy of a new social order based on liberty unrestricted by manmade law; the theory that all forms of government rest on violence, and are therefore wrong and harmful, as well as unnecessary.

The new social order rests, of course, on the materialistic basis of life; but while all Anarchists agree that the main evil today is an economic one, they maintain that the solution of that evil can be brought about only through the consideration of *every phase* of life,—individual, as well as the collective; the internal, as well as the external phases.

A thorough perusal of the history of human development will disclose two elements in bitter conflict with each other; elements that are only now beginning to be understood, not as foreign to each other, but as closely related and truly harmonious, if only placed in proper environment: the individual and social instincts. The individual and society have waged a relentless and bloody battle for ages, each striving for supremacy, because each was blind to the value and importance of the other. The individual and social instincts,—the one a most potent factor for individual endeavor, for growth, aspiration, self-realization; the other an equally potent factor for mutual helpfulness and social well-being.

The explanation of the storm raging within the individual, and between him and his surroundings, is not far to seek. The primitive man, unable to understand his being, much less the unity of all life, felt himself absolutely dependent on blind, hidden forces ever ready to mock and taunt him. Out of that attitude grew the religious concepts of man as a mere speck of dust dependent on superior powers on high, who can only be appeased by complete surrender. All the early sagas rest on that idea, which continues to be the *leit-motif* of the biblical tales dealing with the relation of man to God, to the State, to society. Again and again the same motif, *man is nothing, the powers are everything*. Thus Jehovah would only endure man on condition of complete surrender. Man can have all the glories of the earth, but he must not become conscious of himself. The State, society, and moral laws all sing the same refrain: Man can have all the glories of the earth, but he must not become conscious of himself.

Anarchism is the only philosophy which brings to man the consciousness of himself; which maintains that God, the State, and society are non-existent, that their promises are null and void, since they can be fulfilled only through man's subordination. Anarchism is therefore the teacher of the unity of life; not merely in nature, but in man. There is no conflict between the individual and the social instincts, any more than there is between the heart and the lungs: the one the receptacle of a precious life essence, the other the repository of the element that keeps the essence pure and strong. The individual is the heart of society, conserving the essence of social life; society is the lungs which are distributing the element to keep the life essence—that is, the individual—pure and strong.

"The one thing of value in the world," says Emerson, "is the active soul; this every man contains within him. The soul active sees absolute truth and utters truth and creates." In other words, the individual instinct is the thing of value in the world. It is the true soul that sees and creates the truth alive, out of which is to come a still greater truth, the re-born social soul.

Anarchism is the great liberator of man from the phantoms that have held him captive; it is the arbiter and pacifier of the two forces for individual and social harmony. To accomplish that unity, Anarchism has declared war on the pernicious influences which have so far prevented the harmonious blending of individual and social instincts, the individual and society.

Religion, the dominion of the human mind; Property, the dominion of human needs; and Government, the dominion of human conduct, represent the stronghold of man's enslavement and all the horrors it entails. Religion! How it dominates man's mind, how it humiliates and degrades his soul. God is everything, man is nothing, says religion. But out of that nothing God has created a kingdom so despotic, so tyrannical, so cruel, so terribly exacting that naught but gloom and tears and blood have ruled the world since gods began. Anarchism rouses man to rebellion against this black monster. Break your mental fetters, says Anarchism to man, for not until you think and judge for yourself will you get rid of the dominion of darkness, the greatest obstacle to all progress.

Property, the dominion of man's needs, the denial of the right to satisfy his needs. Time was when property claimed a divine right, when it came to man with the same refrain, even as religion, "Sacrifice! Abnegate! Submit!" The spirit of Anarchism has lifted man from his prostrate position. He now stands erect, with his face toward the light. He has learned to see the insatiable, devouring, devastating nature of property, and he is preparing to strike the monster dead.

"Property is robbery," said the great French Anarchist, Proudhon. Yes, but without risk and danger to the robber. Monopolizing the accumulated efforts of man, property has robbed him of his birthright, and has turned him loose a pauper and an outcast. Property has not even the time-worn excuse that man does not create enough to satisfy all needs. The A B C student of economics knows that the productivity of labor within the last few decades far exceeds normal demand a hundredfold. But what are normal demands to an abnormal institution? The only demand that property recognizes is its own gluttonous appetite for greater wealth, because wealth means power: the power to subdue, to crush, to exploit, the power to enslave, to outrage, to degrade. America is particularly boastful of her great power, her enormous national wealth. Poor America, of what avail is all her wealth, if the individuals comprising the nation are wretchedly poor? If they live in squalor, in filth, in crime, with hope and joy gone, a homeless, soilless army of human prey.

It is generally conceded that unless the returns of any business venture exceed the cost, bankruptcy is inevitable. But those engaged in the business of producing wealth have not yet learned even this simple lesson. Every year the cost of production in human life is growing larger (50,000 killed, 100,000 wounded in America last year); the returns to the masses, who help to create wealth, are ever getting smaller. Yet America continues to be blind to the inevitable bankruptcy of our business of production. Nor is this the only crime of the latter. Still more fatal is the crime of turning the producer into a mere particle of a machine, with less will and decision than his master of steel and iron. Man is being robbed not merely of the products of his labor, but of the power of free initiative, of originality, and the interest in, or desire for, the things he is making.

Real wealth consists in things of utility and beauty, in things that help to create strong, beautiful bodies and surroundings inspiring to live in. But if man is doomed to wind cotton around a spool, or dig coal, or build roads for thirty years of his life, there can be no talk of wealth. What he gives to the world is only gray and hideous things, reflecting a dull and hideous existence,—too weak to live, too cowardly to die. Strange to say, there are people who extol this deadening method of centralized production as the proudest achievement of our age. They fail utterly to realize that if we are to continue in machine subserviency, our slavery is more complete than was our bondage to the King. They do not want to know that centralization is not only the death knell of liberty, but also of health and beauty, of art and science, all these being impossible in a clocklike, mechanical atmosphere.

Anarchism cannot but repudiate such a method of production: its goal is the freest possible expression of all the latent powers of the individual. Oscar Wilde defines a perfect personality as "one who develops under perfect conditions, who is not wounded, maimed, or in danger." A perfect personality, then, is only possible in a state of society where man is free to choose the mode of work, the conditions of work, and the freedom to work. One to whom the making of a table, the building of a house, or the tilling of the soil, is what the painting is to the artist and the discovery to the scientist,—the result of inspiration, of intense longing, and deep interest in work as a creative force. That being the ideal of Anarchism, its economic arrangements must consist of voluntary productive and distributive associations, gradually developing into free communism, as the best means of producing with the least waste of human energy. Anarchism, however, also recognizes the right of the individual, or numbers of individuals, to arrange at all times for other forms of work, in harmony with their tastes and desires.

83   **Herbert Read, from 'The Paradox of Anarchism',**
     in *Anarchy and Order: Essays in Politics*
     (Faber & Faber, 1965), pp. 132–7

Born in Yorkshire, Read (1893–1968) was educated at Leeds University. He served during the First World War as a captain in the British army, and was awarded the Military Cross for bravery. He published two volumes of poetry and two autobiographical accounts of life on the Western front based on his wartime experiences. After the war he was assistant keeper of the Victoria and Albert Museum (1922–31), and subsequently Professor of Art at Edinburgh

University and editor of the *Burlington Magazine* from 1933 to 1939. He wrote widely on both art and literature, becoming a champion of a wide range of European art in the twentieth century and of a new generation of British artists, such as Henry Moore, Ben Nicholson, and Barbara Hepworth. He helped found the Institute of Contemporary Art in 1947, and was knighted for services to literature in 1953. He became a convert to anarchism in 1937, as a result of the Spanish Civil War, and was closely associated with the anarchist Freedom Press.

Suppose we were to ignore these boundaries, or abolish them. The realities are, after all, human beings with certain desires: with certain primitive needs. These human beings, according to their needs and sympathies, will *spontaneously* associate themselves into groups for mutual aid, will *voluntarily* organize an economy which ensures the satisfaction of their needs. This is the principle of mutual aid, and it has been explained and justified with much historical and scientific evidence by Kropotkin. It is this principle which the anarchist makes the foundation of his social order, and upon which he believes he can build that democratic form of society which Rousseau felt was reserved for the gods.

It is not necessary here to repeat the empirical evidence for this belief: Kropotkin's great book is a work whose scholarship is acknowledged by sociologists of all schools. The difficulty is not to justify a principle which has sound psychological and empirical evidence to support it, but to apply this principle to the existing state of society.

This we do tentatively by taking the voluntary organizations that already exist and seeing to what extent they are capable of becoming the units in a democratic society. Such organizations are trade unions, syndicates, professional unions, academies, etc.—all those groups which crystallize around a human function. We then consider the functions which are now performed by the State, and which are necessary for our well-being, and we ask ourselves to what extent these functions could be entrusted to such voluntary organizations. We come to the conclusion that there are no *essential* functions which could not thus be transferred. It is true that there are functions like making war and charging rent which are not the expression of an impulse towards mutual aid, but it does not need much consideration of such functions to see that they would naturally disappear if the central authority of the State was abolished.

The mistakes of every political thinker from Aristotle to Rousseau have been due to their use of the abstract conception *man*. Their systems assume the substantial uniformity of this creature of their imaginations, and what they actually propose are various forms of authority to enforce uniformity on man.

But the anarchist recognizes the uniqueness of the person, and only allows for organization to the extent that the person seeks sympathy and mutual aid among his fellows. In reality, therefore, the anarchist replaces the *social* contract by the *functional* contract, and the authority of the contract only extends to the fulfilling of a specific function.

The political unitarian or authoritarian conceives society as one body compelled to uniformity. The anarchist conceives society as a balance or harmony of groups, and most of us belong to one or more such groups. The only difficulty is their harmonious interrelation.

But is it so difficult? It is true that trade unions sometimes quarrel with one another, but analyse these quarrels and you will find, either that they proceed from causes outside their function (such as their different conceptions of their place in a non-functional, i.e., capitalist society) or from personal rivalries, which are a reflection of the struggle for survival in a capitalist world. Such differences of aim bear no relation to the principle of voluntary organization and are indeed excluded by that very concept. In general, trade unions can agree with one another well enough even in a capitalist society, in spite of all its incitement to rivalry and aggressiveness.

If we go outside our own time to the Middle Ages, for example, we find that the functional organization of society, though imperfectly realized, was proved to be quite possible, and its gradual perfection was only thwarted by the rise of capitalism. Other periods and other forms of society, as Kropotkin has shown, fully confirm the possibility of the harmonious inter-relationships of functional groups.

Admitted, it may be said, that we can transfer all the economic functions of the State in this way, what about other functions—the administration of criminal law, relationships with foreign countries not at the same stage of social development, education, etc.?

To this question the anarchist has two replies. In the first place he argues that most of these non-functional activities are incidental to a non-functional State—that crime, for example, is largely a reaction to the institution of private property, and that foreign affairs are largely economic in origin and motivation. But it is agreed that there are questions, such as certain aspects of common law, infant education, public morality, which are outside the province of the functional organizations. These, he argues, are matters of common sense, solved by reference to the innate good will of the community. But the community for this purpose need not necessarily be anything so impersonal and so grandiose as a State—in fact, it will be effective in inverse ratio to its size. The most effective community is the smallest—the family. Beyond the family is the parish, the local association of men in contiguous dwellings. Such local associations may form their courts and these courts are sufficient to administer a common law based on common sense. The manor courts in the Middle Ages, for example, dealt with all crimes and misdemeanours save those committed against the artificial entities of the State and the Church.

In this sense anarchism implies a universal decentralization of authority, and a universal simplification of life. Inhuman entities like the modern city will disappear. But anarchism does not necessarily imply a reversion to handicraft and outdoor sanitation. There is no contradiction between anarchism and electric power, anarchism and air transport, anarchism and the division of labour, anarchism and industrial efficiency. Since the functional groups will all be working for their mutual benefit, and not for other people's profit or for destructive armaments, the measure of efficiency will be the appetite for fullness of living. The anarchist collectives in Spain gave a convincing demonstration of this progressive tendency during their brief existence.

There is a further consideration of a more topical and more pressing nature. In a remarkable book, *The Crisis of Civilization*, Alfred Cobban has shown that the disasters which have fallen on the Western world are a direct consequence of the adoption by Germany of the theory of popular or national sovereignty, in place of the theory of natural law which had been evolved by the rational movement of thought in the eighteenth century known as the Enlightenment. German thought, writes Mr. Cobban, 'substituted historical rights for natural rights, and the will of the nation, or the *Volk*, for reason as the basis of law and government . . . The ultimate result of the theory of popular sovereignty was thus the substitution of history for ethics. This tendency was present in the contemporary thought of all countries. It has only achieved a complete triumph in Germany. The distinguishing mark of modern German thought is the dissolution of ethics in the *Volkgeist*; its practical conclusion is that the state is the source of all morality, and the individual must accept the laws and actions of his own state as having ultimate ethical validity.'

I will not repeat the detailed evidence which Mr. Cobban, who is a professional historian, offers in support of this statement, but its truth is obvious enough. 'Sovereignty, whether it adopts the democratic, nationalist, or socialist disguise, or some amalgam of all three, is the political religion of today.' It follows that if we are to rid Europe permanently of the menace to peace which Germany represents, we must first of all destroy the German conception of sovereignty. So long as this conception remains, as a national religion, there will be a continual resurgence of the instruments of such a policy—armed might and arbitrary aggression.

Germany can, of course, be disarmed, but we have tried that remedy once before, and it gave Europe only a short respite. Reparations also proved to be a capitalist illusion, and did no good, least of all to the recipients. A reconstituted democratic republic, once again a member of a reconstituted League of Nations, or European Federation? Nothing in the history of Germany can allow any realist to suppose that Germany would play such a nice political game. So long as her present social structure remains intact, Germany will seek the economic and political advantages which she believes to be her right and destiny.

There is only one way to prevent a third resurgence of German power, and that is the way of anarchism. It is necessary to destroy the German State as such. The German people are made up of as many diverse elements as any other people, but the great majority of them (workers included) are sustained in their fanatical beliefs by the most centralized State in Europe; and the most fanatical of all their beliefs is their belief in the sovereignty of this State. It is difficult for anyone unfamiliar with German thought, or with even the ordinary run of German people, to realize the force and philosophic strength of this belief—a belief common to all parties, from the militarists on the right to the communists on the left. Germany, in all her menace and neurotic frenzy, is obsessed by this uncritical worship of the State, and she can only be immunized and rendered harmless by the systematic destruction of that concept. This can be done in stages, first by the restoration of independence to the provinces whose union made the German State possible, and then by the devolution within these separate provinces of all economic power to trade unions and other voluntary organizations. Other measures, such as the abolition of national banks and national currency, would follow as a matter of course. The principles of anarchism would be introduced into one country in Europe and the demonstration of their pacific and civilizing influence would be so effective that other countries would quickly and voluntarily hasten to follow the same path. Force would have abolished force and individual life would once more expand in freedom and beauty.

It was a great German, already alarmed by the tendencies then taking shape, as an immediate reaction from the French Revolution, who warned his countrymen against the monster they were creating. 'It is thus', wrote Schiller, 'that concrete individual life is extinguished, in order that the abstract whole may continue its miserable life, and the State remains for ever a stranger to its citizens, because feeling does not discover it anywhere.

The governing authorities find themselves compelled to classify, and thereby simplify, the multiplicity of citizens, and only to know humanity in a representative form and at second hand. Accordingly they end by entirely losing sight of humanity, and by confounding it with a simple artificial creation of the understanding, whilst on their part the subject classes cannot help receiving coldly laws that address themselves so little to their personality. At length society, weary of having a burden that the State takes so little trouble to lighten, falls to pieces and is broken up—a destiny that has long since attended most European States. They are dissolved in what may be called a state of moral nature, in which public authority is only one function more, hated and deceived by those who think it necessary, respected only by those who can do without it.' In these prescient words Schiller stated that antagonism between organic freedom and mechanical organizations which has been ignored in the political development of modern Europe with results that we see all round us now.

Anarchism is the final and most urgent protest against this fate: a recall to those principles which alone can guarantee the harmony of man's being and the creative evolution of his genius.

84 Paul Goodman, from (a) 'Reflections on the Anarchist Principle', and (b) 'Anarchism and Revolution', both in *Drawing the Line: Political Essays of Paul Goodman* (ed. T. Stoehr; Free Life Editions, 1978), pp. 176–7, 216–17

Born in New York, Goodman (1911–1972) was brought up by his mother in the urban Jewish intellectual community of the early part of the century. He graduated from City College in 1931, and having gained a number of teaching posts, was fired from several of these for the public affairs he conducted with students. Throughout most of his life he lived as an artist, writing numerous plays, poems and stories. During his middle years, he became a proponent of the idea of Gestalt Therapy and practised as a therapist as his artistic endeavours met with diminishing success. He shot to fame in the 1960s with his *Growing up Absurd,* a powerful critique of the problems of youth in modern society and celebration of the common sense of ordinary people and celebration of America's small-town rural heritage. This work led to his adoption as intellectual guru by the youth and New Left movements of the decade.

(**a**) Anarchism is grounded in a rather definite proposition: that valuable behavior occurs only by the free and direct response of individuals or voluntary groups to the conditions presented by the historical environment. It claims that in most human affairs, whether political, economic, military, religious, moral, pedagogic, or cultural, more harm than good results from coercion, top-down direction, central authority, bureaucracy, jails, conscription, states, pre-ordained standardization, excessive planning, etc. Anarchists want to increase intrinsic functioning and diminish extrinsic power. This is a social-psychological hypothesis with obvious political implications.

Depending on varying historical conditions that present various threats to the anarchist principle, anarchists have laid their emphasis in varying places: sometimes agrarian, sometimes freecity and guild-oriented; sometimes technological, sometimes anti-technological; sometimes Communist, sometimes affirming property; sometimes individualist, sometimes collective; sometimes speaking of Liberty as almost an absolute good, sometimes relying on custom and "nature." Nevertheless, despite these differences, anarchists seldom fail to recognize one another, and they do not consider the differences to be incompatibilities. Consider a crucial modern problem, violence. Guerilla fighting has been a classical anarchist technique; yet where, especially in modern conditions, *any* violent means tends to reinforce centralism and authoritarianism, anarchists have tended to see the beauty of non-violence.

Now the anarchist principle is by and large true. And far from being "utopian" or a "glorious failure," it has proved itself and won out in many spectacular historical crises. In the period of mercantilism and patents royal, free enterprise by joint stock companies was anarchist. The Jeffersonian bill of rights and independent judiciary were anarchist. Congregational churches were anarchist. Progressive education was anarchist. The free cities and corporate law in the feudal system were anarchist. At present, the civil rights movement in the United States has been almost classically decentralist and anarchist. And so forth, down to details like free access in public libraries. Of course, to later historians these things do not seem to be anarchist, but in their own time they were all regarded as such and often literally called such, with the usual dire threats of chaos. But this relativity of the anarchist principle to the actual situation is of the essence of anarchism. There *cannot* be a history of anarchism in the sense of establishing a permanent state of things called "anarchist." It is always a continual coping with the next situation, and a vigilance to make sure that past freedoms are not lost and do not turn into the opposite, as free enterprise turned into wage-slavery and monopoly capitalism, or the independent judiciary turned into a monopoly of courts, cops, and lawyers, or free education turned into School Systems.

. . .

(b) With regard to freedoms, even "eternal vigilance" is not enough. Unless freedoms are extended, they are whittled away, for those in power always have the advantage of organization and state resources, while ordinary people become tired of battle and fragmented. We may vigilantly defend constitutional limitations and privileges that we have won, but new conditions arise that circumvent them. For instance, new technology like wiretapping and new organizations like computerized Interpol must be offset by new immunities, public defenders, etc.; otherwise the adversary system of Runnymede is nullified. Labor leaders become bureaucrats and are co-opted, and union members do not attend meetings, unless new demands revitalize the labor movements—in my opinion, the labor movement can at present only be revitalized by turning to the idea of workers' management. Triumphant science, having won the battles of Galileo and Darwin, has become the new orthodoxy. We see that ecological threats have created a brand new freedom to fight for—the right to have an environment.

On the positive side, the spirit of freedom is indivisible and quick to revive. A good fight on one issue has a tonic effect on all society. In totalitarian countries it is very difficult to control a "thaw," and we have seen how contagious populist protest has been in recent years in the United States. In Czechoslovakia an entire generation was apparently totally controlled since 1948, but—whether because of native human wildness or the spirit of Hus, Comenius and Masaryk—the youth acted in 1968 as if there were no such thing. And in the United States, twenty-five years of affluent consumerism and Organization mentality have not seemed to dampen the youth of the present decade.

Anarchists rely on the inventiveness, courage, and drive to freedom of human nature, as opposed to the proletarian industrialized mentality of Scientific Socialism, which takes it for granted that people are essentially and totally socialized by their historical conditions. But anarchist philosophers disagree sharply on the conditions that encourage freedom. (Characteristically, disagreements among anarchists are taken by them as "aspects" of some common position, rather than as "factions" in a power struggle, leading to internecine strife.) Bakunin, for instance, relies on the unemployed, the alienated, the outcasts, the criminal, the uprooted intelligentsia—those who have nothing to lose, not even their chains. But Kropotkin, by contrast, relies on the competent and independent, the highly skilled—small farmers with their peasant community traditions, miners, artists, explorers, architects, educators. Student anarchism at present tends to be Bakuninist because, in my opinion, the students are inauthentically students; they are exploited and *lumpen* in principle—kept on ice. "Students are niggers." But hopefully the Movement is now beginning to have a more Kropotkinian tendency—authentic young professionals in law, medicine, and ecology. The March 4 (1969) movement of the young scientists at M.I.T. is significant of the new trend.

85   Noam Chomsky, from *Powers and Prospects: Reflections on Human Nature and the Social Order* (Pluto, 1996), pp. 71–3, 75–7

The son of an emigrant Hebrew scholar from Russia, Chomsky (1928–) grew up in Pennsylvania. He attended University there and studied linguistics, mathematics and philosophy. Since completing his doctorate, he has taught at the Massachusetts Institute of Technology, where he now holds a Chair in Modern Language and Linguistics. It was in this latter field that he made his scholarly reputation, particularly for his theories of transformational grammar and natural language, which have influenced much subsequent research on the linguistic abilities of children. He is, however, more widely known for his political writing and campaigning. Well versed in both socialism and anarchism, he has become one of the leading radical critics of U.S. foreign policy, publishing a powerful critique of the war against Vietnam, in his *American Power and the New Mandarins* (1969). His most recent public intervention, *9–11* (2002), offers an analysis of the World Trade Center attack which traces its origins to the actions and power of the 'leading terrorist state', the US.

Goals and visions can appear to be in conflict, and often are. There's no contradiction in that, as I think we all know from ordinary experience. Let me take my own case, to illustrate what I have in mind.

My personal visions are fairly traditional anarchist ones, with origins in the Enlightenment and classical liberalism. Before proceeding, I have to clarify what I mean by that. I do not mean the version of classical liberalism that has been reconstructed for ideological purposes, but the original, before it was broken on the rocks of rising industrial capitalism, as Rudolf Rocker put it in his work on anarchosyndicalism 60 years ago—rather accurately, I think.

As state capitalism developed into the modern era, economic, political and ideological systems have increasingly been taken over by vast institutions of private tyranny that are about as close to the totalitarian ideal as any that humans have so far constructed. 'Within the corporation,' political economist Robert Brady wrote half a century ago, 'all policies emanate from the control above. In the union of this power to determine policy with the execution thereof, all authority necessarily proceeds from the top to the bottom and all responsibility from the bottom to the top. This is, of course, the inverse of "democratic" control; it follows the structural conditions of dictatorial power'. 'What in political circles would be called legislative, executive, and judicial powers' is gathered in 'controlling hands' which, 'so far as policy formulation and execution are concerned, are found at the peak of the pyramid and are manipulated without significant check from its base'. As private power 'grows and expands', it is transformed 'into a community force ever more politically potent and politically conscious', ever more dedicated to a 'propaganda program' that 'becomes a matter of converting the public . . . to the point of view of the control pyramid'. That project, already substantial in the period Brady reviewed, reached an awesome scale a few years later as American business sought to beat back the social democratic currents of the postwar world, which reached the United States as well, and to win what its leaders called 'the everlasting battle for the minds of men', using the huge resources of the public relations industry, the entertainment industry, the corporate media, and whatever else could be mobilised by the 'control pyramids' of the social and economic order. These are crucially important features of the modern world, as is dramatically revealed by the few careful studies.

The 'banking institutions and moneyed incorporations' of which Thomas Jefferson warned in his later years—predicting that if not curbed, they would become a form of absolutism that would destroy the promise of the democratic revolution—have since more than fulfilled his most dire expectations. They have become largely unaccountable and increasingly immune from popular interference and public inspection while gaining great and expanding control over the global order. Those inside their hierarchical command structure take orders from above and send orders down below. Those outside may try to rent themselves to the system of power, but have little other relation to it (except by purchasing what it offers, if they can). The world is more complex than any simple description, but Brady's is pretty close, even more so today than when he wrote.

It should be added that the extraordinary power that corporations and financial institutions enjoy was not the result of popular choices. It was crafted by courts and lawyers in the course of the construction of a developmental state that serves the interests of private power, and extended by playing one state against another to seek special privileges, not hard for large private institutions. That is the major reason why the current Congress, business-run to an unusual degree, seeks to devolve federal authority to the states, more easily threatened and manipulated. I'm speaking of the United States, where the process has been rather well studied in academic scholarship. I'll keep to that case; as far as I know, it is much the same elsewhere.

We tend to think of the resulting structures of power as immutable, virtually a part of nature. They are anything but that. These forms of private tyranny only reached something like their current form, with the rights of immortal persons, early in this century. The grants of rights and the legal theory that lay behind them are rooted in much the same intellectual soil as nourished the other two major forms of twentieth century totalitarianism, Fascism and Bolshevism. There is no reason to consider this tendency in human affairs to be more permanent than its ignoble brethren.

Conventional practice is to restrict such terms as 'totalitarian' and 'dictatorship' to political power. Brady is unusual in not keeping to this convention, a natural one, which helps to remove centres of decision-making from the public eye. The effort to do so is expected in any society based on illegitimate authority—any actual society, that is. That is why, for example, accounts in terms of personal characteristics and failings, vague and unspecific cultural practices, and the like, are much preferred to the study of the structure and function of powerful institutions.

When I speak of classical liberalism, I mean the ideas that were swept away, in considerable measure, by the rising tides of state capitalist autocracy. These ideas survived (or were re-invented) in various forms in the culture of resistance to the new forms of oppression, serving as an animating vision for popular struggles that have considerably expanded the scope of freedom, justice, and rights. They were also taken up, adapted, and developed within libertarian left currents. According to this anarchist vision, any structure of hierarchy and authority carries a heavy burden of justification, whether it involves personal relations or a larger social order. If it cannot bear that burden—sometimes it can—then it is illegitimate and should be dismantled. When honestly posed and squarely faced, that challenge can rarely be sustained. Genuine libertarians have their work cut out for them.

. . .

With this in mind, I'd like to turn to the broader question of visions. It is particularly pertinent today against the background of the intensifying attempt to reverse, undermine, and dismantle the gains that have been won by long and often bitter popular struggle. The issues are of historic importance, and are often veiled in distortion and deceit in campaigns to 'convert the public to the point of view of the control pyramid'. There could hardly be a better moment to consider the ideals and visions that have been articulated, modified, reshaped, and often turned into their opposite as industrial society has developed to its current stage, with a massive assault against democracy, human rights, and even markets, while the triumph of these values is being hailed by those who are leading the attack against them—a process that will win nods of recognition from those familiar with what used to be called 'propaganda' in more honest days. It is a moment in human affairs that is as interesting intellectually as it is ominous from a human point of view.

Let me begin by sketching a point of view that was articulated by two leading twentieth century thinkers, Bertrand Russell and John Dewey, who disagreed on a great many things, but shared a vision that Russell called 'the humanistic conception'—to quote Dewey, the belief that the 'ultimate aim' of production is not production of goods, but 'of free human beings associated with one another on terms of equality'. The goal of education, as Russell put it, is 'to give a sense of the value of things other than domination', to help create 'wise citizens of a free community' in which both liberty and 'individual creativeness' will flourish, and working people will be the masters of their fate, not tools of production. Illegitimate structures of coercion must be unravelled; crucially, domination by 'business for private profit through private control of banking, land, industry, reinforced by command of the press, press agents and other means of publicity and propaganda' (Dewey). Unless that is done, Dewey continued, talk of democracy is largely beside the point. Politics will remain 'the shadow cast on society by big business, [and] the attenuation of the shadow will not change the substance'. Democratic forms will lack real content, and people will work 'not freely and intelligently, but for the sake of the work earned', a condition that is 'illiberal and immoral'. Accordingly, industry must be changed 'from a feudalistic to a democratic social order' based on workers' control, free association, and federal organisation, in the general style of a range of thought that includes, along with many anarchists, G.D.H. Cole's guild socialism and such left Marxists as Anton Pannekoek, Rosa Luxemburg, Paul Mattick, and others. Russell's views were rather similar, in this regard.

Problems of democracy were the primary focus of Dewey's thought and direct engagement. He was straight out of mainstream America, 'as American as apple pie', in the standard phrase. It is therefore of interest that the ideas he expressed not many years ago would be regarded today in much of the intellectual culture as outlandish or worse, if known, even denounced as 'anti-American' in influential sectors.

The latter phrase, incidentally, is interesting and revealing, as is its recent currency. We expect such notions in totalitarian societies. Thus in Stalinist days, dissidents and critics were condemned as 'anti-Soviet', an intolerable crime; Brazilian neo-Nazi generals and others like them had similar categories. But their appearance in much more free societies, in which subordination to power is voluntary, not coerced, is a far more significant phenomenon. In any milieu that retains even the memory of a democratic culture, such concepts would merely elicit ridicule. Imagine the reaction on the streets of Milan or Oslo to a book entitled *Anti-Italianism* or *The Anti-Norwegians*, denouncing the real or fabricated deeds of those who do not show proper respect for the doctrines of the secular faith. In the Anglo-American societies, however—including Australia, so I've noticed— such performances are treated with solemnity and respect in respectable circles, one of the signs of a serious deterioration of ordinary democratic values.

The ideas expressed in the not very distant past by such outstanding figures as Russell and Dewey are rooted in the Enlightenment and classical liberalism, and retain their revolutionary character: in education, the workplace, and every other sphere of life. If implemented, they would help clear the way to the free development of human beings whose values are not accumulation and domination, but independence of mind and action, free association on terms of equality, and cooperation to achieve common goals. Such people would share Adam Smith's contempt for the 'mean' and 'sordid pursuits' of 'the masters of mankind' and their 'vile maxim': 'All for ourselves, and nothing for other people', the guiding principles we are taught to admire and revere, as traditional values are eroded under unremitting attack. They would readily understand what led a pre-capitalist figure like Smith to warn of the grim consequences of division of labour, and to base his rather nuanced advocacy of markets in part on the belief that under conditions of 'perfect liberty' there would be a natural tendency towards equality, an obvious desideratum on elementary moral grounds.

The 'humanistic conception' that was expressed by Russell and Dewey in a more civilised period, and that is familiar to the libertarian left, is radically at odds with the leading currents of contemporary thought: the guiding ideas of the totalitarian order crafted by Lenin and Trotsky, and of the state capitalist industrial societies of the West. One of these systems has fortunately collapsed, but the other is on a march backwards to what could be a very ugly future.

9   Fascism

Introduction

Fascism emerged after the First World War as a reaction against two classical ideological traditions, liberalism and socialism. A relative ideological latecomer, as the political scientist Juan Linz has put it, fascism had to open up new ideological space, but it did so in part by eclectically using materials available, and sometimes by presenting the appearance of novelty rather than through genuine innovation. Rather more than other doctrines discussed in this book, fascism is a term associated with very specific regimes and movements, particularly those of the interwar years in Europe. But here too the label is used in a variety of ways. For example, to think only of the years between the First and Second World Wars, it is used to characterize governments and political groups in Germany, Italy, Austria, Spain, the United Kingdom, Belgium, France, Romania, Spain, Yugoslavia, Hungary, and South Africa, among others. Since the war, the soubriquet fascist (or neo-Nazi) has been applied to a wide range of groups, states, and ideas in Europe, the Americas, the Middle East, South Africa, and elsewhere. Scholars are divided over whether it is useful to apply the label in such varied contexts, and what, if any, content can be given to a concept of 'generic' fascism, which clearly gathers together fascists and marks them off from other sorts of nationalist and authoritarian ideology.

The term itself only hints at its content. It derives from the Italian *fasciare*, to fasten or bind, it is a politics of 'unions' or bundles. The excerpt from Benito Mussolini and Giovanni Gentile [Reading 86] alludes to the significance of this in the Italian context: the *fascii* were the bundles of rods carried by Roman Lictors or magistrates as symbols of their authority. One way of grouping together fascists is through identifying what they opposed. Liberalism is attacked for its individualism, and socialism for pitting social classes against one another. In particular, after the Russian Revolution, communism was perceived as a threat. The menace presented itself not only from the Soviet state but from radical and communist political parties in several of the countries with significant fascist movements, including Italy, Germany, and Spain. Conservatives too are lambasted for a failure to see the necessity of radical and violent political change. In many versions, feminism too is a target, as both the traditional family and the virility of political life are fetishized. Instead, fascists emphasize a populist ultra-nationalism, which pictures the nation or state as unity to which all individuals or groups who belong are subordinate. This is accompanied by a politics of struggle, which glorifies violence and emphasizes theatrical gestures, expressed through mass meetings, film, architecture, and sport. The ideology extols charismatic leadership, a quasi-military 'party army', and the forceful elimination of political opponents. In keeping with the emphasis on social unity, fascists aimed at what the Italian fascists called a totalitarian state, although the precise meaning of this varies. For Gentile, the Italian 'philosopher of fascism', it meant something like the ethical pre-eminence of the state, its having a tutorial role in relation to citizens, rather than a state that intervenes in every aspect of social and political life. Hitler's regime, in spite of its chaos and inefficiency, exemplifies the latter model better. Also in keeping with the vision of social unity, fascists emphasize a national corporatist economic state, in which the state takes the lead in organizing both industrial concerns and trade unions. Finally, the ideology valorizes war, empire, and territorial expansion, aiming radically to transform and strengthen the nation's relationship to other powers.

Many of these themes appear in Mussolini's and Gentile's statement of the fundamental ideas of fascism. Fascism is here viewed as spiritual doctrine or form of civil religion, urging an active politics on behalf of the 'higher personality' of the state. Fascism is opposed to the disintegrative forces of liberalism, socialism, and democracy. Instead, the ethical primacy of the state must be acknowledged, and whatever social groupings or 'corporations' that people belong to must be viewed as subordinate to the state. It is worth noting that these authors reject the 'naturalistic' view of the nation as the foundation of the political institutions of the state. Rather, the nation is viewed as the creation of the state, to which citizens should fundamentally be loyal and which gives the people its unity as a national community.

This is one of the important ideological differences between Italian fascism and German National Socialism. In the excerpt reproduced here from Adolf Hitler's autobiography *Mein Kampf*, the state is viewed as a servant of a nation conceived in highly 'naturalistic' terms, through a blend of racism and social Darwinism [Reading 87]. For Nazism, the fundamental unit of history and politics is not the state but the race. Racial membership is the key determinant of human characteristics, and the different races are ordered in a hierarchy with the Aryan or Nordic race at the summit. History is viewed as a process of struggle among races. The task of the state is to expel foreign elements and to strengthen the racial purity of the nation. This requires, as Hitler spells out elsewhere in the book, expansion of the German empire to the east, in order to have sufficient *Lebensraum* for the race to flourish, and the elimination of the danger posed to racial purity by the Jews, although he does not explain exactly what this would mean.

The first excerpt from the National Socialist Party ideologue Alfred Rosenberg's writings bring out the sense of civilisational collapse for which National Socialism was meant to provide a remedy [Reading 88], in the wake of the catastrophe of the First World War, the devastating experience of which was crucial for the initial development of fascist movements. A new myth of the race-soul is needed to fill the void created by the war's destruction of old values. The second excerpt is a brief expression of the rhetoric of Nazi anti-semitism: the Jew is viewed as embodying the alienating and bestial materialism of modern life. The final excerpt, written during the period of the so-called 'harmonization' of the state by the Nazi Party, articulates an important tension that afflicted the National Socialist State, between a view of the state as an instrument of the Party (itself the key representative of the *Volk*) and as itself a source of authority.

In 'Spain or Barbarism', the leader of the political movement Falange Española (Spanish Phalanx) José Primo de Rivera distances his own brand of authoritarian nationalism from both German and Italian variants, and indeed draws distinctions between them [Reading 89]. What he shares with the Germans and Italians is the call for a new order, grounded in a new spiritual vision of the individual, in order to repel the barbarity of Russian communism. His national syndicalism (by the stage he wrote this text) was moving to the 'left' of Italian fascism, finding the latter too conservative and the excerpt here emphasizes the need for fundamental agricultural and industrial reform. Whether the scepticism about total dictatorship and stress on individualism evident in a text such as this represents a qualitative break with fascism or a continuation of it in a different cultural and political context is an open question.

A different minority variant of fascism is represented by Oswald Mosley's 'Ten Points of Fascist Policy' [Reading 90]. The document, a manifesto for Mosley's British Union of Fascists published in the year after its formation in 1932, presents fascism as a patriotic movement, loyal to King and Country, which through its passionate ideal of national service is capable of offering policies to remedy the depression. Since Britain is already in possession of a vast empire, economic autarchy rather than expansion is the key element of foreign policy, and, as in José Antonio's declaration, the rhetoric of a radical corporatism is prominent—accompanied, in an idea borrowed from guild socialists, with an occupational franchise. In spite of the ominous warnings about the alien menace, anti-semitism was initially not a significant element in the BUF (indeed, in the early days its strong-arm squads were trained by the Jewish boxer 'Kid' Lewis), although it became prominent by 1936.

The final two readings represent different forms of contemporary authoritarian populism. The Movimento Sociale Italiano, dissolved and reformed as the Alleanza Nationale in 1995, embodies an explicit nostalgia for Mussolini's fascism. For example, in 1992 it celebrated the seventieth anniversary of the March on Rome with a well-attended demonstration. In the chaotic Italian political scene of the early 1990s, when the collapse of communism and a series of massive corruption scandals destabilized the settled forms of Italian electoral politics, the party surprised many observers by moving from being a minority to a relatively mainstream political force. Under the leadership of the popular Gianfranco Fini, the MSI/AN established itself as the 'third force' in Italian politics through strong showings in the 1994 and 1996 elections and as a key part of the prime minister Silvio Berlusconi's right-wing 'Freedom Alliance'. While descended from the Partito fascista repubblicano, the MSI alienated its own hard-liners by adopting the language and practice of electoral democracy. However, the themes invoked in the manifesto excerpted here—a new Italy, a new state that overcomes the corruption and ineptitude of the past, revised borders with Dalmatia, a stress on youth and moral and spiritual renewal—possess evident continuities with older fascist themes [Reading 91].

In Russia, Vladimir Zhirinovsky's spectacularly misnamed Liberal Democratic Party also enjoyed electoral success in the early 1990s, forming the third largest parliamentary faction (albeit one prone to splits and in-fighting). Campaigning on a populist, anti-market, and ultra-nationalist platform, Zhirinovsky has been attributed with giving these ideas legitimacy in the post-Soviet political climate. The article excerpted here, from the newspaper 'Zhirinovsky's Falcon', supports the racist and irredentist redrawing of boundaries and expulsion of aliens in order to stave off the disaster of racial intermingling [Reading 92]. The key threat facing European civilization is racial mixing, to be met by Russians in alliance with Germany against the internationalizing force of the United States, with the goal of establishing a healthier racial balance on the continent of Europe.

FURTHER READING

There is a useful array of primary sources in Roger Griffin (ed.) *Fascism* (Oxford University Press, 1995). Other useful general works which focus on or offer careful treatments of the ideological aspects of fascism include Roger Griffin, *The Nature of Fascism* (London, 1991), Roger Griffin (ed.), *International Fascism: Theories, Causes and the New Consensus* (Edward Arnold, 1998), Noël O'Sullivan, *Fascism* (Dent, 1983), Stanley G. Payne, *A History of Fascism, 1914–1945* (University College London Press, 1995), Zeev Sternhell, *Neither Left Nor Right* (University of California Press, 1986), Zeev Sternhell, Mario Sznajder and Maia Asheri, *The Foundations of Fascist Ideology* (Princeton University Press, 1993).

86 Benito Mussolini and Giovanni Gentile, from 'The Doctrine of Fascism', in *Italian Fascism* (ed. Adrian Lyttleton; Cape, 1973), pp. 39–44

Benito Mussolini (1883–1945) started his career as a journalist and radical Marxist critic of parliamentary socialism from the left. The experience of the First World War was decisive in persuading him that nations, rather than economic classes, were the key historical actors. He founded the Fasci Italiani di Combattimento in 1919. The Fascist movement grew in size and power to such an extent that Mussolini could seize control of the Italian government in 1922. He aimed to strengthen Italy's industrial and military power and to build a new Italian empire.

Giovanni Gentile (1875–1944) was an Italian philosopher and educator. Initially an idealist follower of the Italian liberal philosopher Benedetto Croce, Gentile was an early supporter of Mussolini's fascism. He was made a senator in 1922 and served as the minister of education. 'The Doctrine of Fascism' was published, under Mussolini's name, in the *Enciclopedia Italiana* in 1932.

1. Like every sound political conception, Fascism is both practice and thought; action in which a doctrine is immanent, and a doctrine which, arising out of a given system of historical forces, remains embedded in them and works there from within. Hence it has a form correlative to the contingencies of place and time, but it has also a content of thought which raises it to a formula of truth in the higher level of the history of thought. In the world one does not act spiritually as a human will dominating other wills without a conception of the transient and particular reality under which it is necessary to act, and of the permanent and universal reality in which the first has its being and its life. In order to know men it is necessary to know man; and in order to know man it is necessary to know reality and laws. There is no concept of the State which is not fundamentally a concept of life: philosophy or intuition, a system of ideas which develops logically or is gathered up into a vision or into a faith, but which is always, at least virtually, an organic conception of the world.

2. Thus Fascism could not be understood in many of its practical manifestations as a party organization, as a system of education, as a discipline, if it were not always looked at in the light of its whole way of conceiving life, a spiritualized way. The world seen through Fascism is not this material world which appears on the surface, in which man is an individual separated from all others and standing by himself, and in which he is governed by a natural law that makes him instinctively live a life of selfish and momentary pleasure. The man of Fascism is an individual who is nation and fatherland, which is a moral law, binding together individuals and the generations into a tradition and a mission, suppressing the instinct for a life enclosed within the brief round of pleasure in order to restore within duty a higher life free from the limits of time and space: a life in which the individual, through the denial of himself, through the sacrifice of his own private interests, through death itself, realizes that completely spiritual existence in which his value as a man lies.

3. Therefore it is a spiritualized conception, itself the result of the general reaction of modern times against the flabby materialistic positivism of the nineteenth century. Anti-positivistic, but positive: not sceptical, nor agnostic, nor pessimistic, nor passively optimistic, as are, in general, the doctrines (all negative) that put the centre of life outside man, who with his free will can and must create his own world. Fascism desires an active man, one engaged in activity with all his energies: it desires a man virilely conscious of the difficulties that exist in action and ready to face them. It conceives of life as a struggle, considering that it behoves man to conquer for himself that life truly worthy of him, creating first of all in himself the instrument (physical, moral, intellectual) in order to construct it. Thus for the single individual, thus for the nation, thus for humanity. Hence the high value of culture in all its forms (art, religion, science), and the enormous importance of education. Hence also the essential value of work, with which man conquers nature and creates the human world (economic, political, moral, intellectual).

4. This positive conception of life is clearly an ethical conception. It covers the whole of reality, not merely the human activity which controls it. No action can be divorced from moral judgment; there is nothing in the world which can be deprived of the value which belongs to everything in its relation to moral ends. Life, therefore, as conceived by the Fascist, is serious, austere, religious: the whole of it is poised in a world supported by the moral and responsible forces of the spirit. The Fascist disdains the 'comfortable' life.

5. Fascism is a religious conception in which man is seen in his immanent relationship with a superior law and with an objective Will that transcends the particular individual and raises him to conscious membership of a spiritual society. Whoever has seen in the religious politics of the Fascist regime nothing but mere opportunism has not understood that Fascism besides being a system of government is also, and above all, a system of thought.

6. Fascism is an historical conception, in which man is what he is only in so far as he works with the spiritual process in which he finds himself, in the family or social group, in the nation and in the history in which all nations collaborate. From this follows the great value of tradition, in memories, in language, in customs, in the standards of social life. Outside history man is nothing. Consequently Fascism is opposed to all the individualistic abstractions of a materialistic nature like those of the eighteenth century; and it is opposed to all Jacobin utopias and innovations. It does not consider that 'happiness'

is possible upon earth, as it appeared to be in the desire of the economic literature of the eighteenth century, and hence it rejects all teleological theories according to which mankind would reach a definitive stabilized condition at a certain period in history. This implies putting oneself outside history and life, which is a continual change and coming to be. Politically, Fascism wishes to be a realistic doctrine; practically, it aspires to solve only the problems which arise historically of themselves and that of themselves find or suggest their own solution. To act among men, as to act in the natural world, it is necessary to enter into the process of reality and to master the already operating forces.

7. Against individualism, the Fascist conception is for the State; and it is for the individual in so far as he coincides with the State, which is the conscience and universal will of man in his historical existence. It is opposed to classical Liberalism, which arose from the necessity of reacting against absolutism, and which brought its historical purpose to an end when the State was transformed into the conscience and will of the people. Liberalism denied the State in the interests of the individual; Fascism reaffirms the State as the true reality of the individual. And if liberty is to be the attribute of the real man, and not of that abstract puppet envisaged by individualistic Liberalism, Fascism is for liberty. And for the only liberty which can be a real thing, the liberty of the State and of the individual within the State. Therefore, for the Fascist, everything is in the State, and nothing human or spiritual exists, much less has value, outside the State. In this sense Fascism is totalitarian, and the Fascist State, the synthesis and unity of all values, interprets, develops and gives strength to the whole life of the people.

8. Outside the State there can be neither individuals nor groups (political parties, associations, syndicates, classes). Therefore Fascism is opposed to Socialism, which confines the movement of history within the class struggle and ignores the unity of classes established in one economic and moral reality in the State; and analogously it is opposed to class syndicalism. Fascism recognizes the real exigencies for which the socialist and syndicalist movement arose, but while recognizing them wishes to bring them under the control of the State and give them a purpose within the corporative system of interests reconciled within the unity of the State.

9. Individuals form classes according to the similarity of their interests, they form syndicates according to differentiated economic activities within these interests; but they form first, and above all, the State, which is not to be thought of numerically as the sum-total of individuals forming the majority of a nation. And consequently Fascism is opposed to Democracy, which equates the nation to the majority, lowering it to the level of that majority; nevertheless it is the purest form of democracy if the nation is conceived, as it should be, qualitatively and not quantitatively, as the most powerful idea (most powerful because most moral, most coherent, most true) which acts within the nation as the conscience and the will of a few, even of One, which ideally tends to become active within the conscience and the will of all—that is to say, of all those who rightly constitute a nation *by reason of* nature, history of race, and have set out upon the same line of development and spiritual formation as one conscience and one sole will. Not a race, nor a geographically determined region, but as a community historically perpetuating itself, a multitude unified by a single idea, which is the will to existence and to power: consciousness of itself, personality.

10. This higher personality is truly the nation in so far as it is the State. It is not the nation that generates the State, as according to the old naturalistic concept which served as the basis of the political theories of the national States of the nineteenth century. Rather the nation is created by the State, which gives to the people, conscious of its own moral unity, a will and therefore an effective existence. The right of a nation to independence derives not from a literary and ideal consciousness of its own being, still less from a more or less unconscious and inert acceptance of a *de facto* situation, but from an active consciousness, from a political will in action and ready to demonstrate its own rights: that is to say, from a state already coming into being. The State, in fact, as the universal ethical will, is the creator of right.

11. The nation as the State is an ethical reality which exists and lives in so far as it develops. To arrest its development is to kill it. Therefore the State is not only the authority which governs and gives the form of laws and the value of spiritual life to the wills of individuals, but it is also a power that makes its will felt abroad, making it known and respected, in other words, demonstrating the fact of its universality in all the necessary directions of its development. It is consequently organization and expansion, at least virtually. Thus it can be likened to the human will which knows no limits to its development and realizes itself in testing its own limitlessness.

12. The Fascist State, the highest and most powerful form of personality, is a force, but a spiritual force, which takes over all the forms of the moral and intellectual life of man. It cannot therefore confine itself simply to the functions of order and supervision as Liberalism desired. It is not simply a mechanism which limits the sphere of the supposed liberties of the individual. It is the form, the inner standard and the discipline of the whole person; it saturates the will as well as the intelligence. Its principle, the central inspiration of the human personality living in the civil community, pierces into the depths and makes its home in the heart of the man of action as well as of the thinker, of the artist as well as of the scientist: it is the soul of the soul.

13. Fascism, in short, is not only the giver of laws and the founder of institutions, but the educator and promoter of spiritual life. It wants to remake, not the forms of human life, but its content, man, character, faith. And to this end it requires discipline and authority that can enter into the spirits of men and there govern unopposed. Its sign, therefore, is the Lictors' rods, the symbol of unity, of strength and justice.

87   Adolf Hitler, from *Mein Kampf* (trans. by Ralph Mannheim; Hutchinson, 1969), pp. 358–62

Adolf Hitler (1889–1945) was born in Austria, moving with his family to Germany as a small child. He served in the army in the First World War, and joined the anti-semitic right-wing German Workers Party in 1919. His autobiography *Mein Kampf* ('My Struggle') was written during Hitler's imprisonment for his part in the so-called 'Beer Hall Putsch', a failed attempt to overthrow the government of Bavaria in 1924. A charismatic demagogue, his electoral success led to the chancellorship and subsequent authoritarian rule of Germany in 1933. The German military-industrial complex over whose construction he presided helped to pull

Germany out of the Depression of the nineteen-thirties and, at its peak, exercised control over most of Europe. He committed suicide in the closing stages of the European war.

The quality of a state cannot be evaluated according to the cultural level or the power of this state in the frame of the outside world, but solely and exclusively by the degree of this institution's virtue for the nationality involved in each special case.

A state can be designated as exemplary if it is not only compatible with the living conditions of the nationality it is intended to represent, but if in practice it keeps this nationality alive by its own very existence—quite regardless of the importance of this state formation within the framework of the outside world. For the function of the state is not to create abilities, but only to open the road for those forces which are present. *Thus, conversely, a state can be designated as bad if, despite a high cultural level, it dooms the bearer of this culture in his racial composition.* For thus it destroys to all intents and purposes the premise for the survival of this culture which it did not create, but which is the fruit of a culture-creating nationality safeguarded by a living integration through the state. The state does not represent the content, but a form. *A people's cultural level at any time does not, therefore, provide a standard for measuring the quality of the state* in which it lives. It is easily understandable that a people highly endowed with culture offers a more valuable picture than a Negro tribe; nevertheless, the state organism of the former, viewed according to its fulfilment of purpose, can be inferior to that of the Negro. Though the best state and the best state form are not able to extract from a people abilities which are simply lacking and never did exist, a bad state is assuredly able to kill originally existing abilities by permitting or even promoting the destruction of the racial culture-bearer.

Hence our judgment concerning the quality of a state can primarily be determined only by the relative utility it possesses for a definite nationality, and in no event by the intrinsic importance attributable to it in the world.

This relative judgment can be passed quickly and easily, but the judgment concerning absolute value only with great difficulty, since this absolute judgment is no longer determined merely by the state, but by the quality and level of the nationality in question.

If, therefore, we speak of a higher mission of the state, we must not forget that the higher mission lies essentially in the nationality whose free development the state must merely make possible by the organic force of its being.

Hence, if we propound the question of how the state which we Germans need should be constituted, we must first clearly understand what kind of people it is to contain and what purpose it is to serve.

Our German nationality, unfortunately, is no longer based on a unified racial nucleus. The blending process of the various original components has advanced so far that we might speak of a new race. On the contrary, the poisonings of the blood which have befallen our people, especially since the Thirty Years' War, have led not only to a decomposition of our blood, but also of our soul. The open borders of our fatherland, the association with un-German foreign bodies along these frontier districts, but above all the strong and continuous influx of foreign blood into the interior of the Reich itself, due to its continuous renewal, leaves no time for an absolute blending. No new race is distilled out, the racial constituents remain side by side, with the result that, especially in critical moments in which otherwise a herd habitually gathers together, the German people scatters to all the four winds. Not only are the basic racial elements scattered territorially, but on a small scale within the same territory. Beside Nordic men Easterners, beside Easterners Dinarics, beside both of these Westerners, and mixtures in between. On the one hand, this is a great disadvantage: the German people lack that sure herd instinct which is based on unity of the blood and, especially in moments of threatening danger, preserves nations from destruction in so far as all petty inner differences in such peoples vanish at once on such occasions and the solid front of a unified herd confronts the common enemy. This co-existence of unblended basic racial elements of the most varying kind accounts for what is termed *hyper-individualism* in Germany. In peaceful periods it may sometimes do good services, but taking all things together, it has robbed us of world domination. If the German people in its historic development had possessed that herd unity which other peoples enjoyed, the German Reich today would doubtless be mistress of the globe. World history would have taken a different course, and no one can distinguish whether in this way we would not have obtained what so many blinded pacifists today hope to gain by begging, whining, and whimpering: *a peace, supported not by the palm branches of tearful, pacifist female mourners, but based on the victorious sword of a master people, putting the world into the service of a higher culture.*

The fact of the non-existence of a nationality of unified blood has brought us untold misery. It has given capital cities to many small German potentates, but deprived the German people of the master's right.

Today our people are still suffering from this inner division; but what brought us misfortune in the past and present can be our blessing for the future. For detrimental as it was on the one hand that a complete blending of our original racial components did not take place, and that the formation of a unified national body was thus prevented, it was equally fortunate on the other hand that in this way at least a part of our best blood was preserved pure and escaped racial degeneration.

Assuredly, if there had been a complete blending of our original racial elements, a unified national body would have arisen; however, as every racial cross-breeding proves, it would have been endowed with a smaller cultural capacity than the highest of the original components originally possessed. This is the blessing of the absence of complete blending: that today in our German national body we still possess great unmixed stocks of Nordic-Germanic people whom we may consider the most precious treasure for our future. In the confused period of ignorance of all racial laws, when a man appeared to be simply a man, with full equality—clarity may have been lacking with regard to the different value of the various original elements. Today we know that a complete intermixture of the components of our people might, in consequence of the unity thus produced, have given us outward power, but that the highest goal of mankind would have been unattainable, since the sole bearer, whom Fate had clearly chosen for this completion, would have perished in the general racial porridge of the unified people.

But what, through none of our doing, a kind Fate prevented, we must today examine and evaluate from the standpoint of the knowledge we have now acquired.

Anyone who speaks of a mission of the German people on earth must know that it can exist only in the formation of a state which sees its highest task in the preservation and promotion of the most noble elements of our nationality, indeed of all mankind, which still remain intact.

Thus, for the first time the state achieves a lofty inner goal. Compared to the absurd catchword about safeguarding law and order, thus laying a peaceable groundwork for mutual swindles, the task of preserving and advancing the highest humanity, given to this earth by the benevolence of the Almighty, seems a truly high mission.

From a dead mechanism which only lays claim to existence for its own sake, there must be formed a living organism with the exclusive aim of serving a higher idea.

The German Reich as a state embraces all Germans and has the task, not only of assembling and preserving the most valuable stocks of basic racial elements in this people, but slowly and surely of raising them to a dominant position.

88 Alfred Rosenberg, from (a) *Der Mythus des 20. Jahrhunderts* and (b) 'Totaler Staat?', both in *Selected Writings* (ed. R. Pois; Jonathan Cape, 1970), pp. 33–4, 186–9, 191–2

Alfred Rosenberg (1893–1946) was born in Talinn, Estonia. A supporter of the counter-revolutionaries in the Russian Revolution, he emigrated to Germany in 1918. An early member of the National Socialist German Workers Party, he was an important exponent of Nazi beliefs, notably in *Der Mythus des 20. Jahrhunderts* (1938). He was responsible within the Party for cultural and educational organizations, and, following the German invasion of the USSR, he was appointed head of the *Reich* ministry for the Occupied Eastern Territories. He was tried and executed at Nuremberg after the War.

The power struggles of today are manifestations of an inner collapse. Already, *all* the state systems of 1914 have fallen, even if in part they still have formal existence. Furthermore, social, religious and ideological [*Weltan-schauliche*] concepts and values also lie shattered. No commanding principle, no high Idea exercises uncontested dominion over the lives of peoples. Group struggles against group, party against party, national values against internationalistic doctrines, petrified imperialism against encroaching pacifism. Finance entangles states and peoples in its golden fetters, while economics becomes nomadized and life uprooted.

As indicative of world revolution, the World War laid bare the tragic fact that while millions sacrificed their lives these sacrifices accrued to the benefit of forces other than those for which armies were ready to die. The war dead are the victims of a catastrophe-stricken epoch which had long since become valueless; at the same time, however, . . . they are the martyrs of a new day, of a new belief.

The blood that had died is beginning to come to life anew. In its mystical patterns a new cellular-structure of the German *Volk*-soul is developing. Present and past are suddenly appearing in a new light, and as a result we have a new mission for the future. The actions of history and the future no longer signify class struggle or warfare between Church dogmas, but rather the conflict between blood and blood, race and race, people and people. And this means combat between spiritual values.

Observation of history from a racial standpoint is a heuristic principle which will soon become self-explanatory. Worthy individuals are serving this principle already. In the not-too-distant future these hosts will be able to fulfil themselves as the founders of a new world-picture.

However, the values of race-soul, which stand behind the new world-picture as driving forces, still have not been brought to living consciousness. *Soul means race viewed from within. And, vice-versa, race is the externalization of soul.* Awakening the race-soul to life means recognizing its highest value and, under the direction of this value, providing organic configuration for the other values—in state, *Kultur* and religion. This is the task of our century: to create a new human type from a new life-*Mythus*. Courage is needed for this task, courage on the part of each individual member of the race; courage on the part of the entire ascending race; indeed, courage on the part of generations yet unborn. For the dispirited will never master chaos, nor will cowards ever build a world. Whoever wants to strive forward must burn his bridges behind him. Whoever sets out on a great journey must leave behind all old household effects. Whoever strives for the highest must humble the inferior. The new man of the approaching first German Reich will have but one answer for all doubts and questions: Alone, I will!

. . .

Do not misunderstand me. I am not at all maintaining that the Jew bears sole guilt for the bestial materialization of our life; but I am holding strongly to the fact that he placed his entire power, in terms of energy and money, at the disposal of a tendency which was all-alienating, and that he had to do this to remain in harmony with his centuries-old essence. Left to itself, the German character would have achieved a balance. However, this was made impossible due to Jewish strength in the press, theatre, trade and sciences. We ourselves have been guilty—we should not have emancipated the Jews but, as Goethe, Fichte and Herder vainly demanded, should have created insurmountable exceptional laws for them. One does not allow a poison to drift about unobserved, nor grant it parity with medicine; rather one keeps it within careful limits. After 2,000 years, this has finally happened in the National Socialist Reich!

. . .

The revolution of January 30th, 1933, was in no way the continuation of the old absolutist state, even under a new emblem. Rather, the state assumed a different relationship with regard to the *Volk* and *Volkstum* from what it had in 1918; but also one which was different from the one of 1871. What has been completed during this past year, and what remains to be completed over a broader radius, is not the so-called totality of the state, but the totality of the National Socialist movement. The state is no longer an entity which, be it close to the party and the movement or be it a mechanical apparatus, is a ruling instrument; rather it is an instrument of the National Socialist *Weltanschauung*. On the surface, this would appear to be merely a trifling difference in emphasis between state-political and perception-critical forms of thought. And yet, clarification of the intellectual presuppositions is of great importance, because a false conceptual picture will yield—if not right away, then most certainly in the course of time—practical consequences for political action. If we continue to speak of the total state, younger National Socialists and coming generations will gradually shift the state concept into the centre of things, and the activities of state officials will be felt to be the primary ones. If, however, we emphasize with all clarity today that it is a certain political ideology and movement that demands the right of totality, the gaze of generations will be directed upon the movement, and the relationship between state and N.S.D.A.P. will be seen in a totally different light than if one were to designate statishness itself as primary. The National Socialist movement is the moulded strength of twentieth-century thought; moulded for the security of the collective German *Volk* and of its blood and character. The state, as a most powerful and virile instrument, is placed at the disposal of the movement, and its life-strengths and powers are continuously renewed by the movement in order that it remain flexible and capable of resistance while avoiding the dangers of bureaucratization, petrification and estrangement from *Volk*. Only in this connection does the National Socialist state-concept become truly alive, and we even believe that the state itself will gain sanctification through it, and that it will derive inner strength and authority to a greater degree than if it transformed itself into its own goal—even if it were led by energetic individuals, the state would become ossified through this process.

For all these reasons, it behooves National Socialists not to speak any more of the total state, but of the *completion of the National Socialist* Weltanschauung, *of the N.S.D.A.P. as the embodiment of this* Weltanschauung, *and of the National Socialist state as the means by which National Socialism, the mightiest phenomenon originating in the twentieth century, secures soul, intellect and blood.*

89 José Antonio Primo De Rivera, from 'Spain and Barbarism', in *Selected Writings* (ed. Hugh Thomas; Jonathan Cape, 1970), pp. 144–8

José Antonio Primo De Rivera (1903–1936) was born in Madrid and was the son of the Spanish dictator between 1923 and 1930, General Miguel Primo De Rivera. José Antonio was a lawyer and editor of *El Fascio*, and in 1933 founded the Falange Española. A supporter of the military rebellion against the Spanish Republic, he was captured and executed in 1936. A cult of martyrdom around him was fostered in the victorious General Franco's Spain.

That is our new task in the face of Russian communism, which is the barbarian invasion we are threatened with. Communism does contain an element worth taking up: its self-denial and sense of solidarity. However, being as it is a barbarian invasion, Russian communism goes too far and rejects anything that smacks of historical and spiritual values; it is anti-patriotic, devoid of faith in God. Hence our efforts to save the absolute truths, the historic values, so that they may not perish.

How can this ever be achieved? That is a question to which there is beginning to emerge an answer, here in Castile, in Spain.

One of the alleged solutions is social-democracy. Basically, social-democracy preserves capitalism; it just keeps throwing sand into the mechanism. That is sheer madness.

Another alleged solution is the totalitarian state. But there is no such thing as a totalitarian state. Certain nations have found dictators of genius, who have been up to the task of substituting themselves for the state; but that cannot be imitated, and in Spain, for the time being, we shall have to wait for such a genius to appear. Germany and Italy are examples of what is called the totalitarian state, but notice how they are not only not similar, but even radically unlike each other; their totalitarianism can be traced back to opposite points of departure. The totalitarian state of Germany can be traced back to a people's capacity for trusting its racial instinct. The German people are in a frenzy of self-assertion; Germany is experiencing a super-democracy. Rome, on the other hand, is undergoing the experience of having a genius with a classical mind wanting to forge a people from above. The German movement is Romantic in kind, its course is the same as ever; that is where the Reformation sprang from and even the French Revolution, since the Declaration of Human Rights is a replica of the North American constitution fathered by German Protestant thinking.

Neither social-democracy nor any attempt to set up a totalitarian state without a genius would suffice to prevent the catastrophe. There are ointments of another kind, which we in Spain apply lavishly: I am referring to confederations, blocs and coalitions. All of these are based on the assumption that the union of several dwarfs can result in a giant. Such remedies must be approached with caution. And let us not allow their verbiage to take us by surprise. There are some such movements which make a show of religion being the mainstay of their programme, but which take a stand only when material advantages are at issue; which are prepared, in exchange for some moderation in the sphere of agrarian reform or for a nip into the property of the clergy, to forego the crucifix in schools or the abolition of divorce.

Other such blocs claim, for instance, to be corporativists. That is but a hollow phrase; or else, let us ask the first person to broach the subject with us, What do you mean by corporativism? How does it work? What solution does it bring, for example, to international problems? Hitherto, the best attempt has been made in Italy, and there it is only one integrated part of a perfect political mechanism. In order to try and bring about harmonious relations between employers and workers, there exists something like the mixed arbitration we have here, vastly magnified: a confederation of employers and another of workers, and at the top a liaison body. To date, the corporative state does not exist; neither do we know whether it is a good thing. Italy's corporative legislation is, as Mussolini himself has said, a point of departure and not a point of arrival, which is what our politicians claim corporativism to be.

When the world is unhinged, that unhingement cannot be cured by means of technical plasters; it takes an entire new order to achieve that. And this order must spring once again from the individual. May those hear us who accuse us of professing a state-pantheism: we consider the individual to be the basic unit, for this is the meaning of Spain, which has always considered man to be the embodiment of eternal values. Man must be free, but there cannot be freedom except within an order.

Liberalism told men that they could do as they liked, but failed to provide them with an economic order which would guarantee such freedom. An organized economic guaranty is therefore essential; but given the present economic chaos, there cannot be an organized economy without a strong state, and only a state in the service of a unitarian destiny can be strong without being tyrannical. That is how the strong state serving the consciousness of unity is the real guarantor of individual freedom. By contrast, the state which does not feel itself to be the servant of a supreme unity is constantly fearful of seeming tyrannical. That is the case with our Spanish state: what holds back its arm from doing justice after a bloody revolution is the awareness of its lack of an inner justification, its lack of a mission to fulfil.

Spain can have a state that is strong, because Spain in itself is a unitarian destiny of universal dimensions. And the Spanish state can limit itself to carrying out the essential functions of power, leaving not only arbitration but the entire regulation of many economic aspects to entities which can look back on a great tradition: to the unions, which will no longer be parasitic constructions, as they are in the present conception of labour relations, but the vertically integrated association of all those working together in each branch of production.

The new state will have to set about reorganizing the Spanish countryside as a whole. Not all of Spain is fit to live in: many lands, which merely perpetuate the misery of those who till them, will have to revert to desert or in many cases to forest. Large numbers of people will have to be moved to arable lands, where there will have to be a profound economic and social reform of agriculture involving improvement and rationalization of crops, irrigation, educational schemes for farmers, adequate prices, tariff protection for agriculture, and cheap credit on the one hand, and family holdings and union-run farms on the other. That will be a true return to nature, not in the sense of the eclogue, propounded by Rousseau, but in the sense of the georgic, which epitomizes the profound, stern and ritual way of understanding the land.

The same global view employed in the reorganization of agriculture must be applied to the reorganization of the entire economy. What does it mean to harmonize capital and labour? Labour is a human function, just as property is a human attribute. But property is not synonymous with capital; capital is an economic instrument, and, being an instrument, it must be used for the benefit of the whole economy, not for anyone's personal benefit. Reservoirs of capital must be like reservoirs of water; they are intended not for a few to organize boat races on the surface, but for regulating the flow of rivers and for moving the turbines of waterfalls.

Certainly a great deal of resistance will have to be overcome before these things can come to pass. Many selfish interests will oppose us, but it must always be our watchword that we are not concerned with saving material values. Property as we have known it hitherto is coming to an end; it will be eliminated, in one way or another, by the masses, who have not only a certain amount of justification for doing so, but the strength to do it. No one can possibly save the material values; what matters is that the breakdown of things material must be prevented from entailing the destruction of essential spiritual values. These are the values we want to save at all cost, even in exchange for the sacrifice of all economic advantages. They are well worth sacrificing to the glory of seeing Spain, our Spain, halt the final invasion of the barbarians.

90   Oswald Mosley, *Ten Points of Fascist Policy* (British Union of Fascists, 1936), pp. 2–8

Sir Oswald Mosley (1896–1980) began his political career as a Conservative Member of Parliament, but became an Independent, and then a member of the Labour Party. A rising star and noted orator, he resigned in 1930, following the rejection of his radical economic policies, and, after meeting Mussolini, formed the British Union of Fascists in 1932. The party was dissolved at the outset of the Second World War, and Mosley imprisoned. He continued to espouse radical right wing politics after the War.

I. PATRIOTISM AND REVOLUTION

Fascism is a creed of patriotism and revolution. For the first time a strong movement emerges, which on the one hand is loyal to King and Country, and on the other hand stands for far-reaching and revolutionary changes in government, in economics, and in life itself. Hitherto, patriotism has been associated with those who wish to keep things as they are; revolution has been associated with a flabby internationalism which sets the interests of foreign countries before those of Britain. The watch-word of Fascism is "Britain First." We love our country, but we are determined to build a country worthy of that love. Things cannot remain as they are: we must have great changes to adapt modern Britain to modern fact. True patriotism finds expression for the first time in the revolution of Fascism.

II. ACTION

The first necessity of the day is action. Again and again, the people have voted for programmes of action. Again and again they have been betrayed by the existing parties and frustrated by the present system. Conservatives have tried to keep things as they are, and to maintain what they call the stability of the State. For the purpose of resisting change, they have appealed to loyalty and patriotism. But to resist change in an age when change is necessary, is to threaten the stability and safety of the State, and is the reverse of patriotism. Socialists, on the other hand, have talked of progress, but have sought it in the endless discussions of talkative committees. They have rejected and derided the great instruments of leadership and decision by which alone things can be done and progress can be achieved. So their talk of progress has ended in chaos and in flight from responsibility. Fascism combines progress with the executive instruments of loyalty, decision and voluntary discipline, by which alone things can be done and ordered progress can be secured. The true patriotism of Fascism will carry the changes that are necessary, by principles and by methods which bring change with order and efficiency.

III. FASCIST ORGANISATION

Fascists bind themselves together to serve their country in a voluntary discipline, because without discipline they realise that nothing can be done. The black shirts which they wear symbolise their determination to save the nation. They are not afraid to stand out from their fellows as men dedicated to the service and revival of their country. The wearing of the black shirt by our more active members breaks down all barriers of class within our ranks, for all are dressed alike. The salute is the recognition of a brother Fascist who is inspired by the same passionate ideal of national service. Fascism, like every political creed this country has ever known, is common to all great countries, but Fascism is more in keeping with the British character than any other political faith. For the essence of Fascism is team-work, the power to pull together and to sink individual interests in the service of the nation. This we claim has been the leading characteristic of the British people at every great moment of our history.

IV. UNEMPLOYMENT AND THE MODERN PROBLEM

Fascism believes that the cause of the present world trouble of unemployment is the inability of the people to buy and to consume the goods which industry produces. Every day rationalisation and new scientific development enable industry to produce more goods with less labour. The power to produce increases, but the power to consume does not increase. In addition, Britain is faced with a particular problem because she is the greatest exporting nation in the world. Foreign markets are continually closing against us for the simple reason that other nations are now determined themselves to produce the goods which they consume.

V. FASCIST POLICY: THE CORPORATE STATE

Fascism solves the problem of unemployment and poverty by establishing the Corporate State. Industry will be divided into National Corporations governed by representatives of employers, workers and consumers, operating under Fascist government. The State will not attempt to conduct industry as it would under Socialism. Instead, the State will lay down the limits within which industry may operate, and those limits will be the national welfare. Private ownership will be permitted and encouraged, provided such activity enriches the nation as well as the individual. All interests which operate against the nation will be rigorously suppressed. *The function of the Corporations will be to raise wages and salaries over the whole field of industry as science, rationalisation and industrial technique increase the power to produce. Consumption will be adjusted to production, and a Home Market will be provided by the higher purchasing power of our own people.*

VI. THE EXPORT TRADE

The export trade will be supported by the Corporate system in the unification of our buying and selling arrangements abroad, which will enable industry to speak with one voice, and government for the first time to support our export trade. *Our trade motto will be "Britain Buys from Those who Buy from Britain."* We shall transfer elsewhere our purchases of foodstuffs and raw materials if those from whom we buy will not buy from us in return. By these means we will force the entry of our goods into markets now closed against us, until we have built a self-contained Empire which makes us independent of foreign markets.

VII. FASCIST EMPIRE

We seek to build a Britain as far as possible self contained, and an Empire completely self-contained We seek to create a great area of the earth with a far higher standard of civilisation than prevails elsewhere, which is immune from the chaos of world struggle and collapse. For this purpose, Fascism will exclude foreign goods. Tariffs are useless, because they tax the consumer without keeping out foreign goods which are the product of cheap slave labour in foreign countries. Within the Empire we can produce all manufactured goods, food-stuffs and raw materials which we require. Modern science enables us to do it in abundance, for we have passed from the economics of poverty to the economics of plenty, and great nations can be self-contained once they are organised and scientifically protected from the shocks and dislocations of world chaos. Such organisation will help to preserve the peace of this country and the world, for the prime cause of war is the international struggle for markets and raw materials supported by international finance. A self-contained Empire will be withdrawn from that struggle, and the risks of war will be diminished. Britons will not fight again except in defence of their own homes and Empire. Fascist movements now make rapid progress in all the great Dominions, and are federated with the British Union of Fascists in the New Empire Union.

VIII. AGRICULTURE: A FASCIST THREE-YEAR PLAN

Fascism stresses the importance of reviving the great agricultural industry, which has been betrayed by all parties. At present we produce £280,000,000 per annum of our total food supplies in this country, and we import £220,000,000 worth from foreign countries, and £140,000,000 worth from the Dominions. Under a three-year plan, Fascism will nearly double the production of British agriculture by the total exclusion of foreign goods. We can raise home production to £500,000,000 a year, and yet give the Dominions under Fascist government a better market than they enjoy to-day. The prices of farming produce must be fixed in advance, and the profiteering middleman ruthlessly suppressed. The higher purchasing power of the industrial worker under Fascism will afford the farmer an economic price for his product and a living wage for his worker. The higher purchasing power of the farming population when agricultural production is increased will take the place of our vanishing foreign markets in buying many of the products of our present export trade. The countryside shall be restored to prosperity, and shall contribute a healthy, virile manhood to build the Greater Britain of the future.

IX. ALIENS AND INTERNATIONAL FINANCE

Fascism alone will deal with the alien menace, because Fascism alone puts "Britain First." Under Fascism, no alien shall enter this country to take the jobs of Britons, and aliens already here who have abused the hospitality of this nation will be sent back whence they came. Fascism will deal, not only with the poor aliens who are here seeking jobs; Fascism will deal also with the great alien financiers of the City of London who use the financial power of Britain in the interests, not of this country, but of foreign countries. These men are the real alien menace, for by their foreign investments they are using British money to finance our competitors against us all over the world. The interest on the loans they have made to foreign countries come back to them in the shape of cheap goods which under-cut our standard of life and deprive our people of employment. Fascism alone will deal faithfully with the alien menace, in whatever quarter it rears its head.

X. LEADERSHIP—PARLIAMENT—LIBERTY

Fascism is a leadership of the nation. It is not dictatorship in the old sense of the word, which implies government against the will of the people. It is dictatorship in the modern sense of that word, which implies government armed by the people with complete power of action to overcome problems which must be solved if the nation is to live. We seek to achieve our aims by peaceful, legal and constitutional means with the willing consent of the nation declared at a General Election. Fascist Government, however, will at once take power to act by securing from the first Fascist Parliament complete power of action for the Government. Without the power to act and the will to act, nothing can be done. Fascist Government will use the power given it by the first Fascist Parliament for the reconstruction of the nation. At the end of the first Fascist Parliament, another election will be held, *on an occupational and not on a geographical franchise.* Men and women, will vote within their own industries with a real knowledge of the persons and subjects with which they are dealing. Women who are not in industry will vote as wives and mothers, and will thus be represented for the first time by people competent to speak for the great national interest which they represent. Women will not be compelled to retire from industry, but the high wages of their husbands under the Corporate system will make it possible for them to retire if they wish, and the present competition between men and women in industry will thus be ended. In the new Parliament, every interest and aspect of national life will be represented, but every interest will be subordinate to the welfare of the nation as a whole. Thus a technical and not a political Parliament will be elected to assist Government in the problems of a technical age. Thereafter, the policy and personnel of the Government as a whole will be submitted direct to the people to judge by vote. Government will no longer depend on the intrigues and manœuvres of conflicting parties, but on the will of the nation directly expressed. Thus the people will retain full liberty to approve or reject the policy of the Government, but a Government so approved and supported will have power to act and to end economic chaos. Fascism declares that the real liberty is economic liberty, and this cannot come until the end of economic chaos. Government cannot end economic chaos without power to act, and that power to act can only come from Fascism. Good wages, short hours, good houses, opportunities for culture and recreation are the real liberty. The mass of the people are being robbed of that *real liberty* to-day by the *false* liberty of a few old men to talk for ever in the present Parliamentary system. Talk and action do not go together, and action is the necessity of to-day. We will end talk with a new system, in which the whole resources of the nation are mobilised for action. The Blackshirts of Fascism, by their struggle and sacrifice, offer the nation a new leadership on a new road of national salvation. We ask you to follow that lead through the ending of class war, reaction and chaos, to the building of a Britain worthy of our pride and of our love.

91 Movimento Sociale Italiano, excerpt from 'The Programme of the Right for a New Italy', in *Fascism* (ed. Roger Griffin; Oxford University Press, 1995), pp. 386–7

The Movimento Sociale Italiano, dissolved and reformed as the Alleanza Nationale in 1995, has played a prominent role in Italian government, in coalitions led by Silvio Berlusconi, since the early 1990s. This extract is taken from the party's extended 1994 manifesto.

The year 1993 was crucial. It marked the end of the old and the beginning of the new. Until a few years ago in the era of the democracy of parties, the Italians were convinced of exercising sovereignty by always voting 'for someone' or sometimes 'against something', but never 'for something'. It was only in 1993 that the scandal of the irrelevance of their vote as a means of showing who should govern became apparent.[. . .]

The State is the image of the Nation, epitomizing its values by perpetuating hate. It exalts the qualities of the people whose rights it safeguards; it tells them their duties; it promotes development; it is the inspiring force behind national education and the artefact of justice; it is the guarantor of social equilibrium through the principle of solidarity understood as a synthesis of rights and duties. In this indissoluble identity the roots of the Nation-State extend deep into history and tradition, and it identifies the path to progress by pursuing the maximum common good—the good of the nation—on the basis of which it ensures that all individual needs of individuals and groups are met. With the disappearance of the sense of the State and the travesty of the State itself into a regime of parties, the sense of Nation has disappeared, and with it the awareness of the value of the 'national community' so that the State has come to take material form in its worst aspects: bureaucratic centralism, draconian tax regimes, partitocracy.[. . .]

The identity of the Partito democratico della sinistra has been aptly described as a 'radical mass party', that is, a confederation of groupings promoting causes which range from the politicization of homosexuality to the most extreme and irrational forms of ecologism and feminism, and all lead to the complete laicization of the Italian people. In contrast, our identity is based on the integral respect for the reality of the human person and his or her sacredness.[. . .]

Now a great chance for the introduction of a new model of political representation has been created by the failure of the partitocratic system, by the wiping out of the old parties brought about by the electorate, and by new personalities entering the political stage who are more representative and more reliable than their predecessors.[. . .] The concomitant of a government made strong by direct popular investiture is a strong parliament with extensive powers of policy-making and control.[. . .]

The present situation is the result of the total failure of the absurd and suicidal race for the paradise of possessions and appearances instead of pursuing the only world which gives quality and substance to a person, namely the world of 'being'. This is the difference which has always distinguished the Youth Front [Fronte del Gioventù] from other youth organizations.[. . .] It is because of its way of being, its history, its tradition, its presence in the country, that today the Youth Front must form the nucleus of a youth alliance (like the MSI—DN in the national alliance), a broad based movement which enables different souls to identify with a political project in which values such as national identity, freedom, right to life, the family, and solidarity provide the base for the reconstruction of the nation.[. . .]

After German unification, Italian unification with the return, sanctioned through international agreements, of Istria, Fiume, Dalmatia.[. . .] An allied Europe [. . .] no more subordination, but European strength, independence, and autonomy in political and military decisions.[. . .] There is an Italian people living and working beyond the frontiers of the Fatherland [. . .] nearly 60 million of Italian extraction according to the estimates of the Foreign Minister: a huge potential force, totally ignored and even discriminated against by Italian governments and the forces of Italian politics.[. . .] We will obtain their electoral participation for the reconstruction of the Italian state.

92   **Russia's Liberal Democratic Party, from 'The New Order: Parallel Civilisations', in *Fascism* (ed. Roger Griffin; Oxford University Press, 1995), pp. 388–9**

This excerpt, by Andrei Arkhipov, is drawn from an article published in Vladimir Zhirinovsky's (1946–) newspaper 'Zhirinovsky's Falcon' in 1992. Zhirinovsky enjoyed electoral success and grabbed headlines in the 1990s, by advocating military (including nuclear) aggression against Russia's neighbours and praising Hitler in an article in the newspaper *Izvestia*. Andrei Arkhipov has served in Zhirinovsky's 'shadow cabinet' and ran the militarized youth wing of the Liberal Democratic Party, the Falcons. Several issues of 'Zhirinovsky's Falcon' were published in 1992–1993, each with a print run of fifty thousand.

The bearers of white civilization are disappearing. The world is turning yellow, and red, and black. No place is being left on the planet for the White person. As we approach the year 2000 the White race comprises just 7 or 8 per cent of the population of the globe. The old film-clip about King Kong gripping in his paw the beautiful blonde woman carries its ominous subtext: soon—very soon—that is precisely how the European will feel in the face of other races and peoples.

Yes, we can say with pride: contemporary world civilization has been built by the White person; all other peoples aspire to imitate and copy us, feeling through that a humiliating dependence on us and their own second-rateness in the established world order.[. . .]

Two civilizations cannot go on living together in North America.[. . .] White America will be violently swallowed up by non-White ethnic groups; those of Anglo-Saxon, European, and Jewish extraction not worthy of counting themselves amongst Europeans will find themselves amongst a terrified minority facing the huge mass of black, yellow, and red dwellers on this earth. There will come a demand for the setting up of ethnically pure states on the territory of the former USA. The coloured majority subject to such a fearful and destructive aggravation could then receive moral and material support from Russians (in the shape of Russian weapons).[. . .] The Whites can then of course either live as small colonies on reservations in the midst of these deeply antagonistic states, or return to their historic homeland.[. . .] There is another possibility, of course: when the Whites of America, moved by a healthy impulse for survival and by racial instinct, carry through the deportation of the dark part of the population to their historic homeland. Into the space thus freed up, and with the active help of the Russian government, could be sent representatives of those nations and peoples which, under the guise of national right to self-determination, took part in the destruction of the historic Russian state: a section of Ukrainian nationalists; the leftovers of the non-Russian population in the Baltic region; and the refugees of the virtually disappearing Armenia. These immigrants will make a fine sauce for the ethnic stew in America. At the same time, the enforced expulsion of anti-state elements will make room for the development and improvement of the quality of the population of the renewed Russia.[. . .]

In the political long term, there can be no doubt that once the system of occupation in the Greater Germany is complete there will begin a time for new and joyful changes in Europe. The Germans have truly recognized their own position and the lessons of history: the great racial qualities of Russians. Only with Russians will they be able to find genuine support in their struggle against the rottenness of North American civilization. Together with Russians they will be able to wreak revenge on America for its fierce internationalism and anti-Germanism. Russia and Germany together will be able to ensure the violent end of the United States and the establishment of a healthier racial balance on the continent of Europe.[. . .] And, as our leader Vladimir Zhirinovsky truly points out: 'The joint exit (*vykhod*) of Europe's two great powers towards the shores of the warm Indian Ocean can refresh more than one generation of German and Russian youth.'

Effeminate Europe may still not be completely ready for such a turn of events. There's no doubt, however, that with Russian help Germany should be able to return to itself the historic lands of Alsace-Lorraine (Elsass and Lothringia), for which so much German blood was shed, as well as the Sudetenland and the Baltic coasts of Prussia. Together we shall be able to create on the southern shore of France a new Arab state with the population of those derived from the countries of North Africa.[. . .]

For the first time in world history it will also be possible to create a state along sexual lines: homosexuals should permanently get their own little corner of lust where they will feel genuinely at home. Various regions of Holland or even Amsterdam could be converted into such self-nurturing states.[. . .]

Above all, as the first stage of the new politics, there will be a strong return of nations to their own languages—even by an enforced route. We Russians shall need to demand of non-Russian peoples who insist on their own states that they cease the use of our language in all areas of life, or perhaps the introduction of a charge for using our language. The instruction of non-Russians will only be possible in the local language. No more conversations, negotiations, or interviews of local tribal leaders in Russian! Temporary rulers from the margins of Russia must stop it, and never, anywhere (even in their sleep) use Russian words—and must order their relations to do the same. We must bring in severe laws forbidding the use of Russian as a language of international intercourse.[. . .] We Russians shall at long last stop experiencing the feeling of shame for our precious language corrupted by ridiculous accents.

We Europeans must put all our efforts into returning peoples artificially transplanted into our White civilization to their national roots and their natural way of life. Less contact, no technical aid, no instruction of specialists and students! To cultivate in the end a United Nations of peoples of White race.[. . .]

We shall build a world of hope, stability, and happiness, giving the opportunity for all races, nations, and peoples to develop their civilizations IN PARALLEL, without mixing and with minimal interaction. The grievous experience of the past thousand years, and especially of the twentieth century, has shown emphatically that any kind of intermingling and mutual influence is the way only to death and degradation for the White race. But in parallel civilizations lie paths to the achievement of true internationalism and friendship of peoples.

10   New forms

Introduction

Ideologies are not ossified collections of doctrines, but dynamic 'conversations' that both respond to and transform the social and political world around them. The end of the twentieth century and start of the twenty-first has generated currents of thought that do not fit easily into the categories identified in the previous eight chapters of this book. This chapter collects together a set of readings that point to new sets of ideological concerns: with sexuality, cultural identity, the rights of indigenous or aboriginal peoples, and with globalization. Gay activists and queer theorists argue for new conceptions of human sexuality and for a rethinking of the place of sexuality in our view of social identity. Promoters of multiculturalism argue that the distinctive needs and interests of ethnic and cultural minorities have been downplayed by mainstream views of law and politics. Defenders of the rights of indigenous or aboriginal peoples in the Americas, Australia, New Zealand, Europe, and elsewhere, argue for the restoration of traditional practices and authority in the teeth of a history of colonial oppression. Globalizers predict the coming of a borderless world, in which states have little control over transnational flows of goods, capital, and, perhaps, people. On the other side, the anti-globalization movement views the reality of globalization as the undemocratic and oppressive imposition of the interests of powerful states and multinational corporations on vulnerable populations. These various positions are often presented self-consciously as novel expressions of points of view, interests, and concerns that have been neglected or suppressed by the main currents of ideological thinking. At the same time, they share some family resemblances with features of traditional ideologies. They overlap with and draw upon materials (such as terms, rhetoric, concepts, problems, and arguments) from other ideologies. It is perhaps too soon to say whether these are proto-ideologies in their own right or unorthodox amalgams of the traditional doctrines.

The first four selections here share a concern with identity and the proper social and political recognition of people's particularity. At the same time, it is a distinctive feature of this recent wave of ideological thought that it is reluctant to think of a person's identity as a sort of essence inhering in him or her. Rather, we are 'contextual individuals', whose particular identities emerge from the social relations in which we find ourselves. It is worth noting that to some degree these arguments derive from or build on materials found in other ideologies. Liberals argue for the importance of recognizing the individual and providing for individual particularity. In different ways some socialists, nationalists, and feminists have argued that the liberal individual is too abstract and featureless, and that more concrete elements of a person's social identity (economic class, nation, sex or gender) are crucial to understanding society and politics.

The excerpts from Jeffrey Weeks and Judith Butler are concerned with sexuality and sexual identity. Each alludes to the immense influence of the French historian and philosopher Michel Foucault in thinking in this area. As an ideology, gay liberation aims to expose and criticize laws, beliefs, and practices that oppress homosexuals. These may take the form not only of legal obstacles and the cultural prejudices and stereotypes of the straight world, but the internalization of a sense of shame and guilt derived from the prejudices of the rest of society on the part of homosexuals themselves. It aims to criticize homophobic beliefs and practices, and to promote a sense of gay pride and identity. Weeks in the extract here argues that mobilization around a sense of sexual identity emerges not as a result of a peculiar personal obsession but through a reaction to the importance assigned by a wider homophobic society to 'correct' sexual behaviour: which, for example, presents homosexuality as a medical pathology [Reading 93]. This mobilization also requires a specific set of urban social conditions in which a lesbian and gay movement could coalesce. He argues that sexuality is not a fatality, so social recognition or affirmation of an identity is not a matter of affirming an unchanging essence inhering in someone. Rather, identities are always relational, composed out of the materials available to the individual in his or her culture and society.

Butler extends and radicalizes this idea, in a criticism of main currents of feminist thinking [Reading 94]. Feminists who view women as a group with a common set of characteristics and interests make a mistake, she argues. Their approach unwittingly enforces a 'binary' view of gender identity, in which human beings are divided into two clear-cut groups, women and men. But this rides roughshod over the particularity of different women's experiences, 'the workings of gender oppression in the concrete cultural contexts in which it exists'. Gender and sexual desire, she argues, are not caused by underlying biological or cultural features of a person's identity. Identities do not express some authentic inner core self but are the dramatic effect, rather than cause, of performances. Gender and sexuality are not connected to an essence but to a performance. This is the sense in which 'there need not be a "doer behind the deed"' since 'the "doer" is variably constructed in and through the deed'. Certain cultural configurations of identity seize hold or are hegemonic. She calls for the destabilisation of this apparent fixity: the 'gender trouble' of her title consists in the subversion, proliferation and confusion of gender and identity in order to bring to the fore their performed or constructed quality.

A different terrain on which arguments over the recognition of identities have raged is 'multiculturalism'. This is an outlook for which minority ethnic and cultural identities require not (or not merely) the formally equal treatment under the law promised by liberalism by each individual, but various sorts of legal and political rights designed to accommodate and perhaps to promote their specific identities. Exemptions and exceptions in this vein have a long history in western democracies, a standard example being the special consideration for Jewish shopkeepers from Sunday-closing legislation. In the excerpt from *Rethinking Multiculturalism* reproduced here, Bhikhu Parekh argues that equality of treatment should not be identified with uniformity of treatment [Reading 95]. In a significant number of cases, exemptions from laws that apply to the wider society and policies such as affirmative action are required in order to put an ethnic, cultural, or religious minority on an equal footing with the majority community. He gives a number of examples of the variegated treatment that he thinks permissible or necessary, and discusses at some length the argument for state funding in Britain of Muslim schools. Liberal and nationalist critics of multiculturalism worry that such measures violate equal treatment of individuals or the integrity of the political community. Multiculturalists such as Parekh respond that these concerns are misplaced, and that multicultural measures are necessary for authentic equality and community.

Similar concerns are visible in the movement on behalf of indigenous and tribal peoples. This asserts the value of traditional customs and identities that have been overrun by the invasion of European settlers. In the extract here, the Canadian political theorist James Tully argues that this movement shares the anti-imperialism of decolonising nationalism, but with a different goal [Reading 96; see Chapter 5, especially Readings 58, 59, 60, 61]. While nation-alists typically aspire to nation-state status in order to participate fully as a distinct society in the global political economy and international politics, indigenous peoples typically seek to maintain certain traditional practices while participating on their own terms in wider social, economic, and political structures. Indeed, the constitutional states achieved through decol-onization are perceived as themselves part of the problem identified by this movement, eclipsing indigenous modes of self-government and appropriating land. Only through extending the rights of indigenous peoples can this process of what is sometimes called 'ethnocide' be halted. The various forms of recognition and self-rule claimed include, for example, exclusive rights to hunt and fish in particular territories, restrictions on land owner-ship and use on the part of the majority community, as well as structures of self-government, such as the right to enforce traditional family law. Tully looks forward to the revival of a treaty model of relationship between the state and the communities seeking recognition, which will not be regularly violated by the stronger party, as in the colonial past. As in the discourse of multiculturalism, the movement on behalf of indigenous peoples argues for and anticip-ates a plural form of political society, for which group membership affects the duties and entitlements of citizenship.

The last two readings are not centred around the theme of social identity, although, like the extract from Tully's writings, they call into question the conception of the state as a unitary sovereign actor. Economic, political, and cultural globalization became a central theme in the political discourse of the end of the twentieth century. In particular, the perceived loss of nation-states' capacities for action and control over movement of capital flows and the growth of global regulatory regimes through such varied organizations as the United Nations, the European Union, the World Trade Organization, and International Monetary Fund have been thought to constitute the key conditions for contemporary politics. The collapse of communism seemed to some to usher in an era in which the world truly constituted a global marketplace. Kenichi Ohmae, a management theorist and the author of books with titles such as *The Borderless World* and *The End of the Nation-State*, offers a confident prognosis [Reading 97]. Viewing states and other organizations from the standpoint of the global market, globalizers view the fundamental unit of social change to be not the nation-state or national economy but global patterns of production, exchange, and consumption. States cannot resist the influence of global financial markets and flows of trade. Attempts to do so, by subsidizing employment or protecting uncompetitive industries, are doomed to impover-ish the populations subject to these policies and to destabilize the governments that attempt them. From this perspective, the state is becoming increasingly insignificant, their role restricted to winning the competition to offer the best venue for multinational corporations to locate their activities. However, this is all taken to be not only inevitable but benign, ushering in an era of global cosmopolitanism.

Critics are sceptical both of the claims that the global market is a novelty and that it is a brute force external to the political choices of states. One current of criticism itself seems to constitute to a counter-ideology. Primarily a current defined by what it opposes—neo-liberal orthodoxies, the power of global elites, and the free-trade agenda pursued within various global political forums—the anti-globalization movement is characterized by its ideological, as well as territorial, pluralism, and assembles elements of socialism, anarchism, feminism, environmentalism, and the movement on behalf of indigenous peoples. The reading from Naomi Klein exemplifies and comments on this intermingling of ideological traditions and themes [Reading 98]. Klein argues that a distinctively novel phase of capitalism has emerged in the last decade. The fetish of the 'brand' has supplanted the product within the symbolic economy of corporate capitalism. The enormous increase in the wealth and cultural influence of multi-national corporations of the last fifteen years, she maintains, is rooted in the idea propounded by management theorists: that successful corporations must primarily produce brands, not products. One of the major social implications of this process is the colonisation of public space and individual identity by the successful promulgation of brand identities. She is also committed to charting and interpreting the many different kinds of response and rebellion that have sought to deflect the growing power of corporate capitalism. The movement to which she relates is diverse, non-hierarchical, and geographically dispersed. Yet it is the source, she argues, of a distinct and broadly coherent set of alternative values to those that have been promoted by multi-national giants and that have passed into the political institutions that are seeking to manage the global economy.

FURTHER READING

On gender and sexuality, see Judith Squires, *Gender and Political Theory* (Polity Press, 1999), Richard Mohr, *Gays/Justice* (Columbia University Press, 1998), Annemarie Jagone, *Queer Theory: An Introduction* (New York University Press, 1996). On multiculturalism, there is a substantial literature: Will Kymlicka, *Multicultural Citizenship* (Oxford University Press, 1995) and *Finding Our Way* (Oxford University Press, 1998) and Joseph Carens, *Culture, Citizenship and Community* (Oxford University Press, 2000) are excellent, and good places to start. Brian Barry views multiculturalism as something like an ideology in the perjorative sense in *Culture and Equality* (Polity Press, 2001). On indigenous rights, see Duncan Ivison and Paul Patton (eds.), *The Rights of Indigenous Peoples* (Cambridge University Press, 1999), and Leroy Little Bear, Menno Boldt, and Anthony J. Long (eds.), *Pathways to Self-Determination* (University of Toronto Press, 1984). The best introductions to the debates around globalization are David Held and Anthony McGrew, David Goldblatt and Jonathan Perraton, *Global Transformations: Politics, Economics, Culture* (Polity Press, 1999); David Held and Anthony McGrew (eds.), *The Global Transformations Reader* (Polity Press, 2000).

93   Jeffrey Weeks, from *Against Nature* (Rivers Oram, 1991), pp. 77–9, 81–5

Jeffrey Weeks (1945–) is Professor of Sociology at South Bank University in London. A member of the activist groups Gay Liberation Front and Gay Left Collective in the 1970s, his books include the important text chronicling the development of homosexual politics, *Coming Out: Homosexual Politics in Britain from the Nineteenth Century to the Present* (1977), as well as *Sex, Politics and Society: the Regulation of Sexuality Since 1800* (1981), and *Inverted Moralities: Sexual Values in an Age of Uncertainty* (1995).

The most obvious reason for the emphasis on identity as resistance is that for countless numbers of people it was their sexuality that had been denied. Modern society is fractured by many divisions, along lines of class, race, religion, ideology, status, and age. These intersect with, and complicate, but do not cause, two other major divisions, of gender and sexual preference. It is only at certain times, in certain cultures, that these divisions become the central foci of political controversy. Though feminism has swept the West (and parts of the Third World) since the late 1960s, by and large more specific questions of sexual choice have not become major mobilizing issues. In countries like Britain and France active gay movements have successfully inspired thousands of people, but as political forces they have largely been subordinated to more traditional progressive politics. Issues of class and ideology weigh heavier than sexuality. But in the United States, where class loyalties are less fixed, politics more coalition-minded, "minority" politics (especially the struggles of blacks) better established, and social loyalties more fluid, sexuality has become a potent political issue, and sexual communities have become bases for political mobilization.

This is not, however, merely another product of West Coast esotericism. A city like San Francisco has become a forcing house of sexual radicalism because, for a variety of historical reasons, it has been a refuge for those escaping the sexual ethics of moral America. San Francisco, Edmund White wittily argued, became "a sort of gay finishing school, a place where neophytes can confirm their gay identity". Women and men have mobilized around their sense of sexual identity in such a place because it was in their sexuality that they felt most powerfully invalidated.

The resulting preoccupation with identity among the sexually marginal cannot be explained as an effect of a peculiar personal obsession with sex. It has to be seen, more accurately, as a powerful resistance to the organizing principle of traditional sexual attitudes. It has been the sexual radicals who have most insistently politicized the question of sexual identity. But the agenda has been largely shaped by the importance assigned by our culture to "correct" sexual behaviour.

But politicized sexual identities are not automatic responses to negative definitions. For their emergence, they need complex social and political conditions in order to produce a sense of community experience which makes for collective endeavour. Barry Adam has suggested that five conditions are necessary for this: the existence of large numbers in the same situation; geographical concentration; identifiable targets of opposition; sudden events or changes in social position; and an intellectual leadership with readily understood goals. Each of these has been present in the emergence of the most spectacularly successful of politicized sexual identities, the lesbian and gay identities, over the past twenty years. The growth of urban subcultures since the Second World War especially in North America, but also in Europe, the emergence of general currents of hostility, from McCarthyism to moral panics around the impact of "permissiveness" and the sexual revolution, the growth of new social movements with radical sexual agendas, such as feminism and the lesbian and gay movements, not to mention the movements of the "sexual fringe" following in their wake—each of these has helped to make for the emergence of "the modern homosexual" now not so much a curiosity in the fading pages of sexology textbooks but the bearer of a fully blown social and human identity.

. . .

Identity is not a destiny but a choice. But in a culture where homosexual desires, female or male, are still execrated and denied, the adoption of lesbian or gay identities inevitably constitutes a *political* choice. These identities are not expressions of secret essences. They are self-creations, but they are creations on ground not freely chosen but laid out by history. So homosexual identities illustrate the play of constraint and opportunity, necessity and freedom, power and pleasure. Sexual identities seem necessary in the contemporary world as starting-points for a politics around sexuality. But the form they take is not pre-determined. In the end, therefore, they are not so much about who we really are, what our sex dictates. They are about what we want to be and could be. But this means they are also about the morality of acts and the quality of relations. We live in a world of proliferating "sexual identities" as specific desires (paedophile, sado-masochistic, bisexual) become the focus either for minute subdivisions of well-established notions (gayness or lesbianism) or spin off into wholly new ones. Can we therefore say that all identities are of equal value, and that minute subdivisions of desire, however apparently bizarre and esoteric, deserve social recognition on the basis of the right to erotic difference and sexual identity?

Such questions have led to the development of what may be termed a "relationship paradigm" as opposed to the traditional "identity paradigm" as a way of thinking through some of the conceptual—and political—issues. If, as many advocates of gay politics have suggested, identity is a constraint, a limitation on the flux of possibilities and the exploration of desires, if it is only an historical acquisition, then surely its assertion should be historically junked or at least modified. The difficulty is to find a replacement that would equally satisfactorily provide a basis for personal coherence and social recognition. One possibility is to celebrate the flux, to indulge in a glorification of the "polysexualities" to which, on a radical reading of the Freudian tradition, we are all heirs. The unfortunate difficulty with this is that most individuals do not feel "polymorphously perverse". On the contrary they feel their sexual desires are fairly narrowly organized, whatever use they make of those desires in real life. Moreover, a social identity is no less real for being historically formed. Sexual identities are no longer arbitrary divisions of the field of possibilities; they are encoded in a complex web of social practices—legal, pedagogic, medical, moral, and personal. They cannot be willed away.

The aim of the "relationship paradigm", in contrast, is not to ignore questions of identity but to displace them, by stressing instead the need to examine relationships. If this is done we can look again both at our sexual history and our sexual presence. Historically, we need no longer look for the controversial emergence of identities. Instead we can see the complicated net of relationships through which sexuality is always expressed, changing over time. Looked at from a contemporary point of view, we see not the culmination of a process of identity development but the formation of new types of relationships, validating hitherto execrated sexualities, in complex communities of interest around sex.

This is a very tempting position to adopt. In particular it potentially allows sexual thinking to move away from a "morality of acts", where all debate is about the merits of this form of sexuality as opposed to that, to an "ethics of choice", where the question becomes one of the quality of involvement and the freedom of relationships. This puts the whole debate on quite a new footing, allowing questions of power, diversity and sexual pluralism to be brought in.

The difficulty with the "relationship paradigm" is that it is offered as an alternative to questions of identity. This is a false antinomy. Identities are always "relational" in the general sense that they only exist in relation to other potential identities. More crucially, identities must always be about relationships: to ourselves, precarious unities of conflicting desires and social commitments, "composed of heterogeneous fragments of fossilized cultures"; and to others, who address us and call upon our recognition in diverse ways and through whom our sense of self is always negotiated. A sense of identity is essential for the establishment of relationships. As Foucault has argued, "sex is not a fatality, it's a possibility for creative life". For a variety of historical reasons that possibility is mediated through a recognition of identity. Identity may well be a historical fiction, a controlling myth, a limiting burden. But it is at the same time a necessary means of weaving our way through a hazard-strewn world and a complex web of social relations. Without it, it seems, the possibilities of sexual choice are not increased but diminished.

94   Judith Butler, from *Gender Trouble* (Routledge, 2000), pp. 4–8, 181

Judith Butler (1956–) is the Maxine Elliot Professor in the Departments of Rhetoric and Comparative Literature at the University of California, Berkeley, and has written on a range of topics in philosophy and social theory. Her books include *Subjects of Desire: Hegelian Reflection in Twentieth Century France* (1987), *Bodies That Matter: On the Discursive Limits of 'Sex'* (1993), *The Psychic Life of Power: Theories of Subjection* (1997), and *Antigone's Claim: Kinship Between Life and Death* (2000).

Foucault points out that juridical systems of power *produce* the subjects they subsequently come to represent. Juridical notions of power appear to regulate political life in purely negative terms—that is, through the limitation, prohibition, regulation, control, and even "protection" of individuals related to that political structure through the contingent and retractable operation of choice. But the subjects regulated by such structures are, by virtue of being subjected to them, formed, defined, and reproduced in accordance with the requirements of those structures. If this analysis is right, then the juridical formation of language and politics that represents women as "the subject" of feminism is itself a discursive formation and effect of a given version of representational politics. And the feminist subject turns out to be discursively constituted by the very political system that is supposed to facilitate its emancipation. This becomes politically problematic if that system can be shown to produce gendered subjects along a differential axis of domination or to produce subjects who are presumed to be masculine. In such cases, an uncritical appeal to such a system for the emancipation of "women" will be clearly self-defeating.

The question of "the subject" is crucial for politics, and for feminist politics in particular, because juridical subjects are invariably produced through certain exclusionary practices that do not "show" once the juridical structure of politics has been established. In other words, the political construction of the subject proceeds with certain legitimating and exclusionary aims, and these political operations are effectively concealed and naturalized by a political analysis that takes juridical structures as their foundation. Juridical power inevitably "produces" what it claims merely to represent; hence, politics must be concerned with this dual function of power: the juridical and the productive. In effect, the law produces and then conceals the notion of "a subject before the law" in order to invoke that discursive formation as a naturalized foundational premise that subsequently legitimates that law's own regulatory hegemony. It is not enough to inquire into how women might become more fully represented in language and politics. Feminist critique ought also to understand how the category of "women," the subject of feminism, is produced and restrained by the very structures of power through which emancipation is sought.

Indeed, the question of women as the subject of feminism raises the possibility that there may not be a subject who stands "before" the law, awaiting representation in or by the law. Perhaps the subject, as well as the invocation of a temporal "before," is constituted by the law as the fictive foundation of its own claim to legitimacy. The prevailing assumption of the ontological integrity of the subject before the law might be understood as the contemporary trace of the state of nature hypothesis, that foundationalist fable constitutive of the juridical structures of classical liberalism. The performative invocation of a nonhistorical "before" becomes the foundational premise that guarantees a presocial ontology of persons who freely consent to be governed and, thereby, constitute the legitimacy of the social contract.

Apart from the foundationalist fictions that support the notion of the subject, however, there is the political problem that feminism encounters in the assumption that the term *women* denotes a common identity. Rather than a stable signifier that commands the assent of those whom it purports to describe and represent, *women*, even in the plural, has become a troublesome term, a site of contest, a cause for anxiety. As Denise Riley's title suggests, *Am I That Name?* is a question produced by the very possibility of the name's multiple significations. If one "is" a woman, that is surely not all one is; the term fails to be exhaustive, not because a pregendered "person" transcends the specific paraphernalia of its gender, but because gender is not always constituted coherently or consistently in different historical contexts, and because gender intersects with racial, class, ethnic, sexual, and regional modalities of discursively constituted identities. As a result, it becomes impossible to separate out "gender" from the political and cultural intersections in which it is invariably produced and maintained.

The political assumption that there must be a universal basis for feminism, one which must be found in an identity assumed to exist cross-culturally, often accompanies the notion that the oppression of women has some singular form discernible in the universal or hegemonic structure of patriarchy or masculine domination. The notion of a universal patriarchy has been widely criticized in recent years for its failure to account for the workings of gender oppression in the concrete cultural contexts in which it exists. Where those various contexts have been consulted within such theories, it has been to find "examples" or "illustrations" of a universal principle that is assumed from the start. That form of feminist theorizing has come under criticism for its efforts to colonize and appropriate non-Western cultures to support highly Western notions of oppression, but because they tend as well to construct a "Third World" or even an "Orient" in which gender oppression is subtly explained as symptomatic of an essential, non-Western barbarism. The urgency of feminism to establish a universal status for patriarchy in order to strengthen the appearance of feminism's own claims to be representative has occasionally motivated the shortcut to a categorial or fictive universality of the structure of domination, held to produce women's common subjugated experience.

Although the claim of universal patriarchy no longer enjoys the kind of credibility it once did, the notion of a generally shared conception of "women," the corollary to that framework, has been much more difficult to displace. Certainly, there have been plenty of debates: Is there some commonality among "women" that preexists their oppression, or do "women" have a bond by virtue of their oppression alone? Is there a specificity to women's cultures that is independent of their subordination by hegemonic, masculinist cultures? Are the specificity and integrity of women's cultural or linguistic practices always specified against and, hence, within the terms of some more dominant cultural formation? If there is a region of the "specifically feminine," one that is both differentiated from the masculine as such and recognizable in its difference by an unmarked and, hence, presumed universality of "women"? The masculine/feminine binary constitutes not only the exclusive framework in which that specificity can be recognized, but in every other way the "specificity" of the feminine is once again fully decontextualized and separated off analytically and politically from the constitution of class, race, ethnicity, and other axes of power relations that both constitute "identity" and make the singular notion of identity a misnomer.

My suggestion is that the presumed universality and unity of the subject of feminism is effectively undermined by the constraints of the representational discourse in which it functions. Indeed, the premature insistence on a stable subject of feminism, understood as a seamless category of women, inevitably generates multiple refusals to accept the category. These domains of exclusion reveal the coercive and regulatory consequences of that construction, even when the construction has been elaborated for emancipatory purposes. Indeed, the fragmentation within feminism and the paradoxical opposition to feminism from "women" whom feminism claims to represent suggest the necessary limits of identity politics. The suggestion that feminism can seek wider representation for a subject that it itself constructs has the ironic consequence that feminist goals risk failure by refusing to take account of the constitutive powers of their own representational claims. This problem is not ameliorated through an appeal to the category of women for merely "strategic" purposes, for strategies always have meanings that exceed the purposes for which they are intended. In this case, exclusion itself might qualify as such an unintended yet consequential meaning. By conforming to a requirement of representational politics that feminism articulate a stable subject, feminism thus opens itself to charges of gross misrepresentation.

. . .

The foundationalist reasoning of identity politics tends to assume that an identity must be in place in order for political interests to be elaborated and, subsequently, political action to be taken. My argument is that there need not be a "doer behind the deed," but that the "doer" is variably constructed in and through the deed. This is not a return to an existential theory of the self as constituted through its acts, for the existential theory maintains a prediscursive structure for both the self and its acts. It is precisely the discursively variable construction of each in and through the other that has interested me here.

95 Bhikhu Parekh, from *Rethinking Multiculturalism: Cultural Diversity and Political Theory* (Macmillan, 2000), pp. 234–42, 254–7

Bhikhu Parekh (1935–) is Professor Emeritus of Political Theory at the University of Hull. He has written books on Bentham, Marx, Gandhi, and Hannah Arendt, as well as working on the policy dilemmas and opportunities presented by multi-ethnic Britain for the Commission on Racial Equality and the Runnymede Trust. He entered the House of Lords in 2000. His books include *Hannah Arendt and the Search for a New Public Philosophy* (1981), *Rethinking Multiculturalism* (2000), and *Gandhi* (2001).

Much of the traditional discussion of equality suffers from a weakness derived from the mistaken theory of human nature in which it is grounded. As we saw earlier, many philosophers understand human beings in terms of a substantive theory of human nature and treat culture as of no or only marginal importance. Broadly speaking they maintain that human beings are characterized by two sets of features, some common to them all such as that they are made in the image of God, have souls, are noumenal beings, have common capacities and needs or a similar natural constitution; and others varying from culture to culture and individual to individual. The former are taken to constitute their humanity and are ontologically privileged. Human beings are deemed to be equal because of their shared features or similarity, and equality is taken to consist in treating them in more or less the same way and giving them more or less the same body of rights.

I have argued that this view of human beings is deeply mistaken. Human beings are at once both natural and cultural beings, sharing a common human identity but in a culturally mediated manner. They are similar and different, their similarities and differences do not passively coexist but interpenetrate, and neither is ontologically prior or morally more important. We cannot ground equality in human uniformity because the latter is inseparable from and ontologically no more important than human differences. Grounding equality in uniformity also has unfortunate consequences. It requires us to treat human beings equally in those respects in which they are similar and not those in which they are different. While granting them equality at the level of their shared human nature, we deny it at the equally important cultural level. In our discussions of the Greek, Christian and liberal philosophers we have seen that it is also easy to move from uniformity to monism. Since human beings are supposed to be basically the same, only a particular way of life is deemed to be worthy of them, and those failing to live up to it either do not merit equality or do so only after they are suitably civilized. The idea of equality thus becomes an ideological device to mould humankind in a certain direction. A theory of equality grounded in human uniformity is both philosophically incoherent and morally problematic.

Human beings do share several capacities and needs in common, but different cultures define and structure these differently and develop new ones of their own. Since human beings are at once both similar and different, they should be treated equally because of both. Such a view, which grounds equality not in human uniformity but in the interplay of uniformity and difference, builds difference into the very concept of equality, breaks the traditional equation of equality with similarity, and is immune to monist distortion. Once the basis of equality changes so does its content. Equality involves equal freedom or opportunity to be different, and treating human beings equally requires us to take into account both their similarities and differences. When the latter are not relevant, equality entails uniform or identical treatment; when they are, it requires differential treatment. Equal rights do not mean identical rights, for individuals with different cultural backgrounds and needs might require different rights to enjoy equality in respect of whatever happens to be the content of their rights. Equality involves not just rejection of irrelevant differences as is commonly argued, but also full recognition of legitimate and relevant ones.

Equality is articulated at several interrelated levels. At the most basic level it involves equality of respect and rights, at a slightly higher level that of opportunity, self-esteem, self-worth and so on, and at a yet higher level, equality of power, well-being and the basic capacities required for human flourishing. Sensitivity to differences is relevant at each of these levels. We can hardly be said to respect a person if we treat with contempt or abstract away all that gives meaning to his life and makes him the kind of person he is. Respect for a person therefore involves locating him against his cultural background, sympathetically entering into his world of thought, and interpreting his conduct in terms of its system of meaning. A simple example illustrates the point. It was recently discovered that Asian candidates for jobs in Britain were systematically underscored because their habit of showing respect for their interviewers by not looking them in the eye led the latter to conclude that they were shifty and devious and likely to prove unreliable. By failing to appreciate the candidates' system of meaning and cultural practices, interviewers ended up treating them unequally with their white counterparts. Understandably but wrongly, they assumed that all human beings shared and even perhaps ought to share an identical system of meaning which predictably turned out to be their own. This relatively trivial example illustrates the havoc we can easily cause when we uncritically universalize the categories and norms of our culture.

Like the concept of equal respect, that of equal opportunity, too, needs to be interpreted in a culturally sensitive manner. Opportunity is a subject-dependent concept in the sense that a facility, a resource, or a course of action is only a mute and passive possibility and not an opportunity for an individual if she lacks the capacity, the cultural disposition or the necessary cultural knowledge to take advantage of it. A Sikh is in principle free to send his son to a school that bans turbans, but for all practical purposes it is closed to him. The same is true when an orthodox Jew is required to give up his yarmulke, or the Muslim woman to wear a skirt, or a vegetarian Hindu to eat beef as a precondition for certain kinds of jobs. Although the inability involved is cultural not physical in nature and hence subject to human control, the degree of control varies greatly. In some cases a cultural inability can be overcome with relative ease by suitably reinterpreting the relevant cultural norm or practice; in others it is constitutive of the individual's sense of identity and even self-respect and cannot be overcome without a deep sense of moral loss. Other things being equal, when a culturally derived incapacity is of the former kind, the individuals involved may rightly be asked to overcome it or at least bear the financial cost of accommodating it. When it is of the latter kind and comes closer to a natural inability, society should bear at least most of the cost of accommodating it. Which cultural incapacity falls within which category is often a matter of dispute and can only be resolved by a dialogue between the parties involved.

Equality before the law and equal protection of the law, too, need to be defined in a culturally sensitive manner. Formally a law banning the use of drugs treats all equally, but in fact it discriminates against those for whom some drugs are religious or cultural requirements as is the case with Peyote and Marijuana respectively for the American Indians and Rastafarians. This does not mean that we might not ban their use, but rather that we need to appreciate the unequal impact of the ban and should have strong additional reasons for denying exemption to these two groups. The United States government showed the requisite cultural sensitivity when it exempted the ceremonial use of wine by Jews and Catholics during Prohibition.

Equal protection of the law, too, may require different treatment. Given the horrible reality of the Holocaust and the persistent streak of anti-semitism in German cultural life, it makes good sense for that country to single out physical attacks on Jews for harsher punishment or ban utterances denying the Holocaust. In other societies, other groups such as blacks, Muslims and gypsies might have long been demonized and subjected to hostility and hatred, and then they too might need to be treated differently. Although the differential treatment of these groups might seem to violate the principle of equality, in fact it only equalizes them with the rest of their fellow-citizens.

In a culturally homogenous society, individuals share broadly similar needs, norms, motivations, social customs and patterns of behaviour. Equal rights here mean more or less the same rights, and equal treatment involves more or less identical treatment. The principle of equality is therefore relatively easy to define and apply, and discriminatory deviations from it can be identified without much disagreement. This is not the case in a culturally diverse society. Broadly speaking equality consists in equal treatment of those judged to be equal in relevant respects. In a culturally diverse society citizens are likely to disagree on what respects are relevant in a given context, what response is appropriate to them, and what counts as their equal treatment. Furthermore, once we take cultural differences into account, equal treatment would mean not identical but differential treatment, raising the question as to how we can ensure that it is really equal across cultures and does not serve as a cloak for discrimination or privilege.

. . .

In Britain the state funds thousands of Anglican, Catholic and Jewish religious schools, but it has until recently rejected Muslim requests for similar schools. Its real reasons, often stated in private and sometimes hinted at in public, are mainly two. First, the state funds religious schools because it expects that in addition to grounding their pupils into the basic principles of their religion, they will also develop their analytical and critical faculties, provide secular knowledge, and prepare them for life in a democratic and secular society. This is a difficult balance to strike, which non-Muslim religious schools have been able to achieve after a long struggle. Since Muslim schools are likely to become nurseries of reactionary ideas in the current fundamentalist phase of Islam, they are unlikely to achieve the basic objectives of education. Second, state funding of religious schools in Britain is the result of particular historical circumstances. British society now realizes that such schools lead to ghettoization and are in general undesirable. Since it cannot renege on its past commitments to existing schools, it can at least stop perpetuating the problem by refusing to fund new ones.

Opponents of Muslim schools therefore argue that no inequality is involved in denying state funding to Muslim schools while continuing to provide it to other religious schools. Equality requires equal treatment of those who are equal in relevant respects. The relevant respect here is the capacity to provide a balanced religious and secular education. Since Muslim schools lack that capacity, they cannot be treated on a par with other religious schools. The second argument has a different thrust. It does not say anything about whether or not the two kinds of schools are equal in relevant respects, but it asserts that the state has decided to change its policy on funding religious schools. Since it cannot abrogate its past commitments, it must continue to fund Christian and Jewish schools. Although this involves treating Muslims unequally, such inequalities are inherent in social life and cannot be avoided. Long-established groups often enjoy rights based on past commitments and policies. When the policies are changed, they retain rights that are no longer available to newcomers.

Opponents of state funding for Muslim schools make the important theoretical point that equality should not be understood in purely formal and abstract terms. Just because some religious communities enjoy state-funded schools, it does not *necessarily* follow that denying them to Muslims amounts to inequality, for they might not be able to fulfil the socially prescribed objectives of education or the state might sincerely wish to discontinue such schools. Rather than accuse their opponents of being anti-Muslim, racists, and so forth on the basis of an abstract and untenable view of equality, we need to ask if their arguments have any merit.

The first argument is suspect. To say that Islam is currently going through a fundamentalist phase is a gross exaggeration, true at best of some but not of all Muslim countries. More to the point, it is not at all true of British Islam. Since the

British government allows privately-funded Muslim schools, it evidently shares this view and is wrong to raise the bogey of fundamentalism only when state funding is involved. There is also a rise in Christian and Jewish fundamentalism, but the British government has shown no interest in acquiring greater control over or issuing suitable warnings to state-funded Christian and Jewish schools. It is, of course, possible that Muslim schools could become nurseries of fundamentalism and fail to achieve their objectives. However, there are ways of guarding against this. The government has the right to inspect and regulate schools including their curriculum, pedagogy and general ethos, and has enough power to counter such forms of fundamentalism as might arise in Muslim schools. The power is bound to be greater, and its exercise more acceptable, if the state also funds them.

The second argument is no better. The British state certainly has the right to change its policy on funding religious schools. This involves not only denying state funding to new schools, but also phasing out the existing ones over a mutually agreed period of time, something which the British state shows not the slightest sign of doing. There is no evidence either that it is putting pressure on them to become secular or even to reduce the religious content of their curriculum. Since neither of the two arguments advanced by the government is valid, the denial of state funding to Muslim schools is unjustified.

In the light of our discussions of the *hijab* controversy in France and the state funding of Muslim schools in Britain, it should be clear that equal treatment of cultural communities is logically different from that of individuals. Unlike the latter, it is deeply embedded in and inseparable from the wider cultural and political relations between the communities involved. Besides, cultural communities often contain a wide variety of views on a subject and cannot be homogenized and reified. The case for intercultural equality should not therefore be made in such abstract and ahistorical terms that it ignores genuine differences between and within the communities involved or fails to address the deepest anxieties of the wider society. We should take a contexualized view of equality, identify what respects are relevant, and demand equal treatment of those shown to be equal in these respects. *If* the *hijab* really is different from the cross (which it is not), then Muslim girls may legitimately be denied the right to wear it without incurring the charge of discriminating against them. And *if* Muslim schools do really run the risk that their critics fear (which they do not), or if the British state does really wish to discontinue religious schools (which it does not), then they may legitimately be denied state funding without offending against the principle of equality.

Taking such a contextualized and politically and historically sensitive view of equality, no doubt, creates its own problems. We leave too much space for specious reasoning and alarmist fears, and run the risk of not knowing how to compare differences, how to separate relevant from irrelevant differences, how to determine and assess the context, and so on. It is therefore tempting to take the more dependable route of insisting on the general right to equality, and argue that since Christians and Jews have a right to their schools, Muslims too must have a right to state-funded schools. In the light of what I have said, the temptation should be resisted. If we ask the law to take such a mechanical and simplistic view of equality, then we cannot consistently ask it to take cultural differences into account in the case of the Sikhs and the marriage of the Asian girl discussed earlier. The question therefore is not whether Muslims have a right to religious freedom but what, if anything, that right entails in a specific context, and that involves deciding *what* features of the context are relevant and whether Muslims are equal in respect to *them*. The movement from a general right to equality to the right to a specific treatment in a specific context, that is, from a general right to religion to the right to wear the *hijab* in the school, is not direct and deductive but contexually mediated.

The danger that such a contextualized view of equality might encourage discrimination and disingenuous reasoning is real. The French ban on the *hijab* and the British government's denial of publicly funded Muslim schools were at least in part motivated by anti-Muslim sentiments, and we need to guard against this. We can do so in two ways. We should insist that equality requires identical treatment and place the onus of justification on those seeking to depart from it. Thus British Muslims should be assumed to be entitled to state-funded schools, and it is up to the government to show to the satisfaction of all concerned why such schools might legitimately be denied to them. Secondly, it should be possible for the unconvinced minorities to appeal against government decisions to such public bodies as the courts or the Commission on Human Rights. The reason why the controversy dragged on for years in France and Britain and still remains unresolved in France has to do with the fact that Muslims had no recourse to such a body. Neither country has a Commission on Human Rights although Britain is now moving in that direction, and allows appeal against such 'administrative matters'.

96   James Tully, from *Strange Multiplicity: Constitutionalism in an Age of Diversity* (Cambridge University Press, 1995), pp. 15–17, 127–9, 136–7

James Tully (1953–) is Professor of Political Science, Law, Indigenous Governance, and Philosophy at the University of Victoria, British Columbia. Educated at the Universities of British Columbia and Cambridge, he built a reputation as a scholar of early modern political thought, before publishing widely in political philosophy, with particular focus on articulating the concerns of the multinational Canadian polity. His recent work has tried to show how a political identity can be forged for culturally diverse societies without suppressing that diversity. His books include *A Discourse on Property: John Locke and His Adversaries* (1980), *An Approach to Political Philosophy: Locke in Contexts* (1993), and *Strange Multiplicity: Constitutionalism in an Age of Diversity* (1995).

Modern constitutionalism developed over the last four centuries around two main forms of recognition: the equality of independent, self-governing nation states and the equality of individual citizens. It also developed in opposition to imperialism. First, in Europe, constitutional nation states defined themselves in opposition to the *imperium* of the papacy and the Holy Roman Empire without, and to the feudal and absolutist society of ranks within. European nations in turn constructed their own imperial systems over the non-European world, thus adding an imperial dimension to modern constitutionalism.

Second, constitutionalism came into prominence throughout the world as former colonies freed themselves from European imperialism, built equal and independent constitutional nation states, and grappled with their older customs and traditions, while citizens struggled for equal recognition within and the new states created their own empires over Indigenous peoples. The global movement of anti-imperialism, modern constitutionalism and neo-imperialism began with the thirteen colonies in 1776 and continued through the monumental wars of liberation and decolonisation in the nineteenth and twentieth centuries, down to the overthrow of the Soviet imperial system after 1989 and South Africa today. No doubt it will continue.

The politics of cultural recognition constitutes a third movement of anti-imperialism and constitutionalism, this time by the peoples and cultures who have been excluded and suppressed by the first two movements of decolonisation and constitutional state build-ing. Aboriginal peoples, women, linguistic and ethnic minorities, intercultural groups, suppressed nations and supranational associations experience the constitution of modern nation states as an imperial yoke imposed over their cultures, in a manner analogous to the way in which the proponents of the first two movements of constitutionalism experienced the old imperial systems they overthrew. This continuity among the three movements explains why the older language of imperial oppression and liberation has reappeared in the newer struggles and why they are often called struggles against cultural imperialism.

The second continuity is, as I mentioned above, that the people wish to govern them-selves constitutionally by their own cultural ways. The difference from the first two movements is that, for the most part, they do not seek to build independent nation states in order to gain independence and self government. Rather, they seek forms of cultural recognition and degrees of self rule on the culturally various common ground within and across existing nation states. Seen in this light, the politics of cultural recognition is a con-tinuation of the anti-imperialism of modern constitutionalism, and thus the expression of a genuinely post-imperial age.

. . .

The Two Row Wampum Treaty of the *Haudenosaunee* confederacy is one of the most famous exemplars of treaty constitutionalism between Aboriginal and non-Aboriginal peoples in America. The constitutional negotiations and relations between them are symbolised by belts of wampum beads exchanged at treaty discussions from 1664 to the negotiations between the *Haudenosaunee* confederacy and the Canadian and Québec governments at Kanehsatake, Québec, in 1990. The two row wampum belt is the diplomatic *lingua franca* of Aboriginal and non-Aboriginal constitutionalism, recording the form of agreement reached and expressing the good will the agreement embodies.

A background of white wampum beads symbolises the purity of the agreement; that is, the convention of consent. Two rows of purple beads represent the nations involved in the dialogue. Three beads separating the two rows stand for peace, friendship and respect; the values necessary to an uncoerced and lasting agreement. The two parallel rows of purple beads, Chief Michael Mitchell explicates,

symbolize two paths or two vessels, travelling down the same river together. One, a birch bark canoe, will be for the Indian people, their laws, their customs and their ways. The other, a ship, will be for the white people and their laws, their customs and their ways. We shall each travel the same river together, side by side, but in our own boats. Neither of us will try to steer the other's vessel.

Aboriginal peoples and European Americans are recognised as equal and co-existing nations, each with their own forms of government, traditions of interpretation and ways. This is the convention of *kahswentha*, the mutual recognition of equality. While not in the same canoe, as in the Haida symbol, the people are in the same river. They agree to co-operate in various ways—travelling 'together', presumably mentioned twice for emphasis. But, notwithstanding the agreements they reach, their status as equal and co-existing nations continues. It is never part of the agreement to try 'to steer the other's vessel', or, in Marshall's description, 'to interfere with the internal affairs' of the other. For example, the treaty signed at Canandaigua, New York, in 1794 between President George Washington's official agent, Colonel Timothy Pickering, and the six chiefs of the *Haudenosaunee* recognises the confederacy as a sovereign nation and guarantees that the United States will never encroach on their remaining lands in western and central New York.

The capacity to delegate to, or share various powers of self government with the protecting government (either the United States or Canada) while retaining their sovereignty is extremely important to the Aboriginal peoples. It enables each Aboriginal nation to work out by mutual consent the degree of self government appropriate to their population, land base and particular circumstances, without fear of subordination or discontinuity.

The convention of continuity through relations of protection and interdependency is also a common feature of Aboriginal constitutionalism. Article 84 of the constitution of the *Haudenosaunee* confederacy of six nations, for example, states that, 'whenever a foreign nation has been conquered or has by their own will accepted the Great Peace [confederated with the other nations], their own system of internal government may continue, but they must cease all warfare against other nations'. True to form, each of the six nations of the confederacy has its own language, customs and government. The confederation itself was founded by the mediation of Deganawidah, who brought the original five warring nations together and guided them to reach agreement through dialogue on a form of association to protect their differences and similarities.

. . .

As the settlers gained the upper hand in the nineteenth century, the Aboriginal and common-law system was overwhelmed by the theory and practice of modern constitutionalism. Within its horizons, the relationship of protection, which continued Aboriginal self government according to Marshall, was reinterpreted. Treaties were said to be mere private contracts and Aboriginal rights mere individual rights to hunt and fish on Crown land. The European—American governments were unilaterally recognised as superior guardians whose burden it was to protect Aboriginal people who were recognised as inferior wards incapable of consent and whose primitive ways had to be discontinued and reformed for their own good. When the wards resisted, they were depicted as 'obstacles to progress' and removed to disappear, by neglect, starvation or, as at Wounded Knee, by slaughter.

Although the Aboriginal nations protested throughout this century of the 'gradual civilisation of the Indian tribes', it is only in recent decades that their claims for recognition have started to be effectively heard. They have revived the Aboriginal and common-law system hidden beneath the empire of modern constitutionalism to reclaim self government and control of their territories. From 1972 to 1975, the first contemporary treaty constitution was negotiated between the Cree, Naskapi and Inuit nations and the Québec and Canadian governments. The James Bay and Northern Québec Agreement, while far from ideal, is a precedent that has helped to set the 'world reversal' in motion. Since then, the justice of Aboriginal claims for recognition has begun to be acknowledged in the courts of common-law countries and in the United Nations draft Declaration on the Rights of Indigenous Peoples. In this post-imperial dawn, treaties and agreements have begun to take on some of their former lustre and the Crown has started to discern its fiduciary responsibility in the relationship of protection. Even the mighty leviathans who have extended their empire of modern constitutionalism over 'stolen continents' are being instructed once again by Royal Commissions to see themselves as the Royal Commission of 1664 recommended: as equal 'partners in confederation' with the Aboriginal nations who have survived and continued through the usurpation.

These partnerships will take many forms, depending on the arrangements the partners reach in discussions guided by the three conventions. By calling these agreements 'treaty constitutionalism' and using the example of the Two Row Wampum Treaty, I do not mean to imply that only one form is possible. This would be another kind of imperialism. The appropriate degree of interdependency and the best sort of agreement vary with the very different circumstances of Aboriginal and non-Aboriginal partners on this earth. Even in Canada, the differences within and among First Nations, Inuit and Métis are legion.

97 Kenichi Ohmae, from *The Borderless World* (Harper Collins, 1990), pp. 11–16

Kenichi Ohmae (1943–) is a management theorist and Professor of Public Policy at UCLA. He was formerly a partner in the influential management consultancy, McKinsey. His many books and other publications include *The Borderless World* (1990), *The End of the Nation-State* (1995) and *The Invisible Continent* (2000).

There is another aspect of the country variable, and that is the role of government, which must change and is changing. Not that long ago, in the "preconsumer" era, "country" was synonymous with a sovereign, isolated island within which its government determined what made most sense to the people who lived there. A government's role was to represent its people's interest, serve their purposes, and protect them from threat of foreigners and foreign corporations. When a country's commercial interests spread outside of its sovereignty, the military was there to back them up. British military forces guarded British interests in the Seven Seas when its plantations were spread all over the world.

American forces were fully behind their corporations in the Banana Republic and in the rest of the world to back up the 1960s' and 1970s' multinationalization process. As with the Roman Catholic church, country and doctrine were synonymous, and corporations used overseas countries to provide resources and/or markets to absorb/accept their one-sided, dogmatic, homegrown monolithic products. This is no longer the case. People have become more informed and clever, as a real consequence of living in a truly global information era. And now governments have become the major obstacle for people to have the best and the cheapest from anywhere in the world.

What the energy crisis has taught us is that for a short term the "have" nations can create a supply shortage if they gang up. However, over a longer period of time, alternative supplies develop and the economic principles of supply and demand prevail. If you look at the prosperous nations today—Switzerland, Singapore, Taiwan, South Korea, and Japan—they are characterized by small land mass, no resources, and well-educated hard-working people who all have the *ambition* to participate in the global economy. Having an abundance of resources has truly slowed down a country's development, because bureaucrats there still think that money could solve all problems. In a truly interlinked, global economy, the key success factor shifts from resources to the marketplace, in which you have to participate in order to prosper. It also means *people* are the only true means to create wealth.

As for companies, the prosperity of countries depends on their ability to *create value* through their people, and not by husbanding resources and technologies. While developing countries in particular must learn this lesson, so too must old bureaucrats in the United States, Japan, and the European Community (EC).

In a truly interlinked economy, a country can't fail single-handedly, nor can it win alone. Winning becomes increasingly expensive, as currency and wages are rapidly adjusted and an incremental gain costs dearly in terms of competitiveness. That is the stage Japan and West Germany have entered. Even if a country is outside of the Triad, or the Organization for Economic Cooperation and Development (OECD), or the EC, as long as it an link its economy freely with the rest of the world, it can take advantage of the global economy. Singapore and Hong Kong are doing exactly that. Because neither country has farmers, each has virtually no tariffs on agricultural products. That means people there can buy the best products at the lowest price. The fact that food costs are *cheaper* in Singapore than in Japan because Singapore doesn't produce domestically is a good example of what I am talking about. Even in the isolationist, resource-based economy of Australia, entrepreneurs such as Rupert Murdoch and John Elliot (of Elders IXL) can flourish by reaching out to the ILE. Thus the prosperity of the ILE is not only for its residents but for anyone ambitious enough to interlink.

The government's role, then, is to ensure that its people have a good life by ensuring stable access to the best and the cheapest goods and services from anywhere in the world—not to protect certain industries and certain clusters of people. Contemporary governments must become transparent to their people with respect to the rest of the world. Every time governments try to protect resources, markets, industries, and jobs, they cost taxpayers dearly. Only two decades ago when multinational companies had a colonial attitude, they took advantage of the privileges and licenses allotted to them by governments. They were exploitative. But consumers in today's world are much better informed, and the surviving global corporations are there to serve their needs. If they don't, they will be eliminated by the customers, not by the host governments.

Unfortunately, old-style governments still license and regulate foreign corporations to come in and operate. Once they are inside, corporations take advantage of their special position. So we see cars in developing countries whose doors do not shut when slammed, a model that is at least a decade old introduced as a new model, components and spare parts not available, and so on; none of this happens in a truly open market, where competitors eliminate poor performers. Government officials exercise power by regulating and deregulating the market, but their new role is to assume a backseat, not the driver's position, and to make sure that their country is benefiting fully from the best-performing corporations and producers in the world, at the lowest possible cost to their people on a long-term basis.

THE MYTH OF NATIONAL SECURITY

Under Cold War assumptions, government officials fall back on arguments that countries have to be prepared for emergencies—that is, war. Inefficient industries are subsidized in the name of national security. Even with the Cold War subsiding, government and special-interest groups are still trying to build their cases on these old assumptions. Japan is producing rice, just in case the what if happens. But it is costing its people dearly, in terms of subsidies to farmers and the nation's limited flat land that could be used for housing and pleasure.

Meanwhile, Singapore and Hong Kong don't worry about what ifs. In theory, Singapore can't exist because it has no insurance, either in the form of military forces or strategic (read protected) industries. Yet it enjoys current prosperity. I believe the Singaporean solution is the right one, because in the global economy, economic interlinkage increases security. Nixon's soybean embargo against Japan is often cited as evidence of America's possible clout and Japan's excessive dependence on imported agricultural products. But here again, buyers and markets have the upper hand today. The embargo lasted only a few weeks. Commodity producers need markets, just as developed markets need products. Interlinked and secure supply-demand relationships will have inherent checks and balances. For most commodity suppliers, there are short-term and longer-term alternatives. Soybeans, cotton seeds, and palm oil could all end up being salad oil and detergent. Right-wing politicians in Japan need to recognize this too when they threaten to cut off the supply of advanced chips to the United States. They are ignorant of the fact that more than half of semiconductor production machinery and software to design complicated chips are American made. Moreover, the supply-demand relationships in this industry are much more complex than the right-wingers realize. They know nothing about rare gases, photo resists, and other materials necessary for production—most of which are American controlled. Where there is a market, there will be a producer, and no boycott will last long.

DEVELOPED VERSUS DEVELOPING COUNTRIES

We tend to think that a country's economy consists of primary, secondary, and tertiary industries. Yet we should now think of the interlinked part of the world as having that spectrum of industries *collectively* instead of individually. This viewpoint really forces the interlinkage into our economic interdependence, and thus there will be no black sheep among us. In this way the people of developing nations can have the products of the developed world at the same price as in the United States, and the developed countries can liberate their taxpayers from having to carry their old industries forever.

A modern government's concern is *jobs*. One of the key reasons for governments' protectionism against foreign products and capital is job security. But what we have observed over the past decade is that this conventional wisdom is wrong. During Reagan's eight years when American imports soared, the United States created more jobs than ever in its history. Japan, forced by its fellow OECD members, has opened one market after another. Unemployment in Japan didn't soar. On the contrary, today the labor shortage is so acute that some people are organizing to import *gastarbeiter*, or foreign workers, from Asian neighbors. Other rapidly growing economies have had the same experience. As markets are liberalized, wage rates go up. The consuming habit caves in, and the economy rapidly shifts to the service sector. The service sector occupies more and more of the total employment. In the United States 70 percent of the work force works in the service sector; in Japan, 60 percent; and in Taiwan, 50 percent. These are not necessarily busboys and live-in maids. They are earning as much as manufacturing workers, and often more. In an interlinked global economy, the fact that primary (agricultural, forestry, fishery) industries slip out of a country and even secondary (manufacturing) industries go overseas is not the end of the world from an employment point of view.

Most governments want foreign producers to come in and build factories. Government officials frequently ask me to help them attract Japanese manufacturers. What they don't realize is that the cost of manufacturing today is typically 25 percent of the end-user price. Production per se adds very little value in the eyes of the customer. It is usually just labor that creates no more value than it costs. Furthermore, the leading-edge producers have all but eliminated simple labor and work from production, and steel-collar workers (robots) do most of the jobs. The "production" such firms have attracted typically consists of watching the robots, quality checks, shipments, and factory maintenance. Countries will gain a lot more important and profitable parts of businesses if they can attract R&D, engineering, financing, and marketing functions. But no government official has ever asked me to bring in those functions.

Governments around the world have tried to protect their markets, industries, and jobs and have failed to do so, because they don't understand the value-added chain in globally interlinked economies. The most value added is in the marketplace today. By opening the market for the most competitive products from anywhere in the world, a country can take advantage of the most opportunities for job creation. Such functions as distribution, warehousing, financing, retail marketing, systems integration, and services are all legitimate parts of the business system and can create as many, and often more, jobs than simply manufacturing operations. Preoccupation with production typically forces governments to hang onto old, incompatible industries and hence do disservice to their taxpayers and consumers (often the same people). Each job thus maintained from the old times discourages the dynamic growth of new industries. There is no need to worry about Tokyo, New York, and Los Angeles becoming service-based tertiary economies, nor to worry about a country becoming a Tokyo or New York. In the interlinked global economy, the producing nation must accept whatever money Tokyoites and New Yorkers use to buy "real" products. That means that the money will come back to buy something from New York or Tokyo, perhaps software, design, technology, real estate, or a brand name. It's no different from a person from California buying a high-rise office building in Manhattan. We are all part of the same interlinked economy.

98   Naomi Klein, from 'Reclaiming the Commons', in *New Left Review* (2nd series, 9, May–June 2001), pp. 81–9

Naomi Klein (1970–) was born in Montreal. A columnist and journalist, and a former fellow of the London School of Economics, she came to prominence in the English-speaking world because of her writings about and support of the fledgling anti-globalization movement that has come to the fore since the early 1990s. Her books include *No Logo* (1998), and *Fences and Windows: Dispatches from the Frontline of the Globalization Debate* (2002).

What is 'the anti-globalization movement'? I put the phrase in quote-marks because I immediately have two doubts about it. Is it really a movement? If it is a movement, is it anti-globalization? Let me start with the first issue. We can easily convince ourselves it is a movement by talking it into existence at a forum like this—I spend far too much time at them—acting as if we can see it, hold it in our hands. Of course, we have seen it—and we know it's come back in Quebec, and on the US–Mexican border during the Summit of the Americas and the discussion for a hemispheric Free Trade Area. But then we leave rooms like this, go home, watch some TV, do a little shopping and any sense that it exists disappears, and we feel like maybe we're going nuts. Seattle—was that a movement or a collective hallucination? To most of us here, Seattle meant a kind of coming-out party for a global resistance movement, or the 'globalization of hope', as someone described it during the World Social Forum at Porto Alegre. But to everyone else Seattle still means limitless frothy coffee, Asian-fusion cuisine, e-commerce billionaires and sappy Meg Ryan movies. Or perhaps it is both, and one Seattle bred the other Seattle—and now they awkwardly coexist.

This movement we sometimes conjure into being goes by many names: anti-corporate, anti-capitalist, anti-free trade, anti-imperialist. Many say that it started in Seattle. Others maintain it began five hundred years ago—when colonialists first told indigenous peoples that they were going to have to do things differently if they were to 'develop' or be eligible for 'trade'. Others again say it began on 1 January 1994 when the Zapatistas launched their uprising with the words *Ya Basta!* on the night NAFTA became law in Mexico. It all depends on whom you ask. But I think it is more accurate to picture a movement of many movements—coalitions of coalitions. Thousands of groups today are all working against forces whose common thread is what might broadly be described as the privatization of every aspect of life, and the transformation of every activity and value into a commodity. We often speak of the privatization of education, of healthcare, of natural resources. But the process is much vaster. It includes the way powerful ideas are turned into advertising slogans and public streets into shopping malls; new generations being target-marketed at birth; schools being invaded by ads; basic human necessities like water being sold as commodities; basic labour rights being rolled back; genes are patented and designer babies loom; seeds are genetically altered and bought; politicians are bought and altered.

At the same time there are oppositional threads, taking form in many different campaigns and movements. The spirit they share is a radical reclaiming of the commons. As our communal spaces—town squares, streets, schools, farms, plants—are displaced by the ballooning marketplace, a spirit of resistance is taking hold around the world. People are reclaiming bits of nature and of culture, and saying 'this is going to be public space'. American students are kicking ads out of the classrooms. European environmentalists and ravers are throwing parties at busy intersections. Landless Thai peasants are planting organic vegetables on over-irrigated golf courses. Bolivian workers are reversing the privatization of their water supply. Outfits like Napster have been creating a kind of commons on the internet where kids can swap music with each other, rather than buying it from multinational record companies. Billboards have been liberated and independent media networks set up. Protests are multiplying. In Porto Alegre, during the World Social Forum, José Bové, often caricatured as only a hammer of McDonald's, travelled with local activists from the Movimento Sem Terra to a nearby Monsanto test site, where they destroyed three hectares of genetically modified soya beans. But the protest did not stop there. The MST has occupied the land and members are now planting their own organic crops on it, vowing to turn the farm into a model of sustainable agriculture. In short, activists aren't waiting for the revolution, they are acting right now, where they live, where they study, where they work, where they farm.

But some formal proposals are also emerging whose aim is to turn such radical reclamations of the commons into law. When NAFTA and the like were cooked up, there was much talk of adding on 'side agreements' to the free trade agenda, that were supposed to encompass the environment, labour and human rights. Now the fight-back is about taking them out. José Bové—along with the Via Campesina, a global association of small farmers—has launched a campaign to remove food safety and agricultural products from all trade agreements, under the slogan 'The World is Not for Sale'. They want to draw a line around the commons. Maude Barlow, director of the Council of Canadians, which has more members than most political parties in Canada, has argued that water isn't a private good and shouldn't be in any trade agreement. There is a lot of support for this idea, especially in Europe since the recent food scares. Typically these anti-privatization campaigns get under way on their own. But they also periodically converge—that's what happened in Seattle, Prague, Washington, Davos, Porto Alegre and Quebec.

BEYOND THE BORDERS

What this means is that the discourse has shifted. During the battles against NAFTA, there emerged the first signs of a coalition between organized labour, environmentalists, farmers and consumer groups within the countries concerned. In Canada most of us felt we were fighting to keep something distinctive about our nation from 'Americanization'. In the United States, the talk was very protectionist: workers were worried that Mexicans would 'steal' away 'our' jobs and drive down 'our' environmental standards. All the while, the voices of Mexicans opposed to the deal were virtually off the public radar—yet these were the strongest voices of all. But only a few years later, the debate over trade has been transformed. The fight against globalization has morphed into a struggle against corporatization and, for some, against capitalism itself. It has also become a fight for democracy. Maude Barlow spearheaded the campaign against NAFTA in Canada twelve years ago. Since NAFTA became law, she's been working with organizers and activists from other countries, and anarchists suspicious of the state in her own country. She was once seen as very much the face of a Canadian nationalism. Today she has moved away from that discourse. 'I've changed', she says, 'I used to see this fight as saving a nation. Now I see it as saving democracy.' This is a cause that transcends nationality and state borders. The real news out of Seattle is that organizers around the world are beginning to see their local and national struggles—for better funded public schools, against union-busting and casualization, for family farms, and against the widening gap between rich and poor—through a global lens. That is the most significant shift we have seen in years.

How did this happen? Who or what convened this new international people's movement? Who sent out the memos? Who built these complex coalitions? It is tempting to pretend that someone did dream up a master plan for mobilization at Seattle. But I think it was much more a matter of large-scale coincidence. A lot of smaller groups organized to get themselves there and then found to their surprise just how broad and diverse a coalition they had become part of. Still, if there is one force we can thank for bringing this front into being, it is the multinational corporations. As one of the organizers of Reclaim the Streets has remarked, we should be grateful to the CEOs for helping us see the problems more quickly. Thanks to the sheer imperialist ambition of the corporate project at this moment in history—the boundless drive for profit, liberated by trade deregulation, and the wave of mergers and buyouts, liberated by weakened anti-trust laws—multinationals have grown so blindingly rich, so vast in their holdings, so global in their reach, that they have created our coalitions for us.

Around the world, activists are piggy-backing on the ready-made infrastructures supplied by global corporations. This can mean cross-border unionization, but also cross-sector organizing—among workers, environmentalists, consumers, even prisoners, who may all have different relationships to one multinational. So you can build a single campaign or coalition around a single brand like General Electric. Thanks to Monsanto, farmers in India are working with environmentalists and consumers around the world to develop direct-action strategies that cut off genetically modified foods in the fields and in the supermarkets. Thanks to Shell Oil and Chevron, human rights activists in Nigeria, democrats in Europe, environmentalists in North America have united in a fight against the unsustainability of the oil industry. Thanks to the catering giant Sodexho-Marriott's decision to invest in Corrections Corporation of America, university students are able to protest against the exploding US for-profit prison industry simply by boycotting the food in their campus cafeteria. Other targets include pharmaceutical companies who are trying to inhibit the production and distribution of low-cost AIDS drugs, and fast-food chains. Recently, students and farm workers in Florida have joined forces around Taco Bell. In the St Petersburg area, field hands—many of them immigrants from Mexico—are paid an average $7,500 a year to pick tomatoes and onions. Due to a loophole in the law, they have no bargaining power: the farm bosses refuse even to talk with them about wages. When they started to look into who bought what they pick, they found that Taco Bell was the largest purchaser of the local tomatoes. So they launched the campaign *Yo No Quiero Taco Bell* together with students, to boycott Taco Bell on university campuses.

It is Nike, of course, that has most helped to pioneer this new brand of activist synergy. Students facing a corporate take-over of their campuses by the Nike swoosh have linked up with workers making its branded campus apparel, as well as with parents concerned at the commercialization of youth and church groups campaigning against child labour—all united by their different relationships to a common global enemy. Exposing the underbelly of high-gloss consumer brands has provided the early narratives of this movement, a sort of call-and-response to the very different narratives these companies tell every day about themselves through advertising and public relations. Citigroup offers another prime target, as North America's largest financial institution, with innumerable holdings, which deals with some of the worst corporate malefactors around. The campaign against it handily knits together dozens of issues—from clear-cut logging in California to oil-and-pipeline schemes in Chad and Cameroon. These projects are only a start. But they are creating a new sort of activist: 'Nike is a gateway drug', in the words of Oregon student activist Sarah Jacobson.

By focusing on corporations, organizers can demonstrate graphically how so many issues of social, ecological and economic justice are interconnected. No activist I've met believes that the world economy can be changed one corporation at a time, but the campaigns have opened a door into the arcane world of international trade and finance. Where they are leading is to the central institutions that write the rules of global commerce: the WTO, the IMF, the FTAA, and for some the market itself. Here too the unifying threat is privatization—the loss of the commons. The next round of WTO negotiations is designed to extend the reach of commodification still further. Through side agreements like GATS (General Agreement on Trade and Services) and TRIPS (Trade-Related Aspects of Intellectual Property Rights), the aim is to get still tougher protection of property rights on seeds and drug patents, and to marketize services like health care, education and water-supply.

The biggest challenge facing us is to distil all of this into a message that is widely accessible. Many campaigners understand the connexions binding together the various issues almost intuitively—much as Subcomandante Marcos says, 'Zapatismo isn't an ideology, it's an intuition.' But to outsiders, the mere scope of modern protests can be a bit mystifying. If you eavesdrop on the movement from the outside, which is what most people do; you are liable to hear what seems to be a cacophony of disjointed slogans, a jumbled laundry list of disparate grievances without clear goals. At the Democratic National Convention in Los Angeles last year, I remember being outside the Staples Centre during the Rage Against the Machine concert, just before I almost got shot, and thinking there were slogans for everything everywhere, to the point of absurdity.

MAINSTREAM FAILURES

This kind of impression is reinforced by the decentralized, nonhierarchical structure of the movement, which always disconcerts the traditional media. Well-organized press conferences are rare, there is no charismatic leadership, protests tend to pile on top of each other. Rather than forming a pyramid, as most movements do, with leaders up on top and followers down below, it looks more like an elaborate web. In part, this web-like structure is the result of internet-based organizing. But it is also a response to the very political realities that sparked the protests in the first place: the utter failure of traditional party politics. All over the world, citizens have worked to elect social democratic and workers' parties, only to watch them plead impotence in the face of market forces and IMF dictates. In these conditions, modern activists are not so naive as to believe change will come from electoral politics. That's why they are more interested in challenging the structures that make democracy toothless, like the IMF's structural adjustment policies, the WTO's ability to override national sovereignty, corrupt campaign financing, and so on. This is not just making a virtue of necessity. It responds at the ideological level to an understanding that globalization is in essence a crisis in representative democracy. What has caused this crisis? One of the basic reasons for it is the way power and decision-making has been handed along to points ever further away from citizens: from local to provincial, from provincial to national, from national to international institutions, that lack all transparency or accountability. What is the solution? To articulate an alternative, participatory democracy.

If you think about the nature of the complaints raised against the World Trade Organization, it is that governments around the world have embraced an economic model that involves much more than opening borders to goods and services. This is why it is not useful to use the language of anti-globalization. Most people do not really know what globalization is, and the term makes the movement extremely vulnerable to stock dismissals like: 'If you are against trade and globalization why do you drink coffee?' Whereas in reality the movement is a rejection of what is being bundled along with trade and so-called globalization—against the set of transformative political policies that every country in the world has been told they must accept in order to make themselves hospitable to investment. I call this package 'McGovernment'. This happy meal of cutting taxes, privatizing services, liberalizing regulations, busting unions—what is this diet in aid of? To remove anything standing in the way of the market. Let the free market roll, and every other problem will apparently be solved in the trickle down. This isn't about trade. It's about using trade to enforce the McGovernment recipe.

So the question we are asking today, in the run up to the FTAA, is not: are you for or against trade? The question is: do we have the right to negotiate the terms of our relationship to foreign capital and investment? Can we decide how we want to protect ourselves from the dangers inherent in deregulated markets—or do we have to contract out those decisions? These problems will become much more acute once we are in a recession, because during the economic boom so much has been destroyed of what was left of our social safety net. During a period of low unemployment, people did not worry much about that. They are likely to be much more concerned in the very near future. The most controversial issues facing the WTO are these questions about self-determination. For example, does Canada have the right to ban a harmful gasoline additive without being sued by a foreign chemical company? Not according to the WTO's ruling in favour of the Ethyl Corporation. Does Mexico have the right to deny a permit for a hazardous toxic-waste disposal site? Not according to Metalclad, the US company now suing the

Mexican government for $16.7 million damages under NAFTA. Does France have the right to ban hormone-treated beef from entering the country? Not according to the United States, which retaliated by banning French imports like Roquefort cheese—prompting a cheese-maker called Bové to dismantle a McDonald's; Americans thought he just didn't like hamburgers. Does Argentina have to cut its public sector to qualify for foreign loans? Yes, according to the IMF—sparking general strikes against the social consequences. It's the same issue everywhere: trading away democracy in exchange for foreign capital.

On smaller scales, the same struggles for self-determination and sustainability are being waged against World Bank dams, clear-cut logging, cash-crop factory farming, and resource extraction on contested indigenous lands. Most people in these movements are not against trade or industrial development. What they are fighting for is the right of local communities to have a say in how their resources are used, to make sure that the people who live on the land benefit directly from its development. These campaigns are a response not to trade but to a trade-off that is now five hundred years old: the sacrifice of democratic control and self-determination to foreign investment and the panacea of economic growth. The challenge they now face is to shift a discourse around the vague notion of globalization into a specific debate about democracy. In a period of 'unprecedented prosperity', people were told they had no choice but to slash public spending, revoke labour laws, rescind environmental protections—deemed illegal trade barriers—defund schools, not build affordable housing. All this was necessary to make us trade-ready, investment-friendly, world-competitive. Imagine what joys await us during a recession.

We need to be able to show that globalization—this version of globalization—has been built on the back of local human welfare. Too often, these connexions between global and local are not made. Instead we sometimes seem to have two activist solitudes. On the one hand, there are the international anti-globalization activists who may be enjoying a triumphant mood, but seem to be fighting far-away issues, unconnected to people's day-to-day struggles. They are often seen as elitists: white middle-class kids with dreadlocks. On the other hand, there are community activists fighting daily struggles for survival, or for the preservation of the most elementary public services, who are often feeling burnt-out and demoralized. They are saying: what in the hell are you guys so excited about?

The only clear way forward is for these two forces to merge. What is now the anti-globalization movement must turn into thousands of local movements, fighting the way neoliberal politics are playing out on the ground: homelessness, wage stagnation, rent escalation, police violence, prison explosion, criminalization of migrant workers, and on and on. These are also struggles about all kinds of prosaic issues: the right to decide where the local garbage goes, to have good public schools, to be supplied with clean water. At the same time, the local movements fighting privatization and deregulation on the ground need to link their campaigns into one large global movement, which can show where their particular issues fit into an international economic agenda being enforced around the world. If that connexion isn't made, people will continue to be demoralized. What we need is to formulate a political framework that can both take on corporate power and control, and empower local organizing and self-determination. That has to be a framework that encourages, celebrates and fiercely protects the right to diversity: cultural diversity, ecological diversity, agricultural diversity—and yes, political diversity as well: different ways of doing politics. Communities must have the right to plan and manage their schools, their services, their natural settings, according to their own lights. Of course, this is only possible within a framework of national and international standards—of public education, fossil-fuel emissions, and so on. But the goal should not be better far-away rules and rulers, it should be close-up democracy on the ground.

The Zapatistas have a phrase for this. They call it 'one world with many worlds in it'. Some have criticized this as a New Age non-answer. They want a plan. 'We know what the market wants to do with those spaces, what do *you* want to do? Where's your scheme?' I think we shouldn't be afraid to say: 'That's not up to us'. We need to have some trust in people's ability to rule themselves, to make the decisions that are best for them. We need to show some humility where now there is so much arrogance and paternalism. To believe in human diversity and local democracy is anything but wishy-washy. Everything in McGovernment conspires against them. Neoliberal economics is biased at every level towards centralization, consolidation, homogenization. It is a war waged on diversity. Against it, we need a movement of radical change, committed to a single world with many worlds in it, that stands for 'the one no and the many yesses'.

11   The ends of ideology

....

Introduction

Is ideology something we can hope to be rid of? Is it something we are rid of already? The ferocity of ideological debate of the past has been intertwined with the brutal if sometimes exhilarating history of the twentieth century: with wars, concentration camps, and profound social, political, and economic revolutions. Perhaps, however, ideology is on the wane. The thesis that we are entering into a new phase, in which ideology is fading as an important feature of political life has recently seized many imaginations. The collapse of the Soviet empire, the spread of 'democratisation' and onward march of the global market has led some writers to envisage an end to the deep ideological conflicts that have characterized modern politics.

This is not the first moment at which it has been thought that ideology is coming to a halt. The first reading, from the American political scientist Seymour Martin Lipset offers a version of the famous 'end of ideology' thesis that several writers, also including Daniel Bell, Edward Shils, and Raymond Aron, espoused in the late 1950s and early 1960s [Reading 99]. These writers argued that extremist ideologies were withering away. In particular, the conflict between socialist and liberal ideologies in Western Europe and North America had been decisively resolved in favour of a pragmatic and socially concerned version of liberalism. While the Soviet Union and communist bloc posed an external threat, it offered no serious internal ideological challenge to the West. For these authors (different although they are) ideology is understood in terms we encountered in the excerpts from Giovanni Sartori and Kenneth Minogue [Readings 5 and 7]. Ideologies essentially embody an attempt on the part of an intellectual elite to construct a dogmatic and rationalist blueprint for social life and to impose it on the pluralism of social life. In part, 'ideology' was a code for socialism for these authors, and the orthodox Marxist-Leninist view of historical process leading to the inevitable collapse of capitalism under the vanguard leadership of the communist party was viewed as the central case of the ideological world-view. Indeed, some such as Bell had been Marxists and for them the end-of-ideology thesis expressed disillusion with a god that had failed. But the thesis grouped together the communism of the Soviet Union with other doctrines, such as Mussolini's fascism and particularly National Socialism as a common set of ideological political systems, characterized by brutal totalitarian states. Ideological politics was contrasted with the pragmatic and consensual politics of the post-War democracies, and a non-ideological style of liberal thought that was undogmatic and open to criticism.

For Lipset, post-war societies in the West eliminate the *functional* need for ideologies, since they have solved the fundamental political problems of the industrial revolution that generated these ideologies in the first place. For this perspective, the classical ideologies of the nineteenth and early part of the twentieth century arose as reactions to, and ways of coping with, the turbulent social and economic changes in this period. For example, socialism could be viewed as a response to the traumatic dislocation of the peasantry as they moved from the countryside to the city, and from a traditional way of life to the more insecure status of wage labourers. And fascism could be viewed as the response of an economically and socially insecure lower middle class, which feels itself squeezed between working class movements and the higher echelons of capitalist society. An irony in this is that a version of a functional view of ideology is adopted by orthodox Marxism, for which the strains inherent in a class-divided society generate ideologies as a means for coping with them. As a distorted worldview specific to a class-divided society, ideology is something to be overcome, by the 'universal' class consciousness of the proletariat or the establishment of a classless society [see Reading 1 and the Introduction to chapter 1]. However, for the post-war democracies the traumatic processes of change that give rise to ideological conflict have reached a conclusion. The working class has achieved social and political citizenship, the conservatives have accepted the welfare state, and the democratic left has recognized that an excessive increase in state power carries with it more dangers to freedom than opportunities for solving economic problems. These conditions do not eliminate the 'democratic class struggle', since political parties represent different social interests. But this conflict, in Lipset's pluralist vision, takes place on the basis of a deeper consensus on the rules of the political game and the institutions that govern it: 'it will be a fight without ideologies, without red flags, without May Day parades'. In the mixed and managed post-War economies, mainstream political parties are thought able to represent all the major social interests without the need for ideological blueprints picturing alternative social and economic orders.

Critics of the end-of-ideology thesis retorted that the thesis itself was ideological, expressing a vision of a particular, desirable liberal social order. In the later 1960s and 1970s the thesis fell out of favour. Experiences such as the defeat of the United States in Vietnam and anti-colonial wars against European powers in Africa made a sharp separation between the politics of the prosperous, post-ideological West and the 'Third World' (still necessarily sought susceptible to the ravages of ideology by proponents of the end-of-ideology thesis) seem less plausible. The consensual pluralism expressed by Lipset also came under attack, from groups who questioned the rules of the game through which political conflicts were tamed. For critics, the political structures of the Western democracies were skewed to promote the interests of business corporations and to neglect or marginalize many social groups. Dissenters from the pluralist vision included the New Left, anti-racist movements such as the Civil Rights movement in the United States, feminists, and environmentalists. These criticisms intensified as the post-War 'long boom' shuddered to a halt in the early nineteen-seventies, throwing into crisis the managed mixed economies on whose success the end-of-ideology thesis was premised. Perhaps the most powerful expression of this 're-ideologised' politics, and certainly its most electorally successful incarnation, was the New Right, which self-consciously sought to inject conservative politics with a renewed ideological content and vigour.

Francis Fukuyama's original article 'The End of History' was published in 1989, some thirty years after the emergence of the end-of-ideology thesis, and, with striking prescience, a few months before the Berlin Wall fell. Both its timing and the boldness of its thesis helped to give his claims a wide, if sometimes incredulous, readership. The excerpt here is from his book *The End of History and the Last Man* published three years later [Reading 100]. For Fukuyama, as for the earlier generation of 'endists', the end of history is in part a more specific claim about the triumph of Western liberal capitalism over Soviet communism, and socialism more generally. At the same time, Fukuyama seeks to explain a more general movement toward democracy and capitalism evident in the collapse in the course of the nineteen-seventies and nineteen-eighties of authoritarian regimes in Greece, Spain, Portugal, Argentina, Brazil, and elsewhere, which preceded the spectacular dissolution of the communist bloc. His claim that history has reached an end is not, as he emphasizes in the excerpt here, a claim that the course of events, even momentous ones, has somehow ground to a halt. Rather, it is history in the specialized sense of a single, coherent, and progressive process that has reached its finishing point.

Central to Fukuyama's thesis is the doctrine of liberal historicism: that history is a process with a meaning and purpose that we can discover, and with intelligible processes leading to an ultimate goal. The *end* of history is not merely a terminus but an underlying purpose that makes meaningful all that has gone before. As Fukuyama notes here, he derives this historicism from the German philosopher G. W. F. Hegel, particularly as interpreted by a twentieth century commentator, Alexandre Kojève, but the most prominent figure associated with this style of thinking is Marx. There are two ways in which Fukuyama fleshes out this historicist claim in order to spell out what he means by the end of history. The first is an argument about progress in the natural sciences. The modern natural sciences are by common consensus cumulative and directional, increasing our understanding of nature. This form of progress imposes certain constraints on modern societies, if they are not to be swept aside by military weakness or economic backwardness. This then compels a certain level of homogenization on all societies, which tends to disrupt traditional ties, strengthen the central state, open the societies up to the global market, and adopt a consumer culture.

At the same time, there is no economically necessary reason why advanced industrialization should accompany political liberty. There are many examples of technologically advanced capitalism coexisting with political authoritarianism, from Meiji Japan and Bismarck's Germany to contemporary Thailand and Singapore. In rejecting a purely economic determinism, he offers a second and parallel account of historical process as a struggle for recognition. Here he draws heavily on his account of Hegel. Human beings have a fundamental interest in being 'recognized', that is, in receiving acknowledgement of their dignity and status. Authoritarian or hierarchical societies offer only a damaged form of recognition, which provokes reactions of shame and anger. For Fukuyama, this need for recognition explains why people are not merely content to live in market-oriented authoritarian states such as Franco's Spain, South Korea or Brazil under military rule. In offering a defective form of recognition, such societies are therefore unstable when compared to liberal and democratic societies that allow equal recognition. Communism is being superseded by liberal democracy not only because its command economy hampers economic and technological growth, but because it offers an inadequate form of recognition to its subjects.

In one respect, therefore, Fukuyama offers an end-of-ideology thesis that is broadly continuous with Lipset's: liberalism is viewed as triumphing over socialism, which is no longer thought to represent a credible ideological opponent. However, his way of arriving at this conclusion is quite different. For ideology is not viewed as merely a functional offshoot of deeper social and economic forces. Instead, the explanation of the end of history is specifically ideological. Only through understanding the ideological superiority of liberalism over its rivals can we grasp why it represents the terminus and ultimate purpose of the historical process. In a further twist, we can only understand liberalism's ideological superiority if we adopt a theory, historicism, which was viewed by the earlier generation as itself the acme of ideological dogma. For some critics of Fukuyama, the implausibility of historicism damns his thesis. For others, he asks the right question, about the deep structures of modern experience, which shape what seems ideologically possible or plausible at any given time, but gives an arbitrary answer. Ideologies are in a state of upheaval, but there has been no definitive resolution in favour of liberalism.

The British sociologist and influential theorist of 'third way' politics Anthony Giddens offers a different and more unsettled version of the claim that the ideological traditions are exhausted [Reading 101]. This is based on a view of social change in what he calls 'high modernity'. Three sets of sociological developments in particular have emptied ideological traditions of their credibility. The first is globalization, understood in a very broad sense as the range of processes that connect geographically separate individuals and groups. The second is the emergence of 'post-traditional social order', a world in which traditions are under threat and have to be decided about rather than may be taken for granted. The third is the expansion of 'social reflexivity'. In a detraditionalizing society, individuals are less able to rely on habit, authority, and routine and must engage with and filter information in making decisions. These three phenomena together erode the bases of the main ideological traditions. Socialism was based on 'cybernetic model' of social life as a system that can be subordinated to a directive intelligence. Contemporary societies are too complex for such management, however: the range of information that needs to be processed is too complex and reflexive agents too unpredictable to be organized in this way. This does not leave the ideological field clear for the right, however, since conservatism too is in crisis. It is torn between enthusiasm for liberalization, markets, and an aggressive individualism that dissolves customs and traditions, on the one hand, and an attachment to the nation-state, cultural traditions, and traditional institutions such as the family, on the other. At the same time, Giddens tries to offer hope to a version of radical politics which seeks to mobilize reflexive individuals through extending the scope for dialogue within and across societies.

There is a different and bleaker response to liberal triumphalism, which has also gained notoriety through appearing to have recent history on its side, in Samuel Huntington's vision of a 'clash of civilizations' [Reading 102]. Agreeing that ideological and economic conflicts are in decline at the world level, Huntington envisages a reconfiguration of global politics on principally cultural lines. Conflict is not being superseded. Rather 'alignments defined by ideology and superpower relations are giving way to alignments defined by culture and civilisation', and the principal conflicts of global politics will take place between nations and groups of different civilizations. In the excerpt here, he sketches these alignments, emphasizing the importance of primordial religious affiliations, nation, and ethnicity. Conflicts on these lines are potentially more incendiary than material or even ideological conflicts, he suggests, since the latter can at least be debated and resolved in a way that cultural differences cannot. Here too in effect one of the traditional axes of ideological identification, nationalism, is picked out as the key wave of the future. Critics argue that Huntington offers too undifferentiated a picture of civilizations (there is little internal agreement over what makes up the identity of either 'Islam' or the 'West', for example).

More generally, we can see that, set alongside one another, the claims of Fukuyama, Giddens, and Huntington make it hard to believe that ideological debate is on the wane. Contemporary ideological debate may be tipping on its axis, moving from debates over the state direction of the economy to questions of identity, ethnicity, and nationality. However, as we have shown, these are themselves not entirely novel ideological traditions. Prognostication, as the fate of the earlier end-of-ideology thesis suggests, is a tricky business. But this reorientation of ideology hardly suggests that ideological debate is coming to an end. Furthermore, characterizations of the end of ideology are themselves contributions to shaping a political agenda, offering a contentious vision of a changing world and of how best for societies and individuals to cope with it. In a perfectly intelligible sense, then, they are themselves ideological, and further illustration of the continuing relevance of ideological contention to modern social and political life.

FURTHER READING

The texts cited for Further Reading in Chapter 1, 'The Concept of Ideology', contain discussions of the end of ideology thesis, which tend to be sceptical. Important mid-century texts include Daniel Bell, *The End of Ideology* (The Free Press, 1960: a 1988 edition contains a reflective Afterword), Raymond Aron, *The Opium of the Intellectuals* (Norton, 1962; French edn, 1955). Andrew Gamble, *After Politics* (Polity Press, 2000), is a lucid discussion of what the author calls 'endism' in political thought, including the theses of the end of ideology and the end of history. Also useful are J.-F. Lyotard, *The Postmodern Condition* (Minnesota, 1979), and A. Shtromas (ed.), *The End of 'Isms'* (Basil Blackwell, 1993).

99   Seymour Martin Lipset, from *Political Man* (Heinemann, 1969), pp. 406–8

Seymour Martin Lipset (1922–) was born in New York. His reputation is founded on work on political sociology, trade unions, social stratification, comparative dimensions of democratic theory, and political extremism. He is currently Professor of Public Policy at George Mason University and a Senior Fellow at the Hoover Institution, Stanford University. His many books include *Political Man: The Social Bases of Politics* (1960), *The First New Nation: The United States in Historical and Comparative Perspective* (1963), and *American Exceptionalism: A Double-Edged Sword* (1996).

The fact that the differences between the left and the right in the Western democracies are no longer profound does not mean that there is no room for party controversy. But as the editor of one of the leading Swedish newspapers once said to me, "Politics is now boring. The only issues are whether the metal workers should get a nickel more an hour, the price of milk should be raised, or old-age pensions extended." These are important matters, the very stuff of the internal struggle within stable democracies, but they are hardly matters to excite intellectuals or stimulate young people who seek in politics a way to express their dreams.

This change in Western political life reflects the fact that the fundamental political problems of the industrial revolution have been solved: the workers have achieved industrial and political citizenship; the conservatives have accepted the welfare state; and the democratic left has recognized that an increase in over-all state power carries with it more dangers to freedom than solutions for economic problems. This very triumph of the democratic social revolution in the West ends domestic politics for those intellectuals who must have ideologies or utopias to motivate them to political action.

Within Western democracy, this decline in the sources of serious political controversy has even led some to raise the question as to whether the conflicts that are so necessary to democracy will continue. Barrington Moore, Jr., a Harvard sociologist, has asked whether

> . . . as we reduce economic inequalities and privileges, we may also eliminate the sources of contrast and discontent that put drive into genuine political alternatives. In the United States today, with the exception of the Negro, it is difficult to perceive any section of the population that has a vested material interest on behalf of freedom. . . . There is, I think, more than a dialectical flourish in the assertion that liberty requires the existence of an oppressed group in order to grow vigorously. Perhaps that is the tragedy as well as the glory of liberty. Once the ideal has been achieved, or is even close to realization, the driving force of discontent disappears, and a society settles down for a time to a stolid acceptance of things as they are. Something of the sort seems to have happened to the United States.

And David Riesman has suggested that "the general increase of wealth and the concomitant loss of rigid distinctions make it difficult to maintain the Madisonian [economic] bases for political diversity, or to recruit politicians who speak for the residual oppressed strata." The thesis that partisan conflict based on class differences and left-right issues is ending is based on the assumption that "the economic class system is disappearing . . . that redistribution of wealth and income . . . has ended economic inequality's political significance."

Yet one wonders whether these intellectuals are not mistaking the decline of ideology in the domestic politics of Western society with the ending of the class conflict which has sustained democratic controversy. As the abundant evidence on voting patterns in the United States and other countries indicates, the electorate as a whole does not see the end of the domestic class struggle envisioned by so many intellectuals. A large number of surveys of the American population made from the 1930s to the 1950s report that most people believe that the Republicans do more for the wealthy and for business and professional people and the Democrats do more for the poor and for skilled and unskilled workers. Similar findings have been reported for Great Britain.

These opinions do not simply represent the arguments of partisans, since supporters of both the left and the right agree on the classes each party basically represents—which does not mean the acceptance of a bitter class struggle but rather an agreement on the representation functions of the political parties similar to the general agreement that trade-unions represent workers, and the Chamber of Commerce, businessmen. Continued class cleavage does not imply any destructive consequences for the system; as I indicated in an early chapter, a stable democracy requires consensus on the nature of the political struggle, and this includes the assumption that different groups are best served by different parties.

The predictions of the end of class politics in the "affluent society" ignore the relative character of any class system. The decline of objective deprivation—low income, insecurity, malnutrition—does reduce the potential tension level of a society, as we have seen. But as long as some men are rewarded more than others by the prestige or status structure of society, men will feel *relatively* deprived. The United States is the wealthiest country in the world, and its working class lives on a scale to which most of the middle classes in the rest of the world aspire; yet a detailed report on the findings of various American opinion surveys states; "The dominant opinion on polls before, during, and after the war is that the salaries of corporation executives are too high and should be limited by the government." And this sentiment, prevalent even among prosperous people, finds increasing support as one moves down the economic ladder.

The democratic class struggle will continue, but it will be a fight without ideologies, without red flags, without May Day parades. This naturally upsets many intellectuals who can participate only as ideologists or major critics of the *status quo*.

100 Francis Fukuyama, from *The End of History and the Last Man* (Penguin Books, 1992), pp. xii, xiv–xx

Francis Fukuyama (1952–) is Professor of International Political Economy at Johns Hopkins University. Educated at Cornell and Harvard, he was previously at the Rand Corporation and a member of the Policy Planning Staff of the US State Department, where he wrote his essay on 'The End of History'. His books include *The End of History and the Last Man* (1992), *Trust: The Social Virtues and the Creation of Prosperity* (1995), and *State-Building: Governance and World Order in the Twenty-First Century* (2004).

And yet what I suggested had come to an end was not the occurrence of events, even large and grave events, but History: that is, history understood as a single, coherent, evolutionary process, when taking into account the experience of all peoples in all times. This understanding of History was most closely associated with the great German philosopher G. W. F. Hegel. It was made part of our daily intellectual atmosphere by Karl Marx, who borrowed this concept of History from Hegel, and is implicit in our use of words like "primitive" or "advanced," "traditional" or "modern," when referring to different types of human societies. For both of these thinkers, there was a coherent development of human societies from simple tribal ones based on slavery and subsistence agriculture, through various theocracies, monarchies, and feudal aristocracies, up through modern liberal democracy and technologically driven capitalism. This evolutionary process was neither random nor unintelligible, even if it did not proceed in a straight line, and even if it was possible to question whether man was happier or better off as a result of historical "progress."

Both Hegel and Marx believed that the evolution of human societies was not open-ended, but would end when mankind had achieved a form of society that satisfied its deepest and most fundamental longings. Both thinkers thus posited an "end of history": for Hegel this was the liberal state, while for Marx it was a communist society.

This did not mean that the natural cycle of birth, life, and death would end, that important events would no longer happen, or that newspapers reporting them would cease to be published. It meant, rather, that there would be no further progress in the development of underlying principles and institutions, because all of the really big questions had been settled.

. . .

The unfolding of modern natural science has had a uniform effect on all societies that have experienced it, for two reasons. In the first place, technology confers decisive military advantages on those countries that possess it, and given the continuing possibility of war in the international system of states, no state that values its independence can ignore the need for defensive modernization. Second, modern natural science establishes a uniform horizon of economic production possibilities. Technology makes possible the limitless accumulation of wealth, and thus the satisfaction of an ever-expanding set of human desires. This process guarantees an increasing homogenization of all human societies, regardless of their historical origins or cultural inheritances. All countries undergoing economic modernization must increasingly resemble one another: they must unify nationally on the basis of a centralized state, urbanize, replace traditional forms of social organization like tribe, sect, and family with economically rational ones based on function and efficiency, and provide for the universal education of their citizens. Such societies have become increasingly linked with one another through global markets and the spread of a universal consumer culture. Moreover, the logic of modern natural science would seem to dictate a universal evolution in the direction of capitalism. The experiences of the Soviet Union, China, and other socialist countries indicate that while highly centralized economies are sufficient to reach the level of industrialization represented by Europe in the 1950s, they are woefully inadequate in creating what have been termed complex "post-industrial" economies in which information and technological innovation play a much larger role.

But while the historical mechanism represented by modern natural science is sufficient to explain a great deal about the character of historical change and the growing uniformity of modern societies, it is not sufficient to account for the phenomenon of democracy. There is no question but that the world's most developed countries are also its most successful democracies. But while modern natural science guides us to the gates of the Promised Land of liberal democracy, it does not deliver us to the Promised Land itself, for there is no economically necessary reason why advanced industrialization should produce political liberty. Stable democracy has at times emerged in pre-industrial societies, as it did in the United States in 1776. On the other hand, there are many historical and contemporary examples of technologically advanced capitalism coexisting with political authoritarianism, from Meiji Japan and Bismarckian Germany to present-day Singapore and Thailand. In many cases, authoritarian states are capable of producing rates of economic growth unachievable in democratic societies.

Our first effort to establish the basis for a directional history is thus only partly successful. What we have called the "logic of modern natural science" is in effect an economic interpretation of historical change, but one which (unlike its Marxist variant) leads to capitalism rather than socialism as its final result. The logic of modern science can explain a great deal about our world: why we residents of developed democracies are office workers rather than peasants eking out a living on the land, why we are members of labor unions or professional organizations rather than tribes or clans, why we obey the authority of a bureaucratic superior rather than a priest, why we are literate and speak a common national language.

But economic interpretations of history are incomplete and unsatisfying, because man is not simply an economic animal. In particular, such interpretations cannot really explain why we are democrats, that is, proponents of the principle of popular sovereignty and the guarantee of basic rights under a rule of law. It is for this reason that the book turns to a second, parallel account of the historical process in . . . an account that seeks to recover the whole of man and not just his economic side. To do this, we return to Hegel and Hegel's non-materialist account of History, based on the "struggle for recognition."

According to Hegel, human beings like animals have natural needs and desires for objects outside themselves such as food, drink, shelter, and above all the preservation of their own bodies. Man differs fundamentally from the animals, however, because in addition he desires the desire of other men, that is, he wants to be "recognized." In particular, he wants to be recognized as a *human being*, that is, as a being with a certain worth or dignity. This worth in the first instance is related to his willingness to risk his life in a struggle over pure prestige. For only man is able to overcome his most basic animal instincts—chief among them his instinct for self-preservation—for the sake of higher, abstract principles and goals. According to Hegel, the desire for recognition initially drives two primordial combatants to seek to make the other "recognize" their humanness by staking their lives in a mortal battle. When the natural fear of death leads one combatant to submit, the relationship of master and slave is born. The stakes in this bloody battle at the beginning of history are not food, shelter, or security, but pure prestige. And precisely because the goal of the battle is not determined by biology, Hegel sees in it the first glimmer of human freedom.

The desire for recognition may at first appear to be an unfamiliar concept, but it is as old as the tradition of Western political philosophy, and constitutes a thoroughly familiar part of the human personality. It was first described by Plato in the *Republic*, when he noted that there were three parts to the soul, a desiring part, a reasoning part, and a part that he called *thymos*, or "spiritedness." Much of human behavior can be explained as a combination of the first two parts, desire and reason: desire induces men to seek things outside themselves, while reason or calculation shows them the best way to get them. But in addition, human beings seek recognition of their own worth, or of the people, things, or principles that they invest with worth. The propensity to invest the self with a certain value, and to demand recognition for that value, is what in today's popular language we would call "self-esteem." The propensity to feel self-esteem arises out of the part of the soul called *thymos*. It is like an innate human sense of justice. People believe that they have a certain worth, and when other people treat them as though they are worth less than that, they experience the emotion of *anger*. Conversely, when people fail to live up to their own sense of worth, they feel *shame*, and when they are evaluated correctly in proportion to their worth, they feel *pride*. The desire for recognition, and the accompanying emotions of anger, shame, and pride, are parts of the human personality critical to political life. According to Hegel, they are what drives the whole historical process.

By Hegel's account, the desire to be recognized as a human being with dignity drove man at the beginning of history into a bloody battle to the death for prestige. The outcome of this battle was a division of human society into a class of masters, who were willing to risk their lives, and a class of slaves, who gave in to their natural fear of death. But the relationship of lordship and bondage, which took a wide variety of forms in all of the unequal, aristocratic societies that have characterized the greater part of human history, failed ultimately to satisfy the desire for recognition of either the masters or the slaves. The slave, of course, was not acknowledged as a human being in any way whatsoever. But the recognition enjoyed by the master was deficient as well, because he was not recognized by other masters, but slaves whose humanity was as yet incomplete. Dissatisfaction with the flawed recognition available in aristocratic societies constituted a "contradiction" that engendered further stages of history.

Hegel believed that the "contradiction" inherent in the relationship of lordship and bondage was finally overcome as a result of the French and, one would have to add, American revolutions. These democratic revolutions abolished the distinction between master and slave by making the former slaves their own masters and by establishing the principles of popular sovereignty and the rule of law. The inherently unequal recognition of masters and slaves is replaced by universal and reciprocal recognition, where every citizen recognizes the dignity and humanity of every other citizen, and where that dignity is recognized in turn by the state through the granting of *rights*.

This Hegelian understanding of the meaning of contemporary liberal democracy differs in a significant way from the Anglo-Saxon understanding that was the theoretical basis of liberalism in countries like Britain and the United States. In that tradition, the prideful quest for recognition was to be subordinated to enlightened self-interest—desire combined with reason—and particularly the desire for self-preservation of the body. While Hobbes, Locke, and the American Founding Fathers like Jefferson and Madison believed that rights to a large extent existed as a means of preserving a private sphere where men can enrich themselves and satisfy the desiring parts of their souls, Hegel saw rights as ends in themselves, because what truly satisfies human beings is not so much material prosperity as recognition of their status and dignity. With the American and French revolutions, Hegel asserted that history comes to an end because the longing that had driven the historical process—the struggle for recognition—has now been satisfied in a society characterized by universal and reciprocal recognition. No other arrangement of human social institutions is better able to satisfy this longing, and hence no further progressive historical change is possible.

The desire for recognition, then, can provide the missing link between liberal economics and liberal politics that was missing from the economic account of History in Part II. Desire and reason are together sufficient to explain the process of industrialization, and a large part of economic life more generally. But they cannot explain the striving for liberal democracy, which ultimately arises out of *thymos*, the part of the soul that demands recognition. The social changes that accompany advanced industrialization, in particular universal education, appear to liberate a certain demand for recognition that did not exist among poorer and less educated people. As standards of living increase, as populations become more cosmopolitan and better educated, and as society as a whole achieves a greater equality of condition, people begin to demand not simply more wealth but recognition of their status. If people were nothing more than desire and reason, they would be content to live in market-oriented authoritarian states like Franco's Spain, or a South Korea or Brazil under military rule. But they also have a thymotic pride in their own self-worth, and this leads them to demand democratic governments that treat them like adults rather than children, recognizing their autonomy as free individuals. Communism is being superseded by liberal democracy in our time because of the realization that the former provides a gravely defective form of recognition.

An understanding of the importance of the desire for recognition as the motor of history allows us to reinterpret many phenomena that are otherwise seemingly familiar to us, such as culture, religion, work, nationalism, and war. . . . A religious believer, for example, seeks recognition for his particular gods or sacred practices, while a nationalist demands recognition for his particular linguistic, cultural, or ethnic group. Both of these forms of recognition are less rational than the universal recognition of the liberal state, because they are based on arbitrary distinctions between sacred and profane, or between human social groups. For this reason, religion, nationalism, and a people's complex of ethical habits and customs (more broadly "culture") have traditionally been interpreted as obstacles to the establishment of successful democratic political institutions and free-market economies.

But the truth is considerably more complicated, for the success of liberal politics and liberal economics frequently rests on irrational forms of recognition that liberalism was supposed to overcome. For democracy to work, citizens need to develop an irrational pride in their own democratic institutions, and must also develop what Tocqueville called the "art of associating," which rests on prideful attachment to small communities. These communities are frequently based on religion, ethnicity, or other forms of recognition that fall short of the universal recognition on which the liberal state is based. The same is true for liberal economics. Labor has traditionally been understood in the Western liberal economic tradition as an essentially unpleasant activity undertaken for the sake of the satisfaction of human desires and the relief of human pain. But in certain cultures with a strong work ethic, such as that of the Protestant entrepreneurs who created European capitalism, or of the elites who modernized Japan after the Meiji restoration, work was also undertaken for the sake of recognition. To this day, the work ethic in many Asian countries is sustained not so much by material incentives, as by the recognition provided for work by overlapping social groups, from the family to the nation, on which these societies are based. This suggests that liberal economics succeeds not simply on the basis of liberal principles, but requires irrational forms of *thymos* as well.

101 Anthony Giddens, from *Beyond Left and Right: the Future of Radical Politics* (Polity Press, 1994), pp. 3–11

Anthony Giddens (1938–) was born in London and spent most of his academic career at the University of Cambridge, where he was Professor of Sociology. He was the Director of the London School of Economics and Political Science from 1996 until 2002. In 2004, he was ennobled, becoming Lord Giddens of Southgate. He is the author of a large number of sociological tracts, including *Capitalism and Modern Social Theory* (1971), *The Class Structure of Advanced Societies* (1973), *Central Problems in Social Theory* (1979), *A Contemporary Critique of Historical Materialism* (1981), *The Nation-State and Violence* (1986), and *Politics, Sociology and Social Theory* (1996). An important and controversial contributor to discussion of the 'third way', he has written more explicitly political texts, including *Beyond Left and Right* (1994), *The Third Way* (1998), and *The Global Third Way Debate* (2001).

The world of the late twentieth century, one must conclude, has not turned out as the founders of socialism anticipated when they sought to give direction to history by overcoming tradition and dogma. They believed, reasonably enough, that the more we, as collective humanity, get to know about social and material reality, the more we shall be able to control them in our own interests. In the case of social life in particular, human beings can become not just the authors but the masters of their own destiny.

Events have not borne out these ideas. The world we live in today is not one subject to tight human mastery—the stuff of the ambitions of the left and, one could say, the nightmares of the right. Almost to the contrary, it is one of dislocation and uncertainty, a 'runaway world'. And, disturbingly, what was supposed to create greater and greater certainty—the advance of human knowledge and 'controlled intervention' into society and nature—is actually deeply involved with this unpredictability. Examples abound. Consider, for instance, the debate about global warming, which concerns the possible effects of human activities on climatic change. Is global warming happening, or is it not? Probably the majority of scientists agree that it is; but there are others who question either the very existence of the phenomenon or the theory advanced to account for it. If global warming is indeed taking place, its consequences are difficult to assess and problematic—for it is something which has no real precedents.

The uncertainties thus created I shall refer to generically as *manufactured uncertainty*. Life has always been a risky business. The intrusion of manufactured uncertainty into our lives doesn't mean that our existence, on an individual or collective level, is more risky than it used to be. Rather, the sources, and the scope, of risk have altered. Manufactured risk is a result *of* human intervention into the conditions of social life and into nature. The uncertainties (and opportunities) it creates are largely new. They cannot be dealt with by age-old remedies; but neither do they respond to the Enlightenment prescription of more knowledge, more control. Put more accurately, the sorts of reactions they might evoke today are often as much about *damage control* and *repair* as about an endless process of increasing mastery.

The advance of manufactured uncertainty is the outcome of the long-term maturation of modern institutions; but it has also accelerated as the result of a series of developments that have transformed society (and nature) over no more than the past four or five decades. Pinpointing these is essential if we are to grasp the altered context of political life. Three sets of developments are particularly important; they affect especially the industrialized countries, but are also to an increasing degree worldwide in their impact.

GLOBALIZATION, TRADITION, UNCERTAINTY

First, there is the influence of intensifying *globalization*—a notion much bandied about but as yet only poorly understood. Globalization is not only, or even primarily, an economic phenomenon; and it should not be equated with the emergence of a 'world system'. Globalization is really about the transformation of space and time. I define it as *action at distance*, and relate its intensifying over recent years to the emergence of means of instantaneous global communication and mass transportation.

Globalization does not only concern the creation of large-scale systems, but also the transformation of local, and even personal, contexts of social experience. Our day-to-day activities are increasingly influenced by events happening on the other side of the world. Conversely, local lifestyle habits have become globally consequential. Thus my decision to buy a certain item of clothing has implications not only for the international division of labour but for the earth's ecosystems.

Globalization is not a single process but a complex mixture of processes, which often act in contradictory ways, producing conflicts, disjunctures and new forms of stratification. Thus, for instance, the revival of local nationalisms, and an accentuating of local identities, are directly bound up with globalizing influences, to which they stand in opposition.

Second, and partly as a direct result of globalization, we can speak today of the emergence of a *post-traditional social order*. A post-traditional order is not one in which tradition disappears—far from it. It is one in which tradition changes its status. Traditions have to explain themselves, to become open to interrogation or discourse. At first sight, such a statement might seem odd. For haven't modernity and traditions always been in collision? Wasn't overcoming tradition the main impetus of Enlightenment thought in the first place?

As expressed in the expansion of modernity, Enlightenment thought did destabilize traditions of all sorts. Yet the influence of tradition remained strong: more than this, in earlier phases of the development of modern societies a refocusing of tradition played a major part in consolidating the social order. Grand traditions were invented or reinvented, such as those of nationalism or of religion. No less important were reconstructed traditions of a more down-to-earth kind, to do with, among other areas of social life, the family, gender and sexuality. Rather than being dissolved, these became reformed in such a way as to plant women firmly in the home, reinforce divisions between the sexes and stabilize certain 'normal' canons of sexual behaviour. Even science itself, seemingly so wholly opposed to traditional modes of thought, became a sort of tradition. Science, that is, became an 'authority' which could be turned to in a relatively unquestioning way to confront dilemmas or cope with problems. In a globalizing, culturally cosmopolitan society, however, traditions are forced into open view: reasons or justifications have to be offered for them.

The rise of *fundamentalism* has to be seen against the backdrop of the emergence of the post-traditional society. The term 'fundamentalism' has only come into wide currency quite recently—as late as 1950 there was no entry for the word in the *Oxford English Dictionary*. In this case, as elsewhere, the appearance of a new concept signals the emergence of new social forces. What is fundamentalism? It is, so I shall argue, nothing other than tradition defended in the traditional way—but where that mode of defence has become widely called into question. The point about traditions is that you don't really have to justify them: they contain their own truth, a ritual truth, asserted as correct by the believer. In a globally cosmopolitan order, however, such a stance becomes dangerous, because essentially it is a refusal of dialogue. Fundamentalism tends to accentuate the purity of a given set of doctrines, not only because it wishes to set them off from other traditions, but because it is a rejection of a model of truth linked to the dialogic engagement of ideas in a public space. It is dangerous because edged with a potential for violence. Fundamentalisms can arise in all domains of social life where tradition becomes something which has to be *decided about* rather than just taken for granted. There arise not only fundamentalisms of religion but of ethnicity, the family and gender, among other forms.

The transformation of tradition in the present day is closely linked to the transformation of nature. Tradition and nature used to be relatively fixed 'landscapes', as it were, structuring social activity. The dissolution of tradition (understood in the traditional way) interlaces with the disappearance of nature, where 'nature' refers to environments and events given independently of human action. Manufactured uncertainty intrudes into all the arenas of life thus opened up to decision-making.

The third basic change affecting contemporary societies is the expansion of *social reflexivity*. In a detraditionalizing society individuals must become used to filtering all sorts of information relevant to their life situations and routinely act on the basis of that filtering process. Take the decision to get married. Such a decision has to be made in relation to an awareness that marriage has changed in basic ways over the past few decades, that sexual habits and identities have altered too, and that people demand more autonomy in their lives than ever before. Moreover, this is not just knowledge about an independent social reality; as applied in action it influences what that reality actually *is*. The growth of social reflexivity is a major factor introducing a dislocation between knowledge and control—a prime source of manufactured uncertainty.

A world of intensified reflexivity is a world of *clever people*. I don't mean by this that people are more intelligent than they used to be. In a post-traditional order, individuals more or less have to engage with the wider world if they are to survive in it. Information produced by specialists (including scientific knowledge) can no longer be wholly confined to specific groups, but becomes routinely interpreted and acted on by lay individuals in the course of their everyday actions.

The development of social reflexivity is the key influence on a diversity of changes that otherwise seem to have little in common. Thus the emergence of 'post-Fordism' in industrial enterprises is usually analysed in terms of technological change—particularly the influence of information technology. But the underlying reason for the growth of 'flexible production' and 'bottom-up decision-making' is that a universe of high reflexivity leads to greater autonomy of action, which the enterprise must recognize and draw on.

The same applies to bureaucracy and to the sphere of politics. Bureaucratic authority, as Max Weber made clear, used to be a condition for organizational effectiveness. In a more reflexively ordered society, operating in the context of manufactured uncertainty, this is no longer the case. The old bureaucratic systems start to disappear, the dinosaurs of the post-traditional age. In the domain of politics, states can no longer so readily treat their citizens as 'subjects'. Demands for political reconstruction, for the eliminating of corruption, as well as widespread disaffection with orthodox political mechanisms, are all in some part expressions of increased social reflexivity.

SOCIALISM, CONSERVATISM AND NEOLIBERALISM

It is in terms of these changes that we should look to explain the troubles of socialism. In the shape of Soviet Communism (in the East) and the Keynesian 'welfare compromise' (in the West), socialism worked tolerably well when most risk was external (rather than manufactured) and where the level of globalization and social reflexivity was relatively low. When these circumstances no longer apply, socialism either collapses or is turned on to the defensive—it is certainly not any more in the vanguard of 'history'.

Socialism was based on what might be called a 'cybernetic model' of social life, one which strongly reflects the Enlightenment outlook mentioned at the beginning. According to the cybernetic model, a system (in the case of socialism, the economy) can best be organized by being subordinated to a directive intelligence (the state, understood in one form or another). But while this set-up might work reasonably effectively for more coherent systems—in this case a society of low reflexivity, with fairly fixed lifestyle habits—it doesn't do so for highly complex ones.

Such systems depend on a large amount of low-level input for their coherence (provided in market situations by a multiplicity of local pricing, production and consumption decisions). The human brain probably also works in such a manner. It was once thought that the brain was a cybernetic system, in which the cortex was responsible for integrating the central nervous system as a whole. Current theories, however, emphasize much more the significance of low-level inputs in producing effective neural integration.

The proposition that socialism is moribund is much less controversial now than it was even a few short years ago. More heterodox, I think, is a second assertion I want to make: that conservative political thought has become largely dissolved just at the point at which it has become particularly relevant to our current condition. How can this be, for hasn't conservatism triumphed worldwide in the wake of the disintegrating project of socialism? Here, however, we must distinguish conservatism from the right. 'The right' means many different things in differing contexts and countries. But one main way in which the term is used today is to refer to neoliberalism, whose links with conservatism are at best tenuous. For if conservatism means anything, it means the desire to conserve—and specifically the conserving of tradition, as the 'inherited wisdom of the past'. Neoliberalism is not conservative in this (quite elemental) sense. On the contrary, it sets in play radical processes of change, stimulated by the incessant expansion of markets. As noted earlier, the right here has turned radical, while the left seeks mainly to conserve—trying to protect, for example, what remains of the welfare state.

In a post-traditional society, the conserving of tradition cannot sustain the sense it once had, as the relatively unreflective preservation of the past. For tradition defended in the traditional way becomes fundamentalism, too dogmatic an outlook on which to base a conservatism which looks to the achievement of social harmony (or 'one nation') as one of its main *raisons d'être*.

Neoliberalism, on the other hand, becomes internally *contradictory* and this contradiction is increasingly plain to see. On the one hand neoliberalism is hostile to tradition—and is indeed one of the main forces sweeping away tradition everywhere, as a result of the promotion of market forces and an aggressive individualism. On the other, it *depends upon* the persistence of tradition for its legitimacy and its attachment to conservatism—in the areas of the nation, religion, gender and the family. Having no proper theoretical rationale, its defence of tradition in these areas normally takes the form of fundamentalism. The debate about 'family values' provides a good example. Liberal individualism is supposed to reign in the marketplace, and the purview of markets becomes greatly extended. The wholesale expansion of a market society, however, is a prime force promoting those very disintegrative forces affecting family life which neoliberalism, wearing its fundamentalist hat, diagnoses and so vigorously opposes. This is an unstable mix indeed.

If socialism and conservatism have disintegrated, and neoliberalism is paradoxical, might one turn to liberalism *per se* (capitalism plus liberal democracy, but shorn of New Right fundamentalisms) in the manner, say, of Francis Fukuyama? Although I don't deal in the book with liberal political theory in any detail, I don't think so, and for reasons documented at greater length later. An ever-expanding capitalism runs up not only against environmental limits in terms of the earth's resources, but against the limits of modernity in the shape of manufactured uncertainty; liberal democracy, based on an electoral party system, operating at the level of the nation-state, is not well equipped to meet the demands of a reflexive citizenry in a globalizing world; and the combination of capitalism and liberal democracy provides few means of generating social solidarity.

All this reveals plainly enough the exhaustion of received political ideologies. Should we therefore perhaps accept, as some of the postmodernists say, that the Enlightenment has exhausted itself and that we have to more or less take the world as it is, with all its barbarities and limitations? Surely not. Almost the last thing we need now is a sort of new medievalism, a confession of impotence in the face of forces larger than ourselves. We live in a radically damaged world, for which radical remedies are needed.

There is a very real and difficult issue to be faced, however: the problematic relation between knowledge and control, exemplified by the spread of manufactured risk. Political radicalism can no longer insert itself, as socialism did, in the space between a discarded past and a humanly made future. But it certainly cannot rest content with neoliberal radicalism—an abandonment of the past led by the erratic play of market forces. The possibility of, even the necessity for, a radical politics has not died along with all else that has fallen away—but such a politics can only be loosely identified with the classic orientations of the left.

What might be called 'philosophic conservatism'—a philosophy of protection, conservation and solidarity—acquires a new relevance for political radicalism today. The idea of living with imperfection, long an emphasis of philosophic conservatism, here might be turned to radical account. A radical political programme must recognize that confronting manufactured risk cannot take the form of 'more of the same', an endless exploration of the future at the cost of the protection of the present or past.

It is surely not accidental that these are exactly the themes of that political force which can lay greatest claim to inherit the mantle of left radicalism: the green movement. This very claim has helped to obscure the otherwise rather obvious affinities between ecological thinking, including particularly 'deep ecology', and philosophic conservatism.

In each case there is an emphasis on conservation, restoration and repair. Green political theory, however, falls prey to the 'naturalistic fallacy' and is dogged by its own fundamentalisms. In other words, it depends for its proposals on calling for a reversion to 'nature'. Yet nature no longer exists! We cannot defend nature in the natural way any more than we can defend tradition in the traditional way—yet each quite often *needs* defending.

The ecological crisis is at the core of this book, but understood in a quite unorthodox manner. That crisis, and the various philosophies and movements which have arisen in response to it, are expressions of a modernity which, as it becomes globalized and 'turned back against itself', comes up against its own limits. The practical and ethical considerations thus disclosed, for the most part, are not new, although novel strategies and proposals are undoubtedly required to resolve them. They express moral and existential dilemmas which modern institutions, with their driving expansionism and their impetus to control, have effectively repressed or 'sequestered'.

102 Samuel Huntington, from *The Clash of Civilizations and the Recasting of World Order* (Touchstone Books, 1998), pp. 125–30

Samuel Huntington (1927–) is Professor of Government at Harvard University. Among his other appointments, he served at the White House as the Coordinator of Security Planning for the National Security Council in 1977–1978. His books include *The Soldier and the State: The Theory and Politics of Civil-Military Relations* (1957), *American Politics: The Promise of Disharmony* (1981), *The Third Wave: Democratization in the Late Twentieth Century* (1991), *The Clash of Civilizations and the Remaking of World Order* (1996), and *Who are We? The Challenges to American National Identity* (2004).

Spurred by modernization, global politics is being reconfigured along cultural lines. Peoples and countries with similar cultures are coming together. Peoples and countries with different cultures are coming apart. Alignments defined by ideology and superpower relations are giving way to alignments defined by culture and civilization. Political boundaries increasingly are redrawn to coincide with cultural ones: ethnic, religious, and civilizational. Cultural communities are replacing Cold War blocs, and the fault lines between civilizations are becoming the central lines of conflict in global politics.

During the Cold War a country could be nonaligned, as many were, or it could, as some did, change its alignment from one side to another. The leaders of a country could make these choices in terms of their perceptions of their security interests, their calculations of the balance of power, and their ideological preferences. In the new world, however, cultural identity is the central factor shaping a country's associations and antagonisms. While a country could avoid Cold War alignment, it cannot lack an identity. The question,

"Which side are you on?" has been replaced by the much more fundamental one, "Who are you?" Every state has to have an answer. That answer, its cultural identity, defines the state's place in world politics, its friends, and its enemies.

The 1990s have seen the eruption of a global identity crisis. Almost everywhere one looks, people have been asking, "Who are we?" "Where do we belong?" and "Who is not us?" These questions are central not only to peoples attempting to forge new nation states, as in the former Yugoslavia, but also much more generally. In the mid-1990s the countries where questions of national identity were actively debated included, among others: Algeria, Canada, China, Germany, Great Britain, India, Iran, Japan, Mexico, Morocco, Russia, South Africa, Syria, Tunisia, Turkey, Ukraine, and the United States. Identity issues are, of course, particularly intense in cleft countries that have sizable groups of people from different civilizations.

In coping with identity crisis, what counts for people are blood and belief, faith and family. People rally to those with similar ancestry, religion, language, values, and institutions and distance themselves from those with different ones. In Europe, Austria, Finland, and Sweden, culturally part of the West, had to be divorced from the West and neutral during the Cold War; they are now able to join their cultural kin in the European Union. The Catholic and Protestant countries in the former Warsaw Pact, Poland, Hungary, the Czech Republic, and Slovakia, are moving toward membership in the Union and in NATO, and the Baltic states are in line behind them. The European powers make it clear that they do not want a Muslim state, Turkey, in the European Union and are not happy about having a second Muslim state, Bosnia, on the European continent. In the north, the end of the Soviet Union stimulates the emergence of new (and old) patterns of association among the Baltic republics and between them, Sweden, and Finland. Sweden's prime minister pointedly reminds Russia that the Baltic republics are part of Sweden's "near abroad" and that Sweden could not be neutral in the event of Russian aggression against them.

Similar realignments occur in the Balkans. During the Cold War, Greece and Turkey were in NATO, Bulgaria and Romania were in the Warsaw Pact, Yugoslavia was nonaligned, and Albania was an isolated sometime associate of communist China. Now these Cold War alignments are giving way to civilizational ones rooted in Islam and Orthodoxy. Balkan leaders talk of crystallizing a Greek-Serb-Bulgarian Orthodox alliance. The "Balkan wars," Greece's prime minister alleges, ". . . have brought to the surface the resonance of Orthodox ties. . . . this is a bond. It was dormant, but with the developments in the Balkans, it is taking on some real substance. In a very fluid world, people are seeking identify and security. People are looking for roots and connections to defend themselves against the unknown." These views were echoed by the leader of the principal opposition party in Serbia: "The situation in southeastern Europe will soon require the formation of a new Balkan alliance of Orthodox countries, including Serbia, Bulgaria, and Greece, in order to resist the encroachment of Islam." Looking northward, Orthodox Serbia and Romania cooperate closely in dealing with their common problems with Catholic Hungary. With the disappearance of the Soviet threat, the "unnatural" alliance between Greece and Turkey becomes essentially meaningless, as conflicts intensify between them over the Aegean Sea, Cyprus, their military balance, their roles in NATO and the European Union, and their relations with the United States. Turkey reasserts its role as the protector of Balkan Muslims and provides support to Bosnia. In the former Yugoslavia, Russia backs Orthodox Serbia, Germany promotes Catholic Croatia, Muslim countries rally to the support of the Bosnian government, and the Serbs fight Croatians, Bosnian Muslims, and Albanian Muslims. Overall, the Balkans have once again been Balkanized along the religious lines. "Two axes are emerging," as Misha Glenny observed, "one dressed in the garb of Eastern Orthodoxy, one veiled in Islamic raiment" and the possibility exists of "an ever-greater struggle for influence between the Belgrade/Athens axis and the Albanian/Turkish alliance."

Meanwhile in the former Soviet Union, Orthodox Belarus, Moldova, and Ukraine gravitate toward Russia, and Armenians and Azeris fight each other while their Russian and Turkish kin attempt both to support them and to contain the conflict. The Russian army fights Muslim fundamentalists in Tajikistan and Muslim nationalists in Chechnya. The Muslim former Soviet republics work to develop various forms of economic and political association among themselves and to expand their ties with their Muslim neighbors, while Turkey, Iran, and Saudi Arabia devote great effort to cultivating relations with these new states. In the Subcontinent, India and Pakistan remain at loggerheads over Kashmir and the military balance between them, fighting in Kashmir intensifies, and within India, new conflicts arise between Muslim and Hindu fundamentalists.

In East Asia, home to people of six different civilizations, arms buildups gain momentum and territorial disputes come to the fore. The three lesser Chinas, Taiwan, Hong Kong, and Singapore, and the overseas Chinese communities in Southeast Asia become increasingly oriented toward, involved in, and dependent on the mainland. The two Koreas move hesitatingly but meaningfully toward unification. The relations in Southeast Asian states between Muslims, on the one hand, and Chinese and Christians, on the other, become increasingly tense and at times violent.

In Latin America, economic associations—Mercosur, the Andean Pact, the tripartite pact (Mexico, Colombia, Venezuela), the Central American Common Market—take on a new life, reaffirming the point demonstrated most graphically by the European Union that economic integration proceeds faster and further when it is based on cultural commonality. At the same time, the United States and Canada attempt to absorb Mexico into the North American Free Trade Area in a process whose long-term success depends largely on the ability of Mexico to redefine itself culturally from Latin American to North American.

With the end of the Cold War order, countries throughout the world began developing new and reinvigorating old antagonisms and affiliations. They have been grouping for groupings, and they are finding those groupings with countries of similar culture and the same civilization. Politicians invoke and publics identify with "greater" cultural communities that transcend nation state boundaries, including "Greater Serbia," "Greater China," "Greater Turkey," "Greater Hungary," "Greater Croatia," "Greater Azerbaijan," "Greater Russia," "Greater Albania," "Greater Iran," and "Greater Uzbekistan."

Will political and economic alignments always coincide with those of culture and civilization? Of course not. Balance of power considerations will at times lead to cross-civilizational alliances, as they did when Francis I joined with the Ottomans against the I Hapsburgs. In addition, patterns of association formed to serve the purposes of states in one era will persist into a new era. They are, however, likely to become weaker and less meaningful and to be adapted to serve the purposes of the new age. Greece and Turkey will undoubtedly remain members of NATO but their ties to other NATO states are likely to attenuate. So also are the alliances of the United States with Japan and Korea, its de facto alliance with Israel, and its security ties with Pakistan. Multicivilizational international organizations like ASEAN could face increasing difficulty in maintaining their coherence. Countries such as India and Pakistan, partners of different superpowers during the Cold War, now redefine their interests and seek, new associations reflecting the realities of cultural politics. African countries which were dependent on Western support designed to counter Soviet influence look increasingly to South Africa for leadership and succor.

Why should cultural commonality facilitate cooperation and cohesion among people and cultural differences promote cleavages and conflicts?

First, everyone has multiple identities which may compete with or reinforce each other: kinship, occupational, cultural, institutional, territorial, educational, partisan, ideological, and others. Identifications along one dimension may clash with those along a different dimension: in a classic case the German workers in 1914 had to choose between their class identification with the international proletariat and their national identification with the German people and empire. In the contemporary world, cultural identification is dramatically increasing in importance compared to other dimensions of identity.

Along any single dimension, identity is usually most meaningful at the immediate face-to-face level. Narrower identities, however, do not necessarily conflict with broader ones. A military officer can identify institutionally with his company, regiment, division, and service. Similarly, a person can identify culturally with his or her clan, ethnic group, nationality, religion, and civilization. The increased salience of cultural identity at lower levels may well reinforce its salience at higher levels. As Burke suggested: "The love to the whole is not extinguished by this subordinate partiality. . . . To be attached to the subdivision, to love the little platoon we belong to in society, is the first principle (the germ, as it were) of public affections." In a world where culture counts, the platoons are tribes and ethnic groups, the regiments are nations, and the armies are civilizations. The increased extent to which people throughout the world differentiate themselves along cultural lines means that conflicts between cultural groups are increasingly important; civilizations are the broadest cultural entities; hence conflicts between groups from different civilizations become central to global politics.

Second, the increased salience of cultural identity is in large part, as is argued in chapters 3 and 4, the result of social-economic modernization at the individual level, where dislocation and alienation create the need for more meaningful identities, and at the societal level, where the enhanced capabilities and power of non-Western societies stimulate the revitalization of indigenous identities and culture.

Third, identity at any level—personal, tribal, racial, civilizational—can only be defined in relation to an "other," a different person, tribe, race, or civilization. Historically relations between states or other entities of the same civilization have differed from relations between states or entities of different civilizations. Separate codes governed behavior toward those who are "like us" and the "barbarians" who are not. The rules of the nations of Christendom for dealing with each other were different from those for dealing with the Turks and other "heathens." Muslims acted differently toward those of *Dar al-Islam* and those of *Dar al-harb*. The Chinese treated Chinese foreigners and non-Chinese foreigners in separate ways. The civilizational "us" and the extracivilizational "them" is a constant in human history. These differences in intra-and extracivilizational behavior stem from:

1. feelings of superiority (and occasionally inferiority) toward people who are perceived as being very different;
2. fear of and lack of trust in such people;
3. difficulty of communication with them as a result of differences in language and what is considered civil behavior;
4. lack of familiarity with the assumptions, motivations, social relationships, and social practices of other people.

In today's world, improvements in transportation and communication have produced more frequent, more intense, more symmetrical, and more inclusive interactions among people of different civilizations. As a result their civilizational identities become increasingly salient. The French, Germans, Belgians, and Dutch increasingly think of themselves as European. Middle East Muslims identify with and rally to the support of Bosnians and Chechens. Chinese throughout East Asia identify their interests with those of the mainland. Russians identify with and provide support to Serbs and other Orthodox peoples. These broader levels of civilizational identity mean deeper consciousness of civilizational differences and of the need to protect what distinguishes "us" from "them."

Fourth, the sources of conflict between states and groups from different civilizations are, in large measure, those which have always generated conflict between groups: control of people, territory, wealth, and resources, and relative power, that is the ability to impose one's own values, culture, and institutions on another group as compared to that group's ability to do that to you. Conflict between cultural groups, however, may also involve cultural issues. Differences in secular ideology between Marxist-Leninism and liberal democracy can at least be debated if not resolved. Differences in material interest can be negotiated and often settled by compromise in a way cultural issues cannot. Hindus and Muslims are unlikely to resolve the issue of whether a temple or a mosque should be built at Ayodhya by building both, or neither, or a syncretic building that is both a mosque and a temple. Nor can what might seem to be a straight-forward territorial question between Albanian Muslims and Orthodox Serbs concerning Kosovo or between Jews and Arabs concerning Jerusalem be easily settled, since each place has deep historical, cultural, and emotional meaning to both peoples. Similarly, neither French authorities nor Muslim parents are likely to accept a compromise which would allow schoolgirls to wear Muslim dress every other day during the school year. Cultural questions like these involve a yes or no, zero-sum choice.

Fifth and finally is the ubiquity of conflict. It is human to hate. For self-definition and motivation people need enemies: competitors in business, rivals in achievement, opponents in politics. They naturally distrust and see as threats those who are different and have the capability to harm them. The resolution of one conflict and the disappearance of one enemy generate personal, social, and political forces that give rise to new ones. "The 'us' versus 'them' tendency is," as Ali Mazrui said, "in the political arena, almost universal." In the contemporary world the "them" is more and more likely to be people from a different civilization. The end of the Cold War has not ended conflict but has rather given rise to new identities rooted in culture and to new patterns of conflict among groups from different cultures which at the broadest level are civilizations. Simultaneously, common culture also encourages cooperation among states and groups which share that culture, which can be seen in the emerging patterns of regional association among countries, particularly in the economic area.

Name Index

Subject Index